BASIC AND CLINICAL SCIENCE COURSE

Retina and Vitreous

Section 12

2013–2014

(Last major revision 2012–2013)

Funded in part by the Educational
Trust Fund/Retina Research Foundation

**AMERICAN ACADEMY
OF OPHTHALMOLOGY**
The Eye M.D. Association

The American Academy of Ophthalmology is accredited by the Accreditation Council for Continuing Medical Education to provide continuing medical education for physicians.

The American Academy of Ophthalmology designates this enduring material for a maximum of 15 *AMA PRA Category 1 Credits*™. Physicians should claim only the credit commensurate with the extent of their participation in the activity.

Originally released June 2012; CME expiration date: June 1, 2015. *AMA PRA Category 1 Credits*™ may be claimed only once during this period.

The BCSC is designed to increase the physician's ophthalmic knowledge through study and review. Users of this activity are encouraged to read the text and then answer the study questions provided at the back of the book.

To claim *AMA PRA Category 1 Credits*™ upon completion of this activity, learners must demonstrate appropriate knowledge and participation in the activity by taking the post-test for Section 12 and achieving a score of 80% or higher. For further details, please see the instructions for requesting CME credit at the back of the book.

The Academy provides this material for educational purposes only. It is not intended to represent the only or best method or procedure in every case, nor to replace a physician's own judgment or give specific advice for case management. Including all indications, contraindications, side effects, and alternative agents for each drug or treatment is beyond the scope of this material. All information and recommendations should be verified, prior to use, with current information included in the manufacturers' package inserts or other independent sources, and considered in light of the patient's condition and history. Reference to certain drugs, instruments, and other products in this course is made for illustrative purposes only and is not intended to constitute an endorsement of such. Some material may include information on applications that are not considered community standard, that reflect indications not included in approved FDA labeling, or that are approved for use only in restricted research settings. **The FDA has stated that it is the responsibility of the physician to determine the FDA status of each drug or device he or she wishes to use, and to use them with appropriate, informed patient consent in compliance with applicable law.** The Academy specifically disclaims any and all liability for injury or other damages of any kind, from negligence or otherwise, for any and all claims that may arise from the use of any recommendations or other information contained herein.

Cover image courtesy of Michael F. Marmor, MD.

Basic and Clinical Science Course

Section 12

Faculty Responsible for This Edition

Hermann D. Schubert, MD, *Chair,* New York, New York
Neal H. Atebara, MD, Honolulu, Hawaii
Richard S. Kaiser, MD, Philadelphia, Pennsylvania
Adam A. Martidis, MD, Ventura, California
Colin A. McCannel, MD, Los Angeles, California
David N. Zacks, MD, PhD, Ann Arbor, Michigan
Hardeep S. Dhindsa, MD, Reno, Nevada
  Practicing Ophthalmologists Advisory Committee for Education

The Academy wishes to acknowledge Neil M. Bressler, MD, *Committee on Aging,* and Janet S. Sunness, MD, *Vision Rehabilitation Committee,* for their reviews of this edition.

The Academy also wishes to acknowledge the American Society of Retina Specialists, the Macula Society, and the Retina Society for recommending faculty members to the BCSC Section 12 committee.

Financial Disclosures

The Academy staff members who contributed to the development of this product state that they have no significant financial interest or other relationship with the manufacturer of any commercial product discussed in this course or with the manufacturer of any competing commercial product.

The authors state the following financial relationships:

Dr Kaiser: Alimera Sciences, consultant; Neovista, consultant, equity owner; Ophthotech, consultant, equity owner

Dr Martidis: Genentech, lecture fees; Ophthalmic Imaging Systems, consultant

Dr McCannel: Genentech, grant support; Savient Pharmaceuticals, consultant, equity owner

Dr Zacks: ONL Therapeutics, equity owner, patent/royalty

Reviewers:

Dr Bressler: grant support from the following: Abbott Medical Optics, Alimera Sciences, Allergan USA, Bausch & Lomb, Carl Zeiss Meditec, DIAGNOS, EMMES, ForSight Labs, Genentech, Genzyme, Lumenis, Notal Vision, Novartis Pharmaceuticals, Pfizer, Quark Biotech, Regeneron Pharmaceuticals, Research to Prevent Blindness, Steba Biotech

Dr Sunness: consultant for the following: Acucela, Alcon Laboratories, Cell Cure Neurosciences, Genentech, GlaxoSmithKline, Neurotech Pharmaceuticals, Novartis Pharmaceuticals, Potentia Pharmaceuticals, Shire, Sucampo Pharmaceuticals

The POACE reviewer and other authors state that they have no significant financial interest or other relationship with the manufacturer of any commercial product discussed in the chapters that they contributed to this course or with the manufacturer of any competing commercial product.

Recent Past Faculty

Nancy M. Holekamp, MD
Mark W. Johnson, MD
Peter K. Kaiser, MD
Carl D. Regillo, MD
Ursula M. Schmidt-Erfurth, MD
Richard F. Spaide, MD

In addition, the Academy gratefully acknowledges the contributions of numerous past faculty and advisory committee members who have played an important role in the development of previous editions of the Basic and Clinical Science Course.

American Academy of Ophthalmology Staff

Richard A. Zorab, *Vice President, Ophthalmic Knowledge*
Hal Straus, *Director, Publications Department*
Christine Arturo, *Acquisitions Manager*
Stephanie Tanaka, *Publications Manager*
D. Jean Ray, *Production Manager*
Ann McGuire, *Medical Editor*
Maureen Bourbin, *Administrative Coordinator*

**AMERICAN ACADEMY
OF OPHTHALMOLOGY**
The Eye M.D. Association

655 Beach Street
Box 7424
San Francisco, CA 94120-7424

Contents

General Introduction xiii

Objectives 1
Introduction 3

PART I   Fundamentals and Diagnostic Approaches 5

1 Basic Anatomy 7
The Vitreous 7
Neurosensory Retina 8
Retinal Pigment Epithelium 14
Bruch Membrane 17
Choroid 17
Sclera 18

2 Diagnostic Approach to Retinal Disease 19
Techniques of Examination 19
Retinal Angiographic Techniques 20
   Fluorescein Angiography 20
   Indocyanine Green Angiography 25
Optical Coherence Tomography 26
Scanning Laser Ophthalmoscopy 29
Fundus Autofluorescence 30
Infrared Reflectance Imaging 30
Fundus Near-Infrared Autofluorescence 31
Conditions Commonly Diagnosed Using Imaging Technology 32

3 Retinal Physiology and Psychophysics 33
Electroretinogram 33
   Recording and Interpreting the Response 33
   Specialized Types of ERG 37
   Applications and Cautions 39
Electro-oculogram and RPE Responses 42
   Electro-oculogram 42
Cortical Evoked Potentials 44
   Visually Evoked Potentials 44
   Electrically Evoked Potentials 45

Psychophysical Testing 45
   Dark Adaptation 46
   Color Vision 46
   Contrast Sensitivity 50

PART II   Disorders of the Retina and Vitreous 53

4   **Age-Related Macular Degeneration and Other Causes of Choroidal Neovascularization** 55
  Age-Related Macular Degeneration 55
   Genetics and AMD 56
   Nonneovascular Abnormalities in AMD 57
   Neovascular AMD 63
  Other Causes of Choroidal Neovascularization 80
   Ocular Histoplasmosis Syndrome 80
   Idiopathic CNV 83
   Angioid Streaks 84
   Pathologic Myopia 85
   Miscellaneous Causes of CNV 87
   Anti-VEGF Therapy for Secondary Causes of CNV 87

5   **Retinal Vascular Disease: Diabetic Retinopathy** 89
  Terminology and Classification 89
   Diabetes Terminology 89
   Diabetic Retinopathy Terminology 89
  Epidemiology of Diabetic Retinopathy 90
   The Wisconsin Epidemiologic Study of Diabetic Retinopathy 90
  Pathogenesis of Diabetic Retinopathy 90
  Systemic Medical Management of Diabetic Retinopathy 91
  Conditions Associated With Vision Loss From Diabetic Retinopathy 95
  Nonproliferative Diabetic Retinopathy 95
   Diabetic Macular Edema 95
   Diabetic Macular Ischemia 103
   Severe Nonproliferative Diabetic Retinopathy 104
  Proliferative Diabetic Retinopathy 105
   Nonsurgical Management of Proliferative Diabetic Retinopathy 106
   Surgical Management of Proliferative Diabetic Retinopathy 106
   Vitrectomy Surgery for Complications of Diabetic Retinopathy 109
  Cataract Surgery in Patients With Diabetes Mellitus 111
  Recommended Diabetes-Related Ophthalmic Examinations 111

6   **Other Retinal Vascular Diseases** 113
  Systemic Arterial Hypertension 113
   Hypertensive Retinopathy 113
   Hypertensive Choroidopathy 114
   Hypertensive Optic Neuropathy 115

Sickle Cell Retinopathy 115
    Nonproliferative Sickle Cell Retinopathy 118
    Proliferative Sickle Cell Retinopathy . . . . ; . . . 119
    Other Ocular Abnormalities in Sickle Cell Hemoglobinopathies 120
    Management of Sickle Cell Retinopathy 120
Peripheral Retinal Neovascularization 121
Venous Occlusive Disease 121
    Branch Retinal Vein Occlusion 121
    Central Retinal Vein Occlusion 127
Ocular Ischemic Syndrome and Retinopathy of Carotid
    Occlusive Disease 133
    Symptoms and Signs. 133
    Etiology and Course. 133
    Treatment of Ocular Ischemic Syndrome 134
Arterial Occlusive Disease 135
    Capillary Retinal Arteriole Obstruction (Cotton-Wool Spots) 135
    Branch Retinal Artery Occlusion 136
    Cilioretinal Artery Occlusion 137
    Central Retinal Artery Occlusion 138
    Ophthalmic Artery Occlusion. 140
Vasculitis 140
Cystoid Macular Edema 142
    Etiologies for CME 142
    Incidence of CME 143
    Treatment for CME 143
Coats Disease 143
Parafoveal (Juxtafoveal) Retinal Telangiectasia 145
Arterial Macroaneurysms 147
Phakomatoses 148
    Retinal Angiomatosis 148
    Congenital Retinal Arteriovenous Malformations 151
    Retinal Cavernous Hemangioma 151
Radiation Retinopathy. 151
Valsalva Retinopathy 153
Purtscher Retinopathy and Purtscherlike Retinopathy 154
Terson Syndrome 155

7 Retinopathy of Prematurity **157**
Introduction 157
    Epidemiology. 157
Classification and Terminology. 157
Pathogenesis. 162
    Natural Course 163
    Associated Conditions and Late Sequelae. 163
Screening Recommendations. 164
    Screening Criteria. 164
    Screening Intervals 164
    Fundus Photographic Screening of ROP 165

Prevention and Risk Factors 165
Treatment 166
   Laser and Cryoablation Surgery 167
   Anti-VEGF Drugs 169
   Vitrectomy and Scleral Buckling Surgery 170

8   Choroidal Disease. 171

Central Serous Chorioretinopathy. 171
   Fluorescein Angiography of CSC 172
   Other Imaging Modalities for CSC. 173
   Differential Diagnosis of CSC. 174
   Natural Course and Management of CSC. 175
Choroidal Perfusion Abnormalities 176
   Increased Venous Pressure 176
   Hypertension. 176
   Inflammatory Conditions 177
   Thromboembolic Disease 179
   Iatrogenic Abnormalities. 180
Choroidal Hemangioma 180
Uveal Effusion Syndrome 182
Bilateral Diffuse Uveal Melanocytic Proliferation 183

9   Focal and Diffuse Choroidal and Retinal Inflammation. 185

Noninfectious Retinal and Choroidal Inflammation 185
   White Dot Syndromes 185
   Acute Macular Neuroretinopathy 193
   Acute Idiopathic Maculopathy 193
   Acute Retinal Pigment Epitheliitis 193
   Solitary Idiopathic Choroiditis 194
   Inflammatory Vasculitis 194
   Intermediate Uveitis. 196
   Panuveitis 196
   Uveitis Masquerade 199
Infectious Retinal and Choroidal Inflammation. 200
   Cytomegalovirus Infection 200
   Necrotizing Herpetic Retinitis 201
   Endogenous Bacterial Endophthalmitis 202
   Fungal Endophthalmitis 203
   Tuberculosis 204
   Syphilitic Chorioretinitis 205
   Cat-Scratch Disease 206
   Toxoplasmic Chorioretinitis 206
   Toxocariasis 209
   Lyme Disease. 210
   Diffuse Unilateral Subacute Neuroretinitis 210
   West Nile Virus Chorioretinitis 211

10 Congenital and Stationary Retinal Disease **213**
Color Vision (Cone System) Abnormalities. 213
    Congenital Color Deficiency 213
    Achromatopsia 214
Night Vision (Rod System) Abnormalities 215
    Congenital Night-Blinding Disorders With Normal Fundi 215
    Congenital Night-Blinding Disorders With Prominent
        Fundus Abnormality 218

11 Hereditary Retinal and Choroidal Dystrophies **221**
Diagnostic and Prognostic Testing 223
Diffuse Photoreceptor Dystrophies 223
    Retinitis Pigmentosa. 223
    Cone Dystrophies 232
    Cone–Rod Dystrophies 233
Macular Dystrophies 234
    Stargardt Disease 234
    Vitelliform Degenerations 236
    Familial (Dominant) Drusen 239
    Pattern Dystrophies 240
    Sorsby Macular Dystrophy 241
Choroidal Dystrophies 242
    Diffuse Degenerations 242
    Regional and Central Choroidal Dystrophies 244
Inner Retinal and Vitreoretinal Dystrophies 246
    X-Linked Retinoschisis 246
    Goldmann-Favre Syndrome 248

12 Retinal Degenerations Associated With
Systemic Disease. **249**
Disorders Involving Other Organ Systems 251
    Infantile-Onset to Early Childhood–Onset Syndromes 251
    Bardet-Biedl Complex of Diseases 252
    Hearing Loss and Pigmentary Retinopathy 253
    Neuromuscular Disorders 254
    Other Organ System Disorders 254
    Paraneoplastic Retinopathy. 256
Metabolic Diseases 257
    Albinism. 257
    Central Nervous System Metabolic Abnormalities 259
    Amino Acid Disorders. 264
    Mitochondrial Disorders. 265
Systemic Drug Toxicity 266
    Chloroquine Derivatives 266
    Phenothiazines 267
    Other Drugs 268

13 Retinal Detachment and Predisposing Lesions **271**
Retinal Breaks 271
   Traumatic Breaks 272
Posterior Vitreous Detachment 274
   Examination and Management of PVD. 276
Lesions Predisposing Eyes to Retinal Detachment 276
   Lattice Degeneration. 276
   Vitreoretinal Tufts. 278
   Meridional Folds, Enclosed Ora Bays, and Peripheral
     Retinal Excavations 280
Lesions Not Predisposing Eyes to Retinal Detachment 281
   Paving-Stone, or Cobblestone, Degeneration 281
   Retinal Pigment Epithelial Hyperplasia. 282
   Retinal Pigment Epithelial Hypertrophy 282
   Peripheral Cystoid Degeneration 282
Prophylactic Treatment of Retinal Breaks 282
   Symptomatic Retinal Breaks 283
   Asymptomatic Retinal Breaks. 284
   Prophylactic Treatment of Lattice Degeneration 284
   Aphakia and Pseudophakia 285
   Fellow Eye in Patients With Retinal Detachment. 285
   Subclinical Retinal Detachment 285
Retinal Detachment. 286
   Rhegmatogenous Retinal Detachment 286
   Tractional Retinal Detachment 291
   Exudative Retinal Detachment 291
Differential Diagnosis of Retinal Detachment. 292
   Retinoschisis 292
Optic Pit Maculopathy 294

**14 Diseases of the Vitreous and Vitreoretinal
Interface** **297**
Posterior Vitreous Detachment 297
   Epiretinal Membranes 298
   Vitreomacular Traction Syndrome. 302
   Idiopathic Macular Holes. 304
Developmental Abnormalities 307
   Tunica Vasculosa Lentis 307
   Prepapillary Vascular Loops 307
   Persistent Fetal Vasculature. 307
Hereditary Hyaloideoretinopathies With Optically Empty Vitreous:
   Wagner and Stickler Syndromes 309
Familial Exudative Vitreoretinopathy 310
Vitreous Opacities 311
   Asteroid Hyalosis 311
   Cholesterolosis 311

Amyloidosis 312
Spontaneous Vitreous Hemorrhage 313
Pigment Granules 314
Vitreous Abnormalities Secondary to Surgery. 314

15 Posterior Segment Manifestations of Trauma **317**
Evaluation of the Patient After Ocular Trauma 317
Blunt Trauma 318
Vitreous Hemorrhage 319
Commotio Retinae 319
Choroidal Rupture 320
Posttraumatic Macular Hole 321
Traumatic Chorioretinal Disruption (Retinal Sclopetaria). 323
Scleral Rupture 323
Lacerating and Penetrating Injuries 324
Perforating Injuries 325
Intraocular Foreign Bodies 325
Surgical Techniques for Removal of Intraocular Foreign Bodies 326
Retained Intraocular Foreign Bodies. 327
Posttraumatic Endophthalmitis 328
Sympathetic Ophthalmia 329
Shaken Baby Syndrome/Nonaccidental Trauma 330
Avulsion of the Optic Disc 331
Photic Damage 332
Solar Retinopathy 332
Phototoxicity From Ophthalmic Instrumentation 333
Ambient Light 334
Occupational Light Toxicity 334

PART III   Selected Therapeutic Topics **335**

16 Laser Therapy for Posterior Segment Diseases **337**
Basic Principles of Photocoagulation 337
Choice of Laser Wavelength 337
Practical Aspects of Laser Photocoagulation 339
Indications 340
Complications of Photocoagulation 341
Transpupillary Thermotherapy 343
Photodynamic Therapy 343
Complications of Photodynamic Therapy. 344

17 Vitreoretinal Surgery **345**
Pars Plana Vitrectomy 345
Vitrectomy for Selected Macular Diseases 346
Macular Epiretinal Membranes 346
Vitreomacular Traction Syndrome. 346
Idiopathic Macular Holes. 349

Submacular Hemorrhage. 349
Subfoveal Choroidal Neovascularization 351
Vitrectomy for Complications of Diabetic Retinopathy. 352
Vitreous Hemorrhage 352
Diabetic Tractional Retinal Detachment 352
Diabetic Macular Edema 353
Vitrectomy for Posterior Segment Complications of Anterior
Segment Surgery. 354
Postoperative Endophthalmitis 354
Retained Lens Fragments After Phacoemulsification 357
Posteriorly Dislocated Intraocular Lenses. 359
Cystoid Macular Edema 360
Suprachoroidal Hemorrhage 360
Needle Penetration of the Globe. 362
Retinal Detachment Surgery 362
Techniques for Surgical Repair of Retinal Detachments. 364
Complications of Pars Plana Vitrectomy 368

Basic Texts. 369
Related Academy Materials 371
Requesting Continuing Medical Education Credit. 373
CME Posttest Request Form 375
Study Questions 377
Answer Sheet for Section 12 Study Questions. 385
Answers. 387
Index 393

General Introduction

The Basic and Clinical Science Course (BCSC) is designed to meet the needs of residents and practitioners for a comprehensive yet concise curriculum of the field of ophthalmology. The BCSC has developed from its original brief outline format, which relied heavily on outside readings, to a more convenient and educationally useful self-contained text. The Academy updates and revises the course annually, with the goals of integrating the basic science and clinical practice of ophthalmology and of keeping ophthalmologists current with new developments in the various subspecialties.

The BCSC incorporates the effort and expertise of more than 80 ophthalmologists, organized into 13 Section faculties, working with Academy editorial staff. In addition, the course continues to benefit from many lasting contributions made by the faculties of previous editions. Members of the Academy's Practicing Ophthalmologists Advisory Committee for Education serve on each faculty and, as a group, review every volume before and after major revisions.

Organization of the Course

The Basic and Clinical Science Course comprises 13 volumes, incorporating fundamental ophthalmic knowledge, subspecialty areas, and special topics:

1. Update on General Medicine
2. Fundamentals and Principles of Ophthalmology
3. Clinical Optics
4. Ophthalmic Pathology and Intraocular Tumors
5. Neuro-Ophthalmology
6. Pediatric Ophthalmology and Strabismus
7. Orbit, Eyelids, and Lacrimal System
8. External Disease and Cornea
9. Intraocular Inflammation and Uveitis
10. Glaucoma
11. Lens and Cataract
12. Retina and Vitreous
13. Refractive Surgery

In addition, a comprehensive Master Index allows the reader to easily locate subjects throughout the entire series.

References

Readers who wish to explore specific topics in greater detail may consult the references cited within each chapter and listed in the Basic Texts section at the back of the book. These references are intended to be selective rather than exhaustive, chosen by the BCSC faculty as being important, current, and readily available to residents and practitioners.

Related Academy educational materials are also listed in the appropriate sections. They include books, online and audiovisual materials, self-assessment programs, clinical modules, and interactive programs.

Study Questions and CME Credit

Each volume of the BCSC is designed as an independent study activity for ophthalmology residents and practitioners. The learning objectives for this volume are given on page 1. The text, illustrations, and references provide the information necessary to achieve the objectives; the study questions allow readers to test their understanding of the material and their mastery of the objectives. Physicians who wish to claim CME credit for this educational activity may do so by following the instructions given at the end of the book.

Conclusion

The Basic and Clinical Science Course has expanded greatly over the years, with the addition of much new text and numerous illustrations. Recent editions have sought to place a greater emphasis on clinical applicability while maintaining a solid foundation in basic science. As with any educational program, it reflects the experience of its authors. As its faculties change and as medicine progresses, new viewpoints are always emerging on controversial subjects and techniques. Not all alternate approaches can be included in this series; as with any educational endeavor, the learner should seek additional sources, including such carefully balanced opinions as the Academy's Preferred Practice Patterns.

The BCSC faculty and staff are continually striving to improve the educational usefulness of the course; you, the reader, can contribute to this ongoing process. If you have any suggestions or questions about the series, please do not hesitate to contact the faculty or the editors.

The authors, editors, and reviewers hope that your study of the BCSC will be of lasting value and that each Section will serve as a practical resource for quality patient care.

Objectives

Upon completion of BCSC Section 12, *Retina and Vitreous,* the learner should be able to

- describe the basic structure and function of the retina and its relationship to the pigment epithelium, choroid, and vitreous

- select appropriate methods of examination and ancillary studies for the diagnosis of vitreoretinal disorders

- identify specific pathologic processes that affect the retina or vitreous

- describe the principles of medical and surgical treatment of vitreoretinal disorders

- incorporate data from major prospective clinical trials in the management of selected vitreoretinal disorders

Introduction

The retina is a delicate neuroepithelium that lines the posterior aspect of the eye, adhering firmly to the optic nerve head and to the ora serrata anteriorly. Divided into central and extra-areal periphery, this layer of modified sensory cilia serves various kinds of visual function:

- detail discrimination
- color perception
- vision in dim illumination
- peripheral vision

BCSC Section 12, *Retina and Vitreous,* has 3 parts. Part I, Fundamentals and Diagnostic Approaches, covers retinal anatomy, imaging, and functional evaluation in 3 chapters. Chapter 1 provides an overview of the anatomy of the posterior segment. Chapter 2 discusses techniques of biomicroscopy and examination of the retina through transparent ocular media. Routine diagnostic techniques include slit-lamp biomicroscopy and direct and indirect ophthalmoscopy. Slit-lamp biomicroscopy in combination with precorneal non–contact or contact lenses is useful in examining both the posterior pole of the retina and the retinal periphery. Biomicroscopy is also crucial in the diagnosis of macular thickening, as well as in the diagnosis of specific vitreoretinal and choroidal diseases. Examination of the posterior segment is facilitated by maximal pupillary dilation, which usually allows evaluation of the retina from the posterior pole to its anterior margin at the ora serrata. Scleral indentation, combined with indirect ophthalmoscopy, is a valuable technique for observing the peripheral retina and examining it in profile. Ancillary tests, such as fundus autofluorescence, fluorescein angiography, indocyanine green angiography, optical coherence tomography (OCT), scanning laser ophthalmoscopy (SLO), microperimetry, and electrophysiology, may provide additional diagnostic information in eyes with transparent media. Fluorescein angiography is a commonly employed ancillary tool, and indocyanine green angiography is another technique that adds to the understanding of the pathophysiology of chorioretinal vascular diseases, especially age-related macular degeneration. Documenting clinical findings, either descriptively or by illustration, is an essential element of a complete posterior segment examination.

Chapter 3 reviews electrophysiologic tests and their significance in diagnosis. Ultrasonography, or echography, employing both A- and B-scan techniques, is useful for patients with clear or opaque media. Echography is particularly important in determining axial length, but it may also help diagnose choroidal lesions. Furthermore, it is a quantitative measurement that can be used for follow-up evaluation. However, the physician must use consistent techniques of examination and documentation to allow for meaningful comparisons.

X-ray techniques are useful to determine the presence of intraocular calcification or bone formation. Plain-film x-ray and computed tomography (CT) can reveal the presence, number, and location of radiopaque intraocular foreign bodies. Magnetic resonance imaging (MRI) can be helpful in determining orbital disease processes that affect the posterior segment, such as thyroid eye disease, or inflammatory diseases of the posterior segment itself, such as posterior scleritis. However, MRI is *contraindicated* if there is a possibility that the patient has an intraocular, orbital, or intracranial metallic foreign body.

Depending on their location, developmental or acquired alterations in the posterior segment may or may not be symptomatic. Some diseases, such as diabetic retinopathy, may be asymptomatic until advanced stages are reached. Symptoms caused by posterior segment abnormalities may include the following:

- transient or persistent reduction in visual acuity
- alterations in color perception
- photophobia
- metamorphopsia
- floaters
- photopsia
- scotomata
- loss of visual field
- night blindness

Part II, Disorders of the Retina and Vitreous, discusses specific diseases of and trauma to the posterior segment in Chapters 4 through 15. Appropriate diagnostic techniques are indicated throughout these discussions. Management of and therapy for the retinal disorders covered in Part II are complemented by descriptions of many related clinical trials being conducted or interpreted. Descriptions of selected trials and studies are set off from the main text for easy reference.

Part III, Selected Therapeutic Topics, offers more detailed information on 3 important posterior segment treatments: photocoagulation, photodynamic therapy, and vitreoretinal surgery. Treatment strategies, complications, and outcomes are covered in detail. Accompanying clinical illustrations provide further understanding of these basic tools of the retinal surgeon.

Throughout this volume, primary reference sources are supplemented by appropriate and up-to-date text references; additional references appear at the end of the book under Basic Texts and Related Academy Materials.

PART I

Fundamentals and Diagnostic Approaches

CHAPTER 1

Basic Anatomy

The Vitreous

The vitreous is a transparent gel composed of water, collagen, and hyaluronan; it occupies 80% of the volume of the eye. The vitreous body is divided into 2 main topographic areas: the central, or core, and the peripheral, or cortical, vitreous. The vitreous gel is composed of collagen fibrils separated by hydrated hyaluronan molecules, which act as fillers and separators between adjacent collagen fibrils.

The anterior surface of the vitreous body is called the anterior cortical gel, a condensation of collagenous fibers that attach to the posterior lens capsule, forming the ligament of Wieger (Fig 1-1A). The retrolental indentation of the anterior vitreous is called the patellar fossa. The potential space between lens and anterior cortical gel bordered by the Wieger ligament is called the Berger space. In the vitreous base, the collagen fibers are especially dense; they insert firmly into a ringlike area that extends 2 mm anterior and 3 mm posterior to the ora serrata. The vitreous is not only attached to its base; it is also firmly attached to the lens capsule, retinal vessels, optic nerve, and macula. The collagen fibrils in

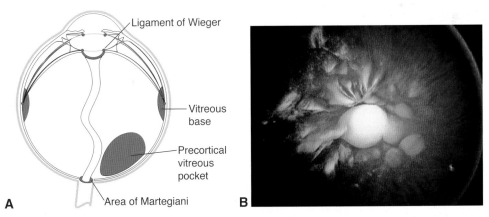

A   **B**

Figure 1-1 **A,** The vitreous is firmly attached to the posterior lens capsule, vitreous base, macula, and optic nerve. A prominent liquefaction of the premacular vitreous gel is called the premacular bursa, or precortical vitreous pocket. **B,** During vitrectomy, triamcinolone can be introduced into the vitreous cavity to highlight these cavities, that is, the posterior precortical vitreous pocket, cisterns, and canals. *(Part A illustration by Daniel Casper, MD, PhD; Part B reproduced with permission from Fine HF, Spaide RF. Visualization of the posterior precortical vitreous pocket in vivo with triamcinolone. Arch Ophthalmol. 2006;124(11):1663.)*

the cortical vitreous are densely packed, forming the cortical gel. Posteriorly, fibers course in a direction roughly parallel to the inner surface of the retina, forming the preretinal tract. Thus, the vitreous may be regarded as transparent connective tissue surrounded by a basal laminar bag provided by the lens and retina. There is no basement membrane between the vitreous base and lens, an area called the annular gap, which is a ringlike zone important for diffusion between the aqueous and vitreous compartments. The posterior attachment of the vitreous to the macula forms a space known as the premacular bursa, or the precortical vitreous pocket (see Fig 1-1A). Attachment of the collagenous vitreous to the disc is at the area of Martegiani. The anatomy of the vitreous is difficult to delineate in vivo, but the vitreous appears to contain interconnected cisterns and canals, most notably the ciliobursal canal connecting the ciliary body and macula and possibly mediating some forms of cystoid macular edema (Fig 1-1B).

Neurosensory Retina

The central area, or macula, measures 5.5 mm in diameter and is centered between the disc and the temporal vascular arcades. Histologically, it is an area featuring 2 or more layers of ganglion cells, totaling half of all the ganglion cells in the retina. Oxygenated carotenoids, in particular lutein and zeaxanthin, accumulate within the central macula and contribute to its yellow color.

The central 1.5 mm of the macula is called the *fovea* (or *fovea centralis*), which is specialized for high spatial acuity and for color vision. The fovea has a margin, declivity, and floor known as the *foveola*, a 0.35-mm-diameter region where cones are slender, elongated, and densely packed. The very center of the foveola is a small depression, 150 μm in diameter, known as the *umbo*. Within the fovea is a region devoid of retinal vessels known as the *foveal avascular zone (FAZ)*. The geometric center of the FAZ is often taken to be the center of the macula and thus the point of fixation; it is an important landmark in fluorescein angiography. Surrounding the fovea is a ring 0.5 mm in width called the *parafovea*, where the ganglion cell layer, inner nuclear layer, and outer plexiform layer are thickest. Surrounding this zone is a ring approximately 1.5 mm wide termed the *perifovea* (Table 1-1). Thus, the umbo forms the center, and the periphery of the perifovea forms the margin, of the area centralis, or macula (Fig 1-2).

The retina outside the macula, the extra-areal periphery, is commonly divided into a few concentric regions, starting with a 1.5-mm ring peripheral to the temporal major vascular arcades called the *near periphery*. The retina around the equator is called the *equatorial retina*, and the region anterior to it is called the *peripheral retina*. In the far periphery, the border between the retina and the pars plana is called the *ora serrata*. The posterior border of the vitreous base is located between the ora serrata and the equator of the eye. This is where most retinal tears occur. Jetties of retinal tissue, called *dentate processes*, extend anteriorly into the pars plana. These are more prominent nasally. *Ora bays* are posterior extensions of the pars plana toward the retinal side. On occasion, dentate processes may wrap around a portion of ora bay to form an enclosed ora bay. A *meridional fold* is a radially oriented, prominent thickening of retinal tissue extending into the pars plana. When aligned with a ciliary process, such folds are known as a *meridional complex* (Fig 1-3).

Table 1-1 Anatomical Terminology of the Macula (Area Centralis)

Term	Synonym	Histologic Definition	Clinical Observation (Size)
Macula	Posterior pole Area centralis	Contains 2 or more ganglion cell layers	Area between vascular arcades 5.5 mm in diameter centered 3.0 mm temporal and 0.8 mm inferior to the center of the optic disc
Fovea	Fovea centralis	A depression in the inner retina, has a margin, slope, and floor, the photoreceptor layer of which is entirely cones	A concave central retinal depression seen on slit-lamp examination 1.5 mm in diameter (about 1 disc diameter, or 5°)
Foveola		The floor of the fovea features cones only, arranged in the shape of a cake (gâteau nucléaire), where the inner nuclear layer and ganglion cell layer are laterally displaced	0.35 mm in diameter, usually smaller than the foveal avascular zone
Umbo	Fixation Light reflex	Small (150–200 μm) center of the floor of the foveola; features elongated cones forming a bouquet of cones	Observed point corresponding to the normal light reflex but not solely responsible for this light reflex
Parafovea		Margin, where the ganglion cell layer, inner nuclear layer, and Henle layer are thickest (ie, the retina is thickest)	Ring 0.5 mm in width surrounding the fovea
Perifovea		From the outermost limit of the parafovea to the outer limit of the macula	Ring 1.5 mm in width surrounding the parafovea

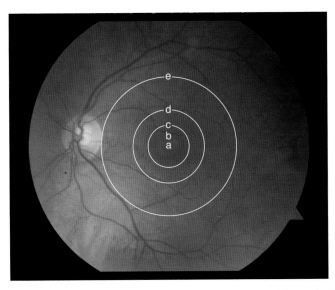

Figure 1-2 Anatomical macula, also called *area centralis* or *posterior pole*. The anatomical fovea and foveola are contained within the center of the anatomical macula. Letters indicate borders of: a = umbo; b = foveola; c = fovea; d = parafovea; e = perifovea. *(Courtesy of Hermann D. Schubert, MD.)*

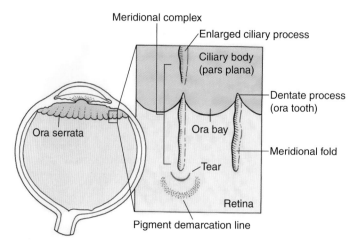

Figure 1-3 Schematic of the ora serrata, showing an ora bay and dentate process. Meridional folds are pleats of redundant retina. Tears may occur at the posterior end of such folds. *(Redrawn from Federman JL, Gouras P, Schubert H, et al. Retina and vitreous. In: Podos SM, Yanoff M, eds. Textbook of Ophthalmology. Vol 9. London: Mosby; 1988.)*

The layers of the retina can be seen in cross-sectional histologic preparations. They are listed here in order from the inner to outer retina (Fig 1-4):

- internal limiting membrane (ILM)
- nerve fiber layer (NFL; the axons of the ganglion cell layer)
- ganglion cell layer (GCL)
- inner plexiform layer (IPL)
- inner nuclear layer (INL)
- middle limiting membrane (MLM)
- outer plexiform layer (OPL)
- outer nuclear layer (ONL; the nuclei of the photoreceptors)
- external limiting membrane (XLM)
- rod and cone inner and outer segments (IS/OS)

Light must travel through the full thickness of the retina to reach the photoreceptors. The density and distribution of photoreceptors vary with topographic location. In the fovea, densely packed cones are predominantly red- and green-sensitive, with a density exceeding 140,000 cones/mm². The fovea has no rods; it contains only cones and processes of Müller cells. The number of cone photoreceptors decreases rapidly away from the center, even though 90% of cones overall reside outside the foveal region. The rods have their greatest density in a zone lying approximately 20° from fixation, where they reach a peak density of about 160,000 rods/mm². The density of rods also decreases toward the periphery.

The light-sensitive molecules in rods and cones are derived from vitamin A and are contained in the disc membranes of the photoreceptor outer segments. The discs are attached to a cilium, which is rooted through neurotubules in the ellipsoid and myoid of the inner segment. The ellipsoid, which is adjacent to the cilium, contains mitochondria and is responsible for the cone shape. The myoid, which is closer to the photoreceptor nucleus, contains endoplasmic reticulum. The mitochondria, cilia, and inner discs together form

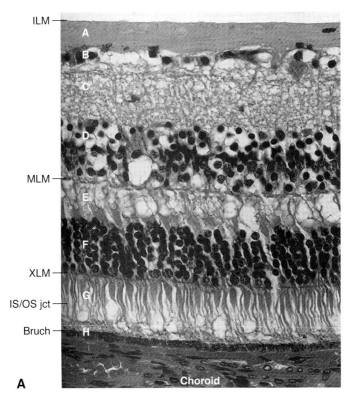

ILM —
MLM —
XLM —
IS/OS jct —
Bruch —

A

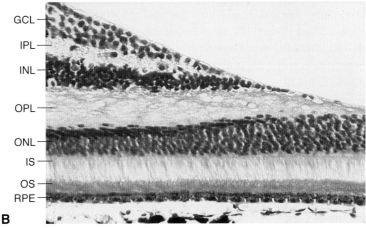

GCL —
IPL —
INL —
OPL —
ONL —
IS —
OS —
RPE —

B

Figure 1-4 **A,** Cross section of the retina and choroid. *A,* Nerve fiber layer. *B,* Ganglion cell layer. *C,* Inner plexiform layer. *D,* Inner nuclear layer. *E,* Outer plexiform layer. *F,* Outer nuclear layer. *G,* Photoreceptor outer segments. *H,* Retinal pigment epithelium. ILM = internal limiting membrane; MLM = middle limiting membrane; XLM = external limiting membrane; IS/OS jct = inner/outer segment junction; Bruch = Bruch membrane. **B,** In the fovea, the inner cellular layers are laterally displaced, and there is an increased density of pigment in the retinal pigment epithelium (RPE). The incident light falls directly on the photoreceptor outer segments, reducing the potential for scattering of light by overlying tissue elements. GCL = ganglion cell layer; IPL = inner plexiform layer; INL = inner nuclear layer; OPL = outer plexiform layer; ONL = outer nuclear layer; IS = inner segment of photoreceptors; OS = outer segment of photoreceptors.

(Part A reproduced with permission from Spaide RF, Miller-Rivera NE. Anatomy. In: Spaide RF, ed. Diseases of the Retina and Vitreous. Philadelphia: Saunders;1999; Part B courtesy of David J. Wilson, MD.)

the IS/OS junction, which is apparent with optical coherence tomography (OCT) and provides evidence of the origin of the photoreceptor as a modified sensory cilium prone to the full range of ciliopathies. Rod outer segments may contain up to 1000 discs stacked like coins. These discs are renewed in and shed from the outer retina and are phagocytosed by the retinal pigment epithelium (RPE) for processing and recycling of components (Fig 1-5).

Cone photoreceptors have a 1-to-1 synapse with a type of bipolar cell known as a *midget bipolar cell*. Other types of bipolar cells also synapse with each cone. Conversely, more than 1 rod—and sometimes more than 100 rods—converge on each bipolar cell. Bipolar cells, the first neurons of the visual pathway, synapse with ganglion cells, the second neurons of the visual pathway in the IPL. The ganglion cells summate responses from bipolar and amacrine cells and develop action potentials that are conducted to the dorsolateral geniculate nucleus and the third neuron in the brain. Amacrine cells on the inside of the INL help in signal processing by responding to specific alterations in retinal stimuli, such as sudden changes in light intensity or the presence of certain sizes of stimuli. Horizontal cells are on the outside of the INL. In the NFL, axons of the GCL course along the inner portion of the retina to form the optic nerve, a brain tract. The ILM, which is formed by the footplates of Müller cells, is attached to the posterior cortical gel of the vitreous (Fig 1-6).

Two additional intraretinal "membranes," the XLM and MLM, were identified by histologists but in actuality are not true membranes but junctional systems. At the outer extent of the Müller cells, zonular attachments between photoreceptors and Müller cells create the XLM, a structure visible with both light microscopy and OCT. Thus, the Müller cells whose nuclei reside in the INL course through almost the entire thickness of the retina. The inner third of the OPL has a linear density where synaptic and desmosomal connections occur between the photoreceptor inner fibers and the processes of the bipolar cells. This linear density, which is also apparent with OCT, is the junctional system that has been called the MLM.

The central retinal artery (a branch of the ophthalmic artery) enters the eye and divides into 4 branches, each supplying blood to a quadrant of the retina. These branches are located in the inner retina. Occasionally, a cilioretinal artery, derived from the ciliary circulation, will supply a portion of the inner retina between the optic nerve and the center of the macula (Fig 1-7). On a tissue level, the retina is supplied by up to 4 layers of capillaries, 1 superficial in the NFL (the radial peripapillary network) and 2 on either side of the INL as a superficial and a deep capillary plexus. The metabolic needs of the outer retina are met by the choriocapillaris, a capillary system of the choroidal arteries supplied by the short posterior ciliary arteries. The boundary between the retinal vascular supply and the diffusion from the choriocapillaris varies according to the topographic location, retinal thickness, and amount of light present. The retinal vasculature, including its capillaries, retains the blood–brain barrier with tight junctions between capillary endothelial cells. Blood collected from the capillaries accumulates within a branch retinal vein, which in turn forms the central retinal vein. The retinal vascular system is thought to supply about 5% of the oxygen used in the fundus; the choroid supplies the rest. See also Part I, Anatomy, of BCSC Section 2, *Fundamentals and Principles of Ophthalmology*.

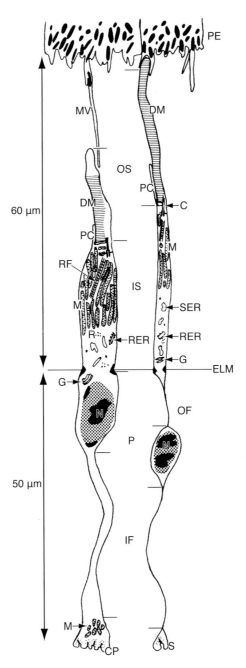

Figure 1-5 Schematic of a cone cell *(left)* and a rod cell *(right)* in the peripheral retina. C = cilium; CP = cone cell pedicle; DM = membranous discs; ELM = external limiting membrane; G = golgi apparatus; IF = inner fiber; IS = inner segment; M = mitochondria; MV = microvilli of pigment epithelial cells; N = nucleus; OF= outer fiber; OS = outer segment; P = perikaryon; PC = processus calycoides; PE = pigment epithelium; R = free ribosomes; RER = rough endoplasmic reticulum; RF = rootlet fiber; S = rod cell spherule; SER = smooth endoplasmic reticulum. *(Reproduced with permission from Krebs W, Krebs I. Primate Retina and Choroid. Atlas of Fine Structure in Man and Monkey. New York: Springer Verlag; 1991.)*

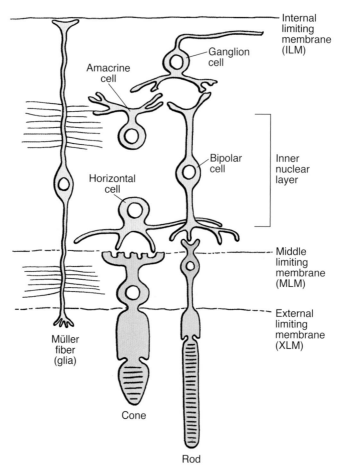

Figure 1-6 Schematic of the neuronal connections in the retina and participating cells. *(Redrawn from Federman JL, Gouras P, Schubert H, et al. Retina and vitreous. In: Podos SM, Yanoff M, eds. Textbook of Ophthalmology. Vol 9. London: Mosby; 1988.)*

Retinal Pigment Epithelium

The RPE is a monolayer of pigmented cells derived from the outer layer of the optic cup and thus maintains the apex-to-apex arrangement with müllerian glia (Fig 1-8). This layer is continuous with the pigment epithelium of the ciliary body and iris. Each RPE cell has an apex and base, the apical portion enveloping the outer segments of the photoreceptor cells with villous processes. RPE cells are hexagonal, cuboidal cells approximately 16 μm in diameter. In the macula, however, the cells are taller and denser than in the periphery. The lateral surfaces of adjacent cells are closely apposed and joined by tight junctional complexes (zonulae occludentes) near the apices, forming apical girdles and the outer blood–ocular barrier. The basal surface of the cells shows a rich infolding of the plasma membrane. The basement membrane does not follow these infoldings. The RPE contributes to retinal function in several ways; it

- absorbs light
- phagocytoses rod and cone outer segments

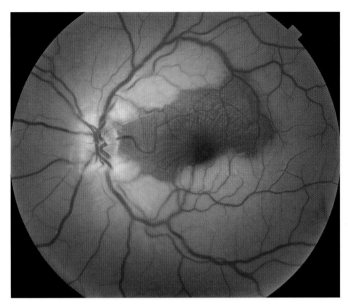

Figure 1-7 A central retinal artery occlusion in a young patient with a previously unknown patent foramen ovale. Fortunately, the patient had a patent cilioretinal artery. Note the inner retinal ischemic whitening in the distribution of the central retinal artery but preservation of the normal retinal transparency in the zone supplied by the cilioretinal artery. *(Reproduced with permission from Ho IV, Spaide RF. Central retinal artery occlusion associated with a patent foramen ovale. Retina. 2007;27(2):259–260.)*

- participates in retinal and polyunsaturated fatty acid metabolism
- forms the outer blood–ocular barrier
- maintains the subretinal space
- heals and forms scar tissue

The typical RPE cell has a number of melanosomes, each designed to be a biological light absorber. Melanosomes are spheroidal, with their melanin distributed on protein fibers.

RPE cells serve a phagocytic function, continually ingesting the membranes, or discs, shed by the outer segments of the photoreceptor cells. Over the course of a lifetime, each RPE cell is thought to phagocytose billions of outer segments. This process of shedding, phagocytosis, and photoreceptor renewal follows a daily (circadian) rhythm. Rods shed discs at dawn, and cones shed them at dusk. The ingested outer segments are digested gradually through the action of enzymes within cytoplasmic organelles known as *lysosomes*.

Visual pigments contain 11-*cis*-retinaldehyde that is converted to 11-*trans*-retinaldehyde. Most of the steps of regeneration of the 11-*cis* configuration occur in the RPE. A variety of pathologic changes may develop if this process of phagocytosis and renewal is impaired by genetic defects, drugs, dietary insufficiency (of vitamin A), or senescence.

The barrier function of the RPE prevents diffusion of metabolites between the choroid and the subretinal space. Because of this barrier, the environment of the photoreceptors is largely regulated by the selective transport properties of the RPE. The RPE has a high capacity for water transport, so fluid does not accumulate in the subretinal space

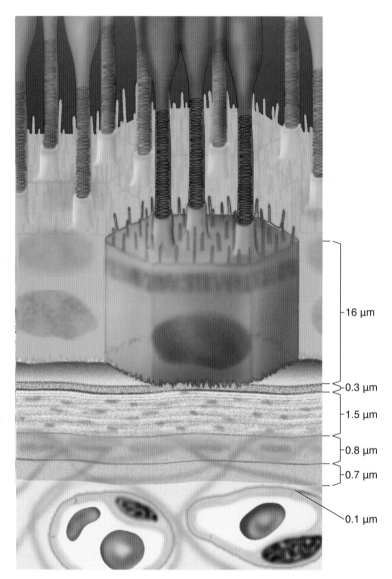

16 μm

0.3 μm

1.5 μm

0.8 μm

0.7 μm

0.1 μm

Figure 1-8 RPE and Bruch membrane. The folded plasmalemma of the RPE rests on its smooth basement membrane (0.3 μm thick) bordering the inner collagenous layer (1.5 μm thick). The outer collagenous layer (0.7 μm thick) borders the elastic layer (0.8 μm thick) and is continuous with intercapillary bridges and the subcapillary fibrous tissue. *(Illustration by Daniel Casper, MD, PhD.)*

under normal circumstances. This RPE-mediated dehydration of the subretinal space also modulates the bonding properties of the interphotoreceptor matrix, which bridges between the RPE and photoreceptors and helps bond the neurosensory retina to the RPE. With deterioration or loss of the RPE, there is corresponding atrophy of the overlying photoreceptors and underlying choriocapillaris.

Bruch Membrane

The basal portion of the RPE is attached to the Bruch membrane, which has 4 to 5 layers. Starting with the innermost, these layers are the

- basement membrane of the RPE
- inner collagenous zone
- middle layer of elastic fibers
- outer collagenous zone
- basement membrane of the endothelium of the choriocapillaris

Throughout life, lipids and oxidatively damaged materials build up within the Bruch membrane. Some disease states, such as pseudoxanthoma elasticum, are associated with increased fragility of the Bruch membrane, presumably caused by abnormalities within the membrane's collagen or elastic portions.

Choroid

Blood enters the choroid through the posterior ciliary arteries (Fig 1-9). The outer layer of large-caliber choroidal vessels, known as the Haller layer, is relatively thick. The choroidal vessels in this layer divide into smaller-diameter vessels and precapillary arterioles in a layer known as the Sattler layer. These vessels distribute the blood over the extent of the choroid, reducing arterial pressure to the relatively low pressure found in the choriocapillaris. The choroid has a maximal thickness posteriorly, where it is 0.22 mm thick, becoming progressively thinner anteriorly; at the ora serrata, it is 0.1 mm thick. In the posterior pole, the choriocapillaris forms a plexus of capillaries that functionally act as endarterioles, even though the capillaries themselves are not arranged strictly into lobules. The

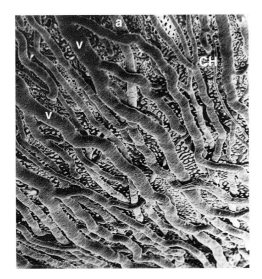

Figure 1-9 Scanning electron micrograph of the choroid. Vascular cast of the choroid from the posterior pole of a 62-year-old man, demonstrating arteries *(a)*, veins *(v)*, and the choriocapillaris *(CH)*. (70×) *(Courtesy of A. Fryczkowski, MD.)*

capillary arrangement becomes more irregular toward the periphery, where the capillaries are arranged more radially.

After passing through the choriocapillaris, the blood is collected in venules, which coalesce into collecting channels, or ampullae, of the vortex veins. Most eyes have 4 or 5 vortex veins, which leave the eye at or posterior to the equator. The vortex veins drain into the superior and inferior ophthalmic veins. The retina has one of the highest metabolic rates per gram of tissue in the body; it is served by the choroid, which has the highest blood flow of any tissue. The venous blood exiting the choroid still has a very high oxygen tension. The RPE cells, which are based on the choriocapillaris, are exposed to the highest oxygen tensions of any perfused tissue, increasing the risk of oxidative damage. The rapid flow in the choroid acts as a heat sink to remove thermal energy from light absorption. Interspersed between the vessels of the choroid are loose connective tissue, fibroblasts, and melanocytes.

Sclera

The sclera is composed of collagen and a few elastic fibers embedded in a matrix of proteoglycans. Compared with the cornea, the sclera has less hydration and a more irregular arrangement of fibers. It terminates at the histologists' limbus and is thinnest near the limbus and equator and in the peripapillary area. The sclera is normally permeable to the passage of molecules in both directions. Fluid is thought to leave the eye through the sclera. Scleral permeability allows drugs to be delivered to the eye by means of injection into the Tenon space.

Hogan MJ, Alvarado JA, Weddell JE. *Histology of the Human Eye.* Philadelphia: Saunders; 1971:chap 5, 8, 9, 11.

Polyak SL. *The Retina.* Chicago: University of Chicago Press; 1941.

Rochon-Duvigneaud A. Recherches sur la fovea de la rétine humaine et particulièrement sur le bouquet des cônes centraux. *Arch Anat Microsc.* 1907(IX):315–342.

Worst JGF, Los LI. *Cisternal Anatomy of the Vitreous.* Amsterdam: Kugler; 1995.

CHAPTER 2

Diagnostic Approach to Retinal Disease

Techniques of Examination

Diagnosing retinal disease requires a combination of careful clinical examination and specialized imaging techniques. The macula can be examined without pupillary dilation, but to perform a complete retinal examination, the pupil should be fully dilated. Pupil dilation is accomplished through a variety of pharmacologic agents, including 1% tropicamide, 2.5% phenylephrine, and 1% cyclopentolate. In general, longer-acting dilating drugs are not required.

The simplest examination technique is to use the direct ophthalmoscope, which provides an upright, monocular, high-magnification (15×) image of the retina. However, the instrument's lack of stereopsis, small field of view, and poor view of the retinal periphery limit its use. These shortcomings are circumvented by using the binocular indirect ophthalmoscope (BIO) in combination with a handheld magnifying lens that dramatically increases the field of view with lower magnification (2–3×). This combination yields an inverted, binocular image of most of the retina; however, to see the entire retina (especially pathology near the ora serrata), the BIO examination must be combined with scleral depression. In general, 20, 28, and 30 D lenses are used to view the retina. Because the field of view is inversely proportional to the power of the lens, the 30 D lens has the widest field and lowest magnification. Clinicians can easily correct for the image reversal by turning the page upside down to draw the retina and the pathology as seen through the lens.

Magnification of even the lowest power BIO lens is insufficient to evaluate subtle retinal changes or abnormalities of the vitreous body. To evaluate these structures, slit-lamp biomicroscopy is required. A variety of lenses are available for viewing the retina with the slit lamp; the type frequently used is the 3-mirror contact lens. Contact lenses offer the advantage of better stereopsis and higher resolution. They require topical corneal anesthesia and are placed directly on the cornea to eliminate its power and the cornea–air interface. Fluids used range from contact lens wetting solutions to viscous clear gel solutions. The more viscous the solution, however, the more it interferes with the quality of any photography or angiography performed shortly after the examination. In contrast, non–contact lenses use the power of the lens in combination with the cornea to produce an inverted image with a wider field of view. The biconvex indirect lenses used with the slit lamp do not touch the cornea, and thus topical anesthesia is not necessary. In general, high-plus optical power lenses such as a 60 D lens with 1:1 image magnification and 78 and 90 D lenses are used. Lenses with lower dioptric power offer more axial resolution and better stereopsis. Non–contact lenses are easier to use and offer more rapid evaluation of the retina. Finally, a Hruby lens, an external planoconcave lens with high-negative optical power attached to the slit-lamp frame, is another option if a contact or non–contact lens is not available. Like the biconvex indirect lenses, it does not require topical anesthesia or placement of other drops on the cornea. Although the Hruby lens does not give an inverted image, it is less versatile than the biconvex indirect lenses for viewing the central area.

Detection of diffuse retinal thickening and cystic spaces in cystoid macular edema or of subretinal fluid in choroidal neovascularization (CNV) is enhanced by using a thin slit beam, ideally at a 45° angle, and a lens with high magnification. The inner aspect of the beam is directed at the surface of the retina and retinal vessels, the outer aspect at the retinal pigment epithelium (RPE). The distance between the inner and outer aspects is recognized as the thickness of the retina. Once the normal thickness of the retina is known for a given location within the macula, abnormal thicknesses may be evaluated in other areas. The same technique is useful for determining the level of hemorrhage—preretinal, intraretinal, or subretinal. Careful examination of the beam as it intersects with the retina can differentiate between elevation and depression of a retinal lesion. Transillumination is another technique that may help highlight cystic changes of the neurosensory retina or help detect pigment epithelial detachments where the edge of the beam appears to glow. Red-free (green) light may be used to help detect small vessels (such as intraretinal micro-vascular abnormalities or retinal neovascularization) or dots of hemorrhage that may be difficult to see against an orange background when viewed with the normal slit beam. A lighter color to the retina with red-free light may correspond to the presence of fluid, fibrin, or fibrous tissue associated with CNV.

Friberg TR. Examination of the retina: ophthalmoscopy and fundus biomicroscopy. In: Albert DM, Miller JW, Azar DT, Blodi BA, eds. *Albert & Jakobiec's Principles and Practice of Ophthalmology.* 3rd ed. Philadelphia: Saunders; 2008:chap 127.

Retinal Angiographic Techniques

Fluorescein Angiography

Fluorescein angiography (FA) allows study of the circulation of the retina and choroid in normal and diseased states. Photographs of the retina are taken after intravenous injection of sodium fluorescein, an orange-red crystalline hydrocarbon with a molecular weight of 376 that diffuses through most of the body fluids. It is available as 2–3 mL of 25% concen-tration or 5 mL of 10% concentration in a sterile aqueous solution. It is eliminated primar-ily through the liver and kidneys within 24–36 hours via the urine. Eighty percent of the fluorescein is protein-bound, primarily to albumin, and not available for fluorescence; the remaining 20% is unbound and circulates in the vasculature and tissues of the retina and choroid, where it can be visualized.

Fluorescence occurs when a molecule is excited by light of a certain wavelength that raises the molecule to a higher energy state and then allows it to release a photon of light to bring it back to its original state. To image this fluorescence, special excitation and barrier filters are required. Sodium fluorescein fluoresces at a wavelength of 520–530 nm (green) after excitation by a light of 465–490 nm (blue). To obtain a fluorescein angiogram, white light from the camera flash unit is passed through a blue (excitatory) filter, and blue light enters the eye. The blue light, with its wavelength of 465–490 nm, excites the unbound fluorescein molecules circulating in the retinal and choroidal layers or unbound molecules that have leaked out of the vasculature, stimulating them to emit a longer-wavelength yellow-green light (520–530 nm). Both the emitted yellow-green fluorescence and reflected blue light from structures that do not contain fluorescein exit the eye and return to the camera. A yellow-green (barrier) filter on the camera lens blocks the reflected blue light, permitting only the yellow-green light, which has originated from the fluorescein molecules, into the camera. Digital imaging systems allow easy image archiving and retrieval, thus offering the capability of quickly comparing images longitudinally.

To interpret a fluorescein angiogram, it is vital to understand retinal vasculature. The retina has a dual blood supply. The central retinal artery and derived retinal capillary plexus serve the inner half of the retina, and the endothelial cell tight junctions provide the inner blood–retinal barrier. Normally, neither bound nor unbound fluorescein can pass this barrier. The choroidal circulation serves the outer half of the retina, and the tight junctional girdles of the RPE provide the outer blood–retinal barrier. Fluorescein particles that are not bound to protein can pass through the fenestrated walls of the choriocapillaris but do not normally pass through the RPE or the zonulae occludentes joining RPE cells to gain access to the subretinal space. Therefore, fluorescein from the choroid cannot enter the neurosensory retina unless the RPE is defective. Although the fluorescence in the choroid is blocked by pigment in the RPE, it is usually visible as deep, diffuse background fluorescence.

Fluorescein is injected into a peripheral vein and enters the ocular circulation via the ophthalmic artery 8–12 seconds later, depending on the rate of injection and the patient's age and cardiovascular health. The retinal and choroidal vessels fill during the transit phase, which lasts 10–15 seconds. Choroidal filling is characterized by a patchy choroidal flush, with choriocapillary lobules often visible. The choroid has a higher flow rate than that of the retinal vessels. The arterial phase of the angiographic study occurs after the choroidal phase, and dye fills the retinal arteries. The arteriovenous phase begins with complete filling of the retinal arteries and capillaries and concludes with laminar filling of the retinal veins. This phase, which usually occurs approximately 1 minute after dye injection, is considered the peak phase of fluorescence, the point in time at which the most capillary detail is shown in the fovea. Over the next few minutes, the dye recirculates and fluorescence gradually declines. In the late phases of the angiographic study, the choroid, Bruch membrane, and sclera stain. The larger choroidal vessels frequently appear as hypofluorescent areas against the hyperfluorescent choroidal interstitium.

Fluorescein can leak out of retinal capillaries into the retina only when the capillary endothelium is damaged, as in diabetic retinopathy, for example. Similarly, fluorescein can leak from the choriocapillaris through pigment epithelial cells into the subretinal space and the retinal interstitium only when the pigment epithelial cells or intercellular junctions are abnormal, as in central serous chorioretinopathy. Thus, patterns of hyperfluorescence combined with stereoscopic images yield valuable information about leakage from retinal vessels or from abnormal pigment epithelium. Abnormalities observed with FA can be grouped into 3 categories, associated with one of the following types of fluorescence:

- autofluorescence
- hypofluorescence
- hyperfluorescence

Autofluorescence is fluorescence that appears before the fluorescein dye is injected; it is caused by naturally highly reflective substances such as optic disc drusen. *Hypofluorescence* occurs when normal fluorescence is reduced or absent; it is present in 2 major patterns:

- vascular filling defect
- blocked fluorescence

Vascular filling defects are those in which retinal or choroidal vessels cannot fill, as in nonperfusion of an artery, vein, or capillary in the retina or choroid. These defects show either a delay in or complete absence of filling of the involved vessels. *Blocked fluorescence* occurs when the stimulation or visualization of the fluorescein is blocked by fibrous tissue or another barrier, such as pigment or blood, obstructing normal retinal or choroidal fluorescence in the area.

Blocked fluorescence is easily differentiated from hypofluorescence that is caused by hypoperfusion by ophthalmoscopy, which may show that a lesion corresponds to the area of blocked fluorescence. If it does not correspond, the problem is likely a vascular filling defect rather than blocked fluorescence. The depth of a lesion can be determined by relating the level of the blocked fluorescence to details of the retinal circulation. For example, when lesions block the choroidal circulation but retinal vessels are present on top of this blocking defect, then the lesions are located above the choroid and below the retinal vessels.

*Hyper*fluorescence occurs when there is an excess of normal fluorescence; it is present in several major patterns:

- leakage
- staining
- pooling
- transmission, or window, defect
- autofluorescence

Leakage refers to a gradual, marked increase in fluorescence throughout the study; it results from seepage of fluorescein molecules through the pigment epithelium into the subretinal space or neurosensory retina, out of retinal blood vessels into the retinal interstitium, or from retinal neovascularization into the vitreous. The borders of hyperfluorescence become increasingly blurred, and the greatest intensity of hyperfluorescence is found in the late phases of the study, when the only fluorescein dye remaining in the eye is extravascular. Leakage occurs, for example, in CNV (Fig 2-1), in diabetic macular edema (via microaneurysms or intraretinal microvascular abnormalities [IRMAs]), and in neo-vascularization of the disc.

Staining refers to a pattern of hyperfluorescence in which the fluorescence gradually increases in intensity through transit views and persists in late views, but its borders remain fixed throughout the study. Staining results from fluorescein entry into a solid tissue or material that retains the fluorescein, such as a scar, drusen, optic nerve tissue, or sclera (see Fig 2-1B).

Pooling refers to the accumulation of fluorescein in a fluid-filled space in the retina or choroid. At the beginning of the study, the fluid in the space contains no fluorescein and is invisible. As fluorescein leaks into the space, the margins of the space trap the fluorescein and appear distinct, as seen, for example, in an RPE detachment in central serous chorioretinopathy (Fig 2-2). As more fluorescein enters the space, the entire area fluoresces.

A *transmission defect,* or *window defect,* refers to a view of the normal choroidal fluorescence through a defect in the pigment or loss of pigment in the RPE, such as shown in Figures 2-1A and 2-1B. In a transmission defect, the hyperfluorescence occurs early, corresponding to filling of the choroidal circulation, and reaches its greatest intensity with the peak of choroidal filling. The fluorescence does not increase in intensity or shape and usually fades in the late phases, as the choroidal fluorescence becomes diluted by blood that does not contain fluorescein. The fluorescein remains in the choroid and does not enter the retina.

Autofluorescence describes the appearance of fluorescence from the fundus captured *before* intravenous fluorescein injection. It delineates structures that fluoresce naturally, such as optic nerve drusen and lipofuscin.

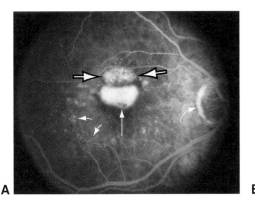 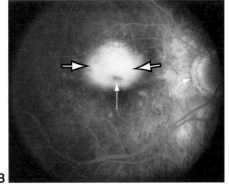

A **B**

Figure 2-1 Classic and occult CNV in age-related macular degeneration. **A,** Early-phase angiogram demonstrates classic CNV *(solid straight arrow)* and the boundaries of occult CNV *(open arrows). Small curved arrows* show a slight transmission of fluorescence (window defect) from drusen. The *large curved arrow* shows transmission resulting from RPE atrophy around the optic nerve. **B,** Late-phase angiogram demonstrates leakage of dye from classic CNV *(solid straight arrow)* and occult CNV *(open arrows).* The transmission of fluorescence from drusen (see the *small curved arrows* in **A**) has faded. The *large curved arrow* shows staining of the sclera around the optic nerve. *(Reproduced with permission from Bressler SB. Management of a small area of choroidal neovascularization in an eye with age-related macular degeneration [AMD] and relatively good visual acuity. The Wilmer Retina Update. 1995;1:3–7.)*

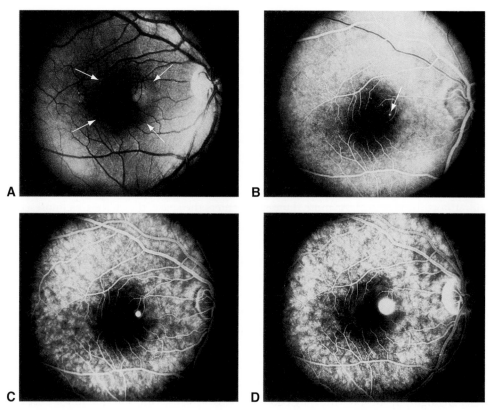

Figure 2-2 Images of typical central serous chorioretinopathy. **A,** The red-free, black-and-white photograph of the right macula reveals a well-demarcated serous detachment of the sensory retina *(arrows)*. **B,** Early transit frame of the angiogram reveals the pinpoint focus of hyperfluorescence, indicating early fluorescein leakage *(arrow)* through the RPE, nasal to the foveal avascular zone. **C,** A late-venous-phase frame of the angiogram reveals increasing fluorescence from continuing leakage. **D,** A later frame of the angiogram demonstrates pooling of fluorescein in a pigment epithelial detachment. Also note the mild hyperfluorescence caused by generalized staining of the serous fluid beneath the sensory retina. The RPE outside the fovea typically is mottled and hyperfluorescent.

Adverse effects of fluorescein angiography

All patients injected with fluorescein have temporary yellowing of the skin and conjunctiva, lasting 6–12 hours after injection, as well as orange-yellow discoloration of the urine, which lasts 24–36 hours. Fluorescein is a relatively safe, injectable drug. Adverse effects include

- nausea, vomiting, or vasovagal reactions, which are associated with approximately 10% of injections; more severe vasovagal reactions, including bradycardia, hypotension, shock, and syncope, are rare
- extravasation with subcutaneous granuloma, toxic neuritis, or local tissue necrosis—these are extremely rare
- urticarial *(anaphylactoid)* reactions in about 1% of cases
- *anaphylactic* reactions (cardiovascular shock) at a rate of probably less than 1 in 100,000 injections

Prior urticarial reactions increase a patient's risk of having a similar reaction after subsequent injections; however, premedicating the individual with antihistamines, corticosteroids, or both decreases the risk.

If the dye extravasates into the skin during injection, local pain may develop. Ice-cold compresses should be placed on the affected area for 5–10 minutes. The patient may be reassessed over hours or days as necessary until the edema, pain, and redness resolve. Although teratogenic effects have not been identified, many ophthalmologists avoid using FA in pregnant women in the first trimester unless absolutely necessary. Also of note, fluorescein is transmitted to breast milk in lactating women. Lower doses of fluorescein should be used in patients with renal insufficiency.

Berkow JW, Flower RW, Orth DH, Kelley JS. *Fluorescein and Indocyanine Green Angiography: Technique and Interpretation.* 2nd ed. Ophthalmology Monograph 5. San Francisco: American Academy of Ophthalmology; 1997.

Kwiterovich KA, Maguire MG, Murphy RP, et al. Frequency of adverse systemic reactions after fluorescein angiography: results of a prospective study. *Ophthalmology.* 1991;98(7): 1139–1142.

Indocyanine Green Angiography

Indocyanine green (ICG) is a water-soluble, tricarbocyanine dye with a molecular weight of 775 that is almost completely protein-bound (98%) after intravenous injection. Because the dye is protein-bound, diffusion through the small fenestrations of the choriocapillaris is limited. The intravascular retention of ICG, coupled with low permeability, makes ICG angiography ideal for imaging choroidal vessels. ICG is metabolized in the liver and excreted into the bile.

ICG fluoresces in the near-infrared range (790–805 nm). Thus, it can be injected immediately before or after FA. Because its fluorescence efficacy is only 4% that of fluorescein dye, ICG can be detected only with specialized infrared video angiography using modified fundus cameras, a digital imaging system, or a scanning laser ophthalmoscope (SLO). ICG angiography uses a diode laser illumination system with an output of 805 nm and barrier filters at 500 and 810 nm. With advances in computer technology, high-speed ICG angiography can produce up to 30 frames per second in a continuous recording of the angiogram. This system has been used to help visualize structures that appear only briefly during the angiogram, such as feeder vessels of CNV. In addition, confocal SLO can eliminate out-of-focus reflections from the ocular media by using a confocal filter in the imaging path, which improves imaging contrast and speed. Newer systems can even obtain fluorescein angiographic and ICG images simultaneously.

Because of its longer operating wavelength, a theoretical advantage of ICG is its ability to fluoresce better through pigment, fluid, lipid, and hemorrhage than fluorescein dye, thereby increasing the detection of abnormalities that may be blocked by an overlying thin, subretinal hemorrhage or hyperplastic RPE such as CNV. This feature allows enhanced imaging of occult CNV and pigment epithelial detachments. CNV appears on ICG angiograms as a plaque, a focal hot spot, or a combination of both. *Plaques* are formed by late-staining vessels and usually correspond to occult CNV. *Focal hot spots* are well-delineated fluorescent spots less than 1 disc diameter in size; their presence often suggests retinal angiomatous proliferations (RAP) or polypoidal vasculopathy, the latter of which is a variant of CNV. However, ICG angiographic imaging of eyes with these features has not consistently produced patterns of well-defined CNV that resemble the traditional CNV imaged by FA.

ICG angiography also delineates the abnormal aneurysmal outpouchings of the inner choroidal vascular network representing idiopathic polypoidal choroidal vasculopathy as well as the focal areas of choroidal hyperpermeability in central serous chorioretinopathy. It also differentiates abnormal vasculature in intraocular tumors and distinguishes the abnormal fluorescence patterns of choroidal inflammatory conditions such as serpiginous choroidopathy, acute multifocal placoid pigment epitheliopathy (AMPPE), multiple evanescent white dot syndrome (MEWDS), birdshot retinochoroidopathy, and multifocal choroiditis.

Indications for ICG angiography may include the following:

- CNV
- pigment epithelial detachment
- polypoidal choroidal vasculopathy
- RAP
- central serous chorioretinopathy
- intraocular tumors
- choroidal inflammatory conditions

Adverse effects of indocyanine green angiography

ICG appears to have a lower rate of adverse effects than fluorescein dye. Unlike for fluorescein dye, nausea and vomiting are rare. Mild adverse events occur in less than 1% of patients. Allergic reactions are less frequent with ICG than with fluorescein, but the dye should be used with caution in individuals with a history of allergy to iodides or shellfish because ICG contains 5% iodide. Angiographic facilities should have emergency plans and establish protocols to manage complications associated with either fluorescein or ICG administration. Contraindications to ICG may include liver disease or use of the drug metformin to control type 2 diabetes.

American Academy of Ophthalmology. Indocyanine green angiography. *Ophthalmology.* 1998;105(8):1564–1569.

Hope-Ross M, Yannuzzi LA, Gragoudas ES, et al. Adverse reactions due to indocyanine green. *Ophthalmology.* 1994;101(3):529–533.

Optical Coherence Tomography

Optical coherence tomography (OCT) is a noninvasive, noncontact imaging modality that produces micrometer-resolution, cross-sectional images of ocular tissue. OCT is based on imaging reflected light (Fig 2-3). The technique produces a 2-dimensional image of the backscattered light from different layers in the retina, analogous to ultrasonic B-scan and radar imaging. The only difference is that OCT, using the principle of low-coherence interferometry, measures optical rather than acoustic or radio wave reflectivity. Using light instead of sound, the resolution is enhanced and the speed is much

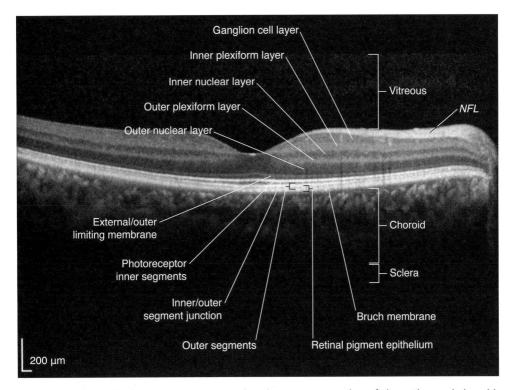

Figure 2-3 Optical coherence tomogram, showing a cross section of the retina and choroid. NFL = nerve fiber layer. *(Courtesy of Colin A. McCannel, MD.)*

greater. Current commercial OCT scanners offer a resolution of 8–10 μm that is at least 10 times better than ultrasound. More advanced OCT imaging, such as spectral-domain (SD) technology, delivers a 100-fold improvement in speed over time-domain OCT scanners. With SD-OCT images, the axial resolution is typically less than 7 μm, represented by 2048 pixels per A-scan, and the scan velocity is 18,000–55,000 A-scans per second. Thus, with SD-OCT, images are captured faster with higher resolution and with reduced motion artifact. In addition, a large amount of image data is obtained at each session, allowing for intricate 3-D reconstruction and point-to-point registration for better reproducibility during follow-up scans. Furthermore, the density of scans over a given area is greater, resulting in far fewer imaging gaps throughout the posterior pole, reducing the likelihood of missing subtle retinal defects.

OCT single-scan, cross-sectional views (tomograms) of the retina appear similar to histologic specimens and have been termed "optical biopsies" (Fig 2-4). Tissues with higher reflectivity, such as the RPE, appear in brighter colors (red-white); less reflective structures, such as the vitreous and intraretinal fluid, appear in darker colors (blue-black). OCT is useful for differentiating lamellar from pseudo- and full-thickness macular holes, diagnosing vitreomacular traction syndrome, differentiating various presentations of traction-related diabetic macular edema, monitoring the course of central serous chorioretinopathy, making treatment decisions in the management of age-related macular

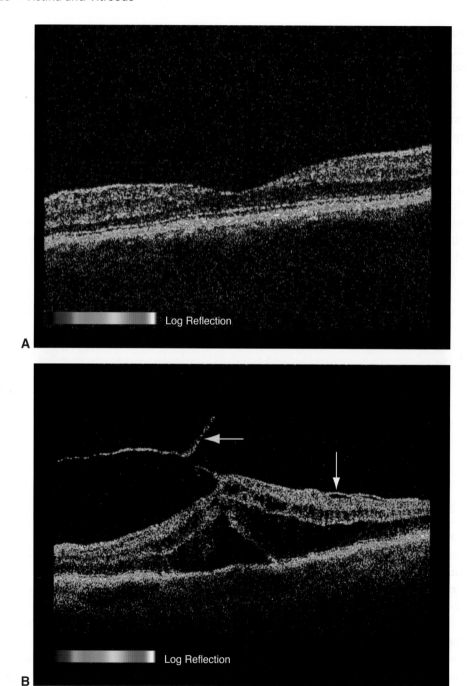

Figure 2-4 Optical coherence tomography (OCT). **A,** OCT scan showing normal foveal depression and retinal thickness. Note that the RPE/Bruch membrane appears red and the vitreous appears dark. **B,** Scan of a patient with diabetic macular edema and vitreous traction. Note the posterior hyaloid *(yellow arrow)* pulling on the retina, a fine epiretinal membrane *(white arrow)* on the retinal surface, and the increased retinal thickness. *(Courtesy of Peter K. Kaiser, MD.)*

degeneration (AMD), and evaluating eyes for subtle subretinal fluid that is not visible with FA. A benefit of higher-resolution systems is the ability to better delineate retinal layers, including the internal, middle, and external limiting membranes and the junction between the inner and outer photoreceptor segments.

OCT can also produce a retinal thickness map. The OCT software automatically determines the inner and outer retinal boundaries and produces a false-color topographic map showing areas of increased thickening in brighter colors and areas of lesser thickening in darker colors. An assessment of macular volume can also be obtained from the retinal thickness map. By evaluating differences in retinal volume over time, the clinician can judge the efficacy of therapy. Time-domain OCT produces retinal thickness maps from 6 × 6-mm radial scans centered on the fovea, with interpolation between the scan lines, to produce a map of the macula. In contrast, Fourier-domain OCT can image the entire macula through its increased scanning speed and improved accuracy of thickness and volume measurements; it also improves registration, allowing for repeated imaging of the same area during follow-up visits.

Dillworth B, Kagemann L, Wollstein G, et al. From the operator's perspective. In: Schuman JS, Puliafito CA, Fujimoto JG, eds. *Everyday OCT*. Thorofare, NJ: Slack; 2006:1–3.

Hee MR, Puliafito CA, Wong C, et al. Optical coherence tomography of macular holes. *Ophthalmology*. 1995;102(5):748–756.

Hee MR, Puliafito CA, Wong C, et al. Quantitative assessment of macular edema with optical coherence tomography. *Arch Ophthalmol*. 1995;113(8):1019–1029.

Huang D, Swanson EA, Lin CP, et al. Optical coherence tomography. *Science*. 1991;254(5035): 1178–1181.

Kiernan DF, Mieler WF, Hariprasad SM. Spectral-domain optical coherence tomography: a comparison of modern high-resolution retinal imaging systems. *Am J Ophthalmol*. 2010;149(1):18–31.

Scanning Laser Ophthalmoscopy

A confocal SLO uses a near-infrared (675 nm) diode laser beam that rapidly scans the posterior pole in a raster fashion—similar to the way in which a television creates an image on a monitor. The reflected light is detected by a confocal photodiode that is conjugate to the retinal plane, and the digitized image is stored in a computer. The confocal filter ensures that only light reflected from the narrow spot illuminated by the laser is recorded.

Stereoscopic high-contrast images can be produced with and without dyes such as fluorescein or ICG, and altering the laser wavelength permits selective examination of different tissue depths. The SLO is capable of imaging structures at very high magnification and high frame rate, which allows accurate diagnosis of retinal structures poorly imaged by ordinary fundus cameras, and it does so using low levels of light exposure and improved contrast. In addition, a topographic 3-dimensional map with optical slices can be made digitally from 32 consecutive and equidistant optical section images obtained from the SLO. From this topographic map, retinal thickness can be estimated. Clinically, however, SLO has been used more in the objective evaluation of the surface contour of the optic nerve head in glaucoma than in the diagnosis of retinal disease.

Infrared imaging is utilized with OCT. It demonstrates different layers of the retina and is highly efficient at imaging separate layers of the retina.

Freeman WR, Bartsch DU, Mueller AJ, Banker AS, Weinreb RN. Simultaneous indocyanine green and fluorescein angiography using a confocal scanning laser ophthalmoscope. *Arch Ophthalmol.* 1998;116(4):455–463.

Ip MS, Duker JS. Advances in posterior segment imaging techniques. *Focal Points: Clinical Modules for Ophthalmologists.* San Francisco: American Academy of Ophthalmology; 1999, module 7.

Fundus Autofluorescence

Fundus autofluorescence (AF) is a rapid, noncontact, noninvasive way to evaluate RPE function. Autofluorescence is the intrinsic fluorescence emitted by a substance after being stimulated by excitation energy. Ocular structures that normally autofluoresce include the corneal epithelium and endothelium and lens, macular, and RPE pigments. Some pathologic conditions that autofluoresce are optic nerve drusen, and in Best disease, subretinal deposits from photoreceptor outer segments. The clinical use of fundus AF relies on the fact that the predominant source of autofluorescence in the macula is lipofuscin. When the RPE phagocytoses photoreceptor outer segments, which consist of retinoids, fatty acids, and proteins, lipofuscin accumulates as an oxidative by-product within the RPE cells. The pigment within lipofuscin that causes autofluorescence is A2E, named for its derivation from 2 molecules of vitamin A aldehyde and 1 molecule of ethanolamine. A loss of RPE cells has been shown to be accompanied by substantial loss of autofluorescent content.

Fundus AF can be imaged using an SLO that uses blue laser excitation (488 nm) and a 500-nm barrier filter to isolate light from other ocular autofluorescent structures. By examining fundus AF images and thus lipofuscin accumulation, clinicians can evaluate selected pathologies of the RPE. For example, with the loss of RPE containing lipofuscin, areas of geographic atrophy appear dark with AF. Surrounding this dark area is a ring of increased autofluorescence due to pathologic lipofuscin accumulation. Some evidence suggests that such hyper-autofluorescence, especially at the edge of this dark area, may predict expansion of geographic atrophy. Autofluorescence has also been helpful in assessing RPE in exudative AMD and can consistently delineate serous pigment epithelial detachment. However, reports on the use of AF in the diagnosis and management of AMD are preliminary at best and sometimes conflicting. Further data are also needed to clarify the relationship of AF patterns to the formation and expansion of geographic atrophy.

Spaide RF. Fundus autofluorescence and age-related macular degeneration. *Ophthalmology.* 2003;110(2):392–399.

Infrared Reflectance Imaging

Some SD-OCT devices use an infrared (IR), or more precisely near-infrared (NIR) spectrum scanning laser to generate an image of the fundus. NIR, also known as infrared A, light is the initial third of the infrared spectrum (approximately 700–1400 nm). NIR reflectance images provide different information from that provided by red-free, color photography, blue-light, or NIR autofluorescence images. Differences include that NIR reflectance imaging demonstrates more clearly some abnormalities of the outer retina, RPE, and Bruch membrane, as well as the presence of subretinal fluid. This difference results from the ocular tissue's different absorption characteristics for visible light versus for light of longer wavelengths such as NIR. Lesions of acute macular neuroretinopathy are extremely difficult to appreciate on fundus photographs, a characteristic of the condition, and are much more easily visible with NIR reflectance imaging. Similarly, the presence of subretinal fluid in central serous chorioretinopathy is difficult to appreciate on fundus photographs but is quite apparent with IR reflectance imaging (Fig 2-5).

Fundus Near-Infrared Autofluorescence

Near-infrared fundus AF (NIA) imaging (with excitation, 787 nm; emission, >800 nm) is an alternative imaging technology. The fluorophore is thought to be melanin, and RPE cells contribute the majority of the signal compared with the choroidal cells. Fundus characteristics of disease states imaged with NIA are somewhat different from those revealed by fundus AF. One major difference is that subretinal fluid causes much greater signal attenuation in NIA than in fundus AF. This difference is believed to stem from the more pronounced scattering of NIR light than of the AF signal in the subretinal fluid. NIR AF imaging is less commonly used than fundus AF imaging. There is considerable interest in AF imaging in general, however, as it appears to demonstrate some pathologic changes more precisely and reproducibly than a clinical examination or a standard fundus photograph can, and may therefore be of value in longitudinal studies of disease progression.

Kellner U, Kellner S, Weinitz S. Fundus autofluorescence (488 NM) and near-infrared autofluorescence (787 NM) visualize different retinal pigment epithelium alterations in patients with age-related macular degeneration. *Retina*. 2010;30(1):6–15.

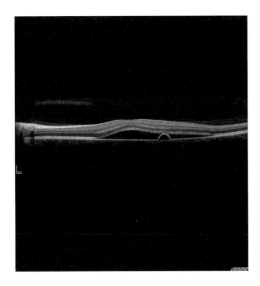

Figure 2-5 Optical coherence tomogram of central serous chorioretinopathy showing a small elevation of the pigment epithelium (pigment epithelial detachment, PED) and subretinal fluid. *(Courtesy of Adam Martidis, MD.)*

Conditions Commonly Diagnosed Using Imaging Technology

Imaging technology is commonly used to diagnose the following conditions:

- CNV
- chorioretinal inflammatory conditions
- subretinal fluid accumulation
- retinal perfusion abnormalities
- macular edema
- vitreomacular interface changes

CHAPTER 3

Retinal Physiology and Psychophysics

Clinical electrophysiologic and psychophysical testing allows for assessment of nearly the entire length of the visual pathway. Most electrophysiologic tests are of evoked responses. By adjusting stimulus conditions and techniques of recording, a representation can be made of the sequence of events along the visual pathway, from changes in the retinal pigment epithelium (RPE) to cortical potentials of the occipital lobes. However, because an abnormality at a proximal location usually gives an abnormal signal farther along the visual pathway, test results can be misleading if interpreted in isolation from the clinical findings or tests specific to other areas of the visual pathway. For instance, an abnormal visually evoked response might be found in macular degeneration or a cone dystrophy, but it could be misinterpreted as a central pathway conduction defect unless a fundus examination or an *electroretinogram (ERG)* is also performed. A careful history and eye examination done before electrophysiologic and psychophysical tests are ordered help the clinician determine the appropriate tests and thus increase the tests' usefulness in diagnosing the level of dysfunction. BCSC Section 5, *Neuro-Ophthalmology,* discusses and illustrates the entire visual pathway.

> Fishman GA, Birch DG, Holder GE, Brigell MG. *Electrophysiologic Testing in Disorders of the Retina, Optic Nerve, and Visual Pathway.* Ophthalmology Monograph 2. 2nd ed. San Francisco: American Academy of Ophthalmology; 2001.
> Ogden TE. Clinical electrophysiology. In: Ryan SJ, Hinton DR, Schachat AP, Wilkinson CP, eds. *Retina.* 4th ed. Philadelphia: Elsevier/Mosby; 2006:351–371.

Electroretinogram

Recording and Interpreting the Response

The clinical ERG is a mass response evoked from the entire retina by a brief flash of light. Five different responses are the basis of most clinical evaluations and are standardized internationally so that ERG results can be interpreted easily at different medical centers (Fig 3-1):

1. "rod response" (scotopic; dark-adapted)
2. maximal combined response (dark-adapted)

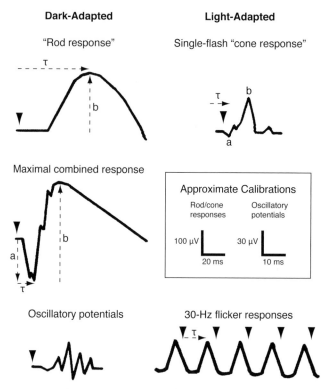

Figure 3-1 Diagram of the 5 basic ERG responses defined by the International Standard for Electroretinography. These waveforms and calibrations are exemplary only, as there is a moderate range of normal values. The *large arrowheads* indicate the stimulus flash, and the *dashed lines* show how to measure a-wave and b-wave amplitude and time-to-peak (implicit time, τ). The implicit time of a flicker response is normally less than the distance between peaks for stimulation at 30 Hz. *(Modified from Marmor MF, Zrenner E. Standard for clinical electroretinography [1994 update]. Doc Ophthalmol. 1995;89(3):199–210.)*

3. oscillatory potentials (dark-adapted)
4. single-flash "cone response" (photopic; light-adapted)
5. 30-Hz flicker responses (light-adapted)

In general, the ERG is characterized by a negative waveform *(a-wave)* that represents the response of the photoreceptors, followed by a positive waveform *(b-wave)* generated by a combination of cells in the Müller/bipolar cell layer. The entire response usually lasts less than 150 milliseconds. A-wave amplitude is measured from baseline to the a-wave trough; b-wave amplitude is measured from the a-wave trough to the b-wave peak. The implicit time (τ), the time to reach a peak, is measured from the onset of the stimulus to the trough of the a-wave or the peak of the b-wave. Figure 3-1 shows typical response amplitudes and durations, but normal values vary with recording technique and should be provided by each laboratory. The use of standardized conditions is essential for meaningful interpretation of the ERG because variations in lighting and recording conditions, the intensity of flashes, or the degree of light and dark adaptation can all greatly affect the test results.

Use of a corneal contact lens electrode to record the ERG gives the most accurate and reproducible results. The pupils should be dilated and light flashes presented full-field to the entire retina. A bowl similar to that of a perimeter is used to illuminate the entire retina. Signals are evoked either by a single flash or by repetitive flashes (with computer averaging if available). To record light-adapted (photopic) ERGs, a uniform background light is projected within the bowl. It is important, especially in evaluating hereditary and other retinal degenerations, to test the rod and cone systems separately.

The 5 responses are obtained as follows:

1. *Rod response:* The rod response *(scotopic)* ERG shown in Figure 3-1 is produced by dark-adapting the patient for at least 20 minutes and stimulating the retina with a dim white flash that is below the cone threshold. The resulting waveform has a prominent b-wave but almost no detectable a-wave.
2. *Maximal combined response* (dark-adapted bright flash): A larger waveform is generated by using a bright flash in the dark-adapted state, which maximally stimulates both cones and rods and results in large a- and b-wave amplitudes with oscillatory potentials superimposed on the ascending b-wave.
3. *Oscillatory potentials:* These (dark-adapted) responses can be isolated by filtering out the slower ERG components. Oscillatory potentials are believed to be the result of feedback interactions among the integrative cells of the inner retina. They are reduced in retinal ischemic states and in some forms of congenital stationary night blindness.
4. *Single-flash cone response:* The *photopic* ERG is obtained by maintaining the patient in a light-adapted state and stimulating the retina with a bright white flash. The rods are suppressed by light adaptation and do not contribute to the waveform.
5. *30-Hz flicker response:* Light-adapted cone responses can also be elicited with a flickering stimulus light. In theory, rods can respond to a stimulus up to 20 Hz, or cycles per second, although in most clinical situations, 8 Hz is their practical limit. Thus, a stimulus rate of 30 Hz is used to screen out the rod response and measure cone responses.

ERG interpretation

Examples of ERG patterns in specific diseases are illustrated in Figure 3-2. The ERG evoked by a full-field (ganzfeld) stimulus measures the response of the entire retina, but retinal cells are unevenly distributed; the density of cones is very high in the fovea and macula, whereas rods are most numerous about 15° away from the fovea. It might seem intuitive that the ERG would distinguish between macular and peripheral lesions on the basis of cone and rod signals. However, this is *not* true. Even though cones are more populous in the fovea, fully 90% of them lie peripheral to the macula.

In a patient with a large atrophic macular lesion and an otherwise normal retina, the photopic (cone) ERG b-wave amplitude would be reduced by only about 10%. This small decrease is not recognizable clinically because the range of normal values for the ERG

Electroretinogram Patterns

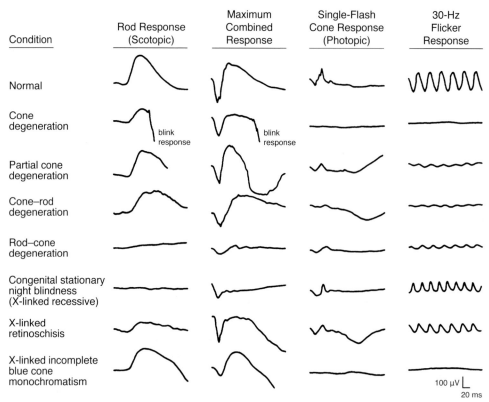

Condition	Rod Response (Scotopic)	Maximum Combined Response	Single-Flash Cone Response (Photopic)	30-Hz Flicker Response
Normal				
Cone degeneration				
Partial cone degeneration				
Cone–rod degeneration				
Rod–cone degeneration				
Congenital stationary night blindness (X-linked recessive)				
X-linked retinoschisis				
X-linked incomplete blue cone monochromatism				

Figure 3-2 Examples of ERG changes in retinal diseases. Note that some diseases are selective for the cone system, the rod system, or the inner retina (b-wave).

varies widely. Conversely, when a patient with a macular lesion has a reduced photopic ERG, the patient must have a diffuse degeneration affecting cones in the extra-areal periphery. Because the ERG measures a panretinal response, it does not necessarily correlate with visual acuity, which is a function of the fovea.

A number of factors may influence the amplitude and timing of the normal ERG, including the intensity of the stimulus, pupil size, and the area of retina stimulated. The ERG is relatively insensitive to refractive error, except for eyes with high myopia, which can have somewhat reduced signals but generally not to the extent shown by patients with hereditary retinal degeneration. Elderly individuals often show signals that are slightly reduced in amplitude compared with signals from a younger population. Newborns have a small ERG signal, which rises rapidly in the first few months of life to a magnitude that allows most clinical distinctions to be made. Debate continues as to whether optic nerve lesions occasionally enhance the ERG, possibly because centrifugal inhibitory signals are interrupted.

Marmor MF, Zrenner E. Standard for clinical electroretinography (1994 update). *Doc Ophthalmol.* 1995;89(3):199–210.

Specialized Types of ERG

Early receptor potentials and c-wave

The *early receptor potential (ERP)* is a small response that occurs with no detectable latency before the a-wave (Fig 3-3). It is evoked by an intense stimulus flash and has been, in part, correlated with electrical changes in the cell membrane that occur during the conversion of lumirhodopsin to metarhodopsin. (This process is discussed and illustrated in Chapter 13, Retina, of BCSC Section 2, *Fundamentals and Principles of Ophthalmology.*) In humans, 60%–80% of the ERP amplitude is generated by cones. The ERP has been used primarily in research settings to measure visual-pigment bleaching and regeneration.

The *c-wave* is a late positive response occurring 2–4 seconds after the stimulus and is generated by the RPE. It is discussed later in this chapter in conjunction with other RPE responses.

Focal and multifocal ERG testing

It is possible to stimulate only the foveal or the parafoveal cones while presenting a bright light on the rest of the retina to suppress the rod system and prevent interference. A rapidly flickering stimulus is typically used so that several hundred small ERG responses can be summated. *Foveal ERG testing* is used primarily for cases in which the physical findings do not correlate clearly with a patient's loss of acuity. The foveal ERG can provide objective information about the presence or absence of organic disease in the macula.

A topographic ERG map of the retina can be produced using a specialized technology known as *multifocal ERG*. Multifocal ERG tests cone-generated responses that subtend 25° radially from fixation. For patients with stable and accurate fixation, results of this test can determine objectively whether macular dysfunction is present—for example, in the early detection of hydroxychloroquine toxicity (Fig 3-4). Such tests may also help evaluate or compare treatment responses in various macular conditions.

Bright-flash ERG

The ability to perform vitrectomies and repair severely traumatized globes has encouraged the evaluation of retinal function in eyes with opaque media. The *bright-flash ERG* is performed with a flash stimulus that is brighter than usual, generated by a high-intensity photographic strobe. An unrecordable ERG indicates widespread retinal damage and a poor prognosis, whereas a moderate signal (eg, 50 μV) suggests that some salvageable retina remains. The test gives no direct information about visual acuity or possible damage to the optic nerve.

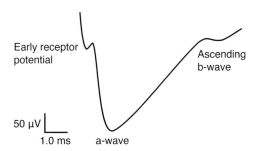

Early receptor potential

Ascending b-wave

50 μV

1.0 ms a-wave

Figure 3-3 Early receptor potential (ERP). The response is very small and occurs before the a-wave. *(Modified from Berson EL, Goldstein EB. Early receptor potential in dominantly inherited retinitis pigmentosa. Arch Ophthalmol. 1970;83(4):412–420.)*

Field View

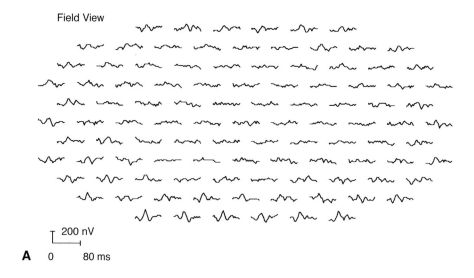

A   0   80 ms   200 nV

Field View

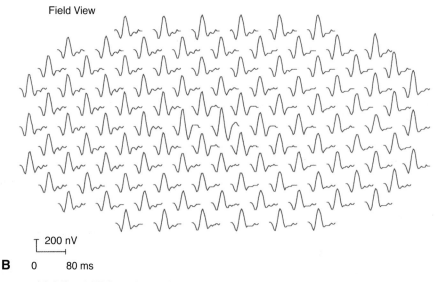

B   0   80 ms   200 nV

Figure 3-4   Multifocal ERG tracings of the right eye of a patient with hydroxychloroquine toxicity. The central macular region has marked decreased waveform amplitudes **(A)** compared with the reference traces **(B)**. *(Courtesy of Carl Regillo, MD.)*

Pattern ERG

The *pattern ERG (PERG)* can be elicited from the retina by an alternating checkerboard stimulus presented to the central retina. The responses to several hundred stimuli (alternations) are averaged to obtain a measurable signal (Fig 3-5). The PERG correlates with the integrity of the optic nerve and thus gives information about the ganglion cells and their retinal interactions. Initial work suggested that comparison of the focal ERG and PERG might distinguish between outer and inner retinal pathology and that the PERG

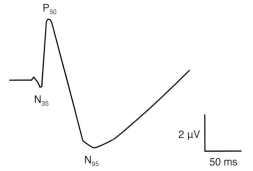

Figure 3-5 Diagram of the pattern ERG (PERG), elicited by alternation of a checkerboard pattern. The major negative (N) and positive (P) waves are labeled according to their typical latencies. *(Reprinted by permission of Kluwer Academic Publishers from Marmor MF, Holder GE, Porciatti V, Trick GL, Zrenner E. Guidelines for basic pattern electroretinography. Recommendations by the International Society for Clinical Electrophysiology of Vision. Doc Ophthalmol. 1995–1996;91(4):291–298.)*

could be a specific test for the early recognition of glaucoma. In practice, however, the PERG has proven difficult to record reproducibly, and the signals have proven very sensitive to confounding factors such as blurring of retinal images (including cataract) and maculopathy. PERGs are typically recorded with a conductive fiber or foil electrode that touches the cornea.

Fishman GA, Birch DG, Holder GE, Brigell MG. *Electrophysiologic Testing in Disorders of the Retina, Optic Nerve, and Visual Pathway.* Ophthalmology Monograph 2. 2nd ed. San Francisco: American Academy of Ophthalmology; 2001.

Scholl HP, Zrenner E. Electrophysiology in the investigation of acquired retinal disorders. *Surv Ophthalmol.* 2000;45(1):29–47.

Tzekov R. Ocular toxicity due to chloroquine and hydroxychloroquine: electrophysiological and visual function correlates. *Doc Ophthalmol.* 2005;110(1):111–120.

Applications and Cautions

The ERG is important for diagnosing and following the course of retinal dystrophies and degenerations (see Chapter 11, Table 11-1). Although not a direct measure of macular function (because it is a mass response), the ERG can be invaluable in determining whether or not pathology is limited to the macula. Macular disorders with peripheral involvement have more serious visual implications for the patient. The ERG is also useful in assessing disorders of dark adaptation, color vision, and visual acuity, and it may be a part of the evaluation of hysteria or malingering.

The ERG can often help distinguish between retinal damage caused by diffuse disease, such as a hereditary dystrophy or drug toxicity, and that caused by focal disease, such as branch vascular occlusion or regional uveitic damage. Panretinal disorders not only reduce ERG amplitude but also cause delayed and abnormal waveforms that reflect the malfunction of cells throughout the retina (Fig 3-6). Focal disease, which typically has a better long-term prognosis, reduces ERG amplitude in proportion to the area of damaged retina, but the remaining signal from healthy areas of retina shows normal waveform and timing. ERG timing is most easily assessed using the 30-Hz flicker response, which normally shows a b-wave implicit time (stimulus-to-peak interval) of less than 32 milliseconds.

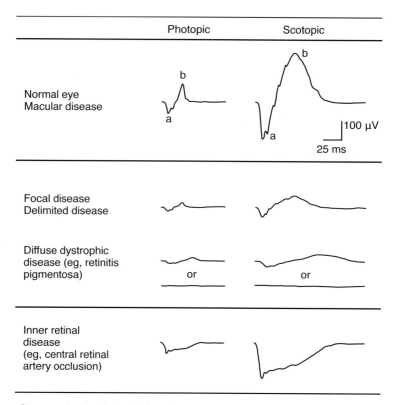

Figure 3-6 Characteristics of the ERG patterns with different types of retinal damage. Disease that damages only parts of the retina reduces the ERG amplitude, but the unaffected areas of retina produce a normal waveform. Diffuse disease leads to responses that are delayed as well as reduced in amplitude. Inner retinal disease may selectively diminish the b-wave. *(Reprinted with permission from Marmor MF. The management of retinitis pigmentosa and allied diseases.* Ophthalmol Digest. *1979;41:13–29.)*

The ERG can be useful in evaluating chronic ischemic damage from vascular disease. Retinal capillary loss or vascular insufficiency causes abnormalities of the b-wave and oscillatory potentials, such as a delay in the implicit time or a reduction of amplitude (Fig 3-7). Normally, the b-wave is larger in amplitude than the a-wave, and inversion of the b-wave:a-wave ratio or a delay in the 30-Hz cone flicker response is a potentially ominous sign in eyes with central retinal vein occlusion.

The ERG may aid in the detection of certain hereditary diseases in affected family members as well. Particularly in X-linked conditions, such as choroideremia, the fundus in female carriers is often a mosaic of normal and abnormal areas, and the ERG may show subtle abnormalities. The ERG may reveal retinal abnormalities in children long before symptoms or clear-cut ophthalmoscopic signs become evident. ERGs can be recorded in children of all ages, although interpretation can be difficult in the first few months of life, before adult waveforms have developed. Pediatric ERGs can be performed without general anesthesia, although oral sedation is sometimes necessary (Fig 3-8). Anesthesia can depress the ERG responses.

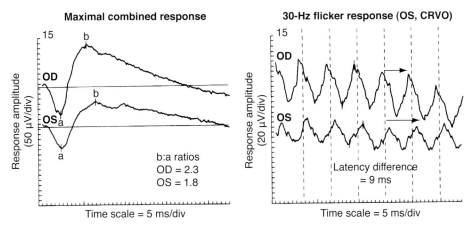

Figure 3-7 ERG in central retinal vein occlusion (CRVO). The right eye is normal. The affected left eye shows a mild reduction in b-wave amplitude but a striking delay in the latency of the flicker responses. The implicit time *(arrows)* of the responses from the left eye is longer than the interval between peaks, a sign that is strongly suggestive of diffuse damage to the retina. *(Modified from Breton ME, Quinn GE, Keene SS, Dahmen JC, Brucker AJ. Electroretinogram parameters at presentation as predictors of rubeosis in central retinal vein occlusion patients.* Ophthalmology. *1989;96(9):1343–1352.)*

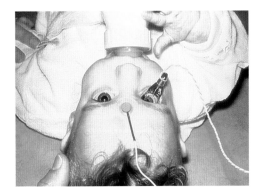

Figure 3-8 A 5-month-old infant with a contact lens electrode in place for ERG recording. The child was quite comfortable and required little restraint until the bottle was empty. *(Reprinted with permission from Marmor MF. Corneal electroretinograms in children without sedation.* J Pediatr Ophthalmol. *1976;13(2):112–116.)*

The ERG can also be used to estimate the extent of damage from trauma or drug toxicity. A reasonable ERG signal behind opaque media, especially when a bright flash is used, indicates that the retina is attached and functional. Cataracts do not appreciably affect the ERG, but the bright-flash technique is necessary for eyes filled with blood. The ERG can help determine whether a retained foreign body is causing siderosis or other toxic damage and can document damage from drugs such as thioridazine or chloroquine. A series of follow-up recordings may be needed to determine whether the damage is continuing and (in cases of trauma) to differentiate the toxic effects of a foreign body from the physical effects of an injury.

Johnson MA, Marcus S, Elman MJ, McPhee TJ. Neovascularization in central retinal vein occlusion: electroretinographic findings. *Arch Ophthalmol.* 1988;106(3):348–352.

Electro-oculogram and RPE Responses

Electro-oculogram

As described in Chapter 1, the RPE is a monolayer of cells that are linked by tight junctional girdles near the apical surface. These junctions separate the apical and basal membranes of the pigment epithelium, which have different ionic permeability characteristics that lead to the generation of a voltage differential across the cell (Fig 3-9). This voltage differential, called the *standing potential,* is positive at the cornea and measures 6–10 mV.

Although the RPE itself is not a light receptor, activation of the photoreceptors in the neurosensory retina can lead to changes in the ionic composition of the extracellular (subretinal) space or to the release of transmitter substances that produce an electrical response in the RPE. For example, when a dark-adapted eye is exposed to steady light, the standing potential across the RPE rises very slowly and reaches a peak 5–10 *minutes* after the onset of light. The voltage change of this *light response* originates across the basal membrane of the RPE. The substance that mediates between the capture of light by the photoreceptors and the slow voltage changes in the RPE remains unknown, although current evidence suggests that the messenger substance may be derived from the photoreceptors.

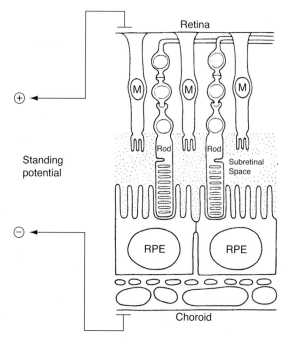

Figure 3-9 Electrical circuit of the standing potential. The RPE cells generate a voltage from apex to base because of the different ionic permeability characteristics on each surface and the presence of impermeable tight junctions between the cells. Changes in the voltage across the apical or basal RPE membrane are reflected in the standing potential and are measurable clinically as the c-wave on ERG or with electro-oculography. M = Müller cells. *(Modified from Steinberg RH. Monitoring communications between photoreceptors and pigment epithelial cells: effects of "mild" systemic hypoxia. Friedenwald Lecture.* Invest Ophthalmol Vis Sci. *1987;28(12):1888–1904.)*

The light response of the standing potential develops so slowly that it is hard to measure directly without artifacts from movement or electrical drift. To circumvent this problem, clinicians use the indirect technique of electro-oculography, in which electrodes are placed at either side of the eye (usually on the skin at the canthi), and the voltage differential between them is recorded as the patient looks back and forth (Fig 3-10). The amplitude of these voltage shifts is proportional to the actual voltage differential across the eye. An international standard technique for recording the *electro-oculogram (EOG)* defines the optimal placement of electrodes, the time of adaptation, and the intensity of the light stimulus, which depends on whether the pupils are dilated.

Arden proposed that, for clinical purposes, a ratio be derived from the highest point of the light peak standing potential and the lowest point of the baseline standing potential in the dark. This light–dark ratio, or Arden ratio, is normally 1.85 or above, although variation among individuals is considerable. Values below 1.85 are generally termed subnormal, and those less than about 1.30 are severely subnormal or nearly extinguished. The amplitude of the EOG is dominated by the rod system, and, like the ERG, the EOG is a mass response.

Arden GB, Constable PA. The electro-oculogram. *Prog Retin Eye Res.* 2006;25(2):207–248.

Ogden TE. Clinical electrophysiology. In: Ryan SJ, Hinton DR, Schachat AP, Wilkinson CP, eds. *Retina.* 4th ed. Philadelphia: Elsevier/Mosby; 2006:351–371.

Uses and limitations of EOG

The major limitation of the EOG as a clinical tool is that the origin and significance of this electrical response are not well understood. The EOG depends not only on the integrity

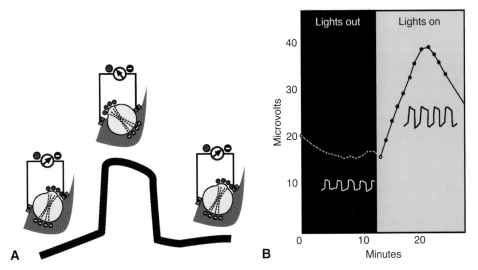

Figure 3-10 The clinical EOG. **A,** The voltage between skin electrodes at either side of an eye varies as the eye turns, in proportion to the size of the standing potential. **B,** Plot of the amplitude of the oscillations, showing how the standing potential diminishes to a trough in the dark and then rises to a peak after light is turned on. In clinical practice, the EOG is often evaluated as the ratio between this peak and trough. *(Modified from Arden GB, Fojas MR. Electrophysiological abnormalities in pigmentary degenerations of the retina. Assessment of value and basis. Arch Ophthalmol. 1962;68:369–389.)*

of the RPE but also on the activity of the photoreceptors and possibly of the inner retinal layers. Thus, the EOG is not useful for most disorders in which the retina itself is damaged; it is most specific for involvement of the RPE when other studies have shown the retina to be normal.

The relationship of the EOG to physiologic functions of the RPE is unclear because it does not correlate closely with either pigmentary changes in the RPE or visual function. For example, the EOG light–dark ratio is normal or only mildly subnormal in some diseases (eg, diffuse fundus flavimaculatus or pattern dystrophy) in which the RPE seems to be primarily involved. However, it is severely reduced in Best disease, in which most of the retina appears normal and functions well. In rubella retinopathy, the RPE can be diffusely altered, but the EOG is normal.

The EOG is most specific for diagnosing Best vitelliform dystrophy and any yellow lesions or macular scars that might be manifestations of this condition. Its use in evaluating diffuse RPE diseases is less clear because patients who show an abnormal EOG usually exhibit fundus changes that make the diagnosis. Some authors believe the EOG can be a sensitive indicator of early chloroquine toxicity, but others argue that mass electrical responses like the EOG or ERG are not sensitive to early toxicity. Serial testing or multifocal ERG may show early and progressive changes.

Cortical Evoked Potentials

Visually Evoked Potentials

The *visually evoked cortical potential (VECP;* also abbreviated *VEP* or *VER,* for *visually evoked potential* or *response)* is an electrical signal generated by the occipital visual cortex in response to stimulation of the retina by either light flashes or patterned stimuli (typically alternating checkerboards or stripes on a TV monitor). The response to many alternations (or flashes) is recorded and averaged. The use of a checkerboard stimulus is preferable when the eye is optically correctable because the occipital cortex is very sensitive to sharp edges and contrast, whereas it is relatively insensitive to diffuse light.

Because most of the visual cortex represents the central area of the retina, the VECP is primarily a method of determining macular function. There is some extra-areal retinal input, but it is minimal. Because the VECP represents the endpoint of the visual pathway, it can indicate an abnormality that is located anywhere from the retina to the cortex.

A normal pattern-evoked VECP is represented in Figure 3-11. The signal is recorded with electroencephalogram electrodes; often, recordings from the inion (back of the occiput) are compared with those from locations to its right and left, although different recording sites may be used in different laboratories. The VECP is characterized by 2 negative (N) and 2 positive (P) peaks, whose amplitude and implicit times depend on the check size, contrast, and alternation frequencies of the stimulus. Although absolute amplitudes of the VECP can be measured, using them as a clinical distinction is difficult because of variability among normal responses. The temporal (delay in peak appearance) aspect of the VECP is less variable and more reliable as a clinical measure.

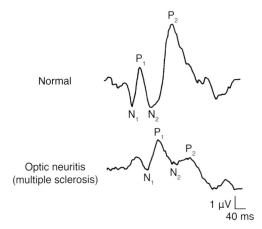

Figure 3-11 Visually evoked cortical responses showing a normal pattern *(top)* and one from a patient with optic neuropathy due to multiple sclerosis *(bottom)*. The diseased response shows not only reduced amplitude but marked delay in the appearance of the negative (N) and positive (P) peaks.

VECPs have mainly been used clinically to confirm the diagnosis of optic neuropathy and other demyelinating disease. They also have the following uses:

- assessing misprojection of optic nerve fibers, such as may occur in albinism, which produces asymmetric VECPs between left and right recording positions
- estimating visual acuity in infants and nonverbal children by using a checkerboard stimulus of decreasing size, in which increased visual acuity corresponds to responses to decreased stimuli
- detecting and locating visual field defects by comparing responses to stimuli in different locations
- evaluating the potential for improvement of visual acuity in patients with opacities of the ocular media

The VECP can also be an important tool in the detection of malingering.

Electrically Evoked Potentials

Responses in the visual system can be evoked by mechanical and electrical stimuli as well as by light. Passage of a small, brief electric current (roughly 0.5 mA) through the eye generates a neural signal that is transmitted to the visual cortex and causes a sensation of light (phosphene). The cortical response is recorded in a manner similar to that of the VECP and is an indicator of the integrity of the retina as well as the subsequent structural components of the visual pathway. The primary clinical use of the electrically evoked response is the functional evaluation and salvageability of traumatized eyes with hemorrhage and possible retinal detachment in which even the bright-flash ERG is unrecordable.

Psychophysical Testing

Although electrophysiologic testing objectively measures cell layers and cell types in the visual pathway, it does not always allow testing of localized responses and may not be sensitive to small degrees of visual dysfunction. Psychophysical tests can be exceedingly sensitive, but they are always subjective and are usually not tissue-specific because perception represents an integration of information provided by different parts of the visual pathway. Psychophysical tests relevant to retinal disease include

- visual acuity
- visual field
- dark adaptation
- color vision
- contrast sensitivity

The last 3 tests are discussed in this chapter. See BCSC Section 10, *Glaucoma,* for extensive discussion of visual field testing.

Pokorny J, Smith VC. Color vision and night vision. In: Ryan SJ, Hinton DR, Schachat AP, Wilkinson CP, eds. *Retina.* 4th ed. Philadelphia: Elsevier/Mosby; 2006:209–225.

Dark Adaptation

The sensitivity of the human eye extends over a range of 10–11 $\log_{10}$ units. Cones and rods adapt to different levels of background light through neural mechanisms and through the bleaching and regeneration of visual pigments. Clinical dark adaptometry primarily measures the absolute thresholds of cone and rod sensitivity.

Dark adaptation is most commonly tested with the *Goldmann-Weekers adaptometer* (Fig 3-12). The patient is first light-adapted to a bright background light. This light is then extinguished, and the patient, now in the dark, is presented with a series of dim-light targets approximately 11° below fixation. The intensity of the test lights is controlled by neutral-density filters, and the threshold at which the test light is first perceived is plotted against time. Under these conditions, the dark-adaptation curve, illustrated in Figure 3-12, shows 2 plateaus: the first represents the cone threshold, which is usually reached in 5–10 minutes, and the second plateau represents the rod threshold, which is reached after about 30 minutes. If the clinical interest is limited to rod sensitivity in the dark, the test can be shortened by eliminating the first step of adaptation to bright light and recording only an endpoint rod threshold, which is normally reached within about 10 minutes of dark adaptation.

Dark adaptometry is useful in evaluating night blindness. Although the test is subjective, poor cooperation or malingering is easily recognized. A record of dark adaptation is complementary to the ERG because adaptometry is a *focal test* (a point to remember in interpreting results from patients with patchy, as opposed to diffuse, retinal disease), and thus it may in some instances be a more sensitive indicator of pathologic conditions than the ERG. Dark adaptometry can also demonstrate the degree of cone adaptation in the evaluation of cone dysfunction syndromes.

Color Vision

The perception of color is a response to electromagnetic energy at wavelengths between 400 and 700 nm, which is absorbed by cone outer segment visual pigments. Each cone contains 1 of 3 types of photolabile pigments. Blue-sensitive (short-wavelength),

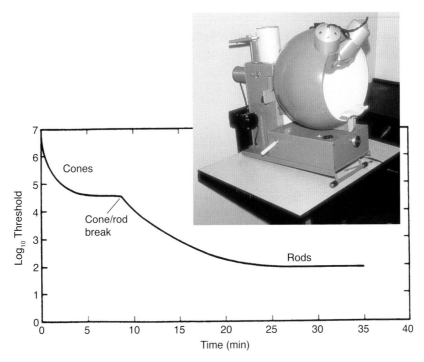

Figure 3-12 Dark-adaptation testing with the Goldmann-Weekers adaptometer *(inset)* yields a biphasic curve after preadaptation to bright light. *(Adapted with permission from Marmor MF. Clinical physiology of the retina. In: Peyman GA, Sanders DR, Goldberg MF. Principles and Practice of Ophthalmology. Philadelphia: Saunders; 1980:823–856.)*

green-sensitive (middle-wavelength), and red-sensitive (long-wavelength) cones are commonly referred to as the initiators of color vision. However, the integrative cells in the retina and higher visual centers are organized primarily to recognize *contrasts* between light or colors, and the receptive fields of color-sensitive cells typically have regions that compare the intensity of red versus green or blue versus yellow.

The classification and the testing of dysfunctional color vision are rooted in this contrast-recognition physiology. Red-green color deficiency, which occurs commonly through X-linked inheritance in males, has traditionally been separated into protan and deutan categories, referring to absent or defective red-sensitive pigment or green-sensitive pigment, respectively. These distinctions have some clinical value in terms of what patients perceive, even though individuals with normal color vision often have a duplication of pigment genes, and color-deficient individuals do not necessarily have single or simple gene defects. Blue-yellow color deficiency, exceedingly rare as a congenital condition, is frequently associated with acquired diseases and thus can be an important marker for them. Inherited color vision defects are described in Chapter 10.

The most accurate instrument for classifying congenital red-green color defects is the *anomaloscope*, but it is not widely used. The patient views a split screen and is asked to match the yellow appearance of one half by mixing varying proportions of red and green light in the other half. Individuals with red-green color deficiency use abnormal proportions of red and green to make the match.

Testing of color vision

The most common tests of color vision use colored tablets or diagrams. These color tests are accurate only in proper lighting, usually blue-white illumination that mimics sunlight. Pseudoisochromatic plates such as the *Ishihara* and *Hardy-Rand-Rittler* plates depict colored numbers or figures that stand out from a background of colored dots (Fig 3-13). The colors of the test figure and background are purposely pale and carefully chosen from hues that are difficult for a color-deficient patient to distinguish. Individuals with defective color vision see either no pattern at all or an alternative pattern based on brightness rather than hue. The pseudoisochromatic plate tests can be done quickly and are sufficiently sensitive for screening color-deficient people, but they are not effective in classifying the deficiency. Patients with normal color vision may have difficulty with the pseudoisochromatic plate tests if they have macular disease severe enough to interfere with spatial integration of the image.

The panel tests, including the Farnsworth Panel D-15 and Farnsworth-Munsell 100-hue tests, are much more accurate in classifying color deficiency. The *Farnsworth-Munsell 100-hue test* is very sensitive because the difference in hues between adjacent tablets approximates the minimum that a normal observer is able to distinguish (1–4 nm). The spectrum is divided into 4 parts during testing, and the patient is asked to discriminate between subtle shades of similar colors. However, the test is fatiguing and time-consuming.

The *Farnsworth Panel D-15 test* (Fig 3-14) is considerably quicker and more convenient for routine clinical use because it consists of only a single box of 15 colored tablets. The hues are more saturated, and they cover the spectrum so that patients will confuse colors for which they have deficient perception (such as red and green). The patient is asked to arrange the tablets in sequence, and errors can be plotted very quickly on a simple circular diagram to define the nature of the color deficiency (Fig 3-15). The D-15 test is not very sensitive and may miss mildly affected individuals, but its speed and accuracy

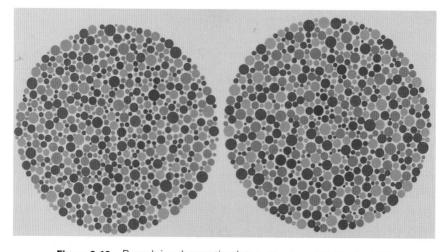

Figure 3-13 Pseudoisochromatic plates. *(Courtesy of Carl Regillo, MD.)*

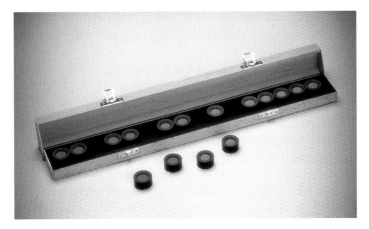

Figure 3-14 Panel D-15 test. *(Courtesy of Luneau Ophtalmologie.)*

make it useful. The relative insensitivity can also be an asset in judging the practical significance of mild degrees of color deficiency. For example, individuals who fail the Ishihara plates but pass the D-15 test will probably not have color discrimination problems under most circumstances and in most jobs. Desaturated versions of the D-15 test, which recognize more subtle degrees of color deficiency, are also available.

The D-15 test is probably the most useful color test in assessing retinal diseases because it discriminates well between congenital and acquired defects. Individuals with major congenital color deficiencies typically make errors that show a very precise protan or deutan pattern on the D-15 scoring graph, whereas those with acquired optic nerve or retinal disease show an irregular pattern of errors (see Fig 3-15). The D-15 test shows tritan (blue-yellow confusion) errors very clearly; these almost always signify acquired disease. The blue cones are fewer in number than the red and green cones and seem to be

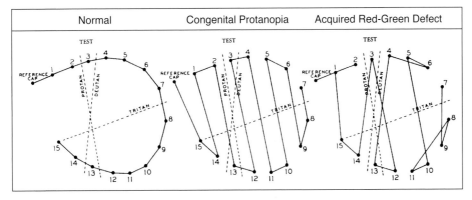

Figure 3-15 Graphed results of the Farnsworth Panel D-15 test. Individuals with congenital red-green defects make errors that show a well-defined axis of confusion. Individuals with acquired defects tend to make irregular errors. *(Modified from Marmor MF. The management of retinitis pigmentosa and allied diseases. Ophthalmol Digest. 1979;41:13–29.)*

preferentially affected in many diseases. Although it is sometimes stated that optic nerve disease usually causes red-green defects and retinal disease blue-yellow defects, this distinction is not reliable.

The Nagel anomaloscope tasks the patient with mixing red and green lights to match a yellow light. Patients with protanopia or deuteranopia can be distinguished from patients with normal color vision because they must give a different brightness to the yellow light to obtain a match.

The Sloan achromatopsia test is designed to test for complete achromatopsia. The test consists of 7 plates, each with a series of gray rectangles whose reflection increases gradually across the card. In the center of each rectangle appears a colored circle of fixed hue and reflectance. Patients with complete achromatopsia can find an exact match of the colored circle with 1 of the rectangles on each card. Observers who do not have complete achromatopsia can make only a brightness match of the colored circle to a rectangle.

Neitz M, Green DG, Neitz J. Visual acuity, color vision, and adaptation. In: Albert DM, Miller JW, Azar DT, Blodi BA, eds. *Albert & Jakobiec's Principles and Practice of Ophthalmology*. 3rd ed. Philadelphia: Saunders; 2008:chap 123.

Contrast Sensitivity

Visual acuity measures only one component of the visual process. The visual system codes most of what individuals see on the basis of *contrast* rather than spatial resolution. Subtleties of light and dark provide much of the richness of visual perception. When dusk, fog, or smoke reduces contrast, it becomes very difficult to resolve ordinary objects. Reduced contrast sensitivity results in significant challenges in reading newspapers and navigating stairways. Patients with retinal disease may have poor contrast sensitivity, which causes them to report dim vision or show poor object recognition even though they can still read small letters under ideal test conditions. Thus, contrast sensitivity is an independent test of visual function.

Testing of contrast sensitivity

Several clinical contrast sensitivity tests are available. Most relate contrast sensitivity to *spatial frequency*, which refers to the size of the light–dark cycles. Individuals are normally most sensitive to contrast for objects that have a spatial frequency between 2 and 5 cycles per degree (Fig 3-16), but this sensitivity can change in disease. Some contrast sensitivity tests use letters or optotypes of varying dimness and size to provide a more clinical context.

Contrast sensitivity testing shows clearly why some patients with nominal good acuity have subjective visual difficulties. The vast majority of patients with retinitis pigmentosa, for example, show reduced contrast sensitivity even when their visual acuity is good (20/25 or better). However, this is also true for patients with media opacities, optic nerve disease, and ill-defined age-related eye disease. Because disease-specific diagnostic patterns of contrast deficiency have not yet emerged, the main value of contrast sensitivity testing is to demonstrate or corroborate visual disability rather than to diagnose disease.

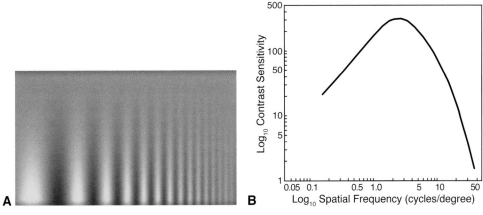

Figure 3-16 Contrast sensitivity. **A,** Grating in which the contrast diminishes from bottom to top, and the spatial frequency of the pattern increases from left to right. The pattern appears to have a hump in the middle at the frequencies for which the human eye is most sensitive to contrast. **B,** Plot of the contrast sensitivity function. *(Part A courtesy of Brian Wandell, PhD.)*

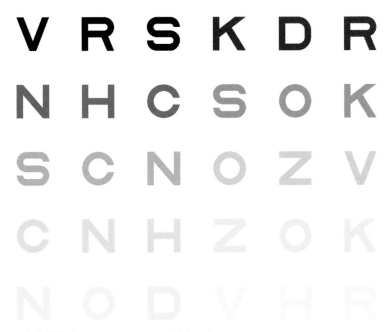

Figure 3-17 A Pelli-Robson contrast sensitivity chart. *(Reprinted with permission from Pelli DG, Robson JG, Wilkins AJ. The design of a new letter chart for measuring contrast sensitivity. Clin Vision Sci. 1988;2(3):187–199.)*

The Pelli-Robson test measures contrast sensitivity using a single, large letter size (20/60 optotype), with contrast varying across groups of letters (Fig 3-17). Patients read the letters, starting with the highest contrast and continue until they are unable to read 2 or 3 letters in a single group. The subject is assigned a score based on the contrast of the last group in which 2 or 3 letters were correctly read. The Pelli-Robson score is a logarithmic measure of the subject's contrast sensitivity. Thus, a score of 2 means that the subject was able to read at least 2 of the 3 letters with a contrast of 1% (contrast sensitivity = 100%, or $\log_{10} 2$). That is, a score of 2.0 indicates normal contrast sensitivity of 100%. A Pelli-Robson contrast sensitivity score of less than 1.5 is consistent with visual impairment, and a score of less than 1.0 represents visual disability.

Contrast sensitivity testing is discussed further in BCSC Section 3, *Clinical Optics,* and Section 5, *Neuro-Ophthalmology.*

Owsley C. Contrast sensitivity. *Ophthalmol Clin North Am.* 2003;16(2):171–177.

Rubin GS. Visual acuity and contrast sensitivity. In: Ryan SJ, Hinton DR, Schachat AP, Wilkinson CP, eds. *Retina.* 4th ed. Philadelphia: Elsevier/Mosby; 2006:227–233.

PART II

Disorders of the Retina and Vitreous

Age-Related Macular Degeneration and Other Causes of Choroidal Neovascularization

This chapter reviews age-related macular degeneration and other diseases commonly associated with choroidal neovascularization.

Age-Related Macular Degeneration

Age-related macular degeneration (AMD) is the leading cause of severe central visual acuity loss in 1 or both eyes in people over 50 years of age in the United States. It is estimated that 15 million North Americans (85%–90% of all AMD patients) currently have "dry" (nonneovascular, or nonexudative) AMD and 1.7 million people (10%–15% of all AMD patients) have "wet" (neovascular) AMD. An estimated 200,000 new cases of wet AMD develop each year.

Normal aging results in a spectrum of changes in the macula, many clinically undetected, that affect the outer retina, retinal pigment epithelium (RPE), Bruch membrane, and choriocapillaris:

- Photoreceptors are reduced in density and distribution.
- Ultrastructural changes in the pigment epithelium include loss of melanin granules, formation of lipofuscin granules, and accumulation of residual bodies.
- Basal laminar/linear deposits accumulate; these consist of granular, lipid-rich material and widely spaced collagen fibers collecting between the plasma membrane of the RPE cell and the inner collagenous layer of Bruch membrane on either side of the basement membrane of the RPE (Fig 4-1; see below).
- Progressive involutional changes occur in the choriocapillaris.

All of these changes represent aging but may not be part of AMD. Abnormalities associated with AMD that are not necessarily part of normal aging may be classified as nonneovascular or neovascular.

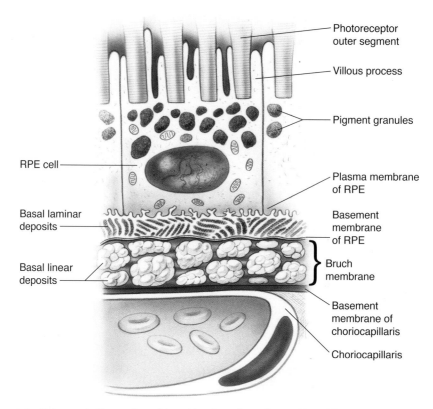

Photoreceptor
outer segment

Villous process

Pigment granules

RPE cell

Plasma membrane
of RPE

Basal laminar
deposits

Basement
membrane
of RPE

Basal linear
deposits

Bruch
membrane

Basement
membrane of
choriocapillaris

Choriocapillaris

Figure 4-1 Schematic illustration of basal laminar deposits and basal linear deposits that result in a thickened inner collagenous layer of the Bruch membrane. *(Illustration by Christine Gralapp.)*

Population-based studies have demonstrated that risk factors for AMD include positive family history, cigarette smoking, hyperopia, light iris color, hypertension, hypercholesterolemia, female sex, and cardiovascular disease.

Genetics and AMD

The etiology of AMD remains poorly understood despite the disease's prevalence. However, recent genetic-association studies have revealed allelic variants of genes encoding the alternate complement pathway, particularly of the *CFH* gene (which encodes complement factor H). Mutations at band 1q31, *HTRA1* (a serine protease) at 10q26 (Tyr402His), and a hypothetical gene called *LOC387715* (Ala69Ser) at 10q statistically significantly increase a patient's risk of AMD. The presence of Tyr402His increases the risk of AMD about 5-fold, and Ala69Ser about 7-fold. Together, these 2 genes may explain 75% of the genetic risk of AMD. Another associated locus is at the complement factor B/complement component 2 locus in the major histocompatibility complex (MHC) class III region on 6p21. There is a variant of complement C3 that increases the risk of AMD. Although these predisposing loci have been clearly validated in white populations, they do not seem to confer the same risk of AMD to other racial groups.

Functional studies of these genes offer insights into the pathogenesis of AMD and provide possible targets for therapeutic intervention. Ongoing whole-genome association studies may reveal further susceptibility genes associated with AMD. These and other genetic discoveries will give clinicians the ability to test for a patient's risk of AMD, allowing for better prevention and treatment of this blinding disease.

Nonneovascular Abnormalities in AMD

The prototypical lesion of the nonneovascular (nonexudative) form of AMD is the druse, named after a geode because of its inward glistening appearance. Other indicators are abnormalities of the RPE, including areas of hyperpigmentation and geographic atrophy.

Drusen

Clinically, drusen are small, round, yellow lesions located at the level of the RPE mostly in the postequatorial retina (Fig 4-2). Histologically, this material corresponds to the abnormal thickening of the inner aspect of the Bruch membrane shown in Figure 4-1. Ultrastructurally, basal *laminar* deposits (granular, lipid-rich material and widely spaced collagen fibers between plasma membrane and basement membrane of the RPE cell) and basal *linear* deposits (phospholipid vesicles and electron-dense granules *within* the inner collagenous zone of the Bruch membrane) are present. Both are illustrated in Figure 4-1.

The thickened inner aspect of the Bruch membrane, along with the RPE, may separate from the rest of the Bruch membrane, resulting in a pigment epithelial detachment (PED). When small, such a detachment may be identified as a large, often soft, druse. When the detachment covers a relatively large area, it may be recognized as a detachment of the RPE that is sometimes called a drusenoid PED. Whether small or large, these areas of detachment may fill rapidly with fluorescein as the dye leaks out of the choriocapillaris and pools within the area of detached RPE.

Because drusen variably affect the photoreceptors overlying the area of abnormal material, they may not cause symptoms unless the central fovea is involved. However, most patients will have some photoreceptor loss, resulting in reduced vision or difficulties with dark adaptation.

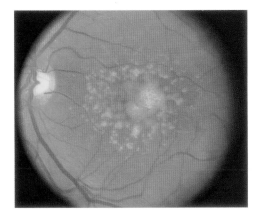

Figure 4-2   Soft, confluent drusen in AMD.

In fundus photographs of populations over the age of 50 years, it is common to see tiny yellow deposits—drusen—at the level of the outer retina. Because not all drusen will carry the same risk of vision loss from subsequent geographic atrophy or choroidal neovascularization (CNV), various classifications have been developed to distinguish the yellow deposits that will likely lead to atrophy or CNV from those that will not. Drusen have been categorized as

- *small* (usually <64 μm in diameter)
- *intermediate* (usually 64–124 μm in diameter)
- *large* (usually ≥125 μm in diameter)

Small drusen are well-defined focal areas of lipidization in the RPE or accumulations of hyaline material in the Bruch membrane. In the Age-Related Eye Disease Study (AREDS), the risk of progression to advanced AMD over a 5-year period for patients with early AMD (many small drusen or few intermediate drusen) was 1.3%. By contrast, the risk in patients with many intermediate or larger drusen was 18%. Patients in the latter group were also more likely to show RPE abnormalities and geographic atrophy or CNV than were patients with a few small or medium drusen.

In addition, the boundaries of drusen have been described as

- *hard* (discrete and well demarcated)
- *soft* (amorphous and poorly demarcated; see Fig 4-2)
- *confluent* (contiguous boundaries between drusen)

Soft drusen are associated with the presence of diffuse thickening of the inner aspects of the Bruch membrane, that is, basal linear deposits. An eye with soft, and perhaps *confluent,* drusen is more likely to progress to atrophy or CNV than an eye with only *hard* drusen. On fluorescein angiography (FA), drusen will stain in late views, or fluorescein may pool in areas of diffuse thickening.

Abnormalities of the RPE

Several patterns of RPE abnormalities characterize nonneovascular AMD:

- focal hyperpigmentation
- nongeographic atrophy
- geographic atrophy

Characteristic abnormalities Increased pigmentation at the level of the outer retina corresponds to *focal hyperpigmentation* of the RPE. On FA, these areas typically show blockage. The incidence of focal hyperpigmentation increases with age, and the presence of focal clumps of hyperpigmentation increases the risk of progression to the more advanced forms of AMD. If the atrophy does not cover a contiguous area, it may appear as a mottled area of depigmentation called *nongeographic atrophy,* or RPE degeneration. When the area in which the RPE is either absent or attenuated is contiguous, the condition is known as *geographic atrophy* of the RPE. In areas of geographic atrophy, the unmasked choroidal vessels are more readily visible, and the overlying outer retina may appear thin (Fig 4-3). Often, the choriocapillaris will be attenuated or atrophied as well. Photoreceptors cannot be seen by biomicroscopy, but they are usually attenuated or absent in areas overlying atrophied RPE. On FA, geographic atrophy shows a characteristic window defect.

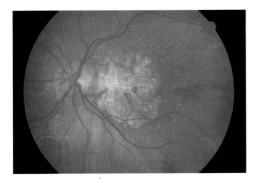

Figure 4-3 A well-demarcated area of geographic atrophy of the RPE; choroidal vessels can be seen easily within the atrophied area. *(Courtesy of Neil M. Bressler, MD.)*

Geographic atrophy often spares the fovea until late in the course of the disease. It may first present as one or more areas of atrophy near the fovea. These enlarge and coalesce to form a horseshoe and later a ring of atrophy surrounding the fovea. Areas with geographic atrophy feature a dense scotoma. Patients with geographic atrophy may demonstrate good visual acuity as measured on a visual acuity chart until late in the course of the disease when the parafovea and fovea become progressively atrophic. Related to the ring of atrophy, patients may have great difficulty reading or recognizing faces because the associated scotoma does not let a full word or face "fit" within the spared seeing area. Once the fovea becomes atrophic, visual acuity generally decreases to the legal blindness level, and the patient is forced to use the eccentric retina for reading and other visual tasks.

Although not all eyes with drusen or PED will develop atrophy, the incidence of atrophy appears to increase with age. The incidence of legal blindness resulting from central geographic atrophy is 12%–20% of patients with geographic atrophy.

Other abnormalities As atrophy develops, other abnormalities of the RPE may become recognizable. For example, the material that makes up the drusen may begin to disappear, a condition sometimes referred to as *regressed drusen*. In addition, dystrophic lipidization and calcification (refractile drusen) may occur, resulting in pinpoint glistening within the area of atrophy or remaining drusen material. Furthermore, pigment or pigment-laden cells (either RPE cells or macrophages that have ingested the pigment) may migrate to the photoreceptor level, resulting in focal clumps or a reticulated pattern of hyperpigmentation.

Fluorescein angiographic patterns of AMD

The patterns of AMD on FA are varied and can be categorized into hyper- and hypofluorescent lesions:

Hyperfluorescent Lesions	*Hypofluorescent Lesions*
Hard and soft drusen	Hemorrhage at any level
RPE atrophy	Lipid
RPE tear	Pigment proliferation
CNV (discussed further later in the chapter)	
Serous PED	
Subretinal fibrosis	
Laser scars	

Bressler SB, Do DV, Bressler NM. Age-related macular degeneration: drusen and geographic atrophy. In: Albert DM, Miller JW, Azar DT, Blodi BA, eds. *Albert & Jakobiec's Principles and Practice of Ophthalmology*. 3rd ed. Philadelphia: Saunders; 2008:chap 144.

Differential diagnosis of nonneovascular AMD

A variety of conditions may have abnormalities of the RPE that mimic the nonneovascular changes in AMD. Central serous choroidopathy (CSC) (discussed in Chapter 8) may cause RPE changes similar to those in AMD; the diagnosis may not be difficult to establish in individuals younger than 50 years of age. In individuals older than 50 years, the absence of drusen, mottled RPE atrophy, and/or multiple small serous detachments of the RPE may help differentiate CSC from nonneovascular changes in AMD. Pattern dystrophy of the RPE may include one or more areas of focal pinpoint or reticular hyperpigmentation surrounded by yellowish subretinal material (called vitelliform detachments) underneath the outer retina. FA shows early blocked fluorescence with a surrounding zone of hyperfluorescence. Late staining of the yellow material may occur and may help distinguish these cases of pattern dystrophy from AMD. These features may occur in "younger" individuals (defined as those who are under 50 years of age). On the other hand, these changes may be present in older individuals who have the more typical drusen and abnormalities of the RPE associated with AMD.

Basal laminar, or *cuticular, drusen,* a clinical syndrome that may occur in patients in their 30s or 40s, consists of innumerable and homogeneous, round drusen that can be small or large. Drusen are more apparent on angiography than on biomicroscopy, and give a "starry-night appearance," often with a vitelliform accumulation of yellow material in the fovea. The retinal signs of *drug toxicity,* such as the mottled hypopigmentation that may occur in chloroquine toxicity, may resemble nongeographic atrophy (RPE degeneration); a history of specific drug ingestion and lack of large drusen may help differentiate these abnormalities from AMD (see Chapter 12).

Management of nonneovascular AMD

Education and follow-up Eyes with soft drusen and RPE hyperpigmentation are at increased risk of developing geographic atrophy and CNV. Patients with drusen or abnormalities of the RPE in 1 or both eyes should be taught how to recognize symptoms of advanced AMD and instructed to contact an ophthalmologist promptly if such symptoms occur. Office staff should be educated to respond promptly to reports of new symptoms. If vision loss is found to be caused by geographic atrophy in both eyes, a low vision evaluation should be considered. Periodic examinations are advised to monitor for intercurrent, treatable eye disease (eg, cataract, glaucoma) and to reevaluate progressive low vision needs. To assist patients whose visual function could be aided or enhanced by vision rehabilitation, refer to resources listed at the American Academy of Ophthalmology SmartSight website (http://one.aao.org/ce/educationalcontent/smartsight.aspx).

Amsler grid It is important that patients self-test for visual changes daily. The Amsler grid is a test card with white grid lines on a black background and a central dot for fixation. Each eye is tested *individually* with reading glasses on and at reading distance to check for any new metamorphopsia, scotoma, or other significant changes in central vision using the specialized grid. Any changes noted should be evaluated.

Micronutrients Ophthalmologists should counsel patients that several epidemiologic studies have demonstrated positive associations between the intake of certain micronutrients and a decreased risk of AMD, although only some micronutrients have been studied.

The AREDS was a randomized, clinical trial that enrolled 4757 patients at 11 centers to evaluate the effect of high-dose micronutrient supplements consisting of antioxidants and vitamins (500 mg vitamin C, 400 IU vitamin E, and 15 mg beta carotene) and zinc (80 mg zinc oxide and 2 mg cupric oxide to prevent zinc-induced anemia) on AMD and vision loss. The results showed that individuals with intermediate AMD (extensive intermediate or at least 1 large druse, or nonsubfoveal geographic atrophy) or advanced unilateral AMD (vision loss due to AMD in 1 eye) who had been randomly assigned to the combination supplement group had a 25% reduction of risk for progression to advanced AMD and a 19% risk reduction in rates of moderate vision loss (≥3 lines of visual acuity) by 5 years. Subjects with no AMD or only early AMD (a few small drusen) did not derive any benefit. Patients were treated a median of 6.5 years, but the treatment effect was present even 10 years later. At 10 years, 44% of placebo recipients compared with 34% of the supplement recipients had advanced AMD (a 27% risk reduction). There was no increased mortality among patients taking the AREDS formula.

A simplified grading scale was developed by the AREDS group for classifying the severity of AMD. The scale was based on the presence or absence in each eye of easily identified retinal abnormalities:

- presence of one or more large (>125-μm diameter) drusen (1 point)
- presence of any pigment abnormalities (1 point)
- for patients with no large drusen, presence of bilateral intermediate (64–124 μm) drusen (1 point)
- presence of neovascular AMD (2 points)

Risk factors were summed across both eyes to add up to a number between 0 and 4 that could be used to estimate the 5- and 10-year risk of developing advanced AMD:

Number of Risk Factors	5-Year Risk	10-Year Risk
0	0.5%	1%
1	3%	7%
2	12%	22%
3	25%	50%
4	50%	67%

The risk of developing advanced AMD increases between years 5 and 10. Patients with increasing scores have increasing risk.

Recommendations of the AREDS group included the following:

- Identify individuals at high risk of AMD progression and vision loss, including those with
  - extensive intermediate drusen
  - at least 1 large druse
  - noncentral geographic atrophy
  - advanced AMD in 1 eye

- Consider supplementation with a combined antioxidant and mineral formulation to decrease rates of disease progression and vision loss for these patients. (Supplementation without beta carotene is preferable for patients who smoke, because large clinical trials sponsored by the National Cancer Institute demonstrated that beta carotene increases the risk of lung cancer in current smokers. In these trials, most of the smokers were heavy smokers. However, in the only other large clinical trial evaluating beta carotene, the Physicians' Health Study, no evidence of increased cancer risk was found in those randomly assigned to receive beta carotene, but few participants were active smokers. Also, no evidence was found of an increased risk of lung cancer in former smokers. Based on these clinical trials, it is reasonable to expect that beta carotene may slightly increase the risk of cancer, at least for several years after cessation of smoking.)
- For patients with early AMD, supplementation was not shown to be beneficial. For patients without AMD but who are at high risk of AMD (including family members), AREDS supplementation has not been tested; therefore, these patients should be advised to maintain a balanced diet and avoid smoking.

Large population-based studies suggest that the xanthophylls lutein and zeaxanthin, as well as omega-3 long-chain polyunsaturated fatty acids (LCPUFAs: docosahexaenoic acid [DHA] and eicosapentaenoic acid [EPA]), may also help reduce AMD progression. Lutein and zeaxanthin are members of the carotenoid family (like beta carotene) and are the only 2 carotenoids present in the macula. They are much more concentrated there than anywhere else in the body; the retinal tissue levels of these compounds depend on intake and are thus modifiable. Carotenoids may protect against light damage because they are efficient absorbers of blue light. Several large studies examining the association of dietary lutein and zeaxanthin intake with advanced AMD have yielded inverse relationships that were statistically significant. Omega-3 polyunsaturated fatty acids are found mainly in fish and nuts and have been shown to have anti-inflammatory and possibly anti-angiogenic properties. In AREDS, a 50% reduction in advanced AMD was found in the group that had the highest consumption of omega-3 LCPUFAs compared with the group that had the lowest.

The National Eye Institute is now administering AREDS2, a clinical trial that is fully enrolled with more than 4000 participants. The goals of this 5-year study are to examine the effects of high supplemental doses of dietary xanthophylls (10 mg lutein and 2 mg zeaxanthin) and omega-3 LCPUFAs on the development of advanced AMD; to study the effects of these supplements on the development of cataract and moderate vision loss; to examine the effects of eliminating beta carotene from the original AREDS formulation on the development and progression of AMD; and to study the effects on the development and progression of AMD of reducing the zinc component to 25 mg from the original AREDS formulation of 80 mg.

Age-Related Eye Disease Study Research Group. A randomized, placebo-controlled, clinical trial of high-dose supplementation with vitamins C and E, beta carotene, and zinc for age-related macular degeneration and vision loss: AREDS report no. 8. *Arch Ophthalmol.* 2001;119(10):1417–1436.

Ferris FL, Davis MD, Clemons TE, et al; Age-Related Eye Disease Study (AREDS) Research Group. A simplified severity scale for age-related macular degeneration: AREDS report no. 18. *Arch Ophthalmol.* 2005;123(11):1570–1574.

Lifestyle changes With increasing evidence that environment and lifestyle influence the development and progression of AMD, patients should be counseled to reduce behaviors that put them at risk. Of particular importance are obesity reduction, smoking cessation, and blood pressure control. Cataract surgery has not been linked to the progression of AMD. Furthermore, there is no strong evidence linking UV light (UV-A or UV-B) to the progression of AMD. It should be noted, however, that there are no negative effects of wearing UV-protective glasses.

Ineffective treatments for nonneovascular AMD

Laser photocoagulation The National Eye Institute sponsored the Complications of Age-Related Macular Degeneration Prevention Trial (CAPT), which enrolled 1052 patients at 22 clinical centers (mean age, 71 years; 99.3% white); the aim was to determine if photo-coagulation with a 514-nm argon green laser reduces vision loss from advancing AMD. At 5 years' follow-up, the cumulative incidence of late AMD was 19.7% in treated eyes and 20.4% in untreated eyes; the incidence of CNV was 13.3% in both groups. Based on this trial and similar studies, prophylactic laser treatment has not been shown to offer any benefit in AMD.

Rheopheresis Differential membrane filtration, or rheopheresis, is an extracorporeal blood-filtration procedure that removes circulating macromolecules from the blood. A phase 3 clinical trial failed to show any clinical benefit from the procedure.

Experimental treatments for nonneovascular AMD

Many drugs and strategies are being evaluated for the treatment of nonexudative AMD or prevention of progression to exudative AMD. Some experimental protocols are currently testing the delivery of ciliary neurotrophic factor by encapsulated cell intraocular implants, and others are evaluating complement inhibitors and retinoid inhibitors. Several studies are currently recruiting participants for evaluations of molecules designed to inhibit complement factors III, V, and H. In addition, ongoing studies are evaluating if RPE cells can be transplanted to treat geographic atrophy; stem cells are being tested for this condition as well.

Neovascular AMD

The hallmark of the neovascular form of AMD is the presence of CNV. Any disturbance of the Bruch membrane, such as the presence of drusen, thickening of the inner aspect, or conditions similar to the nonneovascular changes associated with AMD, can increase the likelihood that a break will occur, allowing buds of capillaries originating from the choriocapillaris to perforate the outer aspect of the Bruch membrane. These new vessels are accompanied by fibroblasts, resulting in a fibrovascular complex (Fig 4-4). This fibro-vascular complex can disrupt and destroy the normal architecture of the choriocapillaris,

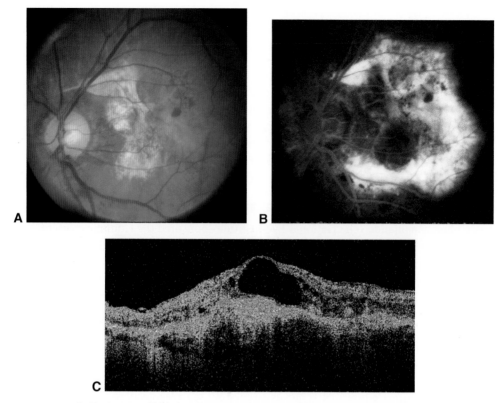

Figure 4-4 **A,** End-stage CNV that has progressed to fibrovascular scar, often called a *disciform scar*. **B,** Late-phase fluorescein angiogram showing staining of the subretinal fibrous tissue and extensive leakage from the disciform scar. **C,** Optical coherence tomogram of the same patient, illustrating disorganization and edema of the retina and underlying fibrous tissue. **D** and **E,** Histologic specimens from a disciform scar. **F,** Schematic cross section of a disciform scar. Note the partial loss of the photoreceptor layer overlying the scar and disturbance of the RPE and Bruch membrane. *(Parts A–C courtesy of Peter K. Kaiser, MD; parts D–E courtesy of Hermann D. Schubert, MD; part F illustration by Christine Gralapp.)*

(Continued on next page)

Bruch membrane, RPE, photoreceptors, and outer retina, leading to the formation of a disciform scar.

Signs and symptoms of neovascular AMD

Patients with neovascular AMD describe the sudden onset of decreased vision, metamorphopsia, and paracentral scotomata. Amsler grid self-testing by patients is highly effective for detecting early neovascular AMD. Clinical signs may include elevation of the RPE; the presence of subretinal or intraretinal lipid, fluid, or blood; PED; and retinal pigment epithelial tears; occasionally, the gray-green CNV lesion itself is visible. The presence of an intraretinal hemorrhage may be an early sign of a retinal angiomatous proliferation (RAP) lesion, with blood flow from the retinal circulation connecting to the CNV. FA is the gold standard for diagnosing CNV. In cases with overlying blood or occult CNV, indocyanine green (ICG) angiography may better demonstrate the vascular lesion.

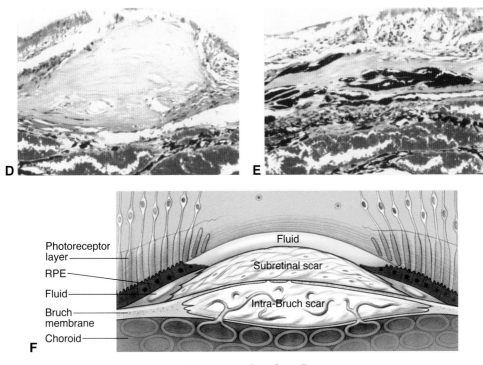

Figure 4-4 *(continued)*

Choroidal neovascularization

CNV in the fovea is the major cause of severe central vision loss in AMD. A variety of clinical symptoms suggests a diagnosis of CNV. Patients often present with an otherwise unexplained, fairly sudden decrease in visual acuity; central metamorphopsia; or a relative central scotoma. Signs of CNV may include the presence of

- subretinal fluid
- subretinal or sub–pigment epithelial blood
- subretinal or intraretinal lipid
- a subretinal pigment ring
- an irregular elevation of the pigment epithelium
- a subretinal gray-white lesion
- cystoid macular edema
- a sea fan pattern of subretinal small vessels

CNV is an ingrowth of new vessels from the choriocapillaris into the sub–pigment epithelial space through a defect in the outer aspect of the Bruch membrane, gaining access to the inner collagenous layer and/or subretinal space (Fig 4-5). Within this space, the CNV can leak fluid and blood and may be accompanied by a serous or hemorrhagic detachment of the RPE. The blood may resorb, dissect under the retina, or in rare instances, migrate into the vitreous cavity. In addition to vascularization from the choroid, fibrovascular tissue may grow within the Bruch membrane (type 1) and, less commonly, between the

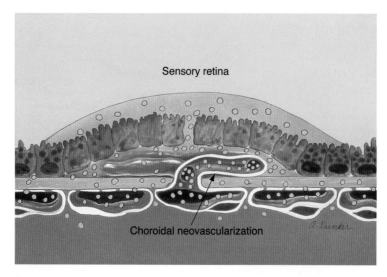

Figure 4-5 Schematic drawing of CNV originating from the choriocapillaris. Neovascularization proliferates within the diffusely thickened inner collagenous layer of the Bruch membrane. Fibrosis accompanies the CNV beneath the RPE, and fibrovascular tissue has replaced normal RPE in some areas. Fibroglial tissue can be seen between the RPE and the photoreceptors; some of the photoreceptors have been replaced by fibrovascular or fibroglial tissue. *(Reproduced with permission from Bressler NM, Bressler SB, Fine SL. Age-related macular degeneration.* Surv Ophthalmol. *1988;32(6):375–413.)*

neurosensory retina and the RPE (type 2). Ultimately, this process results in a disciform granulomatous scar that replaces the normal architecture of the outer retina and leads to permanent loss of central vision (see Fig 4-4).

Fluorescein angiographic patterns of CNV FA patterns of CNV vary because the CNV lesion may be a complex of several components that may include classic CNV, occult CNV, and features that may obscure CNV. Two major patterns of CNV are visible on FA:

1. classic CNV
2. occult CNV

Classic CNV is an area of bright, fairly uniform hyperfluorescence identified in the early phase of the FA study that progressively intensifies throughout the transit phase, with leakage of dye obscuring the boundaries of this area by the late phases of the study (Fig 4-6; see also Fig 2-1).

Occult CNV consists of 2 forms:

1. fibrovascular PED
2. late leakage from an undetermined source

Fibrovascular PED refers to an irregular elevation of the RPE with stippled or granular irregular fluorescence first apparent early in the angiographic study, usually by 1–2 minutes after dye injection. The irregular elevation of the RPE is best observed with stereo views

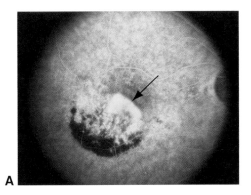 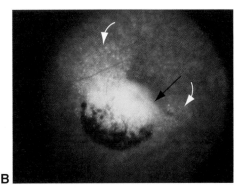

A B

Figure 4-6 **A,** Classic CNV *(arrow)* appears during early transit as intense hyperfluorescence, with early leakage manifested as blurred margins. **B,** Occult CNV *(curved arrows)* manifested as late leakage from an undetermined source lies adjacent to the classic CNV component of this lesion *(black arrow).* The late leakage marked by the curved arrows creates poorly defined boundaries for the lesion. Furthermore, it does not correspond to classic CNV or to irregular elevation of the RPE in the early or midphase frames of the study. *(Reproduced with permission from Subfoveal neovascular lesions in age-related macular degeneration. Guidelines for evaluation and treatment in the macular photocoagulation study. Macular Photocoagulation Study Group. Arch Ophthalmol. 1991;109(9):1242–1257.)*

on the angiogram. As the study progresses, there is progressive leakage from these regions, with a stippled hyperfluorescent pattern that is not as diffuse as that observed in classic CNV (see Fig 2-1B). *Late leakage from an undetermined source* refers to regions of fluorescence at the level of the RPE that are best appreciated in the late phases of an angiographic study; they do not correspond to classic CNV or to areas of irregular elevation of the RPE during the early or midphases of the study.

The distinction between classic and occult CNV used to be extremely important because the benefits of laser treatment and photodynamic therapy (PDT) varied depending on the portion of classic CNV in the lesion. The treatment regimen used currently, anti–vascular endothelial growth factor (anti-VEGF), does not change depending on the classic or occult components of the CNV lesion. However, there is a prognostic distinction between classic and occult CNV: classic CNV tends to be much more aggressive and rapidly progressive without prompt treatment than occult CNV.

If lesion components such as thick blood, pigment, scar tissue, or a serous PED lie adjacent to hyperfluorescence from classic or occult CNV, they may either block fluorescence (blood, pigment, or scar) or intensify hyperfluorescence (serous PED) and thus obscure the underlying CNV.

When determining the size of a CNV lesion, the examiner must take into account all areas of classic and occult CNV, as well as areas with obscured features. Recognition of blood, pigment, or scar tissue as a lesion component depends on clinical examination and blocked fluorescence during the FA study. Identification of a serous PED as a lesion component requires a smooth or dome-shaped area of RPE elevation with rapid, early, homogeneous, and intense fluorescence that retains its same boundaries and intensity throughout the study. In contrast to a serous PED, a fibrovascular PED or occult CNV has irregular topography of the RPE elevation, a stippled and nonhomogeneous pattern of fluorescence, and a slow rate of filling with fluorescein dye. Such areas fluoresce between 1 and 3 minutes rather than between 20 and 60 seconds, and they may either leak or stain in the late phase.

The terms *predominantly classic, minimally classic,* and *occult with no classic* are terms to describe CNV lesions. Predominantly classic lesions are those in which the CNV occupies more than 50% of the lesion—including contiguous blood, pigment, scar, and staining—not just 50% of the CNV. Minimally classic CNV is present when the proportion of classic CNV occupies between 1% and 49% of the entire lesion. Occult with no classic CNV means no classic CNV is present in the lesion—only occult CNV.

The terms *poorly defined* or *poorly demarcated CNV* and *well-defined* or *well-demarcated CNV* should not be used as synonyms for *classic* and *occult CNV,* respectively. "Classic" and "occult" describe *fluorescein patterns* of CNV. "Poorly defined" and "well-defined" describe how distinct the boundaries are between the entire CNV lesion and the uninvolved retina. In poorly defined CNV, the boundaries separating CNV from normal retina cannot be readily distinguished (see Fig 4-6); in well-defined CNV, the boundaries can easily be determined (see Fig 2-1A). Occult CNV can have well-defined borders, and classic CNV can have poorly defined boundaries. This distinction was more important in the past because laser therapy had to be applied to the entire area of CNV, and that area could be identified only when the boundaries of the entire lesion were well demarcated. The distinction is not as important when performing PDT.

The appearance, shape, and size of a disciform lesion are related to a variety of factors, including the amount of fibrovascular tissue, the extent of RPE proliferation, and continued leakage from CNV. Massive exudation may occur beneath the neurosensory retina, resulting in an extensive nonrhegmatogenous retinal detachment.

Other imaging modalities, including high-speed angiography, ICG angiography, and optical coherence tomography (OCT) can also image CNV. OCT in particular plays a key role in the diagnosis of CNV and is crucial for evaluating lesions undergoing treatment with anti-VEGF therapy. OCT can demonstrate intraretinal edema, subretinal fluid, and RPE elevation.

Differential diagnosis of neovascular AMD

A variety of conditions can mimic the neovascular changes of AMD. These clinical entities are listed in Table 4-1.

Retinal arterial macroaneurysms may be associated with preretinal, intraretinal, or subretinal hemorrhage. Because sudden vision loss occurs when blood involves the macula, the clinical appearance may resemble hemorrhage from CNV. In many cases, the

---

Table 4-1 Differential Diagnosis of Neovascular AMD

Macroaneurysms
Vitelliform detachments
Polypoidal choroidal vasculopathy
Central serous chorioretinopathy
Inflammatory conditions
Small tumors such as choroidal melanoma

subretinal hemorrhage surrounds the macroaneurysm, and FA and ICG angiography may demonstrate the dilated lumen of the macroaneurysm along a retinal arteriole (Fig 4-7).

Adult vitelliform dystrophy may resemble a retinal PED or a fundus with large confluent drusen. In vitelliform macular dystrophy, the staining of the vitelliform material in an eye with *pattern dystrophy of the RPE* or in a patient with *basal laminar drusen* may be mistaken for the leakage observed in CNV. Usually, the staining of the vitelliform material is associated with marked blocked fluorescence in the early phase of the angiographic study (Fig 4-8). Furthermore, even though the lesion often involves the foveal center, visual acuity remains relatively good.

Polypoidal choroidal vasculopathy, also known as *posterior uveal bleeding syndrome,* is a variant of choroidal neovascularization (type 1) characterized by multiple and recurrent serosanguineous RPE detachments. The first description of this syndrome was the occurrence of lesions in individuals of African American or Asian ancestry, typically middle-aged women. It is now believed to occur in all races and in men. The areas of serosanguineous detachment are often peripapillary, multifocal, orange, and nodular. Vitreous

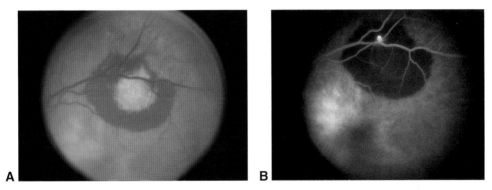

Figure 4-7 Retinal arterial macroaneurysm with subretinal hemorrhage resembling AMD. **A,** Clinical photograph shows subretinal hemorrhage surrounding the macroaneurysm. **B,** Fluorescein angiogram shows a characteristic hyperfluorescence of the macroaneurysm with blockage from the surrounding blood. *(Courtesy of Harry W. Flynn Jr, MD.)*

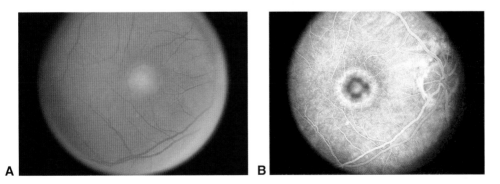

Figure 4-8 Adult vitelliform macular dystrophy. **A,** Patient with 20/50 visual acuity. The macular changes have been present for many years, and yet the patient has maintained relatively good visual acuity. **B,** Fluorescein angiogram shows a hyperfluorescent central lesion surrounded by a halo of retinal pigment epithelial atrophy. *(Courtesy of Harry W. Flynn Jr, MD.)*

hemorrhage may occur more frequently than in AMD, and the typical soft drusen of AMD are not usually present. The natural history and visual acuity outcomes of polypoidal vasculopathy may be better than those of CNV associated with AMD (Fig 4-9).

CSC with subretinal fluid can occasionally mimic the subretinal fluid associated with CNV and AMD. However, patients with CSC are usually younger and usually do not exhibit a subretinal hemorrhagic process. CSC can be further differentiated by characteristic signs, including patches of mottled RPE atrophy (which sometimes assume a gutterlike configuration) or multiple PEDs (Fig 4-10). The areas of pigment epithelial atrophy remaining after reabsorption of subretinal fluid are often geographic in their pattern and may extend below the inferior temporal arcade from the gravitational effect.

A variety of *inflammatory conditions* may cause changes in the outer retina with subretinal fluid accumulation in the macula. These include Vogt-Koyanagi-Harada syndrome, posterior scleritis, and systemic lupus erythematosus. These diseases generally have other distinguishing ocular and systemic features.

Choroidal tumors, such as a small choroidal melanoma or choroidal hemangioma, may present with a mass effect and, occasionally, CNV on the surface that resembles AMD. Ultrasonography can help differentiate the low reflectivity of a choroidal melanoma from the moderate to high reflectivity of a disciform scar.

Levin MR, Gragoudas ES. Retinal arterial macroaneurysms. In: Albert DM, Jakobiec FA, eds. *Principles and Practice of Ophthalmology.* 2nd ed. Philadelphia: Saunders; 2000:1950–1957.

Spaide RF, Noble K, Morgan A, Freund KB. Vitelliform macular dystrophy. *Ophthalmology.* 2006;113(8):1392–1400.

Yannuzzi LA, Wong DW, Sforzolini BS, et al. Polypoidal choroidal vasculopathy and neovascularized age-related macular degeneration. *Arch Ophthalmol.* 1999;117(11): 1503–1510.

Management of neovascular AMD

If neovascular AMD is suspected on clinical grounds, FA should be obtained and interpreted promptly. Stereoscopic angiography and late-phase angiograms (2, 5, and 10 minutes after dye injection) may facilitate identification of occult CNV. Interpretation of fluorescein angiographic patterns of CNV associated with AMD can be complex (see

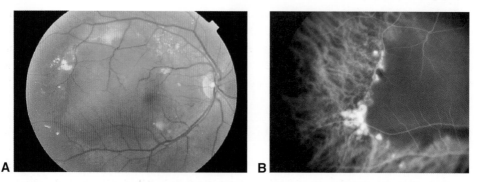

Figure 4-9 Polypoidal choroidal vasculopathy. **A,** Clinical photograph shows a large RPE detachment with multiple yellow-orange nodular lesions temporally. **B,** The ICG angiogram demonstrates the characteristic polypoidal lesions temporally. *(Courtesy of Lawrence A. Yannuzzi, MD.)*

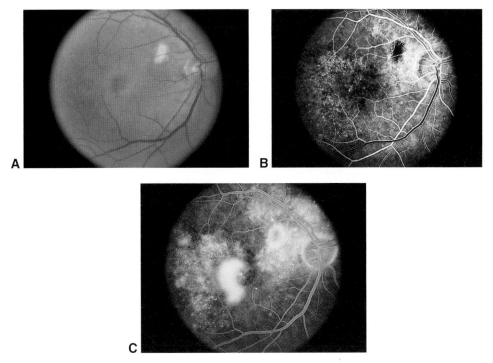

Figure 4-10 Chronic central serous chorioretinopathy. **A,** A 45-year-old patient with visual acuity of 20/200. A PED is present in the center of the macula, and there is extensive but shallow subretinal fluid inside the temporal arcades. **B,** The early-phase fluorescein angiogram shows a window defect corresponding to the location of chronic subretinal fluid. **C,** The late-phase angiogram shows the centrally located PED and a diffusely abnormal RPE. *(Courtesy of Harry W. Flynn Jr, MD.)*

choroidal neovascularization discussion earlier in this chapter), and correct interpretation may be a challenge. With the advent of antiangiogenesis therapy, OCT has taken a larger role than FA in re-treatment decisions.

Laser photocoagulation (thermal laser) From the 1980s through 2001, laser treatment was the primary treatment for classic CNV with well-demarcated boundaries and for lesions with classic and occult CNV components in which the lesion boundary was well demarcated. Although it is now used less frequently, laser photocoagulation remains an option for extrafoveal lesions for which the treating physician believes it is safe and will not damage the foveal center. In general, based on the results of the Macular Photocoagulation Study (MPS), laser photocoagulation is rarely used because pharmacologic therapy has been found to be more beneficial.

Photodynamic therapy PDT was introduced in 2000 as a less-destructive modality of treating CNV than thermal laser treatment. It is a 2-step process that entails the systemic administration of a photosensitizing drug followed by an application of light of a particular wavelength to the affected tissue to incite a localized photochemical reaction. This reaction generates reactive oxygen species that can lead to capillary endothelial cell damage and vessel thrombosis.

The Treatment of AMD with Photodynamic Therapy (TAP) investigation was conducted at 22 clinical centers and studied 609 patients with new or recurrent subfoveal CNV that exhibited a classic component on FA. At 2 years, 59% of verteporfin-treated eyes versus 31% of placebo-treated eyes avoided at least moderate vision loss. Subgroup analysis revealed that participants with predominantly classic CNV (ie, the area of classic CNV occupied ≥50% of the entire lesion) derived the greatest treatment benefit. Results of another study, the Visudyne in Minimally Classic (VIM) Trial, suggested that smaller (<4 MPS disc areas) minimally classic lesions appeared to benefit from the treatment. In the VIM Trial, eyes with smaller (<6 MPS disc areas) minimally classic lesions receiving verteporfin showed a statistically significant difference in vision from those receiving the sham treatment.

The Verteporfin in Photodynamic Therapy (VIP) study, conducted at 28 clinical centers, evaluated 459 patients with AMD and new or recurrent subfoveal CNV measuring up to 5400 μm at its greatest linear dimension. At the 2-year endpoint, verteporfin-treated eyes were statistically significantly less likely to have either moderate or severe vision loss. The treatment benefit was greatest for eyes with occult CNV without a classic component, particularly if the lesion was relatively small (≤4 disc areas) or associated with relatively lower levels of visual acuity (≤20/50) at baseline. In this subgroup, verteporfin-treated eyes had 2-year follow-up rates of moderate and severe vision loss of 49% and 21%, respectively, compared with 75% and 48%, respectively, in the placebo-treated group. The US Food and Drug Administration (FDA) approved the use of PDT with verteporfin for eyes with predominantly classic CNV and AMD, as well as for eyes with pathologic myopia and ocular histoplasmosis (see Other Causes of Choroidal Neovascularization later in the chapter). However, with the advent of pharmacotherapy, PDT use has decreased considerably. Combination therapy consisting of PDT plus antiangiogenesis treatment is being explored to determine whether it offers vision gains similar to those of antiangiogenesis treatment alone but with fewer treatments.

Antiangiogenesis *Angiogenesis* is the formation of new blood vessels that occurs via sprouting or splitting from existing vessels; it is characterized by a complex cascade of events. The first step in the cascade is vasodilation of existing vessels and increased vascular permeability. This is followed by degradation of the surrounding extracellular matrix, which facilitates migration and proliferation of endothelial cells. After endothelial cells proliferate, they join together to form a lumen, which becomes a new capillary. The vessels subsequently mature and undergo remodeling to form a stable vascular network. The successful execution of this cascade requires the balanced interplay of growth-promoting and growth-inhibiting angiogenic factors. Identified activators of angiogenesis include vascular endothelial growth factor (VEGF), fibroblast growth factor (FGF) families, transforming growth factor (TGF)-α and TGF-β, angiopoietin-1, and angiopoietin-2. Inhibitors of angiogenesis include thrombospondin, angiostatin, endostatin, and pigment epithelium–derived factor (PEDF).

The majority of recent antiangiogenesis research has focused on the inhibition of VEGF. VEGF expression is increased in pigment epithelial cells during the early stages of AMD, suggesting that VEGF plays a role in the initiation of neovascularization rather than being secondary to it. In addition, high concentrations of VEGF have been observed in excised CNV from AMD patients as well as in vitreous samples from patients with CNV. VEGF is a homodimeric glycoprotein that is a heparin-binding growth factor specific for vascular endothelial cells. It can induce angiogenesis, vascular permeability, and lymphangiogenesis and may act as a survival factor for endothelial cells by preventing apoptosis. There are at least 4 major VEGF isoforms, produced by alternative exon splicing of the human *VEGF* gene on band 6p21.3: $VEGF_{121}$, $VEGF_{165}$, $VEGF_{189}$, and $VEGF_{206}$. The VEGF isoforms have varying degrees of permeability-enhancing and angiogenic properties, with $VEGF_{165}$ thought to be the most dominant in AMD. All isoforms can undergo posttranslation cleavage by plasmin to produce a freely soluble isoform, $VEGF_{110}$.

Pegaptanib In 2004, pegaptanib was approved by the FDA as an RNA oligonucleotide ligand (or aptamer) that binds human $VEGF_{165}$ with high affinity and specificity. It differs from other anti-VEGF therapies in that it binds near the heparin-binding domain of VEGF, thus preventing $VEGF_{165}$ and larger isoforms from attaching to VEGF receptors instead of targeting all active VEGF-A isoforms. The drug is administered via intravitreal injection every 6 weeks. The VEGF Inhibition Study in Ocular Neovascularization (VISION) was a prospective, randomized, double-masked, controlled, dose-ranging phase 3 clinical trial in which AMD patients with subfoveal CNV received 1 of 3 doses of pegaptanib or sham injections every 6 weeks for 48 weeks. Of the 1196 patients enrolled worldwide, 70% lost less than 3 lines of vision and 10% lost more than 6 lines, compared with 55% and 22%, respectively, among patients who received sham injections at 12 months. Vision gain of 3 or more lines was observed in 6% of treated patients versus 2% of control subjects at 1 year. The drug appeared safe; however, endophthalmitis was reported in 12 patients (1.3% risk/patient/year). Pegaptanib therapy does not slow disease progression. In general, patients still lose vision with pegaptanib therapy, and there is less use of this drug as newer antiangiogenesis drugs have been developed.

Ranibizumab Ranibizumab is a recombinantly produced, humanized antibody fragment (Fab) that binds VEGF. Unlike pegaptanib, ranibizumab binds to and inhibits all active forms of VEGF-A and their active degradation products. The Minimally Classic/Occult Trial of the Anti-VEGF Antibody Ranibizumab in the Treatment of Neovascular AMD (MARINA) study was a randomized, double-masked, sham-controlled clinical trial of ranibizumab in patients with minimally classic or occult CNV secondary to AMD. Subjects were treated with 1 of 2 different doses of intravitreal ranibizumab or with sham injections administered every 4 weeks for 24 months (Clinical Trial 4-1). The MARINA results demonstrated that 95% of ranibizumab-treated patients experienced vision improvement or stabilization compared with 62% of sham-treated patients after 12 months. More important, almost 40% of ranibizumab-treated patients experienced vision improvement of 15 letters or more compared with sham-treated patients.

Another study, the Anti-VEGF Antibody for the Treatment of Predominantly Classic Choroidal Neovascularization in AMD (ANCHOR) study, was a randomized, double-masked, sham-controlled clinical trial of patients with predominantly classic CNV secondary to AMD treated with ranibizumab and sham verteporfin PDT or sham injection and verteporfin PDT (Clinical Trial 4-2). Approximately 95% of ranibizumab-treated patients maintained or improved vision (less than a 15-letter loss in visual acuity)

> **CLINICAL TRIAL 4-1**
>
> **Minimally Classic/Occult Trial of the Anti-VEGF Antibody Ranibizumab in the Treatment of Neovascular AMD (MARINA)**
>
> *Objective:* To determine if monthly ranibizumab administration can reduce the risk of vision loss in patients with subfoveal, minimally classic or occult with no classic CNV compared with placebo-controlled sham treatment.
>
> *Participants:* Eyes with new or recurrent subfoveal CNV, minimally classic or occult with no classic CNV with evidence of recent disease progression defined as new subretinal hemorrhage, recent growth of CNV on FA, or recent visual acuity loss, CNV >50% of lesion, size ≤12 disc areas, no prior PDT, blood <50% of the lesion, and visual acuity of 20/40 to 20/320.
>
> *Outcome measures:* Visual acuity loss of <15 letters at 1 year. Secondary outcomes included visual acuity loss of <30 letters, quality of life, and morphologic outcomes.
>
> *Results:* 95% of study eyes experienced visual acuity improvement or stabilization vs 62% of control eyes. Close to 40% of study eyes had visual acuity improvement of >15 letters compared with control eyes.
>
> *Present status:* Study completed. The HORIZON extension study of MARINA patients demonstrated that repeated injections over 2 years did not result in an increased incidence of adverse effects. Visual acuity demonstrated a 5.1-letter loss at 12 months, but a 2-letter gain at 24 months.

compared with 64% of patients treated with PDT after 12 months; after 24 months, 90% of ranibizumab-treated patients lost less than 15 letters in visual acuity compared with 65.7% of patients treated with PDT. There was a mean improvement of 11 letters, with 41% of patients improving more than 3 lines after 24 months (Fig 4-11). Almost 80% of patients maintained or improved vision after 24 months. Ranibizumab received FDA approval in 2006.

Both the MARINA and ANCHOR studies evaluated monthly ranibizumab dosing. A phase 3b trial, the PIER study examined a different dosing regimen; it evaluated the efficacy and safety of ranibizumab administered monthly for 3 months and then quarterly in patients with subfoveal CNV secondary to AMD. The mean changes in vision from baseline at 12 months were –16.3, –1.6, and –0.2 letters for the sham, 0.3-mg ranibizumab, and 0.5-mg ranibizumab recipients, respectively ($P \leq .0001$; each ranibizumab dose vs sham). Similar to the MARINA and ANCHOR study results, the mean change in visual acuity from baseline in PIER improved over the first 3 months; however, the treatment effect declined in the ranibizumab recipients during quarterly dosing.

To study other dosing schemes, Rosenfeld and colleagues performed an investigator-sponsored trial that evaluated a regimen beginning with 3 consecutive monthly intravitreal injections of ranibizumab (0.5 mg). Thereafter, re-treatment with ranibizumab was performed if one of the following changes occurred between visits: a loss of 5 letters in conjunction with fluid in the macula as detected by OCT, an increase in OCT

CLINICAL TRIAL 4-2

Anti-VEGF Antibody for the Treatment of Predominantly Classic Choroidal Neovascularization in AMD (ANCHOR) Study

Objective: To determine if monthly intravitreal ranibizumab administration can reduce the risk of vision loss in patients with predominantly classic subfoveal CNV compared with photodynamic therapy with verteporfin treatment.

Participants: Eyes with new or recurrent subfoveal CNV, predominantly classic CNV, CNV >50% of lesion, size ≤9 disc areas, no prior PDT, blood <50% of the lesion, and visual acuity of 20/40 to 20/320.

Outcome measures: Visual acuity loss of <15 letters at 1 year. Secondary outcomes included visual acuity loss of <30 letters, contrast threshold function, quality of life, and morphologic outcomes.

Results: 95% of ranibizumab-treated eyes vs 64% of PDT-treated eyes maintained or improved vision (<15-letter loss in visual acuity) at 12 months. 90% of ranibizumab-treated patients lost <15 letters of visual acuity compared with 65.7% of PDT-treated eyes at 24 months. 41% of ranibizumab-treated eyes improved >3 lines after 24 months. Almost 80% of patients maintained or improved vision after 24 months.

Present status: Study completed. The HORIZON extension study of ANCHOR patients is ongoing.

central retinal thickness of at least 100 μm, new-onset classic CNV, new macular hemorrhage, or persistent macular fluid detected by OCT at least 1 month after the previous injection of ranibizumab. With this OCT-guided therapy, the mean visual acuity

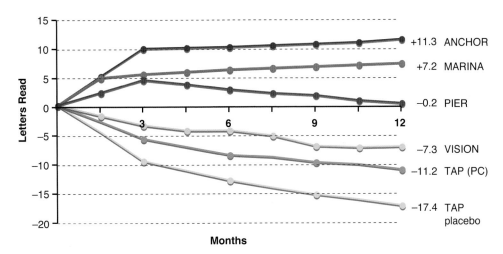

Figure 4-11 Graph illustrating the mean change in vision (letters read) from several phase 3 clinical trials. PC = predominantly classic; TAP = Treatment of Age-Related Macular Degeneration with Photodynamic Therapy; VISION = VEGF Inhibition Study in Ocular Neovascularization. *(Courtesy of Peter K. Kaiser, MD.)*

improved by 9.3 letters ($P < .001$) and the mean OCT central retinal thickness decreased by 178 μm ($P < .001$) in the 40 patients studied. Visual acuity improved 15 or more letters in 35% of patients. These visual acuity and OCT outcomes were achieved with an average of 5.6 injections over 12 months. After a fluid-free macula was achieved, the mean injection-free interval was 4.5 months before another injection was necessary.

In a study to compare various dosing regimens, a randomized, controlled trial called EXCITE tested 3 monthly injections of ranibizumab followed by maintenance injections every 3 months. The 12- and 24-month results showed an initial mean improvement in visual acuity during the initiation phase of monthly dosing; however, after month 3, there was a gradual decline in mean visual acuity during the maintenance phase that eventually fell below the pretreatment visual acuity. The EXCITE study had an additional treatment group comparing the PIER regimen (3 monthly doses followed by quarterly dosing) to the fixed-monthly regimens of the MARINA and ANCHOR studies. Although, on average, the subjects in EXCITE's quarterly dosing groups fared better at 12 months than the patients in the PIER study, the results were not as good as for subjects in the monthly dosing studies (ANCHOR and MARINA).

These data clarified that quarterly treatment is suboptimal; thus, it is not incorporated into clinical practice. In general, there are 2 accepted treatment schemes that deviate from the FDA-approved labeling of monthly injections: "treat-and-observe" and "treat-and-extend" approaches to anti-VEGF therapy. In the treat-and-observe method, regular treatment is performed until the macula is mostly free of exudation, followed by treatment only for signs of recurrent exudation during the maintenance phase. This approach is in contrast to the treat-and-extend regimen in which regular monthly treatment is continued until the macula is dry, after which treatment continues at gradually increasing intervals. In this second approach, injections are administered whether there appears to be active CNV or not. The goal of this therapy is to cautiously extend the time between injections as far apart as tolerated as long as there are no signs of recurrence.

Several clinical trials are evaluating as-needed approaches to anti-VEGF therapy: the PrONTO, SAILOR, SUSTAIN, and HORIZON studies. All of these studies utilize 3 monthly injections followed by various as-needed treatment regimens. Each study has a unique re-treatment regimen based on vision status and OCT findings. The PrONTO study showed the best results of these studies; it assessed the efficacy of 3 consecutive monthly injections followed by a variable-dosing regimen. During the first year, re-treatment with ranibizumab was performed at any monthly visit in which one of the listed criteria occurred; criteria included an increase in OCT central retinal thickness of at least 100 μm or a visual acuity loss of 5 letters or more. During the second year, the re-treatment criteria were amended to include re-treatment if any qualitative increase in the amount of fluid was detected using OCT. A total of 40 patients were enrolled. At month 24, the mean visual acuity improved by 11.1 letters ($P < .001$), and the OCT central retinal thickness decreased by 212 μm ($P < .001$). Visual acuity improved by 15 letters or more in 43% of patients. These visual acuity and OCT outcomes were achieved with an average of 9.9 injections over 24 months; the results were comparable with those of fixed-monthly treatment regimens. The SAILOR study results were not as good. Patients were treated using a similar protocol as in PrONTO, with 3 monthly injections followed by additional injections only if patients met certain clinical specifications. Patients gained between 0.5 letters and 2.3 letters through 1 year. Criticisms of the protocol included restrictive re-treatment criteria that did not reflect the prevailing standard of care, which currently uses more liberal re-treatment criteria. The SUSTAIN trial results were slightly better than those of SAILOR but were still not as good as those of the phase 3 monthly dosage trials (ANCHOR and MARINA).

The HORIZON study was a continuation trial of patients enrolled in prior ranibizumab AMD trials. The patients were allowed to continue ranibizumab treatment on a traditional as-needed basis. The results showed a statistically significant decline in vision. Eyes that had gained 10.2 letters on the ETDRS (Early Treatment Diabetic Retinopathy Study) eye chart during ANCHOR or MARINA after 2 years of monthly injections, declined in visual acuity and ended up with only a mean 2.0-letter gain compared with baseline (ie, they lost nearly 8 letters once the regimen was switched from monthly injections to an as-needed protocol). Experts believed that the major reason the HORIZON study showed such a decline in visual acuity was because of its protocol: unlike the other treatment-as-needed studies, HORIZON included no re-treatment guidelines for investigators, and patients received only a mean of 3.6 ranibizumab injections in the 12 months of the extension trial.

The HARBOR study is an ongoing phase 3 clinical trial comparing higher-dose (2.0 mg) ranibizumab with standard-dose (0.5 mg) ranibizumab therapy. The results of this trial could play a key role in the future treatment of AMD.

Abraham P, Yue H, Wilson L. Randomized, double-masked, sham-controlled trial of ranibizumab for neovascular age-related macular degeneration: PIER study year 2. *Am J Ophthalmol.* 2010;150(3):315–324.e1. Epub 2010 Jul 3.

Boyer DS, Heier JS, Brown DM, Francom SF, Ianchulev T, Rubio RG. A phase IIIb study to evaluate the safety of ranibizumab in subjects with neovascular age-related macular degeneration. *Ophthalmology.* 2009;116(9):1731–1739.

Lalwani GA, Rosenfeld PJ, Fung AE, et al. A variable-dosing regimen with intravitreal ranibizumab for neovascular age-related macular degeneration: year 2 of the PrONTO Study. *Am J Ophthalmol.* 2009;148(1):43–58.e1. Epub 2009 Apr 18.

Schmidt-Erfurth U, Eldem B, Guymer R, et al; EXCITE Study Group. Efficacy and safety of monthly versus quarterly ranibizumab treatment in neovascular age-related macular degeneration: the EXCITE study. *Ophthalmology.* 2011;118(5):831–839. Epub 2010 Dec 13.

VEGF Trap *VEGF Trap* is a soluble protein that acts as a VEGF receptor decoy but is smaller than immunoglobulin G (IgG). VEGF Trap is a fusion protein that combines the ligand-binding elements from the extracellular domains of *VEGFR1* and *VEGFR2* fused to the Fc constant region of IgG. VEGF Trap binds both VEGF and placental-like growth factor *(PIGF)* and fully penetrates all retinal layers.

In the VIEW 1 and 2 (VEGF Trap-Eye: Investigation of Efficacy and Safety in Wet Age-Related Macular Degeneration 1 and 2) studies, patients received VEGF Trap in monthly or bimonthly regimens. Patients achieved a statistically significantly greater mean improvement in visual acuity at week 52 versus baseline (secondary endpoint) than did patients administered ranibizumab 0.5 mg monthly. Specifically, those receiving VEGF Trap 2 mg monthly gained 10.9 letters on average, whereas those receiving ranibizumab 0.5 mg monthly had a mean 8.1-letter gain ($P < .01$). All other dose groups of VEGF Trap-Eye in the VIEW 1 study and all dose groups in the VIEW 2 study had results that were not statistically different from results for patients receiving ranibizumab at this secondary endpoint. A generally favorable safety profile was observed for both VEGF

Trap and ranibizumab. In the second year of the studies, currently under way, patients in VIEW 1 and VIEW 2 are continuing treatment with the same dose per injection as in the first year but administered only every 3 months, or more often for any worsening of AMD, as defined by protocol criteria.

Bevacizumab *Bevacizumab* is a full-length monoclonal antibody against VEGF that was approved by the FDA in February 2004 for the treatment of metastatic colorectal cancer. It has recently been described for "off-label" use via intravitreal and intravenous administration for the treatment of AMD. Both bevacizumab and ranibizumab are manufactured by the same pharmaceutical company, and there are important differences between the drugs: bevacizumab has 2 antigen-binding domains, whereas ranibizumab has only 1, and there are substantial cost differences that may affect access to treatment for some patients. Because fragment antibodies in general have shorter systemic half-lives than full-length antibodies do (2.2 hours for ranibizumab and approximately 21 days for bevacizumab), it is reasonable to assume that intravitreal injections of ranibizumab have a shorter systemic half-life than intravitreal injections of bevacizumab. Studies of bevacizumab in patients with AMD suggest that it is efficacious and relatively safe (no serious ocular or systemic adverse events have been reported), although some patients experience mildly elevated blood pressure.

The Comparison of Age-Related Macular Degeneration Treatments Trials (CATT) was a multicenter, randomized clinical trial to assess the relative safety and efficacy of ranibizumab and bevacizumab for the treatment of subfoveal neovascular AMD, which usually causes severe, irreversible vision loss. CATT was funded by the National Eye Institute and conducted in 44 clinical centers; results were released in 2011. The initial 1-year results demonstrated no statistically significant difference in outcomes between bevacizumab and ranibizumab in monthly or as-needed delivery schedules. The final, 2-year results were still pending at the time of this writing.

Combination treatment CNV is a multifactorial condition that involves all components of a wound-healing response including inflammation, angiogenesis, and fibrosis. Thus, it is unlikely that monotherapy would successfully treat the condition. Combination therapy with treatments that have different modes of action has the potential for additive or synergistic effects. In general, the goal of combination therapy is to maximize the strengths and minimize the weaknesses of individual medications and procedures.

In the past several years, PDT has often been used in conjunction with intravitreal triamcinolone to reduce post-PDT inflammation in retinal tissues. Combination therapy, or triple therapy, combines anti-VEGF pharmacotherapy with dexamethasone and reduced-fluence PDT. A number of studies evaluated 3 different verteporfin/ranibizumab combination regimens against ranibizumab monotherapy, and ongoing studies will help determine the most efficacious protocol. The overall results showed that fewer re-treatment visits were required with the combination therapies than with the ranibizumab monotherapy, and the differences were statistically significant. One such study was the phase 2 Reduced Fluence Visudyne Anti-VEGF-Dexamethasone In Combination for AMD Lesions (RADICAL) study. This study showed that the combination of verteporfin with ranibizumab reduced re-treatment rates compared with ranibizumab monotherapy while maintaining similar vision outcomes and an acceptable safety profile.

Another combination-therapy study was the DENALI study, a 24-month randomized and double-masked, multicenter trial of patients with CNV treated with either reduced- or standard-fluence PDT combined with ranibizumab. At month 12, patients in the standard-fluence combination group gained, on average, 5.3 letters from baseline and those in the reduced-fluence combination group gained, on average, 4.4 letters. Patients in the ranibizumab monthly monotherapy group gained an average of 8.1 letters at month 12. In general, these combination therapies have not been shown to be superior to monotherapy and thus are not the current standard of care.

Other treatment modalities Other treatment modalities that have been studied for AMD are transpupillary thermotherapy (TTT); radiotherapy; submacular surgery to remove subretinal blood, the CNV, or both; macular translocation; pneumatic displacement of hemorrhages; and pharmacologic therapies. Macular translocation procedures have evolved over the years; however, because of limited efficacy and safety data as well as the introduction of anti-VEGF drugs, they have not been used to any appreciable degree. The Submacular Surgery Trials reported no benefit to surgical removal of CNV in AMD. The Transpupillary Thermotherapy for CNV Trial reported no benefit over sham administration of TTT in occult with no classic CNV less than 3000 μm in size. Studies with radiation therapy are ongoing.

Other management considerations The fellow eye of an individual with unilateral neovascular maculopathy is at high risk of developing CNV, especially if it shows evidence of multiple drusen, large drusen, or focal clumps of hyperpigmentation of the RPE, or if the patient has definite systemic hypertension. If CNV does develop in the second eye, the patient is likely to become legally blind with or without treatment to the second eye. However, if CNV does not develop in the fellow eye, the average visual acuity of the fellow eye is likely to remain 20/40 or better over a 5-year period, even with drusen and abnormalities of the RPE.

When central vision in both eyes is markedly affected by AMD, the patient's functional abilities may be improved through low vision rehabilitation and the use of optical and nonoptical devices (see BCSC Section 3, *Clinical Optics*). Patients who have undergone successful anti-VEGF treatment often still have reduced acuity, in the 20/50 to 20/70 range, and will often need to use magnification and good lighting. The magnification is needed because, unlike the fovea, the peripheral retina is not specialized for good visual acuity. The use of good lighting and improved contrast will help patients whose contrast sensitivity is reduced. These patients may also have scotomas in the central visual field despite the absence of obvious scarring on clinical examination. Thus, they need to learn how to make adjustments to move the scotoma away from what they are trying to see to compensate for the blind spot in their vision. The American Academy of Ophthalmology SmartSight website (available at http://one.aao.org/CE/EducationalContent/Smartsight .aspx) provides guidelines for recognizing the need for vision rehabilitation and for implementing some interventions; it also provides a patient handout and information for referring patients for additional vision rehabilitation beyond those interventions provided by the ophthalmologist.

In summary, clinical trials for the treatment of AMD are evolving, and knowledge of this disease is rapidly advancing. Treatment options will likely expand in the coming years as the number of biologic drugs increases beyond anti-VEGF therapy. However, the root cause of the condition is still not fully elucidated, and there is currently no means of prevention.

American Academy of Ophthalmology. SmartSight website. Available at http://one.aao.org/CE/EducationalContent/Smartsight.aspx. Accessed August 29, 2011.

Argon laser photocoagulation for neovascular maculopathy: five-year results from randomized clinical trials. Macular Photocoagulation Study Group. *Arch Ophthalmol.* 1991;109:1109–1114.

Bressler NM; Treatment of Age-Related Macular Degeneration with Photodynamic Therapy (TAP) Study Group. Photodynamic therapy of subfoveal choroidal neovascularization in age-related macular degeneration with verteporfin: two-year results of 2 randomized clinical trials. TAP report 2. *Arch Ophthalmol.* 2001;119(2):198–207.

Brown DM, Kaiser PK, Michels M, et al; ANCHOR Study Group. Ranibizumab versus verteporfin for neovascular age-related macular degeneration. [1-year results of the ANCHOR Study]. *N Engl J Med.* 2006;355(14):1432–1444.

Fung AE, Lalwani GA, Rosenfeld PJ, et al. An optical coherence tomography–guided, variable dosing regimen with intravitreal ranibizumab (Lucentis) for neovascular age-related macular degeneration. *Am J Ophthalmol.* 2007;143(4):566–583.

Gragoudas ES, Adamis AP, Cunningham ET Jr, Feinsod M, Guyer DR; VEGF Inhibition Study in Ocular Neovascularization Clinical Trial Group. Pegaptanib for neovascular age-related macular degeneration. *N Engl J Med.* 2004;351(27):2805–2816.

Laser photocoagulation for juxtafoveal choroidal neovascularization. Five-year results from randomized clinical trials. Macular Photocoagulation Study Group. *Arch Ophthalmol.* 1994;112(4):500–509.

Photodynamic therapy of subfoveal choroidal neovascularization in age-related macular degeneration with verteporfin: one-year results of 2 randomized clinical trials—TAP report. Treatment of Age-Related Macular Degeneration with Photodynamic Therapy (TAP) Study Group. *Arch Ophthalmol.* 1999;117:1329–1345.

Rosenfeld PJ, Brown DM, Heier JS, et al. Ranibizumab for neovascular age-related macular degeneration. [2-year results of the MARINA study]. *N Engl J Med.* 2006;355(14):1419–1431.

Verteporfin in Photodynamic Therapy (VIP) Study Group. Verteporfin therapy of subfoveal choroidal neovascularization in age-related macular degeneration: two-year results of a randomized clinical trial including lesions with occult with no classic choroidal neovascularization. VIP report 2. *Am J Ophthalmol.* 2001;131(5):541–560.

Other Causes of Choroidal Neovascularization

Ocular Histoplasmosis Syndrome

Infection with the yeast form of the fungus *Histoplasma capsulatum* is endemic to certain areas of the United States, including states containing the Mississippi and Ohio River valleys. The fungus is carried on the feathers of chickens, pigeons, and blackbirds, as well as in droppings from infected bats. Humans inhale the fungus, which is then disseminated into the bloodstream. The systemic infection eventually subsides, leaving ocular scarring. Most of the visual symptoms occur years after initial infection.

The condition, *ocular histoplasmosis syndrome (OHS)*, has also been called *presumed ocular histoplasmosis syndrome (POHS)* because previously the causal relationship between the fungus and the eye disease had been considered tenuous; however, the relationship is supported by epidemiologic and histologic data. For example, more than 90% of patients with the typical fundus appearance react positively to histoplasmin skin testing, and the highest prevalence of OHS is found where the population has the greatest percentage of positive skin reactors. In one community with endemic histoplasmosis (where 60% of the total population reacted positively to histoplasmin skin testing), the characteristic peripheral lesions of OHS occurred in 2.6% of the total population surveyed and in 4.4% of the positive skin test responders. Only 1 individual with peripheral lesions showed disciform macular disease. The organism has been identified histologically in the choroids of 5 patients with OHS. Nevertheless, other etiologies besides *H capsulatum* may produce a similar phenotype.

There are 4 signs of OHS:

1. "punched-out" chorioretinal lesions ("histo spots")
2. juxtapapillary atrophic pigmentary changes
3. no vitritis
4. CNV

The clinical appearance of OHS includes small, atrophic, "punched-out" chorioretinal scars in the midperiphery and posterior pole ("histo spots"), linear peripheral atrophic tracks, and juxtapapillary chorioretinal scarring with or without CNV in the macula (Fig 4-12). The changes are bilateral in more than 60% of patients. No vitreous inflammation appears. Most patients with OHS are asymptomatic until CNV develops. Vision loss, metamorphopsia, and paracentral scotomata are the sequelae of CNV. If CNV is suspected, patients should undergo FA to determine the size, location, and characteristics of the CNV and receive appropriate treatment. Other diseases with features similar to those of OHS include multifocal choroiditis, birdshot choroidopathy, acute posterior multifocal placoid pigment epitheliopathy, and diffuse unilateral subacute neuroretinopathy (DUSN), as discussed in BCSC Section 9, *Intraocular Inflammation and Uveitis.*

Management of OHS

Results of the MPS showed that untreated eyes with OHS and extrafoveal CNV have a 44% cumulative risk of severe vision loss (losing at least 6 lines of vision) at 5 years. Photocoagulation of the CNV lesion reduces the risk to 9%. The MPS also showed treatment to be beneficial for juxtafoveal CNV. Although the initial visual acuities at the time of randomization ranged from 20/20 to 20/400, after 5 years the proportion of eyes with severe visual acuity loss was 28% in the untreated group and 12% in the treated group. Even when the CNV originated from a peripapillary scar or when photocoagulation was applied nasal to the fovea or in the papillomacular bundle, treatment was beneficial compared with observation.

As for AMD, recurrent CNV represents an important ongoing risk to central vision after effective photocoagulation for OHS. Unlike for AMD, however, OHS has not been shown to benefit from laser treatment that involves the foveal center in either new or

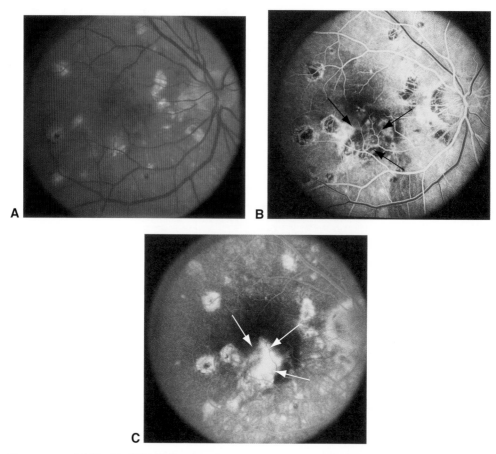

Figure 4-12 OHS with CNV. **A,** Fundus photograph shows peripapillary atrophy and numerous atrophic scars. **B,** Transit frame of the angiographic study reveals blocked fluorescence from blood and pigment as well as hyperfluorescence resulting from the CNV *(arrows)* and choroidal transmission in areas of atrophy. **C,** Leakage from the choroidal neovascular membrane *(arrows)* late in the study, as well as staining of the sclera beneath atrophic scars.

recurrent subfoveal CNV lesions. Even though small, short-term, uncontrolled case series of submacular surgery of subfoveal histoplasmosis–related CNV lesions have suggested possible benefits in vision outcome, recurrence rates have remained high after surgery. The Submacular Surgery Trials evaluated whether surgical removal of these lesions was beneficial compared with observation over a period of 4 years. The study found that in patients with visual acuity of 20/100 or better, submacular surgery was not beneficial. Although patients with worse visual acuity than 20/100 had an increased chance of retaining or improving visual acuity for at least 2 years after surgery, there were additional risks, including a high rate of recurrent CNV, cataract formation in older patients, and retinal detachment.

If 1 eye has OHS with CNV or disciform scarring, the risk of vision loss in the fellow eye is related to but not limited by the presence or absence of focal macular histoplasmosis spots. If no findings of OHS are present in the fellow eye, the risk is 1%. However, when peripapillary atrophy is present, the risk increases to 4%, and if focal macular histoplasmosis spots are present, the risk rises to 25%. Management of eyes with nonneovascular manifestations of OHS consists of instructing patients to monitor their central vision, often with the assistance of an Amsler grid, and evaluating patients promptly with FA if vision loss or metamorphopsia occurs.

Although eyes without macular lesions have a much better prognosis, new histoplasmosis spots, which represent areas where CNV may develop later, can develop in either the peripheral or macular region. The mainstay of clinical treatment for CNV secondary to histoplasmosis is anti-VEGF therapy. In general, most clinicians follow the same principals utilized in treating macular degeneration for histoplasmosis CNV.

> Holekamp NM, Thomas MA, Dickinson JD, Valluri S. Surgical removal of subfoveal choroidal neovascularization in presumed ocular histoplasmosis: stability of early visual results. *Ophthalmology.* 1997;104(1):22–26.
>
> Martidis A, Miller DG, Ciulla TA, Danis RP, Moorthy RS. Corticosteroids as an antiangiogenic agent for histoplasmosis-related subfoveal choroidal neovascularization. *J Ocul Pharmacol Ther.* 1999;15(5):425–428.
>
> Saperstein DA, Rosenfeld PJ, Bressler NM, et al; Verteporfin in Ocular Histoplasmosis (VOH) Study Group. Photodynamic therapy of subfoveal choroidal neovascularization with verteporfin in the ocular histoplasmosis syndrome: one-year results of an uncontrolled, prospective case series. *Ophthalmology.* 2002;109(8):1499–1505.

Idiopathic CNV

CNV and subsequent disciform scarring may develop in the absence of any other ophthalmoscopic abnormality or disease known to be associated with CNV. Such CNV lesions are termed *idiopathic* and are currently viewed as a distinct group. These disorders may represent a number of etiologies, including OHS without histoplasmosis spots and AMD without characteristic drusen or RPE abnormalities. The MPS showed benefits of laser treatment for extrafoveal or juxtafoveal idiopathic CNV that are consistent with the results of the larger trials studying extrafoveal or juxtafoveal CNV associated with OHS or AMD. Likewise, PDT should be considered for treatment of idiopathic subfoveal classic CNV. In addition, the off-label use of anti-VEGF drugs (approved for treatment of neovascular AMD), including pegaptanib, ranibizumab, and bevacizumab, has been described (see section below on anti-VEGF therapy for secondary causes of CNV).

> Krypton laser photocoagulation for idiopathic neovascular lesions. Results of a randomized clinical trial. Macular Photocoagulation Study Group. *Arch Ophthalmol.* 1990;108(6):832–837.
>
> Persistent and recurrent neovascularization after krypton laser photocoagulation for neovascular lesions of ocular histoplasmosis. Macular Photocoagulation Study Group. *Arch Ophthalmol.* 1989;107(3):344–352.
>
> Sickenberg M, Schmidt-Erfurth U, Miller JW, et al. A preliminary study of photodynamic therapy using verteporfin for choroidal neovascularization in pathologic myopia, ocular histoplasmosis syndrome, angioid streaks, and idiopathic causes. *Arch Ophthalmol.* 2000;118(3):327–336.

Angioid Streaks

Dark red to brown bands of irregular contour that radiate from the optic nerve head are known as *angioid streaks*. They represent discontinuities or breaks in a thickened and calcified Bruch membrane. It is possible to confuse angioid streaks with retinal vessels until their location deep to the retina is recognized (Fig 4-13).

Because the RPE overlying angioid streaks is often atrophic, the streaks appear hyperfluorescent *(window defect)* in the early phase of FA. As in other conditions with defects in the Bruch membrane, choroidal neovascular ingrowth may occur, resulting in exudative macular detachment and loss of central visual acuity. FA is not required for diagnosis of angioid streaks but is vital for ruling out CNV.

The systemic disease most commonly associated with angioid streaks is *pseudoxanthoma elasticum (PXE)*, or Grönblad-Strandberg syndrome. PXE is predominantly an autosomal recessive disorder inherited through mutation in the *ABCC6* gene located on band 16p13.1. Additional fundus findings in this condition include optic disc drusen, peripheral round atrophic scars, and a lighter orange appearance against the darker orange color of the normal RPE and choroid. At the interface between the abnormal light color and the normal darker color, the fundus, shown in Figure 4-13, has a fine, stippled appearance referred to as *peau d'orange* ("the skin of an orange"). Small, round subretinal depigmented dots, known as crystalline spots, are also frequently present in the midperiphery. They may also have an associated depigmented "comet tail."

Paget disease of bone, *beta thalassemia*, and *sickle cell anemia (SS)* also may be associated with angioid streaks, as may a number of other, less common, systemic disorders such as *Ehlers-Danlos syndrome* (this syndrome is discussed in a number of BCSC volumes; consult the *Master Index*). Streaklike changes also appear to develop from degenerative factors alone in some elderly patients. Any patient whose angioid streaks are more extensive than would normally be expected given the patient's age should receive a thorough workup for an associated condition; however, some patients with streaks have no demonstrable systemic disease.

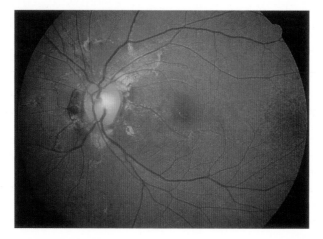

Figure 4-13 Fundus of patient with pseudoxanthoma elasticum shows angioid streaks, "peau d'orange" appearance temporal to the macula, and focal drusenlike lesions (inferotemporal arcade).

Angioid streaks usually are asymptomatic. Visual disturbances may occur if a streak opens under the macula, resulting in subretinal hemorrhages, but these hemorrhages often resolve spontaneously without evidence of CNV. The most significant visual complication of angioid streaks is the development of CNV from breaks in the Bruch membrane. Given that hemorrhages can occur without CNV, it is important to verify the presence of CNV before considering treatment.

No treatment is known to prevent this condition in eyes at risk. In considering laser treatment for CNV associated with angioid streaks, ophthalmologists may decide to extrapolate from the MPS results for CNV associated with other etiologies. In particular, thermal treatment is not appropriate for subfoveal lesions. Patients with extrafoveal or juxtafoveal lesions being considered for treatment should understand that the MPS results may or may not apply to their particular circumstances. The results are more likely to correspond to those for CNV in AMD than to CNV in OHS, because angioid streaks probably resemble a diffuse degenerative process like AMD more closely than they do a focal degenerative process like OHS. PDT alone or in combination with other therapies may also be considered for eyes with subfoveal CNV, although no prospective clinical study has addressed vision outcomes in this scenario.

As mentioned, the off-label use of anti-VEGF agents, including pegaptanib, ranibizumab, and bevacizumab, has been described (see section below on the use of anti-VEGF treatments for secondary causes of CNV). The use of safety glasses may be advised for patients with angioid streaks because their eyes are particularly susceptible to choroidal rupture after even minor blunt injury.

Clarkson JG, Altman RD. Angioid streaks. *Surv Ophthalmol.* 1982;26(5):235–246.

Lim JI, Bressler NM, Marsh MJ, Bressler SB. Laser treatment of choroidal neovascularization in patients with angioid streaks. *Am J Ophthalmol.* 1993;116(4):414–423.

Pathologic Myopia

Myopia is the most common ocular abnormality, affecting 25% of the US population. In contrast, *pathologic myopia,* also known as *high myopia* or *degenerative myopia,* is uncommon, occurring in roughly 2% of the population. Incidence rates are higher in Asians and lower in African Americans. Eyes with pathologic myopia have progressive elongation of the eye and associated thinning and degeneration of the retina, RPE, and choroid. The spherical equivalents of an eye with high myopia are more than –6.00 D, or an axial length greater than 26.5 mm, whereas eyes with pathologic myopia are more than –8.00 D, or an axial length greater than 32.5 mm. Fundus manifestations in pathologic myopia may include the following:

- tilting of the optic disc
- peripapillary chorioretinal atrophy
- lacquer cracks—spontaneous ruptures of the elastic lamina of the Bruch membrane that appear yellowish white, are usually located in the posterior pole, and exhibit linear or stellate patterns (Fig 4-14); FA may be useful in detecting subtle lacquer cracks
- isolated, round, deep subretinal hemorrhages that clear spontaneously and usually result from the occurrence or extension of a lacquer crack and not from CNV

- Forster-Fuchs spots—dark spots due to subretinal or intraretinal RPE hyperplasia, presumably developing in response to a small CNV that does not progress
- posterior staphyloma—localized ectasia of the sclera, choroid, and RPE
- elongation and atrophy of the ciliary body
- gyrate areas of atrophy of the RPE and choroid
- cystoid, paving-stone, and lattice degeneration
- thinning or hole formation in the peripheral retina
- thinning and rearrangement of the collagen layers of the sclera
- CNV

CNV in myopia

CNV may develop in 5%–10% of eyes with an axial length of more than 26.5 mm, often in conjunction with widespread chorioretinal degeneration and lacquer cracks in the posterior pole. In considering laser treatment for CNV that is outside the foveal center and associated with pathologic myopia, the ophthalmologist may cautiously extrapolate from the MPS results for CNV associated with other etiologies. In addition, laser therapy can have a long-term negative effect because laser scars expand; thus, the scar from treatment of a juxtafoveal lesion can extend into the fovea over time. Laser treatment is not appropriate for subfoveal lesions. PDT of subfoveal lesions in eyes with pathologic myopia was investigated in the VIP Pathologic Myopia Trial. This randomized trial found a benefit in preventing vision loss with PDT up to 3 years after initiating treatment. The off-label use of anti-VEGF drugs, including ranibizumab and bevacizumab has been described (see section below on anti-VEGF therapy for secondary causes of CNV) with promising results. A small prospective trial in 54 patients compared the effects on visual acuity of laser treatment, PDT with verteporfin, and intravitreal bevacizumab administration for patients with juxtafoveal choroidal neovascularization secondary to pathologic myopia. Overall, bevacizumab treatment offered the best functional results at the 2-year follow-up.

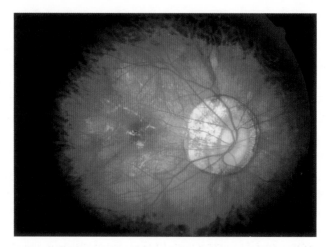

Figure 4-14 Pathologic myopia with tilted disc and peripapillary atrophy of RPE and choroid. Lacquer cracks are visible in the macula. Other features include a scleral crescent and a "blond" fundus, allowing visualization of choroidal vessels.

Another prospective trial evaluated the efficacy of intravitreal bevacizumab administration for CNV secondary to pathologic myopia. The 6-month outcomes suggested that this treatment may be promising, as it resulted in both visual and anatomical improvements. At 3 months, 90.9% of treated eyes showed complete absence of angiographic leakage. Further studies to evaluate the safety, efficacy, and optimal treatment regimen for bevacizumab are justified (see section below on the use of anti-VEGF therapy for secondary causes of CNV).

Blinder KJ, Blumenkranz MS, Bressler NM, et al. Verteporfin therapy of subfoveal choroidal neovascularization in pathologic myopia: 2-year results of a randomized clinical trial. VIP report no. 3. *Ophthalmology.* 2003;110(4):667–673.

Chan WM, Lai TY, Liu DT, Lam DS. Intravitreal bevacizumab (Avastin) for myopic choroidal neovascularization: six-month results of a prospective pilot study. *Ophthalmology.* 2007;114(12):2190–2196. Epub 2007 Jun 28.

Hampton GR, Kohen D, Bird AC. Visual prognosis of disciform degeneration in myopia. *Ophthalmology.* 1983;90(8):923–926.

Parodi MB, Iacono P, Papayannis A, Sheth S, Bandello F. Laser photocoagulation, photodynamic therapy, and intravitreal bevacizumab for the treatment of juxtafoveal choroidal neovascularization secondary to pathologic myopia. *Arch Ophthalmol.* 2010;128(4):437–442.

Tabandeh H, Flynn HW Jr, Scott IU, et al. Visual acuity outcomes of patients 50 years of age and older with high myopia and untreated choroidal neovascularization. *Ophthalmology.* 1999;106(11):2063–2067.

Verteporfin in Photodynamic Therapy Study Group. Photodynamic therapy of subfoveal choroidal neovascularization in pathologic myopia with verteporfin. 1-year results of a randomized clinical trial. VIP report no. 1. *Ophthalmology.* 2001;108(5):841–852.

Miscellaneous Causes of CNV

CNV may complicate a variety of conditions that damage the Bruch membrane, including choroidal rupture, optic disc drusen, and others (Table 4-2). In general, the ophthalmologist deciding whether to extend the MPS results to CNV arising from these other causes should probably avoid treating the foveal center but consider treating lesions outside the foveal center. Both the ophthalmologist and the patient must understand that because the natural histories are different for CNV of different etiologies, the exact risks and benefits for a particular circumstance may not be analogous to those in the MPS reports. After laser treatment, all patients must be carefully monitored for recurrent disease.

Anti-VEGF Therapy for Secondary Causes of CNV

A recent clinical trend has emerged in which CNV from non-AMD conditions is being treated with anti-VEGF drugs on an off-label basis. Because of its availability, bevacizumab (FDA approved for the treatment of some metastatic cancers) has generally been the drug most commonly selected. Several recent reports have described the benefits of anti-VEGF therapy for CNV from non-AMD conditions such as pathologic myopia, POHS, angioid streaks, and other causes of CNV. A prospective trial using ranibizumab showed benefits of treating all of these conditions with monthly or as-needed protocols

Table 4-2 Conditions Associated With CNV

Degenerative
Age-related macular degeneration
Myopic degeneration
Angioid streaks

Heredodegenerative
Vitelliform macular dystrophy
Fundus flavimaculatus
Optic nerve head drusen

Inflammatory
Ocular histoplasmosis syndrome
Multifocal choroiditis
Serpiginous choroiditis
Toxoplasmosis
Toxocariasis
Rubella
Vogt-Koyanagi-Harada syndrome
Behçet syndrome
Sympathetic ophthalmia

Tumor
Choroidal nevus
Choroidal hemangioma
Metastatic choroidal tumors
Hamartoma of the RPE

Traumatic
Choroidal rupture
Intense photocoagulation

Idiopathic

similar to those used in treating AMD. Further investigations are needed to establish the role of anti-VEGF drugs in the treatment of secondary causes of CNV.

Heier JS, Brown D, Ciulla T, Abraham P, Bankert JM, Chong S, Daniel PE Jr, Kim IK. Ranibizumab for choroidal neovascularization secondary to causes other than age-related macular degeneration: a phase I clinical trial. *Ophthalmology.* 2011;118(1):111–118. Epub 2010 Aug 3.

CHAPTER 5

Retinal Vascular Disease: Diabetic Retinopathy

A frequent cause of blindness in the United States, diabetic retinopathy is the leading cause in patients aged 20–64 years. This chapter provides a foundation for the evaluation and treatment of diabetic retinopathy; additional information is available in the following selected references.

American Academy of Ophthalmology Retina/Vitreous Panel. Preferred Practice Pattern Guidelines. *Diabetic Retinopathy.* San Francisco: American Academy of Ophthalmology; 2008. Available at www.aao.org/ppp.

Scott IU, Flynn HW Jr, Smiddy WE, eds. *Diabetes and Ocular Disease: Past, Present, and Future Therapies.* 2nd ed. Ophthalmology Monograph 14. San Francisco: American Academy of Ophthalmology; 2009.

Terminology and Classification

Diabetes Terminology

The terminology used for types of diabetes mellitus has evolved over the years. The American Diabetes Association (ADA) classifies diabetes mellitus as *type 1 diabetes mellitus,* formerly known as *insulin-dependent diabetes mellitus (IDDM),* and *type 2 diabetes mellitus,* formerly known as *non–insulin-dependent diabetes mellitus (NIDDM).* In type 1 diabetes mellitus there is β-cell destruction, usually leading to absolute insulin deficiency. This process is either idiopathic or immune mediated. Type 2 diabetes mellitus ranges from a condition characterized as predominantly insulin resistance with relative insulin deficiency to one that is predominantly an insulin secretory defect with insulin resistance. Other forms of diabetes mellitus are recognized, including a genetically mediated form secondary to endocrinopathies and drug- or chemical-induced diabetes mellitus.

Diabetic Retinopathy Terminology

The classification of diabetic retinopathy is based on clinical features. *Nonproliferative diabetic retinopathy (NPDR)* refers to the presence of intraretinal vascular changes without the presence of extraretinal fibrovascular tissue; it is further subdivided into mild, moderate, and severe. NPDR is also referred to as *background diabetic retinopathy,* a term that is still commonly used but not recommended. *Clinically significant diabetic macular edema (CSDME)* is present when minimal severity criteria for macular edema have been met. In *proliferative diabetic retinopathy (PDR),* ischemia-induced neovascularization from diabetes and the associated complications are noted. PDR is further described as early, high-risk, or advanced. In describing study results, the BCSC uses the terminology used by the individual studies, even if it does not conform to current terminology.

Epidemiology of Diabetic Retinopathy

The prevalence of all types of diabetic retinopathy in the diabetic population increases with the duration of diabetes mellitus and patient age. Diabetic retinopathy is rare in children younger than 10 years of age. The risk of developing diabetic retinopathy increases after puberty.

The Wisconsin Epidemiologic Study of Diabetic Retinopathy

The Wisconsin Epidemiologic Study of Diabetic Retinopathy (WESDR), an ongoing epidemiologic study on the progression of diabetic retinopathy, involved assessments using 7-field stereoscopic fundus photography, measurements of glycosylated hemoglobin levels, and recording of visual acuity. The WESDR reported important epidemiologic findings, including that the duration of diabetes mellitus was directly associated with an increased prevalence of diabetic retinopathy in both type 1 and type 2 diabetes mellitus. After 20 years of diabetes mellitus, nearly 99% of patients with type 1 and 60% with type 2 had some degree of diabetic retinopathy, and 3.6% of younger-onset patients (aged <30 years at diagnosis, an operational definition of type 1 diabetes mellitus) and 1.6% of older-onset patients (aged ≥30 years at diagnosis, an operational definition of type 2 diabetes mellitus) were found to be legally blind. Diabetic retinopathy caused legal blindness in 86% and 33% for the younger-onset and older-onset groups, respectively.

WESDR epidemiologic data were limited primarily to white populations of northern European descent and therefore are not entirely applicable to other racial groups. The National Health and Nutrition Examination Survey III of type 2 diabetes mellitus showed that the frequency of diabetic retinopathy in patients over 40 years of age was higher among non-Hispanic blacks (27%) and Mexican Americans (33%) than among non-Hispanic whites (18%).

Klein R, Klein BE, Moss SE, Davis MD, DeMets DL. The Wisconsin Epidemiologic Study of Diabetic Retinopathy. II. Prevalence and risk of diabetic retinopathy when age at diagnosis is less than 30 years. *Arch Ophthalmol.* 1984;102(4):520–526.

Pathogenesis of Diabetic Retinopathy

The exact cause of diabetic microvascular disease is unknown. It is believed that exposure to hyperglycemia over an extended period results in biochemical and physiologic changes that ultimately cause endothelial damage. Specific retinal capillary changes include selective loss of pericytes and basement membrane thickening, changes that favor capillary occlusion and retinal nonperfusion (Fig 5-1), as well as decompensation of the endothelial

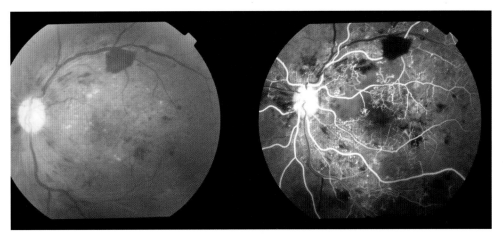

Figure 5-1 Fundus photograph of a patient with early proliferative diabetic retinopathy. Corresponding early-phase fluorescein angiogram shows severe capillary nonperfusion. Clinically difficult to appreciate, evidence of early neovascularization is revealed on the angiogram by dye leakage at the disc. *(Courtesy of Colin A. McCannel, MD.)*

barrier function, which allows serum leakage and retinal edema to occur. The stages of disease represent a continuous progression of the retinovascular damage with a seemingly stepwise clinical progression from mild stages to advanced proliferative changes. The pace of the progression varies among patients and depends mainly on systemic factors such as control of blood pressure, blood lipid concentrations, and glucose levels, among others.

Numerous hematologic and biochemical abnormalities have been correlated with the prevalence and severity of retinopathy:

- increased platelet adhesiveness
- increased erythrocyte aggregation
- abnormal levels of serum lipids
- defective fibrinolysis
- abnormal levels of growth hormone
- upregulation of vascular endothelial growth factor (VEGF)
- abnormalities in serum and whole-blood viscosity
- local and systemic inflammation

The precise roles of these abnormalities—individually or in combination—in the pathogenesis of retinopathy are not well defined, however.

Systemic Medical Management of Diabetic Retinopathy

The most important factor in the medical management of diabetic retinopathy is maintenance of good glycemic control. The Diabetes Control and Complications Trial (DCCT; Clinical Trial 5-1) and the United Kingdom Prospective Diabetes Study (UKPDS; Clinical Trial 5-2) showed that intensive glycemic control was associated with a reduced risk of newly diagnosed retinopathy and reduced progression of existing retinopathy in people with diabetes mellitus (type 1 diabetes mellitus in the DCCT and type 2 diabetes mellitus in the

CLINICAL TRIAL 5-1

Diabetes Control and Complications Trial (DCCT)

Study questions:

1. Primary prevention study: Will intensive control of blood glucose level slow development and subsequent progression of diabetic retinopathy (neuropathy and nephropathy)?
2. Secondary intervention study: Will intensive control of blood glucose level slow progression of diabetic retinopathy (neuropathy and nephropathy)?

Enrollment:

1. 726 patients with type 1 diabetes mellitus (1–5 years' duration) and no diabetic retinopathy.
2. 715 patients with type 1 diabetes mellitus (1–15 years' duration) and mild to moderate diabetic retinopathy.

Study groups: Intensive control of blood glucose level (multiple daily insulin injections or insulin pump) vs conventional management.

Outcome variables: Development of diabetic retinopathy or progression of retinopathy by 3 steps using a modified Airlie House classification scale; neuropathy, nephropathy (albuminuria, microalbuminuria), and cardiovascular outcomes were also assessed.

Results: In the primary prevention cohort, intensive control reduced the risk of developing retinopathy by 76% and in the secondary intervention cohort slowed progression of retinopathy by 54%. In the 2 cohorts combined, intensive control reduced the risk of clinical neuropathy by 60% and albuminuria (nephropathy) by 54%.

UKPDS). Furthermore, the DCCT showed that intensive glycemic control (compared with conventional treatment) was associated with reductions in progression to severe NPDR and PDR, incidence of macular edema, and need for panretinal and focal photocoagulation. The UKPDS showed that control of hypertension was also beneficial in reducing progression of retinopathy and loss of vision. Figure 5-2, adapted from published results of the DCCT, illustrates the interplay of sustained glycemic control, as represented by hemoglobin A_{1c} (HbA_{1c}) levels, time, and progression of diabetic retinopathy. Even small changes in sustained HbA_{1c} levels were found to have a large impact on diabetic retinopathy progression.

The effect of intensive treatment of diabetes on the development and progression of long-term complications in insulin-dependent diabetes mellitus. Diabetes Control and Complications Trial Research Group. *N Engl J Med.* 1993;329(14):977–986.

Intensive blood-glucose control with sulphonylureas or insulin compared with conventional treatment and risk of complications in patients with type 2 diabetes (UKPDS 33). United Kingdom Prospective Diabetes Study Group. *Lancet.* 1998;352(9131):837–853.

Klein R, Klein BE, Moss SE, Cruickshanks KJ. Association of ocular disease and mortality in a diabetic population. *Arch Ophthalmol.* 1999;117(11):1487–1495.

CLINICAL TRIAL 5-2

United Kingdom Prospective Diabetes Study (UKPDS)

Study questions:

1. Will intensive control of blood glucose level, in patients with type 2 diabetes, reduce the risk of microvascular complications of diabetes, including the risk of retinopathy progression?
2. Will intensive control of blood pressure, in patients with type 2 diabetes and elevated blood pressure, reduce the risk of microvascular complications of diabetes, including the risk of retinopathy progression?

Enrollment:

1. 4209 patients with newly diagnosed type 2 diabetes.
2. 1148 patients with hypertension and newly diagnosed type 2 diabetes.

Randomization:

1. Patients were randomly assigned to conventional policy starting with diet (1138 patients) or to intensive policy starting with a sulfonylurea—chlorpropamide (788 patients), glibenclamide (615 patients), or glipizide (170 patients)—or with insulin (1156 patients). If overweight and in the intensive group, patients were assigned to start treatment with metformin (342 patients).
2. Patients were randomly assigned to tight control of blood pressure (400 with angiotensin-converting enzyme [ACE] inhibitor and 398 with beta blockers) or to less tight control (390 patients).

Outcome variables: Development of any of 3 aggregate adverse outcomes and specific retinopathy-related outcomes (worsening of retinopathy on a modified Airlie House scale, retinal photocoagulation, vitreous hemorrhage, and worsening of visual acuity).

Results:

1. Intensive control of blood glucose level slowed progression of retinopathy and reduced the risk of other microvascular complications of diabetes. Sulfonylureas did not increase the risk of cardiovascular disease.
2. Intensive control of blood pressure slowed progression of retinopathy and reduced the risk of other microvascular and macrovascular complications of diabetes. No clinically or statistically significant difference was found in the comparison of blood pressure lowering with ACE inhibitors versus beta blockers.

Progression of retinopathy with intensive versus conventional treatment in the Diabetes Control and Complications Trial. Diabetes Control and Complications Trial Research Group. *Ophthalmology.* 1995;102(4):647–661.

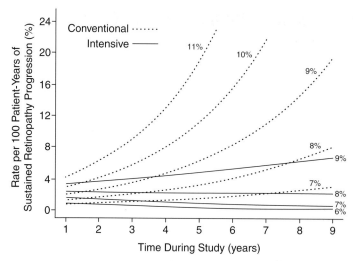

Figure 5-2 Results from the DCCT showing the risk of sustained retinopathy progression as a function of the mean HbA$_{1c}$ (percentage) during the study (years), estimated from the risk regression models of sustained progression as a function of time and glycemic exposure during the DCCT. The graph shows results of the intensive *(solid lines)* and conventional *(dotted lines)* treatment groups. *(Reproduced with permission from Lachin JM, Genuth S, Nathan DM, Zinman B, Rutledge BN; DCCT/EDIC Research Group. Effect of glycemic exposure on the risk of microvascular complications in the Diabetes Control and Complications Trial—revisited. Diabetes 2008;57(4):995–1001. Epub 2008 Jan 25.)*

> Tight blood pressure control and risk of macrovascular and microvascular complications in type 2 diabetes: UKPDS 38. UK Prospective Diabetes Study Group. *Br Med J.* 1998;317(7160):703–713.

Hypertension, when poorly controlled over many years, is usually associated with a higher risk of progression of diabetic retinopathy and diabetic macular edema (DME). In *asymmetric carotid artery occlusive disease,* the retinopathy may be further exacerbated by ocular ischemia. Controversy exists as to whether mild or moderate carotid artery occlusive disease has a protective effect on the development and severity of diabetic retinopathy. *Severe carotid artery occlusive disease* may result in advanced PDR as part of the ocular ischemic syndrome. *Advanced diabetic nephropathy* and *anemia* also may be markers of advanced diabetic retinopathy.

Pregnancy is associated with a worsening of retinopathy; therefore, women with diabetes mellitus who become pregnant require more frequent retinal evaluations. Vision loss may occur from NPDR with DME or from the complications of PDR. Although many of these pregnant women will have some regression of retinopathy after delivery, photocoagulation treatment is generally recommended if high-risk PDR develops during pregnancy.

> Brown GC. Arterial occlusive disease. In: Regillo CD, Brown GC, Flynn HW Jr, eds. *Vitreoretinal Disease: The Essentials.* New York: Thieme; 1999:97–117.
>
> Chew EY, Mills JL, Metzger BE, et al. Metabolic control and progression of retinopathy: The Diabetes in Early Pregnancy Study. National Institute of Child Health and Human Development Diabetes in Early Pregnancy Study. *Diabetes Care.* 1995;18(5):631–637.
>
> Davis MD, Fisher MR, Gangnon RE, et al. Risk factors for high-risk proliferative diabetic retinopathy and severe visual loss: Early Treatment Diabetic Retinopathy Study report 18. *Invest Ophthalmol Vis Sci.* 1998;39(2):233–252.

Conditions Associated With Vision Loss From Diabetic Retinopathy

Vision loss in patients with diabetic retinopathy can be associated with the following conditions:

- capillary leakage (macular edema)
- capillary occlusion (macular ischemia, diabetic papillopathy)
- sequelae from ischemia-induced neovascularization (vitreous hemorrhage, traction retinal detachment, neovascular glaucoma)

Nonproliferative Diabetic Retinopathy

Retinal microvascular changes that occur in NPDR are limited to the retina and do not extend beyond the internal limiting membrane (ILM). Characteristic findings in NPDR include microaneurysms, areas of capillary nonperfusion, nerve fiber layer (NFL) infarcts (also called "cotton-wool spots"), intraretinal microvascular abnormalities (IRMAs), "dot-and-blot" intraretinal hemorrhages, retinal edema, hard exudates, arteriolar abnormalities, and dilation and beading of retinal veins. NPDR can affect visual function through 2 mechanisms:

- increased intraretinal vascular permeability, resulting in macular edema
- variable degrees of intraretinal capillary closure, resulting in macular ischemia

Chew EY, Ferris FL III. Nonproliferative diabetic retinopathy. In: Ryan SJ, Hinton DR, Schachat AP, Wilkinson CP, eds. *Retina*. 4th ed. Philadelphia: Elsevier/Mosby; 2006: 1271–1284.

Diabetic Macular Edema

Retinal edema threatening or involving the fovea often results in vision loss. It is an important consequence of abnormal retinal vascular permeability in diabetic retinopathy (Fig 5-3). The diagnosis of DME is made when retinal thickening is noted by slit-lamp biomicroscopy or optical coherence tomography (OCT). Important observations include

- location of retinal thickening relative to the foveal center
- presence and location of exudates
- presence of cystoid macular edema

Fluorescein angiography is useful in demonstrating the breakdown of the blood–retinal barrier by showing retinal capillary leakage. However, angiography is *not* the appropriate test to evaluate eyes for the presence or absence of macular edema. Leakage shown on the angiogram may occur in the *absence* of macular retinal thickening and is thus not diagnostic of macular edema.

DME may manifest as focal or diffuse retinal thickening, with or without exudates. Although an overlap of categories often occurs, 2 general categories of macular edema—focal and diffuse—are recognized. *Focal macular edema* is characterized by areas of focal

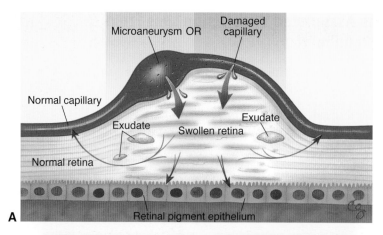

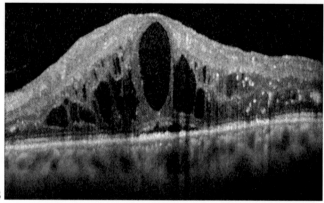

Figure 5-3 **A,** Artist's rendering of the mechanism of diabetic macular edema, demonstrating development of thickening from a breakdown of the blood–retinal barrier. **B,** Spectral-domain optical coherence tomogram of diabetic macular edema. Note the foveal detachment. *(Part A reproduced with permission from Ginsburg LH, Aiello LM. Diabetic retinopathy: classification, progression, and management.* Focal Points: Clinical Modules for Ophthalmologists. *San Francisco: American Academy of Ophthalmology; 1993, module 7. Illustration by Christine Gralapp. Part B courtesy of Colin A. McCannel, MD.)*

fluorescein leakage from capillary lesions, such as microaneurysms (Fig 5-4A, B). Focal macular edema may be associated with hard exudates, that is, precipitated plasma lipoproteins. Resorption of aqueous occurs at a greater rate than that of the lipid plasma components, resulting in the accumulation of lipid residues. The lipid usually accumulates in the outer and inner plexiform layers but occasionally underneath the sensory retina itself. These residues are the yellow to white deposits described as *hard exudates.*

Diffuse macular edema is characterized by widespread retinal capillary leakage and extensive breakdown of the blood–retinal barrier, often with cystoid fluid accumulation in the perifoveal macula (cystoid macular edema) (Fig 5-4C, D). Aside from whether the pattern of macular edema is focal or diffuse, criteria have been developed to determine clinical significance, which is the basis of treatment decisions.

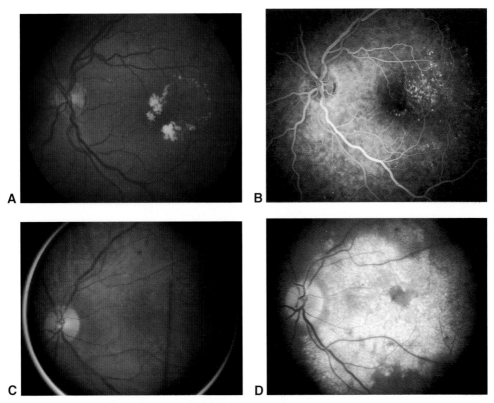

Figure 5-4 Focal macular edema. **A,** The color photograph shows circinate hard exudates surrounding a group of microaneurysms. **B,** The fluorescein angiogram confirms the microaneurysms, which appear as a group of punctate foci of hyperfluorescence. Diffuse macular edema. **C,** The color photograph shows diffuse thickening of the retina with glistening surface. **D,** The fluorescein angiogram confirms the diffuse intraretinal leakage. *(Courtesy of Hermann D. Schubert, MD.)*

Clinically significant diabetic macular edema

Many of the current treatment paradigms for managing DME were derived from the Early Treatment Diabetic Retinopathy Study (ETDRS), a prospective, randomized clinical trial evaluating photocoagulation of patients with diabetes who had less than high-risk PDR in both eyes (Clinical Trial 5-3).

The ETDRS defined clinically significant macular edema (CSME) and recommended treatment with focal laser photocoagulation using the following criteria:

- retinal edema located at or within 500 μm of the center of the macula (Fig 5-5)
- hard exudates at or within 500 μm of the center if associated with thickening of adjacent retina (Fig 5-6)
- a zone of thickening larger than 1 disc area if located within 1 disc diameter of the center of the macula (Fig 5-7)

CLINICAL TRIAL 5-3

Early Treatment Diabetic Retinopathy Study (ETDRS)

Study questions:

1. Is photocoagulation effective for treating DME?
2. Is photocoagulation effective for treating diabetic retinopathy?
3. Is aspirin effective for preventing progression of diabetic retinopathy?

Eligibility: Mild nonproliferative diabetic retinopathy through early proliferative diabetic retinopathy, with visual acuity 20/200 or better in each eye.

Randomization: 3711 participants: 1 eye randomly assigned to photocoagulation (scatter and/or focal) and 1 eye assigned to no photocoagulation; patients randomly assigned to 650 mg/day aspirin or placebo.

Outcome variables: Visual acuity less than 5/200 for at least 4 months; visual acuity worsening by doubling of initial visual angle (eg, 20/40 to 20/80); retinopathy progression.

Aspirin use results:

1. Aspirin use did not alter progression of diabetic retinopathy.
2. Aspirin use did not increase risk of vitreous hemorrhage.
3. Aspirin use did not affect visual acuity.
4. Aspirin use reduced risk of cardiovascular morbidity and mortality.

Early scatter photocoagulation results:

1. Early scatter photocoagulation resulted in a small reduction in the risk of severe vision loss (<5/200 for at least 4 months).
2. Early scatter photocoagulation is not indicated for eyes with mild to moderate diabetic retinopathy.
3. Early scatter photocoagulation may be most effective in patients with type 2 diabetes.

Macular edema results:

1. Focal photocoagulation for DME decreased risk of moderate vision loss (doubling of initial visual angle).
2. Focal photocoagulation for DME increased chance of moderate vision gain (halving of initial visual angle).
3. Focal photocoagulation for DME reduced retinal thickening.

Treatment of diabetic macular edema

Treatment strategies for DME encompass lifestyle modifications including weight reduction, increased level of exercise, and smoking cessation, as well as better control of blood sugar levels, blood pressure, blood lipid levels, and body mass index. Once a patient's medical management has been optimized, ocular therapies should be considered

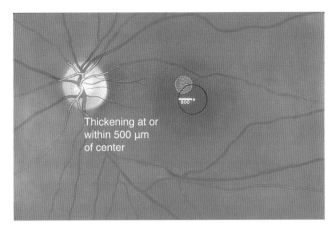

Figure 5-5 Clinically significant macular edema (CSME). Retinal edema located at or within 500 μm of the center of the macula. *(Courtesy of the ETDRS.)*

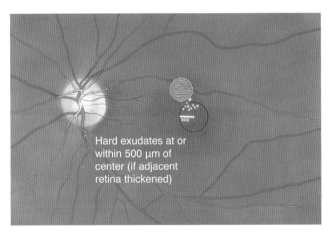

Figure 5-6 CSME. Hard exudates at or within 500 μm of the center of the macula, if associated with thickening of the adjacent retina. *(Courtesy of the ETDRS.)*

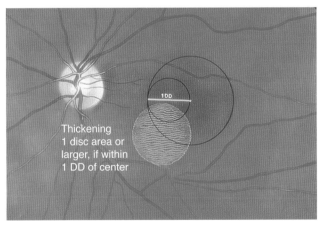

Figure 5-7 CSME. A zone of thickening larger than 1 disc area, if located within 1 disc diameter (DD) of the center of the macula. *(Courtesy of the ETDRS.)*

to prevent progressive vision loss and optimize the patient's vision. These include ocular pharmacologic management and laser photocoagulation treatment.

Ocular pharmacologic management of DME Both corticosteroids and anti-VEGF drugs continue to be investigated for use in managing DME.

CORTICOSTEROIDS In patients with refractory DME, a posterior sub-Tenon injection of triamcinolone acetonide improved visual acuity at 1 month and stabilized vision for up to 1 year in a retrospective, interventional case series. A rise in intraocular pressure (IOP) was rare, as was ptosis. The Diabetic Retinopathy Clinical Research Network (DRCR.net) prospectively evaluated sub-Tenon injection of triamcinolone acetonide as an adjunct to macular laser photocoagulation in the management of mild DME and failed to show any benefit.

Similarly, in patients with refractory CSME, intravitreal administration of corticosteroids improved vision modestly in the short term and reduced macular thickness for up to 2 years of follow-up. However, when the use of intravitreal triamcinolone acetonide (IVTA) was compared with macular laser treatment in the DRCR.net Standard Care Versus Corticosteroid for Retinal Vein Occlusion (SCORE) trial at 2 and 3 years of follow-up, eyes treated with focal macular laser had better visual acuity outcomes than did those treated with IVTA on an every-3-months basis. Although effective, sustained-release implants containing fluocinolone and dexamethasone for the treatment of DME have been plagued by cataract progression and corticosteroid-induced glaucoma. These adverse effects are shared by all local ocular corticosteroid treatments and need to be considered.

ANTI-VEGF DRUGS Currently available anti-VEGF drugs include ranibizumab, bevacizumab, and pegaptanib. Several studies are assessing the efficacy of these drugs for the treatment of DME, but most are uncontrolled and have relatively short follow-up periods. However, a number of prospective studies are emerging. In a prospective, randomized trial, the DRCR.net evaluated the efficacy and safety of ranibizumab plus prompt or deferred laser photocoagulation or triamcinolone plus prompt laser photocoagulation for DME. Intravitreal ranibizumab administration with prompt or deferred laser photocoagulation was shown to be more effective at improving visual acuity through at least 1 year than was prompt laser photocoagulation alone for the treatment of DME involving the central macula.

In another prospective, randomized study, the Ranibizumab for Edema of the Macula in Diabetes 2 (READ-2) trial, ranibizumab administration alone was compared with laser photocoagulation (focal or grid pattern) alone and with laser photocoagulation combined with ranibizumab administration. At the 6-month time point, ranibizumab treatment alone resulted in a 7-letter improvement over treatment with laser photocoagulation alone, and the combination of the 2 treatments had an intermediate effect. By 2 years, there was no statistically significant difference in mean visual acuity among the 3 treatment groups, although macular thickness was most improved in the ranibizumab group (Fig 5-8).

There are many studies suggesting bevacizumab may be similarly useful in the treatment of DME and CSME; however, there are no prospective, randomized trials with long-term follow-up. The exact role of anti-VEGF drugs in the treatment of DME and CSME is rapidly evolving, with promising outcomes reported thus far.

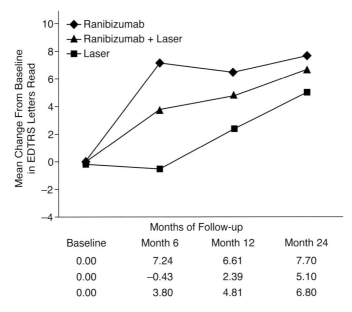

Figure 5-8 Results from the READ-2 Study showing the mean change from baseline in best-corrected visual acuity at several time points for each treatment group. Each point shows the mean change from baseline in best-corrected visual acuity measured in letters read at 4 meters on an Early Treatment Diabetic Retinopathy (ETDRS) chart for each treatment group: ranibizumab injection alone *(diamonds)*, focal or grid laser photocoagulation alone *(rectangles)*, or ranibizumab plus laser photocoagulation *(triangles)*. For each time point, data were included for all patients who remained in the trial at that time. *(From Nguyen QD, Shah SM, Khwaja AA, et al; READ-2 Study Group. Two-year outcomes of the ranibizumab for edema of the macula in diabetes (READ-2) study. Ophthalmology. 2010;117(11):2146–2151. Epub 2010 Sep 19.)*

Diabetic Retinopathy Clinical Research Network (DRCR.net), Beck RW, Edwards AR, Aiello LP, Bressler NM, Ferris F, et al. Three-year follow-up of a randomized trial comparing focal/grid photocoagulation and intravitreal triamcinolone for diabetic macular edema. *Arch Ophthalmol.* 2009;127(3):245–251.

Diabetic Retinopathy Clinical Research Network, Elman MJ, Aiello LP, Beck RW, Bressler NM, Bressler SB, et al. Randomized trial evaluating ranibizumab plus prompt or deferred laser or triamcinolone plus prompt laser for diabetic macular edema. *Ophthalmology.* 2010;117(6):1064–1077. Epub 2010 Apr 28.

Gillies MC, Sutter FK, Simpson JM, Larsson J, Ali H, Zhu M. Intravitreal triamcinolone for refractory diabetic macular edema: two-year results of a double-masked, placebo-controlled, randomized clinical trial. *Ophthalmology.* 2006;113(9):1533–1538.

Nguyen QD, Shah SM, Khwaja AA, Channa R, Hatef E, Do DV, et al; READ-2 Study Group. Two-year outcomes of the Ranibizumab for Edema of the Macula in Diabetes (READ-2) study. *Ophthalmology.* 2010;117(11):2146–2151. Epub 2010 Sep 19.

Surgical management of DME In the management of DME, laser surgery is a well-proven treatment with very good efficacy, whereas the exact role of vitrectomy continues to evolve.

LASER TREATMENT OF DME The ETDRS demonstrated that eyes with CSME benefited from focal- or grid-pattern macular argon laser photocoagulation treatment (macular laser) compared with untreated eyes in a control group. The primary outcome measurement in the ETDRS was moderate visual loss (MVL), comparing baseline with follow-up visual acuities. MVL was defined as a doubling of the visual angle (eg, a decrease from 20/20 to 20/40 or from 20/50 to 20/100), a decrease of 15 or more letters on ETDRS visual acuity charts, or a decrease of 3 or more lines of Snellen visual acuity equivalent. Thus, laser photocoagulation treatment for CSME reduced the risk of MVL, increased the chance of visual improvement, and was associated with only minor losses of visual field. Eyes without CSME showed no statistically significant difference between treated eyes and control eyes during the first 2 years. In clinical practice, therefore, treatment of such eyes can be delayed until progression of edema threatens the center of the macula.

For patients with CSME who are asymptomatic and have normal visual acuity, the decision as to when to begin treatment may be complex. It can be influenced by the proximity of exudates to the fovea, the status and course of the fellow eye, anticipated cataract surgery, or the presence of high-risk PDR. It is preferable to initiate photocoagulation for DME before performing scatter photocoagulation for high-risk PDR. Likewise, it is preferable to treat DME prior to cataract surgery because of the potential progression of retinopathy and macular edema after surgery.

The ETDRS also demonstrated that subretinal fibrosis occurred less often in laser-treated eyes than in untreated control eyes. Subretinal fibrosis was associated with the presence and severity of hard exudates in the macula. Table 5-1 lists the adverse effects of photocoagulation for macular edema.

Clinical features associated with poorer visual acuity outcomes after photocoagulation treatment for DME include the following:

- diffuse macular edema with center (foveal) involvement
- diffuse fluorescein leakage
- macular ischemia (extensive perifoveal capillary nonperfusion)
- hard exudates in the fovea
- marked cystoid macular edema

In general, the ophthalmologist views the patient's fluorescein angiogram to guide treatment for CSME. For focal leakage, direct laser therapy using green or yellow wavelengths

---

Table 5-1 Focal Laser Photocoagulation: Adverse Effects and Complications

Paracentral scotomata

Transient increase of edema/decrease in vision

Choroidal neovascularization

Subretinal fibrosis

Photocoagulation scar expansion

Inadvertent foveolar burns

Modified from Kim JW, Al E. Diabetic retinopathy. In: Regillo CD, Brown GC, Flynn HW Jr, eds. *Vitreoretinal Disease: The Essentials.* New York: Thieme; 1999:147.

is applied to all leaking microaneurysms between 500 and 3000 μm from the center of the macula. Focal treatment typically includes the following parameters:

- 50- to 100-μm spot size
- duration of 0.1 second or less
- attempt to whiten or darken microaneurysms

For diffuse leakage or zones of capillary nonperfusion adjacent to the macula, a light-intensity grid pattern using green or yellow laser is applied to all areas of diffuse leakage more than 500 μm from the center of the macula and 500 μm from the temporal margin of the optic disc. Parameters for local treatment in a grid pattern include the following:

- 50- to 100-μm spot size
- duration of 0.1 second or less
- spots spaced at least 1 burn width apart

Subthreshold intensity may be effective and may reduce retinal pigment epithelial and choroidal atrophy. Treatment sessions repeated over many months are frequently necessary for resolution of DME.

Treatment techniques and clinical guidelines for photocoagulation of diabetic macular edema. ETDRS report number 2. Early Treatment Diabetic Retinopathy Study Research Group. *Ophthalmology.* 1987;94:761–774.

PARS PLANA VITRECTOMY FOR DME   Pars plana vitrectomy and detachment of the posterior hyaloid may also be useful for treating DME, particularly when there is evidence of posterior hyaloidal traction and diffuse DME. In a prospective observational case series, the DRCR.net investigated whether there is benefit of vitrectomy for the treatment of DME in eyes with at least moderate vision loss and vitreomacular traction. The study determined that after vitrectomy, retinal thickening was reduced in most eyes, but the median visual acuity remained unchanged over the 6-month follow-up period. However, the exact role of vitrectomy in the treatment of DME remains to be determined.

Diabetic Retinopathy Clinical Research Network Writing Committee, Haller JA, Qin H, et al. Vitrectomy outcomes in eyes with diabetic macular edema and vitreomacular traction. *Ophthalmology.* 2010;117(6):1087–1093. Epub 2010 Mar 17.

Kaiser PK, Riemann CD, Sears JE, Lewis H. Macular traction detachment and diabetic macular edema associated with posterior hyaloidal traction. *Am J Ophthalmol.* 2001;131(1):44–49.

Diabetic Macular Ischemia

Retinal capillary nonperfusion is a feature commonly associated with moderate to severe NPDR. Fluorescein angiography can show the extent of capillary nonperfusion. The foveal avascular zone may become irregular and enlarged because of nonperfusion of the marginal capillaries. Microaneurysms tend to cluster at the margins of zones of capillary nonperfusion. Closure of retinal arterioles may result in larger areas of nonperfusion and progressive ischemia. A foveal avascular zone of greater than 1000 μm in diameter generally correlates with central vision loss.

Severe Nonproliferative Diabetic Retinopathy

Historically, the term *preproliferative diabetic retinopathy* included NFL infarcts (cotton-wool spots) as well as the features defined by the ETDRS under severe or very severe NPDR. NFL infarcts can be identified easily on clinical examination, and their presence suggests that a careful search for features predicting progression to PDR is indicated, including for systemic factors such as hypertension. However, the ETDRS reported that the presence of NFL infarcts was less helpful in predicting progression to PDR than were other characteristics of severe NPDR.

Severe NPDR, as defined by the ETDRS (see Clinical Trial 5-1) in the *4:2:1 rule,* is characterized by any 1 of the following:

- diffuse intraretinal hemorrhages and microaneurysms in *4* quadrants (Fig 5-9)
- venous beading in *2* quadrants (Fig 5-10)
- IRMAs in *1* quadrant (Fig 5-11)

The ETDRS investigators developed this 4:2:1 rule to help clinicians identify patients at greatest risk of progression to PDR and high-risk PDR. The ETDRS found that severe NPDR had a 15% chance of progression to high-risk PDR within 1 year. Very severe NPDR, defined by the presence of any 2 of these features, had a 45% chance of progression to high-risk PDR within 1 year. Patients with severe NPDR or worse should be considered for early treatment with panretinal photocoagulation.

As the retinopathy progresses, the degree of capillary damage and nonperfusion increases, which leads to retinal ischemia and release of vasoproliferative factors. One vasoproliferative factor, VEGF, has been isolated from vitrectomy specimens of patients with PDR. This factor can stimulate neovascularization of the retina, optic nerve head, or anterior segment.

Aiello LP, Avery RL, Arrigg PG, et al. Vascular endothelial growth factor in ocular
fluid of patients with diabetic retinopathy and other retinal disorders. *N Engl J Med.*
1994;331(22):1480–1487.

Early photocoagulation for diabetic retinopathy. ETDRS report number 9. Early Treatment
Diabetic Retinopathy Study Research Group. *Ophthalmology.* 1991;98(5 suppl):766–785.

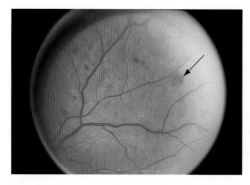 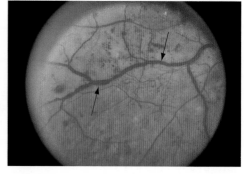

Figure 5-9 Diffuse intraretinal hemorrhages *(arrow)* and microaneurysms in NPDR. *(Standard photograph 2A, courtesy of the ETDRS.)*

Figure 5-10 Venous beading in NPDR *(arrows). (Standard photograph 6B, courtesy of the ETDRS.)*

IRMA

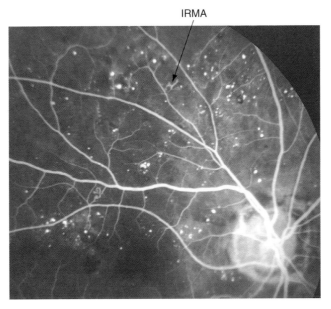

Figure 5-11 Intraretinal microvascular abnormalities (IRMAs) in NPDR. Fluorescein angiogram showing microaneurysms, areas of nonperfusion, and intraretinal capillary remodeling *(arrow)*. *(Courtesy of Hermann D. Schubert, MD.)*

Proliferative Diabetic Retinopathy

Extraretinal fibrovascular proliferation is present in varying stages of development in PDR. The new vessels evolve through 3 stages:

1. Fine new vessels with minimal fibrous tissue cross and extend beyond the ILM.
2. The new vessels increase in size and extent, with an increased fibrous component.
3. The new vessels regress, leaving residual fibrovascular tissue that uses the posterior hyaloid as a scaffold.

Based on the extent of proliferation, PDR is graded into early, high-risk, or advanced categories. By definition, the location of neovascular proliferations is categorized to be either on the disc (neovascularization of the disc, or NVD) or elsewhere (neovascularization elsewhere, or NVE). High-risk PDR was defined in the Diabetic Retinopathy Study (DRS) as either (a) the presence of any 1 of the following findings:

- mild NVD with vitreous hemorrhage (Fig 5-12)
- moderate to severe NVD with or without vitreous hemorrhage (≥DRS standard 10A, showing 1/4 to 1/3 disc area of NVD)
- moderate (1/2 disc area) NVE with vitreous hemorrhage (Fig 5-13)

OR (b) any 3 of the 4 following findings:

1. presence of vitreous or preretinal hemorrhage
2. presence of new vessels

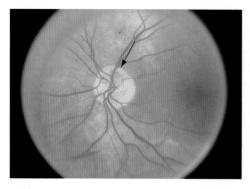

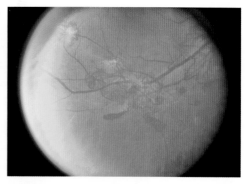

Figure 5-12 Neovascularization of the disc (NVD) with small vitreous hemorrhage *(arrow)*. Even without vitreous hemorrhage, this amount of NVD is the lower limit of moderate NVD and is considered high-risk PDR. *(Standard photograph 10A, courtesy of the DRS.)*

Figure 5-13 Moderate neovascularization elsewhere (NVE) with preretinal hemorrhage. *(Standard photograph 7, courtesy of the DRS.)*

3. location of new vessels on or near the optic disc
4. moderate to severe extent of new vessels

Advanced diabetic retinopathy is associated with cardiovascular disease risk factors. Patients with PDR are at increased risk of myocardial infarction, cerebrovascular accident, diabetic nephropathy, amputation, and death.

Nonsurgical Management of Proliferative Diabetic Retinopathy

Anti-VEGF drugs

Numerous, mostly uncontrolled, studies involving bevacizumab collectively suggest that anti-VEGF drugs may have a role in the management of PDR. Intravitreal anti-VEGF drugs can temporarily decrease leakage and cause regression of diabetic neovascular complexes in newly diagnosed and refractory disease. Anti-VEGF drugs may expedite resolution of vitreous hemorrhage and have been reported to cause regression of anterior segment neovascularization. These drugs may be helpful as an adjunct to vitrectomy for diabetic traction retinal detachment by reducing intraoperative bleeding and allowing for easier dissection when administered preoperatively. Potential complications from anti-VEGF drugs in the management of PDR include precipitating traction retinal detachments, causing retinal tears and combined tractional-rhegmatogenous retinal detachments related to the induced rapid contracture of the fibrovascular tissue, as well as increasing macular ischemia.

Surgical Management of Proliferative Diabetic Retinopathy

Laser surgery

The mainstay of treatment for PDR is thermal laser photocoagulation in a panretinal pattern to induce regression of neovascularization. For patients with high-risk PDR, panretinal photocoagulation (PRP) treatment is almost always recommended. The goal of

PRP is to destroy ischemic retina and increase oxygen tension in the eye. Ischemic retina is known to produce growth factors, such as VEGF, that promote disease progression. Increased oxygen tension is achieved by 2 mechanisms: decreased consumption resulting from the purposeful retinal destruction, and increased diffusion of oxygen from the choroid in the areas of the photocoagulation scars. Collectively, these changes cause regression of existing neovascular tissue and prevent progressive neovascularization. The exact amount of treatment necessary to achieve these endpoints is not always predictable; regardless, the treatment endpoint is regression of neovascularization. Although treatments may be spread over a number of sessions, the DRCR.net found no apparent long-term vision benefit from administering full PRP over several sessions versus in a single session, except for a transient decrease in vision in the latter. After the initial PRP, additional therapy can be applied incrementally in an attempt to achieve complete regression of persistent or recurrent neovascularization.

Full PRP, as used in the DRS (Clinical Trial 5-4) and ETDRS, included 1200 or more 500-μm burns using argon green or blue/green laser, separated from each other by one-half burn width (Fig 5-14). Because PRP promotes contracture of fibrovascular tissue, treatment may be followed by increased vitreoretinal traction, vitreous hemorrhage, tractional retinal detachment, and combined tractional-rhegmatogenous retinal detachment. In addition, contracting fibrovascular tissue and resultant traction can result in recurrent vitreous hemorrhages.

Adverse effects of scatter PRP include decreased night vision, color vision, contrast sensitivity, and peripheral vision. Some patients may lose 1 or 2 lines of visual acuity or experience glare. Transient adverse effects include loss of accommodation, loss of corneal sensitivity, and photopsias. Macular edema may also be precipitated or worsened by PRP. Using more peripheral laser placement may be sufficient to arrest disease progression, as it preserves the largest central visual field. Sparing the horizontal meridians, that is, the path of the long ciliary vessels and nerves, protects accommodation and corneal innervation. Heavy treatment, when necessary, should be performed in areas of retina where vision loss is less noticed by patients or is associated with less morbidity. In particular, the nasal and superior retina should receive heavy treatment last, as those areas correspond

CLINICAL TRIAL 5-4

Diabetic Retinopathy Study (DRS)

Study question: Is photocoagulation (argon or xenon arc) effective for treating diabetic retinopathy?

Eligibility: PDR or bilateral severe NPDR, with visual acuity 20/100 or better in each eye.

Randomization: 1742 participants. One eye randomly assigned to photocoagulation (argon or xenon arc) and 1 eye assigned to no photocoagulation.

Outcome variable: Visual acuity less than 5/200 for at least 4 months.

Results: Photocoagulation (argon or xenon) reduces risk of severe vision loss compared with no treatment. Treated eyes with high-risk PDR achieved the greatest benefit.

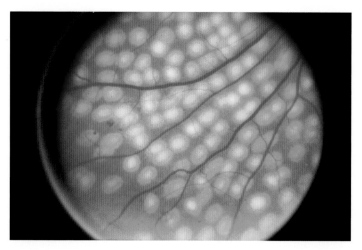

Figure 5-14 Full-scatter panretinal photocoagulation (PRP) treatment used in the DRS and the ETDRS. Included are 1200 or more 500-µm burns, separated by one-half burn width. The burns in this photograph have a surrounding ring of edema, making many of the burns appear confluent. *(Courtesy of Harry W. Flynn, Jr, MD.)*

to important temporal and inferior peripheral vision. Great care must be taken to avoid foveal photocoagulation, especially when using image-inverting contact lenses.

Early photocoagulation for diabetic retinopathy. ETDRS report number 9. Early Treatment Diabetic Retinopathy Study Research Group. *Ophthalmology.* 1991;98(5 suppl):766–785.

Diabetic Retinopathy Study findings

The DRS was a prospective, randomized clinical trial evaluating PRP treatment of 1 eye in patients with clear media and advanced NPDR or PDR in both eyes (see Clinical Trial 5-4). The primary outcome measurement in the DRS was severe visual loss (SVL), defined as a visual acuity of less than 5/200 on 2 consecutive follow-up examinations 4 months apart. At 5 years of follow-up, eyes treated with PRP had a 50% or greater reduction in rates of SVL compared with untreated control eyes (Fig 5-15). As a result, the DRS recommended prompt treatment of eyes with high-risk PDR because this group had the highest risk of SVL. The complications of argon laser PRP in the DRS were generally mild but included a decrease in visual acuity by 1 or more lines in 11% and visual field loss in 5%.

Photocoagulation treatment of proliferative diabetic retinopathy. Clinical application of Diabetic Retinopathy Study (DRS) findings, DRS report number 8. The Diabetic Retinopathy Study Research Group. *Ophthalmology.* 1981;88(7):583–600.

Neovascularization of the iris or anterior chamber angle

Small, isolated tufts of neovascularization at the pupillary border are relatively common in eyes of patients with diabetes mellitus. Eyes with small, isolated tufts can have treatment withheld and be carefully monitored with relatively short intervals between slit-lamp *and*

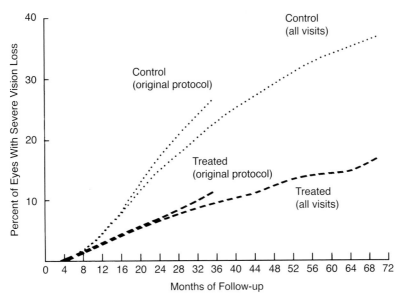

Figure 5-15 The cumulative percentage of eyes experiencing severe vision loss during the period of follow-up in the Diabetic Retinopathy Study, including and excluding observations made after 1976 protocol change, for argon laser and xenon arc treatment groups combined. *(From Photocoagulation treatment of proliferative diabetic retinopathy. Clinical application of Diabetic Retinopathy Study (DRS) findings. DRS report number 8. Diabetic Retinopathy Study Research Group.* Ophthalmology. *1981;88(7):583–600.)*

gonioscopic examinations. Patients with contiguous neovascularization of the pupil and iris collarette with or without inclusion of the anterior chamber angle generally require prompt PRP whether or not high-risk PDR is present. Intravitreal injection of anti-VEGF drugs can be used as a temporizing measure to reduce neovascularization until definitive PRP is administered.

Vitrectomy Surgery for Complications of Diabetic Retinopathy

The following are indications for pars plana vitrectomy in patients with diabetes mellitus:

- dense, nonclearing (>3 months) vitreous hemorrhage
- tractional retinal detachment involving or threatening the macula
- combined tractional and rhegmatogenous retinal detachment
- diffuse DME associated with posterior hyaloidal traction
- significant recurrent vitreous hemorrhage despite maximal PRP
- fibrovascular proliferation
- anterior hyaloidal fibrovascular proliferation
- red blood cell–induced (erythroclastic) glaucoma and "ghost cell" glaucoma
- anterior segment neovascularization with media opacities preventing photocoagulation
- dense premacular subhyaloid hemorrhage

Vitreous hemorrhage

The Diabetic Retinopathy Vitrectomy Study (DRVS) was a prospective, randomized clinical trial investigating the role of vitrectomy in managing eyes with severe PDR. Two outcome measurements in the DRVS were the percentages of eyes with 10/20 and 10/50 visual acuity on DRVS standardized visual acuity charts at the 2- and 4-year follow-up examinations.

The DRVS evaluated the benefit of early (1–6 months after onset of vitreous hemorrhage) versus late (1 year after onset) vitrectomy for eyes with severe vitreous hemorrhage and vision loss (≤5/200 visual acuity). Patients with type 1 diabetes mellitus and severe vitreous hemorrhage clearly demonstrated the benefit of early vitrectomy, but no such advantage was found in patients with mixed or type 2 diabetes mellitus. The DRVS also showed an advantage of early vitrectomy over conventional management for eyes with very severe PDR.

To evaluate the presence or absence of retinal detachment in patients with dense, nonclearing vitreous hemorrhage, echography (ultrasound) is required. If a retinal detachment is present, the timing of vitrectomy is dictated by the anatomical characteristics. Patients with bilateral severe vitreous hemorrhage generally should undergo vitrectomy in 1 eye as soon as possible for visual rehabilitation.

Advances in vitreoretinal surgery, including the routine use of the endolaser during surgery, have resulted in modifications of surgical indications, which are no longer strictly based on DRVS results. Patients with previous, well-placed, complete PRP treatment who exhibit vitreous hemorrhage can be observed for a longer period. If PRP has not been performed, early intervention is usually recommended for patients with vitreous hemorrhage secondary to PDR regardless of the class of diabetes.

Early vitrectomy for severe proliferative diabetic retinopathy in eyes with useful vision. Results of a randomized trial—DRVS report 3. Diabetic Retinopathy Vitrectomy Study Research Group. *Ophthalmology.* 1988;95(10):1307–1320.

Early vitrectomy for severe vitreous hemorrhage in diabetic retinopathy. Two-year results of a randomized trial. DRVS report 2. The Diabetic Retinopathy Vitrectomy Study Research Group. *Arch Ophthalmol.* 1985;103(11):1644–1652.

Tractional retinal detachment

Complications from PDR are exacerbated by vitreal attachment to and traction on fibrovascular proliferative tissue, often elevating it. Partial posterior vitreous detachment frequently develops in eyes with fibrovascular proliferation, resulting in traction on the new vessels and vitreous or preretinal hemorrhage. Tractional complications such as vitreous hemorrhage, retinal schisis, retinal detachment, or macular heterotopia may ensue, as may progressive fibrovascular proliferation. Contraction of the fibrovascular proliferation and vitreous may result in retinal breaks and subsequent rhegmatogenous retinal detachment. The presence of chronic retinal detachment in eyes with PDR contributes to retinal ischemia and may account for the increased risk of anterior segment neovascularization in such eyes.

Tractional retinal detachment not involving the macula may remain stable for many years. When the macula becomes involved, immediate vitrectomy is generally recommended. Combined tractional and rhegmatogenous retinal detachment may progress rapidly, and early surgery should be considered for these patients.

A more extensive discussion of the surgical management of tractional retinal detachments secondary to PDR appears in Chapter 17.

Davis M, Blodi B. Proliferative diabetic retinopathy. In: Ryan SJ, Hinton DR, Schachat AP, Wilkinson CP, eds. *Retina.* 4th ed. Philadelphia: Elsevier/Mosby; 2006:1285–1322.

Cataract Surgery in Patients With Diabetes Mellitus

Patients with diabetes enrolled in the ETDRS who underwent cataract surgery usually had improved visual acuity postoperatively. However, various studies suggest that diabetic retinopathy may progress after cataract surgery. Patients about to undergo cataract surgery who have CSME, severe NPDR, or PDR should be considered for photocoagulation before undergoing cataract removal if the ocular media are sufficiently clear to allow for treatment. If the density of the cataract precludes adequate evaluation of the retina or treatment, prompt postoperative retinal evaluation and treatment are recommended. In general, all patients with preexisting diabetic retinopathy should be reevaluated after cataract surgery.

Cataract surgeons should be mindful of the need for regular retinal evaluations and the possibility of future surgical interventions in eyes of patients with diabetes; thus, they need to plan their capsulorrhexis accordingly to avoid capsular phimosis and a resultant, very small, anterior capsular opening that may limit the view of the posterior segment. Because vitrectomy may be necessary in the future, the cataract surgeon should not place silicone lenses in the eye, as these develop condensation in an air-filled eye as well as silicone oil adherence. Both of these situations interfere with intraoperative visibility.

BCSC Section 11, *Lens and Cataract,* briefly discusses considerations that the cataract surgeon must take into account in patients with diabetes mellitus.

Recommended Diabetes-Related Ophthalmic Examinations

Retinopathy is rare in patients with type 1 diabetes mellitus in the first 5 years after diagnosis. By contrast, a large percentage of patients with type 2 diabetes mellitus have established retinopathy at the time of initial diagnosis and should undergo an ophthalmic examination at that time. Pregnancy poses a risk of progression of diabetic retinopathy. An eye examination is generally recommended for pregnant patients in the first trimester and thereafter at the discretion of the ophthalmologist (Table 5-2). The frequency of follow-up visits depends on the severity of the retinopathy, systemic factors such as history of blood glucose control, and blood pressure, as well as the threat to visual function from potentially missed opportunities to treat (Table 5-3).

Table 5-2 Recommended Eye Examination Schedule for Patients With Diabetes Mellitus

Diabetes Type	Recommended Time of First Eye Examination	Routine Minimum Follow-up Interval
Type 1	3–5 years after diagnosis	Annually
Type 2	Upon diagnosis	Annually
Type 1 or 2 and Pregnancy	Before conception or early in first trimester	No retinopathy to mild or moderate NPDR: every 3–12 months Severe NPDR or worse: every 1–3 months

NPDR = nonproliferative diabetic retinopathy.

Modified from American Academy of Ophthalmology Retina/Vitreous Panel. Preferred Practice Pattern Guidelines. *Diabetic Retinopathy.* San Francisco: American Academy of Ophthalmology; 2008:7. Available at www.aao.org/ppp.

Table 5-3 Recommended Eye Examination Schedule Based on Diabetic Retinopathy Severity

Diabetic Retinopathy Severity	CSME Present?	Suggested Follow-up Interval (months)
Normal or minimal NPDR	No	12
Mild to moderate NPDR	No	6–12
	Yes*	2–4
Severe NPDR[†]	No	2–4
	Yes*	2–4
Non–high-risk PDR[†]	No	2–4
	Yes*	2–4
High-risk PDR[†]	No	2–4
	Yes*	2–4
Inactive/involuted PDR	No	6–12
	Yes*	2–4

CSME = clinically significant diabetic macular edema; NPDR = nonproliferative diabetic retinopathy; PDR = proliferative diabetic retinopathy.
*Consider macular laser surgery.
[†] Consider panretinal scatter laser surgery.

Modified from American Academy of Ophthalmology Retina/Vitreous Panel. Preferred Practice Pattern Guidelines. *Diabetic Retinopathy.* San Francisco: American Academy of Ophthalmology; 2008:12. Available at www.aao.org/ppp.

American Academy of Ophthalmology Retina/Vitreous Panel. Preferred Practice Pattern Guidelines. *Diabetic Retinopathy.* San Francisco: American Academy of Ophthalmology; 2008. Available at www.aao.org/ppp.

CHAPTER 6

![gray bar]

Other Retinal Vascular Diseases

Systemic Arterial Hypertension

Systemic arterial hypertension affects more than 65 million Americans. It is currently defined by a series of stages: prehypertension encompasses blood pressure readings of 120–139 mm Hg systolic or 80–89 mm Hg diastolic; stage 1 hypertension includes readings of 140–159 mm Hg systolic or 90–99 mm Hg diastolic pressure; and stage 2 hypertension is 160 mm Hg or higher systolic and 100 mm Hg or higher diastolic pressure. Isolated systolic hypertension occurs with a systolic blood pressure of 160 mm Hg or higher and a diastolic blood pressure below 90 mm Hg.

Together with heart, kidneys, and brain, the eye is a target organ of systemic hypertension. Ocular effects of hypertension can be observed in the retina, choroid, and optic nerve. Retinal changes can be described and classified using ophthalmoscopy and angiography. Recognition of the posterior segment vascular changes by the ophthalmologist may prompt the initial diagnosis of hypertension and alert the patient to potential complications from this condition. BCSC Section 1, *Update on General Medicine,* discusses hypertension in detail and includes several tables that describe drugs and drug interactions of antihypertensive therapy.

Kim SK, Mieler WF, Jakobiec F. Hypertension and its ocular manifestations. In: Albert DM, Miller JW, Azar DT, Blodi BA, eds. *Albert & Jakobiec's Principles and Practice of Ophthalmology.* 3rd ed. Philadelphia: Saunders; 2008:4367–4384.

Hypertensive Retinopathy

Hypertension affects precapillary arterioles and capillaries, the anatomical loci of autoregulation and nonperfusion. An acute hypertensive episode may produce focal intraretinal periarteriolar transudates (FIPTs). FIPTs are at the precapillary level and, therefore, are deeper, smaller, and less white than cotton-wool spots, which correspond to ischemia in the superficial radial capillary net (Fig 6-1). Uncontrolled systemic hypertension leads to nonperfusion at various retinal levels and to neuronal loss and related scotomata. Other, more chronic, hypertensive retinal lesions include microaneurysms, intraretinal microvascular abnormalities (IRMAs), blot hemorrhages, "hard exudates," venous beading, and new retinal vessels; the latter 2 are signs of an ischemic retinopathy. The relationship between hypertensive vascular changes and the changes of arteriosclerotic vascular disease is complex, with wide variation related to duration of hypertension, severity of dyslipidemia, age, and history of smoking. Hence, classification of retinal vascular changes caused

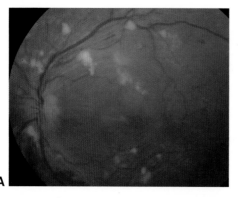
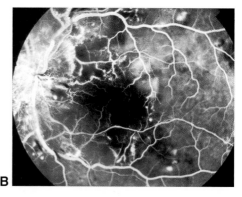

A **B**

Figure 6-1 Severe hypertension retinopathy. **A,** Fundus of a 25-year-old man with renal hypertension, showing large superficial and white cotton-wool spots, contrasting with small, tan, and deep focal intraretinal periarteriolar transudates (FIPTs). **B,** The angiogram shows areas of nonperfusion corresponding to the cotton-wool spots and punctuate hyperfluorescence corresponding to the FIPTs. *(Courtesy of Hermann D. Schubert, MD.)*

strictly by hypertension is difficult. The often-cited focal arteriolar narrowing and arterial venous nicking are related to vascular sclerosis and have been shown to have little predictive value for actual hypertension. One historical classification of mostly arteriolosclerotic retinopathy is the Modified Scheie Classification of "Hypertensive Retinopathy":

Grade 0	No changes
Grade 1	Barely detectable arterial narrowing
Grade 2	Obvious arterial narrowing with focal irregularities
Grade 3	Grade 2 plus retinal hemorrhages and/or exudates
Grade 4	Grade 3 plus disc swelling

Hypertension may be complicated by branch retinal artery occlusion (BRAO), branch retinal vein occlusion (BRVO), central retinal vein occlusion (CRVO), and retinal arterial macroaneurysms (all discussed later in the chapter). The coexistence of hypertension and diabetes mellitus results in more severe retinopathy because precapillary and capillary insults act in combination.

Murphy RP, Lam LA, Chew EY. Hypertension. In: Ryan SJ, Hinton DR, Schachat AP,
   Wilkinson CP, eds. *Retina.* 4th ed. Philadelphia: Elsevier/Mosby; 2006:1377–1382.
Wong TY, Mitchell P. The eye in hypertension. *Lancet.* 2007;369(9559):425–435.

Hypertensive Choroidopathy

Hypertensive choroidopathy typically occurs in young patients who experience an episode of acute hypertension associated with preeclampsia, eclampsia, pheochromocytoma, or renal hypertension. Lobular nonperfusion of the choriocapillaris may occur and initially results in tan, lobule-sized patches that, in time, become hyperpigmented and surrounded by margins of hypopigmentation; these are known as *Elschnig spots* (Fig 6-2). Linear configurations of similar-appearing hyperpigmentations known as *Siegrist streaks* follow the

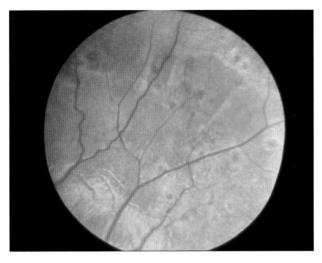

Figure 6-2 Elschnig spots. *(Courtesy of Harry W. Flynn, Jr, MD.)*

meridional course of choroidal arteries in patients with acute, uncontrolled hypertension. Fluorescein angiography shows focal choroidal hypoperfusion in early phases and multiple subretinal areas of leakage in late phases (Fig 6-3). Focal retinal pigment epithelium (RPE) detachments may occur, and extensive bilateral exudative retinal detachments may develop in severe cases on rare occasions.

Hypertensive Optic Neuropathy

Depending less on the degree than on the chronicity of the hypertension, hypertensive optic neuropathy has a variable presentation. Patients with severe hypertension may have linear peripapillary flame-shaped hemorrhages, blurring of the disc margins, florid disc edema with secondary retinal venous stasis, and macular exudates (Fig 6-4). The differential diagnosis for patients with this clinical appearance includes diabetic papillopathy, radiation papillopathy, CRVO, anterior ischemic optic neuropathy, and neuroretinitis. Treatment of systemic arterial hypertension is essential for reducing or reversing these ocular manifestations of the disease.

Sickle Cell Retinopathy

The sickle cell hemoglobinopathies of greatest ocular importance are those in which mutant hemoglobins S, C, or both are inherited as alleles of normal hemoglobin A. These disorders result from a mutant gene that defines the sequence of amino acids in the β-polypeptide chain of adult hemoglobin. In sickle cell hemoglobin (Hb S), the sixth position in the β-polypeptide chain is occupied by valine instead of the normally present glutamic acid—the result of a substitution of adenine for thymine. This seemingly small alteration causes a profound reduction in solubility when hemoglobin is deoxygenated, leading to deformation of red blood cells into a characteristic sickle shape when the partial

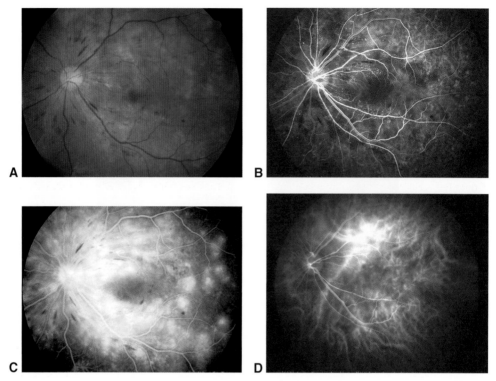

Figure 6-3 Malignant hypertension. **A,** The color fundus photograph shows typical features of hypertensive retinopathy and choroidopathy. The hypertensive retinopathy manifests as a shallow detachment of the macula with striae of the internal limiting membrane (ILM), splinter hemorrhages in the radial peripapillary net, slight hyperemia of the optic nerve, and a few lipid exudates in the macula. The hypertensive choroidopathy is evident as multiple tan patches at the level of the RPE and inner choroid. The fluorescein angiogram shows numerous abnormalities of the retinal and choroidal circulation. **B,** Early in the angiographic study, areas of retinal capillary nonperfusion and microaneurysm formation are seen, as well as a dendritic pattern of choroidal filling defects. **C,** Late in the angiographic study, intense leakage of dye from the retinal vessels as well as from some, but not all, of the yellowish tan patches shown in part **A** can be seen. **D,** Early in the corresponding indocyanine green (ICG) angiogram, a "moth-eaten" appearance of the choriocapillaris is demonstrated. *(Courtesy of Richard Spaide, MD.)*

pressure of oxygen is low. Hemoglobin C (Hb C) disease is caused by a substitution of glutamic acid by lysine in the same position.

Sickle cell hemoglobinopathies are most prevalent in the African American population. Sickle cell trait (Hb AS) affects 8% of African Americans; 0.4% have sickle cell disease (Hb SS), and 0.2% have hemoglobin SC disease (Table 6-1). Thalassemia, in which the α- or β-polypeptide chain is defective, is rare; however, it frequently causes retinopathy. Although sickling and solubility tests (sickle cell preparations) are reliable indicators of the presence of hemoglobin S and are therefore excellent for screening, they do not distinguish between heterozygous and homozygous states. Hemoglobin electrophoresis testing should be performed for patients testing positive on sickle cell preparations. This process is described in Part III, Genetics, of BCSC Section 2, *Fundamentals and Principles of Ophthalmology,* along with detailed explanations of allelic gene defects.

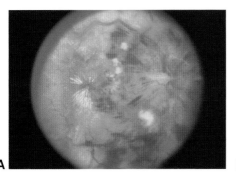 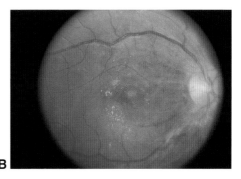

Figure 6-4 Severe hypertension retinopathy with improvement. **A,** Fundus photograph of a 25-year-old patient with severe hypertension (210/140 mm Hg) and visual acuity loss to the 2/200 level. Note the disc edema, macular exudates, intraretinal hemorrhage with nerve fiber layer (NFL) infarct, and venous congestion. **B,** Fundus of the same patient 10 weeks later, after treatment of hypertension and normalization of blood pressure. The optic disc is now normal, and minimal residual macular exudates are present. The visual acuity has returned to 20/50. *(Courtesy of Harry W. Flynn, Jr, MD.)*

Sickle cell ocular abnormalities are caused by intravascular sickling, hemolysis, hemostasis, and thrombosis. The initial event in the pathogenesis of sickle cell retinopathy is peripheral arteriolar occlusion with capillary nonperfusion, which may progress to retinal neovascularization, usually at the border between perfused and nonperfused retina.

The incidence of substantial vision loss from sickle cell retinopathy is variable but appears to be relatively low in natural history studies. Serious ocular complications of proliferative sickle cell retinopathy (PSR)—including retinal neovascularization, vitreous hemorrhage, and tractional retinal detachment—are more characteristic of sickle cell hemoglobin C (SC) and sickle cell thalassemia (SThal) than of SS disease, although SS disease results in more systemic complications.

Emerson GG, Harlan JB Jr, Fekrat S, Lutty GA, Goldberg MF. Hemoglobinopathies. In: Ryan SJ, Hinton DR, Schachat AP, Wilkinson CP, eds. *Retina.* 4th ed. Philadelphia: Elsevier/ Mosby; 2006:1429–1445.

Table 6-1 Incidence of Sickle Cell Hemoglobinopathies in North America

Hemoglobinopathy	Incidence in Population (%)	Incidence of Proliferative Retinopathy in Subgroups
Any sickle hemoglobin	10	—
Sickle cell trait (AS)	8	Uncommon
Hemoglobin C trait (AC)	2	Uncommon
Sickle cell homozygote (SS)	0.4	3%*
Sickle cell hemoglobin C (SC)	0.2	33%*
Sickle cell thalassemia (SThal)	0.03	14%*
Homozygous C (CC)	0.016	Unknown

*Approximate.

Modified from Fekrat S, Goldberg MF. Sickle retinopathy. In: Regillo CD, Brown GC, Flynn HW Jr, eds. *Vitreoretinal Disease: The Essentials.* New York: Thieme; 1999:333.

Nonproliferative Sickle Cell Retinopathy

The retinal changes found in nonproliferative sickle cell retinopathy (NPSR) are caused by arteriolar and capillary occlusion, similar to white or hemorrhagic infarcts of the central nervous system. Anastomosis and remodeling occur in the periphery, as does the resorption of the blood in the area of the infarct (Fig 6-5). Retinal findings of NPSR include

- salmon patch hemorrhages
- refractile (iridescent) deposits or spots
- black "sunburst" lesions

Clinical and histologic studies have shown that *salmon patch hemorrhages* represent areas of intraretinal hemorrhage occurring after a peripheral retinal arteriolar occlusion. *Refractile spots* are old, resorbed hemorrhages with hemosiderin deposition within the inner retina just beneath the internal limiting membrane (ILM). *Black sunburst lesions* are localized areas of retinal pigment epithelial hypertrophy, hyperplasia, and pigment migration into the retina. These lesions often have a spiculated appearance and are usually found in a perivascular location in the periphery. The presence of hemosiderin deposition in the lesion suggests that retinal hemorrhage with extension into the subretinal space plays a role in the pathogenesis of the black sunburst lesions.

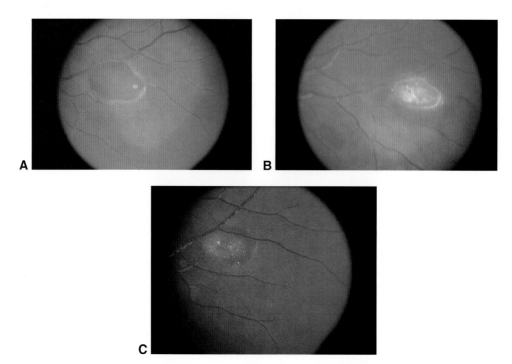

Figure 6-5 Evolution of retinal changes found in nonproliferative sickle cell retinopathy. **A,** Retinal and preretinal orange-red hemorrhage obscures the retinal vasculature. **B,** Two weeks later, the hemorrhage is smaller, has a central grayish white color, and is surrounded by a yellow granular halo. **C,** Two years later, the hemorrhage has resolved and an iridescent spot is visible. *(Reproduced with permission from Gagliano DA, Goldberg MF. Evolution of salmon-patch hemorrhages in sickle cell retinopathy. Arch Ophthalmol. 1989;107(12):1814–1815.)*

Occlusion of parafoveal capillaries and arterioles is one cause of decreased visual acuity in sickle cell retinopathy. Spontaneous occlusion of the central retinal artery may also develop in patients with sickle cell hemoglobinopathies. Vascular occlusions do not inevitably lead to infarction in sickle cell retinopathy.

Proliferative Sickle Cell Retinopathy

PSR has been classified into 5 stages based on the following pathogenetic sequence (Fig 6-6):

1. Peripheral arteriolar occlusions (stage 1) lead to peripheral nonperfusion and
2. peripheral arteriovenular anastomoses (stage 2), which appear to be dilated, preexisting capillary channels. Sequential fluorescein angiograms show dynamic remodeling of the peripheral retinal vasculature.
3. Preretinal *sea fan neovascularization* (stage 3) may occur at the posterior border of areas of nonperfusion and lead to
4. vitreous hemorrhage (stage 4) and
5. tractional retinal detachment (stage 5).

PSR is one of many retinal vascular diseases in which extraretinal fibrovascular proliferation occurs in response to retinal ischemia. Whereas the neovascularization in proliferative diabetic retinopathy (PDR) generally begins postequatorially, that in PSR is located more peripherally. Another way in which PSR differs from PDR is in the frequent occurrence in PSR of autoinfarction of the peripheral neovascularization, resulting in a white "sea fan" neovascularization (Fig 6-7).

Elagouz M, Jyothi S, Gupta B, Sivaprasad S. Sickle cell disease and the eye: old and new concepts. *Surv Ophthalmol.* 2010;55(4):359–377. Epub 2010 May 10.

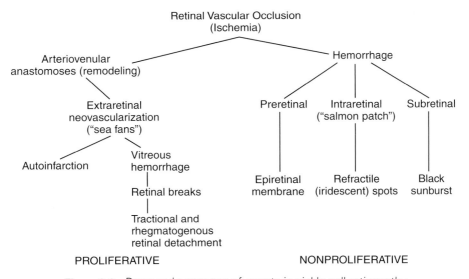

Figure 6-6 Proposed sequence of events in sickle cell retinopathy.

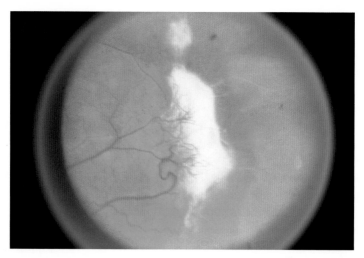

Figure 6-7 Peripheral neovascularization ("sea fan" neovascularization) with autoinfarction, as illustrated by the white atrophic vessels. *(Courtesy of Harry W. Flynn, Jr, MD.)*

Other Ocular Abnormalities in Sickle Cell Hemoglobinopathies

Another clinical finding found in many patients with SS or SC disease is segmentation of blood in the conjunctival blood vessels. Numerous comma-shaped thrombi dilate and occlude capillaries, most often in the inferior bulbar conjunctiva and fornix (the *comma sign*). Similarly, small vessels on the surface of the optic disc can exhibit intravascular occlusions, manifested as dark red spots (the *disc sign* of sickling). Angioid streaks have been reported clinically in up to 6% of cases of SS disease and in persons with AS trait. The pathogenetic basis of this association is uncertain.

Management of Sickle Cell Retinopathy

All African American patients presenting with a traumatic hyphema should be screened for a sickling hemoglobinopathy (including trait) because of the increased risk of complications in the presence of rigid sickled erythrocytes. Intraocular pressure (IOP) control may be difficult, and ischemic optic neuropathy may result from short intervals of a modest increase in IOP. Some authors have recommended early anterior chamber washout in the presence of a hyphema with increased IOP. In addition, the physician must be cautious when using carbonic anhydrase inhibitors, which may worsen sickling through the production of systemic acidosis.

McLeod DS, Merges C, Fukushima A, Goldberg MF, Lutty GA. Histopathologic features of neovascularization in sickle cell retinopathy. *Am J Ophthalmol.* 1997;124(4):455–472.

Photocoagulation

Therapeutic approaches to PSR have included diathermy, cryopexy, and photocoagulation. Peripheral scatter photocoagulation, applying lower-intensity light burns to the ischemic peripheral retina, may cause regression of neovascular fronds and thus decrease the risk of vitreous hemorrhage. The decision to treat with scatter photocoagulation should be made cautiously, as retinal tears and subsequent rhegmatogenous retinal detachment are more common in this proliferative condition than in PDR, for example.

Farber MD, Jampol LM, Fox P, et al. A randomized clinical trial of scatter photocoagulation of proliferative sickle cell retinopathy. *Arch Ophthalmol.* 1991(3);109:363–367.

Vitreoretinal surgery in PSR

Surgery may be indicated for nonclearing vitreous hemorrhage and for rhegmatogenous, tractional, schisis, or combined retinal detachment. Retinal detachment usually begins in the ischemic peripheral retina. The tears typically occur at the base of sea fans and are often precipitated by photocoagulation treatment. Anterior segment ischemia or necrosis has been reported in association with 360° scleral buckling procedures, particularly when combined with extensive diathermy or cryopexy. For this reason, the following precautions should be taken when treating retinal detachments:

- Use local anesthesia without adjunctive epinephrine.
- Avoid encircling buckles.
- Do not remove extraocular muscles.
- Use cryopexy judiciously.
- Ensure adequate patient hydration.
- Use supplementary nasal oxygen.

Precautions for vitrectomy also include the cautious use of expansile gases to minimize IOP elevations postoperatively, which increase the risk of vascular occlusions. Exchange transfusion is no longer favored before vitreoretinal surgery.

Peripheral Retinal Neovascularization

Apart from sickling disorders, a number of entities can cause peripheral neovascularization; see Table 6-2 for a differential diagnosis.

Venous Occlusive Disease

Branch Retinal Vein Occlusion

The ophthalmoscopic findings of acute BRVO include intraretinal hemorrhages, retinal edema, and sometimes cotton-wool spots (nerve fiber layer [NFL] infarcts) in a sector of retina drained by the affected vein (Fig 6-8). The occlusion of the vein occurs most commonly at an arteriovenous crossing, and the degree of macular involvement determines the level of visual impairment. When the occlusion does not occur at an arteriovenous crossing, the possibility of an underlying retinochoroiditis or retinal vasculitis should be considered. The mean age for patients at the time of occurrence is in the seventh decade. The obstructed vein is dilated and tortuous and, with time, the corresponding artery may become narrowed and sheathed. The quadrant most commonly affected is the superotemporal (63%); nasal vascular occlusions detected clinically are rare.

Table 6-2 Differential Diagnosis of Peripheral Retinal Neovascularization

Vascular diseases with ischemia
Proliferative diabetic retinopathy (PDR)
Branch retinal vein occlusion (BRVO)
Branch retinal arteriolar occlusion (BRAO)
Carotid cavernous fistula
Sickling hemoglobinopathies (eg, SC, SS)
Other hemoglobinopathies (eg, AC, AS)
Idiopathic retinal vasculitis, aneurysms, and neuroretinitis (IRVAN)
Retinal embolization (eg, talc emboli)
Retinopathy of prematurity (ROP)
Familial exudative vitreoretinopathy (FEVR)
Hyperviscosity syndromes (eg, chronic myelogenous leukemia)
Aortic arch syndromes/ocular ischemic syndromes
Eales disease

Inflammatory diseases with possible ischemia
Sarcoidosis
Retinal vasculitis (eg, systemic lupus erythematosus)
Uveitis, including pars planitis
Birdshot retinochoroidopathy
Toxoplasmosis
Multiple sclerosis

Miscellaneous conditions
Incontinentia pigmenti
Long-standing retinal detachment
Choroidal melanoma
Retinitis pigmentosa
Retinoschisis
Chronic retinal detachment

Modified from Jampol LM, Ebroon DA, Goldbaum MH. Peripheral proliferative retinopathies: an update on angiogenesis, etiologies, and management. *Surv Ophthalmol.* 1994;38(6):519–540.

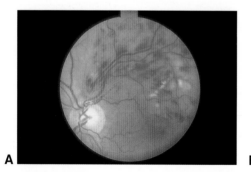 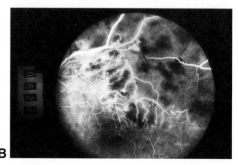

Figure 6-8 Branch retinal vein occlusion with ischemia. **A,** Superotemporal branch retinal vein occlusion (BRVO). **B,** Fluorescein angiogram corresponding to **A** reveals pronounced retinal capillary nonperfusion in the distribution of the retina drained by the obstructed vein. *(Courtesy of Gary C. Brown, MD.)*

Histologic studies suggest that common adventitia binds the artery and the vein together at the arteriovenous crossing and that thickening of the arterial wall compresses the vein. Resultant turbulence of flow results in endothelial cell damage and thrombotic occlusion. The thrombus may extend histologically to the capillary bed. Secondary arterial narrowing often develops in the area of occlusion.

Risk factors for the development of BRVO

The Eye Disease Case-Control Study identified the following abnormalities as risk factors for the development of BRVO:

- history of systemic arterial hypertension
- cardiovascular disease
- increased body mass index at 20 years of age
- history of glaucoma

Diabetes mellitus was not a major independent risk factor.

Visual prognosis

Visual prognosis in BRVO is most closely related to the extent of capillary damage and retinal ischemia in the macula. Fluorescein angiography is used to assess the extent and location of retinal capillary nonperfusion, as shown in Figure 6-8. The integrity of the parafoveal capillaries is an important prognostic factor for visual acuity. Vision may be reduced in acute cases from macular edema, retinal hemorrhage, or perifoveal retinal capillary occlusion. The hemorrhage resolves over time, and capillary compensation and collateral formation may permit restitution of flow with resolution of the edema and improvement in visual function. In other eyes, however, progressive capillary closure may occur.

Extensive retinal ischemia (greater than 5 disc diameters of retinal involvement) results in neovascularization from the retina or optic nerve in approximately 40% of eyes, and preretinal bleeding will develop in 60% of such eyes if laser photocoagulation is not performed. Overall, approximately 50%–60% of patients with all types of BRVO will maintain visual acuity of 20/40 or better after 1 year.

Findings in eyes with permanent vision loss from BRVO include the following:

- macular ischemia
- cystoid macular edema
- macular edema with hard lipid exudates
- pigmentary macular disturbance
- subretinal fibrosis
- epiretinal membrane formation

Less commonly, vision is lost from vitreous hemorrhage or tractional or rhegmatogenous retinal detachment, which typically develops after a break occurs in the retina adjacent to, or underlying, an area of retinal neovascularization.

Argon laser scatter photocoagulation for prevention of neovascularization and vitreous hemorrhage in branch vein occlusion. A randomized clinical trial. Branch Vein Occlusion Study Group. *Arch Ophthalmol.* 1986(1);104:34–41.

Frangieh GT, Green WR, Barraquer-Somers E, Finkelstein D. Histopathologic study of nine branch retinal vein occlusions. *Arch Ophthalmol.* 1982;100(7):1132–1140.

Risk factors for branch retinal vein occlusion. The Eye Disease Case-Control Study Group. *Am J Ophthalmol.* 1993;116(3):286–296.

Evaluation and management of BRVO

The ophthalmic evaluation of BRVO involves a complete ocular examination to exclude vasculitis and macular edema and to assess for glaucoma. If BRVO appears to have been present for some time, gonioscopic evaluation should be performed to check for angle neovascularization. Systemic evaluation should include assessment of blood pressure and possible referral to the primary care provider for evaluation of cardiovascular risk factors.

Evidence in support of new therapies for the treatment of BRVO has become available. In the coming years, considerable attention will be paid to elucidating the optimal management of BRVO patients, that is, determining the best combinations of treatments.

Surgical management of BRVO Laser surgery has been shown to be efficacious, whereas pars plana vitrectomy is less well established in the treatment of BRVO.

Laser Surgery Photocoagulation surgery is considered for treating the 2 major complications of BRVO: (1) chronic macular edema in eyes with intact perifoveal retinal capillary perfusion and (2) posterior segment neovascularization. For eyes with macular edema, it is suggested that therapy be delayed for at least 3 months to permit the maximum spontaneous resolution of the edema and intraretinal blood. Photocoagulation for macular edema accompanying BRVO is usually administered to eyes with vision declining to a visual acuity range of 20/40–20/200. Treatment is focused on edematous retina within the arcades drained by the obstructed vein (Fig 6-9). Areas of capillary leakage as identified by recent fluorescein angiography are treated with a light grid pattern using 100- and 200-μm spots. Leaking microvascular abnormalities may be treated directly, but prominent collateral vessels should be avoided.

Neovascularization of the iris is present in approximately 1% of eyes with BRVO. Scatter laser photocoagulation in the distribution of the occluded vein can be considered in such instances to prevent the development of neovascular glaucoma.

The Branch Vein Occlusion Study (BVOS) demonstrated that argon laser photocoagulation improved the vision outcome significantly in eyes with BRVO in which the foveal vasculature was intact but macular edema had reduced vision to a visual acuity in the 20/40–20/200 range. Treated eyes were more likely to gain 2 lines of visual acuity (65%) than were untreated eyes (37%). Furthermore, treated eyes were more likely than untreated eyes to have 20/40 or better vision at 3 years' follow-up (60% vs 34%, respectively), with a mean visual acuity improvement of 1.3 ETDRS lines versus 0.2 line, respectively. Overall, mean visual acuity in the treated group was in the 20/40–20/50 range; in the untreated group, it was 20/70.

Panretinal photocoagulation to the area of retinal capillary nonperfusion was effective in causing regression of the new vessels in eyes with retinal or disc neovascularization (Fig 6-10). The BVOS showed that scatter argon laser photocoagulation reduced the risk of developing neovascularization from 22% to 12% in eyes that had recently sustained a BRVO involving a retinal area of at least 5 disc diameters. Although patients with large areas of nonperfusion, such as that shown in Figure 6-8, were found to be at significant risk of developing neovascularization, the BVOS concluded that ischemia alone was not an indication for treatment provided that follow-up could be maintained. Rather,

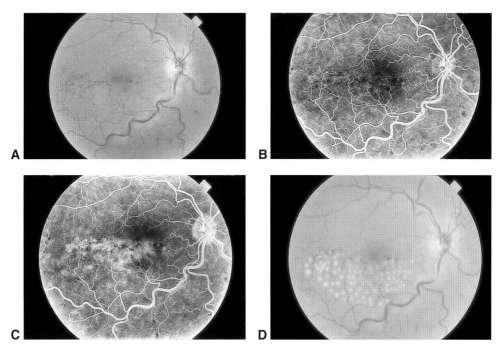

Figure 6-9 BRVO. **A,** Fundus photograph of inferotemporal BRVO. Corresponding fluorescein angiograms show, at 49 seconds after injection **(B),** that the perifoveal capillary bed is essentially intact, and at 393 seconds after injection **(C),** intraretinal leakage of dye from the capillaries in macular distribution of the vein occlusion *(white)*. **D,** Fundus photograph after treatment shows a grid of macular photocoagulation lesions in the affected area but sparing the foveal region. *(Courtesy of Gary C. Brown, MD.)*

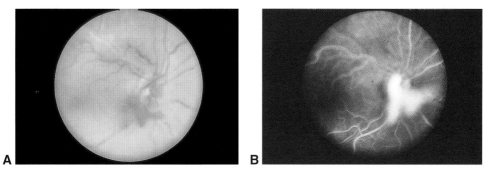

Figure 6-10 BRVO with neovascularization. **A,** Neovascularization of the disc occurring secondary to a superotemporal BRVO. **B,** Corresponding fluorescein angiogram at 18 seconds after injection reveals marked hyperfluorescence of the new vessels originating on the optic disc. *(Courtesy of Gary C. Brown, MD.)*

it recommended that patients be monitored for the development of neovascularization, which was an indication for photocoagulation.

The BVOS also showed that scatter argon laser photocoagulation reduced the risk of vitreous hemorrhage from 60% to 30% in eyes with a recent BRVO in which neovascularization was already detectable. Clinically, it is important to distinguish collateral vessels from neovascularization of the disc or retina.

Argon laser photocoagulation for macular edema in branch vein occlusion. The Branch Vein Occlusion Study Group. *Am J Ophthalmol.* 1984;98(3):271–282.

Fuller JJ, Mason JO III. Retinal vein occlusions: update on diagnostic and therapeutic advances. *Focal Points: Clinical Modules for Ophthalmologists.* San Francisco: American Academy of Ophthalmology; 2007, module 5.

PARS PLANA VITRECTOMY Vitrectomy may be indicated for eyes that develop nonresorbing vitreous hemorrhage or retinal detachment (see also Chapters 13 and 17). Pars plana vitrectomy with arteriovenous sheathotomy has been reported in small, uncontrolled series of cases with decreased vision due to BRVO and macular edema that was either unresponsive to laser treatment or did not meet BVOS criteria for laser treatment (eg, macular ischemia, persistent and extensive macular hemorrhage). Studies have suggested that the vitrectomy is the major positive intervention rather than the sheathotomy component of the surgery. The exact role of vitrectomy in the management of BRVO remains controversial.

Pharmacotherapy of BRVO Intravitreal corticosteroids and anti-VEGF therapy have both been shown to be effective for the management of BRVO in clinical trials.

INTRAVITREAL CORTICOSTEROIDS The SCORE (Standard Care Versus Corticosteroid for Retinal Vein Occlusion) study, a prospective, randomized, controlled clinical trial, investigated the safety and efficacy of intravitreal triamcinolone compared with macular grid laser treatment in patients with macular edema associated with BRVO and CRVO. In the BRVO arm of the study, after 1 year, 29% of patients in the laser treatment group, 26% of patients in the 1-mg-corticosteroid injection group, and 27% of patients in the 4-mg-injection group experienced a substantial visual acuity gain of 3 or more lines. Eyes receiving either dose of corticosteroid were more likely to develop a cataract or experience elevated IOP than were eyes receiving laser treatment. The study investigators pointed out that macular grid laser therapy remains the benchmark against which other treatments should be compared.

A dexamethasone (0.7 mg) intravitreal implant was approved in 2009 by the US Food and Drug Administration for the treatment of macular edema in BRVO and CRVO. In a multicenter, prospective, randomized control trial, after 3 months, the eyes treated with the implant had a statistically significantly greater percentage of those with at least a 15-letter improvement than did sham-injected eyes. The effect was greater in CRVO eyes than in BRVO eyes.

Trials are under way to evaluate efficacy of an injectable fluocinolone implant over 18–24 months and for a surgically implanted device for drug delivery of up to 30 months.

Haller JA, Bandello F, Belfort R Jr, et al; OZURDEX GENEVA Study Group. Randomized, sham-controlled trial of dexamethasone intravitreal implant in patients with macular edema due to retinal vein occlusion. *Ophthalmology.* 2010;117(6):1134–1146. Epub 2010 Apr 24.

Scott IU, Ip MS, VanVeldhuisen PC, et al; SCORE Study Research Group. A randomized trial comparing the efficacy and safety of intravitreal triamcinolone with standard care to treat vision loss associated with macular edema secondary to branch retinal vein occlusion: the Standard Care vs Corticosteroid for Retinal Vein Occlusion (SCORE) study report 6. *Arch Ophthalmol.* 2009;127(9):1115–1128.

INTRAVITREAL ANTI-VEGF THERAPY In the Branch Retinal Vein Occlusion (BRAVO) study, ranibizumab was administered to eyes with BRVO with macular edema. A total of 397 patients were randomly assigned to receive either monthly injections of 0.5 or 0.3 mg of ranibizumab or sham injection. At 6 months, there was a mean gain from baseline of 18.3, 16.6, and 7.3 ETDRS letters, respectively. Overall, 61.1%, 55.2%, and 28.8%, respectively, gained 15 or more letters (3 lines of vision) at 6 months. Uncontrolled studies of bevacizumab have also demonstrated substantial resolution of macular edema and visual improvement. However, robust visual acuity data are not available for bevacizumab. Many practitioners use the 2 anti-VEGF drugs interchangeably, despite lack of evidence of equivalence for this indication. Further studies are under way, including one for another anti-VEGF drug, VEGF Trap.

> Campochiaro PA, Heier JS, Feiner L, et al; BRAVO Investigators. Ranibizumab for macular edema following branch retinal vein occlusion: six-month primary end point results of a phase III study. *Ophthalmology*. 2010;117(6):1102–1112. Epub 2010 Apr 15.

Central Retinal Vein Occlusion

Long associated with a characteristic fundus appearance of dilated and tortuous retinal veins, a swollen optic disc, intraretinal hemorrhages, and retinal edema, CRVO is now classified by 2 ends of the spectrum of disease:

- a mild, *nonischemic* form sometimes referred to as *partial, perfused*, or *venous stasis retinopathy*
- a severe, *ischemic* form characterized by the fluorescein angiographic demonstration of at least 10 disc areas of retinal capillary nonperfusion on a posterior pole view, also known as *nonperfused, complete*, or *hemorrhagic retinopathy*

An intermediate, or indeterminate, form also exists, but more than 80% of these eyes progress to the severe ischemic form.

A *hemicentral* or *hemispheric retinal vein occlusion*, a variant of CRVO, is associated with congenital variation in central vein anatomy; it may involve either the superior or inferior half of the retina (Fig 6-11).

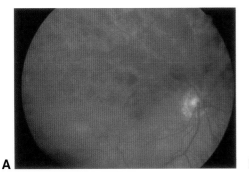 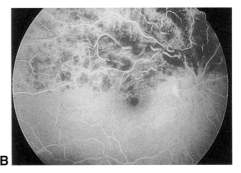

Figure 6-11 Hemispheric retinal vein occlusion. **A,** Photograph shows superior involvement with intraretinal hemorrhage. **B,** Fluorescein angiogram shows blockage of underlying details in areas of hemorrhage; ischemia is probably minimal. Note that the foveal avascular zone is intact.

Histologic studies suggest that most forms of CRVO share a common mechanism: thrombosis of the central retinal vein at and posterior to the level of the lamina cribrosa. It is postulated that, in some cases, a thickened central retinal artery may impinge on the central retinal vein, causing turbulence, endothelial damage, and thrombus formation.

Nonischemic (mild) CRVO is characterized by good visual acuity, a mild or no afferent pupillary defect, and mild visual field changes. Ophthalmoscopy shows mild dilation and tortuosity of all branches of the central retinal vein as well as dot- and flame-shaped hemorrhages in all quadrants of the retina (Fig 6-12). Macular edema with decreased visual acuity and mild optic disc swelling may or may not be present. If disc edema is prominent in younger patients, a combined inflammatory and occlusive mechanism may be present that has been termed *papillophlebitis*. Fluorescein angiography usually demonstrates prolongation of the retinal circulation time with breakdown of capillary permeability but minimal areas of nonperfusion. Anterior segment neovascularization is rare in mild CRVO.

Ischemic (severe) CRVO is usually associated with poor vision, an afferent pupillary defect, and dense central scotoma. Marked venous dilation is present, and more extensive 4-quadrant hemorrhage, retinal edema (Fig 6-13), and variable numbers of cotton-wool spots are frequently found as well. Fluorescein angiography typically shows widespread capillary nonperfusion, as well as prolonged retinovascular circulation times. A decreased electroretinographic bright-flash, dark-adapted b-wave:a-wave amplitude ratio is characteristic. The visual prognosis is generally poor in ischemic CRVO, with approximately 10% of eyes achieving vision better than 20/400. In addition, the incidence of iris neovascularization is high (up to 60%) in very ischemic eyes, usually occurring at a mean of 3–5 months after the onset of symptoms.

Iris neovascularization in CRVO

The Central Vein Occlusion Study (CVOS) found that the most important risk factor predictive of iris neovascularization in central venous occlusive disease is poor visual acuity. Other risk factors associated with the development of iris neovascularization included large areas of retinal capillary nonperfusion and intraretinal blood.

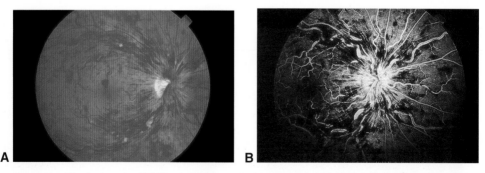

A   **B**

Figure 6-12 Nonischemic CRVO. **A,** Mild nonischemic, or perfused, CRVO in an eye with 20/40 vision. Dilated retinal veins and retinal hemorrhages are present, as well as occasional cotton-wool spots, but a foveolar reflex is still present. **B,** Fluorescein angiogram corresponding to **A** at 33 seconds after injection reveals perfusion of the retinal capillary bed. *(Courtesy of Gary C. Brown, MD.)*

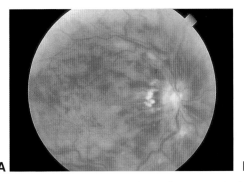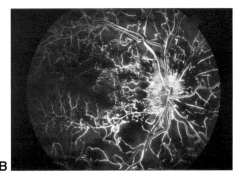

A **B**

Figure 6-13 Ischemic CRVO. **A,** Severe, or ischemic, CRVO in an eye with hand motions vision. The veins are dilated, and retinal hemorrhages are present. Unlike with the mild variant, marked retinal edema casts a yellow hue to the background fundus appearance and obscures the foveolar reflex. **B,** Fluorescein angiogram corresponding to **A** at 18 seconds after injection reveals widespread retinal capillary nonperfusion, which causes the midsize and larger retinal vessels to stand out in relief from the gray, nonperfused areas. *(Courtesy of Gary C. Brown, MD.)*

Baseline and early natural history report. The Central Vein Occlusion Study. *Arch Ophthalmol.* 1993;111(8):1087–1095.

Risk factors for the development of CRVO

Patients may have premonitory symptoms of transient obscuration of vision before overt retinal manifestations appear; however, the vision loss is more commonly of sudden onset. Both types of CRVO are similar with regard to patient age at onset (although mild forms generally occur at a younger age), associated local and systemic findings, and laboratory test results. Although CRVO can occur at younger ages and lead to severe vision loss, 90% of patients are older than 50 years at the time of onset. The Eye Disease Case-Control Study found the following associations with CRVO:

- systemic arterial hypertension
- diabetes mellitus
- open-angle glaucoma

Increased IOP is a rare but potentially important cause of central vein occlusion.

It is common for patients presenting with CRVO to have elevated IOP or frank open-angle glaucoma in the affected eye only or in both eyes. CRVO can also be followed by a transient shallowing of the anterior chamber that, in some instances, leads to angle-closure glaucoma.

Oral contraceptives and diuretics have been implicated in CRVO. Unusual diseases that affect the blood vessel wall or cause alteration in clotting mechanisms and blood viscosity may be associated with a CRVO-like picture. Examples include blood dyscrasias (polycythemia vera), dysproteinemias, and causes of vasculitis (eg, sarcoidosis, systemic lupus erythematosus), and such hypercoagulable conditions as hyperhomocysteinemia, protein S deficiency, and protein C deficiency.

It is particularly important to recognize that *hyperviscosity retinopathy* can mimic a typical CRVO. However, the retinal findings in hyperviscosity retinopathy are generally bilateral and usually related to dysproteinemia such as Waldenström macroglobulinemia or multiple myeloma. In many cases, the hyperviscosity can be reversed by plasmapheresis. Diagnostic testing includes serum protein electrophoresis and measurements of whole blood viscosity.

Fuller JJ, Mason JO III. Retinal vein occlusions: update on diagnostic and therapeutic advances. *Focal Points: Clinical Modules for Ophthalmologists.* San Francisco: American Academy of Ophthalmology; 2007, module 5.

Natural history and clinical management of central retinal vein occlusion. The Central Vein Occlusion Study Group. *Arch Ophthalmol.* 1997;115(4):486–491.

Risk factors for central retinal vein occlusion. The Eye Disease Case-Control Study Group. *Arch Ophthalmol.* 1996;114(5):545–554.

Evaluation and management of CRVO

The ocular evaluation of CRVO requires measurement of IOP to help detect glaucoma. Gonioscopy should be performed in both eyes to determine a predilection for angle-closure glaucoma, evidence of previous angle-closure glaucoma, or signs of iris neovascularization. Any elevation of IOP in the affected or fellow eye should be treated (see also BCSC Section 10, *Glaucoma*).

The examiner should try to determine whether the vein occlusion is of the mild, nonischemic or the severe, ischemic type. Assessments of visual acuity, visual fields, and relative afferent defect, as well as electroretinography, ophthalmoscopy, and fluorescein angiography are helpful in making this determination. The retinopathy associated with carotid occlusive disease may simulate CRVO and should be differentiated by determining retinal artery pressure and evaluating the carotid.

It is advisable to refer patients with CRVO for medical evaluation. Common associated medical conditions include hypertension, diabetes mellitus, elevated cholesterol levels, and hyperhomocysteinemia, as well as a history of smoking. If the evaluation indicates that common risk factors for CRVO are absent, or the patient is less than 50 years of age, a thorough investigation should be considered, possibly including a workup for thrombophilia.

Patients with CRVO should be warned of the possibility of worsening vision, because eyes with initially perfused CRVO sometimes progress to an ischemic pattern. In the first 4 months of follow-up in the CVOS, 15%, and after 36 months, 34%, of initially perfused eyes converted to ischemia.

Follow-up In the absence of treatment, patients with CRVO should be monitored on a monthly basis for progression and for at least 6 months for the development of anterior segment neovascularization or neovascular glaucoma. If anti-VEGF drugs are used, patients should be observed for a similar duration after discontinuation of these drugs.

Complications The most common complications of CRVO are vitreous hemorrhage, anterior segment neovascularization, and neovascular glaucoma. Vitreous hemorrhage may occur in the absence of neovascularization and can be managed with vitrectomy. Anterior segment neovascularization and neovascular glaucoma are usually managed with pan-retinal photocoagulation, and glaucoma must be treated if present (see BCSC Section 10, *Glaucoma*).

Evaluation of grid pattern photocoagulation for macular edema in central vein occlusion. The Central Vein Occlusion Study Group M report. *Ophthalmology.* 1995;102(10):1425–1433.

Lahey JM, Tunc M, Kearney J, et al. Laboratory evaluation of hypercoagulable states in patients with central retinal vein occlusion who are less than 56 years of age. *Ophthalmology.* 2002;109(1):126–131.

Treatment of CRVO

Pharmacotherapy of CRVO Systemic anticoagulation for the treatment or prevention of CRVO has been attempted and is now discouraged. No evidence has demonstrated a benefit; to the contrary, publications have documented poorer outcomes from such treatment due to more extensive intraretinal hemorrhages. Recently, evidence has been accumulating in support of using local pharmacotherapies for CRVO and is changing how CRVO is managed.

INTRAVITREAL CORTICOSTEROIDS In the SCORE-CRVO study, at 1 year, 27% of patients treated with 1-mg triamcinolone and 26% with 4-mg triamcinolone had an improvement of 15 ETDRS letters or more compared with 7% of patients in the observation group. A study of sustained delivery of fluocinolone acetonide over 36 months demonstrated visual acuity and anatomical improvement in macular edema from CRVO. Evaluation of a dexamethasone injectable intravitreal implant for the management of CRVO similarly improved visual acuity outcomes over a 6-month period. In the latter study, however, rates of steroid-induced glaucoma or cataract formation were lower.

INTRAVITREAL ANTI-VEGF THERAPY In the Central Retinal Vein Occlusion (CRUISE) study, ranibizumab was administered to eyes with CRVO and related macular edema. A total of 392 patients were randomly assigned to receive monthly injections of either 0.5 or 0.3 mg of ranibizumab for 6 months or "standard of care" (observation). At 6 months, study subjects in the 3 groups had a mean gain from baseline of 14.9, 12.7, and 0.8 ETDRS letters, respectively. Overall, 47.7%, 46.2%, and 16.9%, respectively, gained 15 or more letters (3 lines of vision) at 6 months. Uncontrolled studies of bevacizumab administration have also demonstrated substantial resolution of macular edema as well as improvement in visual acuity (Fig 6-14). However, robust visual acuity data are not available for bevacizumab. Many practitioners use the 2 anti-VEGF drugs interchangeably, despite a lack of evidence for their equivalency. A third anti-VEGF drug, aflibercept (also called VEGF Trap), has also been shown to be effective in the treatment of vision loss and macular edema secondary to CRVO.

Intravitreal anti-VEGF drugs may also be used to reduce iris neovascularization and treat neovascular glaucoma in the short term.

Surgical management of CRVO A number of laser and other surgical methods have been explored for the treatment of CRVO.

LASER SURGERY Grid-pattern photocoagulation for macular edema in CRVO was evaluated prospectively by the CVOS investigators. The initial median visual acuity was 20/160 in treated eyes and 20/125 in control eyes, and the final median acuity was 20/200 and 20/160, respectively. Thus, even though grid laser treatment of the macula reduced angiographic evidence of macular edema, it yielded no benefit in improved visual acuity. However, a trend was revealed in the CVOS that grid laser treatment might be beneficial in younger patients in improving visual acuity in eyes with macular edema.

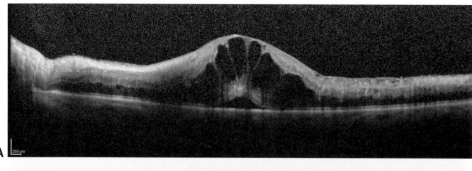

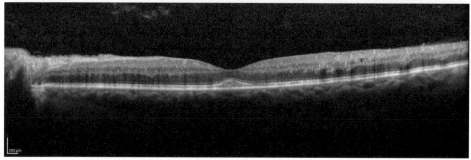

Figure 6-14 CME secondary to CRVO before and after treatment. **A,** Spectral-domain optical coherence tomogram showing severe cystoid macular edema with foveal detachment in a patient with a nonischemic CRVO. Visual acuity was 20/200. **B,** One month after bevacizumab 1.25-mg intravitreal injection, the cystic changes and foveal detachment have resolved, and the visual acuity measured 20/25. *(Courtesy of Colin A. McCannel, MD.)*

The CVOS reported that scatter panretinal photocoagulation (PRP)—when applied before any iris neovascularization had developed—failed to show a statistically significant decrease in the incidence of iris neovascularization, even though the participants assigned to receive it had a greater average amount of retinal capillary nonperfusion than did control participants. Because 20% of participants who had received scatter PRP before any signs of iris neovascularization still developed it despite the prophylactic laser treatment, close monitoring of patients at high risk of iris neovascularization is necessary. A dense central scotoma is common in ischemic CRVO, and laser PRP may add a peripheral scotoma, possibly leaving less useful retina and visual field. Therefore, the CVOS investigators recommended waiting until undilated gonioscopic examination revealed at least 2 clock-hours of iris neovascularization before performing PRP. In clinical practice, however, PRP is often performed at the first sign of iris neovascularization, particularly when close follow-up is not possible or seems unlikely.

Natural history and clinical management of central retinal vein occlusion. The Central Vein Occlusion Study Group. *Arch Ophthalmol.* 1997;115(4):486–491.

A randomized clinical trial of early panretinal photocoagulation for ischemic central vein occlusion. The Central Vein Occlusion Study Group N report. *Ophthalmology.* 1995;102(10):1434–1444.

OTHER SURGICAL TREATMENTS Several surgical approaches have been attempted for the treatment of CRVO. These include attempting to create an anastomotic connection between the retinal vein and the choroidal circulation with a high-power laser application; radial optic neurotomy involving sectioning of the posterior scleral ring to decompress the central retinal vein; and retinal vein cannulation with an infusion of tissue plasminogen activator (tPA). None of these procedures has stood the test of time, despite uncontrolled studies suggesting their efficacy; they are therefore currently considered to be of questionable benefit.

Ocular Ischemic Syndrome and Retinopathy of Carotid Occlusive Disease

Ocular ischemic syndrome is the term for the ocular symptoms and signs attributable to chronic, severe carotid artery obstruction, although chronic ophthalmic artery obstruction can cause a similar clinical picture.

Symptoms and Signs

Typical symptoms are vision loss usually over a period of weeks to months, aching pain localized to the orbital area of the affected eye, and prolonged recovery after exposure to a bright light. Anterior segment signs include iris neovascularization in two-thirds of eyes and an anterior chamber cellular response in about one-fifth of eyes. Although iris neovascularization is very prevalent, only one-half of the eyes with this condition show an increase in IOP; the low or normal IOP in the other half is most likely caused by impaired aqueous production.

Ocular ischemic syndrome can cause a retinopathy similar in appearance to a partial occlusion of the central retinal vein; therefore, it was originally called venous stasis retinopathy. Typical retinal findings include narrowed arteries, dilated but not very tortuous veins, hemorrhages, microaneurysms, and neovascularization of the optic disc, retina, or both (Fig 6-15). The retinal hemorrhages in carotid occlusive disease are commonly deep, round, and more often located in the midperipheral retina. A helpful method for differentiating between the 2 entities is to measure the retinal artery pressure by ophthalmodynamometry, or by gently pushing on the eye during the examination and observing the central retinal artery. An eye with CRVO will have normal artery pressure, whereas one with carotid occlusive disease will have low artery pressure and collapse easily.

Fluorescein angiography reveals delayed choroidal filling in 60% of eyes, delayed arteriovenous transit time in 95% of eyes, and prominent vascular staining (particularly of the arteries) in 85% of eyes. Electroretinography often discloses diminished amplitude of the a- and b-waves as a result of outer and inner layer retinal ischemia, respectively.

Etiology and Course

Atherosclerosis is the most common etiology, but other possible causes include Eisenmenger syndrome, giant cell arteritis, and other inflammatory conditions. Most patients

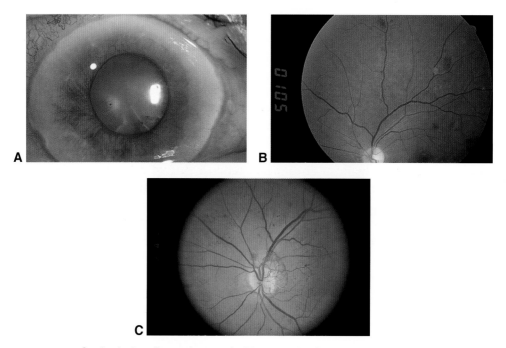

Figure 6-15 Ocular ischemic syndrome. **A,** Photograph of the anterior segment shows iris neovascularization. Patients with anterior chamber angle involvement may develop neovascular glaucoma. Fundus photographs show typical findings of, **B,** intraretinal hemorrhages in the midperiphery, narrowed retinal arteries, and, **C,** optic disc neovascularization. *(Used with permission from Quillen DA, Blodi BA, eds.* Clinical Retina. *Chicago: AMA Press; 2002:143. Copyright 2002, American Medical Association. All rights reserved.)*

are older than 55 years. Typically, a 90% or greater ipsilateral obstruction is necessary to cause the ocular ischemic syndrome. Both eyes are involved in about 20% of cases.

The natural history of vision in eyes with ocular ischemic syndrome is uncertain, but when rubeosis iridis is present, more than 90% of eyes are legally blind within 1 year after the disease is diagnosed. For this reason, timely diagnosis is essential. Full-scatter PRP is effective in eradicating rubeosis in about 35% of eyes.

Approximately one-half of patients with ocular ischemic syndrome also have ischemic cardiovascular disease; one-fourth have had a previous cerebrovascular accident; and one-fifth have peripheral atherosclerotic vascular disease so severe that a previous surgical procedure was necessary. The stroke rate is increased over that in the general population, and the 5-year mortality is approximately 40%, mostly from complications of cardiovascular disease.

Treatment of Ocular Ischemic Syndrome

The most definitive treatment for ocular ischemic syndrome appears to be carotid artery stenting and endarterectomy, although visual results are variable. Unfortunately, the procedures are ineffective when there is 100% obstruction, which is often the case. Extracranial to intracranial bypass surgery has been attempted in such cases but has been shown to be ineffective for preventing vision loss or stroke. In eyes with iris neovascularization and low or normal IOP as a result of impaired ciliary body perfusion and decreased aqueous formation, carotid reperfusion can lead to increased aqueous formation and a severe rise in IOP.

Sharma S, Brown GC. Ocular ischemic syndrome. In: Ryan SJ, Hinton DR, Schachat AP, Wilkinson CP, eds. *Retina.* 4th ed. Philadelphia: Elsevier/Mosby; 2006:1491–1502.

Arterial Occlusive Disease

The blood supply to the inner layers of the retina is derived entirely from the central retinal artery, unless a cilioretinal artery is present (15%–30% of eyes). Retinal ischemia results from disease processes affecting the afferent vessels anywhere from the common carotid artery to the intraretinal arterioles. The signs and symptoms of arterial obstruction depend on the vessel involved: occlusion of a peripheral extramacular arteriole may be asymptomatic, but ophthalmic artery disease can cause total blindness.

Capillary Retinal Arteriole Obstruction (Cotton-Wool Spots)

Acute obstruction in the distribution of radial peripapillary capillary net leads to the formation of an NFL infarct, or cotton-wool spot, thus inhibiting axoplasmic transport in the NFL. These inner retinal ischemic spots are superficial, white, typically 1/4 disc area or less in size, and perpendicular to the optic disc. They usually fade in 5–7 weeks, although spots in association with diabetic retinopathy often persist longer (Fig 6-16). A subtle retinal depression caused by inner retinal ischemic atrophy may develop in the area of prior ischemia. The effect on visual function, including loss of visual acuity and field defects, is related to the size and location of the occluded area.

Diabetic retinopathy, the most common cause of cotton-wool spots, is discussed in Chapter 5. Although the clinical findings are similar, many other diverse causes of inner retinal ischemic spots have been identified:

- sickle cell retinopathy
- radiation retinopathy
- HIV-associated retinopathy
- systemic arterial hypertension
- cardiac embolic disease

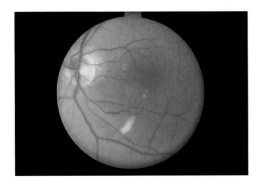

Figure 6-16   Cotton-wool spot. *(Courtesy of Gary C. Brown, MD.)*

- carotid artery obstructive disease
- vasculitis
- collagen-vascular disease
- leukemia
- anemia (severe)

The observation of even 1 cotton-wool spot in the fundus in an otherwise apparently healthy eye should alert the clinician to initiate a workup for an underlying etiology.

Brown GC, Brown MM, Hiller T, Fischer D, Benson WE, Magargal LE. Cotton-wool spots. *Retina*. 1985;5(4):206–214.

Branch Retinal Artery Occlusion

Although an acute BRAO may not initially be apparent ophthalmoscopically, within hours to days it leads to an edematous opacification caused by infarction of the inner retina in the distribution of the affected vessel (Fig 6-17). With time, the occluded vessel recanalizes, perfusion returns, and the edema resolves; however, a permanent field defect remains. Beyond the posterior pole, occlusion may be clinically silent.

Occlusion at any site is a result of embolization or thrombosis of the affected vessel. Three main varieties of emboli are recognized:

1. cholesterol emboli (Hollenhorst plaques) arising in the carotid arteries (Fig 6-18)
2. platelet-fibrin emboli associated with large-vessel arteriosclerosis
3. calcific emboli arising from diseased cardiac valves

Rare causes of emboli include cardiac myxoma, fat emboli from long-bone fractures, septic emboli from infective endocarditis, and talc emboli in intravenous drug users. Though rare, migraine in patients younger than 30–40 years of age can cause ocular arterial occlusions. Other associations include

- trauma
- coagulation disorders
- sickle cell disease
- oral contraceptive use or pregnancy
- mitral valve prolapse

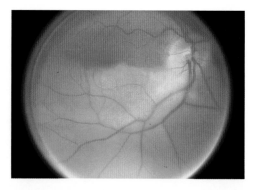

Figure 6-17 Inferotemporal branch retinal artery obstruction. The fundus photograph shows opacification of the retina in the distribution of the occluded vessel (inferior macula). In this case, the visual acuity was initially 20/30 at presentation but returned to 20/20 over several weeks. *(Courtesy of Gary C. Brown, MD.)*

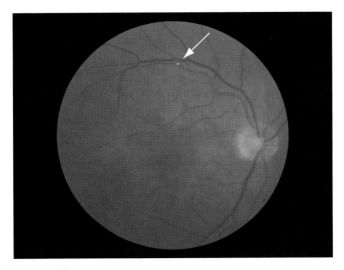

Figure 6-18 Hollenhorst plaque. Note the Hollenhorst plaque lodged at a bifurcation of the superior arcade arteriole *(arrow).* Hollenhorst plaques do not typically cause vascular obstruction and can remain at the bifurcation indefinitely. Occasionally, they can be observed to move with blood flow. *(Courtesy of Tara A. McCannel, MD, PhD.)*

- arrhythmias
- inflammatory and infectious etiologies such as toxoplasmic retinochoroiditis and syphilis
- connective tissue disorders, including giant cell arteritis

Management is directed toward determining systemic etiologic factors. Retinal arterial emboli have been linked with an increased risk of mortality; therefore, a systemic and vascular evaluation should be considered. No specific ocular therapy has been found to be effective in improving the visual prognosis. Pressure on the globe may dislodge an embolus from a large central vessel toward a more peripheral location, but the efficacy of this maneuver in improving vision outcomes is unknown.

Arruga J, Sanders MD. Ophthalmologic findings in 70 patients with evidence of retinal embolism. *Ophthalmology.* 1982;89(12):1336–1347.

Wang JJ, Cugati S, Knudtson MD, et al. Retinal arteriolar emboli and long-term mortality: pooled data analysis from two older populations. *Stroke.* 2006;37(7):1833–1836. Epub 2006 Jun 1.

Cilioretinal Artery Occlusion

A distinct clinical entity is the occlusion of the cilioretinal artery. As their name suggests, cilioretinal arteries arise from the short posterior ciliary vessels rather than the central retinal artery. They occur in approximately 32% of eyes and contribute to some portion of the macular circulation in 15% of eyes. Most commonly, their occlusion occurs in the setting of a central retinal vein occlusion. It is postulated that the increased hydrostatic pressure associated with CRVO can reduce blood flow in the cilioretinal artery to the point of functional occlusion and retinal infarction.

When cilioretinal artery occlusion occurs in isolation, giant cell arteritis should be considered strongly.

Hayreh SS, Fraterrigo L, Jonas J. Central retinal vein occlusion associated with cilioretinal artery occlusion. *Retina*. 2008;28(4):581–594.

Justice J Jr, Lehmann RP. Cilioretinal arteries. A study based on review of stereo fundus photographs and fluorescein angiographic findings. *Arch Ophthalmol*. 1976;94(8): 1355–1358.

Central Retinal Artery Occlusion

Sudden, complete, and painless loss of vision in 1 eye is characteristic of central retinal artery occlusion (CRAO). The retina becomes opaque and edematous, particularly in the posterior pole, where the nerve fiber and ganglion cell layers are thickest (Fig 6-19). The orange reflex from the intact choroidal vasculature beneath the foveola thus stands out in contrast to the surrounding opaque neural retina, producing the *cherry-red spot*. Some degree of macular vision can be preserved by a cilioretinal artery protecting an area of retina perfused by it (see Fig 1-7).

With time, the central retinal artery reopens or recanalizes and the retinal edema clears; however, the effect on visual acuity is usually permanent because the inner retina has been infarcted. In one study, 66% of eyes had final visual acuity worse than 20/400, and 18% of eyes had 20/40 or better. Most cases of 20/40 or better visual acuity occur in the presence of a patent cilioretinal artery, which can preserve portions of the central macula (see Figs 6-19, 1-7). Loss of vision to the level of no light perception is often associated with choroidal vascular insufficiency (partial or complete ophthalmic artery occlusion) in addition to occlusion of the central retinal artery (Fig 6-20). Studies in nonhuman primates have suggested that irreversible damage to the sensory retina occurs after 90 minutes of complete CRAO. Nevertheless, clinical return of vision can occur in some instances even if the obstruction has persisted for many hours.

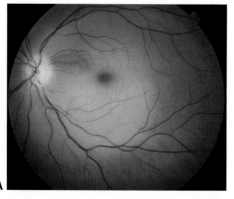
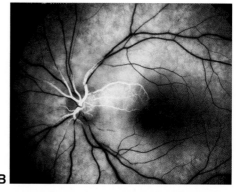

A   B

Figure 6-19 CRAO. **A,** Note the superficial macular opacification and a cherry-red spot in the foveola. **B,** Preservation of a sector of superonasal macula related to cilioretinal vessels, perfused in this angiogram. The patient had hand motion visual acuity. *(Courtesy of Hermann D. Schubert, MD.)*

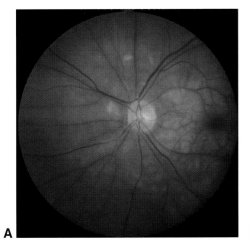
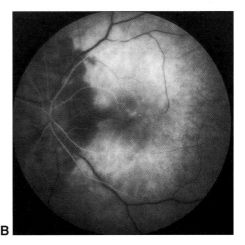

A

B

Figure 6-20 Central retinal and parent ciliary artery occlusion. **A,** Acute central retinal and parent ciliary artery obstruction. Severe retinal opacification is present. The visual acuity was no light perception. **B,** Fluorescein angiogram at 3 minutes after injection reveals hypofluorescence of the retinal vessels, the nasal choroid, and the optic disc, corresponding to an occlusion of the central retinal artery and nasal parent ciliary artery with the vertical watershed of choroidal perfusion. *(Courtesy of Hermann D. Schubert, MD.)*

CRAO is often caused by atherosclerosis-related thrombosis occurring at the level of the lamina cribrosa. Embolization may be important in some cases, as are hemorrhage under an atherosclerotic plaque, thrombosis, spasm, and dissecting aneurysm within the central retinal artery. Overall, emboli are present in the retinal arterial system in approximately 20% of eyes with CRAO.

Emboli within the carotid distribution may cause transient ischemic attacks (TIAs), amaurosis fugax, or both. Bright cholesterol emboli, or Hollenhorst plaques, located typically at retinal arterial bifurcations, suggest a carotid atheromatous origin and, when accompanied by relevant symptoms and findings, may be an indication for carotid artery treatment. Systemic etiologic considerations, as outlined for BRAO, are important and require evaluation. It should be noted that the leading cause of death in patients with retinal arterial obstruction is cardiovascular disease.

Giant cell arteritis (GCA) accounts for approximately 1%–2% of cases of CRAO. In cases of CRAO in which emboli are not readily visible, a thorough evaluation for GCA should be considered. The erythrocyte sedimentation rate (ESR) and C-reactive protein levels— markers of inflammation—are usually elevated and should be checked. A complete blood count may detect elevated platelet counts, which are also suggestive of GCA, and aids in the interpretation of the ESR. If GCA is suspected as a cause, corticosteroid therapy should be instituted promptly because the second eye can become involved by ischemia within hours to days after the first; in addition, a temporal artery biopsy should be performed. See BCSC Section 5, *Neuro-Ophthalmology*, for further discussion of giant cell arteritis.

Hayreh SS, Kolder HE, Weingeist TA. Central retinal artery occlusion and retinal tolerance time. *Ophthalmology.* 1980;87(1):75–78.

Management of CRAO

If therapy for CRAO is to be instituted, it should be undertaken without delay. Unfortunately, treatment efficacy is questionable. Simple therapeutic approaches should be performed, such as reducing IOP by ocular massage, administering IOP-lowering medications, and performing anterior chamber paracentesis. Vasodilatory inhalation therapy with a mixture of 95% oxygen and 5% carbon dioxide or having the patient breathe in a paper bag is no longer recommended. Hyperbaric oxygen therapy, catheterization of the ophthalmic artery with tPA infusion, and transvitreal Nd:YAG embolysis have been described as successful management options, but all lack good evidence of efficacy.

Iris neovascularization develops after acute CRAO in approximately 18% of eyes 1–12 weeks after the event, with a mean time interval of approximately 4–5 weeks. PRP is effective in eradicating the new iris vessels in about two-thirds of cases.

Ophthalmic Artery Occlusion

Ophthalmic artery occlusion is very rare. Clinically, ophthalmic artery occlusion typically produces vision loss to the level of light perception or no light perception because of the simultaneous ischemia of the choroid and retina. This simultaneous occlusion of the choroidal and retinal circulation leaves all layers of the retina ischemic or infarcted. A cherry-red spot is usually not present, as both the inner retina and outer retina become opacified from the infarction, and thus there is no contrast difference between foveola and fovea that would lead to such a spot.

In autopsy studies of patients who died during active GCA, as many as 76% of cases had some degree of ophthalmic artery affected by vasculitis; clinically, however, occlusion is rare in this condition. Other known causes of ophthalmic artery occlusion are dissection of the internal carotid artery, orbital mucormycosis, embolization, and as a complication of surgical interventions and injections in or near the area.

Vasculitis

Retinal vasculitis from any cause can lead to similar pathologic sequelae; it may be primarily ocular or be associated with inflammatory disease elsewhere in the body. The early clinical manifestations are generally nonspecific, consisting of perivascular infiltrates and sheathing of the retinal vessels (vascular wall thickening with vessel involution; Fig 6-21). Involvement of exclusively retinal arteries or veins is uncommon. Veins tend to be inflamed earlier and more frequently than arterioles, and combinations are the rule. Causes of retinal vasculitis include

- giant cell arteritis
- polyarteritis nodosa
- systemic lupus erythematosus
- Behçet disease
- inflammatory bowel diseases
- multiple sclerosis
- pars planitis
- sarcoidosis

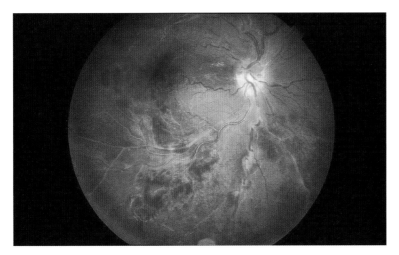

Figure 6-21 Retinal vasculitis in an eye of a patient with Crohn disease. Retinal hemorrhages and edema are present, as is prominent sheathing of the retinal vessels. *(Courtesy of Gary C. Brown, MD.)*

- syphilis
- toxoplasmosis
- viral retinitides
- Lyme disease
- cat-scratch disease
- medications, such as rifabutin

The masquerade syndromes should also be considered. See BCSC Section 9, *Intraocular Inflammation and Uveitis,* for further discussion of most of these conditions and Section 5, *Neuro-Ophthalmology,* for discussion of multiple sclerosis and giant cell arteritis.

A primary occlusive retinal vasculopathy for which no cause can be found has been termed *Eales disease.* This condition is an occlusive vasculopathy that usually involves the peripheral retina of both eyes and often results in extraretinal neovascularization with vitreous hemorrhage. It usually occurs in males, and an associated tuberculin hypersensitivity may be present.

Susac syndrome is characterized by multiple branch retinal arterial occlusions and can be associated with hearing loss and, though rare, with strokes. The syndrome is most commonly diagnosed in women in their third decade, and there is no known cause. Treatment is with corticosteroids or immunosuppression.

A clinical picture indistinguishable from past retinal vasculitis may result from chronic embolism or thrombosis without inflammation. Evaluation includes a search for possible causes: cardiac valvular disease, cardiac arrhythmias, ulcerated atheromatous disease of the carotid vessels, and hemoglobinopathies.

Idiopathic retinal vasculitis, aneurysms, and neuroretinitis (IRVAN) describes a syndrome characterized by the presence of retinal vasculitis, multiple macroaneurysms, neuroretinitis, and peripheral capillary nonperfusion. Systemic investigations are generally noncontributory and oral prednisone has demonstrated little benefit. Capillary nonperfusion is often sufficiently severe to warrant PRP.

Cystoid Macular Edema

Cystoid macular edema (CME) is characterized by intraretinal edema contained in honeycomblike cystoid spaces. Fluorescein angiography shows the source of edema to be abnormal perifoveal retinal capillary permeability, visible as multiple small focal fluorescein leaks and late pooling of the dye in extracellular cystoid spaces. Optical coherence tomography (OCT) findings in CME include diffuse retinal thickening with cystic areas of low reflectivity (reduced reflectivity) more prominently in the inner nuclear and outer plexiform layers. This finding correlates with histologic studies that indicate swelling in and between müllerian glia. On occasion, a nonreflective cavity is present beneath the neurosensory retina that is consistent with subretinal fluid accumulation (see Figs 5-3B, 6-14A). Because of the radial foveal arrangement of both glia and Henle inner fibers, this pooling classically forms a "flower-petal" pattern (Fig 6-22). Severe cases may be associated with vitritis (vitreous cells) and optic nerve head swelling.

Etiologies for CME

Abnormal permeability of the perifoveal retinal capillaries may occur in a wide variety of conditions, including diabetic retinopathy, central and branch retinal vein occlusion, any type of uveitis (particularly pars planitis), and retinitis pigmentosa. CME may occur after any ocular surgery, such as cataract extraction (in which case the CME is termed *Irvine-Gass Syndrome*), retinal detachment surgery, vitrectomy, glaucoma procedures, photocoagulation, and cryopexy. It has been triggered by prostaglandin analogues used to treat glaucoma. Subretinal disease processes (choroidal neovascularization, choroidal hemangioma, subclinical retinal detachment) must also be considered when CME is detected; see Chapter 4. The nutritional supplement niacin has also been implicated as a cause of atypical CME.

Rare causes of cystic macular change of different pathogenesis (such as X-linked hereditary retinoschisis, Goldmann-Favre disease, some cases of retinitis pigmentosa, and nicotinic acid maculopathy) are distinguishable by the clinical setting, family history, and lack of late-phase fluorescein leakage into the cystlike spaces, as well as by OCT.

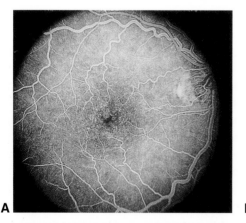 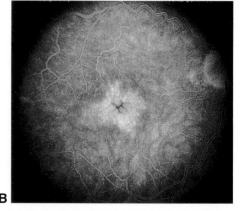

A **B**

Figure 6-22 CME. Fluorescein angiogram demonstrates hyperfluorescent dilated capillaries in early frames **(A)** with late intraretinal accumulation of fluorescein in a petaloid pattern **(B).** Disc staining is also commonly associated.

Incidence of CME

For patients who have undergone intracapsular lens extraction, the incidence of CME is as high as 60%, although the incidence is lower when the posterior capsule remains intact. Intraocular lens implantation at the time of extracapsular surgery does not appear to increase the incidence of CME. The peak incidence occurs 6–10 weeks postoperatively, with spontaneous resolution occurring clinically in approximately 95% of uncomplicated cases, usually within 6 months. Most such cases of CME are mild and asymptomatic, and distinguishing between symptomatic, or *clinical, CME* and edema that is apparent only on fluorescein angiography, termed *angiographic CME,* is relevant. More severe CME may result in permanent vision loss. The incidence of CME increases with degree of postoperative inflammation and with surgical complications such as vitreous loss or iris prolapse. Increased incidence may be related to complications of intraocular lens implantation and to photic effects. See also BCSC Section 11, *Lens and Cataract.*

Berkow JW, Flower RW, Orth DH, Kelley JS. *Fluorescein and Indocyanine Green Angiography: Technique and Interpretation.* 2nd ed. Ophthalmology Monograph 5. San Francisco: American Academy of Ophthalmology; 1997:117–118.

Treatment for CME

The effect of therapy on CME is difficult to evaluate because of the high rate of spontaneous resolution. Pharmacologic therapy using a combination of topical corticosteroids and nonsteroidal anti-inflammatory drugs (NSAIDs) has become commonplace for prophylaxis and is well supported by the medical literature for established edema. If CME is severe or refractory to topical therapy, periocular (eg, posterior sub-Tenon) or intraocular injection of triamcinolone acetonide is an appropriate escalation of treatment. In chronic CME, systemic acetazolamide treatment has been shown to be successful and is very helpful in cases associated with retinitis pigmentosa. For treating CME associated with diabetic retinopathy of ocular venous occlusive disease, also see Chapter 5.

If CME is associated with vitreous adhesions to the iris or a corneoscleral wound, interruption of the vitreous strands by vitrectomy or Nd:YAG laser treatment may be helpful.

Coats Disease

Coats disease is defined by the presence of vascular dilatations (retinal telangiectasia), including ectatic arterioles, microaneurysms, venous dilations (phlebectasias), and fusiform capillary dilatations, frequently associated with exudative retinal detachment. Despite the presence of retinal capillary nonperfusion shown by angiography, posterior segment neovascularization is unusual. The abnormal vessels are incompetent, resulting in the leakage of serum and other blood components, which accumulate in and under the retina. Any portion of the peripheral and macular capillary system may be involved. Variation in the clinical findings is wide, ranging from mild retinal vascular abnormalities and minimal exudation to extensive areas of retinal telangiectasia associated with massive leakage and exudative retinal detachment, as may occur in children presenting with leukocoria (Coats reaction; Fig 6-23). The yellow exudate can also cause a yellow appearance of the pupil, referred to as xanthocoria.

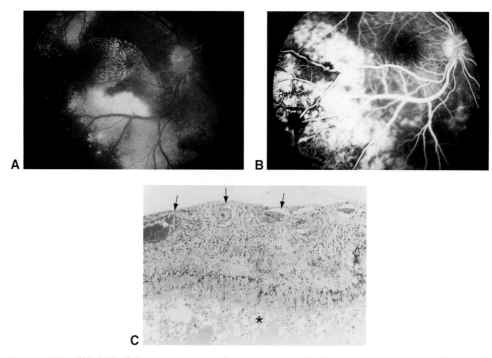

Figure 6-23 "Light bulb" aneurysms in Coats disease. **A,** Retinal telangiectasia, light bulb aneurysms, fusiform telangiectasia, phlebectasia, and massive retinal edema surrounded by subretinal exudate in an 8-year-old boy with Coats disease. **B,** Fluorescein angiogram showing retinal telangiectasia, areas of capillary ectasia and nonperfusion, and light bulb aneurysms typical of Coats disease. **C,** Histology of Coats disease demonstrating intraretinal gliosis, small schisis cavities, and loss of the normal lamellar architecture. Telangiectatic blood vessels *(arrows)* are present in the inner layer of the retina, causing massive intraretinal and subretinal exudation and focal areas of hemorrhage (diapedesis). The retina is detached by subretinal exudate containing numerous foamy, lipid-laden macrophages *(asterisk).* (H&E, ×100.) *(Used with permission from Scott IU, Flynn HW Jr, Rosa RH Jr. Other retinal vascular diseases: hypertensive retinopathy, venous and arterial occlusive disease, retinal artery macroaneurysms, sickle cell retinopathy, Coats disease, juxtafoveal telangiectasis, and Eales disease. In: Parrish RK, ed.* The University of Miami Bascom Palmer Eye Institute Atlas of Ophthalmology. *Philadelphia: Current Medicine; 2000:300.)*

This retinal condition is not hereditary and is not associated with systemic vascular abnormalities, even though an associated gene has been located on chromosome 4. Entities such as retinitis pigmentosa and others may occasionally be associated with retinal telangiectasia. Usually only 1 eye is involved, and there is a marked male predominance (85%). Gradual progression with increasing exudation occurs over time. The severity and rate of progression appear greater in children under the age of 4 years, in whom massive exudative retinal detachment with retina apposed to the lens may simulate retinoblastoma. Therefore, Coats disease is included in the differential diagnosis of leukocoria. Apart from Coats disease, the differential diagnosis for leukocoria in this age group includes retinoblastoma, retinoma, retinal dysplasia, coloboma, myelinated nerve fibers, astrocytic hamartoma, granuloma, persistent fetal vasculature (PFV), trauma, endophthalmitis, incontinentia pigmenti, retinopathy of prematurity (ROP), familial exudative vitreal retinopathy (FEVR), and Norrie disease. BCSC Section 4, *Ophthalmic Pathology and Intraocular Tumors,* discusses retinoblastoma in depth.

Patients with peripheral areas of leaky vascular anomalies typically present with lipid deposition in an otherwise angiographically normal macula, as hard exudate tends to accumulate in the macula. Similar findings in adults probably represent late decompensation of preexisting vascular anomalies. Occasionally, a submacular lipogranuloma or subretinal fibrosis is the initial finding. The differential diagnosis may include

- dominant (familial) exudative vitreoretinopathy
- facioscapulohumeral muscular dystrophy
- ROP
- capillary hemangioma (von Hippel disease)

For milder cases of lipid exudation, additional considerations are diabetic retinopathy, BRVO, juxtafoveal retinal telangiectasia, and radiation retinopathy.

Treatment of Coats disease generally consists of photocoagulation, cryotherapy, and in severe cases, retinal reattachment surgery. Photocoagulation and cryotherapy are effective in obliterating the vascular anomalies and in halting progression. Several treatments may be necessary, and long-term follow-up is important to detect recurrences.

Parafoveal (Juxtafoveal) Retinal Telangiectasia

Focal retinal gliosis and telangiectasia of the capillary bed, confined to the juxtafoveolar region of 1 or both eyes, may result in vision loss from capillary incompetence and exudation (Fig 6-24). Refractile changes ("retinal crystals") are visible in advanced cases. Histologic evidence suggests that this condition is not a true telangiectasia but rather consists of structural abnormalities similar to those of diabetic microangiopathy, with deposits of excess basement membrane within the retinal capillaries. The entity has been subdivided into 3 types:

Type 1: Unilateral parafoveal telangiectasia, congenital or acquired
Type 2: Bilateral parafoveal telangiectasia (Fig 6-25)
Type 3: Bilateral parafoveal telangiectasia with retinal capillary obliteration

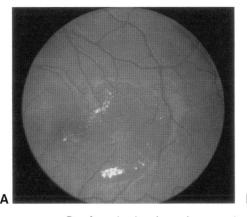 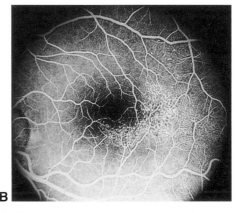

A   **B**

Figure 6-24 Parafoveal telangiectasia, type 1. **A,** Fundus photograph shows typical retinal capillary abnormalities in the temporal macula and retinal exudate. **B,** Fluorescein angiogram demonstrates more clearly the retinal capillary abnormalities.

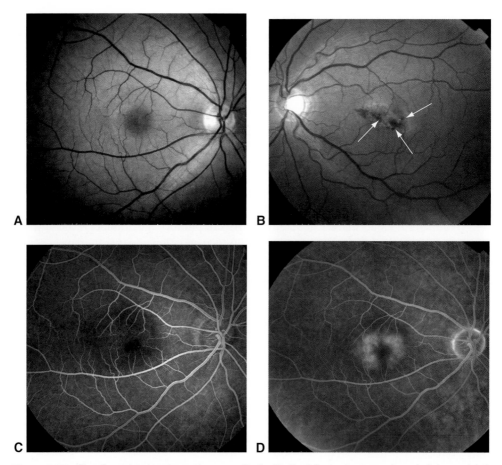

Figure 6-25 Parafoveal telangiectasia, type 2. **A, B,** Red-free photographs of right and left eyes, respectively, show bilateral parafoveal telangiectasia. Early right-angle branching and fine crystals are visible temporal to the fovea in each eye. *Arrows* point to the intraretinal pigment migration in the left eye **(B)** typically present as a late manifestation in this condition. **C, D,** Early and late fluorescein angiograms of the right eye. Early-phase fluorescein angiogram **(C)** demonstrating telangiectatic changes of the retinal capillaries temporal to the fovea. In the late-phase fluorescein angiogram **(D)** there is hyperfluorescence from inner retinal leakage of fluorescein in the perifoveal macula. *(Courtesy of Richard F. Spaide, MD.)*

Type 1, also referred to as aneurysmal telangiectasia, typically occurs in males and resembles a macular variant of Coats disease with a circinate type of exudates, also known as Leber miliary aneurysms. Type 2, or perifoveal telangiectasia, has equal sex predilection and affects both eyes. Perifoveal retinal changes typically include thickening, loss of transparency with grayish appearance, small telangiectatic vessels, and a cystic appearance of the fovea, all most pronounced in the temporal fovea. As the lesion ages, intralesional RPE migration is often present, and choroidal neovascularization may subsequently develop. Vision loss ranges from mild to severe. Approximately one-third of patients with this variant have an abnormal glucose tolerance test result. Cases in type 3 show progressive vision loss from the obliteration of the perifoveal capillaries.

On fluorescein angiography, the telangiectatic vessels are readily apparent and usually leak. OCT imaging typically shows a thinned central macular retina, including the fovea, with inner lamellar oblong foveal cavitations in which the long axis is parallel to the retinal surface.

Photocoagulation treatment may be indicated for type 1 cases and can be successful in resolving exudation. Type 2 and type 3 eyes typically do not respond to photocoagulation because leaky vessels are not the predominant feature. Small, controlled and uncontrolled trials suggest limited success of managing with intravitreal anti-VEGF drugs. The differential diagnosis includes, but is not limited to, branch retinal vein or venule obstruction, diabetes mellitus, radiation retinopathy, cystoid macular edema (especially chronic), and carotid artery disease.

Charbel Issa P, Finger RP, Kruse K, Baumüller S, Scholl HP, Holz FG. Monthly ranibizumab for nonproliferative macular telangiectasia type 2: a 12-month prospective study. *Am J Ophthalmol*. 2011;151(5):876–886.e1. Epub 2011 Feb 19.

Clemons TE, Gillies MC, Chew EY, et al; MacTel Research Group. Baseline characteristics of participants in the natural history study of macular telangiectasia (MacTel) MacTel Project Report No. 2. *Ophthalmic Epidemiol*. 2010;17(1):66–73.

Gass JD, Blodi BA. Idiopathic juxtafoveolar retinal telangiectasis. Update of classification and follow-up study. *Ophthalmology*. 1993;100(10):1536–1546.

Yannuzzi LA, Bardal AM, Freund KB, Chen KJ, Eandi CM, Blodi B. Idiopathic macular telangiectasia. *Arch Ophthalmol*. 2006;124(4):450–460.

Arterial Macroaneurysms

Retinal arterial macroaneurysms are acquired ectasias of mostly second-order retinal arterioles (Fig 6-26). Large macroaneurysms can actually traverse the full thickness of the retina. Vision loss may occur from embolic or thrombotic occlusion of the endarteriole (white infarct); sub-ILM hemorrhage; or intraretinal, subretinal, or vitreous hemorrhage

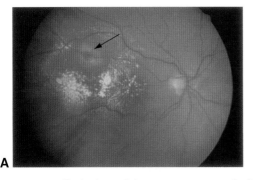 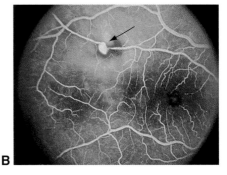

A   B

Figure 6-26 Retinal arterial macroaneurysm. **A,** Arterial macroaneurysm of the distal superior arcade arteriole associated with leakage, manifested as exudate in a partial circinate pattern *(arrow)*, and an early macular star of exudate surrounding the fovea. **B,** Fluorescein angiogram shows a saccular area of bright hyperfluorescence along the distal, superior arcade arteriole, representing the arteriolar macroaneurysm *(arrow)*.

(red infarct). Other retinal findings may include capillary telangiectasia and remodeling, as well as retinal edema involving the macula. Frequently, there are multiple arterial macroaneurysms, although only 10% of cases are bilateral. Arterial macroaneurysms are associated with systemic arterial hypertension in about two-thirds of cases and can follow a CRVO. Sclerosis and spontaneous closure often accompany macroaneurysm-related hemorrhage; bleeding more than once is rare.

Laser photocoagulation treatment may be considered if increasing edema in the macula threatens central visual function. In most instances, moderate-intensity laser treatment of the retina immediately adjacent to the macroaneurysm with 2–3 rows of large-spot-size (200–500 μm) applications results in closure. Direct treatment carries risks of rupture and vascular occlusion and should be avoided. Caution should be used when treating macroaneurysms that occur in macular arterioles because a main complication of the disease and its therapy is thrombosis with retinal arterial obstruction distal to the macroaneurysm.

Brown DM, Sobol WM, Folk JC, Weingeist TA. Retinal arteriolar macroaneurysms: long-term visual outcome. *Br J Ophthalmol.* 1994;78(7):534–538.

Rabb MF, Gagliano DA, Teske MP. Retinal arterial macroaneurysms. *Surv Ophthalmol.* 1988;33(2):73–96.

Phakomatoses

Conventionally, a number of syndromes referred to as *phakomatoses* ("mother spot") are grouped loosely by the common features of ocular and systemic involvement of a congenital nature. Most, but not all, are hereditary. With the exception of Sturge-Weber syndrome, the phakomatoses involve the neuroretina and its circulation. For further discussion of the phakomatoses, see BCSC Section 5, *Neuro-Ophthalmology*, and Section 6, *Pediatric Ophthalmology and Strabismus*.

Retinal Angiomatosis

Capillary hemangioblastomas develop in the retina and optic nerve head in *retinal angiomatosis*. The early lesions are small and easily overlooked clinically but may be more apparent on fluorescein angiography. A fully developed lesion is a spherical orange-red tumor fed by a dilated, tortuous retinal artery and drained by an engorged vein (Fig 6-27). Multiple hemangioblastomas may be present in the same eye, and bilateral involvement occurs in 50% of patients. Angiomas affecting the optic nerve head and peripapillary retina may be more difficult to recognize because of the absence of visible afferent and efferent dilated vessels. Lesions in such locations are predominantly subretinal or epiretinal (exophytic or endophytic).

An angiomatous variant (vasoproliferative tumor) has been described, with the lesion located peripherally and not associated with large feeding and draining vessels or with systemic manifestations. Vasoproliferative tumors have also been reported as late sequelae of ROP and associated with retinitis pigmentosa.

Leakage of plasma constituents from a hemangioblastoma may lead to serous detachment of the retina and accumulation of exudate in the macula, resulting in reduced visual acuity (Fig 6-28). Occasionally, vitreous hemorrhage or tractional detachment may

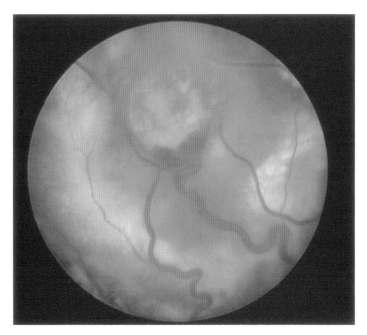

Figure 6-27 Fundus of a patient with von Hippel disease, showing peripheral hemangioblastoma with surrounding exudate and retinal detachment. Note the dilation of the feeder arteriole and draining venule.

occur. Neovascularization may develop in the optic disc, retina, or iris following retinal detachment.

Retinal angiomatosis has hereditary and sporadic forms. The hereditary form is a result of a mutation in a tumor-suppressor gene located on the short arm of chromosome 3

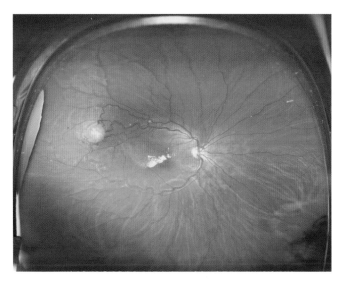

Figure 6-28 Ultra-wide-field fundus photograph of a patient with von Hippel disease, showing hemangioblastoma in near periphery and associated exudative maculopathy. *(Courtesy of Colin A. McCannel, MD.)*

(3p26–p25). The mode of transmission is autosomal dominant, often with incomplete penetrance and variable expression. Retinal and optic disc lesions that are limited to the eye have also been referred to as *von Hippel lesions.* When retinal angiomatosis is associated with central nervous system and visceral involvement, the eponym *von Hippel–Lindau (VHL) disease* is used. For a more extensive discussion of VHL disease, see BCSC Section 6, *Pediatric Ophthalmology and Strabismus.*

Central nervous system tumors (hemangioblastomas of the cerebellum, medulla, pons, and spinal cord) occur in 20% of patients. The visceral lesions include cysts of the kidney, pancreas, liver, epididymis, and ovary. Renal cell carcinoma, meningiomas, and pheochromocytomas have also been associated. When an ocular lesion is discovered, a systemic workup must be considered for possible renal cell carcinoma and pheochromocytoma, as well as for central nervous system lesions. The leading causes of death in patients with VHL disease are cerebellar hemangioblastoma and renal cell carcinoma.

Retinal hemangioblastomas typically enlarge over time, related to an increase in capillaries but also in interstitial cells. Early diagnosis increases the likelihood of successful treatment. Ocular management, therefore, should include treatment of all identified retinal angiomas and careful follow-up to detect recurrence or the development of new lesions. Wide-angle fluorescein angiography can assist in detecting small lesions that may be difficult to spot on examination or with fundus photography (Fig 6-29). The techniques of photocoagulation, photodynamic therapy with verteporfin, and cryotherapy have been used successfully to treat the angiomatous lesions directly. Successful treatment results in shrinkage of the angioma, attenuation of the afferent vessels, and resorption of the subretinal fluid. Cryotherapy treatment in particular can cause a temporary, marked increase in the amount of exudation, which may occasionally lead to development of a total exudative retinal detachment.

Atebara NH. Retinal capillary hemangioma treated with verteporfin photodynamic therapy. *Am J Ophthalmol.* 2002;134(5):788–790.

Gass JD, Braunstein R. Sessile and exophytic capillary angiomas of the juxtapapillary retina and optic nerve head. *Arch Ophthalmol.* 1980;98(10):1790–1797.

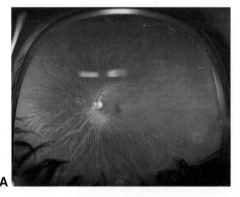 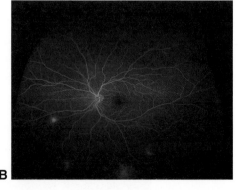

A **B**

Figure 6-29 Ultra-wide-angle fundus image of the left eye of a 26-year-old woman with von Hippel–Lindau disease. **A,** No obvious lesions are visible. **B,** The ultra-wide-angle fluorescein angiogram demonstrates multiple foci of leakage, which are early, small, retinal hemangioblastomas, some of which are not visible on the photograph or clinically. *(Courtesy of Colin A. McCannel, MD.)*

Hardwig P, Robertson DM. von Hippel–Lindau disease: a familial, often lethal, multi-system phakomatosis. *Ophthalmology.* 1984;91(3):263–270.

Congenital Retinal Arteriovenous Malformations

Congenital retinal arteriovenous malformations are rare developmental anomalies in which no intervening capillary bed exists *(racemose angioma).* The abnormalities may range from a single arteriovenous communication to a complex anastomotic system.

Lesions are typically unilateral, nonhereditary, and located in the retina or optic nerve. Typically, they do not show leakage on fluorescein angiography. The retinal lesions may be associated in some cases with similar ipsilateral vascular malformations in the brain, face, orbit, and mandible *(Wyburn-Mason syndrome).* Associated central nervous system vascular malformations tend to be located deeply and follow the optic tract. Many of the retinal malformations remain asymptomatic. In contrast, intraosseous vascular malformations that may occur in the maxilla and mandible can lead to unexpected hemorrhage during dental extractions.

Retinal Cavernous Hemangioma

Although most cases of cavernous hemangioma are sporadic and restricted to the retina or optic nerve head, they may occur in a familial (autosomal dominant) pattern and may be associated with intracranial and skin hemangiomas. For this reason, cavernous hemangioma may be considered one of the phakomatoses.

Retinal cavernous hemangioma is characterized by the formation of grapelike clusters of thin-walled saccular angiomatous lesions in the inner retina or on the optic nerve head (Fig 6-30). The blood flow in these lesions is derived from the retinal circulation and is relatively stagnant, producing a characteristic fluorescein angiographic picture. These dilated saccular lesions fill slowly during angiography, and plasma-erythrocyte layering occurs as a result of the sluggish blood flow. Fluorescein leakage is characteristically absent, correlating with the absence of subretinal fluid and exudate in the retinal cavernous hemangioma and serving to differentiate the condition from retinal telangiectasia, von Hippel retinal angiomatosis, and racemose aneurysm of the retina.

Though rare, the hemangiomas may bleed into the vitreous, but they usually remain asymptomatic. Vitreous traction is thought to be the cause of hemorrhage in these cases. Treatment of retinal cavernous hemangiomas is usually not indicated unless vitreous hemorrhage is recurrent, in which case photocoagulation or cryotherapy may be effective. For further discussion, see BCSC Section 4, *Ophthalmic Pathology and Intraocular Tumors.*

Radiation Retinopathy

Exposure to ionizing radiation can damage the retinal vasculature. Radiation retinopathy typically has a delayed onset, is slowly progressive, and causes microangiopathic changes that clinically resemble diabetic retinopathy. Radiation retinopathy can occur after either external-beam or local plaque therapy, typically within months to years after radiation treatment. In general, radiation retinopathy is observed around 18 months after treatment with external-beam radiation and earlier with brachytherapy. Because radiation

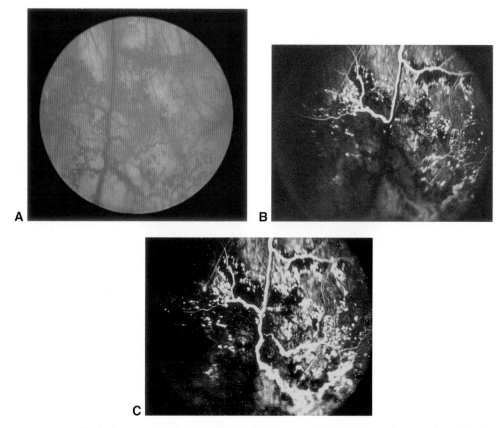

Figure 6-30 Retinal cavernous hemangioma. **A,** Large retinal cavernous hemangioma in the inferior retina of right eye. Note the dilated and tortuous vein with grapelike saccular clusters of angiomatous lesions that could be mistaken for retinal neovascularization. These lesions are usually stable and require no treatment. **B,** Fluorescein angiogram (late transit at 43.3 seconds) shows poor blood flow and uneven filling of the vascular lesion. **C,** Even by 60.8 seconds, the vascular tree is not completely filled. Late phases typically show an accumulation of dye in the saccular lesions with no sign of leakage.

retinopathy is very similar to other vascular diseases, eliciting a history of radiation treatment is important in establishing the diagnosis. An exposure to doses of 30–35 grays (Gy) or more is usually required to induce clinical symptoms; occasionally, however, retinopathy may develop after as little as 15 Gy of external-beam radiation. Studies have shown retinal damage in 50% of patients receiving 60 Gy and in 85%–95% of patients receiving 70–80 Gy. The total dose, volume of retina irradiated, and fractionation scheme are important in determining the threshold dose for radiation retinopathy. See BCSC Section 4, *Ophthalmic Pathology and Intraocular Tumors,* for further discussion of these therapies, including sample dosages.

Clinically, affected patients may be asymptomatic or may describe decreased visual acuity. Ophthalmic examination may reveal signs of retinal vascular disease, including cotton-wool spots, retinal hemorrhages, microaneurysms, perivascular sheathing, capillary telangiectasis, macular edema, and disc edema. Capillary nonperfusion, documented by fluorescein angiography, is commonly present, and extensive retinal ischemia can lead

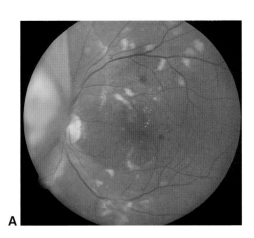
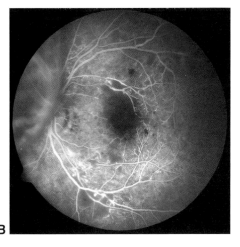

A **B**

Figure 6-31 Radiation retinopathy. Images of an eye that has undergone plaque brachytherapy for treatment of choroidal melanoma. The melanoma can be seen nasally, obscuring part of the disc. Typical radiation retinopathy changes are apparent. **A,** In the fundus photograph, cotton-wool spots, exudates ("hard exudates"), and intraretinal blot hemorrhages are visible. **B,** The fluorescein angiogram shows microvascular abnormalities (representative of capillary nonperfusion) superior to the fovea and adjacent to an enlarged foveal avascular zone. Additional areas of nonperfusion are noted in the macula and near periphery. *(Courtesy of Tara A. McCannel, MD, PhD.)*

to neovascularization of the retina, iris, or disc (Fig 6-31). Other complications may occur, such as optic atrophy, central retinal artery occlusion, central retinal vein occlusion, choroidal neovascularization, vitreous hemorrhage, neovascular glaucoma, and tractional retinal detachment. Vision outcome is primarily related to the extent of macular involvement with cystoid macular edema, exudative maculopathy, or capillary nonperfusion. Occasionally, vision loss may be caused by acute optic neuropathy. Although no clinical trials have been performed, the management of radiation retinopathy is similar to that for diabetic retinopathy and includes focal laser therapy to reduce macular edema or panretinal photocoagulation to treat zones of ischemia and neovascularization. Intravitreal administration of triamcinolone acetonide or anti-VEGF drugs can stabilize or improve visual acuity in some patients, but the effect might not be lasting.

Patel SJ, Schachat AP. Radiation retinopathy. In: Albert DM, Miller JW, Azar DT, Blodi BA, eds. *Albert & Jakobiec's Principles and Practice of Ophthalmology.* 3rd ed. Philadelphia: Saunders; 2008:chap 175.

Shields CL, Demirci H, Dai V, et al. Intravitreal triamcinolone acetonide for radiation maculopathy after plaque radiotherapy for choroidal melanoma. *Retina.* 2005;25(7): 868–874.

Valsalva Retinopathy

A sudden rise in intrathoracic or intraabdominal pressure (such as accompanies coughing, vomiting, lifting, or straining for a bowel movement) may raise intraocular venous pressure sufficiently to rupture small superficial capillaries in the macula. The hemorrhage is typically located under the ILM, where it may create a hemorrhagic detachment of the

ILM. Vitreous hemorrhage and subretinal hemorrhage may be present. Vision is usually only mildly reduced and the prognosis is excellent, with spontaneous resolution usually occurring within months after onset. The differential diagnosis of Valsalva retinopathy includes posterior vitreous separation, which may cause an identical hemorrhage or a macroaneurysm. Therefore, in all cases, a peripheral retinal tear or an aneurysm along an arteriole must be ruled out.

Purtscher Retinopathy and Purtscherlike Retinopathy

After acute compression injuries to the thorax or head, a patient may experience loss of vision associated with Purtscher retinopathy in 1 or both eyes. Large cotton-wool spots, hemorrhages, and retinal edema are found most commonly surrounding the optic disc, and fluorescein angiography shows evidence of arteriolar obstruction and leakage (Fig 6-32). Occasionally, patients present with disc edema and an afferent pupillary defect. Vision may be permanently lost from this infarction, and optic atrophy may develop.

Purtscher retinopathy is thought to be a result of injury-induced complement activation, which causes granulocyte aggregation and leukoembolization. This process in turn occludes small arterioles such as those found in the peripapillary retina.

Even in the absence of trauma, various other conditions may activate complement and produce a similar fundus appearance. Because Purtscher's original description involved trauma, cases with similar fundus findings are termed *Purtscherlike retinopathy* (Table 6-3). For example, the retinopathy associated with acute pancreatitis, which appears identical to traumatic Purtscher retinopathy, is probably also caused by complement-mediated leukoembolization. Other conditions that may cause these changes include collagen-vascular diseases (such as systemic lupus erythematosus), childbirth, and amniotic fluid embolism.

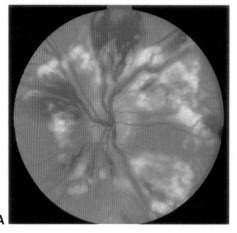 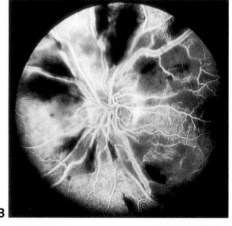

A   B

Figure 6-32 Purtscher retinopathy following trauma to the head and face. **A,** Extensive cotton-wool spots and retinal hemorrhage. **B,** Fluorescein angiogram showing capillary nonperfusion in areas of cotton-wool spots. *(Reproduced from Burton TC. Unilateral Purtscher's retinopathy. Ophthalmology. 1980;87(11):1096–1105.)*

Table 6-3 Conditions Associated With Purtscher or Purtscherlike Retinopathy

Trauma
    Head injury
    Chest compression
    Long-bone fractures (fat embolism syndrome)
Acute pancreatitis
Chronic renal failure
Autoimmune diseases
    Systemic lupus erythematosus
    Thrombotic thrombocytopenic purpura
    Scleroderma
    Dermatomyositis
    Sjögren syndrome
Amniotic fluid embolism
Retrobulbar anesthesia
Orbital steroid injection

Modified from Regillo CD. Posterior segment manifestations of systemic trauma. In: Regillo CD, Brown GC, Flynn HW Jr, eds. *Vitreoretinal Disease: The Essentials.* New York: Thieme; 1999:538.

Fat embolism following crushing injuries or long-bone fractures may cause similar retinal findings. Usually, intraretinal hemorrhages are scattered in the paramacular area, and the cotton-wool spots of fat embolism are generally smaller and situated more peripherally in the retina than they are in Purtscher retinopathy.

Terson Syndrome

Terson syndrome is recognized as vitreous and sub-ILM or subhyaloid hemorrhage caused by an abrupt intracranial hemorrhage. Although the exact mechanism is not known, it is suspected that the acute intracranial hemorrhage causes an acute rise in the intraocular venous pressure, resulting in a rupture of peripapillary and retinal vessels. Approximately one-third of patients with subarachnoid or subdural hemorrhage have associated intraocular hemorrhage, which may include intraretinal and subretinal bleeding. Terson syndrome occurs primarily in individuals between 30 and 50 years old, but it can occur at any age. In most cases, visual function is unaffected once the hemorrhage clears. Spontaneous improvement generally occurs, although vitrectomy is occasionally required to clear the ocular media.

Gass JDM. *Stereoscopic Atlas of Macular Diseases: Diagnosis and Treatment.* 4th ed. St Louis: Mosby; 1997:452–455.

CHAPTER 7

Retinopathy of Prematurity

Introduction

Retinopathy of prematurity (ROP) is a complex disease process initiated in part by a lack of complete or normal retinal vascularization in premature infants. ROP has a typical progression pattern, but earlier disease stages may regress spontaneously at any time. The absence of retinal vessels in portions of the immature retina can result in retinal ischemia, leading to the release of growth factors that promote vascular growth. Instead of the normal process in which retinal vessels continue to vascularize the avascular retina, the growth pattern becomes disturbed. At the border of vascular and avascular retina, blood vessels grow into the vitreous cavity, a process driven by the growth factors. As the disease progresses, vitreous hemorrhage and tractional retinal detachment occur. The end stage of untreated ROP is the development of a dense, white fibrovascular plaque behind the lens and complete tractional retinal detachment. The former name of this condition, *retrolental fibroplasia,* is descriptive of the end stage of ROP. The main risk factors for developing this condition are prematurity and low birth weight.

Epidemiology

Estimates are that ROP causes some degree of vision loss in approximately 1300 newborns per year in the United States and severe visual impairment in 250–500 of those children. Approximately 300 children per million live births have at least 1 eye blinded by ROP. In resource-limited regions of the world, there has recently been a rise in the incidence of ROP, and affected infants are often of more advanced gestational age and higher birth weight than is typical for ROP patients in more resource-rich regions. This difference is important to note, as screening criteria and study findings from more highly resourced regions may not be applicable to others.

Classification and Terminology

For the purpose of consistently describing, staging, and studying ROP, an International Classification of ROP was developed (Table 7-1). Four classification concepts have prognostic and pathophysiologic importance: the location or *zone* of involvement, the disease severity or *stage,* the *extent* of disease in clock-hours of involvement, and whether or not *plus disease* is present.

Table 7-1 Acute ROP (International Committee on Classification of Acute ROP)

Location

Zone I: posterior retina within a 60° circle centered on the optic nerve

Zone II: from the posterior circle (zone 1) to the nasal ora serrata anteriorly

Zone III: remaining temporal peripheral retina

Extent: number of clock-hours involved

Severity

Stage 1: presence of a demarcation line between vascularized and nonvascularized retina

Stage 2: presence of a demarcation line that has height, width, and volume (ridge). Small, isolated tufts of neovascular tissue lying on the surface of the retina, commonly called "popcorn," may be present.

Stage 3: a ridge with extraretinal fibrovascular proliferation (may be mild, moderate, or severe, as judged by the amount of proliferative tissue present)

Stage 4: partial retinal detachment
      A. extrafoveal
      B. retinal detachment including fovea

Stage 5: total retinal detachment with funnel configuration (combinations are listed in order of frequency: top row is the most common and bottom row the least common configuration):

Anterior	Posterior
Open	Open
Narrow	Narrow
Open	Narrow
Narrow	Open

Plus disease: vascular dilatation (venous) and tortuosity (arteriolar) of posterior retinal vessels in at least 2 quadrants of the eye; iris vascular dilatation and vitreous haze may be present

Modified from International Committee for the Classification of Retinopathy of Prematurity. The International Classification of Retinopathy of Prematurity revisited. *Arch Ophthalmol.* 2005;123(7):991–999.

Regarding the zones, the retina is divided into 3 areas. *Zone I* encompasses the area included in a circle twice the radius of the distance from the optic disc to the foveola. *Zone II* encompasses the area included in a circle centered on the optic disc with a radius of the distance from the optic disc to the nasal ora serrata, and *zone III* includes the remainder of the fundus outside zones I and II.

ROP is classified into 5 stages, 1 through 5. Sometimes, the term *stage 0 ROP* is used for immature retinal vasculature without pathologic changes; however, this term is not part of the International Classification. Stages 1 through 3 describe the appearance of the interface of normally vascularized and avascular retina, and stages 4 and 5 describe degrees of retinal detachment. In *stage 1* ROP, the shunt at the interface of vascular and avascular retina is essentially flat, and a *demarcation line* is visible (Fig 7-1), whereas in *stage 2*, the border thickens and appears elevated *(ridge)*; small tufts of vessels may be present (Fig 7-2). *Stage 3* ROP is distinguished by the presence of a ridge with extraretinal fibrovascular proliferation, and blood vessels grow through the ILM of the retina at the ridge into the vitreous (Fig 7-3). *Stage 3* ROP can be mild, moderate, or severe. *Stage 4* ROP denotes the presence of a tractional retinal detachment. If the detachment is extramacular (known as "fovea-on"), the category is *stage 4A*, whereas if the fovea is detached ("macula-off"), the ROP is referred to as *stage 4B* (Fig 7-4). *Stage 5* ROP is a complete tractional retinal detachment and is further subclassified according to the configuration of the central

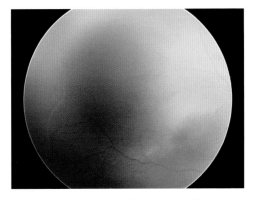

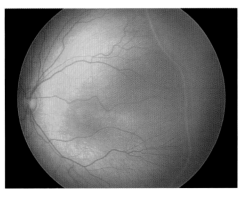

Figure 7-1 Stage 1 ROP. Temporally, a faint demarcation line can be appreciated. *(Courtesy of Colin A. McCannel, MD.)*

Figure 7-2 Stage 2 ROP. An elevated ridge of mesenchymal tissue is present at the border of the vascularized (reddish) and avascular (grayish) retina. *(Courtesy of Colin A. McCannel, MD.)*

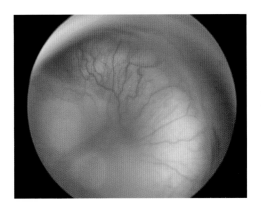

Figure 7-3 Stage 3 ROP. Severe stage 3 ROP with marked preretinal proliferations. Some vitreous and preretinal hemorrhage is visible in the lower right side of the image. *(Courtesy of Colin A. McCannel, MD.)*

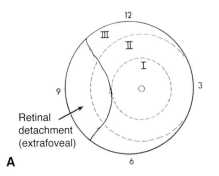

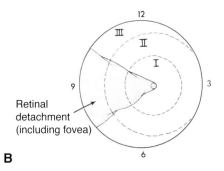

Figure 7-4 **A,** Stage 4A ROP. **B,** Stage 4B ROP. The roman numerals in each circle indicate the zones, as per the international classification. *(Courtesy of J. Arch McNamara, MD.)*

retinal "funnel": open or closed anteriorly, open or closed posteriorly (Fig 7-5). If the retinal detachment progresses to a closed funnel anteriorly, fibrosis is often associated with the central funnel cavity and retina. These structures may be visible immediately behind the lens and resemble a white mass (Fig 7-6).

Figure 7-5 Stage 5 ROP. A "macula-off" ROP retinal detachment can be appreciated. The marked contraction of the preretinal fibrosis can be seen to act like a purse string. Even at this stage—an open-funnel stage 5 retinal detachment—the arborizing pattern of the retinal blood vessels approaching the pre-retinal proliferation can be seen. Additionally, tortuous dilated vessels, also called plus disease, are present. *(Courtesy of Colin A. McCannel, MD.)*

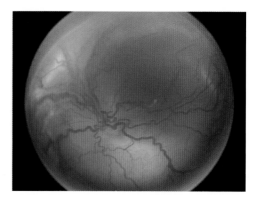

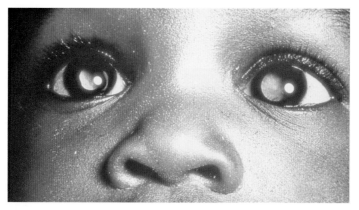

Figure 7-6 Stage 5 ROP. Bilateral total retinal detachments are present, with the retinal tissue drawn up behind the clear lens, forming a retrolental mass in each eye. *(Courtesy of Gary C. Brown, MD.)*

The *extent* describes in clock-hours the amount of interface between vascular and avascular retina involved with pathologic changes. *Plus disease* is characterized by the presence of retinal vascular dilation and tortuosity in the posterior pole (Fig 7-7). Plus disease is indicative of an actively progressing phase of the disease. In some cases, plus disease is difficult to diagnose, leading to interobserver variation in making the diagnosis by both bedside and photographic screening methods. If vascularization ends in zone I or very posterior zone II and is accompanied by plus disease, very rapid progression *("rush" disease)* poses a significant risk.

Additional terminology is helpful in treatment considerations. *Threshold disease* is characterized by more than 5 contiguous clock-hours of extraretinal neovascularization or 8 cumulative clock-hours of extraretinal neovascularization in association with plus disease and location of the retinal vessels within zone I or II (Fig 7-8). *Prethreshold disease* is a term coined by the Early Treatment for Retinopathy of Prematurity (ETROP) study; it encompasses all zone 1 and zone 2 ROP changes, except stage 1, that do not meet threshold treatment criteria. It is further divided into high-risk prethreshold ROP, or *type 1 ROP*, and lower-risk prethreshold ROP, or *type 2 ROP*.

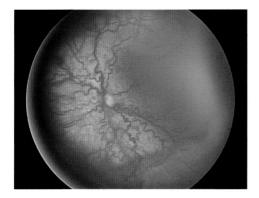

Figure 7-7 Pronounced plus disease in an eye with ROP. The retinal arteries and veins are dilated, and the arteries in particular are tortuous. The avascular retina and preretinal proliferations can be seen inferiorly and inferotemporally (bottom right). *(Courtesy of Colin A. McCannel, MD.)*

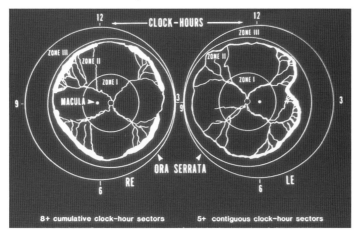

Figure 7-8 Examples of threshold disease, as characterized in the Multicenter Trial of Cryotherapy for Retinopathy of Prematurity. *(Reprinted by permission of American Medical Association from Multicenter trial of cryotherapy for retinopathy of prematurity. Preliminary results. Cryotherapy for Retinopathy of Prematurity Cooperative Group.* Arch Ophthalmol. *1988;106(4):474.)*

Type 1 ROP is defined to include:

- zone I, any stage ROP with plus disease
- zone I, stage 3 ROP without plus disease
- zone II, stage 2 or 3 ROP with plus disease

Type 2 ROP is defined to include:

- zone I, stage 1 or 2 ROP without plus disease
- zone II, stage 3 ROP without plus disease

An eye is classified according to the most advanced disease noted; however, documentation should reflect all zones and stages observed, including their relative extent. Eyes with ROP in zone III typically have a good visual prognosis. The more posterior the zone at the time of recognition of the disease, the more nonperfused retina there is and thus the more worrisome the prognosis.

International Committee for the Classification of Retinopathy of Prematurity. The International Classification of Retinopathy of Prematurity revisited. *Arch Ophthalmol.* 2005;123(7):991–999.

Pathogenesis

Retinal vascularization normally proceeds from the optic disc to the periphery and is completed in the nasal quadrants by approximately 36 weeks of gestation and on the temporal side by 40 weeks. A vanguard of mesenchymal cells initially grows outward in the nerve fiber layer from the region of the optic disc starting at month 4–5 of gestation. These mesenchymal cells give rise to retinal capillary endothelial cells, which then form the capillary system. Some capillaries enlarge to form arterioles and venules, and some undergo apoptosis as remodeling occurs. Current understanding of ROP is incomplete, but it has been suggested that the vascularization results from 2 distinct processes that differ in time, location, and visual prognosis:

1. *vasculogenesis:* the de novo formation of new vessels by transformation of vascular precursor cells; characterizes zone I disease
2. *angiogenesis:* budding from existing vessels; characterizes zone II disease

The posterior vasculogenic process responds poorly to treatment.

Exposure to excessive concentrations of oxygen can lead to an arrest of vascular development, leaving a variable amount of neurosensory retina without an inner retinal blood supply. Although an important contributing factor, oxygen supplementation is no longer considered the sole factor in the pathogenesis of ROP. Other factors, such as genetic predisposition, low birth weight, and a short gestational period also increase the risk of developing the disease.

Factors such as intercurrent illnesses, blood transfusions, and Pco_2, although statistically associated with the outcome in a univariate sense, failed to maintain a statistically significant association when considered in a multivariate analysis. ROP has been reported in full-term infants, in stillborn infants who had not received supplemental oxygen, in anencephalic infants, and in infants with congenital heart disease and substantial right-to-left shunting whose Pao_2 readings never exceeded 50–60 mm Hg.

Clinically, vascularized retina in the premature infant without ROP normally blends almost imperceptibly into the anterior, gray, nonvascularized retina. With ROP, however, the juncture between the 2 becomes more distinct because of the presence of shunts and variable glial hyperplasia.

Conversely, the more peripheral the shunt is, and the smaller its size and extent on the retina, the better the outlook for spontaneous regression with minimal scarring. An active shunt is associated with dilation and increased tortuosity of the retinal vessels posteriorly. A notable finding in active disease is increased and abnormal terminal arborization of retinal vessels as they approach the shunt or ridge. In addition, microvascular abnormalities (eg, microaneurysms, areas of capillary nonperfusion, and dilated vessels) may be visible behind the shunt.

In the vasoproliferative phase, new vessels varying widely in size and extent arise from retinal vessels just posterior to the shunt. These new vessels can induce contracture of the firmly attached vitreous gel, which results in progressive tractional retinal detachment. Vitreous hemorrhage can occur in stages 3–5, as can exudative retinal detachment.

Flynn JT, Chan-Ling T. Retinopathy of prematurity: two distinct mechanisms that underlie zone 1 and zone 2 disease. *Am J Ophthalmol.* 2006:142(1);46–59.

Natural Course

The systemic or local tissue factors that influence regression or progression of ROP are not known; however, there is a predictable time course. ROP is a transient disease in the majority of infants, with spontaneous regression occurring in 85% of eyes. The initial clinical sign of regression is the development of a clear zone of retina beyond the shunt, followed by the development of straight vessels crossing the shunt, with an arteriovenous feeder extending into the avascular retina.

Threshold ROP eventually develops in approximately 7% of infants with a birth weight of 1250 g or less. Eyes that demonstrate progression undergo a gradual transition from the active to the cicatricial stage of ROP, which is associated with variable degrees of fibrosis, contracture of the proliferative tissue, vitreous and retinal traction, macular distortion, and/or retinal detachment.

Flynn JT, Bancalari E, Bachynski BN, et al. Retinopathy of prematurity. Diagnosis, severity, and natural history. *Ophthalmology.* 1987;94(6):620–629.

Multicenter trial of cryotherapy for retinopathy of prematurity. Preliminary results. Cryotherapy for Retinopathy of Prematurity Cooperative Group. *Arch Ophthalmol.* 1988;106(4):471–479.

Associated Conditions and Late Sequelae

Conditions more likely to occur in eyes with regressed ROP include the following:

- myopia with astigmatism
- anisometropia
- strabismus
- amblyopia
- cataract
- glaucoma
- macular pigment epitheliopathy
- vitreoretinal scarring
- tractional retinal detachment
- anomalous foveal anatomy

Though rare, both angle-closure and pupillary-block glaucoma may occur in myopic eyes with cicatricial ROP. Angle-closure glaucoma has been reported to occur during the second to fifth decades of life, with a mean age of 32 years in affected individuals.

Rhegmatogenous retinal detachment, exudative retinopathy, and recurrent vitreous hemorrhages can also occur later in life. ROP and its sequelae can cause problems throughout a patient's life, and long-term follow-up is crucial. Failure to diagnose and treat ROP and its complications in a timely fashion combined with a statute of limitations of up to 20 years in many US states increases the legal exposure of physicians caring for children with ROP.

Day S, Menke, AM, Abbott RL. Retinopathy of prematurity malpractice claims: the Ophthalmic Mutual Insurance Company experience. *Arch Ophthalmol.* 2009;127(6):794–798.

Screening Recommendations

According to the Cryotherapy for Retinopathy of Prematurity Cooperative Group, signs of ROP were present in 66% of infants with a birth weight 1250 g or less and in 82% of those with a birth weight of less than 1000 g. Recommendations for the screening of premature infants at risk of ROP were issued in a joint statement of the American Academy of Pediatrics, Section on Ophthalmology; the American Association for Pediatric Ophthalmology and Strabismus; and the American Academy of Ophthalmology (available at http://pediatrics.aappublications.org/cgi/content/full/pediatrics;117/2/572).

Screening Criteria

Recommended screenings include at least 2 dilated funduscopic examinations using binocular indirect ophthalmoscopy for all infants with a birth weight of less than 1500 g or with a gestational age of 30 weeks or less, as well as for selected infants with a birth weight between 1500 g and 2000 g or a gestational age greater than 30 weeks with an unstable clinical course who are believed to be at high risk by their attending pediatrician or neonatologist. The first examination should generally be performed between 4 and 6 weeks of postnatal age or, alternatively, within the 31st to 33rd week of postconceptional or postmenstrual age, whichever is later. Examinations are then generally performed every 1–2 weeks (see the following examination schedules) until the retina is fully vascularized. One examination is sufficient only if it demonstrates unequivocally that the retinal periphery is fully vascularized bilaterally.

Screening Intervals

After each evaluation, the follow-up interval should be based on the disease features, with more severe disease having shorter follow-up intervals.

1 Week or Less Follow-up

- zone I retinal vessels ending without ROP, stage 1 or 2 ROP
- zone II, stage 2 or 3 ROP

1- to 2-Week Follow-up

- zone I, regressing ROP
- zone II, stage 1 ROP

2-Week Follow-up

- zone II, stage 1 or regressing ROP

2- to 3-Week Follow-up

- zone II, immature vascularization without ROP
- zone III, stage 1or 2 or regressing ROP

Retinal screening examinations can be discontinued when any one of the following criteria is met:

- Zone III retinal vascularization is attained without previous zone I or II ROP. If there is examiner doubt about the zone or if the postmenstrual age is less than 35 weeks, confirmatory examinations may be warranted.
- There is full retinal vascularization.
- Postmenstrual age of 45 weeks and no prethreshold disease (defined as stage 3 ROP in zone II, any ROP in zone I) or worse ROP is present.
- ROP is regressing. Care must be taken to ensure that no abnormal vascular tissue capable of reactivation and progression is present.

Palmer EA, Flynn JT, Hardy RJ, et al. Incidence and early course of retinopathy of prematurity. The Cryotherapy for Retinopathy of Prematurity Cooperative Group. *Ophthalmology*. 1991;98(11):1628–1640.

Section on Ophthalmology, American Academy of Pediatrics; American Academy of Ophthalmology; American Association for Pediatric Ophthalmology and Strabismus. Screening examination of premature infants for retinopathy of prematurity. Policy Statement. *Pediatrics*. 2006;117(2):572–576.

Fundus Photographic Screening of ROP

Ultra-wide-angle fundus photography (120 degrees) of premature infant eyes is very useful both for documentation of findings and for use in fundus photographic screening. Remote screening of photographic fundus images has established itself as an efficient and cost-effective method for screening premature infants for ROP. The Photo-ROP Cooperative Group concluded that remote interpretation of weekly digital fundus images was a useful adjunct to conventional bedside ROP screening by indirect ophthalmoscopy. The study concluded that because of limitations of image quality in some cases, there continued to be a need for the availability of an ophthalmologist skilled at examining premature infant eyes. The study also established a definition of clinically significant ROP, the presence of which warrants evaluation by an ophthalmologist for assessment and possible treatment.

Prevention and Risk Factors

As ROP, or then-termed retrolental fibroplasia (RLF), became a clinically distinct and recognized entity in the 1950s, supplemental oxygen was implicated as a major causative factor. The drastic reductions in oxygen utilization in neonatal intensive care units that followed indeed reduced the incidence of RLF dramatically. An unintended consequence of oxygen restriction was that many of the infants suffered adverse neurologic outcomes, and infant death rates rose. Once oxygen was utilized more liberally again, neurologic outcomes and survival improved, at the price of a resurgence of RLF.

Years later, the Supplemental Therapeutic Oxygen for Prethreshold ROP (STOP-ROP) study evaluated whether supplemental oxygen administration would decrease the progression to threshold ROP in infants with prethreshold ROP. The STOP-ROP trial demonstrated that use of supplemental oxygen at pulse oximetry saturations of 96%–99% did not cause further progression of prethreshold ROP but also did not statistically significantly reduce the number of infants requiring peripheral ablative surgery. Supplemental oxygen increased the risk of adverse pulmonary events, including pneumonia and exacerbations of chronic lung disease, as well as the need for oxygen, diuretics, and hospitalization at 3 months of corrected age.

Preventing ROP begins with preventing prematurity through optimal pre-, peri-, and postnatal care. Avoiding extremely low birth weight and short gestational ages may be most important. There is mounting evidence that the clinical course alters risk as well; that is, very sick premature infants are at greater risk of developing ROP. Specifically, sepsis, blood transfusion, and slow rate of postnatal weight gain have been shown to increase the risk of ROP. Systemic insulinlike growth factor 1 (IGF-1) levels are also associated with ROP risk. Taken together, the rate of weight gain and IGF-1 levels are more predictive of ROP development than is either value alone. A newer model—the weight, IGF, neonatal ROP (WINROP) algorithm—is being assessed for more targeted screening efforts, replacing the conventional screening criteria. In some studies, this model has been 100% sensitive in detecting at-risk infants while identifying as many as 90% of infants that do not need screening.

Löfqvist C, Andersson E, Sigurdsson J, et al. Longitudinal postnatal weight and insulin-like growth factor I measurements in the prediction of retinopathy of prematurity. *Arch Ophthalmol.* 2006;124(12):1711–1718.

Treatment

In 1988, the Cryotherapy for ROP study demonstrated that ablation of avascular anterior retina in ROP eyes with threshold disease reduced by approximately half the incidence of an unfavorable outcome such as macular dragging, retinal detachment, or retrolental cicatrix formation. These sequelae were reduced from 47% to 25% at 1 year of follow-up, and the visual results in such cases were shown to parallel the anatomical results. At 10 years, eyes that received cryotherapy were still much less likely to be blind than control eyes.

The ETROP trial randomly assigned 1 eye of infants with bilateral, high-risk, prethreshold ROP to receive early ablation of the avascular retina, while the fellow eye was managed conventionally according to Cryotherapy for ROP study methods. High risk was determined using a computational model based on the natural history cohort of the Cryotherapy for ROP study; this model used demographic characteristics of the infants and clinical features of ROP to classify eyes with prethreshold ROP as high risk or low risk. In infants with high-risk prethreshold ROP, earlier treatment was associated with a reduction in unfavorable grating visual acuity outcomes (from 19.5% to 14.5%; $P = .01$) and a reduction in unfavorable structural outcomes (from 15.6% to 9.1%; $P < .001$) at 9 months. The study determined that the clinical categorization of prethreshold eyes into type 1 or type 2 ROP achieved very similar results to the computational model for risk assessment to prethreshold eyes.

Any eyes meeting the criteria for type 1 ROP should be considered for peripheral retinal ablative treatment, whereas type 2 ROP eyes can be monitored in short intervals and laser ablative treatment considered if they progress to type 1 ROP or threshold ROP. The authors of the ETROP study pointed out that the prethreshold treatment algorithm did not take into account all other known risk factors for progression, such as systemic disease, and that, therefore, clinical judgment is still required for optimal management.

American Academy of Pediatrics website. Screening examination of premature infants for retinopathy of prematurity. February 2006. http://aappolicy.aappublications.org/cgi/content/full/pediatrics;117/2/572. Accessed September 14, 2011.

Cryotherapy for Retinopathy of Prematurity Cooperative Group. Multicenter Trial of Cryotherapy for Retinopathy of Prematurity: ophthalmological outcomes at 10 years. *Arch Ophthalmol.* 2001;119(8):1110–1118.

Early Treatment for Retinopathy of Prematurity Cooperative Group. Revised indications for the treatment of retinopathy of prematurity: results of the Early Treatment for Retinopathy of Prematurity Randomized Trial. *Arch Ophthalmol.* 2003;121(12):1684–1694.

Wallace DK. Retinopathy of prematurity. *Focal Points: Clinical Modules for Ophthalmologists.* San Francisco: American Academy of Ophthalmology; 2008, module 12.

Laser and Cryoablation Surgery

Ablation treatment of threshold or prethreshold type 1 ROP should be accomplished whenever possible with laser rather than cryoablation surgery, as laser surgery has less treatment-related morbidity. Treatment should be administered within 72 hours of determining its need and applied using the indirect ophthalmoscope in a confluent or subconfluent scatter fashion to the avascular retina anterior to the ridge (Figs 7-9, 7-10). In the horizontal meridia, laser treatment should be applied in a lighter pattern to avoid damage to the long ciliary vessels and nerves. Damage to these structures can lead to severe anterior segment ischemia. Use of retinal cryoablation (Fig 7-11) is now rare (in the United States), but the technique may still have a role in the treatment of eyes for which visualization of the retina is insufficient for laser treatment because of media opacities or persistent tunica vasculosa lentis, or when a laser is not available. Treatment should be performed in conjunction with pediatric consultation and with systemic monitoring because respiratory or cardiorespiratory arrest can occur in up to 5% of treated infants. Use of systemic analgesia is also advisable to minimize stress and risk to the infant. Some neonatologists prefer that infants undergo treatment in an operating room under general anesthesia.

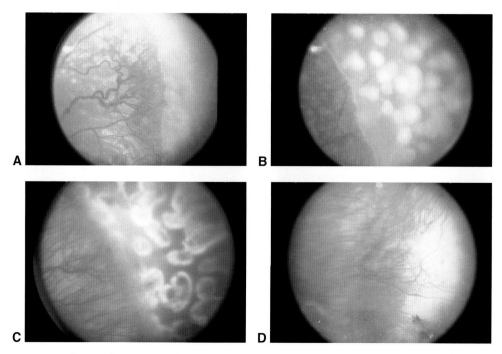

Figure 7-9 Laser photocoagulation for threshold ROP. **A,** Threshold eye before laser therapy. **B,** Immediately after laser therapy. **C,** 1 week after laser therapy. **D,** 3 months after laser therapy. *(Courtesy of Gary C. Brown, MD.)*

Figure 7-10 Wide-angle photographic view of fundus after laser photocoagulation for threshold ROP. Plus disease is visible posteriorly, and avascular retina is apparent in the inferior and inferior temporal fundus (bottom right of image). Arborization of the vasculature leading up to the ridge and associated fibrovascular proliferation is pronounced. *(Courtesy of Colin A. McCannel, MD.)*

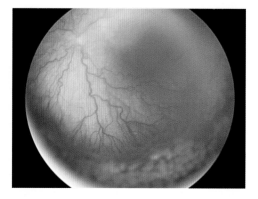

Brown GC, Tasman WS, Naidoff M, Schaffer DB, Quinn G, Bhutani VK. Systemic complications associated with retinal cryoablation for retinopathy of prematurity. *Ophthalmology.* 1990;97(7):855–858.

Connolly BP, McNamara JA, Sharma S, Regillo CD, Tasman W. A comparison of laser photocoagulation with trans-scleral cryotherapy in the treatment of threshold retinopathy of prematurity. *Ophthalmology.* 1998;105(9):1628–1631.

Laser therapy for retinopathy of prematurity. Laser ROP Study Group. *Arch Ophthalmol.* 1994;112(2):154–156.

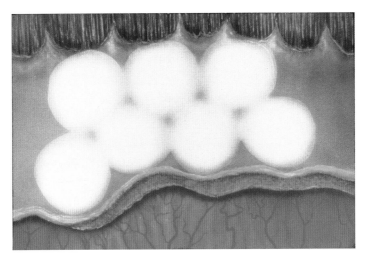

Figure 7-11 Cryotherapy to the avascular anterior retina in an eye with threshold ROP. *(Reprinted by permission of American Medical Association from Multicenter trial of cryotherapy for retinopathy of prematurity. Preliminary results. Cryotherapy for Retinopathy of Prematurity Cooperative Group. Arch Ophthalmol. 1988;106(4):474.)*

Anti-VEGF Drugs

The Bevacizumab Eliminates the Angiogenic Threat of Retinopathy of Prematurity (BEAT-ROP) Cooperative Group conducted a prospective, randomized, multicenter trial to assess intravitreal bevacizumab monotherapy for zone I or zone II posterior stage 3+ (ie, stage 3 with plus disease) ROP. Infants were randomly assigned to receive bilateral intravitreal bevacizumab (0.625 mg in 0.025 mL of solution) or conventional laser therapy. Enrollment consisted of 150 infants (total sample, 300 eyes). After treatment, among the 143 surviving infants, ROP recurred in 4 infants in the bevacizumab group (6 of 140 eyes [4%]) and 19 infants in the laser-therapy group (32 of 146 eyes [22%], $P = .002$). A statistically significant treatment effect for bevacizumab treatment was demonstrated for zone I ROP ($P = .003$), whereas zone II disease had similar outcomes with either treatment ($P = .27$). Development of peripheral retinal vessels continued after treatment with intravitreal bevacizumab, whereas conventional laser therapy led to permanent destruction of the peripheral retina.

It is very likely that the results of this study will lead to a dramatic change in how zone 1 ROP, and probably all ROP, is treated. However, as of late 2011, concerns about the safety of bevacizumab persist. Reported ocular complications of antiangiogenic therapy for ROP include vitreous hemorrhage, retinal detachment, extension of an existing retinal detachment, and choroidal rupture. Concerns over systemic safety of antiangiogenic therapy include the possible effects on infant development, and these have prevented widespread use of bevacizumab for ROP in the United States.

Mintz-Hittner HA, Kennedy KA, Chuang AZ; BEAT-ROP Cooperative Group. Efficacy of intravitreal bevacizumab for stage 3+ retinopathy of prematurity. *N Engl J Med.* 2011;364(7):603–615.

Vitrectomy and Scleral Buckling Surgery

Eyes with stage 4 ROP (progressive, active-phase ROP) require surgical intervention using scleral buckling or a lens-sparing vitrectomy to alleviate the vitreoretinal traction causing retinal detachment. Eyes undergoing surgical intervention at stage 4A rather than at later stages 4B or 5 have more favorable outcomes. Lens-sparing vitrectomy for 4A ROP may reduce the progression to stages 4B and 5 ROP and is therefore the preferred approach, given the improved visual outcome.

For eyes with stage 5 disease, vitrectomy combined with dissection of the fibrovascular membranes and adherent vitreous has been successful in fully or partially reattaching the retina in approximately 30% of eyes. Nevertheless, only 25% of retinas in eyes with initial partial or total reattachment after surgery remained fully attached at a median of 5 years later. Among the patients whose retinas were initially reattached, only 10% will eventually have ambulatory vision. In the United States, use of the "open-sky vitrectomy" approach, in which the cornea is temporarily removed intraoperatively, is rare for treatment of severe stage 5 disease and has given way to a standard vitrectomy approach. If a retinal break occurs during a vitrectomy for ROP, the eye's prognosis is uniformly poor—an adverse outcome of total retinal detachment is almost guaranteed regardless of the additional procedures performed (eg, silicone oil placement, scleral buckle).

For additional information on ROP, also see BCSC Section 6, *Pediatric Ophthalmology and Strabismus*.

Capone A Jr, Trese MT. Lens-sparing vitreous surgery for tractional stage 4A retinopathy of prematurity retinal detachments. *Ophthalmology*. 2001;108(11):2068–2070.

Quinn GE, Dobson V, Barr CC, et al. Visual acuity of eyes after vitrectomy for retinopathy of prematurity: follow-up at 5 1/5 years. The Cryotherapy for Retinopathy of Prematurity Cooperative Group. *Ophthalmology*. 1996;103(4):595–600.

Trese MT, Droste PJ. Long-term postoperative results of a consecutive series of stages 4 and 5 retinopathy of prematurity. *Ophthalmology*. 1998;105(6):992–997.

CHAPTER 8

Choroidal Disease

This chapter describes noninflammatory choroidal diseases that also involve the retina. Inflammatory disorders of the retina and choroid are discussed in Chapter 9. See also BCSC Section 9, *Intraocular Inflammation and Uveitis*. Intraocular tumors, such as melanoma, are covered in BCSC Section 4, *Ophthalmic Pathology and Intraocular Tumors*.

Central Serous Chorioretinopathy

Central serous chorioretinopathy or *choroidopathy (CSC),* also commonly known by the less-preferred name of *central serous retinopathy (CSR),* is an idiopathic condition characterized by the development of a typically well-circumscribed, serous detachment of the sensory retina (neuroepithelium). The detachment results from altered barriers and deficient pumping functions at the level of the retinal pigment epithelium (RPE), even though the primary pathology may involve the choriocapillaris. Some cases may include serous detachment of the RPE, usually underneath the superior half of the serous retinal detachment. Often, small whitish subretinal precipitates or gray-white subretinal sheets may be noted, probably indicating the presence of shed outer segments or fibrin. Fluid continues to accumulate because the primary disease is most likely a diffuse abnormality of the RPE and choroid that impairs fluid removal. Occasionally, a localized serous detachment of the RPE without overlying neurosensory elevation is present. CSC is often bilateral, with asymmetric findings. In many patients, previous episodes are suggested by areas of extramacular RPE atrophy.

Very severe CSC can occur but is uncommon. Some patients may have multifocal disease extending to the periphery. Even though rare, CSC can cause subtotal bullous serous retinal detachment, often bilateral. These severe forms of CSC represent management dilemmas, as any focal treatment may be difficult to administer through detached retina.

CSC occurs primarily in otherwise healthy men between 25 and 55 years of age. Most patients are asymptomatic unless the macula is affected. CSC is common in whites, Asians, and Hispanics and rare in African Americans. Symptomatic patients describe the sudden onset of blurred and dim vision, micropsia (objects appear smaller than they are), metamorphopsia (objects appear distorted), paracentral scotomata, or decreased color vision. In general, visual acuity ranges from 20/20 to 20/200, but in most patients it is better than 20/30. The decreased acuity can often be corrected with a hyperopic correction. In rare cases, these symptoms are accompanied by a migrainelike headache.

Certain personality types and disorders, including "type A" personality, hypochondriasis, hysteria, and conversional neurosis, have been associated anecdotally with CSC, although no association with any personality trait has been proved. Stress has also been implicated as an etiologic factor, but no conclusive proof has been presented.

Systemic associations with CSC include exogenous steroid use, endogenous hypercortisolism (Cushing syndrome), organ transplantation, systemic lupus erythematosus, systemic hypertension, sleep apnea, gastroesophageal reflux disease, use of psychopharmacologic medications, and pregnancy. In pregnancy, the disease can occur quite aggressively and frequently is associated with exudates; it usually resolves after delivery. Whereas the etiology for CSC remains unknown, recent reports emphasize the frequent finding of increased choroidal thickness on optical coherence tomography (OCT).

Carvalho-Recchia CA, Yannuzzi LA, Negrão S, et al. Corticosteroids and central serous chorioretinopathy. *Ophthalmology.* 2002;109(10):1834–1837.

Haimovici R, Koh S, Gagnon DR, Lehrfeld T, Wellik S; Central Serous Chorioretinopathy Case-Control Study Group. Risk factors for central serous chorioretinopathy: a case-control study. *Ophthalmology.* 2004;111(2):244–249.

Maruko I, Iida T, Sugano Y, Ojima A, Ogasawara M, Spaide RF. Subfoveal choroidal thickness after treatment of central serous chorioretinopathy. *Ophthalmology.* 2010;117(9):1792–1799. Epub 2010 May 15.

Fluorescein Angiography of CSC

Three characteristic fluorescein angiographic patterns are observed in CSC:

1. expansile dot pattern
2. smokestack pattern
3. diffuse pattern

An *expansile dot* pattern of hyperfluorescence is the most common presentation. The dot represents a small, focal, hyperfluorescent leak from the choroid through the RPE that appears in the early phase of the fluorescein study and increases in size and intensity as the study progresses (Fig 8-1). Fluorescein dye slowly pools into the subretinal space (epithelioretinal interspace) as the angiographic study progresses. Late-phase angiograms at 10 or 15 minutes are often required to detect very slow leaks or fluorescein pooling in the epithelioretinal interspace. In some patients, several leaking expansile dots may be present. If no expansile dot is observed in the macula, examination should include the near periphery and equatorial retina, especially superiorly.

Fluorescein leakage into the subretinal fluid pocket can produce a memorable pattern of subretinal pooling referred to as a *smokestack*. The fluorescein study starts with a central spot of hyperfluorescence that spreads vertically and finally laterally, in a shape resembling a plume of smoke. This unique pattern is thought to be secondary to convection currents and to a pressure gradient between the protein concentration of the subretinal fluid and the fluorescein dye entering the detachment. Although characteristic, this angiographic presentation is found in only 1 in 10 cases (10%).

In rare cases, an extensive, often gravity-dependent, serous detachment of the retina may develop from one or more leakage points outside the central area or may be associated

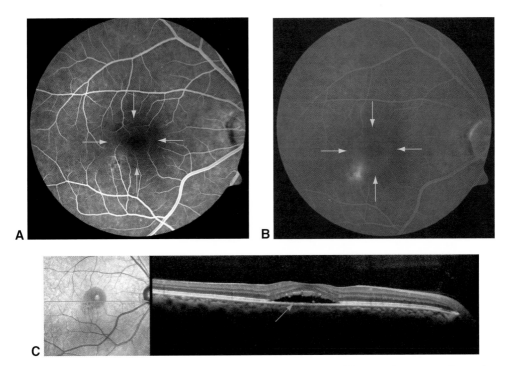

Figure 8-1 **A,** Early-phase fluorescein angiogram of a patient with central serous retinopathy. The *yellow arrows* outline the area of serous retinal detachment. In the inferotemporal aspect of the serous retinal detachment, there is early minimal hyperfluorescence, with diffuse leakage in late views **(B). C,** Corresponding optical coherence tomogram illustrating the subretinal fluid accumulation *(orange arrow)*. Accumulation of deposits on the outer surface of the photoreceptors can be seen. This material is thought to represent shed photoreceptor outer segments or fibrin. The *green arrow* and line on the infrared reflectance imaging shows the scan location of the OCT image. *(Courtesy of Colin A. McCannel, MD.)*

with a *diffuse pattern* of fluorescein leakage, often without any prominent leakage point. Thus, CSC must be considered in the differential diagnosis of nonrhegmatogenous serous retinal detachment.

Other Imaging Modalities for CSC

Optical coherence tomography is an excellent, noninvasive method to diagnose and monitor the resolution of the subretinal fluid and pigment epithelial detachments in CSC. Subtle fluid accumulation beneath the sensory retina and the RPE not evident on fluorescein angiography (FA) or clinical examination can often be imaged using OCT. Recent studies using spectral-domain OCT (SD-OCT) show increased choroidal thickness in most patients with CSC. This is visualized especially well using a SD-OCT technique called enhanced depth imaging (EDI).

Fundus autofluorescence demonstrates hypoautofluorescence corresponding to the site of the focal RPE leak depicted on FA as well as pigment mottling in the area of the RPE disturbance. In addition, central macular autofluorescence patterns correlate with RPE abnormalities. Darker levels of macular autofluorescence are associated with poorer vision.

Fundus autofluorescence has also shown hyperautofluorescent material on the outer surface of the elevated retina. This material, formerly called "subretinic precipitates," is visible with SD-OCT imaging as well. Based on its autofluorescence characteristics, this material is hypothesized to represent accumulation of shed photoreceptor outer segments.

Indocyanine green (ICG) angiography can be used to show choroidal vascular abnormalities, including filling delays in the choroidal arteries and choriocapillaris, venous dilation, hyperpermeability of the choroidal vessels, and characteristic multifocal choroidal hyperfluorescent patches that appear early in the ICG study. These areas slowly enlarge during the angiographic study but are less prominent in late-phase views. In addition, a characteristic "washout pattern" is often evident that remains unchanged during clinically inactive phases. ICG angiography can be useful in helping distinguish atypical diffuse CSC in older patients from both occult choroidal neovascularization (CNV) in exudative age-related macular degeneration and idiopathic polypoidal choroidal vasculopathy.

Imamura Y, Fujiwara T, Margolis R, Spaide RF. Enhanced depth imaging optical coherence tomography of the choroid in central serous chorioretinopathy. *Retina.* 2009;29(10):1469–1473.

Spaide RF, Klancnik JM Jr. Fundus autofluorescence and central serous chorioretinopathy. *Ophthalmology.* 2005;112(5):825–833.

Differential Diagnosis of CSC

The presence of subretinal fluid in older patients with CSC should lead the physician to consider a diagnosis of CNV associated with age-related macular degeneration, idiopathic polypoidal choroidal vasculopathy, optic nerve pits, or idiopathic uveal effusion syndrome (IUES). The following features help differentiate CSC from these other entities:

- A pinpoint leak relative to a large area of subretinal fluid most likely represents CSC, whereas the area of subretinal fluid associated with CNV and idiopathic polypoidal choroidal vasculopathy usually corresponds closely to the area of leakage shown on angiography. The leakage in IUES is usually diffuse.
- Optic nerve pits are often visible on the temporal disc margin and are contiguous with the schisis cavity, subretinal fluid accumulation, or both. No pinpoint leakage is present.
- Multifocal RPE abnormalities, including small serous pigment epithelial detachments (PEDs) in 1 or both eyes, likely represent CSC, whereas the presence of large drusen probably represents age-related macular degeneration.
- The yellow-white lesions of Vogt-Koyanagi-Harada syndrome can appear similar to those of CSC; however, the granulomatous uveitis present in the former helps differentiate the diseases.
- Saccular choroidal vascular outpouchings are characteristic of idiopathic polypoidal choroidal vasculopathy; these can be differentiated from the multifocal hyperfluorescent patches of CSC through ICG angiography.
- Intraocular lymphoma can appear similar to CSC but typically has subretinal infiltrates rather than fluid.

- Absence of blood or significant amounts of lipid is more likely to represent CSC, whereas their presence is more likely to represent CNV or idiopathic polypoidal choroidal vasculopathy.

Older patients presenting with CNV occasionally may show pigment epithelial changes suggestive of previous episodes of CSC.

Natural Course and Management of CSC

The visual prognosis of CSC is generally good except in chronic, recurrent cases and in cases of bullous CSC. Most (80%–90%) eyes with CSC undergo spontaneous resorption of subretinal fluid within 3–4 months; recovery of visual acuity usually follows but can take up to 1 year. Mild metamorphopsia, faint scotomata, abnormalities in contrast sensitivity, and mild color vision deficits frequently persist. Some eyes have permanently reduced visual acuity, and many (40%–50%) experience one or more recurrences. A small subset of patients have poor vision outcomes.

Laser photocoagulation at the site of fluorescein leakage can induce rapid remission; resorption of subretinal fluid may occur within several weeks of therapy. A randomized, controlled clinical study of ruby laser photocoagulation in eyes with active CSC by Watzke and colleagues in 1974 showed a significantly more rapid resorption of subretinal fluid in treated eyes (a 5-week median duration from laser treatment to remission) than in untreated eyes (a 23-week median duration from examination to spontaneous remission). However, this study did not find the final Snellen visual acuity to be any better in treated versus untreated eyes despite the shorter disease duration; nor was there evidence that treatment altered the recurrence rate.

Another option for the treatment of CSC, especially when the leakage site is too close to the center of the fovea, is the use of verteporfin photodynamic therapy (PDT). Using a fluence level ranging from standard treatment (600 mW/cm^2) to reduced fluence (300 mW/cm^2), small retrospective studies have shown PDT leading to resolution of the fluid leakage and improving vision. Some evidence suggests that low-fluence photodynamic therapy is beneficial in resolving acute leaks of subretinal fluid and may have the added effect of thinning the choroid. A recent study of 67 patients with CSC treated using either reduced- or standard-fluence PDT found that 97% responded without recurrence. More studies are needed, however.

Current treatment guidelines recommend observation in most cases. If fluid persists, however, treatment using laser photocoagulation or photodynamic therapy may be indicated for the following scenarios:

- The serous detachment persists beyond 3–6 months.
- The disease recurs in eyes with visual deficits from previous episodes.
- A permanent visual deficit is present from previous episodes in the fellow eye.
- Chronic signs develop, such as cystic changes in the neurosensory retina or widespread RPE abnormalities.
- Occupational or other patient needs require prompt restoration of vision, stereopsis, or both.

If laser photocoagulation is performed, a follow-up examination within 3–4 weeks may help detect the rare complication of postlaser CNV. Though rare, CNV may develop in patients with typical CSC, even without laser treatment.

Loo RH, Scott IU, Flynn HW Jr, et al. Factors associated with reduced visual acuity during long-term follow-up of patients with idiopathic central serous chorioretinopathy. *Retina*. 2002;22(1):19–24.

Ober MD, Yannuzzi LA, Do DV, et al. Photodynamic therapy for focal retinal pigment epithelial leaks secondary to central serous chorioretinopathy. *Ophthalmology*. 2005; 112(12):2088–2094.

Shin JY, Woo SJ, Yu HG, Park KH. Comparison of efficacy and safety between half-fluence and full-fluence photodynamic therapy for chronic central serous chorioretinopathy. *Retina*. 2011;31(1):119–126.

Choroidal Perfusion Abnormalities

Although most of the blood flow to the eye goes to the choroid, perfusion abnormalities in the choroid are more difficult to diagnose. Retinal vascular occlusion is readily visible by ophthalmoscopy and corroborated by FA. Choroidal vascular occlusion, however, may produce changes that are quite subtle. In addition, it is not uncommon for choroidal vascular abnormalities to be obscured by overlying retinal vascular abnormalities such as cotton-wool spots and intraretinal hemorrhages. The entities that cause choroidal vascular abnormalities may affect the circulation from the ophthalmic artery to the choriocapillaris. Areas of ischemia and their watersheds tend to be vertically or horizontally hemispheric if they are caused by an intraorbital vascular occlusion. Intraocular vascular occlusions result in triangular areas of ischemia in the often oblique meridian of the occluded vessel.

Increased Venous Pressure

Though rare, choroidal blood flow abnormalities may be related to venous outflow problems, including those caused by *dural arterial malformations* and *carotid cavernous fistulas*. Diagnosis of choroidal blood flow abnormalities often requires both fluorescein and indocyanine green angiography, and occasionally a stethoscope, to detect a bruit (Fig 8-2).

Hypertension

The most commonly observed diseases that lead to choroidal vascular compromise are those that cause severe, acute elevations in blood pressure, such as in *malignant hypertension, eclampsia,* or *severe cocaine abuse.* In addition to retinal abnormalities, these disorders commonly lead to serous detachment of the retina associated with areas of yellow placoid discoloration of the RPE (Fig 8-3). The perfusion abnormalities may range from focal infarction of the choriocapillaris to fibrinoid necrosis of larger arterioles. Although the choroid has a rich circulation, the blood flows in a functionally terminal fashion at

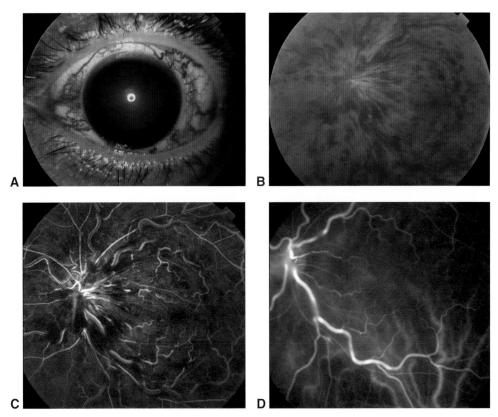

Figure 8-2 **A,** The left eye of this patient was proptotic and had dilated episcleral vessels. **B,** Color fundus photograph of the left eye shows a swollen optic nerve head, dilated and tortuous veins, and intraretinal hemorrhages. **C,** Fluorescein angiography of the left eye shows swelling of the optic nerve, blocking of the background fluorescence from retinal hemorrhages, and a global delay in venous filling. Note how some venous segments show laminar filling whereas others do not. **D,** Indocyanine green (ICG) angiography shows hypovascularity with dilation of the remaining choroidal veins. *(From Chung JE, Spaide RF, Warren FA. Dural arteriovenous malformation and superior ophthalmic vein occlusion. Retina. 2004;24(3):491–492.)*

the level of the choriocapillaris, so there is very little collateral flow after a focal occlusion. Resolution of smaller infarcts, which appear tan in color initially, produces small patches of atrophy and pigmentary hyperplasia called *Elschnig spots*. Linear aggregations of these spots are called *Siegrist streaks*.

Inflammatory Conditions

Various types of arteritis may affect the choroidal circulation as well. *Giant cell arteritis* may cause occlusion of one or more short, posterior ciliary arteries, leading to broad triangular areas of choroidal nonperfusion in any meridian (Fig 8-4). Patients with this condition may have concurrent central retinal artery occlusion combined with nasal choroidal hypoperfusion, suggesting involvement of the first intraorbital segment of the ophthalmic

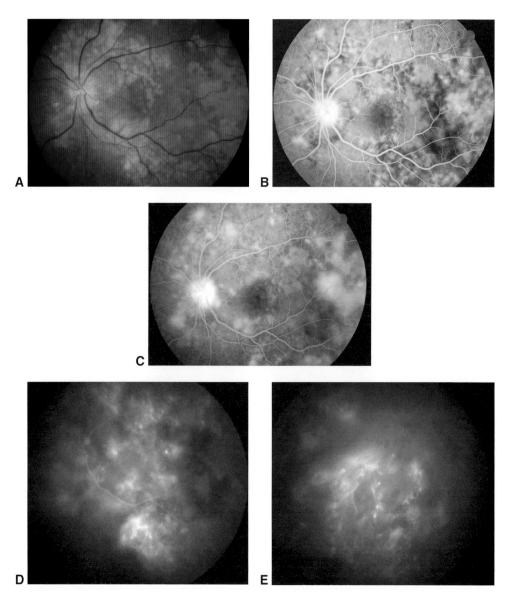

Figure 8-3 Preeclampsia with HELLP (hemolysis, elevated liver enzymes, and low platelet count) syndrome. **A,** This patient had a serous detachment of the retina and multiple yellowish placoid areas at the level of the RPE and inner choroid. **B,** The early-phase fluorescein angiograms showed reticular patterns of decreased choroidal perfusion bordering areas of hyperfluorescence. Early leakage from the level of the RPE is evident and becomes more apparent in the later phases of the fluorescein study **(C).** There is also staining of and leakage from the optic nerve. **D,** The ICG angiogram shows profound choroidal vascular filling defects alternating with areas of abnormal vessel leakage and staining, a rare finding in ICG angiography. **E,** In the late phase, numerous arterioles show staining of their walls, indicative of severe vascular damage. *(From Spaide RF, Goldbaum M, Wong DW, Tang KC, Iida T. Serous detachment of the retina.* Retina. *2003;23(6):820–846.)*

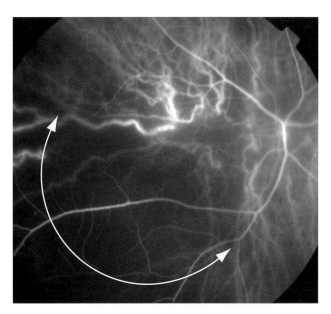

Figure 8-4 Giant cell arteritis. One day after this patient had severe vision loss secondary to arteritic anterior ischemic optic neuropathy, ICG angiography revealed a wedge-shaped area of choroidal nonperfusion *(curved arrow)*. The apex of the wedge points toward the area of the occluded short posterior vessel. *(Courtesy of Richard F. Spaide, MD.)*

artery. *Wegener granulomatosis* is a disorder characterized by necrotizing granulomatous lesions of the upper and lower respiratory tracts, glomerulonephritis, and generalized focal necrotizing vasculitis. Ocular manifestations occur in 30%–50% of patients and may include retinal vascular occlusion, choroidal vascular occlusion, or both (Fig 8-5). Other inflammatory conditions reported to cause choroidal infarction include *systemic lupus erythematosus, polyarteritis nodosa,* and *antiphospholipid syndrome.*

Thromboembolic Disease

Vasoocclusion by microemboli may occur in a variety of diseases. In these entities, the choroidal circulation appears to be more affected than is the retinal circulation. Because of the rapid deceleration of the blood flow and larger volumetric flow within the choroid, platelet emboli may be more likely to become lodged there. *Thrombotic thrombocytopenic purpura* causes a classic pentad of findings: microangiopathic hemolytic anemia, thrombocytopenia, fever, and neurologic and renal dysfunction. Patients with this condition may also have multifocal yellow placoid areas and associated serous detachment of the retina. Similar fundus findings may occur in patients with *disseminated intravascular coagulation,* in which consumption of coagulation proteins, involvement of cellular elements, and release of fibrin degradation products lead to hemorrhage from multiple sites and ischemia from microthrombi.

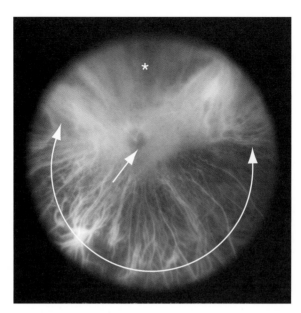

Figure 8-5 Wegener granulomatosis. Early phase of wide-angle ICG angiography of the left eye revealed a widespread filling defect of the arterioles and choriocapillaris in the inferior fundus *(arcuate arrow)* and in a segmental area of the superior fundus *(asterisk)*. Occlusion of the infratemporal retinal artery is also present *(small arrow)*. *(From Iida T, Spaide RF, Kantor J. Retinal and choroidal arterial occlusion in Wegener's granulomatosis. Am J Ophthalmol. 2002;133(1):151–152. Copyright © 2002, with permission from Elsevier.)*

Iatrogenic Abnormalities

Though rare, choroidal ischemia may result from iatrogenic causes. Thermal laser photocoagulation and photodynamic therapy have also, on rare occasions, caused choroidal vascular occlusion with resultant segmental ischemia. Ocular compression related to cataract surgery has caused choroidal ischemia in some patients. Other reported causes of emboli to the choroid include subcutaneous injection of micronized dermal matrix in the forehead region and intracisternal papaverine injection with resultant rapid and dramatic elevation of intracranial pressure.

Gaudric A, Coscas G, Bird AC. Choroidal ischemia. *Am J Ophthalmol.* 1982;94(4):489–498.

Iida T, Spaide RF, Kantor J. Retinal and choroidal arterial occlusion in Wegener's granulomatosis. *Am J Ophthalmol.* 2002;133(1):151–152.

Spaide RF, Goldbaum M, Wong DW, Tang KC, Iida T. Serous detachment of the retina. *Retina.* 2003;23(6):820–846.

Choroidal Hemangioma

Isolated choroidal hemangiomas are reddish orange, well-circumscribed tumors of varying thickness; they may be discovered during routine examinations or because of blurring of vision caused by hyperopia or related to serous detachment induced by the tumor.

Circumscribed hemangiomas transilluminate readily and have distinctive echographic and angiographic characteristics (Fig 8-6). Large choroidal vessels are visible early during ICG angiography, and the tumors show a characteristic "washed-out" pattern in later phases of the study.

By contrast, the hemangioma associated with Sturge-Weber syndrome (encephalo-facial cavernous hemangiomatosis) is diffuse and may present first as glaucoma or amblyopia in children. Biomicroscopically, the areas corresponding to the hemangioma have a typical "tomato catsup" appearance, in which the underlying choroidal markings are not visible. The choroidal hemangiomas in Sturge-Weber syndrome may sometimes be overlooked because they are diffuse and may blend imperceptibly into adjacent normal choroid. An ipsilateral facial nevus flammeus (port-wine stain) is also typically present in patients with this syndrome.

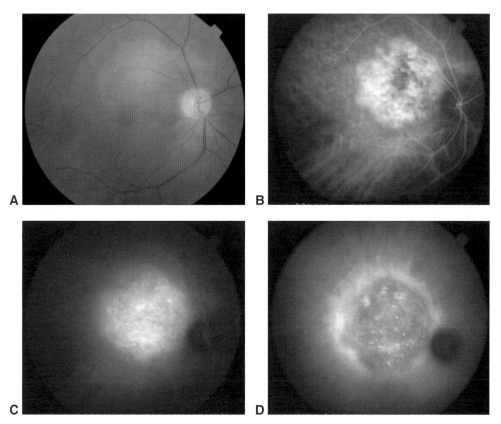

Figure 8-6 Choroidal hemangioma. **A,** The typical reddish orange elevation of a circumscribed choroidal hemangioma. **B,** Soon after ICG injection, the vascular composition of the hemangioma is revealed. **C,** Hyperfluorescence of the tumor occurs in the midphases of the angiogram study, from a combination of dye within and leakage from the vessels of the hemangioma. **D,** In the late phase of the study, the dye washes out of the lesion, leaving hyperfluorescent staining of the adjacent tissues. *(From Spaide RF, Goldbaum M, Wong DW, Tang KC, Iida T. Serous detachment of the retina. Retina. 2003;23(6):820–846.)*

The alterations to retina and pigment epithelium caused by choroidal hemangiomas range from cystic retinal edema to neurosensory detachment to formation of an epichoroidal membrane with calcification and ossification; the particular alterations ultimately determine the ophthalmoscopic appearance, which therefore is quite varied. Retinal vascular leakage in the form of hard exudate is not common.

Hemangiomas have been treated with a variety of modalities, including laser photocoagulation, cryopexy, external-beam and plaque radiation, and photodynamic therapy. When applied before chronic retinal changes occur, each modality has had therapeutic success. Photodynamic therapy with verteporfin may have the lowest risk of treatment-related morbidity.

Barbazetto I, Schmidt-Erfurth U. Photodynamic therapy of choroidal hemangioma: two case reports. *Graefes Arch Clin Exp Ophthalmol.* 2000;238(3):214–221.

Madreperla SA, Hungerford JL, Plowman PN, Laganowski HC, Gregory PT. Choroidal hemangiomas: visual and anatomic results of treatment by photocoagulation or radiation therapy. *Ophthalmology.* 1997;104(11):1773–1779.

Uveal Effusion Syndrome

Net water movement across the vitreous cavity and posterior eye wall can be altered by reduced transscleral aqueous outflow. This alteration may be caused by abnormal scleral composition or thickness, as in nanophthalmos, scleritis, idiopathic uveal effusion syndrome, and other conditions. Hyperopia frequently accompanies such conditions, as does glaucoma. Choroidal and ciliary body thickening, RPE alterations, and exudative retinal detachment may occur transiently or permanently. FA usually shows a leopard spot pattern of hypofluorescence without focal leakage (Fig 8-7).

Posterior pole manifestations in the uveal effusion syndrome may be accompanied by ciliochoroidal detachment and abnormal episcleral vessels. Visual function may fluctuate during the natural course of the disease. Although encouraging anatomical restitution can be obtained with surgical approaches such as scleral window surgery, the visual results

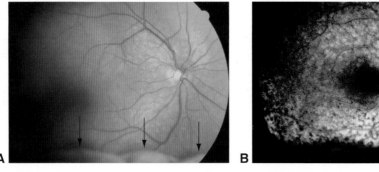

Figure 8-7 Uveal effusion. **A,** Note the inferior exudative detachment *(arrows)*. **B,** The fluorescein angiogram shows a diffuse leopard spot pattern of hypofluorescence but no focal leaks. *(From Spaide RF, Goldbaum M, Wong DW, Tang KC, Iida T. Serous detachment of the retina. Retina. 2003;23(6):820–846.)*

may be less rewarding because of chronic, irreversible changes. A high index of suspicion for uveal effusion syndrome should be maintained for young patients with hyperopia whose disorder has been diagnosed as either central serous chorioretinopathy or a retinal detachment without a retinal hole or tear.

Brockhurst RJ. Nanophthalmos with uveal effusion. A new clinical entity. *Arch Ophthalmol.* 1975;93(12):1989–1999.

Johnson MW, Gass JD. Surgical management of the idiopathic uveal effusion syndrome. *Ophthalmology.* 1990;97(6):778–785.

Bilateral Diffuse Uveal Melanocytic Proliferation

A rare paraneoplastic disorder affecting the choroid, called *bilateral diffuse uveal melanocytic proliferation (BDUMP),* causes diffuse thickening of the choroid, reddish or brownish choroidal discoloration, serous retinal detachment, and cataracts. The bilateral proliferation of benign melanocytes is usually associated with or often heralds a systemic cancer. These proliferations can look like large nevi (Fig 8-8). Some BDUMP lesions appear as reddish areas of depigmentation of the RPE that have associated hyperfluorescence during FA. The more common tumors associated with BDUMP are cancer of the ovaries, uterus, and lung, but BDUMP may also occur with cancer of the colon, pancreas, gallbladder, and esophagus.

Gass JD, Gieser RG, Wilkinson CP, Beahm DE, Pautler SE. Bilateral diffuse uveal melanocytic proliferation in patients with occult carcinoma. *Arch Ophthalmol.* 1990;108(104):527–533.

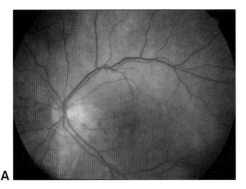 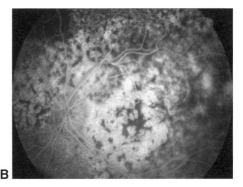

A **B**

Figure 8-8 Bilateral diffuse uveal melanocytic proliferation. **A,** Note the large nevuslike regions of increased pigmentation and thickening of the choroid. **B,** Fluorescein angiography demonstrates decreased fluorescence in the region of the melanocytic proliferation in the superonasal portion of the angiogram. There is a leopard spot pattern to the fluorescence in the posterior pole, secondary to chronic subretinal fluid. *(Courtesy of Mark Johnson, MD.)*

CHAPTER 9

Focal and Diffuse Choroidal and Retinal Inflammation

A variety of inflammatory disorders are associated with funduscopically yellow-white lesions of the retina and choroid. The following descriptions highlight the clinical features, epidemiology, and potential treatments of various focal and diffuse choroidal and retinal inflammatory disorders causing such lesions. BCSC Section 9, *Intraocular Inflammation and Uveitis,* also discusses and illustrates some of the entities covered in this chapter.

Gass JDM. *Stereoscopic Atlas of Macular Diseases: Diagnosis and Treatment.* 4th ed. St Louis: Mosby; 1997:601–736.

Guyer DR, Yannuzzi LA, Chang S, Shields JA, Green WR, eds. *Retina–Vitreous–Macula.* Philadelphia: Saunders; 1999:535–828.

Noninfectious Retinal and Choroidal Inflammation

White Dot Syndromes

The term *white dot syndromes* has been used to describe the following diseases:

- acute posterior multifocal placoid pigment epitheliopathy (APMPPE)
- serpiginous choroidopathy
- multiple evanescent white dot syndrome (MEWDS)
- birdshot retinochoroidopathy
- multifocal choroiditis and panuveitis syndrome (MCP)
- punctate inner choroidopathy (PIC)
- acute zonal occult outer retinopathy (AZOOR)

Table 9-1 provides an overview of these syndromes and their characteristics. Other noninfectious chorioretinal inflammatory disorders are discussed later in this chapter.

Buggage RR. White dot syndrome. *Focal Points: Clinical Modules for Ophthalmologists.* San Francisco: American Academy of Ophthalmology; 2007, module 4.

Acute posterior multifocal placoid pigment epitheliopathy

APMPPE is an acute-onset bilateral inflammatory disease causing decreased vision in 1 eye first and often in the second eye days later. It presents with yellow, creamy, placoid

Table 9-1 Characteristics of White Dot Syndromes

	Sex	Pathology	Laterality	Size	Morphology	Location	Appearance	A/C	VIT	FA	EOG	ERG	Prognosis	Etiology	Treatment
APMPPE	F=M	RPE Choroid	Bi	Large	Placoid	Posterior pole	White scar	+	50%	Early blockage Late stain	↓	↓	80% good	50% viral	None
Serpiginous	F=M	Choroid RPE	Bi	Large	Serpiginous	Disc Macula	Gray-yellow	–	30%	Loss of chorio-capillaries	↓		Poor	?	None Immuno-suppressives
MEWDS	F>M (4:1)	RPE Retina	80% Uni	100–200 μm	Granular macula	Perifoveal	Gray-white	–	+	Early "wreath"	↓	→	Recover	50% viral	None
Birdshot	F>M (2:1)	Choroid RPE	Bi	100–300 μm	Ovoid	Posterior equator	Creamy, no pigment	30%	100%	Vessel leak Mac-ON	↓	→	Chronic	S-Ag CMI	CSA
MCP	F>M (3:1)	Choroid RPE	80% Bi	50–350 μm	Punched out	Multifocal	Yellow pigment ring	52%	98%	Early stain		↑↓	Poor	EBV?	Steroids Acyclovir?
PIC	F>M	Choroid RPE	Bi	50–100 μm	Discrete; well-circum-scribed	Posterior pole	Yellow-white	–	–	Early stain			May develop subretinal fibrosis	EBV?	Steroids?
AZOOR	F>M	Outer retina	Bi	Large	Large zones of RPE	Midperiphery	Bone spicule	–	+/–	Mild leakage	*	↓	Good in 1 eye	?	None

A/C = Anterior chamber infiltrate; CMI = cell-mediated immune response; CSA = cyclosporine; EBV = Epstein-Barr virus; EOG = electro-oculogram findings; ERG = electroretinogram findings; FA = fluorescein angiogram findings; Mac-ON = macula-optic nerve involvement; S-Ag = S-antigen; VIT = vitritis presence.

lesions in the macula at the level of the retinal pigment epithelium (RPE) (Fig 9-1). APMPPE typically occurs in young adults in the second to third decades of life, without sex predilection. The etiology is unknown, but a viral prodrome occurs in about one-third of patients.

Diagnosis is based on clinical history and ophthalmoscopic features. The fluorescein angiogram in the acute phase of the disease characteristically demonstrates lobular hypofluorescence in the early frames, with even, diffuse staining of these same areas in the late frames. Whether APMPPE is a result of primary disease of the pigment epithelium or is caused by obstruction of choriocapillary lobules with secondary pigment epithelial reaction remains unclear. The fundus appearance in most patients starts to show improvement in 1–2 weeks. Visual acuity begins to recover within weeks and continues to improve, with a generally good long-term prognosis. In one series of 30 patients with more than 5 years of follow-up, all but 2 of the eyes had 20/30 or better visual acuity. There is no evidence that corticosteroids or any other medications are beneficial. However, patients must be monitored closely because of the difficulty in distinguishing APMPPE from early serpiginous choroidopathy, which requires aggressive treatment. Despite the improvement in visual acuity, patients with APMPPE do continue to report visual dysfunction. Several case reports have highlighted potential central nervous system vasculitis associated with APMPPE.

Gass, JDM. *Stereoscopic Atlas of Macular Diseases: Diagnosis and Treatment.* St Louis: Mosby; 1997:668–675.

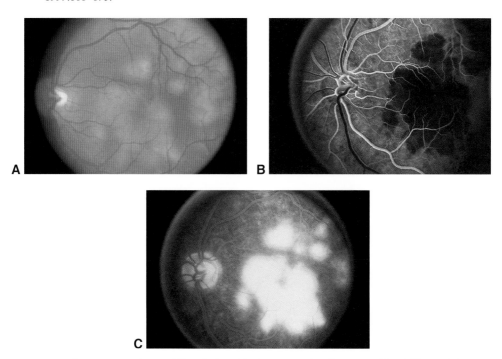

Figure 9-1 Acute posterior multifocal placoid pigment epitheliopathy (APMPPE). **A,** Multiple yellowish placoid lesions in the posterior pole. **B,** Early-phase angiogram demonstrates hypofluorescence from nonperfusion of the choriocapillaris or blocked fluorescence by the RPE lesions. **C,** Late-phase angiogram demonstrates hyperfluorescence in the areas involved. *(Courtesy of J. Donald M. Gass, MD.)*

Serpiginous choroidopathy

Serpiginous choroidopathy, also known as *geographic choroiditis* or *helicoid peripapillary choroidopathy,* is a recurrent inflammatory disease of the choroid that causes a serpiginous (pseudopodial) or geographic (maplike) pattern of scarring in the posterior fundus (Fig 9-2). Patients describe decreased visual acuity and central or paracentral scotomata. Acute lesions have a geographic zone of gray-yellow discoloration of the RPE, which spreads centrifugally outward from the optic disc and macula in a jigsawlike pattern. These lesions are hypofluorescent in the early phases but stain in the later phases of angiographic studies and may appear similar to the lesions of APMPPE. Unlike APMPPE, however, serpiginous choroidopathy affects deeper choroidal levels and is chronic and recurrent. As formerly involved areas become atrophic over weeks to months, new lesions can occur elsewhere or contiguously with atrophic lesions, and the second eye may be affected months or years later. Dense scotomata corresponding to involved areas develop in all patients. Though rare, choroidal neovascularization (CNV) may develop at the margin of an area of chorioretinal atrophy.

Treatment with immunosuppressive drugs, systemic corticosteroids, or acyclovir has been attempted, but the results are generally poor. More potent combination immuno-

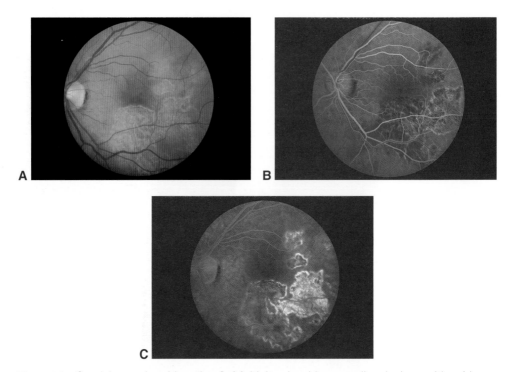

Figure 9-2 Serpiginous choroidopathy. **A,** Multiple, placoid, gray-yellow lesions with evidence of early scar formation. **B,** Early-phase angiogram demonstrates hypofluorescence from blocking by RPE lesions or nonperfusion of the choriocapillaris as occurs in APMPPE; however, early hyperfluorescence is visible at the edges of the lesion, which increases in the late-phase angiogram **(C);** the late phase also shows staining as a result of lesion activity and chorioretinal scarring. *(Courtesy of Russell Van Gelder, MD, PhD.)*

suppressive treatment with mycophenolate, cyclosporine, azathioprine, and prednisone appears to halt disease activity in some patients and should be initiated immediately if serpiginous choroidopathy is suspected. When lesions spread to involve the center of the macula, visual acuity remains at a very low level.

> Tom D, Yannuzzi LA. Serpiginous choroiditis. In: Guyer DR, Yannuzzi LA, Chang S, Shields JA, Green WR, eds. *Retina–Vitreous–Macula.* Philadelphia: Saunders; 1999:553–564.

Multiple evanescent white dot syndrome

MEWDS is an acute-onset syndrome characterized by multiple, small gray-white dots at the level of the deep retina and RPE in the posterior pole (Fig 9-3). In some patients, an unusual transient foveal granularity also develops that is nearly pathognomonic of this condition and consists of tiny yellow-orange dots at the level of the RPE. Vitritis may be present. Patients typically describe a unilateral (80%) decrease in visual acuity. MEWDS occurs in individuals with myopia who are in their second to fifth decades, more often in women than in men. The etiology is unknown, but a viral prodrome has been reported in about 50% of patients.

Diagnosis is made according to the clinical history and ophthalmoscopic findings. Fluorescein angiography demonstrates that each white dot comprises multiple punctate, hyperfluorescent spots in a wreathlike cluster, with staining occurring in the late phases. Indocyanine green angiography shows multiple hypofluorescent dots and

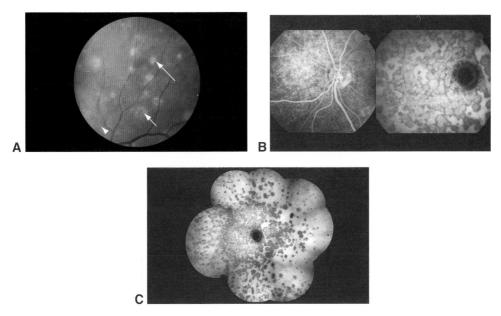

Figure 9-3 The gray-white dots in MEWDS resolve quickly. **A,** The acute lesions are gray-white *(long arrow)*; they start to resolve first centrally *(short arrow)* and then leave a subtle change in color *(arrowhead)*. **B,** The fluorescein angiogram *(left)* shows wreaths of gray-white dots. The corresponding indocyanine green angiogram *(right)* shows darker placoid lesions with bordering darker dots. **C,** Wide-angle indocyanine green angiogram shows that the amount of choroidal involvement in MEWDS is often much more extensive than what is visible using ophthalmoscopy alone. *(Courtesy of Richard F. Spaide, MD.)*

hypofluorescence around the optic nerve. Enlargement of the physiologic blind spot may be revealed through visual field testing, and a transient afferent pupillary defect is sometimes present. Decreased a-wave amplitudes may be demonstrated on the electroretinogram (ERG). Treatment is not required because the fundus appearance starts to improve in most patients in 2–6 weeks, and recovery of central vision usually follows. Though rare, MEWDS can be recurrent or bilateral or have persistent visual-field defects.

A related entity is referred to as *idiopathic enlargement of the blind spot syndrome (IEBSS)*. This condition shares demographic features with MEWDS, but patients do not have retinal lesions.

Jampol LM, Sieving PA, Pugh D, Fishman GA, Gilbert H. Multiple evanescent white dot syndrome. I. Clinical findings. *Arch Ophthalmol.* 1984;102(5):671–674.

Birdshot retinochoroidopathy

Birdshot retinochoroidopathy, or *vitiliginous chorioretinitis,* occurs in patients in the fourth to sixth decades. Women are affected more frequently than men. Early symptoms include floaters, blurred vision, and peripheral photopsia. Nyctalopia and loss of color vision may occur later. Examination reveals vitritis (100%), variable degrees of disc edema and vascular sheathing, and characteristic yellow, ovoid "birdshot" chorioretinal lesions that are most numerous in the nasal retina (Fig 9-4). The choroidal lesions are more visible on ophthalmoscopy than on fluorescein angiography, which often yields unremarkable images. One interesting fluorescein angiographic phenomenon in patients with this condition is the presence of "quenching," whereby dye appears to fade away rapidly from the retinal circulation.

Vision loss may be caused by cystoid macular edema (CME) in approximately one-third of patients, optic atrophy, or, in rare cases, macular CNV. The disease is chronic, bilateral, and prone to recurrent episodes of inflammation. Approximately 90% of patients are HLA-A29 positive. Disease progression may be assessed electroretinographically by monitoring the 30-Hz-flicker implicit time. The ERG response may be reduced or extinguished. Visual acuity outcomes depend on the nature and extent of the disc and macular disease. Intravitreal triamcinolone can control the retinal lesions and improve vision. However, immunomodulatory treatment is often required to control inflammation

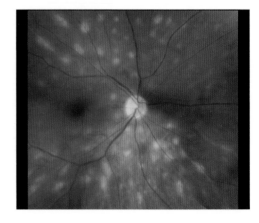

Figure 9-4 Birdshot retinochoroidopathy. *(Courtesy of Richard F. Spaide, MD.)*

and prevent vision loss. Systemic drugs include cyclosporine, mycophenolate mofetil, azathioprine, and methotrexate, all of which have been used successfully. The fluocinolone acetonide intravitreal implant has been shown in prospective studies to decrease recurrences of inflammation and vision loss in birdshot retinochoroidopathy. BCSC Section 9, *Intraocular Inflammation and Uveitis,* discusses the human leukocyte antigens in detail.

Jaffe GJ, Martin D, Callanan D, Pearson PA, Levy B, Comstock T; Fluocinolone Acetonide Uveitis Study Group. Fluocinolone acetonide implant (Retisert) for noninfectious posterior uveitis: thirty-four-week results of a multicenter randomized clinical study. *Ophthalmology.* 2006;113(6):1020–1027. Epub 2006 May 9.

Kiss S, Ahmed M, Letko E, Foster CS. Long-term follow-up of patients with birdshot retinochoroidopathy treated with corticosteroid-sparing systemic immunomodulatory therapy. *Ophthalmology.* 2005;112(6):1066–1071.

Multifocal choroiditis and panuveitis syndrome

MCP is a bilateral disease that predominantly affects women between the second and sixth decades. Symptoms include decreased vision, floaters, photopsia, and visual field defects such as an enlarged blind spot. Patients present with a bilateral vitritis, disruption of the peripapillary RPE, and multifocal choroiditis (Fig 9-5). The multiple yellow choroidal lesions later evolve into chorioretinal scars similar to the "punched-out" lesions present in ocular histoplasmosis (OHS; see Chapter 4). However, unlike in OHS, patients with MCP have some degree of vitritis, often combined with mild anterior segment inflammation. Topical, periocular, and systemic corticosteroids may help reduce the choroidal and vitreous inflammation, whereas more potent immunomodulation may be necessary for lesions threatening fixation. However, MCP is a diagnosis of exclusion, and infectious etiologies such as syphilis and tuberculosis should be ruled out before initiating immunomodulation. Subfoveal CNV occurs in approximately 20% of affected eyes and is the leading cause of vision loss. Epiretinal membrane formation and CME may be late complications. The risk of vision loss may be reduced by controlling inflammation and by prompt treatment of CNV. Visual outcomes in MCP are often poor.

Michel SS, Ekong A, Baltatzis S, Foster CS. Multifocal choroiditis and panuveitis: immunomodulatory therapy. *Ophthalmology.* 2002;109(2):378–383.

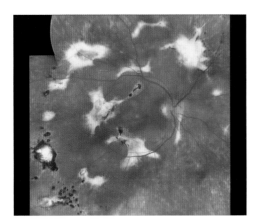

Figure 9-5 Multifocal choroiditis and panuveitis syndrome with subretinal fibrosis. *(Courtesy of Richard F. Spaide, MD.)*

Thorne JE, Wittenberg S, Jabs DA, et al. Multifocal choroiditis with panuveitis incidence of ocular complications and of loss of visual acuity. *Ophthalmology.* 2006;113(12):2310–2316. Epub 2006 Sep 25.

Punctate inner choroidopathy

PIC tends to occur in young patients with myopia. More than 90% are women. Patients present with prominent photopsia and bilateral loss of central visual acuity, as well as scotomata. Fundus examination during the acute phase shows small (100–300 μm), round, yellow-white lesions at the level of the RPE or inner choroid; these lesions may coalesce and cause a serous retinal detachment (Fig 9-6). Mild optic disc edema may be noted in the absence of iritis and vitritis. The lesions fill and stain during the late phase of fluorescein angiography, especially if a serous detachment is present. Lesions later become atrophic yellow-white scars, which may become pigmented or enlarge over time. Scotomata usually correspond to the location of these lesions. These scars appear very similar to those present in OHS and multifocal choroiditis.

Oral and periocular corticosteroids have been used without adverse effects in patients with PIC, but spontaneous improvement usually occurs without treatment. The prognosis for visual acuity is generally good, and the condition does not seem to recur. One-third of eyes develop CNV within a site of previous scarring; however, some of the CNV involutes spontaneously. Photopsia may persist for years.

Watzke RC, Packer AJ, Folk JC, Benson WE, Burgess D, Ober RR. Punctate inner choroidopathy. *Am J Ophthalmol.* 1984;98(5):572–584.

Acute zonal occult outer retinopathy

AZOOR, a presumed inflammatory disorder, damages broad zones of the outer retina in 1 or both eyes. AZOOR typically occurs in young women, with an acute onset in 1 eye. Initial symptoms include photopsia, visual field loss, and sometimes an enlarged blind spot. On initial presentation, the fundus may appear normal, or show evidence of mild vitritis (Fig 9-7). Angiographic findings may include retinal and optic nerve head capillary leakage, especially in patients with evidence of vitritis. The ERG response often shows decreased rod and cone amplitudes under both photopic and scotopic conditions. Visual field testing may show scotomata, which can enlarge over weeks or months.

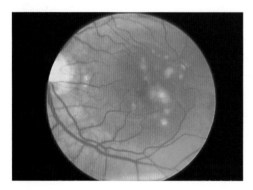

Figure 9-6 Punctate inner choroidopathy.

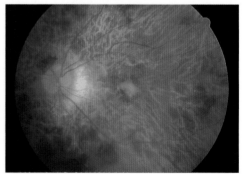

Figure 9-7 Acute zonal occult outer retinopathy. *(Courtesy of J. Donald M. Gass, MD.)*

Some patients recover from AZOOR, whereas others have persistent, large visual field defects. Permanent visual field loss is often associated with late development of fundus changes. Depigmentation of large zones of RPE usually corresponds to scotomata; narrowed retinal vessels may be visible within these areas. The late fundus appearance in some patients may resemble cancer-associated retinopathy or retinitis pigmentosa. Most patients retain good vision in at least 1 eye. No treatment has any proven benefit.

Gass JD. Acute zonal occult outer retinopathy. Donders Lecture: The Netherlands Ophthalmological Society, Maastricht, Holland, June 19, 1992. *J Clin Neuroophthalmol.* 1993;13(2):79–97.

Gass JD, Agarwal A, Scott IU. Acute zonal occult outer retinopathy: a long-term follow-up study. *Am J Ophthalmol.* 2002;134(3):329–339.

Acute Macular Neuroretinopathy

Acute macular neuroretinopathy (AMN) is a bilateral condition that presents with acute central vision loss that typically follows a viral prodrome in younger individuals. Visual acuity is generally reduced to the range of 20/30–20/40. Clinical findings include wedge-shaped, reddish-brown macular lesions in the outer retina. The retinal vessels and optic nerve are unaffected, and there is no vitreous inflammation. Angiography shows faint hypofluorescence of the affected areas; infrared photography may clearly delineate the lesions. Electroretinography may show early photoreceptor potential changes. The lesions typically resolve over several weeks to months with corresponding visual recovery, except in rare cases that remain symptomatic for years.

Bos PJ, Deutman AF. Acute macular neuroretinopathy. *Am J Ophthalmol.* 1975;80(4):573-584.

Acute Idiopathic Maculopathy

Acute idiopathic maculopathy (AIM) presents with sudden central vision loss, typically in younger individuals after a flulike illness. AIM was initially reported as a unilateral disorder, but bilateral cases have since been described. Although most patients have no other associated conditions, AIM has been linked with pregnancy and human immuno-deficiency virus (HIV) infection in some cases. The main clinical finding is an exudative neurosensory macular detachment; there may also be vitreous cells, retinal hemorrhages, subretinal infiltrates, and papillitis. Central lesions were described initially, but eccentric macular lesions have been added to the spectrum. Angiographic findings include staining of the yellowish-white lesions visible on ophthalmoscopy, suggestive of an inflammatory disorder of the RPE. The lesions resolve spontaneously but leave a "bull's-eye" pattern of RPE atrophy. There is near complete recovery of vision over several weeks.

Yannuzzi LA, Jampol LM, Rabb MF, Sorenson JA, Beyrer C, Wilcox LM Jr. Unilateral acute idiopathic maculopathy. *Arch Ophthalmol.* 1991;109(10):1411–1416.

Acute Retinal Pigment Epitheliitis

Acute retinal pigment epitheliitis (ARPE), also known as Krill disease, presents with rapid central vision loss, typically in young adults. On ophthalmoscopic examination, one or both maculae show clusters of dark, round spots surrounded by depigmented haloes at the level of the RPE. Angiographic studies demonstrate hypofluorescence surrounding the dark spots that are apparent biomicroscopically. The disease is self-limited; patients typically have vision recovery and near total resolution of RPE changes. The cause is unknown.

Krill AE, Deutman AF. Acute retinal pigment epitheliitis. *Am J Ophthalmol.* 1972;74(2):193–205.

Solitary Idiopathic Choroiditis

Solitary idiopathic choroiditis is a localized inflammatory condition of the choroid of unknown etiology that can simulate an amelanotic intraocular neoplasm (eg, nevus, melanoma, choroidal metastasis, osteoma, retinoblastoma, or astrocytic hamartoma). It is differentiated from known etiologies of choroidal granuloma such as sarcoidosis, tuberculosis, toxocariasis, and cat-scratch disease. The age range at presentation is 20–50 years. Most cases are asymptomatic or present with mild vision loss. Fundus examination reveals a distinct, yellow-white lesion with well-defined margins at the level of the choroid, usually located posterior to the equator. Signs of inflammation are present in about one-third of cases and may be associated with intraretinal exudation, localized subretinal fluid, and focal retinal hemorrhages that tend to disappear as the inflammation subsides. Fluorescein angiographic findings include hypofluorescence in the early-phase images and hyperfluorescence in the late phases in the area of clinical involvement. Exudative lesions generally improve with or without treatment but do respond favorably to systemic corticosteroids. Scarred lesions tend to remain stable over the long term.

Shields JA, Shields CL, Demirci H, Hanovar S. Solitary idiopathic choroiditis: the Richard B. Weaver lecture. *Arch Ophthalmol.* 2002;120(3):311–319.

Inflammatory Vasculitis

Behçet disease

Behçet disease, a chronic recurrent systemic disease, consists of a classic triad of recurrent aphthous oral ulcers, genital ulcers, and acute iritis with hypopyon. The nonocular manifestations of Behçet disease may predominate and precede ocular involvement; these are characterized by a cyclical systemic occlusive vasculitis. Recurrent oral ulceration occurs in nearly all patients, and cutaneous lesions such as erythema nodosum are common. Central nervous system involvement may occur in more than 50% of patients and should be suspected in any patient with neurologic signs. Other systemic manifestations include arthritis, epididymitis, and intestinal ulcers. It tends to affect men more than women and is particularly common in Japan, Southeast Asia, the Middle East, and the Mediterranean region. The etiology is unknown, but the disease is associated with HLA-B*5101.

Anterior segment involvement is common and includes severe uveitis, often with hypopyon. Posterior segment involvement may include an occlusive retinal vasculitis, intraretinal hemorrhages, macular edema, focal areas of retinal necrosis, ischemic optic neuropathy, and marked vitritis. Recurrent episodes of retinal vasculitis may lead to severe ischemia and retinal neovascularization, which should be treated with panretinal photocoagulation. Corticosteroids are used to treat retinal vasculitis, and in severe and recurrent cases, immunomodulators such as cyclosporine are used to control and prevent inflammation. Despite treatment, the visual prognosis is often poor because of progressive retinal ischemia from recurrent episodes of occlusive vasculitis. Use of biologic agents such as infliximab, which targets tumor necrosis factor, has recently shown benefit in decreasing the recurrence of inflammation in refractory Behçet disease.

Tugal-Tutkun I, Mudun A, Urgancioglu M, et al. Efficacy of infliximab in the treatment of uveitis that is resistant to treatment with the combination of azathioprine, cyclosporine, and corticosteroids in Behçet's disease: an open-label trial. *Arthritis Rheum.* 2005;52(8):2478–2484.

Lupus vasculitis

Systemic lupus erythematosus (SLE) is a systemic autoimmune disorder most commonly affecting women of childbearing age. As a multisystem disease, it can involve almost every ocular and periocular structure. Approximately 3%–10% of patients with SLE will have retinal disease ranging from asymptomatic cotton-wool spots and intraretinal hemorrhages to blinding vasoocclusive disease (Fig 9-8). Lupus choroidopathy is less common and presents as multifocal serous elevations of the neurosensory retina and RPE. The retinal and choroidal pathology is vascular and thought to arise from autoimmune mechanisms: polyclonal B-cell activation, a multitude of autoantibodies, and circulating immune complexes causing microangiopathy. Histologic studies of the damaged vessels show hematoxylin bodies and fibrinoid necrosis.

No treatment is necessary for cotton-wool spots, although their presence may indicate active SLE. Severe vasoocclusive disease is potentially blinding and should be treated. Plasmapheresis, corticosteroids, immunomodulators, and anticoagulation therapy have been tried. Although immunosuppressive therapy is thought to be the mainstay of treatment, plasmapheresis has been reported to be helpful in the acute phase by rapidly removing circulating immune complexes. Panretinal photocoagulation may have a role in treating retinal ischemia and preventing complications of neovascularization. Lupus vasculitis should be managed in conjunction with a rheumatologist. Retinal vasoocclusive

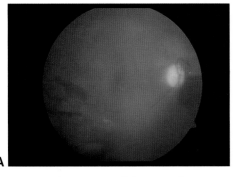 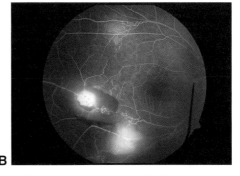

A   **B**

Figure 9-8 Lupus vasculitis secondary to systemic lupus erythematosus. **A,** Vitreous hemorrhage secondary to neovascularization. **B,** Choroidal and retinal nonperfusion, perivascular staining, and leakage due to neovascularization visible on late-phase fluorescein angiogram. *(Courtesy of Matthew A. Thomas, MD.)*

disease has been associated with central nervous system lupus and may also require neurologic consultation.

Papadaki TG, Zacharopoulos IP, Papaliodis G, Iaccheri B, Fiore T, Foster CS. Plasmapheresis for lupus retinal vasculitis. *Arch Ophthalmol.* 2006;124(11):1654–1656.

Intermediate Uveitis

Intermediate uveitis (IU) refers to posterior segment inflammation primarily involving the vitreous cavity. The differential diagnosis of IU includes multiple sclerosis, syphilis, Lyme disease, and sarcoidosis.

Pars planitis

Pars planitis is a specific form of idiopathic bilateral IU that typically affects young adults and children, with peaks occurring in the age ranges of 5–15 years and 25–35 years. Patients with pars planitis may have floaters, decreased vision, or both due to CME. Ocular manifestations include inflammatory exudates on the inferior pars plana ("snowbanking"), aggregates of vitreous cells ("snowballs"), and diffuse vitritis with spillover of cells into the anterior chamber. There may be associated retinal phlebitis or optic nerve head swelling. Fluorescein angiography may show diffuse peripheral venular leakage and late-phase staining. Peripheral neovascularization may form along the inferior snowbank in 5%–10% of cases and can lead to vitreous hemorrhage with tractional or rhegmatogenous retinal detachment in up to 5%. The disease may be chronic or self-limited, and exacerbations of inflammation complicated by CME may respond to topical, oral, sub-Tenon, or intravitreal administration of corticosteroids. CME occurs in one-third of patients with pars planitis and is the leading cause of vision loss. Visual impairment may also be caused by development of epiretinal membrane, posterior subcapsular cataract, large amounts of vitreous debris, and band keratopathy. Peripheral neovascularization can be treated with transcleral cryopexy applied to the snowbanks or, preferably, peripheral laser photocoagulation. Pars plana vitrectomy may be considered for serious complications of the disease, including retinal detachment, uveitis, cataracts, and severe CME. Immunomodulatory therapy should be considered for cases of persistent or refractory inflammation.

Androudi S, Letko E, Meniconi M, Papadaki T, Ahmed M, Foster CS. Safety and efficacy of intravitreal triamcinolone acetonide for uveitic macular edema. *Ocul Immunol Inflamm.* 2005;13(2-3):205–212.

Hooper PL. Pars planitis. *Focal Points: Clinical Modules for Ophthalmologists.* San Francisco: American Academy of Ophthalmology; 1993, module 11.

Panuveitis

Sarcoid panuveitis

Up to 50% of patients with sarcoidosis have ocular manifestations. Anterior segment involvement presents as granulomatous inflammation characterized by mutton-fat keratic precipitates, iris nodules, and posterior synechiae. Posterior segment manifestations of sarcoidosis are numerous and protean. They can include intermediate uveitis with snowbank formation; vitritis with characteristic snowballs in the inferior periphery; retinal periphlebitis, specifically with formation of "candlewax drippings"; multifocal choroiditis; and optic nerve swelling (Fig 9-9). The systemic complications of sarcoidosis should be treated in conjunction with the ocular disease.

See BCSC Section 9, *Intraocular Inflammation and Uveitis,* for information about the workup and treatment of sarcoidosis.

Vogt-Koyanagi-Harada syndrome

Vogt-Koyanagi-Harada (VKH) syndrome is a systemic inflammatory disorder that predominantly affects individuals with darker skin pigmentation and shows a slight female predilection. It is a bilateral granulomatous panuveitis associated with dermatologic and neurologic manifestations, including vitiligo, alopecia, poliosis, and meningeal signs. During workup, any history of previous penetrating ocular injury or ocular surgery must be elicited to rule out sympathetic ophthalmia. HLA-DRB1*0405 has a strong association with VKH syndrome in Japanese patients.

Isolated posterior segment findings in the absence of systemic involvement are frequently referred to as Harada disease. VKH syndrome can be divided into 4 separate phases:

1. The *prodromal phase* is characterized by a flulike illness with symptoms that can include meningismus, headache, tinnitus, and dysacusis.
2. The *uveitic phase,* which follows, is characterized by acute-onset bilateral granulomatous uveitis with vitritis and optic disk edema. Patients present with pain, photophobia, and concomitant vision loss. Posterior segment findings are characterized by yellow-white exudates at the level of the RPE, with serous retinal detachment.
3. The *acute uveitic phase* lasts for 2–6 weeks. During this third, or convalescent, phase, the uveitis subsides, but depigmentation of the skin and uvea may occur. *Sugiura sign,* or perilimbal vitiligo, along with a "sunset glow" fundus and "punched-out"-appearing Dalen-Fuchs nodules may be visible at this time.
4. The *final phase* is characterized by chronic and recurrent inflammation that frequently leads to the development of cataract, glaucoma, and CNV.

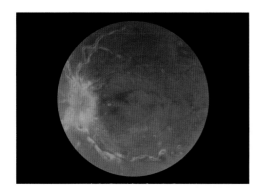

Figure 9-9 Sarcoidosis, with retinal vascular sheathing. *(Courtesy of Ramin Schadlu, MD.)*

Fluorescein angiography is helpful in the diagnosis of VKH syndrome by revealing multiple punctate, hyperfluorescent dots, with leakage of dye into the subretinal space (Fig 9-10). Echography and enhanced-depth optical coherence tomography (OCT) may be useful in demonstrating diffuse choroidal thickening in the acute phase. The disease course is occasionally recurrent, but episodes generally respond well to systemic corticosteroids. Long-term immunomodulation therapy may be required to halt progression of the disease and ocular complications. With treatment, the visual prognosis is generally good, but visual outcomes may be adversely influenced by secondary glaucoma, subfoveal CNV, complicated cataract, and phthisis bulbi.

Sympathetic ophthalmia

Sympathetic ophthalmia is clinically and histologically indistinguishable from VKH syndrome, except that it occurs only after a penetrating ocular injury or ocular surgery; it develops in less than 1% of those patients. Inflammation of the exciting (injured) and sympathizing (fellow) eye may occur days to decades after the initial insult. As in VKH syndrome, the inflammation is a bilateral granulomatous panuveitis with associated optic disk swelling and choroidal thickening. Nonocular findings similar to those in VKH syndrome may also occur in patients with this condition. The risk of sympathetic ophthalmia may be minimized by either meticulous anatomical restoration or enucleation of an

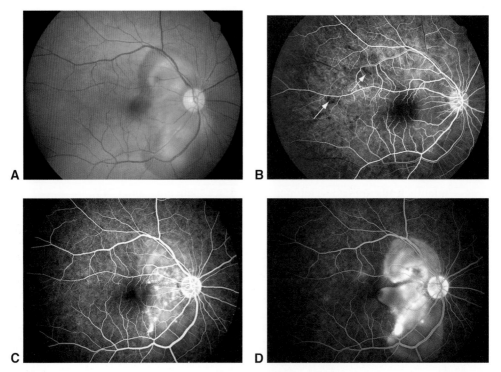

Figure 9-10 Harada disease. **A,** The color fundus photograph shows a multilobed serous detachment of the retina. **B,** The early-phase fluorescein angiogram demonstrates focal areas of choroidal filling delay *(arrows)*. **C,** In the midphase, multiple leaks are apparent, and by the later phases **(D)**, pooling of fluorescein is visible in the subretinal space. *(Courtesy of Richard F. Spaide, MD.)*

injured eye within 2 weeks of the injury. Because the incidence of sympathetic ophthalmia is low, however, only structurally disorganized no-light-perception (NLP) eyes should be enucleated. Once inflammation develops, the visual prognosis is poor, and aggressive treatment with corticosteroids, possibly including intravitreal administration or immunomodulation, is often necessary to prevent bilateral blindness.

Damico FM, Kiss S, Young LH. Sympathetic ophthalmia. *Semin Ophthalmol.* 2005;20(3): 191–197.

Jabs DA, Johns CJ. Ocular involvement in chronic sarcoidosis. *Am J Ophthalmol.* 1986;102(3): 297–301.

Moorthy RS, Inomata H, Rao NA. Vogt-Koyanagi-Harada syndrome. *Surv Ophthalmol.* 1995;39(4):265–292.

Uveitis Masquerade

Intraocular lymphoma

Intraocular lymphoma was previously referred to as *reticulum cell sarcoma, histiocytic lymphoma,* and *non-Hodgkin lymphoma of the central nervous system.* Intraocular lymphoma typically presents in the sixth or seventh decade of life with bilateral iritis, vitritis, retinal vasculitis, and creamy yellow sub-RPE infiltrates (Fig 9-11); it may be mistaken for uveitis. The diagnosis should be suspected if large, solid, confluent RPE detachments are present. These solid RPE detachments can spontaneously involute and are thought to be distinctive for the diagnosis of intraocular lymphoma. Disc edema may be visible. The diagnosis is confirmed through pars plana vitrectomy and cytologic examination of the specimen by an experienced cytopathologist. The cytologic examination is more important in establishing the diagnosis than are immunologic markers. This condition should be suspected in any elderly patient with chronic, nonresponsive uveitis. Systemic evaluation for central nervous system involvement is required. Despite treatment with chemotherapy, radiation, or both, the prognosis is poor, and the disease has a low 5-year survival rate. BCSC Section 4, *Ophthalmic Pathology and Intraocular Tumors,* discusses this condition in greater depth.

Gill MK, Jampol LM. Variations in the presentation of primary intraocular lymphoma: case reports and a review. *Surv Ophthalmol.* 2001;45(6):463–471.

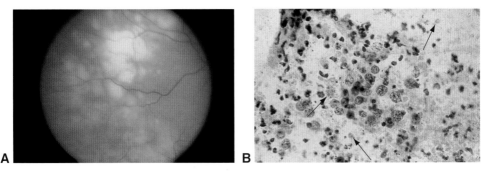

A   **B**

Figure 9-11 **A,** Sub–retinal pigment epithelial infiltrates in a patient with intraocular lymphoma. **B,** Cytologic preparation of vitreous cells in a patient with lymphoma reveals many atypical cells with large nuclei and multiple nucleoli. Cell ghosts *(arrows)* are also present. *(Courtesy of David J. Wilson, MD.)*

Infectious Retinal and Choroidal Inflammation

The following are brief descriptions of some of the infectious diseases that can cause retinal and choroidal inflammation.

Cytomegalovirus Infection

Cytomegalovirus (CMV) retinitis is the most common ocular opportunistic infection in patients with AIDS. Retinal manifestations usually occur in advanced disease, after the patient's CD4$^+$ cell count declines below 50/μL. Patients typically present with decreased visual acuity and floaters. CMV retinitis has a characteristic appearance that consists of opacification of the retina with areas of hemorrhage, exudate, and necrosis (Fig 9-12). There is often an appearance of superficial granularity. Periphlebitis and even frosted branch angiitis may be prominent features. The degree of vitreous inflammation is highly variable and decreases to the extent to which the patient is immunocompromised. Because the diagnosis is not usually made until the lesions enlarge (over 1–2 weeks) to at least 750 μm, CMV retinitis may resemble the cotton-wool spots present in HIV-related retinopathy early in its course. Serologic testing for CMV is of limited value because exposure to CMV is common in the general population.

CMV retinitis is initially managed with intravenous ganciclovir or foscarnet. After high-dose induction of ganciclovir 5 mg/kg twice daily or foscarnet 90 mg/kg twice daily for 2 weeks, patients who respond well may be switched to lower-dose daily intravenous therapy of either ganciclovir or foscarnet or to oral ganciclovir therapy. Ganciclovir and foscarnet can also be injected intravitreally, but this route of administration has not been approved by the US Food and Drug Administration (FDA) and will not treat systemic infection. Because ganciclovir has adverse myelotoxic effects, patients who cannot tolerate systemic administration but respond to the drug may benefit from intravitreal insertion of a ganciclovir implant, which delivers adequate concentrations of the drug for approximately 8 months. Valganciclovir, an oral prodrug of ganciclovir, is an effective alternative to intravenous treatment and is administered at an induction dose of 900 mg twice a day for 3 weeks, followed by 900 mg once a day for maintenance therapy.

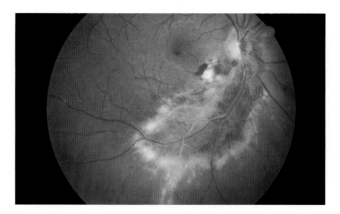

Figure 9-12 Cytomegalovirus retinitis. *(Courtesy of Mark W. Johnson, MD.)*

Within the first year, CMV retinitis is complicated by retinal detachment in 40%–50% of patients. Small peripheral detachments may benefit from laser demarcation, but most patients require pars plana vitrectomy with silicone oil intraocular tamponade. Effective antiretroviral therapy that leads to sustained elevation of the CD4+ T-cell count may reduce or eliminate the need for specific anti-CMV treatment. However, immune recovery uveitis develops in approximately 20% of HIV-infected patients with a history of CMV retinitis once their CD4+ T-cell counts rise to 100/µL or more; the uveitis can be complicated by CME and cataract formation. BCSC Section 9, *Intraocular Inflammation and Uveitis,* discusses CMV in greater detail.

Kempen JH, Min YI, Freeman WR, et al; Studies of Ocular Complications of AIDS Research Group. Risk of immune recovery uveitis in patients with AIDS and cytomegalovirus retinitis. *Ophthalmology.* 2006;113(4):684–694.

Martin DF, Sierra-Madero J, Walmsley S, et al; Valganciclovir Study Group. A controlled trial of valganciclovir as induction therapy for cytomegalovirus retinitis. *N Engl J Med.* 2002;346(15):1119–1126.

Rhegmatogenous retinal detachment in patients with cytomegalovirus retinitis: the Foscarnet-Ganciclovir Cytomegalovirus Retinitis Trial. The Studies of Ocular Complications of AIDS (SOCA) Research Group in Collaboration with the AIDS Clinical Trials Group (ACTG). *Am J Ophthalmol.* 1997;124(1):61–70.

Necrotizing Herpetic Retinitis

Necrotizing herpetic retinitis may present as *acute retinal necrosis (ARN)* syndrome or *progressive outer retinal necrosis* (PORN) syndrome. Herpes simplex and herpes zoster viruses have been identified as the causative agents in these syndromes, and early diagnosis may be achieved by polymerase chain reaction (PCR) analysis of vitreous fluid. In the ARN syndrome, typical presentation is an otherwise healthy patient with ocular pain and reduced vision. Iritis, episcleritis, or vitritis may be visible on initial examination. Subsequently, large areas of retinal whitening and necrosis appear, often in the peripheral retina (Fig 9-13). These areas coalesce and spread centripetally. Optic neuritis, arteriolitis, and vascular occlusions are associated findings. As the retinal opacification clears, large retinal breaks may occur in the necrotic retina, and the risk of retinal detachment is high. The disease is bilateral at onset in 20% of patients; in patients with unilateral onset, subsequent involvement of the fellow eye is very common without treatment. The ARN syndrome may also occur in immunocompromised patients, but PORN syndrome is more typical and may be distinguished by its more rapid progression, lack of vitritis, and characteristic sparing of the retinal vessels. Often, patients with either of these syndromes are found to have a history of herpes zoster ophthalmicus or herpes simplex infection.

In immunocompetent patients, initial therapy involves intravenous acyclovir (800 mg 5 times daily) or oral famciclovir (500 mg 3 times daily) or valaciclovir (1 g 3 times daily). Treatment is continued until there is clinical evidence that the retinitis has resolved. Oral acyclovir (800 mg 5 times daily for 3 months) may decrease the risk of infection in the second eye. In immunocompetent patients with severe, sight-threatening disease, intravitreal injections of foscarnet and ganciclovir may be of benefit. The risk of retinal detachment appears to be highest 8–12 weeks after the onset of the disease. Prophylactic use of laser

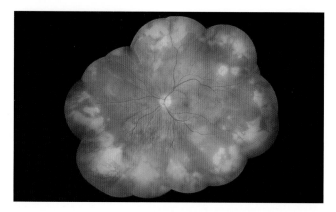

Figure 9-13 Necrotizing herpetic retinitis (acute retinal necrosis) with intraretinal hemorrhage and full-thickness opacification of the retina. *(Courtesy of Mark W. Johnson, MD, and Richard Hackel, CRA. Reproduced with permission from Aizman A, Johnson MW, Elner SG. Treatment of acute retinal necrosis syndrome with oral antiviral medications.* Ophthalmology. *2007;114(2):307–312. Epub 2006 Nov 21.)*

photocoagulation to demarcate the borders of retinal necrosis may decrease the risk of retinal detachment.

> Lau CH, Missotten T, Salzmann J, Lightman SL. Acute retinal necrosis features, management, and outcomes. *Ophthalmology.* 2007;114(4):756–762. Epub 2006 Dec 20.
>
> Scott IU, Luu KM, Davis JL. Intravitreal antivirals in the management of patients with acquired immunodeficiency syndrome with progressive outer retinal necrosis. *Arch Ophthalmol.* 2002;120(9):1219–1222.

Endogenous Bacterial Endophthalmitis

Endogenous bacterial endophthalmitis typically begins as a focal or multifocal chorioretinal lesion that spreads into the vitreous (Fig 9-14). Initially, the lesions are flat or slightly elevated chorioretinal infiltrates. A wide range of bacteria can cause endogenous bacterial endophthalmitis, including *Streptococcus* species, *Staphylococcus aureus, Serratia* species, and *Bacillus* species.

The extraocular source of the infection should be determined through medical consultation and appropriately treated with systemic therapy. Endocarditis and infections of the gastrointestinal or urinary tract are the most commonly associated etiologies. Medical

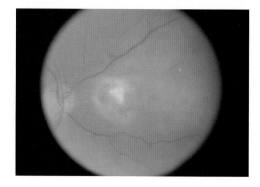

Figure 9-14 Focal endogenous bacterial endophthalmitis. *(Courtesy of Janet L. Davis, MD.)*

evaluation usually includes cultures of the vitreous, blood, and other extraocular sites. Treatment commonly includes intravenous antibiotics and, if there is substantial vitreous involvement, intravitreal antibiotics.

Binder MI, Chua J, Kaiser PK, Procop GW, Isada CM. Endogenous endophthalmitis: an 18-year review of culture-positive cases at a tertiary care center. *Medicine (Baltimore)*. 2003;82(82):97–105.

Fungal Endophthalmitis

Endophthalmitis caused by fungal infections may be either endogenous or exogenous. In India, fungi account for up to one-fifth of culture-positive cases of postoperative endophthalmitis. The causative species is often difficult to diagnose because of poor growth in culture. Treatment is also difficult, resulting from drug resistance, drug toxicity, and poor bioavailability of systemically administered antifungal drugs.

Yeast (Candida) endophthalmitis

Endogenous yeast endophthalmitis is most frequently caused by *Candida* species. Affected patients frequently have had prior use of indwelling catheters, long-term antibiotic treatment, or immunosuppression therapy. Many also have a history of hyperalimentation, recent abdominal surgery, or diabetes mellitus. The initial intraocular inflammation is usually mild to moderate, and yellow-white choroidal lesions may be single or multiple. Subretinal infiltrates may coalesce into a mushroom-shaped white nodule that projects through the retina into the vitreous (Fig 9-15).

The diagnosis is usually based on the clinical history and the presence of characteristic features in the posterior segment. Results of systemic and intraocular cultures help confirm the clinical diagnosis. The ophthalmologist should seek consultation with a specialist in infectious diseases to evaluate the patient for systemic disease and assist with treatment planning. If the macula is not involved, visual prognosis after treatment is generally good. Focal chorioretinal lesions are often successfully treated with systemic medications. Intravenous amphotericin B does not penetrate well into the vitreous, but fluconazole does penetrate well and has fewer systemic adverse effects. Intravenous, oral, or intravitreal voriconazole, alone or in combination with intravenous caspofungin, has also been used.

Intraocular culture specimens are best obtained during pars plana vitrectomy, as it is difficult to culture the localized vitreous clusters of fungus from a diagnostic vitreous tap. After completion of the vitrectomy, intravitreal amphotericin B or voriconazole is usually injected, but successful treatment has been reported by vitrectomy alone in conjunction with systemic fluconazole.

Endogenous mold (Aspergillus) endophthalmitis

Endogenous mold endophthalmitis is a rare but often devastating infection that occurs in immunosuppressed patients and intravenous drug users. Mold is the most frequent cause of endogenous endophthalmitis in patients who have undergone liver transplantation. Symptoms include the acute onset of ocular pain and vision loss. Intraocular inflammation is generally more severe than that associated with the endophthalmitis caused by *Candida* infection. The chorioretinal lesion associated with *Aspergillus* infection is usually

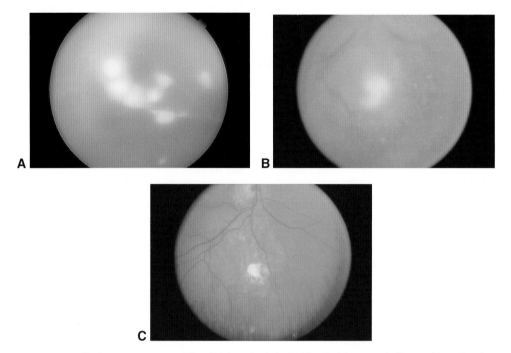

Figure 9-15 Endogenous yeast *(Candida)* endophthalmitis. **A,** Vitreous infiltrates in a "string of pearls" configuration. **B,** Endogenous endophthalmitis before treatment. **C,** Endogenous endophthalmitis resolved after treatment with vitrectomy and intravitreal amphotericin B. *(Courtesy of Harry W. Flynn, Jr, MD.)*

larger and progresses more rapidly, and it is characterized by a large yellow infiltrate in or near the macula. The inflammatory exudate may layer to form a subretinal or subhyaloidal hypopyon. Vitritis, vasculitis, and retinal necrosis are often associated features.

Pars plana vitrectomy with diagnostic cultures and injection of intravitreal amphotericin B are usually recommended, especially if vitritis is present. Visual acuity outcomes are frequently poor as a result of the associated macular lesion (Fig 9-16). However, intravitreal injections of voriconazole have been used with success in the treatment of *Aspergillus* endophthalmitis.

Rao NA, Hidayat AA. Endogenous mycotic endophthalmitis: variations in clinical and histopathologic changes in candidiasis compared with aspergillosis. *Am J Ophthalmol.* 2001;132(2):244–251.

Sen P, Gopal L, Sen PR. Intravitreal voriconazole for drug-resistant fungal endophthalmitis: case series. *Retina.* 2006;26(8):935–939.

Weishaar PD, Flynn HW Jr, Murray TG, et al. Endogenous *Aspergillus* endophthalmitis. Clinical features and treatment outcomes. *Ophthalmology.* 1998;105(1):57–65.

Tuberculosis

Mycobacterium tuberculosis may disseminate hematogenously to the eye, and the choroid is the most common initial site of intraocular tuberculosis. Tuberculous panophthalmitis was more common before the availability of effective antimycobacterial therapy, but even then, it was rare. Ocular involvement was usually associated with disseminated miliary

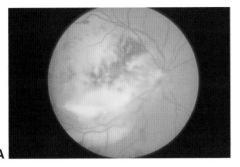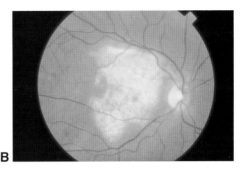

A   B

Figure 9-16 Endophthalmitis caused by infection with *Aspergillus* species. **A,** Features present include mild vitritis, a diffuse macular chorioretinal lesion with subretinal and subhyaloid hypopyon, intraretinal hemorrhage, and papillitis secondary to *Aspergillus* endophthalmitis. **B,** Same eye 2 months after treatment shows macular scar, preserved overlying retinal vessels, temporal disc pallor. Final visual acuity was 20/400. *(Reproduced with permission from Weishaar PD, Flynn HW Jr, Murray TG, et al. Endogenous* Aspergillus *endophthalmitis. Clinical features and treatment outcomes.* Ophthalmology. *1998;105(1):60.)*

tuberculosis and tended to be severe. An upsurge of mycobacterial infection occurred during the initial AIDS epidemic, but the incidence was reduced by the advent of effective antiretroviral therapy.

The patient may present with decreased vision from macular involvement or vitritis. Posterior segment examination shows miliary choroidal tubercles, which appear as single or multiple polymorphous, yellow-white lesions with indistinct borders. The choroidal granulomas are initially flat, are one or several disc diameters in size, and exhibit variable degrees of pigmentation. Vitritis, papillitis, and an overlying serous retinal detachment may be associated with the choroidal lesions (Fig 9-17).

Treatment of ocular tuberculosis is similar to that of the pulmonary disease. A 4-drug regimen of isoniazid, rifampin, pyrazinamide, and either streptomycin or ethambutol is recommended by the US Centers for Disease Control and Prevention. Treatment should be coordinated with a specialist in infectious diseases.

Syphilitic Chorioretinitis

Syphilitic chorioretinitis usually occurs in the secondary stage of syphilis and is often associated with a positive result on rapid plasma reagin (RPR) or Venereal Disease Research Laboratory (VDRL) testing, except in HIV-infected patients. The fluorescent treponemal

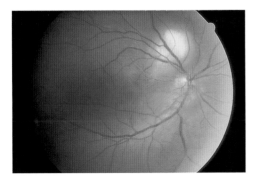

Figure 9-17 A choroidal granuloma caused by tuberculosis is located superior to the optic nerve. *(Courtesy of Janet L. Davis, MD.)*

antibody absorption (FTA-ABS) test may be used to confirm prior exposure to syphilis; however, a positive result does not necessarily indicate active disease. Along with intraocular lymphoma and tuberculosis, syphilis is a masquerade syndrome and thus can present with a wide variety of symptoms and findings; these include choroiditis, retinitis, retinal vasculitis, optic neuritis, neuroretinitis, and even exudative retinal detachment. Characteristic findings are yellow, placoid chorioretinal lesions in the posterior pole (Fig 9-18). Treatment is the same as for neurosyphilis, and most patients respond quickly. Corticosteroids are of value in decreasing posterior segment inflammation, only if combined with appropriate antibiotic cover. In neurosyphilis, a subset of tertiary syphilis, patients may test negative on serum VDRL and RPR screening but positive on cerebrospinal fluid analysis. For this reason, lumbar puncture and analysis of the cerebrospinal fluid should be considered in any patient with suspected syphilitic uveitis who tests positive for FTA-ABS and negative on VDRL/RPR testing, particularly if there is no history of prior treatment.

Tamesis RR, Foster CS. Ocular syphilis. *Ophthalmology.* 1990;97(10):1281–1287.

Cat-Scratch Disease

Cat-scratch disease is characterized by regional lymphadenopathy, fever, and malaise that appear 2 weeks after a cat scratch or bite, although it may occur from any contact between cat saliva and a mucocutaneous surface or open wound. Parinaud oculoglandular syndrome (conjunctival inflammation with preauricular adenopathy) is present in about 7% of patients with cat-scratch disease. *Bartonella henselae* has been isolated as the etiologic agent, and serologic testing for *B henselae* IgG and IgM is now available. The typical retinal findings are similar to those of Leber stellate neuroretinitis: macular star formation and optic disk swelling, as well as yellow-white retinal infiltrates (Fig 9-19). The visual prognosis is good with or without treatment. Antibiotics that have high intracellular penetration, such as doxycycline, ciprofloxacin, and erythromycin, appear to be effective.

Freund KB. Leber's idiopathic stellate neuroretinitis. In: Guyer DR, Yannuzzi LA, Chang S, Shields JA, Green WR, eds. *Retina–Vitreous–Macula.* Philadelphia: Saunders; 1999:885–888.

Gray AV, Michels KS, Lauer AK, Samples JR. *Bartonella henselae* infection associated with neuroretinitis, central retinal artery and vein occlusion, neovascular glaucoma, and severe vision loss. *Am J Ophthalmol.* 2004;137(1):187–189.

Toxoplasmic Chorioretinitis

Toxoplasmic chorioretinitis is probably the most common cause of posterior segment infection worldwide; it accounts for 25% of posterior uveitis cases in the United States. *Toxoplasma gondii* is an obligate, intracellular parasitic protozoan that causes a necrotizing chorioretinitis. Seropositivity for *T gondii* is very common and therefore not useful in diagnosis; however, the absence of antibodies to the organism is often used to rule out disease. Congenital disease occurs via acquisition of the organism by a pregnant woman exposed to tissue cysts or oocytes in uncooked meat or substances contaminated with cat feces. Spontaneous abortion may occur if the disease is acquired during the first trimester. Congenital toxoplasmosis may lead to hydrocephalus, seizures, lymphadenopathy, hepatosplenomegaly, rash, and fever. However, retinochoroiditis is the most common

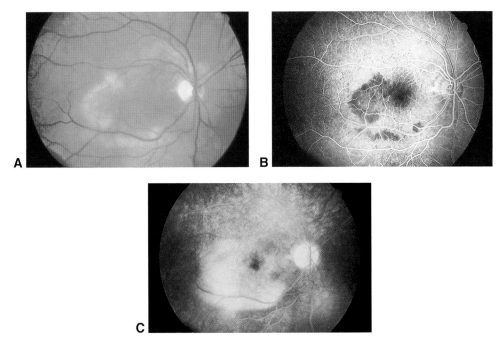

Figure 9-18 Syphilitic chorioretinitis. **A,** Placoid yellow lesion involving the macula. **B,** Early-phase angiogram shows hypofluorescence. **C,** Late-phase angiogram shows diffuse hyper-fluorescence. *(Courtesy of J. Donald M. Gass, MD.)*

manifestation, occurring in three-fourths of cases. In congenital toxoplasmosis, the disease is bilateral in 65%–85% of cases and involves the macula in 58%. A positive serologic test result for maternal IgM supports the diagnosis of congenital toxoplasmosis. Most cases are currently assumed to be acquired but can be distinguished from congenital disease only if there is no scar adjacent to a site of active inflammation or disease occurs after documentation of a previously normal fundus.

A unilateral decrease in visual acuity is the most common presenting symptom of toxoplasmosis. A unifocal area of acute-onset inflammation contiguous with a previous chorioretinal scar is considered pathognomonic for toxoplasmic chorioretinitis (Fig 9-20). Focal condensation of vitreous and inflammatory cells may be visible overlying the pale

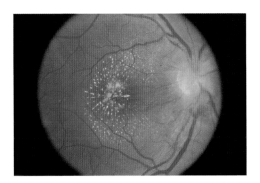

Figure 9-19 Cat-scratch disease *(Bartonella henselae)*. *(Courtesy of George Alexandrakis, MD.)*

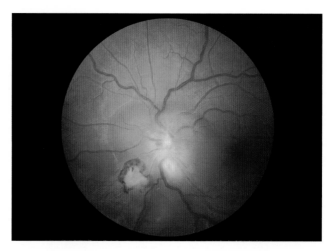

Figure 9-20 Reactivation of inflammation at a site contiguous with a chronic peripapillary toxoplasmosis scar causes sight-threatening infectious papillitis. *(Courtesy of Nancy M. Holekamp, MD.)*

yellow or gray-white raised lesion in the posterior pole. Perivasculitis, arteriolar narrowing, and arteriolar occlusion may be noted near the inflamed area.

In immunocompromised patients (eg, HIV-seropositive, elderly), toxoplasmic chorioretinitis can clinically resemble necrotizing herpetic retinitis; such patients may present with a dense vitritis, active retinitis without an adjacent scar, and negative results on anti-*Toxoplasma* IgG and/or IgM testing. PCR is helpful in making the diagnosis. Neuroimaging is warranted for HIV-infected patients with these findings; intracranial toxoplasmic lesions have been reported in up to 29% of HIV-infected patients with toxoplasmic chorioretinitis.

Small extramacular lesions may be observed in untreated patients. Sight-threatening lesions are treated for 4–6 weeks with triple therapy consisting of pyrimethamine, sulfadiazine, and folinic acid (Table 9-2). Prednisone in low doses of 0.5–1.0 mg/kg per day

Table 9-2 Standard Therapy for Ocular Toxoplasmosis: Drugs and Dosage

Pyrimethamine	75–100 mg loading dose (2 days)
	25–50 mg daily until the lesion is healed (usually 4–6 weeks)
Sulfadiazine	2.0–4.0 g loading dose (2 days)
	0.5–1.0 g 4 times daily until the lesion is healed (usually 4–6 weeks)
Folinic acid	5 mg 3 times a week during pyrimethamine therapy
Prednisone (optional)	0.5–1 mg/kg daily for 3–6 weeks (starting on or after the third day of antibiotic therapy for macula- or optic-nerve–threatening lesions)
	Taper off according to clinical response
	Avoid in immunocompromised patients; avoid without concurrent antibiotic therapy
	Weekly assays of white blood cells and platelets

Modified with permission from Dodds EM. Ocular toxoplasmosis: clinical presentations, diagnosis, and therapy. *Focal Points: Clinical Modules for Ophthalmologists*. San Francisco: American Academy of Ophthalmology; 1999, module 10.

for 3–6 weeks may be added to reduce macular or optic nerve inflammation and can be started on day 3 of antibiotic therapy. Corticosteroids should not be used without concurrent antibiotic treatment or in immunocompromised patients because of the risk of exacerbating the disease. Folinic acid protects against the decrease in platelets and white blood cells induced by pyrimethamine. Trimethoprim/sulfamethoxazole has been shown to be equivalent to triple therapy in the treatment of ocular toxoplasmosis and may be better tolerated by the patient. Clindamycin and azithromycin can also be considered as alternate therapies. HIV-infected patients require long-term maintenance treatment.

Dodds EM. Ocular toxoplasmosis: clinical presentations, diagnosis, and therapy. *Focal Points: Clinical Modules for Ophthalmologists.* San Francisco: American Academy of Ophthalmology; 1999, module 10.

Soheilian M, Sadoughi MM, Ghajarnia M, et al. Prospective randomized trial of trimethoprim/sulfamethoxazole versus pyrimethamine and sulfadiazine in the treatment of ocular toxoplasmosis. *Ophthalmology.* 2005;112(11):1876–1882. Epub 2005 Sep 19.

Toxocariasis

Toxocariasis usually presents as a severe, unilateral, intraocular inflammation in a child or young adult. Although toxocariasis is part of a systemic infestation by the nematode *Toxocara canis,* systemic manifestations such as visceral larval migrans, fever, and eosinophilia are relatively uncommon. *Toxocara canis* is a common intestinal parasite in dogs; it may be acquired by humans after ingestion of soil or vegetables infected with the ova. The parasite migrates to the liver and lungs and may disseminate from there.

Ocular manifestations include a severe uveitis or posterior segment granuloma, often with a fibrocellular stalk extending from the disc to a posterior granuloma (Fig 9-21). Patients usually have elevated intraocular levels of antibodies to *T canis.* Inflammation is exacerbated by the death of the nematode. Antihelminthic therapy is usually not effective in ocular or systemic disease. Intensive local and systemic corticosteroids are necessary

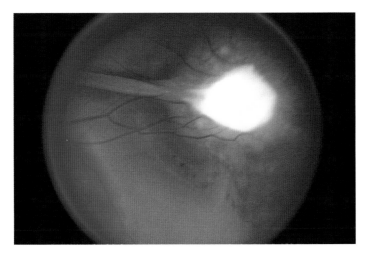

Figure 9-21 Toxocariasis (fibrotic granuloma). *(Courtesy of Harry W. Flynn, Jr, MD.)*

to control the acute intraocular inflammation. The visual prognosis depends on the location of posterior segment inflammation or scar tissue causing macular traction or retinal detachment.

Lyme Disease

Lyme disease is caused by *Borrelia burgdorferi,* which is transmitted to humans by ticks from its usual animal reservoirs: rodents, deer, birds, cats, and dogs. The early stage of Lyme disease may present with a follicular conjunctivitis. Early systemic manifestations consist of myalgias, arthralgias, fever, headache, malaise, and a characteristic annular erythematous skin lesion—the solitary erythema migrans skin lesion with central clearing at the site of the tick bite ("bull's-eye rash"). In later stages, as neurologic or musculoskeletal manifestations develop, the eyes may exhibit keratitis, uveitis, vitritis, retinal vasculitis, and optic neuritis. Chronic iridocyclitis and vitritis in patients who reside in endemic areas or who have had recent tick bites should suggest Lyme disease. Diagnosis is difficult because *B burgdorferi* is fastidious and does not grow on blood agar. Furthermore, serologic testing is plagued by high rates of false-positive and false-negative results. However, the spirochetes may be detected with dark-field microscopy. Typically, laboratory testing for antibodies is performed with a screening enzyme-linked immunosorbent assay (ELISA) followed by a confirmatory Western blot test. Treatment for early disease is with tetracycline, doxycycline, or penicillin; advanced disease may require intravenous ceftriaxone or penicillin.

Karma A, Seppälä I, Mikkilä H, Kaakkola S, Viljanen M, Tarkkanen A. Diagnosis and clinical characteristics of ocular Lyme borreliosis. *Am J Ophthalmol.* 1995;119(2):127–135.

Diffuse Unilateral Subacute Neuroretinitis

Diffuse unilateral subacute neuroretinitis (DUSN) is a rare condition that typically occurs in otherwise healthy, young patients and is due to the presence of a subretinal nematode. Prompt diagnosis and treatment of the condition can help prevent vision loss. The clinical findings in this disease can be divided into acute and end-stage manifestations. In the acute phase, patients frequently have decreased visual acuity, vitritis, papillitis, and crops of gray-white or yellow-white outer retinal lesions. The clustering of the retinal lesions is important because this often helps localize the causative nematode. Left untreated, late sequelae ultimately develop; these include optic atrophy, retinal arterial narrowing, diffuse RPE changes, and an abnormal electroretinogram response. The late findings of this condition are often misinterpreted as unilateral retinitis pigmentosa.

DUSN may be caused by a helminthic infection with *Toxocara canis, Baylisascaris procyonis,* or *Ancylostoma caninum.* The characteristic lesions are believed to result from a single nematode migrating within the subretinal space. If the nematode can be seen, which occurs in less than half of cases, it should be treated with photocoagulation. After the worm is killed, visual acuity loss usually does not progress. In any unilateral presentation of "white dots," it is important that this condition be considered. Although previously thought to be endemic in some areas, that belief was likely the result of underawareness. DUSN has been diagnosed in different climates and residents of many countries.

Gass JDM. *Stereoscopic Atlas of Macular Diseases: Diagnosis and Treatment.* 4th ed. St Louis: Mosby; 1997:622–628.

West Nile Virus Chorioretinitis

West Nile virus infection is most often subclinical but presents with a febrile illness in approximately 20% of cases. The most common ophthalmic manifestation is multifocal chorioretinitis, although in rare cases, occlusive vasculitis may occur. The multifocal choroiditis is usually asymptomatic and presents with a unique fundus appearance. Clinically, active lesions appear as linear clusters of circular, creamy spots; inactive lesions appear targetlike, with hyperpigmented centers surrounded by atrophy. Fluorescein angiographic studies of active lesions show early-phase hypofluorescence and late-phase hyperfluorescence. Inactive lesions have a central hypofluorescence surrounded by hyperfluorescence. The disease is self-limited without treatment.

The authors gratefully acknowledge the contributions of Anita Prasad, MD, to this chapter.

CHAPTER 10

Congenital and Stationary Retinal Disease

Color Vision (Cone System) Abnormalities

Color vision defects can be congenital or acquired. Congenital color vision defects are stationary and usually affect both eyes equally, whereas acquired defects may be progressive and may affect just 1 eye depending on the underlying cause.

Congenital Color Deficiency

Congenital color vision defects are traditionally classified by an individual's color-matching performance. An individual with normal color vision *(trichromatism,* or *trichromacy)* can match any colored light by varying a mixture of 3 different colored lights, or primary colors (eg, a long-wavelength "red," middle-wavelength "green," and short-wavelength "blue" light). Individuals who need only 2 primary colors to make a color match have dichromacy. It is assumed that such individuals lack 1 of the cone photopigments. Approximately 2% of males have dichromacy; 1% are missing the long-wavelength (L-cone) photopigment, a condition termed protanopia, and 1% are missing the medium-wavelength (M-cone) photopigment, a disorder referred to as deuteranopia. Persons with tritanopia lack the short-wavelength (S-cone) photopigment. Congenital tritanopia, an autosomal dominant defect, is a very rare form of dichromacy, occurring in approximately 0.001% of the population.

Individuals with *anomalous trichromatism* make up the largest group of color-deficient persons. Approximately 5%–6% of males have anomalous trichromatism. They require 3 primary colors to match a given color, but because 1 of the cone photopigments has an abnormal absorption spectrum, they use different proportions of the 3 primary colors to make a match from those used by individuals with normal color vision. For approximately 5% of males, the M-cone photopigment has an abnormal absorption spectrum that is closer to that of the L-cone photopigment, a condition referred to as deuteranomalous trichromatism. For 1% of males, the L-cone photopigment has an absorption spectrum that is closer to that of the M-cone photopigment, a disorder referred to as protanomalous trichromatism. Congenital tritanomalous defects are even rarer than tritanopic defects, and there is some question as to whether these defects exist.

Anomalous trichromacy ranges in severity. Some individuals have only a mild abnormality and may, for example, fail some of the sensitive Ishihara test plates but have no trouble naming colors or passing the less-sensitive screening tests such as the Farnsworth Panel D-15 test (see Chapter 3). Others have poor color discrimination and may appear to have dichromacy on some of the color vision tests.

Whereas hereditary congenital color vision defects are most frequently X-linked recessive red-green abnormalities that affect 5%–8% of males and 0.5% of females, acquired defects are more frequently of the blue-yellow, or tritan, variety and affect males and females equally. Table 10-1 shows the traditional classification of color vision deficits on the basis of color-matching test results.

Achromatopsia

An absence of color discrimination, or *achromatopsia,* means that any spectral color can be matched with any other solely by intensity adjustments. Congenital achromatopsias are photoreceptor disorders. The most severe form is complete achromatopsia. It is assumed that persons with complete achromatopsia lack cones and thus have rod monochromatism, but there is some evidence that they have residual cone function. The less severe form of achromatopsia is incomplete achromatopsia. Patients with this form are assumed to have normal rods and S cones but to lack M and L cones; thus, they are considered to have blue-cone monochromatism. Both disorders present typically with congenital nystagmus, poor visual acuity, and photoaversion. The diagnosis may be missed or misjudged as congenital nystagmus unless an electroretinogram (ERG) is obtained. Characteristically, the ERG shows an absence of conventional cone responses, whereas the rod ERG appears relatively normal (see Chapter 3, Fig 3-2). Dark adaptometry shows no cone plateau, and no cone–rod break occurs in the dark-adaptation curve.

Table 10-1 Classification and Male-Population Incidence of Color Vision Defects

Color Vision	Inheritance	Incidence in Male Population (%)
Hereditary		
Trichromatism		
Normal		92.0
Deuteranomalous	XR	5.0
Protanomalous	XR	1.0
Tritanomalous	AD	0.0001
Dichromatism		
Deuteranomalous	XR	1.0
Protanomalous	XR	1.0
Tritanomalous	AD	0.001
Achromatopsia (monochromatism)		
Typical (rod monochromatism)	AR	0.0001
Atypical (blue-cone monochromatism)	XR	Unknown
Acquired		
Tritanomalous (blue-yellow)	Unknown	Unknown
Protanomalous-deuteranomalous (red-green)	Unknown	Unknown

XR = X-linked recessive; AD = autosomal dominant; AR = autosomal recessive.

Rod monochromatism, true color blindness, is inherited as an autosomal recessive trait. Fully affected individuals have no cone function at all and see the world in shades of gray. Patients may have full to partial expression of the disorder, with visual acuity ranging from 20/60 to 20/200. Nystagmus is often present in childhood and usually improves with age. Three candidate genes, *CNGA3, CNGB3,* and *GNAT2,* have been associated with stable rod monochromatism, and mutations of *CNGA3* have also been associated with the progressive forms. The range of severity could imply that different allelic forms of this entity exist. Because these patients may have lightly pigmented fundi and minimal granularity of the macula, their disorder may be misdiagnosed as ocular albinism; an ERG will quickly distinguish between the 2 diagnoses because the cone responses are normal in albinism.

Blue-cone monochromatism is an X-linked recessive congenital disorder of cone dysfunction that can be clinically indistinguishable from rod monochromatism in the absence of a family history or results of specialized color or ERG testing. Patients with this condition have only the blue-sensitive cones, which are so few in number (and normally absent in the central fovea) that visual function mimics rod monochromatism. X-linked recessive inheritance in a male patient with a congenital lack of cone function is the most reliable indicator of this disease. The condition is caused by a loss of function of both red- and green-cone-pigment genes on the X chromosome.

Pokorny J, Smith VC. Color vision and night vision. In: Ryan SJ, Hinton DR, Schachat AP, Wilkinson CP, eds. *Retina.* Vol 1. 4th ed. Philadelphia: Elsevier/Mosby; 2006:209–225.

Sunness JS. Abnormalities of cone and rod function. In: Ryan SJ, Hinton DR, Schachat AP, Wilkinson CP, eds. *Retina.* Vol 1. 4th ed. Philadelphia: Elsevier/Mosby; 2006:509–518.

Night Vision (Rod System) Abnormalities

Congenital Night-Blinding Disorders With Normal Fundi

Congenital stationary night blindness (CSNB) is characterized by a lifelong stable abnormality of scotopic vision (ie, vision at illumination levels at which rods alone are operating). Three genetic subtypes of CSNB have been described:

1. X-linked, the most common
2. autosomal dominant, typified by the large French Nougaret pedigree
3. autosomal recessive

X-linked CSNB has been mapped to the locus Xp11, and mutations in the rhodopsin gene have been documented in some families with autosomal dominant CSNB.

Snellen visual acuities of CSNB patients range from normal to occasionally as poor as 20/200, but most cases of decreased vision are associated with significant myopia. With the exception of myopic changes, the fundus appearance of CSNB patients is usually normal. Children may present with signs of nystagmus, decreased vision, or myopia. Although dark-adaptometry curves are typically 2–3 $\log_{10}$ units above normal, some CSNB patients never complain of nyctalopia, perhaps being accustomed to it as a way of life (Fig 10-1).

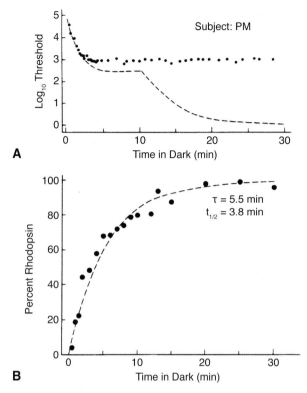

Figure 10-1 Dark-adaptometry curves in congenital stationary night blindness. **A,** Dark adaptometry shows no rod adaptation. **B,** Fundus reflectometry shows a normal rate of rhodopsin regeneration. *(Reprinted with permission from Ripps H. Night blindness revisited: from man to molecules. Proctor Lecture.* Invest Ophthalmol Vis Sci. *1982;23(5):588–609.)*

Electroretinography is important in the diagnosis of CSNB, and several classifications of the disorders are based on the test results. The most common ERG pattern is the *negative ERG* (from the Schubert-Bornschein form of CSNB), in which the maximal dark-adapted response has a large a-wave but an absent or much reduced b-wave (Fig 10-2). The photopic (cone) ERG pattern also shows some abnormalities in this disease. A much rarer type of CSNB shows a reduction of both scotopic a- and scotopic b-waves.

Patients with the more prevalent negative ERG pattern have had their conditions further divided into *complete* and *incomplete* types. Patients with the complete type of CSNB have very poor rod function and psychophysical thresholds that are mediated by cones. The complete form maps to the locus Xp11.4 and results from a mutation in the gene *NYX*, which encodes the protein Nyctalopin. Patients with the incomplete type of CSNB still have some rod function but an elevated dark-adaptation threshold. The incomplete form maps to Xp11.23.

In spite of poor rod vision in CSNB, both the amount and rate of rhodopsin regeneration following a bright-light bleach are normal (see Fig 10-1B). Thus, in contrast to retinitis pigmentosa, which involves a loss of photoreceptor cells, the defect in most cases

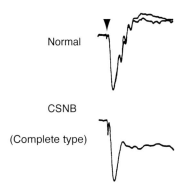

Normal

CSNB

(Complete type)

Figure 10-2 Negative-type ERG pattern typical of congenital stationary night blindness (CSNB). In CNSB, the a-wave is of normal amplitude, whereas the b-wave is absent. *(Reprinted with permission from Miyake Y, Yagasaki K, Horiguchi M, Kawase Y. On- and off-responses in photopic electroretinogram in complete and incomplete types of congenital stationary night blindness. Jpn J Ophthalmol. 1987;31(1):81–87.)*

of CSNB appears to be a communication failure between the proximal end of the photoreceptor and the bipolar cell.

ERG studies have provided insight into the mechanism of CSNB (Fig 10-3). The abnormal cone and rod b-waves in patients with a negative ERG pattern were found to result from a loss of retinal "on-responses." Normally, cones produce a b-wave to both the onset and offset of light, mediated by different neuronal pathways through the retina; the clinical b-wave response to a very brief flash of light is a summation of the 2 responses. Rods, however, stimulate only on-responses. CSNB patients with a selective loss of retinal on-response pathways therefore have no rod vision but still have reasonable cone vision by means of the off-responses. A similar negative ERG pattern has been observed in some patients with Duchenne muscular dystrophy and systemic melanoma (see Chapter 12).

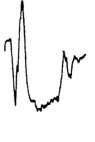

25 µV
50 ms

ON   OFF

Figure 10-3 ERG patterns of on- and off-responses from the human retina. The stimulus here ("On") is a long flash of light (about 0.1 second) so that the ERG responses to onset and offset can be recorded independently. The pattern of a subject without CNSB *(top)* shows an a- and b-wave at the onset of light and a smaller response at the offset. Patients with CSNB have no b-wave at the onset but a large off-response *(bottom)*. *(Reprinted with permission from Miyake Y, Yagasaki K, Horiguchi M, Kawase Y. On- and off-responses in photopic electroretinogram in complete and incomplete types of congenital stationary night blindness. Jpn J Ophthalmol. 1987;31(1):81–87.)*

Congenital Night-Blinding Disorders With Prominent Fundus Abnormality

Fundus albipunctatus is a disorder of the visual pigment regeneration process in which the recovery of normal rhodopsin levels after intense light exposure may take several hours. Affected individuals are symptomatically night blind (and their rod ERG response is minimal) until they have spent several hours in a dark environment; given enough time, however, they adapt to normal sensitivity and the ERG pattern becomes normal. Visual acuity and color vision are typically very good, though often not entirely normal. The fundus shows a striking array of yellow-white dots in the posterior pole (except the fovea) that radiate out toward the periphery (Fig 10-4).

Fundus albipunctatus must be distinguished from *retinitis punctata albescens,* which is a variant of retinitis pigmentosa in which the fundus shows yellow-white dots but has narrowed vessels and a severely depressed ERG pattern that does not recover with dark adaptation. Larger, patchlike flecks and less severe impairment of night vision characterize the *fleck retina of Kandori,* a rare disorder.

Patients who have *Oguchi disease* also adapt very slowly to the dark, but their rhodopsin regeneration is normal. The physiologic defect appears to be in the retinal circuitry rather than the visual pigments. Once these patients are dark-adapted, just a brief flash of light (too short to bleach the visual pigments) can destroy their dark sensitivity. The fundus in Oguchi disease shows a peculiar yellow iridescent sheen after light exposure that disappears after dark adaptation (Mizuo-Nakamura phenomenon; Fig 10-5).

The *enhanced S-cone syndrome* ("S-cone" refers to short-wavelength, or blue-catching, cone) is a rare recessive form of CSNB in which the photopic ERG responses resemble the scotopic ones. Patients with this syndrome lack rod function and have only very weak red- and green-cone function. Their ERG pattern appears to have a greatly magnified blue-cone signal showing minimal differences in waveform between photopic and scotopic ERG responses, and the amplitude of the photopic a-wave tends to be larger than

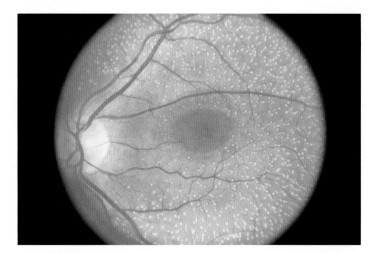

Figure 10-4 Fundus photograph of a patient with fundus albipunctatus, showing multiple spots of unknown material scattered primarily throughout the deep retina. *(Reprinted with permission from Fishman GA, Birch DG, Holder GE, Brigell MG.* Electrophysiologic Testing in Disorders of the Retina, Optic Nerve, and Visual Pathway. Ophthalmology Monograph 2. 2nd ed. San Francisco: American Academy of Ophthalmology; 2001:51.)

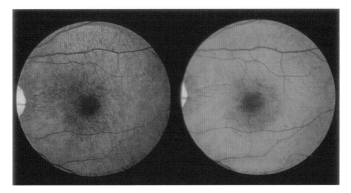

Figure 10-5 The Mizuo-Nakamura phenomenon. The fundus of this patient (with X-linked cone dystrophy) is unremarkable in the dark-adapted state *(right)*, but in the light *(left)*, it has a yellow iridescent sheen.

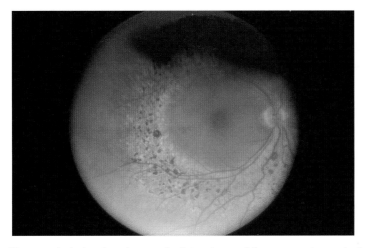

Figure 10-6 Characteristic fundus changes in the enhanced S-cone syndrome include a ring of clumped retinal pigmentation. *(Courtesy of Michael F. Marmor, MD.)*

the amplitude of the 30-Hz flicker response. A ring of retinal pigment epithelium (RPE) degeneration is often observed in the region of the vascular arcades, and foveal schisis may develop (Fig 10-6). Both enhanced S-cone and Goldmann-Favre syndromes have the same genetic basis in that they have been associated with mutations in a nuclear receptor transcription factor gene, *NR2E3,* located on band 15q23 (see Chapter 11).

Carr RE. The generalized heredoretinal disorders. In: Regillo CD, Brown GC, Flynn HW Jr, eds. *Vitreoretinal Disease: The Essentials.* New York: Thieme; 1999:307–332.

Dryja TP. Molecular genetics of Oguchi disease, fundus albipunctatus, and other forms of stationary night blindness. LVII Edward Jackson Memorial Lecture. *Am J Ophthalmol.* 2000;130(5):547–563.

Noble KG. Congenital stationary night blindness. In: Yanoff M, Duker JS, eds. *Ophthalmology.* 2nd ed. St. Louis: Mosby; 2004:840–842.

The authors gratefully acknowledge the contribution of Vivienne Greenstein, PhD, to this chapter.

CHAPTER 11

Hereditary Retinal and Choroidal Dystrophies

The hereditary dystrophies of the posterior segment constitute a large and potentially confusing group of disorders. The *Online Mendelian Inheritance in Man (OMIM)* website, lists over 750 genetic disorders with significant involvement of the retina, choroid, or both. Another excellent online resource, *RetNet,* lists over 200 different retinal degenerations in which the chromosomal site and often the specific gene defect have been identified. Given the large heterogeneity in causative mutations, patients with these diseases can present in a wide variety of ways, with varied symptoms and at various ages. Different levels of organization are useful in approaching these diseases. Traditionally, anatomical classifications have divided the disorders by apparent topography or layer of involvement, such as retina, macula, retinal pigment epithelium (RPE), choroid, and vitreous-retina. This approach is not sufficient, however, because many dystrophies overlap and may involve multiple layers or areas. A second level of organization comes from the family history, to establish the inheritance pattern of the disease. Approximately 60% of thorough pedigrees give useful information. A third approach in diagnostic evaluation is to establish the disease phenotype by clinical examination and electrophysiologic and psychophysical testing. Careful analysis of the information gathered by these 3 approaches allows most conditions to be assigned to a disease group, and many can be given a specific clinical diagnosis that can be confirmed by molecular testing.

Hereditary diseases of the eye, with rare exceptions, have bilateral symmetric involvement. If ocular involvement is unilateral, other causes, such as birth defect, intrauterine or antenatal infection, and inflammatory disease, should be considered before a hereditary dystrophy is diagnosed. Occasionally, a patient presents with clinically uniocular disease that becomes bilateral after several years. In such asymmetric cases, the apparently uninvolved eye was presumably in a subclinical state on the initial examination. Given that retinal degenerations can occur as part of a systemic disorder, obtaining a thorough medical history is crucial, as is ruling out any reversible cause of retinal degeneration or dysfunction, such as vitamin A deficiency (these causes are discussed in greater detail in Chapter 12).

Obtaining an accurate family history is essential to determining the inheritance pattern, which in turn is helpful in selecting candidate genes on which to perform mutational testing. The mendelian patterns of inheritance are well known—namely, autosomal dominant, autosomal recessive, and X-linked recessive. In addition, mitochondrial and

X-linked dominant retinal disorders have been described (see RetNet website). Patients with retinal degenerative disease may have a negative family history. Such a patient may have a *de novo* mutation; alternatively, the disease may be mild in other family members, making them relatively asymptomatic. For this reason, it may be important to examine relatives, if possible, for any signs of retinal degeneration.

The search for gene defects and pathophysiologic mechanisms underlying retinal dystrophies continues at a rapid pace. Perhaps the most important insight gleaned thus far is that *depending on where a mutation lies in a gene, there may be varying expression or even different phenotypes.* This phenomenon has been observed for a number of autosomal dominant genes. For example, mutations in the *RDS/peripherin* gene have been reported to cause cone–rod dystrophy, retinitis pigmentosa (RP), and pattern dystrophy phenotypes; mutations in the *rhodopsin* gene can cause stationary night blindness or RP; and *CRX (cone–rod homeobox-containing gene)* mutations can give rise to a Leber congenital amaurosis phenotype or cone–rod dystrophy phenotype. Autosomal recessive genes also have demonstrated varying phenotypes depending on the location and type of mutation within the gene. For example, mutations in the Stargardt gene result in juvenile or adult macular dystrophy, severe progressive cone–rod dystrophy, RP, or a mild cone–rod dystrophy. In another example, 5% of patients with mutations in the Usher gene, *USH2A,* have RP without the hearing loss characteristic of Usher syndrome. How different mutations in the same gene can cause such varied phenotypes is not well understood. In some instances, interaction with secondary expression genes may influence the phenotype.

Until the mechanisms and implications of these genetic variations are understood, the diseases need to be categorized in a way that helps clinicians recognize topographic patterns of retinal damage and assess prognosis relative to other dystrophies. The classification used here represents a compromise between possible approaches. To aid in clinical identification and management, dystrophies with primary diffuse photoreceptor involvement are classified separately from those with predominantly macular involvement, for which the symptoms and prognoses generally differ. Further distinction is made within the diffuse photoreceptor dystrophy category by separating rod-dominant from cone-dominant syndromes. The choroidal and vitreoretinal dystrophies are separated for ease in clinical description.

Brown J, Webster AR, Sheffield VC, Stone EM. Molecular genetics of retinal disease. In: Ryan SJ, Hinton DR, Schachat AP, Wilkinson CP, eds. *Retina.* Vol 1. 4th ed. Philadelphia: Elsevier/Mosby; 2006:373–392.

Heckenlively JR, Daiger SP. Hereditary retinal and choroidal degenerations. In: Rimoin DL, Connor JM, Pyeritz RE, Korf BR, eds. *Emery and Rimoin's Principles and Practice of Medical Genetics.* 3 vols. 5th ed. Philadelphia: Churchill Livingstone; 2007:chap 137.

McKusick-Nathans Institute of Genetic Medicine, Johns Hopkins University School of Medicine. Online Mendelian Inheritance in Man website. Available at http://www.omim.org. Updated daily. Accessed August 9, 2011.

Sieving PA. Retinitis pigmentosa and related disorders. In: Yanoff M, Duker JS, eds. *Ophthalmology.* 2nd ed. St Louis: Mosby; 2004:813–823.

The University of Texas–Houston Health Science Center. RetNet, the Retinal Information Network website. Available at http://www.sph.uth.tmc.edu/Retnet. Accessed August 9, 2011.

Weleber RG, Gregory-Evans K. Retinitis pigmentosa and allied disorders. In: Ryan SJ, Hinton DR, Schachat AP, Wilkinson CP, eds. *Retina.* Vol 1. 4th ed. Philadelphia: Elsevier/Mosby; 2006:395–498.

Diagnostic and Prognostic Testing

Although a number of tests are helpful in classifying the hereditary retinal and choroidal degenerations, the electroretinogram (ERG) and kinetic visual field examinations have proved the most useful. The ERG is an evoked response test in which a signal generated by the retina in response to a flash of light is recorded by a contact lens or foil electrode on the surface of the eye (see Chapter 3 for further description of the ERG). Certain components of the ERG response are lost or altered depending on the disease and severity of involvement. Comparison of the cone-isolated, rod-isolated, and mixed-cone-and-rod responses shows the diagnostic patterns commonly observed in hereditary retinal diseases (Table 11-1). Results from kinetic (Goldmann) visual field testing are needed for correct interpretation of ERG testing results, particularly for patients with a cone-predominant (cone–rod) loss, as in RP, cone–rod dystrophy, Stargardt disease, and even postinflammatory states.

Diffuse Photoreceptor Dystrophies

Panretinal degeneration is associated with numerous hereditary retinal conditions, most of which are forms of RP. The ERG pattern of loss can be rod-predominant (rod–cone) or cone-predominant (cone–rod); in more advanced cases, the ERG signal may be extinguished.

As noted, *kinetic visual field testing* is needed to further characterize the diagnosis and assess the patient's level of function. Rod–cone RP degenerations show contracted fields, with smaller isopters demonstrating higher thresholds of sensitivity and leaving large spaces between smaller and larger isopters. Partial- to full-ring scotomata are common in midequatorial regions but eventually melt into peripheral isopters, in many cases leaving only a small central island of visual field (Fig 11-1). In cone–rod RP degenerations, isopters contract over time, but they tend to be close to each other (like onion rings), and ring scotomata are closer to fixation. In contrast, patients with primary cone degenerations and (non-RP) cone–rod dystrophies maintain full isopters, although central scotomata are common. Patients with early cone–rod degeneration may need repeated kinetic field testing over time to determine if the field is stable or contracting.

Retinitis Pigmentosa

Pigmentary retinopathy is a general term for a panretinal disturbance of the RPE and retina. Because of the heterogeneity of the pigmentary retinopathies, an overall definition was established by RP specialists in 1984. *Retinitis pigmentosa* was defined as a group of hereditary disorders that diffusely involve photoreceptor and pigment epithelial function

Table 11-1 Basic Guide to Interpreting the Standardized Electroretinogram (ERG)

ERG Finding	Disease or Condition
Nonrecordable ERG	Leber congenital amaurosis
	Retinal aplasia
	Retinitis pigmentosa (RP)
	Total retinal detachment
Abnormal or nonrecordable photopic ERG	
Often mild rod ERG abnormalities	Cone degenerations
	Achromatopsia
	X-linked blue-cone monochromatism
	X-linked cone dystrophy with tapetallike sheen
Nonrecordable rod ERG	
Abnormal dark-adapted bright-flash ERG	
Normal to near-normal photopic ERG	Congenital stationary night blindness
	Early RP (rare), which is progressive
Barely or nonrecordable scotopic ERG	
Abnormal photopic b-wave ERG	Rod–cone degenerations (RP)
	Leber congenital amaurosis
	Choroideremia
	Chorioretinitis (variable)
	Secondary RP, including some storage diseases
	Progressive retinitis punctata albescens
Abnormal cone and rod b-wave amplitudes	
Cones relatively more affected than the rods	Cone–rod degenerations/dystrophies
	Autosomal dominant
	Autosomal recessive
	X-linked recessive
	Postinflammatory degenerations
Negative waveforms: In the dark-adapted bright-flash ERG, the a-wave is normal to attenuated, but the b-wave does not return to the isoelectric point.	X-linked retinoschisis
	Congenital stationary night blindness
	Enhanced S-cone syndrome (Goldmann-Favre syndrome)
	Some autoimmune retinopathies
Nonspecific abnormalities	Metallic foreign bodies
	Chorioretinitis (acute or old)
	Early panretinal degeneration
	Partial retinal vascular occlusion
	Low serum taurine levels
	Vasculitis/diabetic retinopathy

Based on a table in: Rimoin DL, Connor JM, Pyeritz RE, Korf BR, eds. *Emery and Rimoin's Principles and Practice of Medical Genetics*. 3 vols. 4th ed. New York: Churchill Livingstone; 2002:chap 124. Copyright © 2001, with permission from Elsevier.

characterized by progressive visual field loss and abnormal ERG responses. The pigmentary retinopathies can be divided into 2 large groups:

1. *primary RP*, in which the disease process is confined to the eyes, with no other systemic manifestations
2. *secondary pigmentary retinopathy*, in which the retinal degeneration is associated with single or multiple organ system disease. Secondary forms of pigmentary retinopathy are reviewed in Chapter 12.

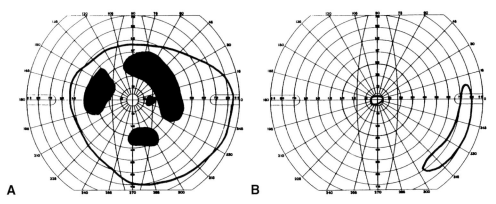

Figure 11-1 Examples of visual fields in RP using a Goldmann III-4 test object. **A,** Early disease: midperipheral scotomata. **B,** Late disease: severe loss, sparing only a central tunnel and far-peripheral island, which may eventually disappear. *(Courtesy of Michael F. Marmor, MD.)*

Clinical features and diagnosis

Typical fundus findings in RP include arteriolar narrowing, variable waxy pallor of the disc, and variable amounts of bone spicule–like pigment changes (Fig 11-2). The peripheral retina and RPE appear atrophic even if spicules are absent *(RP sine pigmento),* and the macula typically shows a loss of the foveal reflex and irregularity of the vitreoretinal interface. Cystoid macular edema (CME) is occasionally present. Vitreous cells and

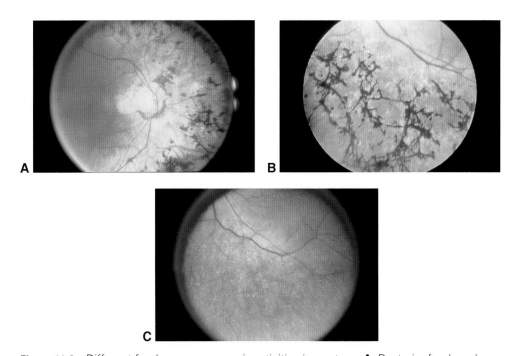

Figure 11-2 Different fundus appearances in retinitis pigmentosa. **A,** Posterior fundus, showing waxy disc pallor, vascular attenuation, and a dull macula. **B,** Fundus with dense, peripheral, bone spicule–like changes. **C,** Fundus featuring peripheral atrophy but virtually no spicules. *(Parts A and C courtesy of Michael F. Marmor, MD; Part B courtesy of Carl D. Regillo, MD.)*

posterior subcapsular cataracts are also commonly observed, although in most patients the cataracts are small and not the main cause of vision loss.

Several RP types have distinctive phenotypes, such as the deep retinal white dots or flecks in *retinitis punctata albescens* (Fig 11-3), choriocapillaris atrophy in choroideremia, macular RPE atrophy in *RDS/peripherin* mutations, or the preserved para-arteriolar RPE in the phenotype *RP12*. Distinctive phenotypes are the exception, however, and most RP cases have diffuse pigment epithelial changes that are secondary effects of the diffuse photoreceptor dysfunction.

For patients newly suspected of having RP, the ERG, in combination with kinetic visual field testing, provides important diagnostic and prognostic information, as previously noted. The ERG in RP typically shows a loss or marked reduction of both rod and cone signals, although rod loss usually predominates. Both a- and b-waves are reduced because the photoreceptors are primarily involved. The b-waves are characteristically prolonged in time as well as diminished in amplitude. The carrier state of X-linked recessive RP often shows a mild reduction or delay in the b-wave responses.

Late in the course of many types of RP, the ERG responses become undetectable with conventional testing. A very small signal can still be recognized in most of these cases by summating a large number of responses, but this procedure is not done routinely in most clinics. An "undetectable" ERG is not diagnostic of RP but simply documents severe retinal degeneration.

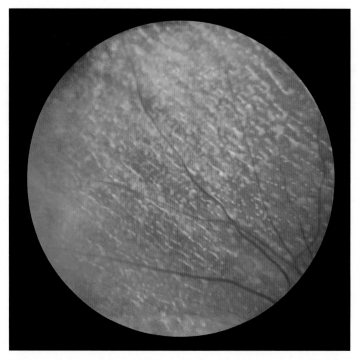

Figure 11-3 Fundus of a patient with retinitis punctata albescens, showing numerous deep retinal white dots. *(Courtesy of John R. Heckenlively, MD.)*

When evaluating suspected RP in a patient with a negative family history (simplex RP), the clinician must consider acquired causes of retinal degeneration that can mimic RP, including previous ophthalmic artery occlusion, diffuse uveitis, infections such as syphilis, paraneoplastic syndromes, and retinal drug toxicity. Secondary forms of pigmentary retinopathy associated with metabolic or other organ system disease must also be considered (see Chapter 12). The differential diagnosis of RP is important because the prognostic implications of the disease are serious, and an error in diagnosis can be devastating in terms of psychological impact or failure to recognize a treatable entity. The clinician should take a careful history from any new patient and consider evaluating for other conditions by tests or nonocular examination.

Heckenlively JR, Yoser SL, Friedman LH, Oversier JJ. Clinical findings and common symptoms in retinitis pigmentosa. *Am J Ophthalmol.* 1988;105(5):504–511.

Sieving PA. Retinitis pigmentosa and related disorders. In: Yanoff M, Duker JS, eds. *Ophthalmology.* 2nd ed. St Louis: Mosby; 2003:813–823.

Weleber RG, Gregory-Evans K. Retinitis pigmentosa and allied disorders. In: Ryan SJ, Hinton DR, Schachat AP, Wilkinson CP, eds. *Retina.* Vol 1. 4th ed. Philadelphia: Elsevier/Mosby; 2006:395–498.

Regional variants of retinitis pigmentosa

Several variants of RP present with unusual or regional distribution of the retinal degeneration. Many of these cases show an unusually sharp demarcation between affected and unaffected areas of the retina, in contrast to the diffuse damage of more typical RP (Fig 11-4). It is important to recognize these forms because some are either nonprogressive or very slowly progressive.

Sectorial RP refers to disease involving only 1 or 2 sectors of the fundus (see Fig 11-4B). The condition is generally symmetric in the 2 eyes, which helps rule out acquired damage (eg, from trauma, vascular insult, or inflammation). Sectorial disease probably comprises a variety of genetic entities, which may account for confusion in the literature about whether sectorial RP is stationary or slowly progressive. Unquestionably, some cases do progress slowly, and all patients should therefore be followed up at intervals of 1–2 years.

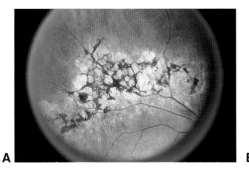 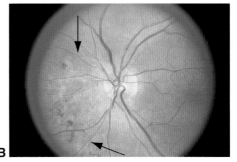

A **B**

Figure 11-4 Delimited forms of RP. Note the sharp demarcation between the areas of degeneration and other regions of the fundus that appear quite healthy. **A,** Fundus with degenerative changes near the arcades. **B,** Fundus with sectorial RP *(between arrows),* showing vascular narrowing and spicules only in the inferonasal quadrant. *(Courtesy of Michael F. Marmor, MD.)*

Carriers of X-linked RP can have fundus findings that appear as a sectorial pigmentary retinopathy. Because there is evidence that the sectorial loss is related to light toxicity in many patients with rhodopsin mutations, UV-light protection and antioxidant vitamins are reasonable recommendations for regional disease.

Some patients with RP-like disease present with macular involvement or markedly reduced acuity very early in the course of disease, which is unusual for RP. Field loss may progress outward from the center rather than inward *(central RP)*. Other patients show a tight ring scotoma within the central 20° or 30° *(pericentral RP)*. This group of regional variants is probably heterogeneous because most of the cases appear sporadic and few are well characterized clinically or genetically.

Unilateral RP is a rare disorder that is usually sporadic. In authentic cases, the clinical presentation and findings in the involved eye are similar to those of typical RP. However, the vast majority of unilateral pigmentary retinal degenerations are likely to have an acquired origin, such as a previous vascular occlusion, prior retinal detachment, trauma, uveitis, infection (such as diffuse unilateral subacute neuroretinitis), or retained metallic intraocular foreign body. To make a diagnosis of true unilateral RP, the clinician must rule out such secondary causes, document a normal ERG response in the unaffected eye, and monitor the patient for at least 5 years to rule out bilateral but highly asymmetric disease.

Weleber RG, Gregory-Evans K. Retinitis pigmentosa and allied disorders. In: Ryan SJ, Hinton DR, Schachat AP, Wilkinson CP, eds. *Retina.* Vol 1. 4th ed. Philadelphia: Elsevier/Mosby; 2006:395–498.

Genetic considerations

Currently, more than 100 different genetic types of RP (or similar degenerations) have been described, and more than 50 genes causing RP have been identified. A full list of mutations causing RP is available on the RetNet website; all inheritance patterns are represented. *Autosomal dominant RP (ADRP)* accounts for 10%–20% of RP cases, depending on the country surveyed. The first mutations discovered to cause RP were in the gene coding for rhodopsin, the visual pigment in rods that mediates night vision. The severity of disease resulting from rhodopsin mutations varies considerably. For example, mild disease (a form of stationary night blindness) is associated with codon 90 mutations, whereas severe forms are associated with mutations that interfere with the attachment of vitamin A to the rhodopsin protein. *RDS/peripherin* mutations have wide disease expression, ranging from RP to pattern macular dystrophies (eg, adult vitelliform dystrophy, butterfly dystrophy). Peripherin is a protein present in the peripheral aspect of the rod and cone photoreceptor discs, and the human peripherin gene has sequence homology with a gene in mice that causes a hereditary retinal degeneration.

Autosomal recessive RP (ARRP) represents about 20% of RP cases, although the percentage increases when the definition includes families with several affected siblings *(multiplex RP)* or consanguinity of parents. *X-linked RP (XLRP)* accounts for about 10% of RP in the United States and up to 25% in England. This number excludes choroideremia, an X-linked, childhood-onset, rod–cone dystrophy, which has visual field loss like that of typical RP.

Up to 40% of cases presenting in the United States have no family history. Most are generally assumed to represent ARRP, although undoubtedly a few are autosomal dominant with reduced penetrance or X-linked recessive, in which the last affected male was several generations past. Rare cases of mitochondrial and X-linked dominant inheritance have been reported in RP (see RetNet website).

Berger W, Kloeckener-Gruissem B, Neidhardt J. The molecular basis of human retinal and vitreoretinal diseases. *Prog Retin Eye Res.* 2010;29(5):335–375.

The University of Texas–Houston Health Science Center. RetNet, the Retinal Information Network website. Available at http://www.sph.uth.tmc.edu/Retnet. Accessed August 9, 2011.

Leber congenital amaurosis

The infantile to early childhood forms of RP have been termed *Leber congenital amaurosis (LCA),* for which there are 9 known causative mutations. Most cases have an autosomal recessive inheritance pattern. LCA is typically characterized by severely reduced vision from birth associated with wandering nystagmus and undetectable or severely impaired ERG responses from both cones and rods. In the early stages, there are seldom obvious fundus changes. Later, round subretinal black pigment clumps develop in many patients, although some cases show bone spicule–like pigment changes. Visual function can range from 20/200 vision to no light perception. Some patients with LCA have been observed to rub or poke their eyes (the *oculodigital reflex*), as do other infants with poor vision. Cataracts and keratoconus may be present in older children.

Most children with LCA have normal intelligence, and some of the psychomotor impairment that has been described may be secondary to sensory deprivation. The systemic disorders that mimic LCA include, among others, the various neuronal ceroid lipofuscinoses and peroxisome disorders (see Chapter 12). The clinician must also rule out other causes of infantile nystagmus, such as albinism, achromatopsia, and congenital stationary night blindness (CSNB).

Electrophysiologic testing is essential in establishing the proper diagnosis. The ERG response is typically minimal or undetectable, differentiating LCA from dystrophic diseases in which the ERG response diminishes with age and from syndromes with similar clinical presentation. One caveat is that because the normal ERG response can be small in the first few months of life, infants with apparently abnormal findings in that period should have the ERG repeated at a later time for confirmation.

den Hollander AI, Roepman R, Koenekoop RK, Crèmers FP. Leber congenital amaurosis: genes, proteins and disease mechanisms. *Prog Retin Eye Res.* 2008:27(4):391–419.

Management

Because of the rarity of these disorders, most ophthalmologists have limited experience working with retinal dystrophy patients. Patients with newly diagnosed RP are inevitably anxious about the possibility of blindness. For most patients, it is reassuring to undergo a complete evaluation by a specialist familiar with hereditary retinal degenerations. Once all the clinical, electrophysiologic, and psychophysical information is assembled, the correct diagnosis should be related to the patient, along with detailed information about the significance of the findings, inheritance pattern, prognosis, and possible treatments.

Popular misconceptions about RP should be dispelled by the ophthalmologist. It is not unusual for RP patients to fear they will be blind within 1 year, when in fact the disease is a chronic degenerative problem, and the majority of patients do very well for decades. Total blindness is an infrequent endpoint, and estimates of prognosis must be individualized according to the clinical findings. Some RP patients believe they should not have children; however, careful scrutiny of most pedigrees shows that offspring are not at immediate risk unless the patient has autosomal dominant disease. Unless an ophthalmologist is very familiar with inheritance patterns, a genetic counselor should assist in genetic counseling of patients. The risk of deafness may be a concern to some patients, but most of the deafness in Usher syndrome is congenital; RP patients who are not born deaf will not ordinarily develop hearing loss later.

Management of RP includes ophthalmic evaluations every 1–2 years. Regular follow-up is important from a research point of view and may help identify the inheritance type in cases for which the family history is incomplete. Although the death of photoreceptor cells in RP cannot at present be arrested or reversed, frequent monitoring allows the clinician to check for progression of visual field effects and ERG responses. It also provides an opportunity to inform patients about new research developments and ensures timely recognition of refractive errors or vision-threatening but treatable complications. For example, cataracts that reduce vision can be extracted, and treatment with intraocular lenses gives RP patients the broadest possible visual field. CME is present in a small percentage of RP patients, but when significant, it may respond to oral or topical carbonic anhydrase inhibitors such as acetazolamide or dorzolamide, respectively (Fig 11-5). CME that is nonresponsive to acetazolamide often shows anatomical resolution after intravitreal injection of triamcinolone acetonide, but the associated visual improvement is variable and recurrences are common.

Many RP patients benefit from counseling to adjust to narrowed visual fields and reduced night vision. Low vision aids frequently help those with subnormal visual acuity. Patients with advanced disease may need vocational rehabilitation and mobility training.

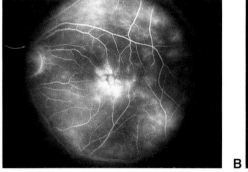 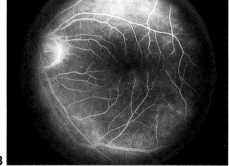

A **B**

Figure 11-5 Cystoid macular edema responsive to treatment in RP. **A,** Dye leakage shown on fluorescein angiography. **B,** Same patient after 2 weeks of oral acetazolamide. *(Courtesy of Michael F. Marmor, MD.)*

Although many patients maintain reasonable central vision for years, some are legally blind (visual field <20°) and may qualify for government disability benefits. Ophthalmologists may refer patients whose visual function could be aided or enhanced by visual rehabilitation to information from the American Academy of Ophthalmology SmartSight website (http://one.aao.org/CE/EducationalContent/Smartsight.aspx).

Various nutritional supplements have been investigated as therapy for RP, and one or more may prove to have merit. However, given the diverse biochemical bases of this disease, it seems unlikely that any one nutritional factor will prove highly beneficial to all RP patients. One large study concluded that high daily doses of vitamin A palmitate (15,000 IU/day) can slow the decline in ERG response in RP by about 20% per year. However, the use of this treatment must be weighed against the unknown risk of long-term adverse effects, especially liver toxicity. Because of the teratogenicity of vitamin A, high doses should not be used by women who might become pregnant. Another nutritional supplement studied for patients with RP is docosahexaenoic acid (DHA), an omega-3 fatty acid found in oily fish and thought to be important for photoreceptor function. Results from 2 clinical trials of DHA supplements for patients with RP failed to show a clear treatment benefit. However, both studies found that patients with the highest concentrations of DHA in red blood cells had the lowest rates of retinal degeneration. In addition, although an earlier clinical trial suggested a possible harmful effect of high-dose vitamin E, increasing laboratory and clinical evidence suggests that an antioxidant mix might benefit RP patients. At present, no conclusive epidemiologic or clinical trial data clarify the role of antioxidant supplements in the treatment of RP.

Light is considered by some to be a source of stress and age-related retinal damage, as well as a possible accelerator of dystrophic injury. Phototoxicity likely plays a role, in particular, in retinal degenerations caused by rhodopsin mutations. No direct evidence demonstrates that light modifies RP, however, and a study in which patients had 1 eye covered with an opaque contact lens failed to show any change in disease progression over time compared with the fellow eye. Nonetheless, prudent advice for dystrophy patients includes protection from high levels of light exposure, as occurs at the beach or in snow, through use of UV-absorbing sunglasses and brimmed hats.

Molecular genetics may someday provide a means for modifying the course of RP. As the genes associated with each type of RP are identified and their functions elucidated, it may become possible in some cases to replace or regulate them or to use the genetic information to employ conventional therapy more effectively. Progress is also being made in transplantation of retinal cells and the use of humoral factors to slow secondary degenerative changes.

Berson EL, Rosner B, Sandberg MA, et al. A randomized trial of vitamin A and vitamin E supplementation for retinitis pigmentosa. *Arch Ophthalmol.* 1993;111(6):761–772.

Fishman GA, Gilbert LD, Fiscella RG, Kimura AE, Jampol LM. Acetazolamide for treatment of chronic macular edema in retinitis pigmentosa. *Arch Ophthalmol.* 1989;107(10):1445–1452.

Genead MA, Fishman GA. Efficacy of sustained topical dorzolamide therapy for cystic macular lesions in patients with retinitis pigmentosa and Usher syndrome. *Arch Ophthalmol.* 2010;128(9):1146–1150.

Hartong DT, Berson EL, Dryja TP. Retinitis pigmentosa. *Lancet.* 2006;368(9549):1795–1809.

Ozdemir H, Karacorlu M, Karacorlu S. Intravitreal triamcinolone acetonide for treatment of cystoid macular oedema in patients with retinitis pigmentosa. *Acta Ophthalmol Scand.* 2005;83(2):248–251.

Sanz MM, Johnson LE, Ahuja S, Ekström PA, Romero J, van Veen T. Significant photoreceptor rescue by treatment with a combination of antioxidants in an animal model for retinal degeneration. *Neuroscience.* 2007;145(3):1120–1129.

Cone Dystrophies

The cone dystrophies should not be confused with congenital color blindness, in which there are color deficits for specific colors but no associated retinal degeneration. Patients with congenital color blindness (protanopia, deuteranopia, and tritanopia) have normal visual acuity and do not show signs of progressive disease. Congenital color deficiency and other congenital stationary cone dysfunction syndromes, including rod monochromatism and blue-cone monochromatism, are discussed in Chapter 10.

The progressive cone dystrophies represent a heterogeneous group of diseases with onset in the teenage or later adult years. In many patients, secondary rod photoreceptor involvement also develops in later life, leading to considerable overlap between progressive cone and cone–rod dystrophies. Cone dystrophies are diagnosed by an abnormal or nonrecordable photopic ERG response and a normal or near-normal rod-isolated ERG response. Peripheral visual fields remain normal. A subset of patients has been described for whom the full-field ERG appears normal, and involvement of only the foveal or central cones has been documented. All 3 mendelian inheritance patterns have been found associated with cone dystrophies. Kinetic visual field testing will help differentiate cone dystrophy from RP cone–rod patterns or cone–rod dystrophy, although in early cases, repeated perimetry testing over several years will help ensure the peripheral fields are stable.

The diagnosis of cone dystrophy is suggested by the progressive loss of visual acuity and color discrimination, often accompanied by hemeralopia (day blindness) and photophobia (light intolerance). Ophthalmoscopy may show a symmetric bull's-eye pattern of macular atrophy (Fig 11-6) or more severe atrophy, such as demarcated circular macular lesions. Mild to severe temporal optic atrophy and tapetal retinal reflexes (glistening greenish or golden sheen) may also be present. Patients with cone dystrophies may have fundi that appear normal, especially early in the course of their disease, and may be mistaken for malingering. Maintaining a high index of suspicion for this entity is important for patients with unexplained vision loss. Dark sunglasses or miotics may help reduce photophobia in some patients with cone dystrophies. Many patients also benefit from low vision aids such as magnifiers, closed-circuit television devices, and software for computer screen text enlargement.

Thus far, mutations causing progressive cone and cone–rod dystrophies have been described in 12 genes. Dominant cone dystrophy linked to 6p21.1 is caused by mutations in the *GUCA1A* gene, which codes for guanylate cyclase activator 1A, a calcium-binding protein expressed in photoreceptor outer segments. Mutations in *GUCY2D* at 17p13.1 were identified in a family with autosomal dominant progressive cone degeneration. Different mutations of both alleles in this same gene cause autosomal recessive LCA (see Ret-Net website). These patients exhibit foveal atrophy that may be misdiagnosed as Stargardt

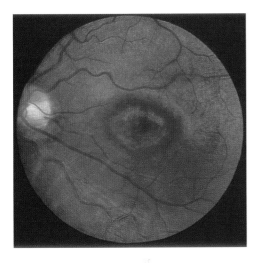

Figure 11-6 Cone dystrophy, showing bull's-eye pattern of central atrophy.

disease, but their ERG shows severely abnormal photopic responses, the scotopic response is maintained, and the Goldmann visual field is full. An adult-onset, X-linked recessive cone dystrophy with a tapetallike sheen (a bright greenish or golden fundus reflex) and Mizuo-Nakamura phenomenon (in which the fundus appearance changes with dark adaptation) has been reported in several pedigrees, but the affected gene has not yet been determined.

American Academy of Ophthalmology. SmartSight website. Available at http://one.aao.org/ CE/EducationalContent/Smartsight.aspx. Accessed August 10, 2011.

Michaelides M, Hardcastle AJ, Hunt DM, Moore AT. Progressive cone and cone-rod dystrophies: phenotypes and underlying molecular genetic basis. *Surv Ophthalmol.* 2006;51(3):232–258.

Nathans J. The evolution and physiology of human color vision: insights from molecular genetic studies of visual pigments. *Neuron.* 1999;24(2):299–312.

Cone–Rod Dystrophies

The term *cone–rod* comes from electroretinographic testing, in which the cone-isolated ERG waveform is proportionately worse than the rod-isolated signal, and both are abnormal. Numerous entities can yield this ERG pattern, from prior inflammatory damage to well-established genetic diseases such as Stargardt disease. Molecular genetics helps differentiate the specific causes among this group. In the past few years, it has become apparent that some of the mutations that result in the severe phenotype of Leber congenital amaurosis will cause a cone–rod dystrophy if there is a different mutation in the same gene or if there is a mutation in only 1 allele. A list of currently known genetic causes of cone–rod dystrophy is available through the RetNet website. Important genes in which mutations are associated with cone–rod degenerations are those for Stargardt disease *(ABCA4)*, Alström disease *(ALMS1)*, and dominant spinocerebellar ataxia *(SCA7)*. Dominant cone–rod dystrophy may result from mutations in *GUCY2D*, whereas recessive mutations cause LCA. Similarly, various mutations in the *CRX* gene can cause RP, LCA, or cone–rod dystrophy.

Patients with progressive cone–rod dystrophy demonstrate expanding central scotomata over time, and severe visual disability may develop to the point that mobility training is necessary. Ophthalmoscopy at later stages may show bone spicule–like (intraretinal) hyperpigmentation and atrophy in the fundus periphery, and patients may report night blindness, poor central acuity, and symptoms of dyschromatopsia. There is a wide variety of expression in this group of disorders, and patients must be monitored over time to determine the disease course.

Hamel CP. Cone rod dystrophies. *Orphanet J Rare Dis.* 2007;2:7–14.

Michaelides M, Hardcastle AJ, Hunt DM, Moore AT. Progressive cone and cone-rod dystrophies: phenotypes and underlying molecular genetic basis. *Surv Ophthalmol.* 2006;51:232–258.

Macular Dystrophies

The macular dystrophies can be difficult to manage. The differential diagnosis is sometimes challenging, and several of the conditions cause legal blindness at a relatively young age. The pathophysiologic processes that result in vision loss in these diseases cannot currently be arrested or reversed, yet patients can be reassured that the disease progresses slowly and they will retain some useful vision. Patients also need proper refraction and education in the use of an Amsler grid to detect symptoms of a complicating choroidal neovascular membrane. In addition, patients may benefit from referral to a low vision specialist. Children with 20/100 or 20/200 vision usually do very well in regular schools, especially if the ophthalmologist is able to communicate with the teacher about the child's visual abilities and limitations.

Stargardt Disease

Stargardt disease, or fundus flavimaculatus, is the most common juvenile macular dystrophy and a common cause of central vision loss in adults under 50 years old. The vast majority of cases are autosomal recessive, but some dominant pedigrees have been reported. Most cases of Stargardt disease are caused by mutations in the *ABCA4* gene, which encodes an ATP-binding cassette (ABC) transporter protein expressed by rod outer segments. Other, less frequent, causes of the phenotype include mutations in the dominant genes *STGD4* and *ELOVL4* (which encodes a photoreceptor-specific component of the fatty acid elongation system) and mutations in the *RDS/peripherin* gene.

The classic Stargardt phenotype is characterized by a juvenile-onset foveal atrophy surrounded by discrete, yellowish, round or pisciform flecks at the level of the RPE (Fig 11-7). If the flecks are widely scattered throughout the fundus, the condition is commonly referred to as *fundus flavimaculatus*. A clinical diagnosis of Stargardt disease is confirmed by the finding of a "dark choroid" with fluorescein angiography. This phenomenon, in which the retinal circulation is highlighted against a hypofluorescent choroid, is present in at least 80% of patients with the disorder (Fig 11-8). Although the absence of this sign does not rule out Stargardt disease, its presence is quite specific for the disease. The dark choroid sign is believed to represent masking of choroidal fluorescence by an

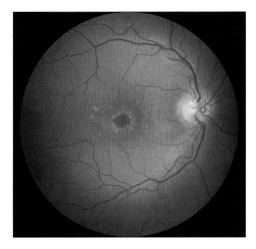

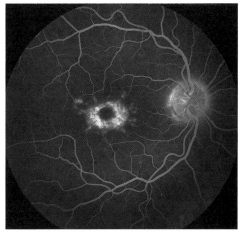

Figure 11-7 Stargardt disease, showing paramacular yellow flecks and "beaten-bronze" central macular atrophy. *(Courtesy of Mark W. Johnson, MD.)*

Figure 11-8 Fluorescein angiogram of the eye from Figure 11-7, showing a dark choroid, hyperfluorescence associated with flecks, and bull's-eye pattern of macular transmission defect. *(Courtesy of Mark W. Johnson, MD.)*

accumulation of lipofuscinlike pigment throughout the RPE (Fig 11-9). The numerous hyperfluorescent lesions observed on angiograms of patients with flecks appear to represent transmission defects around the flecks.

The age of onset and presenting clinical features in Stargardt disease are quite variable, sometimes even among individuals within the same family. A patient may present with vision loss and any combination of the clinical triad of macular atrophy, flecks, and a dark choroid. Signs not present on initial presentation may develop later in the course of the disorder. Although in most patients the condition is slowly progressive, the expressivity can range from mild to a progressive cone–rod dystrophy in which there is an expanding central scotoma over time. Peripheral degenerative changes are severe in occasional cases and associated with progressive visual field changes and loss of ERG response. The differential diagnosis of Stargardt disease includes conditions that may cause a bull's-eye atrophic maculopathy (Table 11-2). Although confirmatory molecular testing

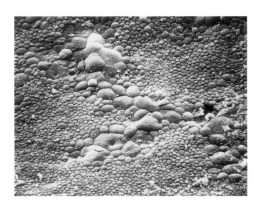

Figure 11-9 Scanning electron micrograph of the RPE in Stargardt disease. The flecks represent regions of RPE cells engorged with abnormal lipofuscinlike material. *(Reproduced with permission from Eagle RC Jr, Lucier AC, Bernardino VB Jr, Yanoff M. Retinal pigment epithelial abnormalities in fundus flavimaculatus: a light and electron microscopic study. Ophthalmology. 1980;87(12):1189–200.)*

Table 11-2 Differential Diagnosis of Bull's-Eye Maculopathy

Stargardt disease
Cone and cone–rod dystrophies
Chloroquine retinal toxicity
Age-related macular degeneration
Chronic macular hole
Central areolar choroidal dystrophy
Olivopontocerebellar atrophy
Ceroid lipofuscinosis

---

may become more available in the future, the gene is very large (52 exons), and sequencing techniques currently are not practical for mass screening.

The visual acuity in Stargardt disease typically ranges from 20/50 to 20/200. Most patients retain fair acuity (eg, 20/70–20/100) in at least 1 eye. Although no medical treatment is available for this condition, low vision therapy referral is usually quite helpful for these patients, and protection from exposure to bright sunlight is prudent.

American Academy of Ophthalmology. SmartSight website. Available at http://one.aao.org/CE/EducationalContent/Smartsight.aspx. Accessed August 10, 2011.

Koenekoop RK, Lopez I, den Hollander AI, Allikmets R, Cremers FP. Genetic testing for retinal dystrophies and dysfunctions: benefits, dilemmas and solutions. *Clin Experiment Ophthalmol.* 2007;35(5):473–485.

Lois N, Holder GE, Bunce C, Fitzke FW, Bird AC. Phenotypic subtypes of Stargardt macular dystrophy–fundus flavimaculatus. *Arch Ophthalmol.* 2001;119(3):359–369.

Walia S, Fishman GA. Natural history of phenotypic changes in Stargardt macular dystrophy. *Ophthalmic Genet.* 2009;30(2):63–68.

Vitelliform Degenerations

Best disease, or Best vitelliform dystrophy

Best disease is an autosomal dominant maculopathy caused by mutations in the *Best1* (or *VMD2*) gene, which is located on the long arm of chromosome 11 and encodes the protein *bestrophin*. This protein localizes to the basolateral plasma membrane of the RPE and functions as a novel, transmembrane chloride channel (see RetNet website). The resulting lipofuscin accumulation may be secondary to abnormal ion flux.

Affected individuals frequently show a yellow, yolklike (vitelliform) macular lesion in childhood, which eventually breaks down, leaving a mottled geographic atrophic appearance (Fig 11-10). Late in the disease, the geographic atrophy may be difficult to distinguish from other types of macular degeneration or dystrophy. Some patients—up to 30% in some series—have extrafoveal vitelliform lesions in the fundus. However, the macular appearance in all stages is deceptive, as most patients maintain relatively good vision throughout the course of the disease. Even patients with the "scrambled egg" stage of the maculopathy typically have 20/30 acuity. In approximately 20% of patients, a choroidal neovascular membrane will develop in 1 eye during the course of the disease; although usually self-limited, it frequently leaves the patient with 20/200 vision. Consideration can

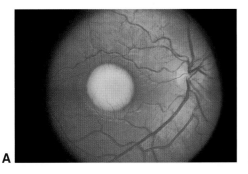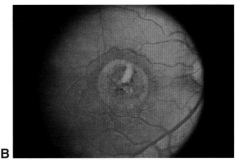

A **B**

Figure 11-10 Best vitelliform dystrophy. **A,** Characteristic yolk stage, during which acuity is typically good. **B,** Atrophy and scarring after the yolk breaks down. *(Courtesy of Mark W. Johnson, MD.)*

be given to treating choroidal neovascular membranes with vascular endothelial growth factor inhibitors. The vision prognosis generally is guarded but optimistic in this group of patients. Parents should be counseled that affected children may retain useful vision but that some vision aids may be required to improve function.

The ERG response is characteristically normal and the electro-oculogram (EOG) result is always abnormal, showing a severe loss of the light response. The Arden ratio (ie, the light peak–dark baseline standing potential ratio) is typically less than 1.5 and often near 1.1 (see Chapter 3). The EOG abnormality is always present in Best disease and serves as a marker for the disease, even in individuals who are asymptomatic with normal fundi. Because of its specificity for Best disease, the EOG may be useful in evaluating poorly defined central macular lesions.

Boon CJ, Klevering BJ, Leroy BP, Hoyng CB, Keunen JE, den Hollander AI. The spectrum of ocular phenotypes caused by mutations in the BEST1 gene. *Prog Retin Eye Res.* 2009;28(3):187–205.

Fishman GA, Baca W, Alexander KR, Derlacki DJ, Glenn AM, Viana M. Visual acuity in patients with Best vitelliform macular dystrophy. *Ophthalmology.* 1993;100(11):1665–1670.

Gass JDM. *Stereoscopic Atlas of Macular Disease: Diagnosis and Treatment.* 4th ed. St Louis: Mosby; 1997:304–313.

Petrukhin K, Koisti MJ, Bakall B, et al. Identification of the gene responsible for Best macular dystrophy. *Nat Genet.* 1998;19(3):241–247.

Adult-onset vitelliform lesions

Several types of symmetric yellow deposits that resemble Best disease may develop in the macula of older adults. The most common disorder, *adult-onset foveomacular vitelliform dystrophy,* is one of the *pattern dystrophies* (discussed later in this chapter), which are usually caused by mutations in the *RDS/peripherin* gene. Adult vitelliform pattern dystrophy is characterized by yellow subfoveal lesions that are bilateral, round or oval, typically one-third disc diameter in size, and often contain a central pigmented spot (Fig 11-11). Occasionally, the lesions may be larger and misdiagnosed as Best disease or even as age-related macular degeneration. This dystrophy generally appears in the fourth to sixth decades in patients who are either visually asymptomatic or have mild blurring and metamorphopsia. Eventually, the lesions may fade, leaving an area of RPE atrophy, but most patients

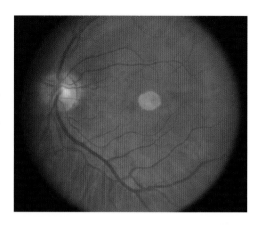

Figure 11-11 Adult vitelliform pattern dystrophy. Note the characteristic small, yellow, round subfoveal lesion. *(Courtesy of Mark W. Johnson, MD.)*

retain reading vision in at least 1 eye throughout their lives. The EOG in these individuals tends to be normal or only mildly subnormal. Autosomal dominant inheritance has been recognized in some families.

Patients with numerous basal laminar (cuticular) drusen may develop an unusual *vitelliform exudative macular detachment* (Fig 11-12). The yellowish subretinal fluid blocks background fluorescence early, often stains late in the angiogram study, and may be mistaken for choroidal neovascularization. Patients with yellowish macular detachments often maintain good visual acuity for many months but may eventually lose central vision because of geographic atrophy or choroidal neovascularization and disciform scarring.

In some patients with large, soft drusen, there is a large, central coalescence of drusen, or *drusenoid RPE detachment,* which may occasionally mimic a macular vitelliform lesion (Fig 11-13). Such lesions often have pigment mottling on their surface and are surrounded by numerous other individual or confluent soft drusen. They may remain stable (and allow for good vision) for many years, but eventually they tend to flatten and evolve into geographic atrophy.

Gass JD, Jallow S, Davis B. Adult vitelliform macular detachment occurring in patients with basal laminar drusen. *Am J Ophthalmol.* 1985;99(4):445–459.

Lim JI, Enger C, Fine SL. Foveomacular dystrophy. *Am J Ophthalmol.* 1994;117:1–6.

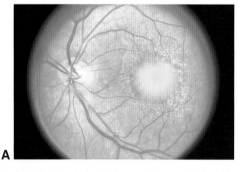
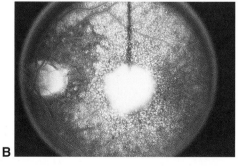

A **B**

Figure 11-12 A, Vitelliform lesion in the setting of numerous cuticular (basal laminar) drusen. **B,** Corresponding late-phase fluorescein angiogram shows staining of drusen and vitelliform lesion. *(Courtesy of Michael F. Marmor, MD.)*

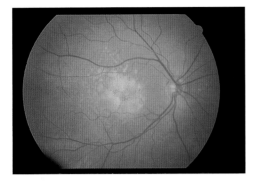

Figure 11-13 Central coalescence of large drusen simulates macular vitelliform lesion. *(Courtesy of Mark W. Johnson, MD.)*

Familial (Dominant) Drusen

Familial drusen typically manifest at younger ages than those in most cases of age-related macular degeneration; it is not uncommon, for example, for affected patients to exhibit drusen in their 20s. In young patients, drusen are usually numerous and of varying size, typically extending beyond the vascular arcades and nasal to the optic disc (Fig 11-14). Although presumed to be genetically determined, the inheritance pattern in the vast majority of young patients with drusen is never established. In well-described pedigrees, the inheritance pattern has been autosomal dominant. The clinical entities that are well documented in the literature are *Doyne honeycomb dystrophy* and *Malattia Leventinese*. Both forms are caused by mutations in the *EFEMP1* gene, which is located on chromosome 2 and codes for an epidermal growth factor (EGF)-containing, fibrillinlike, extracellular matrix protein. The phenotype is distinctive because the drusen develop in a radiating pattern from the fovea. The many phenotypic variations of drusen suggest the likelihood that several genetic defects are capable of causing them. It may be relevant that drusenlike deposits are observed in some hereditary renal disorders that involve basement membrane abnormalities, such as Alport syndrome and membranoproliferative glomerulonephritis type II.

The clinical appearance of familial drusen is variable, ranging from a few large, coarse lesions to numerous tiny dots sometimes called *basal laminar* or *cuticular drusen*. The cuticular drusen phenotype is highly associated with the Tyr402His variant of the

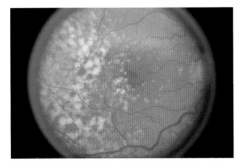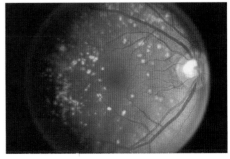

Figure 11-14 Different manifestations of dominant drusen. Variable size and distribution of the drusen are evident. *(Courtesy of Michael F. Marmor, MD.)*

complement factor H gene *(CFH)*. Fluorescein angiography often reveals more extensive drusen and RPE changes than ophthalmoscopy. The ERG and EOG results are typically normal. Central vision is good as long as the drusen are discrete and extrafoveal. However, patients with this phenotype may be at a greater than normal risk of macular degeneration as they age.

Grassi MA, Folk JC, Scheetz TE, Taylor CM, Sheffield VC, Stone EM. Complement factor H polymorphism p. Tyr402His and cuticular drusen. *Arch Ophthalmol.* 2007;125(1):93–97.

Heon E, Munier F, Willoughby C. Dominant drusen. In: Heckenlively JR, Arden GB, eds. *Principles and Practice of Clinical Electrophysiology of Vision.* 2nd ed. Cambridge, MA: MIT Press; 2006:717–725.

Kim DD, Mieler WF, Wolf MD. Posterior segment changes in membranoproliferative glomerulonephritis. *Am J Ophthalmol.* 1992;114(5):593–599.

Stone EM, Lotery AJ, Munier FL, et al. A single EFEMP1 mutation associated with both Malattia Leventinese and Doyne honeycomb retinal dystrophy. *Nat Genet.* 1999;22(2):199–202.

Pattern Dystrophies

The *pattern dystrophies* are a group of disorders characterized by the development, typically in midlife, of a variety of patterns of yellow, orange, or gray pigment deposition at the level of the RPE in the macular area. The inheritance is typically autosomal dominant. These dystrophies may be subdivided into at least 4 major patterns according to the distribution of pigment deposits: *adult-onset foveomacular vitelliform dystrophy* (discussed earlier in this chaper), *butterfly dystrophy* (Fig 11-15), *reticular dystrophy* (Fig 11-16), and *fundus pulverulentus* (coarse pigment mottling). The clinical pattern can vary among affected family members, or even between the 2 eyes of a patient, and it can evolve from one pattern to another over time. The overlapping ophthalmoscopic features of these patterns and their similar clinical implications suggest that they are either closely related or variable expressions of the same genetic defect. Most forms of autosomal dominant pattern dystrophy have been associated with mutations in the *RDS/peripherin* gene.

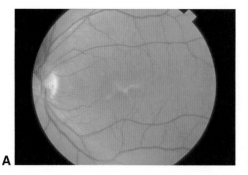
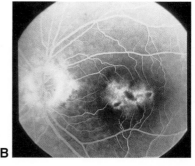

A **B**

Figure 11-15 Butterfly-type pattern dystrophy. **A,** A 56-year-old woman with a typical yellow macular pigment pattern. **B,** Fluorescein angiography shows blocked fluorescence of the pigment lesion itself and a rim of hyperfluorescence from surrounding retinal pigment epithelial atrophy. *(Reproduced with permission from Song M-K, Small KW. Macular dystrophies. In: Regillo CD, Brown GC, Flynn HW Jr, eds.* Vitreoretinal Disease: The Essentials. *New York: Thieme; 1999:297.)*

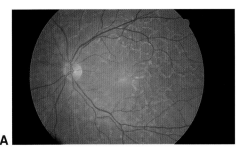
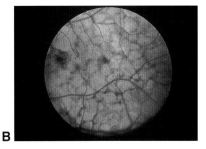

A   **B**

Figure 11-16 Two examples of reticular-type pattern dystrophy, characterized by a fishnet pattern of yellow-orange **(A)** or brown **(B)** pigment deposition in the posterior fundus. *(Courtesy of Mark W. Johnson, MD.)*

The most common presenting symptom of the pattern dystrophies is a slightly diminished visual acuity or mild metamorphopsia. However, patients are often asymptomatic and come to attention with the discovery of unusual macular lesions during routine ophthalmoscopy. Results of functional and electrophysiologic testing are generally normal except for a borderline or mildly reduced EOG consistent with a diffuse RPE disorder. These patients have a small risk of choroidal neovascularization developing later in life. Geographic macular atrophy may develop in patients over 60 years old and can eventually compromise central vision. Most patients retain reading vision in at least 1 eye through late adulthood.

Boon CJ, den Hollander AI, Hoyng CB, Crèmers FP, Klevering BJ, Keunen JE. The spectrum of retinal dystrophies caused by mutations in the peripherin/RDS gene. *Prog Retin Eye Res.* 2008;27(2):213–235.

Gass JDM. *Stereoscopic Atlas of Macular Disease: Diagnosis and Treatment.* 4th ed. St Louis: Mosby; 1997:314–325.

Marmor MF. The pattern dystrophies. In: Heckenlively JR, Arden GB, eds. *Principles and Practice of Clinical Electrophysiology of Vision.* 2nd ed. Cambridge, MA: MIT Press; 2006: 757–761.

Sorsby Macular Dystrophy

The characteristic feature of Sorsby macular dystrophy, a dominantly inherited disease, is the development, at the age of about 40 years, of bilateral subfoveal choroidal neovascular lesions (Fig 11-17). As the macular lesions evolve, they take on the appearance of geographic atrophy, with pronounced clumps of black pigmentation around the central ischemic and atrophic zone (a "pseudoinflammatory" appearance). An early sign of the disease is the presence of numerous, fine drusenlike deposits or a confluent plaque of faintly yellow material beneath the RPE of the posterior pole. Histologic specimens show a lipid-containing deposit between the basement membrane of the RPE and the inner collagenous layers of the Bruch membrane that may impede transport and contribute to the pathogenesis. The gene for Sorsby dystrophy, *TIMP3* (on chromosome 22), codes for a tissue inhibitor of metalloproteinase, which is involved in extracellular matrix remodeling.

Capon MR, Marshall J, Krafft JI, Alexander RA, Hiscott PS, Bird AC. Sorsby's fundus dystrophy. A light and electron microscopic study. *Ophthalmology.* 1989;96(12):1769–1777.

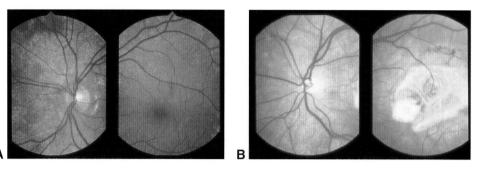

Figure 11-17 Sorsby macular dystrophy. **A,** Characteristic pale drusen. **B,** Late disciform scarring after the development of choroidal neovascularization. *(Courtesy of Alan Bird, MD.)*

Hamilton WK, Ewing CC, Ives EJ, Carruthers JD. Sorsby's fundus dystrophy. *Ophthalmology.* 1989;96(12):1755–1762.

Weber BH, Vogt G, Pruett RC, Stöhr H, Felbor U. Mutations in the tissue inhibitor of metalloproteinases-3 (TIMP3) in patients with Sorsby's fundus dystrophy. *Nat Genet.* 1994;8(4):352–356.

Choroidal Dystrophies

In a number of conditions, a primary retinal or RPE disease results in atrophy of the choriocapillaris. Historically, these conditions were named according to the clinically obvious choroidal involvement, but these names do not reflect current molecular knowledge.

Diffuse Degenerations

Choroideremia

Choroideremia, a hereditary chorioretinal dystrophy, was first identified as a separate entity from "typical" RP by Mauthner in 1871, who reported 2 male patients with pigmentary changes in the fundus, night blindness, and constricted visual fields. The features distinct from typical RP include marked atrophy of the choroid and RPE, normal retinal vessels, and absence of optic atrophy. Choroideremia is an X-linked recessive rod–cone dystrophy that otherwise meets the definition of RP: patients have night blindness and show progressive visual field loss typical of RP over 3 to 5 decades.

The disease is due to mutations in the *CHM* gene, which is located at Xq 21.2 and encodes for a geranylgeranyl transferase Rab escort protein. For many years, the key abnormality in choroideremia was assumed to be a vasculopathy causing primary choriocapillaris atrophy. However, histologic studies of choroideremia and studies of the localization of the *CHM* protein place the basic defect in the RPE.

Choroideremia is characterized by diffuse and progressive degeneration of the RPE and choriocapillaris (Fig 11-18). In affected males, the degeneration first manifests as mottled areas of pigmentation in the anterior equatorial region and macula. The anterior areas gradually degenerate to confluent scalloped areas of RPE and choriocapillaris loss, with preservation of larger choroidal vessels. The fluorescein angiographic changes are

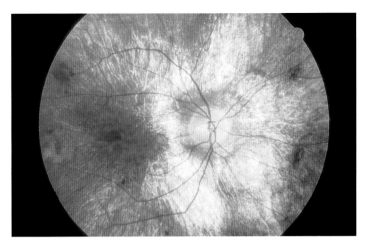

Figure 11-18 Fundus photograph of a patient with choroideremia. *(Reproduced with permission from Fishman GA, Birch DG, Holder GE, Brigell MG. Electrophysiologic Testing in Disorders of the Retina, Optic Nerve, and Visual Pathways. 2nd ed. Ophthalmology Monograph 2. San Francisco: American Academy of Ophthalmology; 2001:67.)*

even more pronounced, with the scalloped areas of missing choriocapillaris appearing hypofluorescent next to brightly hyperfluorescent areas of perfused choriocapillaris. The ERG response is abnormal early in the course of the disease and is generally extinguished by midlife.

Carriers of X-linked choroideremia often show patches of subretinal black mottled pigment, and, on occasion, older female carriers can show a lobular pattern of choriocapillaris and RPE loss. Carriers of choroideremia are usually asymptomatic and have normal electrophysiologic test results.

Although choroideremia has a childhood onset, most patients show a slow course of degeneration. The majority of patients, however, maintain good visual acuity for 4 or 5 decades. Night blindness usually develops in the first or second decade of life, and the visual field progressively contracts and develops ring scotomata similar to other forms of RP. The differential diagnosis of choroideremia includes gyrate atrophy (see the following section), thioridazine hydrochloride retinal toxicity, and Bietti crystalline dystrophy.

Roberts MF, Fishman GA, Roberts DK, et al. Retrospective, longitudinal, and cross sectional study of visual acuity impairment in choroideraemia. *Br J Ophthalmol.* 2002;86(6):658–662.

Seabra MC, Brown MS, Goldstein JL. Retinal degeneration in choroideremia: deficiency of rab geranylgeranyl transferase. *Science.* 1993;259(5093):377–381.

Gyrate atrophy

Gyrate atrophy is an autosomal recessive dystrophy caused by mutations in the gene for ornithine aminotransferase *(OAT),* located on chromosome 10. Originally thought to be a subtype of choroideremia, the disorder is the result of a tenfold elevation in plasma levels of ornithine, which is toxic to the RPE and choroid. Patients with gyrate atrophy have hyperpigmented fundi, with lobular loss of the RPE and choroid. The finding of generalized hyperpigmentation of the remaining RPE helps distinguish gyrate atrophy clinically from choroideremia. In the early stages, patients have large, geographic peripheral

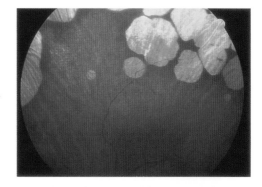

Figure 11-19 Gyrate atrophy.

paving-stone–like areas of atrophy of the RPE and choriocapillaris, which gradually co-alesce to form a characteristic scalloped border at the junction of normal and abnormal RPE (Fig 11-19). Night blindness usually develops during the first decade of life, and pa-tients experience progressive loss of visual field and visual acuity later in the course of the disease. The clinical diagnosis can be confirmed by measuring serum or plasma ornithine levels; molecular confirmation can be obtained by mutational analysis of the *OAT* gene. Occasionally, older patients present with an uncommon syndrome of peripheral chorio-retinal atrophy that closely mimics gyrate atrophy; normal plasma ornithine levels in such patients exclude the diagnosis of gyrate atrophy.

Although dietary restriction of arginine has been used to treat some gyrate atrophy patients, the diet is very difficult to maintain and must be monitored by pediatricians with experience in metabolic disease. Vitamin B_6 ingestion lowers the plasma ornithine levels in a small percentage of patients. Whether or not such a reduction improves the long-term vision outcome is unknown; however, vitamin supplementation is relatively easy to administer, unlike arginine restriction. Long-term vitamin therapy should be considered only for patients whose ornithine levels can be shown to decrease in response to treatment.

Kaiser-Kupfer MI, Caruso RC, Valle D. Gyrate atrophy of the choroid and retina. Long-term reduction of ornithine slows retinal degeneration. *Arch Ophthalmol.* 1991;109(11):1539–1548.

Ramesh V, McClatchey AI, Ramesh N, et al. Molecular basis of ornithine aminotransferase deficiency in B-6-responsive and -nonresponsive forms of gyrate atrophy. *Proc Natl Acad Sci USA.* 1988;85(11):3777–3780.

Weleber RG. Gyrate atrophy of the choroid and retina. In: Heckenlively JR, Arden GB, eds. *Principles and Practice of Clinical Electrophysiology of Vision.* 2nd ed. Cambridge, MA: MIT Press; 2006:705–716.

Regional and Central Choroidal Dystrophies

Several dystrophies show macular or regional choroidal degeneration. Most distinctive ophthalmoscopically are the central atrophies, which include central areolar choroidal dystrophy and North Carolina macular dystrophy, both autosomal dominant disorders. Several genetic types of central choroidal dystrophy likely exist, with overlapping clini-cal features. All are characterized by demarcated atrophy of the RPE and choriocapillaris in the macula and normal full-field electrophysiologic responses; however, there may be differences in onset and progression. The central atrophic lesions must be distinguished from those of acquired disease such as toxoplasmosis and, in older patients, from age-related macular degeneration or late stages of other macular dystrophies that may cause a central round or bull's-eye pattern of RPE atrophy (see Table 11-2).

Central areolar choroidal dystrophy (CACD) has been described as showing nonspecific mottled depigmentation within the macula in younger individuals that develops over time into a round or oval area of sharply demarcated geographic atrophy (Fig 11-20). Visual acuity typically stabilizes at approximately 20/200. Associated choroidal neovascularization rarely develops. A gene associated with this disorder has been mapped to the chromosome arm 17p. Several mutations in the *RDS/peripherin* gene, each affecting an arginine residue, have been reported to cause autosomal dominant CACD. *North Carolina macular dystrophy* begins in infancy with a cluster of peculiar yellow-white lesions at the level of the RPE in the macula. These lesions tend to increase in number and become confluent, in some patients progressing to a severely atrophic macular lesion that can appear excavated or staphylomatous (Fig 11-21). Disease progression appears to stabilize in

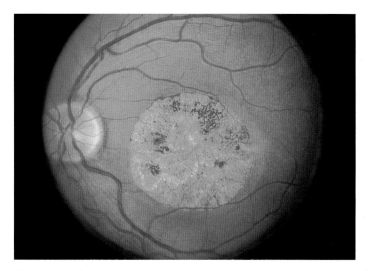

Figure 11-20 Central areolar choroidal dystrophy in a patient with autosomal dominant inheritance pattern. *(Courtesy of Mark W. Johnson, MD.)*

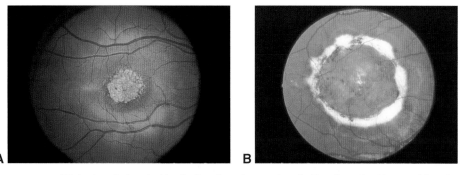

Figure 11-21 Clinical variation in North Carolina dystrophy. **A,** Fundus of a 7-year-old patient with a cluster of peculiar yellow-white atrophic lesions in the macula. **B,** Example of a severe, almost colobomatous, macular defect. *(Part A courtesy of Mark W. Johnson, MD; Part B courtesy of Kent Small, MD.)*

most patients by the early teenage years, and visual acuity is usually better than anticipated from the ophthalmoscopic appearance, typically ranging from 20/20 to 20/200. The gene responsible for this disease has been mapped to the long arm of chromosome 6.

Hughes AE, Lotery AJ, Silvestri G. Fine localisation of the gene for central areolar choroidal dystrophy on chromosome 17p. *J Med Genet.* 1998;35(9):770–772.

Small KW, Hermsen V, Gurney N, Fetkenhour CL, Folk JC. North Carolina macular dystrophy and central areolar pigment epithelial dystrophy. One family, one disease. *Arch Ophthalmol.* 1992;110(4):515–518.

Yanagihashi S, Nakazawa M, Kurotaki J, Sato M, Miyagawa Y, Ohguro H. Autosomal dominant central areolar choroidal dystrophy and a novel Arg195Leu mutation in the peripherin/RDS gene. *Arch Ophthalmol.* 2003;121(10):1458–1461.

Inner Retinal and Vitreoretinal Dystrophies

X-Linked Retinoschisis

Retinoschisis refers to a splitting of the neurosensory retina; at times, the inner retinal elevation may mimic full-thickness retinal detachment. There are 3 forms of retinoschisis:

1. degenerative peripheral retinoschisis with no known inheritance pattern
2. congenital X-linked recessive retinoschisis
3. secondary forms associated with vitreoretinal traction, optic pits, myopic degeneration with staphyloma, or, occasionally, retinal venous occlusion

The phenotype of *congenital X-linked retinoschisis (XLRS)* is somewhat variable, even within families. A constant diagnostic feature, easily seen in pediatric patients, is foveal schisis, which appears as small, cystoid spaces and fine radial striae in the central macula (Fig 11-22). Angiographic studies show no leakage of fluorescein associated with foveal

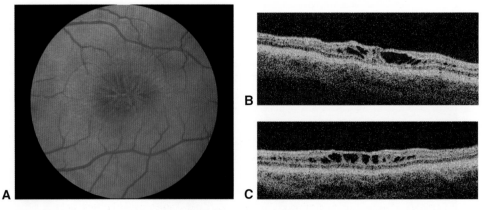

Figure 11-22 Juvenile retinoschisis. **A,** This characteristic pattern of macular schisis is a more consistent finding than peripheral changes. Vertical **(B)** and horizontal **(C)** optical coherence tomographic scans show schisis spaces in the middle layers of the macula. *(Courtesy of Mark W. Johnson, MD.)*

schisis. The central vision may initially be quite good, but with time, degeneration occurs and the acuity typically decreases to 20/200. Peripheral retinoschisis is not a constant feature but occurs in 50% or more of affected males. Histologic studies show that the splitting in peripheral XLRS occurs in the nerve fiber layer, whereas in degenerative retinoschisis, the level of splitting is variable and usually deeper within the retina. Pigmentary deposits may develop in peripheral areas destroyed by the disease process, so advanced cases of XLRS can be mistaken for RP. The clinical diagnosis may have to be confirmed by evaluating younger affected male family members. Boys with XLRS frequently present with vitreous hemorrhages from torn retinal vessels in areas of retinoschisis. These and other tractional complications, such as retinal detachment, sometimes require vitreoretinal surgery.

The panretinal involvement and middle-to-inner retinal location of the disease is reflected in the ERG, in which the a-wave is normal or near normal, and the b-wave is attenuated, typically giving a "negative waveform" (see Fig 3-2). Negative waveforms of the dark-adapted, bright-flash ERG occur in diseases in which the middle retina is affected and the photoreceptors are generally unaffected, yielding an a-wave with no effective b-wave (see Table 11-1). The ERG may become extinguished in cases in which retinal damage is extensive.

The gene associated with XLRS, *RS1*, encodes an adhesion protein called *retinoschisin,* which localizes to all retinal neurons, beginning with ganglion cells in embryonic development. Presumably, *retinoschisin* is essential for Müller cell health because mutations in its coding lead to Müller cell degeneration. Müller cells span the layers of the retina; their endplates form the inner limiting membrane, and their distal ends form the outer limiting membrane between inner segments. Loss of this bridging cellular matrix protein appears to be key to the pathologic changes present in congenital retinoschisis.

Congenital XLRS may leave the retina vulnerable to mechanical injury, and clinical impression suggests that trauma can exacerbate vision loss in this disorder. Prudent medical practice warrants advising patients to avoid boxing and other such contact sports. Although there is no proven medical treatment for this disorder, ophthalmic care should include careful evaluation and treatment of refractive errors, strabismus, and amblyopia; low vision rehabilitation; and genetic counseling. Preliminary clinical experience suggests that use of a topical carbonic anhydrase inhibitor may reduce foveal thickening and cyst-like spaces in affected patients.

American Academy of Ophthalmology. SmartSight website. Available at http://one.aao.org/CE/EducationalContent/Smartsight.aspx. Accessed August 10, 2011.

Apushkin MA, Fishman GA. Use of dorzolamide for patients with X-linked retinoschisis. *Retina.* 2006;26(7):741–745.

Molday LL, Hicks D, Sauer CG, Weber BH, Molday RS. Expression of X-linked retinoschisis protein RS1 in photoreceptor and bipolar cells. *Invest Ophthalmol Vis Sci.* 2001;42(3):816–825.

Sieving PA, MacDonald IM, Trese MT. Congenital X-linked retinoschisis. In: Hartnett ME, Trese M, Capone A Jr, Keats BJB, Steidl SM, eds. *Pediatric Retina: Medical and Surgical Approaches.* Philadelphia: Lippincott Williams & Wilkins; 2004:377–385.

Sieving PA, Yashar BM, Ayyagari R. Juvenile retinoschisis: a model for molecular diagnostic testing of X-linked ophthalmic disease. *Trans Am Ophthalmol Soc.* 1999;97:451–464.

Goldmann-Favre Syndrome

Goldmann-Favre syndrome, also related to the *enhanced S-cone* (or *blue-cone*) *syndrome* (*ESCS*; "S" for short wavelength) was initially described as a vitreoretinal dystrophy. Its most prominent features include night blindness, increased sensitivity to blue light, pigmentary retinal degeneration, an optically empty vitreous, unusual ERG abnormalities, and varying degrees of peripheral to midperipheral visual field loss. The posterior pole frequently shows yellow, sheenlike, round lesions along the arcades, with areas of diffuse degeneration. Macular (and sometimes peripheral) schisis is present, which does not leak during fluorescein angiography. The dark-adapted ERG shows no response to low-intensity stimuli that normally activate the rods, but there are large, slow responses to high-intensity stimuli. These large, slow waveforms persist without change under light adaptation, and there is greater sensitivity to blue-light stimuli.

This autosomal recessive disorder results from mutations in the gene *NR2E3*, which codes for a ligand-dependent transcription factor. There is evidence that the disorder is the result of abnormal cell fate determination, leading to excess S cones at the expense of other photoreceptor subtypes (See Chapter 10). Histologic study of the retina of an ESCS patient demonstrated no rods but an approximately twofold increase in cones, 92% of which were identified as S cones. Only 15% of the cones expressed L/M-cone ("L/M" for long/medium wavelength) opsin, and some of these coexpressed S-cone opsin.

Marmor MF, Jacobson SG, Foerster MH, Kellner U, Weleber RG. Diagnostic clinical findings of a new syndrome with night blindness, maculopathy, and enhanced S cone sensitivity. *Am J Ophthalmol.* 1990;110(2):124–134.

Milam AH, Rose L, Cideciyan AV, et al. The nuclear receptor *NR2E3* plays a role in human retinal photoreceptor differentiation and degeneration. *Proc Natl Acad Sci USA.* 2002;99(1):473–478.

The authors thank John R. Heckenlively, MD, for his significant contributions to this chapter.

CHAPTER **12**

Retinal Degenerations Associated With Systemic Disease

The retina is a highly complex tissue with large metabolic and oxidative demands. Although the retina and retinal pigment epithelium (RPE) receive some protection from systemic toxic elements through the blood–retinal barrier and their relative isolation inside the scleral shell, the retina remains vulnerable to drug toxicities, infections, trauma, and genetic and metabolic insults that can lead to secondary retinal degeneration.

The important diagnostic and prognostic questions that arise in evaluating a patient who presents with retinal degeneration are whether

- the degeneration is primary or secondary
- the condition is stable or progressive
- a precise diagnosis can be made

An appropriate treatment plan, whether intervention for the underlying systemic disease or counseling about the ophthalmic condition, is guided by the most accurate diagnosis and evidence regarding the rate of progression. The term *pigmentary retinopathy* is a broad reference to a panretinal disturbance of the retina and RPE. Pigment deposits define most pigmentary retinopathies, but some diseases have a generalized depigmentation characterized by atrophy and little or no pigment deposition.

Most of the severe secondary pigmentary retinopathies are associated with genetic syndromes, and many have childhood onsets. The number of pigmentary retinopathies reported in association with systemic genetic or acquired disorders is extensive, and the major ones are summarized in Table 12-1. Online resources include the *Online Mendelian Inheritance in Man (OMIM)* database, which allows a search based on physical findings leading to appropriate syndromes, and the *RetNet* website, which lists monogenic hereditary disorders.

Heckenlively JR, Daiger SP. Hereditary retinal and choroidal degenerations. In: Rimoin DL, Connor JM, Pyeritz RE, Korf BR, eds. *Emery and Rimoin's Principles and Practice of Medical Genetics.* 3 vols. 5th ed. Philadelphia: Churchill Livingstone; 2007:chap 137.

McKusick-Nathans Institute of Genetic Medicine, Johns Hopkins University School of Medicine. Online Mendelian Inheritance in Man website. Available at http://www.omim .org. Updated daily. Accessed August 9, 2011.

The University of Texas–Houston Health Science Center. RetNet, the Retinal Information Network website. Available at http://www.sph.uth.tmc.edu/Retnet. Accessed August 9, 2011.

Table 12-1 Systemic Diseases With Pigmentary Retinopathies (Partial List)

Disorder	Features
Autosomal dominant disorders	
Arteriohepatic dysplasia (Alagille syndrome)	Intrahepatic cholestatic syndrome, posterior embryotoxon, Axenfeld anomaly, congenital heart disease, flattened facies and bridge of nose, bony abnormalities, myopia, pigmentary retinopathy
Charcot-Marie-Tooth disease	Pigmentary retinopathy, degeneration of lateral horn of spinal cord, optic atrophy
Myotonic dystrophy (Steinert disease)	Muscle wasting, "Christmas tree" cataract, retinal degeneration, pattern dystrophy; ERG subnormal to abnormal
Oculodentodigital dysplasia syndrome	Thin nose with hypoplastic alae, narrow nostrils, abnormality of fourth and fifth fingers, hypoplastic dental enamel, congenital cataract, colobomas
Olivopontocerebellar atrophy	Retinal degeneration (peripheral and/or macular), cerebellar ataxia, possible external ophthalmoplegia
Stickler syndrome (arthro-ophthalmopathy)	Progressive myopia with myopic retinal degeneration, joint hypermobility, arthritis; retinal detachment common; ERG subnormal to abnormal
Waardenburg syndrome	Hypertelorism, wide bridge of nose, cochlear deafness, white forelock, heterochromia iridis, poliosis, pigment disturbance of RPE; ERG normal to subnormal
Wagner hereditary vitreoretinal degeneration	Narrowed and sheathed retinal vessels, pigmented spots in the retinal periphery and along retinal vessels, choroidal atrophy and optic atrophy, extensive liquefaction and membranous condensation of vitreous body; subnormal ERG; overlapping features with Stickler syndrome
Autosomal recessive disorders	
Bardet-Biedl syndrome	Pigmentary retinopathy, mild cognitive disabilities, polydactyly, obesity, hypogenitalism, progressive visual field loss; ERG severely diminished to nonrecordable
Bietti crystalline retinopathy	Yellow-white crystals limited to posterior pole, round subretinal pigment deposits, confluent loss of choriocapillaris on fluorescein angiogram, possible crystals in limbal cornea
Friedreich ataxia	Spinocerebellar degeneration, limb incoordination, nerve deafness, retinal degeneration, optic atrophy
Homocystinuria	Fine pigmentary or cystic degeneration of retina, marfanoid appearance, myopia, lens subluxation or dislocation, cardiovascular abnormalities (thromboses), glaucoma, cognitive disabilities
Mannosidosis	Resembling Hurler syndrome; macroglossia, flat nose, large head and ears, skeletal abnormalities, possible hepatosplenomegaly, storage material in retina
Mucopolysaccharidosis I H (Hurler syndrome)	Early corneal clouding, gargoyle facies, deafness, cognitive disabilities, dwarfism, skeletal abnormalities, hepatosplenomegaly, optic atrophy; subnormal ERG
Mucopolysaccharidosis I S (Scheie syndrome)	Coarse facies, aortic regurgitation, stiff joints, early clouding of the cornea, normal life span, normal intellect, pigmentary retinopathy
Mucopolysaccharidosis III (Sanfilippo syndrome)	Milder somatic stigmata than Hurler, but severe pigmentary retinopathy
Neonatal adrenoleukodystrophy	Pigmentary retinopathy, optic atrophy, seizures, hypotonia, adrenal cortical atrophy, psychomotor impairment; extinguished ERG

Table 12-1 *(continued)*

Disorder	Features
Neuronal ceroid lipofuscinoses (Batten disease)	Haltia-Santavuori, occurring in infancy with rapid deterioration, fine granular inclusions Jansky-Bielschowsky, onset 2–4 years, rapid CNS deterioration, curvilinear body inclusions Lake-Cavanagh, onset 4–6 years, ataxia, dementia, curvilinear and fingerprint inclusions Spielmeyer-Vogt, onset 6–8 years, slowly progressive, fingerprint inclusions
Refsum disease	Elevations of phytanic acid, pigmentary retinopathy, optic atrophy, partial deafness, cerebellar ataxia, ichthyosis
Usher syndrome	Congenital deafness (profound or partial), pigmentary retinopathy
Zellweger (cerebrohepatorenal) syndrome	Muscular hypotonia, high forehead and hypertelorism, hepatomegaly, deficient cerebral myelination, nystagmus, cataract, microphthalmia, retinal degeneration; nonrecordable ERG
X-linked recessive pigmentary retinopathies	
Incontinentia pigmenti (Bloch-Sulzberger syndrome)	Skin pigmentation in lines and whorls, alopecia, dental anomalies, optic atrophy, falciform folds, cataract, nystagmus, strabismus, patchy mottling of fundi, conjunctival pigmentation
Mucopolysaccharidosis II (Hunter syndrome)	Little corneal clouding, mild clinical course, cognitive disabilities, some retinal arteriolar narrowing; subnormal ERG
Pelizaeus-Merzbacher disease	Infantile progressive leukodystrophy, cerebellar ataxia, limb spasticity, cognitive impairment, possible pigmentary retinopathy with absent foveal reflex
Mitochondrial disorders	
	Progressive external ophthalmoplegia, ptosis, pigmentary retinopathy, heart block (Kearns-Sayre syndrome); ERG normal to abnormal

ERG = electroretinogram; RPE = retinal pigment epithelium; CNS = central nervous system.

Modified from Rimoin DL, Connor JM, Pyeritz RE, Korf BR, eds. *Emery and Rimoin's Principles and Practice of Medical Genetics*. 3 vols. 4th ed. New York: Churchill Livingstone; 2002:chap 124. Copyright © 2001, with permission from Elsevier.

Disorders Involving Other Organ Systems

Infantile-Onset to Early Childhood–Onset Syndromes

Any infant with retinal dysfunction and a diminished electroretinogram (ERG) signal should be screened carefully for congenital syndromes and metabolic disorders that affect the retina when a diagnosis of Leber congenital amaurosis (LCA) is under consideration. Although there are currently 9 known monogenic or primary forms of LCA, systemic diseases that include severe infantile-onset retinal degeneration are grouped under the term *complicated LCA*. Because the site of mutation in a gene may affect the severity and onset of symptoms, the same disease may have a more severe, infantile onset with one mutation and a milder, childhood onset with a different mutation in the same gene. The systemic disorders that mimic LCA include, among others, the neuronal ceroid lipofuscinoses (Batten disease), peroxisome disorders such as Refsum disease, Zellweger (cerebrohepatorenal) syndrome, and neonatal adrenoleukodystrophy. Important diagnostic clues that differentiate these LCA-like disorders from primary LCA are seizures and a deterioration of neurologic and mental function, usually combined with a decline in school performance. Initially, poor eyesight is commonly blamed for the declining cognitive and neuromuscular skills, until subsequently (finally), the metabolic disorder is diagnosed.

Birch DG. Retinal degeneration in retinitis pigmentosa and neuronal ceroid lipofuscinosis: an overview. *Mol Genet Metab.* 1999;66(4):356–366.

den Hollander AI, Roepman R, Koenekoop RK, Crèmers FP. Leber congenital amaurosis: genes, proteins and disease mechanisms. *Prog Retin Eye Res.* 2008:27(4):391–419.

Bardet-Biedl Complex of Diseases

The *Bardet-Biedl syndrome* comprises a number of different diseases with a similar constellation of findings, including pigmentary retinopathy (with or without pigment deposits), obesity, polydactyly, hypogonadism, and cognitive disability. These disorders were previously classified as autosomal recessive, but recent molecular studies strongly suggest that many are multigenic, with 2 or even 3 different mutations contributing to the phenotype. At least 13 causative genes have been identified, which account for approximately 75% of affected families. Increasing evidence suggests that the primary function of the proteins affected in Bardet-Biedl syndrome is to mediate and regulate microtubule-based intracellular transport processes; therefore, the syndrome belongs to the ciliopathies.

Macular pigment mottling and peripheral retinal atrophy are present, usually without bone-spicule pigment clumping (Fig 12-1). A wide spectrum of retinal disease severity is observed, even within a single genotype. Affected patients are most easily recognized by obesity and a history or presence of polydactyly. It may be necessary to inspect feet or hands for signs of scar tissue related to excision of the extra digits in childhood. The hands often appear puffy, making knuckles indistinct. Because these patients tend to have more severe retinopathy and learning disabilities, extra attention should be given to supporting the parents in their efforts to obtain special educational support.

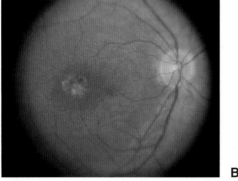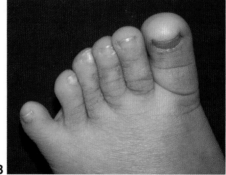

A **B**

Figure 12-1   Bardet-Biedl syndrome. **A,** Macular pigmentary alterations. **B,** Polydactyly. *(Courtesy of John R. Heckenlively, MD.)*

Blacque OE, Leroux MR. Bardet-Biedl syndrome: an emerging pathomechanism of intracellular transport. *Cell Mol Life Sci.* 2006;63(18):2145–2161.

Katsanis N, Lupski JR, Beales PL. Exploring the molecular basis of Bardet-Biedl syndrome. *Hum Mol Genet.* 2001;10(20):2293–2299.

Sheffield VC, Nishimura D, Stone EM. The molecular genetics of Bardet-Biedl syndrome. *Curr Opin Genet Dev.* 2001;11(3):317–321.

Hearing Loss and Pigmentary Retinopathy

Usher syndrome

Usher syndrome is the name most commonly given to the association of retinitis pigmentosa (RP) with *congenital* sensorineural hearing loss, whether partial or profound. The disease was first described in 1906 by Charles Usher, a British ophthalmologist. Although some RP patients acquire deafness in later adult years, this is not usually classified as Usher syndrome. Both the profound (type 1) and partial (type 2) forms show autosomal recessive inheritance and tend to be stable through adult life. The ophthalmologist should be attuned to patients with RP who present with a nasal intonation to their speech or wear hearing aids, suggestive of Usher type 2 patients. A slowly progressive deafness has been identified in one subgroup of Usher patients—those with mutations in *USH3A,* which is a gene encoding clarin-1, a transmembrane protein with a possible role in hair cell and photoreceptor synapses. The hearing level of most Usher patients is typically stable over time, however.

Currently, there are 11 types of Usher syndrome in which the chromosome location is known; of these, 9 have cloned genes (see RetNet website for details and references). The proteins encoded by these genes are part of a dynamic protein complex present in hair cells of the inner ear and in photoreceptor cells of the retina. For example, Usher type 2A is caused by mutations in the gene for *usherin* (at 1q41), which encodes a basement membrane protein found in many tissues, including structural basement membranes in the retina and inner ear. Usher type 1B is caused by defective myosin, a common component of cilia and microvilli. This finding is intriguing because photoreceptors are modified ciliated cells, and cilia are also sensory structures for otologic function. Usher type 1C is caused by mutations in the *harmonin* gene, which encodes a protein expressed in inner ear sensory hair cells.

The exact incidence of Usher syndrome has been difficult to determine, but surveys of RP patients suggest that about 10% are profoundly deaf, and ophthalmic examinations of children in schools for the deaf reveal that approximately 6% have RP. The prevalence of Usher syndrome is thought to be 3 cases per 100,000.

In addition to Usher syndrome, other genetic conditions and environmental insults may lead to pigmentary retinopathy and hearing loss, including Alport syndrome, Alström and Cockayne syndromes, dysplasia spondyloepiphysaria congenita, Hurler syndrome, Refsum disease, and congenital rubella. By careful study of individual patients and families, clinicians can make the diagnosis of Usher syndrome with relative certainty. Molecular testing for specific forms of Usher syndrome can help confirm the diagnosis.

Kremer H, van Wijk E, Märker T, Wolfrum U, Roepman R. Usher syndrome: molecular links of pathogenesis, proteins and pathways. *Hum Mol Genet.* 2006;15(Spec No 2):R262–R270.

Neuromuscular Disorders

Pigmentary retinopathy associated with complex neuromuscular pathology is present in a variety of disorders, including *spinocerebellar degenerations* such as Friedreich ataxia, some of the *olivopontocerebellar atrophies, Charcot-Marie-Tooth disease, myotonic dystrophy, neuronal ceroid lipofuscinosis (Batten disease), progressive external ophthalmoplegia syndromes,* and *peroxisome disorders* (Zellweger syndrome, Refsum disease, neonatal adrenoleukodystrophy) (see Table 12-1). Mitochondrial, autosomal dominant, and autosomal recessive inheritance patterns are all found in this group of disorders. These neurologic conditions vary widely in age of onset and retinal findings, and the diagnosis is normally made in collaboration with a neurologist or medical geneticist. The role of the ophthalmologist is to confirm the pigmentary retinopathy and assist in visual rehabilitation of the patient. The ERG abnormalities found in these neurologic disorders only confirm the presence of retinopathy but are not diagnostic for any one disorder.

Duchenne muscular dystrophy has not traditionally been thought of as a disease involving the retina, and patients do not ordinarily have any visual symptoms. However, recent studies have found a striking ERG abnormality in Duchenne patients that may be useful in diagnosis and relevant to understanding retinal function. The ERG signal shows a negative waveform similar to that found in patients with congenital stationary night blindness (CSNB), who have a normal a-wave but reduced b-wave (see Chapters 3 and 10). This ERG response is suggestive of a defective "on-response" pathway, but these Duchenne patients do not have night blindness. It is interesting that Duchenne muscular dystrophy is caused by mutations in the gene for dystrophin, a protein abundant in muscle but also found in neural synaptic regions and in the retina.

Folz SJ, Trobe JD. The peroxisome and the eye. *Surv Ophthalmol.* 1991;35(5):353–368.

Phelan JK, Bok D. Is the Duchenne muscular dystrophy gene also an X-linked retinitis pigmentosa locus? *Mol Genet Metab.* 2000;70(1):81–83.

Other Organ System Disorders

Most retinopathies associated with other organ systems are rare and genetic, and the OMIM website can be of use in their recognition. Collaboration with pediatric and medical geneticists is often required to identify rare candidate diseases.

Renal diseases

Several forms of congenital renal disease may be associated with retinal degeneration. *Familial juvenile nephronophthisis* is part of a family of renal-retinal dysplasias (and ciliopathies), most of which have autosomal recessive inheritance. Juvenile-onset renal failure related to corticomedullary cysts and tubulointerstitial fibrosis is accompanied by pigmentary retinal degeneration that may be sectorial. Some of these patients have abnormalities of their bony growth plates, leading to shortness of stature. Patients with the Bardet-Biedl complex disorders commonly have urethral reflux with pyelonephritis and kidney damage. Renal disease is also a component of the Alström and Alport syndromes. Type II membranoproliferative glomerulonephritis is associated with a myriad of drusen-like deposits throughout the fundus.

Gastrointestinal disease

Familial adenomatous polyposis (FAP, Gardner syndrome) is associated with pigmented lesions that are somewhat similar to those in congenital hypertrophy of the RPE. The lesions in Gardner syndrome, however, are smaller, ovoid, more variegated, and typically multiple and bilateral (Fig 12-2). More than 4 widely spaced, small (<0.5 disc diameter) lesions per eye and bilateral involvement are suggestive of FAP. Caused by mutations in the adenomatous polyposis *(APC)* gene, FAP is inherited in autosomal dominant fashion with incomplete expression. The pigmented retinal lesions constitute an important marker for identifying family members at risk of colonic polyps, which have a high malignant potential.

Dermatologic diseases

Ichthyosis is abnormal scaling, dryness, and tightness of the skin that may be found in conjunction with the pigmentary retinopathy of Refsum disease and in Sjögren-Larsson syndrome. *Incontinentia pigmenti (Bloch-Sulzberger syndrome)* is a rare, X-linked disorder that causes death in male fetuses and is characterized by a peculiar triphasic dermopathy and variable involvement of the eyes, teeth, and central nervous system (CNS) in females. Ocular involvement occurs in approximately one-third of affected females and includes pigmentary abnormalities as well as deficient peripheral retinal vascularization that may lead to tractional and cicatricial retinal detachment (see also BCSC Section 6, *Pediatric Ophthalmology and Strabismus*). Pseudoxanthoma elasticum is associated with angioid streaks and a peau d'orange fundus appearance (see Chapter 4).

Holmström G, Thorén K. Ocular manifestations of incontinentia pigmenti. *Acta Ophthalmol Scand.* 2000;78(3):348–353.

Traboulsi EI. Ocular manifestations of familial adenomatous polyposis (Gardner syndrome). *Ophthalmol Clin North Am.* 2005;18(1):163–166.

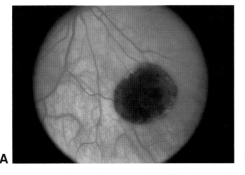 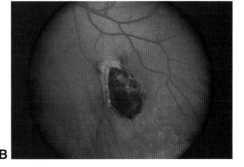

A **B**

Figure 12-2 Hyperpigmented RPE lesions. **A,** Congenital hypertrophy of the RPE. These isolated lesions are typically rounded, with very dense pigmentation (except for occasional lacunae) and a thin depigmented halo. **B,** Pigmented fundus lesions in Gardner syndrome (familial adenomatous polyposis). These lesions are smaller, more ovoid, more variegated in color, and usually multiple and bilateral. The surrounding RPE may be abnormal. *(Part A courtesy of Michael F. Marmor, MD; Part B courtesy of Elias Traboulsi, MD.)*

Paraneoplastic Retinopathy

Retinal degeneration is occasionally a complication of cancer by a paraneoplastic immunologic mechanism. BCSC Section 9, *Intraocular Inflammation and Uveitis,* explains the role of the immune system in this process. The 2 main paraneoplastic retinopathy syndromes are *cancer-associated retinopathy (CAR)* and *melanoma-associated retinopathy (MAR)*. It is hypothesized that a small number of carcinomas and melanomas express protein antigens that are the same as or cross-react with retinal proteins. The immune system is stimulated to produce antibodies that react to the retina and cause progressive retinal degeneration. A third entity, autoimmune retinopathy, refers to an acquired, presumed immunologically mediated, retinal degeneration with symptoms resembling paraneoplastic retinopathy but without any identifiable tumor.

The first retinal protein shown to be the target of the antigenic cross-reactivity in CAR patients was the 23-kDa protein recoverin. Since then, many retinal proteins have been found to be antigenic, including α-enolase, arrestin, transducin, and neurofilament protein. Patients with CAR involving antirecoverin antibodies typically experience rapidly progressive loss of peripheral and central vision, often accompanied by photopsias and a ring scotoma. Fundus examination shows arterial narrowing but may demonstrate no pigmentary alterations early in the disease course (Fig 12-3). Goldmann visual field examinations document dramatic loss of visual field over a few months, in contrast to RP, which typically shows a chronic, slow decline. The ERG signal is severely reduced (for a- and b-waves), with both rods and cones affected, but negative waveforms may occur if the middle retina is affected to a great extent. Paraneoplastic and autoimmune retinopathies associated with antienolase antibodies are characterized predominantly by cone dysfunction, a slow progression of central vision loss, and eventual optic disc pallor.

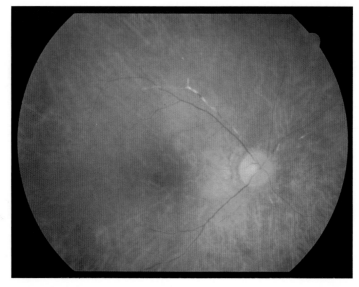

Figure 12-3 Cancer-associated retinopathy (CAR) in patient with ovarian carcinoma. Note severe vascular attenuation without obvious pigmentary alterations. *(Courtesy of John R. Heckenlively, MD.)*

On occasion, the loss of retinal function may precede clinical recognition of the cancer. Therefore, any late-onset, rapidly progressive retinal dysfunction should raise suspicion of an underlying malignancy causing an autoimmune retinopathy. Immunosuppressive therapy, given in close cooperation with the patient's oncologist, may halt and sometimes reverse the vision loss in patients with CAR. If the patient is too ill for systemic immuno-suppression, periocular or intravitreal corticosteroid injections can be considered.

A strong association has been demonstrated between cystoid macular edema and cir-culating antiretinal antibodies in patients with RP. Overall, an estimated 1%–2% of RP patients have antirecoverin antibodies, which may exacerbate their disease.

Patients with MAR experience vision loss and night blindness and show a negative ERG waveform similar to that of CSNB. Their antibodies are directed toward undefined retinal bipolar cell antigens. Confirmation of the diagnosis is obtained by histologic staining.

Alexander KR, Barnes CS, Fishman GA, Milam AH. Nature of the cone ON-pathway dysfunction in melanoma-associated retinopathy. *Invest Ophthalmol Vis Sci.* 2002;43(4):1189–1197.

Heckenlively JR, Ferreyra HA. Autoimmune retinopathy: a review and summary. *Semin Immunopathol.* 2008;30(2):127–134.

Keltner JL, Thirkill CE, Tyler NK, Roth AM. Management and monitoring of cancer-associated retinopathy. *Arch Ophthalmol.* 1992;110(1):48–53.

Keltner JL, Thirkill CE, Yip PT. Clinical and immunologic characteristics of melanoma-associated retinopathy syndrome: eleven new cases and a review of 51 previously published cases. *J Neuroophthalmol.* 2001;21(3):173–187.

Weleber RG, Watzke RC, Shults WT, et al. Clinical and electrophysiologic characterization of paraneoplastic and autoimmune retinopathies associated with antienolase antibodies. *Am J Ophthalmol.* 2005;139(5):780–794.

Metabolic Diseases

It is important to consider metabolic diseases in evaluating patients with retinal degenera-tion, although detailed descriptions of the many metabolic disorders with retinal mani-festations is beyond the scope of this book. Some disorders, such as albinism and the CNS abnormalities, are covered more fully in BCSC Section 6, *Pediatric Ophthalmology and Strabismus.* Other metabolic disorders, such as abetalipoproteinemia and Refsum disease, are among the differential diagnostic concerns for RP, even though their retinopathy may be granular and atypical.

Albinism

Albinism refers to a group of different genetic abnormalities in which the synthesis of melanin is reduced or absent. The current classification scheme is based on the gene mu-tation, replacing the older terminology of complete versus partial and tyrosinase-positive versus tyrosinase-negative disorders (Table 12-2). When the reduction in melanin biosyn-thesis affects the eyes, skin, and hair follicles, the disease is called *oculocutaneous albinism.* These disorders are usually inherited in an autosomal recessive manner. If the skin and

Table 12-2 Molecular Classification of Albinism

	Responsible Gene	Gene Location
Oculocutaneous albinism (OCA)		
OCA1	Tyrosinase	11q14–q21
OCA2	P gene	15q
OCA3	TYRP1*	9q23
OCA4	SLC45A2†	5p
Hermansky-Pudlak syndrome (HPS)		
HPS1	HPS1	10q23.1–q23.3
HPS2	AP3B1	5q14.1
HPS3	HPS3	3q24
HPS4	HPS4	22q11.2–q12.2
HPS5	HPS5	11p15–p13
HPS6	HPS6	10q24.3
HPS7	DTNBP1‡	6p22.3
HPS8	BLOC1S3	19q13
Chédiak-Higashi syndrome (CHS)		
CHS	LYST§	1q42.1–q42.2
Ocular albinism (OA)‖		
OA1	GPR143	Xp22.3

*Tyrosinase-related protein 1.
†Also known as *MATP* gene, encoding membrane-associated transporter protein.
‡Dysbindin protein.
§Lysosomal trafficking regulator.
‖Other types of OA have been shown to represent OCA.

Modified from Summers CG. Albinism: classification, clinical characteristics, and recent findings, Table 1. *Optom Vis Sci.* 2009;86(6):659–662.

hair appear normally pigmented and only the ocular pigmentation is clinically affected, the condition is called *ocular albinism*. This terminology may not be accurate histologically because biopsy specimens from some patients with ocular albinism have shown cutaneous pigmentary dilution as well as giant melanosomes in both the skin and the eye. Ocular albinism is typically inherited in an X-linked pattern. Female carriers of X-linked ocular albinism may show partial iris transillumination and fundus pigment mosaicism.

Regardless of the type of albinism, ocular involvement generally conforms to 1 of 2 clinical patterns: (1) congenitally subnormal visual acuity (typically 20/100–20/400) and nystagmus or (2) normal or minimally reduced visual acuity without nystagmus. The first pattern is true albinism; the second has been termed *albinoidism* because of its milder visual consequences. Both patterns share the clinical features of photophobia, iris transillumination, and hypopigmented fundi. They differ by whether or not the fovea develops normally; in true albinism, the fovea is hypoplastic, with no foveal pit or reflex and no evident luteal pigment (Fig 12-4).

In childhood, all patients with oculocutaneous albinism appear similarly hypopigmented. However, with age, patients with tyrosinase-positive forms gradually accumulate more pigment and exhibit a slow darkening of the skin, hair, and irides that occurs over many years. In general, the more pigmentation the patient demonstrates, such as around

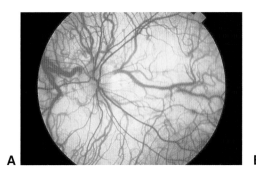
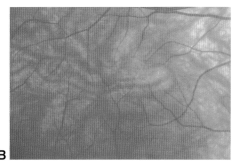

A

B

Figure 12-4 Albinism. **A,** Generalized fundus hypopigmentation. **B,** Foveal hypoplasia: no foveal reflex or luteal pigment evident. *(Courtesy of Carl D. Regillo, MD.)*

hair follicles and in the RPE in the posterior pole, the better the visual prognosis. Many patients have improved nystagmus and visual acuity as pigmentation increases. Genetic counseling includes careful determination of the inheritance pattern and molecular testing in selected cases.

It is important for the clinician to be aware of 2 forms of potentially lethal oculo-cutaneous albinism. In *Chédiak-Higashi syndrome,* albinism is combined with extreme susceptibility to infections and other complications that often lead to death in childhood or youth. *Hermansky-Pudlak syndrome* is characterized by a platelet defect that causes easy bruising and bleeding. Most Hermansky-Pudlak patients in the United States are of Puerto Rican descent. If either of these 2 types of albinism is suspected, hematologic consultation is imperative.

King RA, Jackson IJ, Oetting WS. Human albinism and mouse models. In: Wright AF, Jay B, eds. *Molecular Genetics of Inherited Eye Disorders.* Chur, Switzerland: Harwood Academic; 1994:89–122.

Oetting W, ed. The Albinism Database website. Human Genome Variation Society. Available at http://albinismdb.med.umn.edu/. Last updated September 21, 2009. Accessed August 16, 2011.

Summers CG. Albinism: classification, clinical characteristics, and recent findings. *Optom Vis Sci.* 2009;86(6):659–662.

Central Nervous System Metabolic Abnormalities

A wide range of fundus changes, from pigmentary retinopathy to a cherry-red spot, may be associated with inherited metabolic diseases known to affect the CNS and retina. Although a comprehensive description of them is beyond the scope of this book, the following discussion includes some of the major conditions (see Table 12-1). See BCSC Section 6, *Pediatric Ophthalmology and Strabismus,* for a listing of the ocular findings in inborn errors of metabolism.

Neuronal ceroid lipofuscinosis (Batten disease)

The neuronal ceroid lipofuscinoses (NCLs) are a group of autosomal recessive diseases caused by the accumulation of waxy lipopigments within the lysosomes of neurons and other cells. The accumulation of lipopigments such as ceroid and lipofuscin leads to cellular dysfunction and death, possibly by apoptosis. The disorders are characterized by progressive dementia, seizures, and vision loss, with pigmentary retinopathy in early-onset cases. The diagnosis is made clinically and by demonstrating characteristic curvilinear, fingerprint, or granular inclusions on electron microscopy of a peripheral blood smear or conjunctival or other biopsy tissue.

Several types of NCL have been described, based in part on the age of symptom onset. To date, 8 genes underlying human NCLs have been identified, but there remain disease subgroups whose molecular genetics are unknown. The infantile and juvenile types are associated with pigmentary retinopathies:

- infantile NCL (Haltia-Santavuori disease), with onset occurring between 8 and 18 months of age
- late-infantile NCL (Jansky-Bielschowsky disease), between 2 and 4 years of age
- early-juvenile NCL (Lake-Cavanagh disease), between 4 and 6 years
- juvenile NCL (Spielmeyer-Vogt-Batten disease), between 6 and 8 years

Ocular findings in infantile NCL include optic atrophy, macular pigmentary changes with mottling of the fundus periphery, and reduced or absent ERG signals. Retinal changes in the infantile forms can lead to confusion with LCA. The late-infantile and juvenile cases may show macular granularity or a bull's-eye maculopathy, with variable degrees of peripheral RPE change, optic atrophy, and attenuation of the retinal blood vessels (Fig 12-5). The 2 adult forms of NCL do not have ocular manifestations.

Abetalipoproteinemia and vitamin A deficiency

Abetalipoproteinemia is an autosomal recessive disorder in which apolipoprotein B is not synthesized, leading to fat malabsorption, fat-soluble vitamin deficiencies, and retinal and spinocerebellar degeneration. Red blood cells show acanthocytosis. Supplementation with vitamins A and E is needed to prevent or ameliorate the retinal degeneration. Testing for vitamin A levels is useful diagnostically in these and other retinopathies.

The most common form of vitamin A deficiency retinopathy occurs in patients who have undergone gastric bypass surgery for obesity or small-bowel resection for Crohn disease. These patients have malabsorption of fat-soluble vitamins and may develop a blind loop syndrome, in which an overgrowth of bacteria consumes vitamin A. The patient experiences night blindness, and if the condition remains untreated, eventually demonstrates

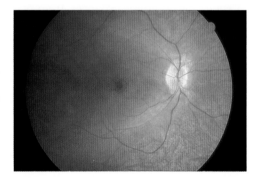

Figure 12-5 Optic atrophy, retinal vascular attenuation, and peripheral pigmentary loss in Batten disease (juvenile neuronal ceroid lipofuscinosis). *(Courtesy of Elias Traboulsi, MD.)*

loss of foveal function and diffuse, drusenlike spots similar to those in retinitis punctata albescens. Before the time at which retinal degeneration develops, the condition is fully reversible through vitamin A supplementation.

Peroxisomal disorders and Refsum disease

The peroxisomal disorders are mostly autosomal recessive diseases caused by dysfunction or absence of peroxisomes or peroxisomal enzymes. The biochemical hallmarks are defective oxidation and accumulation of very long chain fatty acids. *Zellweger syndrome* is the prototype of peroxisomal diseases. Severe, infantile-onset retinal degeneration is associated in this disorder with hypotonia, psychomotor impairment, seizures, characteristic facies, renal cysts, and hepatic interstitial fibrosis. Death usually occurs in infancy. Patients with *neonatal adrenoleukodystrophy* also present in infancy but generally survive until 7–10 years of age (Fig 12-6).

Similar but less severe findings are present in *infantile Refsum disease,* in which serum phytanic acid is elevated. Classic *Refsum disease* (phytanic acid storage disease) may not be a peroxisomal disorder. Sometimes not diagnosed until adulthood, Refsum disease is characterized by pigmentary retinopathy with reduced ERG signals, cerebellar ataxia, polyneuropathy, anosmia, hearing loss, and cardiomyopathy (Fig 12-7). Night blindness

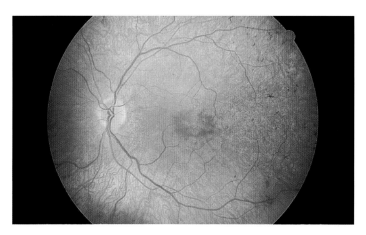

Figure 12-6 Retinal arteriolar attenuation, diffuse pigmentary alterations, and mild optic atrophy in neonatal adrenoleukodystrophy. *(Courtesy of Mark W. Johnson, MD.)*

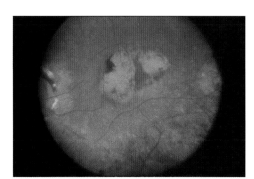

Figure 12-7 Pigmentary retinopathy with macular atrophy in Refsum disease. *(Courtesy of Elias Traboulsi, MD.)*

may be an early symptom. Diagnosis is made by demonstrating elevated plasma levels of phytanic acid or reduced phytanic acid oxidase activity in cultured fibroblasts. Dietary restriction of phytanic acid precursors may slow or stabilize the retinal degeneration.

Mucopolysaccharidoses

The systemic mucopolysaccharidoses (MPSs) are caused by inherited defects in catabolic lysosomal enzymes that degrade the glycosaminoglycans dermatan sulfate, keratan sulfate, and heparan sulfate. Consequently, excessive quantities of incompletely metabolized acid mucopolysaccharides, complex lipids, or both are stored in lysosomes. The MPSs are transmitted as autosomal recessive traits except for type II (Hunter syndrome), an X-linked recessive disorder (see Table 12-1).

Only MPSs in which heparan sulfate is stored are associated with retinal dystrophy. These include MPS I H *(Hurler syndrome)* and MPS I S *(Scheie syndrome),* the clinical features of which include coarse facies, cognitive disabilities, corneal clouding, and retinal degeneration. The retinal pigmentary changes may be subtle, but the ERG response is abnormal. MPS II *(Hunter syndrome)* also features a pigmentary retinopathy but omits corneal clouding; the patients have coarse facies and short stature and may show cognitive disabilities. MPS III *(Sanfilippo syndrome)* shows mild somatic stigmata but severe pigmentary retinopathy.

Other lysosomal metabolism disorders

Tay-Sachs disease (GM$_2$ gangliosidosis type I), caused by a deficient subunit A of hexosaminidase A, is the most common ganglioside storage disease. Glycolipid accumulation in the brain and retina causes cognitive disability and blindness, and death generally occurs between the ages of 2 and 5 years. Ganglion cells surrounding the fovea become filled with ganglioside and appear grayish or white. The subfoveal RPE and choroidal pigmentation thus contrast with the surrounding white fovea and parafovea as a prominent cherry-red spot (Fig 12-8). Sandhoff disease (GM$_2$ gangliosidosis type II) and generalized gangliosidosis (GM$_1$ gangliosidosis type I) can also show cherry-red spots.

The chronic nonneuronopathic adult form of *Gaucher disease* does not have cerebral involvement. This disease is characterized by large accumulations of glucosylceramide in the liver, spleen, lymph nodes, skin, and bone marrow. Some patients have a cherry-red spot; others show whitish subretinal lesions in the midperiphery of the fundus. The various types of *Niemann-Pick disease* are caused by the absence of different sphingomyelinase isoenzymes. Type B (chronic Niemann-Pick disease, sea-blue histiocyte syndrome) is the mildest, and although there is no functional involvement of the CNS, patients have a macular halo that is considered diagnostic (Fig 12-9). Type A (acute neuronopathic) Niemann-Pick disease shows a cherry-red spot in about 50% of cases.

Cherry-red spots are observed in sialidoses and galactosialidoses. These conditions include mucolipidosis I, the cherry-red spot–myoclonus syndrome, and Goldberg-Cotlier syndrome (GM$_1$ gangliosidosis type IV). Mucolipidosis IV causes diffuse retinal degeneration.

Fabry disease (angiokeratoma corporis diffusum) is an X-linked condition caused by mutations in the gene encoding alpha-galactosidase A. Ceramide trihexoside accumulates

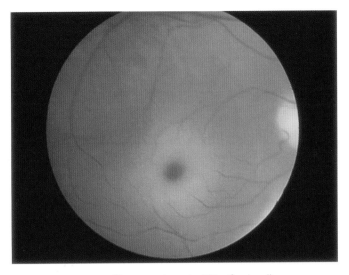

Figure 12-8 Cherry-red spot of Tay-Sachs disease.

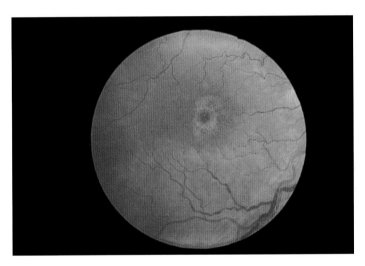

Figure 12-9 Macular halo in chronic Niemann-Pick disease. *(Courtesy of Mark W. Johnson, MD.)*

in the smooth muscle of blood vessels in the kidneys, skin, gastrointestinal tract, CNS, heart, and reticuloendothelial system, leading to various ocular and systemic clinical findings. The first symptom may be burning paresthesias or pain in the extremities in late childhood. Ocular signs include corneal verticillata (whorls), tortuous conjunctival vessels, tortuous and dilated retinal vessels, and lens changes (Fig 12-10). Vascular tortuosity of conjunctival and retinal vessels is also characteristic of fucosidosis.

Folz SJ, Trobe JD. The peroxisome and the eye. *Surv Ophthalmol.* 1991;35(5):353–368.
Haltia M. The neuronal ceroid-lipofuscinoses: from past to present. *Biochim Biophys Acta.* 2006;1762(10):850–856.

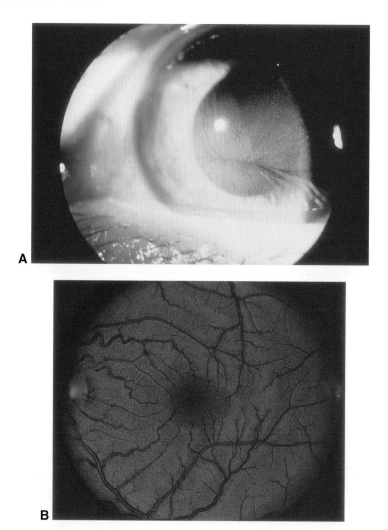

Figure 12-10 Fabry disease. **A,** Corneal whorls (cornea verticillata). **B,** Retinal vascular tortuosity.

Weleber RG, Gregory-Evans K. Retinitis pigmentosa and allied disorders. In: Ryan SJ, Hinton DR, Schachat AP, Wilkinson CP, eds. *Retina*. 4th ed. Philadelphia: Elsevier/Mosby; 2006:395–498.

Amino Acid Disorders

In *cystinosis*, intralysosomal cystine accumulates because of a defect in transport out of lysosomes. Three types are recognized, all autosomal recessive disorders: nephropathic, late-onset (or intermediate), and benign. Cystine crystals accumulate in the cornea and conjunctiva in all 3 types, but retinopathy develops only in patients with the nephropathic type. These patients are asymptomatic until 8–15 months of age, when they present with progressive renal failure, growth retardation, renal rickets, and hypothyroidism. The retinopathy is characterized by areas of patchy depigmentation of the RPE alternating with irregularly distributed pigment clumps. Despite the abnormal fundus appearance, no significant visual disturbance occurs. Treatment with cysteamine, which reacts with lysosomal cystine to form a mixed disulfide that can exit the lysosome, may be beneficial.

Mitochondrial Disorders

Mutations and deletions in mitochondrial DNA are associated with several different retinopathies, many of which are associated with myopathy. *Chronic progressive external ophthalmoplegia* belongs to a group of diseases collectively termed *mitochondrial myopathies*, in which mitochondria are abnormally shaped and increased in number; "ragged-red" fibers may be evident in muscle biopsy specimens. The syndrome is characterized by progressive external ophthalmoplegia, atypical RP, and various systemic abnormalities. When associated with cardiomyopathy, the disorder is known as the *Kearns-Sayre syndrome* (Table 12-3). Onset is usually before age 10. The severity of the pigmentary retinopathy is highly variable; the disease often shows mottled, macular pigmentary changes early in the course and only rarely involves bone-spicule–like changes (Fig 12-11). Many patients retain good visual function and a normal ERG signal; others with more penetrant disease have severe retinopathy with an extinguished ERG signal. Other mitochondrial myopathies with pigmentary retinopathy include *NARP* (neurogenic muscle weakness, ataxia, and retinitis pigmentosa) and *MELAS* (mitochondrial encephalomyopathy, lactic acidosis, and stroke) syndromes.

Brown MD, Lott MR, Wallace DC. Mitochondrial DNA mutations and the eye. In: Wright AF, Jay B, eds. *Molecular Genetics of Inherited Eye Disorders.* Chur, Switzerland: Harwood Academic; 1994:469–490.

Table 12-3 Characteristic Features of Kearns-Sayre Syndrome

Chronic progressive external ophthalmoplegia
Retinal pigmentary degeneration
Heart block

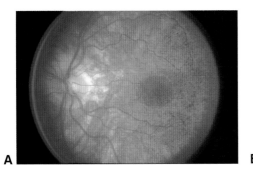 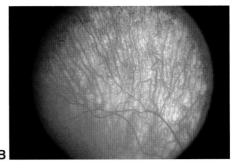

A   B

Figure 12-11 Pigmentary changes in Kearns-Sayre syndrome, a mitochondrial myopathy. Retinal function is often quite good. **A,** Macula. **B,** Periphery. *(Courtesy of Michael F. Marmor, MD.)*

Systemic Drug Toxicity

Chloroquine Derivatives

Although retinal toxicity from chloroquine use remains a problem in many parts of the world, it is rare in the United States, where the drug has largely been replaced by hydroxychloroquine for treatment of rheumatologic and dermatologic conditions. The mechanism of retinal toxicity from these drugs remains unclear. Both drugs bind to melanin in the RPE, which may serve to concentrate them or prolong their effects. Although the incidence of toxicity is very low, it is of serious concern because associated vision loss rarely recovers and may even progress after the drug is discontinued. Patients and their primary care physicians must be made fully aware of the ophthalmic risks and the need for regular screening examinations to detect retinal toxicity at an early stage (before symptomatic vision loss).

The earliest signs of toxicity include bilateral, paracentral visual field changes (best detected with a red test object) and a subtle, granular depigmentation of the paracentral RPE. With continued drug exposure, there is progressive development of a bilateral atrophic bull's-eye maculopathy (Fig 12-12) and paracentral scotomata, which may in severe cases ultimately spread over the entire fundus, causing widespread retinal atrophy and vision loss. In some patients, intraepithelial corneal verticillata develops.

Ophthalmic screening of patients receiving chloroquine or hydroxychloroquine is aimed primarily at early detection and minimization of toxicity. As summarized in a recent Clinical Statement from the American Academy of Ophthalmology (http://one.aao.org/CE/PracticeGuidelines/ClinicalStatements.aspx), the risk of toxicity is low for individuals without complicating conditions taking less than 6.5 mg/kg/day of hydroxychloroquine or 3 mg/kg/day of chloroquine, and/or cumulative doses of less than 1000 g and 460 g (total), respectively, particularly in the first 5 years of treatment. Additional risk factors mandate annual examinations starting with the initiation of the drug. In addition to higher daily and cumulative doses, other risk factors for retinal toxicity include obesity

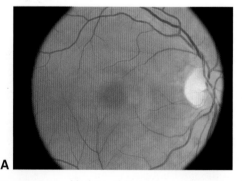 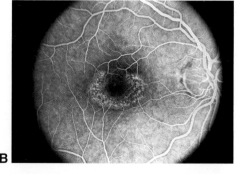

Figure 12-12 Hydroxychloroquine retinopathy. **A,** Fundus photograph shows subtle bull's-eye pattern of depigmented macular atrophy. **B,** Fluorescein angiogram highlights the atrophic maculopathy as a granular RPE transmission defect. *(Courtesy of Mark W. Johnson, MD, and Richard E. Hackel, MA, CRA.)*

("safe" daily doses are based on lean body weight), kidney or liver disease, older age (ie, over 60 years), and possibly concomitant retinal disease. Nevertheless, well-documented cases of hydroxychloroquine maculopathy have occurred with "safe" daily doses and in the absence of other risk factors.

Baseline evaluation for patients beginning treatment with a chloroquine derivative should include a complete ophthalmic examination, fundus photography for follow-up comparisons, and automated threshold field testing with a white pattern (Humphrey white 10-2 protocol), though some authors prefer red for its increased sensitivity. Ideally, central visual field assessment should test the central 10° of vision with a red visual test target because scotomata detected in this fashion may precede symptomatic vision loss and fundus changes and may be reversible. For patients at risk or those with unclear symptomatology, optical coherence tomography (to reveal loss of inner segment/outer segment junctions), fundus autofluorescence (focal hyper-/hypoautofluorescence), and multifocal electroretinography (paracentral mfERG depressions) should be obtained. In contrast to previous teachings, fluorescein angiography, full-field electroretinography, Amsler grid testing, color vision testing, and electro-oculography have been found to be less effective. Cessation of the drug at the first sign of toxicity is recommended.

Elder M, Rahman AM, McLay J. Early paracentral visual field loss in patients taking hydroxychloroquine. *Arch Ophthalmol.* 2006;124(12):1729–1733.

Marmor MF, Kellner U, Lai TY, Lyons JS, Mieler WF; American Academy of Ophthalmology. Revised recommendations on screening for chloroquine and hydroxychloroquine retinopathy. *Ophthalmology.* 2011;118(2):415–422.

Stepien KE, Han DP, Schell J, Godara P, Rha J, Carroll J. Spectral-domain optical coherence tomography and adaptive optics may detect hydroxychloroquine retinal toxicity before symptomatic vision loss. *Trans Am Ophthalmol Soc.* 2009;107:28–33.

Phenothiazines

Phenothiazines, including chlorpromazine and thioridazine, are concentrated in uveal tissue and RPE by binding to melanin granules. High-dose *chlorpromazine* therapy commonly results in abnormal pigmentation of the eyelids, interpalpebral conjunctiva, cornea, and anterior lens capsule; anterior and posterior subcapsular cataracts may develop. However, pigmentary retinopathy from chlorpromazine is rare, if it occurs at all.

In contrast, *thioridazine* causes severe retinopathy that can develop within a few weeks or months of high-dose utilization (Fig 12-13). Retinopathy is rare at doses of 800 mg/day or less. Initially, patients experience blurred vision, and the fundus shows coarse retinal pigment stippling in the posterior pole (see Fig 12-13A). Over time, the retinopathy evolves to widespread but patchy atrophy of the pigment epithelium and choriocapillaris, with a characteristic nummular pattern of involvement (see Fig 12-13B). Fundus changes in the late stages may be confused with choroideremia or Bietti crystalline corneoretinal dystrophy; symptoms include visual field loss and night blindness.

Visual function may improve after the drug is discontinued but will sometimes deteriorate years later if the chorioretinal atrophy progresses slowly. It is not known whether these late atrophic changes occurring after discontinuation of thioridazine or chloroquine

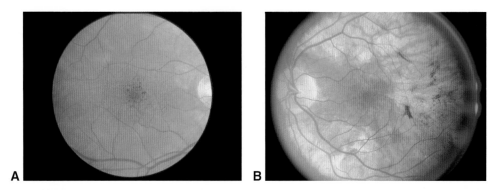

Figure 12-13 Thioridazine toxicity. **A,** The initial change is a coarse, granular maculopathy. **B,** The degeneration evolves into a nummular pattern with patchy areas of hypo- and hyperpigmentation. *(Courtesy of Michael F. Marmor, MD.)*

represent continued toxicity of the drugs or decompensation of cells injured when the drugs were used initially.

Patients taking thioridazine are generally not monitored ophthalmically because toxicity is rare at standard doses. However, suspected cases or patients who have received high doses of the drug should undergo a full evaluation of visual function that includes an ERG and monitoring comparable to that for chloroquine.

Other Drugs

Tamoxifen is an antiestrogen drug that has been used for more than 30 years to treat patients with advanced breast cancer. It is also used as adjuvant therapy following primary treatment for early-stage breast cancer and as prophylactic therapy for women with a high risk of the disease. Retinopathy is rare at the dose levels currently used, but crystalline retinopathy has been reported in patients receiving high-dose therapy (daily doses >200 mg and >100 g, cumulatively). The maculopathy is characterized by crystalline deposits and sometimes macular edema (Fig 12-14). Moderate degrees of both functional loss and morphological degenerative changes can occur.

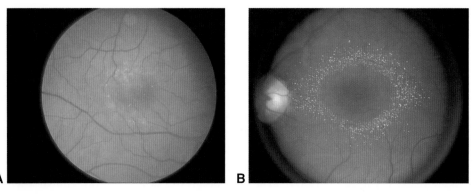

Figure 12-14 Crystalline retinopathies. **A,** Tamoxifen retinopathy. Significant functional damage may be associated with the crystalline changes. **B,** Canthaxanthine retinopathy. Retinal function is usually normal. *(Part A courtesy of Michael F. Marmor, MD; Part B courtesy of William Mieler, MD.)*

A crystalline maculopathy may also occur after ingestion of high doses of *canthaxanthine,* a carotenoid widely available in stores and on the Internet that is used to simulate tanning. Canthaxanthine retinopathy is generally asymptomatic, and the deposits resolve after the drug is discontinued (see Fig 12-14B). Crystalline deposits of oxalate have been noted after the ingestion of *ethylene glycol* and after prolonged administration of *methoxyflurane* anesthesia to patients with renal dysfunction (Table 12-4).

Intravenous administration of *desferrioxamine* in doses of 3–12 g/24 hours for the treatment of transfusional hemosiderosis can result in rapid bilateral vision loss (usually starting 7–10 days after treatment) with nyctalopia, ring scotoma, and reduced ERG signals. The fundi may appear normal initially, developing widespread mottled pigmentary changes within several weeks. Return of visual function occurs over 3–4 months, with most patients recovering normal acuity.

Some patients taking *isotretinoin* for acne have reported poor night vision and been found to have abnormal dark-adaptation curves and ERG responses. Toxicity seems to be infrequent but is more likely in patients undergoing repetitive courses of therapy. The changes are largely reversible.

The use of *rifabutin* in patients with human immunodeficiency virus (HIV) infection as prophylaxis against coinfection with *Mycobacterium avium* complex has been associated with the development of anterior and posterior uveitis. Hypopyon is sometimes present. The inflammation is reversible following discontinuation of the medicine.

In rare cases, the cardiac glycosides (eg, *digitalis*) may produce blurred vision, pericentral scotomata, defective color vision, and xanthopsia ("yellow vision"). The drug's ocular effects result from a cone dysfunction syndrome that reverses with cessation of the drug. Transient blue tinting of vision and temporary abnormal ERG responses have been observed in patients taking high doses of *sildenafil*. The vision symptom may occur in up to 50% of patients ingesting more than 100 mg per dose of sildenafil, but no permanent retinal toxic effects have been reported.

Table 12-4 Causes of Crystalline Retinopathy

Systemic disease
Primary hereditary hyperoxaluria
Cystinosis
Secondary oxalosis as a result of chronic renal failure and hemodialysis
Sjögren-Larsson syndrome

Drug-induced causes
Tamoxifen
Canthaxanthine
Talc (from contamination via intravenous drug abuse)
Nitrofurantoin
Methoxyflurane anesthesia (secondary oxalosis)
Ethylene glycol ingestion (secondary oxalosis)

Ocular diseases
Bietti crystalline dystrophy
Calcific drusen
Gyrate atrophy
Retinal telangiectasia

Callanan D, Williams PD. Retinal toxicity of systemic medications. In: Albert DM, Miller JW, Azar DT, Blodi BA, eds. *Albert & Jakobiec's Principles and Practice of Ophthalmology.* 3rd ed. Philadelphia: Saunders; 2008:chap 176.

Marmor MF. Is thioridazine retinopathy progressive? Relationship of pigmentary changes to visual function. *Br J Ophthalmol.* 1990;74(12):739–742.

Marmor MF. Sildenafil (Viagra) and ophthalmology. *Arch Ophthalmol.* 1999;117(4):518–519.

Mittra RA, Mieler WF. Drug and light ocular toxicity. In: Regillo CD, Brown GC, Flynn HW Jr, eds. *Vitreoretinal Disease: The Essentials.* New York: Thieme; 1999:545.

The authors thank John R. Heckenlively, MD, for his significant contributions to this chapter.

CHAPTER 13

Retinal Detachment and Predisposing Lesions

Retinal Breaks

A retinal break is any full-thickness defect in the neurosensory retina. Breaks are clinically significant in that they may allow liquefied vitreous to enter the potential space between the sensory retina and the retinal pigment epithelium (RPE), the epithelioretinal interspace, and thus cause a rhegmatogenous retinal detachment. Some breaks are caused by atrophy of inner retinal layers (holes); others result from vitreoretinal traction (tears). Breaks resulting from trauma are discussed in the following section. Retinal breaks may be classified as

- flap, or horseshoe, tears
- giant retinal tears
- operculated holes
- dialyses
- atrophic retinal holes

A *flap tear* occurs when a strip of retina is pulled anteriorly by vitreoretinal traction, often in the course of a posterior vitreous detachment or trauma. A tear is considered symptomatic when the patient reports photopsias, floaters, or both. A tear that extends 90° (3 clock-hours) or more circumferentially is classified as a *giant retinal tear*. An *operculated hole* occurs when traction is sufficient to tear a piece of retina completely free from the adjacent retinal surface. *Dialyses* are circumferential, linear breaks that occur along the anterior and posterior vitreous base, commonly as a consequence of blunt trauma. An *atrophic hole* is generally not associated with vitreoretinal traction and has not been associated with an increased risk of retinal detachment.

American Academy of Ophthalmology Retina/Vitreous Panel. Preferred Practice Pattern Guidelines. *Posterior Vitreous Detachment, Retinal Breaks, and Lattice Degeneration.* San Francisco: American Academy of Ophthalmology; 2008. Available at: www.aao.org/ppp.

Regillo CD, Benson WE. *Retinal Detachment. Diagnosis and Management.* 3rd ed. Philadelphia: Lippincott Williams & Wilkins; 1998.

Tiedeman JS. Retinal breaks, holes, and tears. *Focal Points: Clinical Modules for Ophthalmologists.* San Francisco: American Academy of Ophthalmology; 1996, module 3.

Traumatic Breaks

Blunt or penetrating eye trauma can cause retinal breaks by direct retinal perforation, contusion, or vitreous traction. Fibrocellular proliferation occurring later at the site of an injury may cause vitreoretinal traction and subsequent detachment. See also Chapter 15, Posterior Segment Manifestations of Trauma.

Blunt trauma can cause retinal breaks by direct contusive injury to the globe through 2 mechanisms:

1. *coup:* adjacent to the point of trauma
2. *contrecoup:* opposite the point of trauma

Blunt trauma compresses the eye along its anteroposterior axis and expands it in the equatorial plane. Because the vitreous body is viscoelastic, slow compression of the eye has no deleterious effect on the retina. However, rapid compression of the eye results in severe traction on the vitreous base that may tear the retina.

Contusion injury may cause large, ragged equatorial breaks, dialysis, or a macular hole. Traumatic breaks are often multiple, and they are commonly found in the inferotemporal and superonasal quadrants. The most common injuries are dialyses, which may be as small as 1 ora bay (the distance between 2 retinal dentate processes at the latitude of the ora serrata) or may extend 90° or more. Dialyses are usually located at the posterior border of the vitreous base but can also occur at the anterior border (Fig 13-1). Avulsion of the vitreous base may be associated with dialysis and is considered pathognomonic of ocular contusion. The vitreous base can be avulsed from the underlying retina and nonpigmented epithelium of the pars plana without tearing either one; generally, however, one or both are also torn in the process.

Less common types of breaks caused by blunt trauma are horseshoe-shaped tears, which may occur at the posterior margin of the vitreous base, at the posterior end of a meridional fold, or at the equator, and operculated holes (see Fig 13-1, Part 3).

Trauma in young eyes

Although young patients have a higher incidence of eye injury than other age groups, only in rare instances does the retina detach immediately following blunt trauma because young vitreous has not yet undergone syneresis, or liquefaction. The vitreous, therefore, provides an internal "cork," or tamponade, for the retinal tears or dialyses. With time, however, the vitreous may liquefy over a tear, allowing fluid to pass through the break to detach the retina. The clinical presentation of the retinal detachment is usually delayed, as follows:

- 12% of detachments are identified immediately
- 30% are identified within 1 month
- 50% are identified within 8 months
- 80% are identified within 24 months

Traumatic retinal detachments in young patients may be shallow and often show signs of chronicity, including multiple demarcation lines, subretinal deposits, and intraretinal schisis.

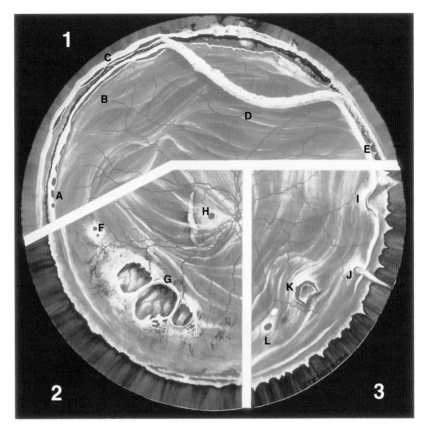

Figure 13-1 *Part 1.* Retinal breaks at borders of vitreous base. *A,* Small breaks at posterior border of vitreous base. *B,* Retinal dialysis at posterior border of vitreous base. *C,* Dialysis at anterior border of vitreous base. *D,* Avulsion of vitreous base that lies free in vitreous cavity. *E,* Tenting-up of retina and epithelium of pars plana ciliaris, forming ridges at posterior and anterior borders of vitreous base.

Part 2. Retinal breaks with no apparent vitreoretinal attachment. *F,* Round holes in atrophic retina. *G,* Irregular retinal hole in equatorial zone, associated with chorioretinal degeneration and vitreous and retinal hemorrhage. *H,* Atrophic macular hole associated with pigmentary changes and a choroidal rupture.

Part 3. Retinal breaks associated with abnormal vitreoretinal attachments. *I,* Horseshoe-shaped tear associated with an anomalous posterior extension of the vitreous base. *J,* Horseshoe-shaped tear at posterior end of meridional fold. *K,* Horseshoe-shaped tear in equatorial zone. *L,* Tear with operculum in overlying vitreous.

(Figure reproduced with permission from Cox MS, Schepens CL, Freeman HM. Retinal detachment due to ocular contusion. Arch Ophthalmol. 1966;76(5):678–685. Copyright 1966, American Medical Association.)

When posterior vitreous separation is present or occurs later after trauma, retinal breaks are often associated with abnormal vitreoretinal attachments and may resemble nontraumatic breaks. Retinal detachments may occur acutely in these patients.

Cox MS, Schepens CL, Freeman HM. Retinal detachment due to ocular contusion. *Arch Ophthalmol.* 1966;76(5):678–685.

Dugel PU, Win PH, Ober RR. Posterior segment manifestations of closed-globe contusion injury. In: Ryan SJ, Hinton DR, Schachat AP, Wilkinson CP, eds. *Retina*. Vol 3. 4th ed. Philadelphia: Elsevier/Mosby; 2006:2365–2377.

Rabena MD, Pieramici DJ, Balles MW. Traumatic retinopathy. In: Albert DM, Miller JW, Azar DT, Blodi BA, eds. *Albert & Jakobiec's Principles and Practice of Ophthalmology*. 3rd ed. Philadelphia: Saunders; 2008:chap 173.

Posterior Vitreous Detachment

The vitreous gel is attached most firmly at the *vitreous base,* a circumferential zone straddling the ora serrata that extends approximately 2 mm anterior and 4 mm posterior to the ora. Vitreous collagen fibers at this base are so firmly attached to the retina and pars plana epithelium that the vitreous cannot be separated without tearing these tissues. The vitreous is also firmly attached at the margin of the optic disc, at the macula, along major vessels, at the margins of lattice degeneration, and at chorioretinal scars.

Most retinal tears result from traction caused by spontaneous or traumatic *posterior vitreous detachment* (PVD; Fig 13-2). The predisposing event is syneresis of the central vitreous. There is growing evidence that age-related PVD is insidious and slowly progressive over many years. A PVD typically begins with a shallow separation in the perifoveal cortical vitreous. Liquid vitreous enters through a cortical tear and detaches the macular vitreous cortex, causing a partial vitreous detachment. The early stages are usually asymptomatic and occult; in most eyes, the evolving PVD remains subclinical for years until separation from the glial disc margin (the area of Martegiani) occurs (this separation from the disc is often accompanied by symptoms associated with the appearance of a Weiss ring). The vitreous gel remains attached at the vitreous base, and the resulting vitreous traction, commonly located at the posterior margin of the vitreous base or other points of firm attachment, can produce a retinal break (Fig 13-3).

The prevalence of PVD increases with the axial length of the eye and with age. Other conditions associated with vitreous syneresis (collapse), synchysis (liquefaction), and PVD include aphakia, inflammatory disease, trauma, vitreous hemorrhage, and myopia. It may be difficult to determine using biomicroscopy whether the vitreous is attached to or separated from the surface of the retina. Clinical studies typically reveal a low incidence of

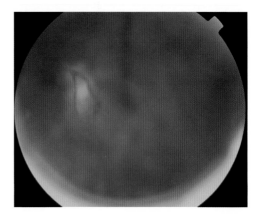

Figure 13-2 Posterior vitreous detachment. This patient has a glial floater (Weiss ring) overlying the area of Martegiani of the optic disc. *(Courtesy of Hermann D. Schubert, MD.)*

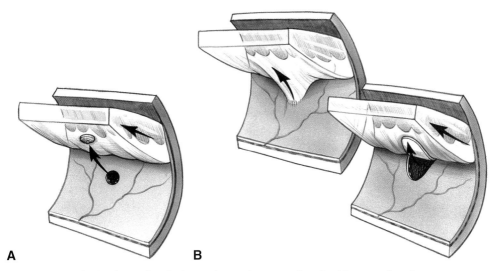

A   **B**

Figure 13-3 Mechanism of retinal tear formation associated with posterior vitreous separation. **A,** Round or oval hole. **B,** Flap tear: posterior extension of vitreous base with firm vitreoretinal attachment. *(Illustration by Christine Gralapp after illustrations by Tim Hengst.)*

PVD in patients less than 50 years of age. Autopsy studies demonstrate PVD in less than 10% of patients under the age of 50 years but in 63% of those over age 70 years.

Aphakia is commonly accompanied by PVD, which occurs in 66%–100% of aphakic eyes. The frequency of PVD was similar in patients undergoing intracapsular cataract extraction (ICCE) (84%) and extracapsular cataract extraction (ECCE) with an open capsule (76%), but it was much lower in eyes undergoing ECCE with an intact posterior capsule (40%).

Many patients do not report acute symptoms when a PVD occurs. Symptoms of PVD at the initial examination include the entoptic phenomena of photopsias (flashing lights), multiple floaters, and a curtain or cloud. Patients with these symptoms should be examined promptly, and office staff should be made aware of the urgency of these symptoms. Flashing lights are caused by the physical stimulus of vitreoretinal traction on the retina. Floaters are caused by vitreous opacities such as blood, glial cells torn from the optic disc, or aggregated collagen fibers, all of which can cast shadows on the retina.

Vitreous hemorrhage may arise from rupture of retinal vessels that cross retinal tears or from avulsion of superficial retinal or prepapillary vessels. Vitreous hemorrhage is an ominous sign. Approximately 15% of all patients with acute symptomatic PVD have a retinal tear. However, 50%–70% of PVD patients who have associated vitreous hemorrhage have retinal tears, whereas only 10%–12% without vitreous hemorrhage have retinal tears. Patients with an acute PVD complicated by a retinal tear are 7 times more likely to present with vitreous pigment or granules than those without a tear. Vitreous hemorrhage at the initial examination and an increase in the number of floaters after the initial examination are important predictors of subsequent new retinal breaks.

van Overdam KA, Bettink-Remeijer MW, Klaver CC, Mulder PG, Moll AC, van Meurs JC. Symptoms and findings predictive for the development of new retinal breaks. *Arch Ophthalmol.* 2005;123(4):479–484.

Examination and Management of PVD

Indirect ophthalmoscopy with scleral depression and slit-lamp biomicroscopy with a 3-mirror lens or indirect contact lens are used to make the clinical diagnosis of PVD and rule out retinal breaks or detachment. The presence of hemorrhage or pigment in the vitreous suggests a possible retinal break and demands a thorough examination. Even in the absence of hemorrhage, pigment, or detectable retinal break, the ophthalmologist may wish to reexamine the patient in 2–4 weeks because breaks may evolve over time, depending on additional risk factors such as aphakia, myopia, family history of retinal detachment, or signs of Stickler syndrome. All patients should be instructed to return to the ophthalmologist immediately if they notice a change in symptoms, such as increasing numbers of floaters or the development of visual field loss.

If a large vitreous hemorrhage precludes a complete examination, bilateral ocular patching and bed rest with the patient's head elevated 45° or more for a few hours or days may clear the vitreous sufficiently to allow breaks in a superior location to be found. This approach is especially important for patients with risk factors for retinal detachment. Echography may be performed to find flap tears and rule out retinal detachment and other fundus lesions. If the cause of the hemorrhage cannot be found, the patient should be reexamined at frequent, regular intervals. A vitrectomy may be considered in the search for an etiology of a nonclearing hemorrhage.

Byer NE. Natural history of posterior vitreous detachment with early management as the premier line of defense against retinal detachment. *Ophthalmology.* 1994:101(9): 1503–1514.

Green WR, Sebag J. Vitreoretinal interface. In: Ryan SJ, Hinton DR, Schachat AP, Wilkinson CP, eds. *Retina.* Vol 3. 4th ed. Philadelphia: Elsevier/Mosby; 2006:1921–1989.

Uchino E, Uemura A, Ohba N. Initial stages of posterior vitreous detachment in healthy eyes of older persons evaluated by optical coherence tomography. *Arch Ophthalmol.* 2001;119(10):1475–1479.

Lesions Predisposing Eyes to Retinal Detachment

Lattice Degeneration

Lattice degeneration, a vitreoretinal interface abnormality, is present in 6%–10% of the general population and is bilateral in one-third to one-half of affected patients. It occurs more commonly in—but is not limited to—myopic eyes; a familial predilection is present.

Lattice degeneration may predispose eyes to retinal breaks and detachment. The most important histologic features include varying degrees of atrophy and irregularity of the inner layers, an overlying pocket of liquefied vitreous, condensation, and adherence of vitreous at the margin of the lesion. (Figs 13-4, 13-5, 13-6).

Although detachment develops in only a small number of patients with lattice degeneration, lattice is found in 20%–30% of all eyes that present with rhegmatogenous retinal detachments. Lattice degeneration progresses to retinal detachment either by means of a

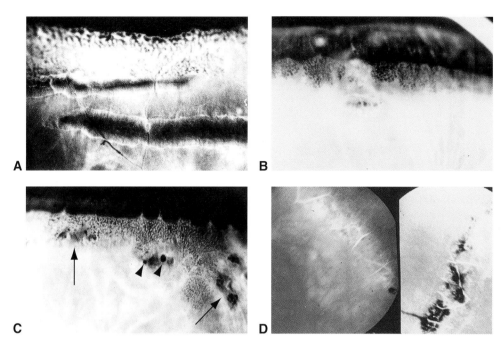

Figure 13-4 Various appearances of lattice degeneration of the retina. **A,** Overlapping linear areas of retinal thinning; condensed vitreous at margin is apparent. **B,** Small area of retinal thinning, with vitreous condensation at margin and pocket of fluid vitreous centrally. **C,** Several areas of retinal thinning *(arrows).* One area has 2 holes *(arrowheads)* within area of thinning. **D,** Ophthalmoscopic appearance of lattice degeneration *(left)* with a linear area of lattice "wicker" caused by sclerotic blood vessels. In addition, photograph at right shows secondary RPE hyperplasia with migration into the retina. *(From Green WR. Retina. In: Spencer WH, ed. Ophthalmic Pathology: An Atlas and Textbook. 3rd ed. Philadelphia: Saunders; 1985:866.)*

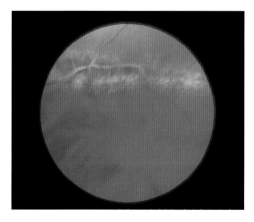

Figure 13-5 Lattice degeneration as viewed without scleral indentation. Vascular sheathing is apparent where the vessel crosses the area of lattice. Characteristic white lattice lines are visible. *(Reproduced with permission from Byer NE. Peripheral Retina in Profile: A Stereoscopic Atlas. Torrance, CA: Criterion Press; 1982.)*

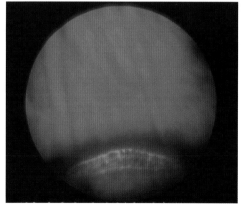

Figure 13-6 Lattice degeneration as viewed with scleral indentation. *(Reproduced with permission from Byer NE. Peripheral Retina in Profile: A Stereoscopic Atlas. Torrance, CA: Criterion Press; 1982.)*

tractional tear at the lateral or posterior margin of the lattice lesion or, less commonly, by means of an atrophic hole within the zone of lattice itself (Figs 13-7, 13-8). Progression to detachment tends to occur in young patients with myopia; they are typically asymptomatic until fixation is involved and do not have vitreous detachment.

> Byer NE. Lattice degeneration of the retina. *Surv Ophthalmol.* 1979;23(4):213–248.
>
> Byer NE. Long-term natural history of lattice degeneration of the retina. *Ophthalmology.* 1989;96(9):1396–1402.

Vitreoretinal Tufts

Peripheral retinal tufts are small, peripheral, focal areas of elevated glial hyperplasia associated with vitreous or zonular attachment and traction. Tractional tufts are classified according to anatomical, pathogenetic, and clinical distinctions into the following groups:

- noncystic retinal tufts (Fig 13-9)
- cystic retinal tufts (Fig 13-10)
- zonular traction retinal tufts (Fig 13-11)

Retinal pigment epithelial hyperplasia may surround the tuft. Cystic and zonular traction retinal tufts, both with firm vitreoretinal adhesions, may predispose eyes to retinal detachment. Flap tears and operculated holes may occur as a result of traction associated with PVD.

> Byer NE. Cystic retinal tufts and their relationship to retinal detachment. *Arch Ophthalmol.* 1981;99(10):1788–1790.

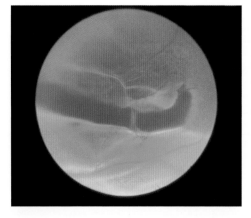

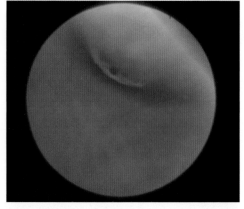

Figure 13-7 Lattice degeneration with large, posteriorly located flap tear and associated detachment. Note vessel bridging the tear. *(Reproduced with permission from Byer NE. Peripheral Retina in Profile: A Stereoscopic Atlas. Torrance, CA: Criterion Press; 1982.)*

Figure 13-8 Lattice degeneration with a small atrophic hole. *(Courtesy of Norman E. Byer, MD.)*

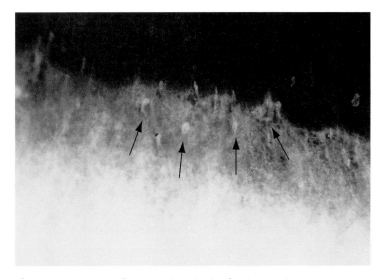

Figure 13-9 Gross appearance of noncystic retinal tufts *(arrows)*. *(From Green WR. Retina. In: Spencer WH, ed. Ophthalmic Pathology: An Atlas and Textbook. 3 vols. 3rd ed. Philadelphia: Saunders; 1985:894.)*

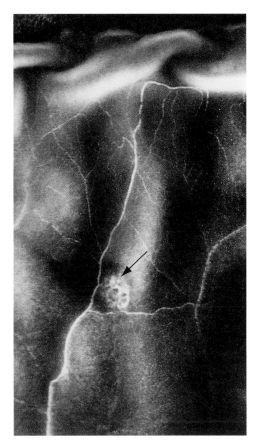

Figure 13-10 Cystic retinal tuft *(arrow)* in the peripheral retina of a 14-year-old boy. Tuft measures 0.47 mm at its circular base, is 3.7 mm from the ora serrata, and contains many microcysts with dense walls. *(From Duane TD, Jaeger EA, eds. Clinical Ophthalmology. Vol 3. Philadelphia: Lippincott; 1990:chap 26, p 24. Photograph courtesy of Robert Y. Foos, MD.)*

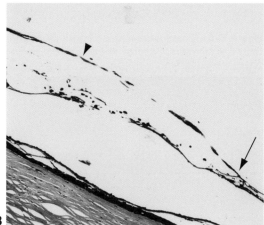

Figure 13-11 A, Zonular traction tuft *(arrow)* extending over the pars plana from the peripheral retina. **B,** Tuft is attached to the peripheral retina *(arrow)* and extends *(arrowhead)* over the pars plana. *(From Green WR. Retina. In: Spencer WH, ed. Ophthalmic Pathology: An Atlas and Textbook. 3 vols. 3rd ed. Philadelphia: Saunders; 1985:897.)*

Meridional Folds, Enclosed Ora Bays, and Peripheral Retinal Excavations

Meridional folds are folds of redundant retina, usually located superonasally. They are most commonly associated with dentate processes but may also extend posteriorly from ora bays. Occasionally, tears associated with PVD occur at the most posterior limit of the folds (see Fig 1-3). Retinal tears can also occur at or near the posterior margins of *enclosed ora bays,* which are oval islands of pars plana epithelium located immediately posterior to the ora serrata and completely or almost completely surrounded by peripheral retina (Fig 13-12). Occasionally, tears may occur at the site of *peripheral retinal excavations.* These lesions may represent a mild form of lattice degeneration. The excavations may have firm vitreoretinal adhesions and are found adjacent to, or up to 4 disc diameters posterior to, the ora serrata. They are often aligned with meridional folds.

Glasgow BJ, Foos RY, Yoshizumi MO. Degenerative diseases of the peripheral retina. In: Tasman W, Jaeger EA, eds. *Duane's Clinical Ophthalmology.* Vol 3. Philadelphia: Lippincott; 1994:chap 26, pp 1–30.

Figure 13-12 Meridional complex, consisting of a dentate process *(arrowhead)* that is continuous with pars plicata and an area of enclosed pars plana and ora bay *(asterisk)*. *(Reproduced from Green WR. Pathology of the retina. In: Frayer WC, ed. Lancaster Course in Ophthalmic Histopathology, unit 9. Philadelphia: FA Davis; 1981.)*

Lesions Not Predisposing Eyes to Retinal Detachment

Paving-Stone, or Cobblestone, Degeneration

Paving-stone (cobblestone) degeneration is characterized by peripheral, small, discrete areas of atrophy of the outer retina that appear in 22% of individuals over 20 years of age (Fig 13-13). They may occur singly or in groups and sometimes are confluent. Histologically, paving stones are characterized by atrophy of the RPE and outer retinal layers, attenuation or absence of the choriocapillaris, and adhesions between the remaining

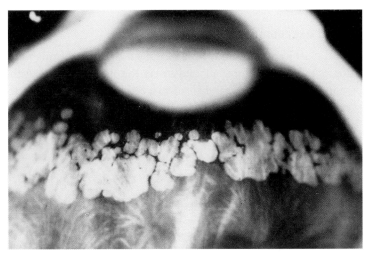

Figure 13-13 Gross appearance of paving-stone degeneration. *(From Green WR. Pathology of the retina. In: Frayer WC, ed. Lancaster Course in Ophthalmic Histopathology, unit 9. Philadelphia: FA Davis; 1981.)*

neuroepithelial layers and Bruch membrane. These lesions are most common in the inferior quadrants, anterior to the equator. Ophthalmoscopically, they appear yellowish white and are sometimes surrounded by a rim of hypertrophic RPE. Because the RPE is absent or hypoplastic, large choroidal vessels are visible beneath the lesions.

Paving-stone degeneration is never the site of a primary retinal break, but some observers have reported that a secondary tear may occur if a retinal detachment caused by an unrelated break puts traction on the margin of the lesion. Such breaks appear to be exceedingly rare. In fact, a zone of paving stones usually limits the spread of a detachment.

> Glasgow BJ, Foos RY, Yoshizumi MO. Degenerative diseases of the peripheral retina. In: Tasman W, Jaeger EA, eds. *Duane's Clinical Ophthalmology.* Vol 3. Philadelphia: Lippincott; 1994:chap 26, pp 1–30.

Retinal Pigment Epithelial Hyperplasia

When stimulated by chronic low-grade traction, RPE cells proliferate abnormally. Diffuse RPE hyperplasia can be observed straddling the ora serrata, in latitudes that correspond roughly to the insertion of the vitreous base or occurring focally on the pars plana and peripheral retina, especially in areas of focal traction such as vitreoretinal tufts and lattice degeneration. Areas of previous inflammation and trauma may also be sites of RPE hyperplasia.

Retinal Pigment Epithelial Hypertrophy

Acquired RPE hypertrophy is an aging and degenerative change that commonly occurs in the periphery, often in a reticular pattern. Histologically, it is characterized by large cells and by large, spherical melanin granules. Hypertrophy is usually observed just posterior to the ora serrata. Similar histologic features are present in congenital hypertrophy of the RPE (grouped pigmentation, or "bear tracks").

Peripheral Cystoid Degeneration

Typical peripheral cystoid degeneration, characterized by zones of microcysts in the far peripheral retina, is present in almost all adults over the age of 20 years. Although retinal holes may form in these areas, they rarely lead to a retinal detachment. Reticular peripheral cystoid degeneration is almost always located posterior to typical peripheral cystoid degeneration. It tends to occur in the inner retina and presents with a linear or reticular pattern following the retinal vessels. This form is found in about 20% of adults and may, in a few instances, develop into reticular degenerative retinoschisis.

Prophylactic Treatment of Retinal Breaks

Any retinal break can cause a retinal detachment by allowing liquid vitreous to pass through it and separate the sensory retina from the RPE. However, the vast majority of retinal breaks do not cause a detachment. Approximately 6% of all eyes have a break, but detachments develop in only 1 in 10,000–15,000 persons per year. Assuming an average life expectancy of 78 years in the United States, an estimated 0.07% or more (depending on local rates of cataract surgery) of the population will incur a retinal detachment over their lifetime.

The ophthalmologist may consider prophylactic treatment of breaks in an attempt to reduce the risk of retinal detachment. Treatment does not eliminate the risk of new tears or detachment.

The goal of prophylactic treatment of retinal breaks is to create a chorioretinal scar around each break to prevent fluid vitreous from entering the subretinal space. Either cryotherapy or photocoagulation can be used to "wall off" the break. If subretinal fluid is present, treatment must surround the area of subretinal fluid. In treating lattice degeneration, the ophthalmologist should take care to surround the entire lesion with treatment, paying particular attention to its posterior margin and lateral extent.

Results of numerous clinical studies have demonstrated that acute, symptomatic breaks are at higher risk of progression than are preexisting, asymptomatic breaks. Acute breaks are sometimes associated with vitreous hemorrhage or intraretinal hemorrhage at the margin of the tear. For some retinal breaks, such as inferior round atrophic holes and operculated holes, the risk of progressing to retinal detachment is minimal, whereas for other breaks, such as superior acute symptomatic flap tears, the risk may be substantial.

In considering prophylaxis, the ophthalmologist must weigh numerous factors, including symptoms, family history, residual traction, size and location of the break, phakic status, refractive error, status of the fellow eye, presence of subretinal fluid, and availability of follow-up evaluation. The following discussion serves only as a broad guideline, as specific recommendations depend on many clinical factors. (See also the discussion of hereditary vitreoretinopathies with optically empty vitreous in Chapter 14.)

American Academy of Ophthalmology Retina/Vitreous Panel. Preferred Practice Pattern Guidelines. *Posterior Vitreous Detachment, Retinal Breaks, and Lattice Degeneration.* San Francisco: American Academy of Ophthalmology: 2008. Available at www.aao.org/ppp.

Hilton GF, McLean EB, Brinton DA. *Retinal Detachment: Principles and Practice.* 2nd ed. Ophthalmology Monograph 1. San Francisco: American Academy of Ophthalmology; 1995.

Smiddy WE, Flynn HW Jr, Nicholson DH, et al. Results and complications in treated retinal breaks. *Am J Ophthalmol.* 1991;112(6):623–631.

Symptomatic Retinal Breaks

Approximately 15% of eyes with a symptomatic PVD are found to have one or more tractional tears, which are likely to cause a retinal detachment. Therefore, *acute symptomatic flap tears* are commonly treated prophylactically (Table 13-1).

Acute operculated holes are less likely to cause detachment because there is no residual traction on the adjacent retina; therefore, such breaks may not require treatment. However, if slit-lamp biomicroscopy reveals persistent vitreous traction at the margin of an operculated hole, that hole is comparable to a flap tear, and prophylaxis should be considered. Additional factors that may weigh in the decision toward treatment are large holes, a superior location, and the presence of vitreous hemorrhage.

Table 13-1 Indications for Treatment of Retinal Tears and Holes in Symptomatic Patients

Type of Lesion	Treatment
Horseshoe tears	Almost always
Dialysis	Almost always
Operculated tear	Sometimes
Atrophic hole	Rarely
Lattice degeneration without horseshoe tears	Rarely

Modified with permission from American Academy of Ophthalmology Retina/Vitreous Panel. Preferred Practice Pattern Guidelines. *Posterior Vitreous Detachment, Retinal Breaks, and Lattice Degeneration.* San Francisco: American Academy of Ophthalmology; 2008. Available at www.aao.org/ppp.

Atrophic holes are often incidental findings in a patient who presents with an acute PVD. Without associated traction, treatment is generally not required.

Asymptomatic Retinal Breaks

Asymptomatic flap tears infrequently cause retinal detachment and generally are not treated in emmetropic, phakic eyes. However, asymptomatic flap tears accompanied by lattice degeneration, myopia, or subclinical detachment or aphakia associated with detachment in the fellow eye all may increase a patient's risk of retinal detachment; under these circumstances, treatment may be considered. Asymptomatic operculated and atrophic holes rarely cause retinal detachment and are generally not treated (Table 13-2).

> Byer NE. What happens to untreated asymptomatic retinal breaks, and are they affected by posterior vitreous detachment? *Ophthalmology.* 1998;105(6):1045–1050.

Prophylactic Treatment of Lattice Degeneration

As mentioned earlier in this chapter, lattice degeneration occurs in approximately 6%–10% of eyes but is found in 20%–30% of eyes with a retinal detachment. Limited data are

Table 13-2 Indications for Treatment of Retinal Tears and Holes in Asymptomatic Patients

Type of Lesion	Types of Eyes			
	Phakic	Highly Myopic	Fellow Eye*	Aphakic or Pseudophakic
Horseshoe tears	Sometimes	Sometimes	Sometimes	Sometimes
Operculated tears	No	Rarely	Rarely	Rarely
Atrophic holes	Rarely	Rarely	Rarely	Rarely
Lattice degeneration with or without holes	No	No	Sometimes	Rarely

*Applies to patients who have had a retinal detachment in the other eye.

Modified with permission from American Academy of Ophthalmology Retina/Vitreous Panel. Preferred Practice Pattern Guidelines. *Posterior Vitreous Detachment, Retinal Breaks, and Lattice Degeneration.* San Francisco: American Academy of Ophthalmology; 2008. Available at www.aao.org/ppp.

available, but an 11-year follow-up study of untreated lattice degeneration patients with no symptomatic tears showed that retinal detachment occurred in approximately 1%. Thus, the presence of lattice, with or without atrophic holes during routine examination, generally does not require prophylaxis in the absence of other risk factors. If lattice degeneration is present in a patient with additional risk factors, such as retinal detachment in the fellow eye, flap tears, or aphakia, prophylactic treatment can be considered.

> Byer NE. Long-term natural history of lattice degeneration of the retina. *Ophthalmology.* 1989;96(9):1396–1402.
>
> Wilkinson CP. Evidence-based analysis of prophylactic treatment of asymptomatic retinal breaks and lattice degeneration. *Ophthalmology.* 2000;107(1):12–18.

Aphakia and Pseudophakia

Because aphakic and pseudophakic eyes have a higher risk of retinal detachment (1%–3%) than do phakic eyes, such patients should be warned of potential symptoms and carefully examined if symptoms occur. The value of prophylactic treatment of asymptomatic breaks is uncertain. Flap tears or eyes with subclinical detachments are sometimes treated in patients with aphakia or pseudophakia.

Fellow Eye in Patients With Retinal Detachment

Approximately 10% of patients with phakic retinal detachment in 1 eye and 20%–36% of patients with aphakic detachment in 1 eye will incur detachment in the fellow eye. Prophylactic treatment of flap tears is often considered, whereas the treatment benefit for round holes has not been conclusively determined. A retrospective study found that the risk of retinal detachment in the fellow eye of patients with phakic lattice retinal detachments was reduced over 7 years of follow-up from 5.1% in untreated eyes to 1.8% in eyes receiving full prophylactic laser treatment of lattice degeneration. However, it is noteworthy that the incidence of retinal detachment was low in both groups; therefore, prophylaxis was not universally recommended, particularly not for eyes with more than 6 D of myopia and more than 6 clock-hours of lattice.

> Folk JC, Arrindell EL, Klugman MR. The fellow eye of patients with phakic lattice retinal detachment. *Ophthalmology.* 1989;96(1):72–79.

Subclinical Retinal Detachment

The definition of a *subclinical retinal detachment* varies. Although the term may refer to an asymptomatic retinal detachment, it more commonly describes a detachment in which subretinal fluid extends more than 1 disc diameter from the break but not more than 2 disc diameters posterior to the equator. Because approximately 30% of such detachments will progress, treatment is often recommended. Treatment is particularly advised for symptomatic patients or those with traction on the break. Patients with demarcation lines may be monitored but should not be considered risk free, as progression may occur through the demarcation line.

> Brod RD, Flynn HW Jr, Lightman DA. Asymptomatic rhegmatogenous retinal detachments. *Arch Ophthalmol.* 1995;113(8):1030–1032.

Retinal Detachment

Retinal detachments are classified as

- rhegmatogenous
- tractional
- exudative

The most common type, *rhegmatogenous retinal detachment (RRD),* is caused by lique-fied vitreous passing through a retinal break into the potential epithelioretinal interspace between the sensory retina and the RPE. The term is derived from the Greek *rhegma,* meaning "break." The less common *tractional detachments* are caused by proliferative membranes that contract and elevate the retina. Combinations of tractional and rheg-matogenous causes may lead to a detachment. *Exudative,* or *secondary, detachments* are caused by retinal or choroidal diseases in which fluid leaks beneath the sensory retina and accumulates. Although exudative detachments commonly occur in limited areas associ-ated with choroidal neovascularization, unlike rhegmatogenous detachments, it is rare for exudative detachments to become extensive.

The differential diagnosis of retinal detachment includes retinoschisis, choroidal tu-mors, and retinal elevation secondary to detachment of the choroid. Diagnostic features of the 3 forms of retinal detachment are listed in Table 13-3.

Rhegmatogenous Retinal Detachment

In 90%–95% of RRDs, a definite retinal break can be found, often with the help of Lincoff rules (Figs 13-14, 13-15). In the remainder, an occult break is presumed to be present. If no break can be found, the ophthalmologist must rule out all other causes of retinal elevation. Fifty percent of patients with RRD have photopsias or floaters. The intraocular pressure is usually lower in the affected eye than in the fellow eye but may occasionally be higher. A Shafer sign, descriptively termed "tobacco dust" for small clumps of pigmented cells, is frequently present in the vitreous or anterior segment. The retina detaches pro-gressively from the ora serrata to the disc; usually it has convex borders and contours and a corrugated appearance, especially in recent retinal detachments, and undulates with eye movements. In a long-standing RRD, however, the retina may appear smooth and thin. Fixed folds resulting from *proliferative vitreoretinopathy (PVR)* almost always indicate a rhegmatogenous retinal detachment. Shifting fluid may occur but is uncommon.

PVR is the most common cause of failure to repair RRD. In PVR, retinal pigment epi-thelial, glial, and other cells grow and migrate on both the inner and outer retinal surfaces and on the vitreous face, forming membranes. Contraction of these membranes causes fixed retinal folds, equatorial traction, detachment of the nonpigmented epithelium from the pars plana, and generalized retinal shrinkage (Fig 13-16). As a result, the causative ret-inal breaks may reopen, new breaks may occur, or a tractional detachment may develop.

To better compare preoperative anatomy with outcomes, a generally accepted clas-sification of PVR was developed (Table 13-4). The 1991 classification has 3 grades of PVR (A, B, C), corresponding to increasing severity of the disease. Anterior and posterior involvement (CA, CP) is distinguished and subclassified into focal, diffuse, subretinal,

Table 13-3 Diagnostic Features of the 3 Types of Retinal Detachments

	Rhegmatogenous (Primary)	Nonrhegmatogenous (Secondary)	
		Tractional	Exudative
History	Aphakia, myopia, blunt trauma, photopsia, floaters, field defect; progressive, generally healthy	Diabetes, prematurity, penetrating trauma, sickle cell disease, venous occlusions	Systemic factors such as malignant hypertension, eclampsia, renal failure
Retinal break	Identified in 90%–95% of cases	No primary break; may develop secondary break	No break, or coincidental
Extent of detachment	Extends ora to disc early, has convex borders and surfaces, gravity-dependent	Frequently does not extend to ora, may be central or peripheral	Volume- and gravity-dependent; extension to ora is variable, may be central or peripheral
Retinal mobility	Undulating bullae or folds	Taut retina, concave borders and surfaces, peaks to traction points	Smoothly elevated bullae, usually without folds
Evidence of chronicity	Demarcation lines, intraretinal macro-cysts, atrophic retina	Demarcation lines	Usually none
Pigment in vitreous	Present in 70% of cases	Present in trauma cases	Not present
Vitreous changes	Frequently syneretic, posterior vitreous detachment, traction on flap of tear	Vitreoretinal traction	Usually clear, except in uveitis
Subretinal fluid	Clear	Clear, no shift	May be turbid and shift rapidly to dependent location with changes in head position
Choroidal mass	None	None	May be present
Intraocular pressure	Frequently low	Usually normal	Varies
Transillumination	Normal	Normal	Blocked transillumination if pigmented choroidal lesion present
Examples of conditions causing detachment	Retinal break	Proliferative diabetic retinopathy, retinopathy of prematurity, toxocariasis, sickle cell retinopathy, posttraumatic vitreous traction	Uveitis, metastatic tumor, malignant melanoma, Coats disease, Vogt-Koyanagi-Harada syndrome, retinoblastoma, choroidal hemangioma, senile exudative maculopathy, exudative detachment after cryotherapy or diathermy

Reproduced with permission from Hilton GF, McLean EB, Brinton DA, eds. *Retinal Detachment: Principles and Practice*. 2nd ed. Ophthalmology Monograph 1. San Francisco: American Academy of Ophthalmology; 1995.

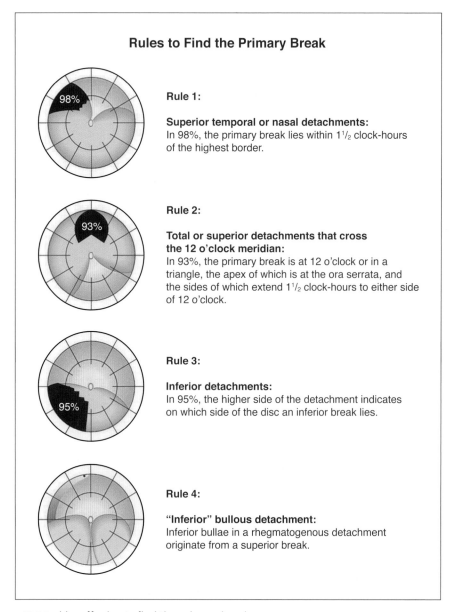

Rules to Find the Primary Break

Rule 1:

Superior temporal or nasal detachments:
In 98%, the primary break lies within 1½ clock-hours of the highest border.

Rule 2:

Total or superior detachments that cross the 12 o'clock meridian:
In 93%, the primary break is at 12 o'clock or in a triangle, the apex of which is at the ora serrata, and the sides of which extend 1½ clock-hours to either side of 12 o'clock.

Rule 3:

Inferior detachments:
In 95%, the higher side of the detachment indicates on which side of the disc an inferior break lies.

Rule 4:

"Inferior" bullous detachment:
Inferior bullae in a rhegmatogenous detachment originate from a superior break.

Figure 13-14 Lincoff rules to find the primary break. *(Reproduced with permission from Kreissig I. A Practical Guide to Minimal Surgery for Retinal Detachment. Vol 1. Stuttgart, New York: Thieme; 2000:13–18.)*

circumferential, and anterior displacement. The extent of the pathology is described in clock-hours.

Han DP, Lean JS. Proliferative vitreoretinopathy. In: Albert DM, Miller JW, Azar DT, Blodi BA, eds. *Albert & Jakobiec's Principles and Practice of Ophthalmology*. Philadelphia: Saunders; 2008:chap 183.

Machemer R, Aaberg TM, Freeman HM, Irvine AR, Lean JS, Michels RM. An updated classification of retinal detachment with proliferative vitreoretinopathy. *Am J Ophthalmol.* 1991;112(2):159–165.

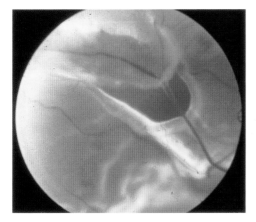

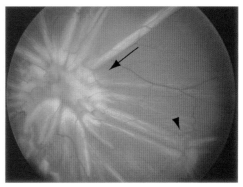

Figure 13-15 Horseshoe retinal tear with associated retinal detachment. Intact retinal vessel bridges the tear, and some vessels crossing the flap tears rupture. Along with photopsia, initial symptoms may include black spots from an intravitreal hemorrhage.

Figure 13-16 Retinal detachment with proliferative vitreoretinopathy (PVR). Revised Retina Society classification CP-12 with diffuse retinal contraction in posterior pole *(arrow)* and single midperipheral starfold *(arrowhead)*. See Table 13-4.

Table 13-4 Classification of Proliferative Vitreoretinopathy, 1991

Grade	Features
A	Vitreous haze, vitreous pigment clumps, pigment clusters on inferior retina
B	Wrinkling of inner retinal surface, retinal stiffness, vessel tortuosity, rolled and irregular edge of retinal break, decreased mobility of vitreous
CP 1–12	Posterior to equator: focal, diffuse, or circumferential full-thickness folds,* subretinal strands*
CA 1–12	Anterior to equator: focal, diffuse, or circumferential full-thickness folds,* subretinal strands,* anterior displacement,* condensed vitreous with strands

*Expressed in number of clock-hours involved.

From Machemer R, Aaberg TM, Freeman HM, Irvine AR, Lean JS, Michels RM. An updated classification of retinal detachment with proliferative vitreoretinopathy. *Am J Ophthalmol.* 1991;112(2):159–165.

Management of rhegmatogenous retinal detachment

The principles of surgery for retinal detachment are as follows:

- Find all breaks.
- Create a chorioretinal irritation around each break.
- Bring the retina and choroid into contact for sufficient time to produce a chorioretinal adhesion that will permanently wall off the subretinal space.

The most important element in management is a careful retinal examination, first preoperatively and then intraoperatively.

The retinal break can be closed by a number of methods. A scleral buckling procedure, which indents the sclera beneath the retinal break, promotes reapposition of the retina to the RPE by reducing vitreous traction and diminishing the flux of vitreous fluid through the retinal tear (Fig 13-17). A balloon device can be used to create a temporary

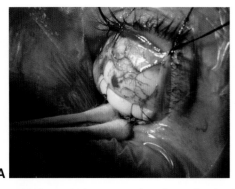
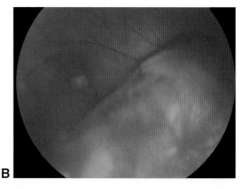

A   **B**

Figure 13-17   **A,** Intraoperative view of scleral buckle, parallel to and 18.75 mm posterior to the limbus. **B,** Interior view after nondrainage reattachment. *(Courtesy of Irene Barbazetto, MD, and Hermann D. Schubert, MD.)*

scleral buckle until a chorioretinal adhesion forms. With either a balloon or a buckle, the scleral indentation "corks" the break from the outside. In cases of PVR, epiretinal membranes pull retinal breaks away from the RPE. The indentation of the scleral buckle may change the vector of the tractional forces exerted by epiretinal membranes and thus permanently reduce traction on the breaks and on the yet-uninvolved retina.

Whereas most buckling procedures produce an indentation from the outside, some breaks, particularly those with minimal or no vitreous traction, can be treated by means of a temporary tamponade from the inside. *Pneumatic retinopexy,* used in selected retinal detachments caused by breaks in the superior two-thirds of the fundus, is a procedure in which a gas bubble is injected into the vitreous cavity to "cork" the retinal breaks internally until the retina is reattached. All retinal reattachment procedures include a firm chorioretinal adhesion around the break produced by cryotherapy, laser, or diathermy. *Vitrectomy* is useful in selected retinal detachments to internally relieve vitreoretinal traction. See Chapter 17.

Brinton DA, Lit ES. Pneumatic retinopexy. In: Ryan SJ, Hinton DR, Schachat AP, Wilkinson CP, eds. *Retina.* Vol 3. 4th ed. Philadelphia: Elsevier/Mosby; 2006:2071–2083.

Haller JA. Retinal detachment. *Focal Points: Clinical Modules for Ophthalmologists.* San Francisco: American Academy of Ophthalmology; 1998, module 5.

Hilton GF, McLean EB, Brinton DA. *Retinal Detachment: Principles and Practice.* 2nd ed. Ophthalmology Monograph 1. San Francisco: American Academy of Ophthalmology; 1995.

Kreissig I. *A Practical Guide to Minimal Surgery for Retinal Detachment.* Vol 1. Stuttgart: Thieme; 2000.

Kreissig I, ed. *Primary Retinal Detachment: Options for Repair.* Berlin: Springer-Verlag; 2005.

Williams GA, Aaberg TM Jr. Techniques of scleral buckling. In: Ryan SJ, Hinton DR, Schachat AP, Wilkinson CP, eds. *Retina.* Vol 3. 4th ed. Philadelphia: Elsevier/Mosby; 2006:2035–2070.

Anatomical reattachment

The overall rate of anatomical reattachment with current techniques is 80%–90%. The prognosis for reattachment is better in patients whose detachments are caused by dialyses or small holes or who have detachments associated with demarcation lines. Aphakic and pseudophakic eyes have a slightly less favorable prognosis. Detachments caused by giant tears or associated with PVR, uveitis, choroidal detachments, or posterior breaks secondary to trauma have the worst prognosis for anatomical reattachment.

Regillo CD, Benson WE. *Retinal Detachment: Diagnosis and Management.* 3rd ed. Philadelphia: Lippincott Williams & Wilkins; 1998:100–134.

Williams GA, Aaberg TM Jr. Techniques of scleral buckling. In: Ryan SJ, Hinton DR, Schachat AP, Wilkinson CP, eds. *Retina.* Vol 3. 4th ed. Philadelphia: Elsevier/Mosby; 2006;2035–2070.

Postoperative visual acuity

The status of the macula—whether it was detached and for how long—is the primary presurgical determinant of postoperative visual acuity. If the macula was detached, degeneration of photoreceptors may prevent good postoperative visual acuity. Although 87% of eyes with retinal detachment sparing the macula recover visual acuity of 20/50 or better, only one-third to one-half with a detached macula attain that level. Among patients with a macular detachment of less than 1 week's duration, 75% will obtain a final visual acuity of 20/70 or better, as opposed to 50% with a macular detachment of 1–8 weeks' duration.

In 10%–15% of successfully repaired retinal detachments with the macula attached preoperatively, visual acuity does not return to the preoperative level. This loss of acuity occurs secondary to factors such as irregular astigmatism, cataract progression, macular edema, or macular pucker. Intraoperative complications such as hemorrhage and preexisting vision loss as a result of underlying ocular pathology may also limit visual recovery.

Tractional Retinal Detachment

Vitreous membranes caused by penetrating injuries or by proliferative retinopathies such as diabetic retinopathy can pull the neurosensory retina away from the RPE, causing a tractional retinal detachment. The retina characteristically has smooth concave surfaces and contours and is immobile. The detachment can be central or peripheral and, in rare cases, extends from the disc to the ora serrata. In most cases, the causative vitreous membrane can be seen biomicroscopically with a 3-mirror contact lens or a 60 D to 90 D indirect lens.

If the traction can be released by vitrectomy, the detachment may resolve. In some cases, traction may tear the retina and cause a rhegmatogenous retinal detachment. The retina then becomes more mobile, assumes convex surfaces and contours modified by residual traction, reaches from the disc to the ora, and has retinal corrugations characteristic of a rhegmatogenous detachment. Treatment may require a combination of vitrectomy to release the traction and a scleral buckling procedure to seal the break.

Exudative Retinal Detachment

It is crucial to properly diagnose a large retinal detachment as exudative because, unlike with other types of retinal detachment, its management is usually not surgical. Exudative detachment occurs when either retinal blood vessels leak or the RPE is damaged, allowing

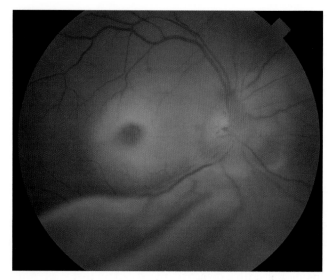

Figure 13-18 Exudative retinal detachment as a result of metastatic breast carcinoma. *(Courtesy of Hermann D. Schubert, MD.)*

fluid to pass into the subretinal space (Fig 13-18). Neoplasia and inflammatory diseases are the leading causes of large exudative detachments.

The presence of shifting fluid is highly suggestive of a large exudative retinal detachment. Because the subretinal fluid responds to the force of gravity, it detaches the area of the retina in which it accumulates. For example, when the patient is sitting, the inferior retina is detached. However, when the patient becomes supine, the fluid moves posteriorly in a matter of seconds or minutes, detaching the macula. Another characteristic of exudative detachments is the smoothness of the detached retinal surface, in contrast to the corrugated appearance in rhegmatogenous retinal detachment. Included in the differential diagnosis is the rhegmatogenous inferior bullous detachment, which may shift and is connected to a small superior tear by a sinus (see Fig 13-14, rule 4). Fixed retinal folds, usually indicative of PVR, are rarely if ever present in exudative detachments. Occasionally, the retina is sufficiently elevated in exudative detachments to be visible directly behind the lens (eg, in Coats disease), a rare occurrence in rhegmatogenous detachments.

Differential Diagnosis of Retinal Detachment

Retinoschisis

Typical peripheral cystoid degeneration is present in virtually all adults. Contiguous with and extending up to 2–3 mm posterior to the ora serrata, the area of degeneration has a bubbly appearance and is best visualized with scleral depression. The cystoid cavities in the outer plexiform layer contain a hyaluronidase-sensitive mucopolysaccharide. The only known complication of typical cystoid degeneration is coalescence and extension of the cavities and progression to typical degenerative retinoschisis.

Reticular peripheral cystoid degeneration is almost always located posterior to and continuous with typical peripheral cystoid degeneration, but it is considerably less common. It has a linear or reticular pattern that corresponds to the retinal vessels and a finely stippled internal surface. The cystoid spaces are in the nerve fiber layer. This condition may progress to reticular degenerative retinoschisis (bullous retinoschisis).

Although degenerative retinoschisis is sometimes subdivided into typical and reticular forms, clinical differentiation is difficult. The complications of posterior extension and progression to retinal detachment are associated with the reticular form. Retinoschisis is bilateral in 50%–80% of affected patients, often occurs in the inferotemporal quadrant, and is commonly associated with hyperopia.

In *typical degenerative retinoschisis,* the retina splits in the outer plexiform layer. The outer layer is irregular and appears pockmarked on scleral depression. The inner layer is thin and appears clinically as a smooth, oval elevation, most commonly found in the inferotemporal quadrant but sometimes located superotemporally (Fig 13-19). Occasionally, small, irregular white dots ("snowflakes") are present; these are footplates of Müller cells and neurons that bridge or formerly bridged the cavity. The retinal vessels appear sclerotic. In all cases, typical bubbly appearing peripheral cystoid degeneration can be found anterior to the schisis cavity. The schisis may extend posteriorly to the equator, but complications such as hole formation, retinal detachment, or marked posterior extension are rare. The split in retina almost never extends as far posteriorly as the macula.

In *reticular degenerative retinoschisis,* the splitting occurs in the nerve fiber layer. The very thin inner layer may be markedly elevated. As in typical retinoschisis, the outer layer appears pockmarked and the retinal vessels sclerotic. Posterior extension is more common

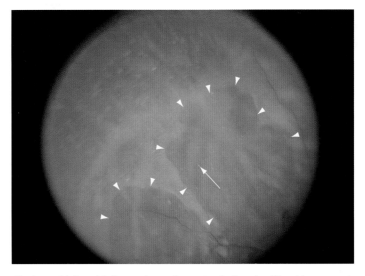

Figure 13-19 Retinoschisis with large, irregular outer holes *(outlined by arrowheads)* and yellow dots on the inner surface *(arrow). (Modified from Lee BL, van Heuvan WAJ. Peripheral lesions of the fundus. Focal Points: Clinical Modules for Ophthalmologists. San Francisco: American Academy of Ophthalmology; 2000, module 8.)*

Table 13-5 Differentiation of Retinal Detachment and Retinoschisis

Clinical Feature	Retinal Detachment	Retinoschisis
Surface	Corrugated	Smooth-domed
Hemorrhage or pigment	Present	Usually absent
Scotoma	Relative	Absolute
Reaction to photocoagulation	Absent	Generally present
Shifting fluid	Variable	Absent

in reticular than in typical retinoschisis. Approximately 23% of cases have outer wall holes that may be large and have rolled edges.

Differentiation of retinoschisis from RRD

Retinoschisis must be differentiated from RRD (Table 13-5). Retinoschisis causes an absolute scotoma, whereas RRD causes a relative scotoma. "Tobacco dust," hemorrhage, or both are rarely present in the vitreous with retinoschisis, whereas they are commonly observed with RRD. Retinoschisis has a smooth surface and usually appears dome-shaped; in contrast, RRD often has a corrugated, irregular surface. In long-standing RRD, however, the retina also may appear smooth and thin, similar to its appearance in retinoschisis. Whereas long-standing RRD may also show atrophy of the underlying RPE, demarcation line(s), and degenerative retinal schisis ("macrocysts"), in retinoschisis the underlying RPE is normal.

Retinoschisis is associated with about 3% of full-thickness retinal detachments. Two types of schisis-related detachments occur. In the first type, if holes are present in the outer but not inner wall of the schisis cavity, the contents of the cavity can migrate through an outer wall hole and slowly detach the retina. Demarcation lines and degeneration of the underlying RPE are common. A demarcation line in an eye with retinoschisis suggests that a full-thickness detachment is or was formerly present and has spontaneously regressed. This type of retinoschisis detachment usually does not progress, or it progresses slowly and seldom requires treatment.

In the second type of schisis detachment, holes are present in both the inner and outer layers. The schisis cavity may collapse, and a progressive RRD may result. Such detachments often progress rapidly and usually require treatment. The causative breaks may be located very posteriorly and thus may be difficult to repair. Vitrectomy may be required.

Byer NE. Long-term natural history study of senile retinoschisis with implications for management. *Ophthalmology.* 1986;93(9):1127–1137.

Tiedeman JS. Retinal breaks, holes, and tears. *Focal Points: Clinical Modules for Ophthalmologists.* San Francisco: American Academy of Ophthalmology; 1996, module 3.

Optic Pit Maculopathy

Optic pits are small, hypopigmented, yellow or whitish, oval or round, excavated colobomatous defects; they are most often found within the inferior temporal portion of the optic disc margin (Fig 13-20). Most are unilateral and asymptomatic; however, optic pits

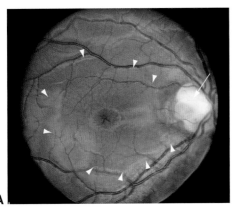
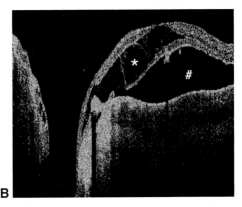

Figure 13-20 Optic nerve pit. **A,** Fundus photograph shows an abnormal temporal optic head appearance with an excavation, or pit *(arrow).* The adjacent retina is thickened and elevated, extending into the macula *(outlined by arrowheads).* **B,** Optical coherence tomogram illustrating retinoschisis cavity *(asterisk)* and subretinal fluid *(pound sign)* associated with the optic pit. *(Part A courtesy of Mark W. Johnson, MD; Part B courtesy of Peter K. Kaiser, MD.)*

may lead to serous macular detachments with a poor prognosis if left untreated. The central retinal elevations extend from the optic pit in an oval shape toward the fovea. The origin of the subretinal fluid is not clear, but liquid vitreous and cerebrospinal fluid have been implicated. Optical coherence tomography reveals macular schisis as well as subretinal fluid. Optic pits are among the few conditions associated with macular schisis. Various successful treatments have been reported, including use of laser treatment along the edge of the optic nerve forming a barrier to fluid, displacement by use of a gas bubble, vitrectomy, and complete intraocular gas tamponade. Because optic pits are included in the differential diagnosis of central retinal elevations, careful examination of the optic nerve margin is vital to rule out this condition.

CHAPTER **14**

Diseases of the Vitreous and Vitreoretinal Interface

Posterior Vitreous Detachment

The vitreous is a transparent connective tissue in a partial basal laminar bag, provided by lens, optic nerve, and retina, to which it is attached. Detachment of the anterior cortical gel from the lens and the ligament of Wieger is called anterior vitreous detachment, in the past frequently induced by intracapsular cataract extraction. More important in practice is the detachment of the posterior cortical gel from its adhesions at the disc (the area of Martegiani), the macula, and blood vessels. Independent from anterior or posterior detachment, the vitreous remains firmly attached to its base, even after severe trauma, which may cause vitreous base avulsion. Because of the firm attachment, the basal cortical vitreous collagen must be "shaved" during vitrectomy. Collagen is the major structural protein component of the vitreous; the other major component is hyaluronan. Hyalocytes, resident macrophages, are located in the posterior cortical gel.

With advancing age, there is both liquefaction (synchysis) and collapse (syneresis) of the vitreous gel. The viscous hyaluronan accumulates in lacunae, which are surrounded by displaced collagen fibers. With increasing destabilization of the gel, contractile forces can develop, possibly related to electrostatic attraction and cross-linking of adjacent collagen fibers in the absence of hyaluronan. Concomitant with liquefaction and collapse, the posterior cortical gel detaches toward the firmly attached vitreous base. The prevalence of posterior vitreous detachment (PVD) increases in patients who have had cataract extractions, particularly if the posterior capsule's integrity has been violated, and in patients with a history of vitritis. The reason is loss or alteration of hyaluronan. Localized regions of the posterior cortical gel can separate slowly over the course of many years. A rent in the posterior wall of the macular precortical vitreous pocket can allow the contained fluid to dissect posteriorly, accelerating the posterior detachment of the vitreous, also known as rhegmatogenous PVD.

The diagnosis of PVD may be made by biomicroscopic examination using a wide-field lens. The posterior vitreous face may be observed a few millimeters in front of the retinal surface. A translucent ring of fibroglial tissue, called a Weiss ring, frequently is torn loose from the surface of the optic nerve head (the area of Martegiani) and serves as a marker of prepapillary PVD. A shallow detachment of the posterior cortical gel may be difficult or impossible to appreciate by biomicroscopy. It may be imaged using contact B-scan ultrasonography, appearing as a thin hyperreflective line bounding the posterior vitreous. Optical coherence tomography (OCT) has shown that PVDs often start as a localized detachment of the vitreous over the perifovea, called a *posterior perifoveal vitreous detachment*. This detachment may spread anteriorly to involve larger areas. Both ultrasound and OCT are helpful in following the progression of partial PVDs. Persistent focal attachment of the vitreous to the retina may induce a number of different pathologic abnormalities. The combined effects of static traction from the contracting vitreous as well as dynamic traction from ocular saccades acting through vitreous inertia may place mechanical stress on the affected retina. Focal traction on the peripheral retina may lead to breaks, particularly at the posterior vitreous base. Persistent attachment to the macula may lead to tractional distortion and possibly elevation of the macula, called *vitreomacular traction syndrome*. OCT has shown that many cases of vitreomacular traction have vitreous attachment only to the foveola, not to the macula as a whole. Such focal attachment can induce foveal cavitation and macular hole formation (Fig 14-1). Remnants of the vitreous often remain on the internal limiting membrane after a posterior vitreous "detachment." For this reason, some authorities state that a presumed PVD often is actually posterior vitreoschisis, internal or external to the layer of hyalocytes (Fig 14-2). Vitreous remnants may have a role in epiretinal membrane or macular hole formation and can contribute to traction detachments in patients with pathologic myopia and to macular edema in patients with diabetes. Plaques of cortical vitreous can be highlighted during vitreous surgery by applying triamcinolone (Fig 14-3).

Balazs EA. The vitreous. *Int Ophthalmol Clin.* 1973;13(3):169–187.

Spaide RF, Wong D, Fisher Y, Goldbaum M. Correlation of vitreous attachment and foveal deformation in early macular hole states. *Am J Ophthalmol.* 2002;133(2):226–229.

Epiretinal Membranes

An epiretinal membrane (ERM) is a semitranslucent, avascular, fibrocellular membrane on the inner retinal surface adhering to and covering the internal limiting membrane (ILM) of the retina. Proliferating glia, retinal pigment epithelium (RPE), or hyalocytes at the vitreoretinal interface, especially at the posterior pole, result in ERM formation. ERMs can be

- idiopathic and presumably related to an abnormality of the vitreoretinal interface in conjunction with a PVD
- secondary to a wide variety of conditions, including retinal vascular occlusions, uveitis, trauma, intraocular surgery, and retinal breaks

Idiopathic ERMs are relatively common; at autopsy, they are discovered in 2% of patients older than 50 years and in 20% older than 75 years. Idiopathic ERMs are most common in patients over age 50 years, and both sexes are equally affected. The incidence of bilaterality is approximately 10%–20%, and severity is usually asymmetric. Detachment or separation of the posterior vitreous is present in almost all eyes with idiopathic membranes. Schisis of the posterior vitreous (see Fig 14-2) may leave variable portions of the posterior cortical

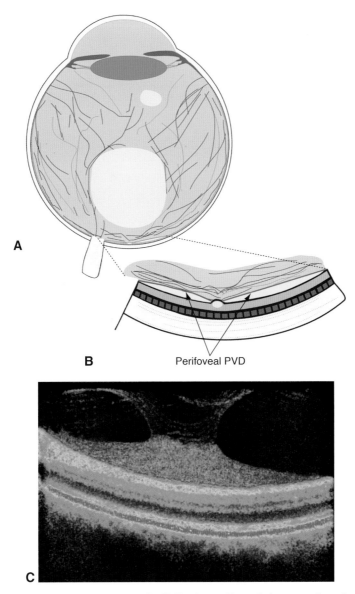

Figure 14-1 **A,** During the development of a PVD, the perifoveal vitreous often detaches first, producing a posterior perifoveal vitreous detachment. **B,** Persistent attachment of the vitreous to a more focal and localized area in the central macula can lead to deformation and structural failure. **C,** A 3-dimensional reconstruction of a spectral OCT rendering of vitreomacular traction syndrome. The cone of vitreous is attached to and elevates the central fovea. *(Courtesy of Richard F. Spaide, MD. Illustrations by Dr Spaide.)*

vitreous attached to the macula, allowing glial cells from the retina to proliferate along the retinal surface and hyalocytes to proliferate on posterior cortical vitreous remnants on the retinal surface. Secondary ERMs occur regardless of age or sex in association with abnormal vitreoretinal adhesions and areas of inflammation, as well as after retinal detachment or retinal bleeding; they are observed in approximately 3.0%–8.5% of patients at autopsy.

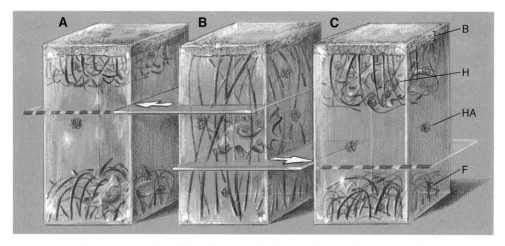

Figure 14-2 Schematic model of the 2 types of vitreoschisis. **A,** External schisis, when the bulk of the cortical gel with the hyalocytes separates from a thin vitreous gel layer and moves toward the center of the vitreous space. The space between the 2 separated gels is filled with liquid vitreous. **B,** Normal vitreous. **C,** Internal schisis, when the hyalocytes and the cortical gel remain attached to the retina. B = basal lamina; F = vitreous fibrils; H = hyalocyte; HA = hyaluronan molecules. *(Modified from Balazs EA. The vitreous.* Int Ophthalmol Clin. *1973;13(3):185.)*

Signs and symptoms

Epiretinal proliferation is generally located in the central area—over, surrounding, or eccentric to the fovea (Fig 14-4). The membranes usually present with a mild sheen or glint on the retinal surface. Over time, ERMs become highly reflective and, when thickened, become more opaque, obscuring underlying retinal details. A "pseudohole" may appear if this preretinal membrane has a gap or hole. OCT is useful in differentiating a full-thickness macular hole from a pseudohole. Occasionally, intraretinal hemorrhages or whitened patches of superficial retina representing delayed axoplasmic flow and edema may be present. The cellular origin of ERMs is still under debate. Histologic examination reveals mainly RPE cells and retinal glial cells (astrocytes and Müller cells); however, myofibroblasts, fibroblasts, hyalocytes, and macrophages have also been identified.

Contracture of ERMs produces distortion and wrinkling of the inner surface of the retina, also called *cellophane maculopathy* or *preretinal macular fibrosis* when mild, and *surface-wrinkling retinopathy* or *retinal striae* when moderate; severe cases are called *macular pucker.* Greater traction may cause shallow detachment, diffuse thickening, or cystic changes of the macula. Furthermore, traction on retinal vessels results in increased vascular tortuosity and straightening of the perimacular vessels. These changes are evident clinically and on fluorescein angiography (FA); optic nerve staining may also be observed. OCT scans illustrate the irregular inner retinal surface and the higher reflectivity of the ERM.

Treatment

In most cases, the symptoms are mild and surgical treatment is not required. Although rare, an ERM can spontaneously detach from the inner retinal surface with a concomitant

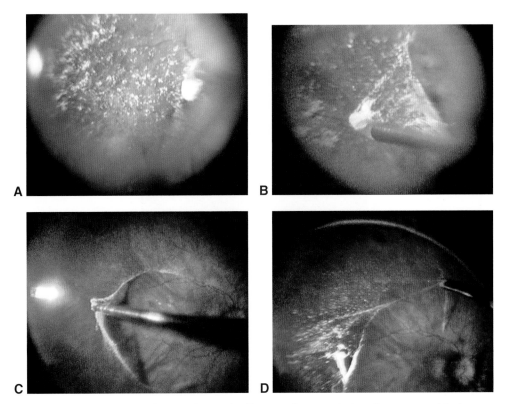

Figure 14-3 Visualization of a thin layer of adherent vitreous during vitrectomy with the use of triamcinolone. This patient appeared to have a PVD and underwent a vitrectomy. **A,** A small amount of triamcinolone was injected into the vitreous cavity, and the excess was aspirated from the surface of the retina, leaving a fine distribution of triamcinolone sticking to the adherent vitreous. **B,** The vitreous membrane was elevated using a diamond-dusted silicone scraper. Note that the vitreous is difficult to see; the sheet of triamcinolone is the clue to its presence. **C,** A wide-angle viewing system then was used to visualize the elevation of the adherent vitreous, and the vitrector was set to suction only. **D,** Note the extent of the adherent vitreous sheet, which was removed, with the vitrector set to cut. *(Courtesy of Richard F. Spaide, MD.)*

resolution of retinal distortion and improvement in symptoms and vision. An eye that loses vision or has an intolerable level of distortion may be a candidate for removal of the ERM by vitrectomy. See Chapter 17 for a discussion on vitrectomy for macular disease.

The goal of surgery is to both optimize visual acuity and reduce metamorphopsia. After surgical removal of the ERM, 50%–75% of patients have some improvement in vision; however, return to normal vision is rare. Sometimes line vision does not improve, but patients experience a significant subjective improvement in the quality of their vision.

Capone A Jr. Macular surface disorders. *Focal Points: Clinical Modules for Ophthalmologists.* San Francisco: American Academy of Ophthalmology; 1996, module 4.

Johnson MW. Epiretinal membrane. In: Yanoff M, Duker J, eds. *Ophthalmology.* 2nd ed. St Louis: Mosby; 2004:947–950.

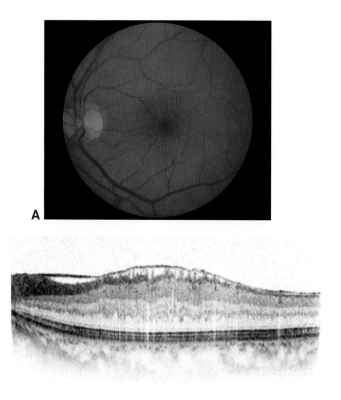

Figure 14-4 Epiretinal membrane. **A,** Color photograph reveals radiating striae of the ILM in the macula, caused by this largely transparent membrane. Note the tortuosity of small vessels in this region. **B,** OCT illustrating increased retinal thickening, with the ERM distorting the retinal surface. *(Part A courtesy of Peter K. Kaiser, MD. Part B courtesy of Hermann D. Schubert, MD.)*

Vitreomacular Traction Syndrome

Vitreomacular traction (VMT) syndrome is a result of incomplete separation of the posterior vitreous at the macula. The abnormal adherence of the vitreous to the posterior pole allows for propagation of tractional forces on the macula. It is not known whether vitreomacular adhesion is primary or secondary to cellular proliferations induced by partial vitreous detachment. In VMT syndrome, abnormal opacities may be present in the central vitreous, usually in association with traction on the macular region and the optic nerve (Fig 14-5). Similar to ERMs, the macular retina may become distorted, cystic, or tented anteriorly with a shallow detachment, although no ERM is present. Angiography may demonstrate leakage of fluorescein dye from macular vessels as well as from the optic nerve (Fig 14-6). OCT is useful to demonstrate the vitreoretinal interface abnormalities and the traction of VMT syndrome. The condition may be bilateral.

Vitrectomy may be considered if a patient's vision decreases. Although the long-term risks and benefits of vitrectomy for VMT syndrome are unknown, they are believed to be similar to those of surgery for ERMs (see Chapter 17). Spontaneous separation of the focal vitreoretinal adhesion may occur, with resolution of all clinical features. With the advent of OCT, it has become apparent that in more than half of these cases, vitreous adhesions

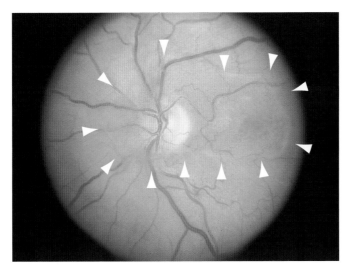

Figure 14-5 VMT syndrome showing an ovoid area of persistent attachment that extends from the nasal aspect of the optic nerve head to a crescent-shaped area of attachment along the temporal macula *(arrowheads)*. *(Reproduced with permission from Capone A. Jr. Macular surface disorders.* Focal Points: Clinical Modules for Ophthalmologists. *San Francisco: American Academy of Ophthalmology; 1996, module 4.)*

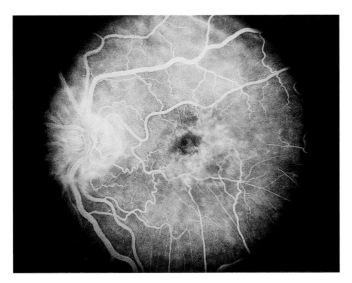

Figure 14-6 Mid–venous phase angiographic image of the eye shown in Figure 14-5, demonstrating disc leakage, vascular distortion, early cystoid macular edema, and diffuse accumulation of dye in the subsensory space as a result of broad, shallow, tractional detachment of the posterior pole. *(Reproduced with permission from Capone A. Jr. Macular surface disorders.* Focal Points: Clinical Modules for Ophthalmologists. *San Francisco: American Academy of Ophthalmology; 1996, module 4.)*

are limited to the foveola, inducing focal cystic edema. This subgroup of patients responds well to surgery.

Hikichi T, Yoshida A, Trempe CL. Course of vitreomacular traction syndrome. *Am J Ophthalmol.* 1995;119(1):55–61.

Johnson MW. Tractional cystoid macular edema: a subtle variant of the vitreomacular traction syndrome. *Am J Ophthalmol.* 2005;140(2):184–192.

McDonald HR, Johnson RN, Schatz H. Surgical results in the vitreomacular traction syndrome. *Ophthalmology.* 1994;101(8):1397–1402.

Idiopathic Macular Holes

Idiopathic macular holes occur mostly in the sixth through eighth decades of life, affect women more frequently than men, and appear at a younger age in myopic eyes. Investigations using OCT and ultrasonography suggest that idiopathic macular holes are caused by the tractional forces associated with perifoveal vitreous detachment, an early stage of age-related PVD (see Fig 14-1B). The observation that an idiopathic macular hole appears to be a complication of the earliest stage of age-related PVD helps explain the age and sex demographics of this condition, which are similar to those of PVD. The following description of the stages of macular hole formation and OCT findings at each stage is useful in interpreting biomicroscopic findings and making management decisions (Fig 14-7):

- A *stage 0* or *premacular hole state* occurs when a perifoveal vitreous detachment develops, and only subtle changes in macular topography, such as loss of the foveal depression, can be observed. Patients usually have normal visual acuity, and most stage 0 holes do not progress to advanced stages.
- Patients with *stage 1* macular holes (also known as *impending macular holes*) have visual symptoms that typically include central vision loss (with visual acuity typically measuring 20/25 to 20/60) and metamorphopsia. Biomicroscopy shows a loss of the foveal depression associated with a small yellow spot (stage 1A) or yellow ring (stage 1B) in the center of the fovea. OCT examination reveals that a stage 1A hole is a foveal "pseudocyst," or horizonal splitting (schisis), associated with a vitreous detachment from the perifoveal retina but not from the foveal center. In stage 1B holes, there is progression of the pseudocyst to include a break in the outer foveal layer, the margins of which constitute the yellow ring noted clinically. As many as 50% of stage 1 holes resolve spontaneously following separation of the vitreofoveal adhesion and spontaneous relief of tractional forces.
- A *stage 2* macular hole represents the progression of foveal schisis (pseudocyst) to a full-thickness dehiscence, as a tractional break develops in the "roof" (inner layer) of the pseudocyst. The small opening in the inner layer (<400 μm diameter) may be either centrally or slightly eccentrically located. Progression to stage 2 typically occurs over several weeks or months, usually accompanied by further decline in visual acuity. OCT typically demonstrates that the posterior hyaloid remains attached to the foveal center in stage 2 holes.
- A *stage 3* macular hole is a fully developed hole (≥400 μm diameter), typically surrounded by a rim of thickened and slightly elevated retina. Visual acuity may range from 20/40 to 5/200 but is generally around 20/200. The posterior hyaloid remains attached to the optic disc, but it is detached from the fovea. An operculum may or may not be present, suspended by the posterior hyaloid overlying the hole.
- A *stage 4* macular hole is a fully developed hole with a complete posterior vitreous detachment evidenced by a Weiss ring.

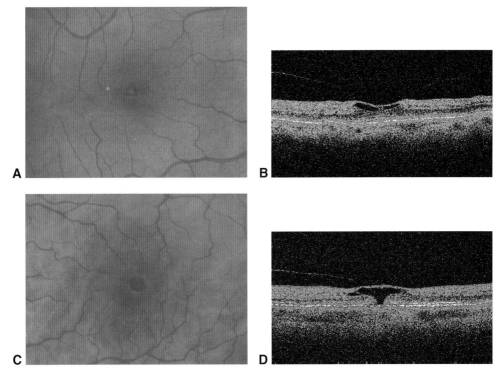

Figure 14-7 Macular hole. **A,** Stage 1A hole with horizontal splitting of retinal layers. **B,** Corresponding OCT showing stage 1A hole. **C,** Stage 1B hole. **D,** Corresponding OCT showing stage 1B hole. **E,** Stage 2 hole with small opening in inner layer eccentrically. **F,** Corresponding OCT of stage 2 hole. **G,** OCT of a stage 3 full-thickness hole with elevation of adjacent retinal edges. **H,** OCT of a stage 4 full-thickness hole with operculum. *(Courtesy of Mark W. Johnson, MD, and Peter K. Kaiser, MD.)*

(Continued on next page)

FA of eyes with stage 2, 3, or 4 holes demonstrates a circular-transmission defect resulting from the loss of xanthophyll at the site of the hole and from RPE depigmentation and atrophy at the base of the hole. However, the gold standard in the diagnosis of the various stages of macular holes is OCT examination.

Retrospective studies have found the incidence of bilaterality in macular holes to be 12%. Patients who present with a full-thickness macular hole in 1 eye that is symptomatic, with loss of foveal depression or stage 1A abnormalities in the other eye, have a substantial risk of progression to a stage 2 hole in the fellow eye. Patients with a full-thickness macular hole in 1 eye and a normal retina with a vitreomacular separation in the other eye have minimal, if any, risk of a macular hole developing in the fellow eye. Patients presenting with a full-thickness macular hole in 1 eye and a normal fellow eye with an attached posterior vitreous probably have an intermediate risk of vitreomacular interface abnormalities developing in the second eye over their lifetimes.

Management options

Investigators in a collaborative multicenter trial designed to assess the benefit of vitrectomy in preventing macular holes suggested that surgery should probably not be

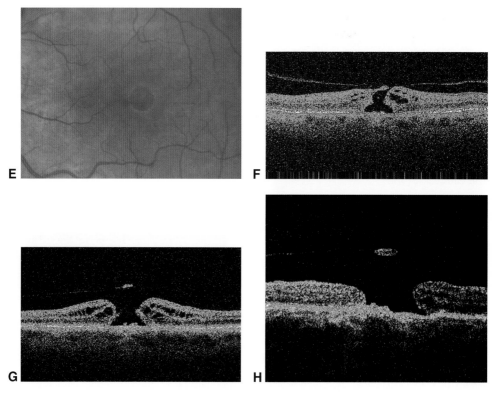

Figure 14-7 *(continued)*

recommended for stage 1 macular holes because of the high rate of spontaneous resolution (approximately 50%) and the failure of surgery to show a benefit. The study was limited by its small sample size and the difficulty, in the absence of OCT, of documenting stage 1 holes to ensure that investigators adhered to the eligibility criteria. Spontaneous resolution of more advanced stages of macular holes (stages 2–4) secondary to fibroglial tissue proliferation on the retinal surface or as a result of RPE hyperplasia is rare (occurring in 5% or less of cases). Most do not spontaneously resolve and should be considered for vitrectomy. The first series of patients undergoing vitrectomy for idiopathic macular hole was reported in 1991. In 58% of eyes, the hole was closed; in 42%, visual acuity improved by 2 lines or more. Subsequent series have reported hole-closure rates after vitrectomy as high as 92%–100%. See Chapter 17 for discussion of vitrectomy for macular holes.

Chew EY, Sperduto RD, Hiller R, et al. Clinical course of macular holes: the Eye Disease Case-Control Study. *Arch Ophthalmol.* 1999;117(2):242–246.

Haouchine B, Massin P, Gaudric A. Foveal pseudocyst as the first step in macular hole formation: a prospective study by optical coherence tomography. *Ophthalmology.* 2001;108(1):15–22.

Johnson MW, Van Newkirk MR, Meyer KA. Perifoveal vitreous detachment is the primary pathogenic event in idiopathic macular hole formation. *Arch Ophthalmol.* 2001;119(2):215–222.

Developmental Abnormalities

Tunica Vasculosa Lentis

Remnants of the tunica vasculosa lentis and hyaloid artery are commonly observed, none visually significant. *Mittendorf dot,* an anterior remnant, is a small, dense, and white round plaque attached to the posterior lens capsule nasally and inferiorly to its posterior pole. A prepapillary remnant known as *Bergmeister papilla* is a fibroglial tuft of tissue extending into the vitreous for a short distance at the margin of the optic nerve head. The entire hyaloid artery may persist from disc to lens as multilayered fenestrated sheaths forming the Cloquet canal.

Prepapillary Vascular Loops

Initially thought to be remnants of the hyaloid artery, prepapillary vascular loops are normal retinal vessels that have grown into Bergmeister papilla before returning to the retina. The loops typically extend less than 5 mm into the vitreous. These vessels may supply one or more quadrants of the retina. FA has shown that 95% are arterial and 5% are venous. Complications include branch retinal artery obstruction, amaurosis fugax, and vitreous hemorrhage (Fig 14-8).

Persistent Fetal Vasculature

The condition originally known as persistent hyperplastic primary vitreous (PHPV) is thought to result from failure of the primary vascular vitreous to regress. "Hyperplasia" referred to dense retrolental fibrovascular tissue, metaplastic cartilage, adipose tissue, smooth muscle, retinal dysplasia, and folds—all of which can be associated with persistent fetal vessels, particularly posteriorly. Currently, the term *persistent fetal vasculature (PFV)* is used to reflect an integrated interpretation of the signs and symptoms originally

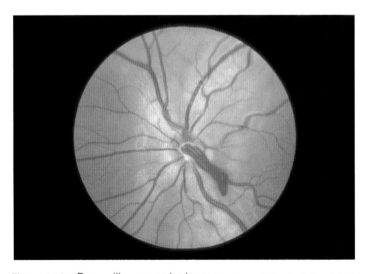

Figure 14-8 Prepapillary vascular loop. *(Courtesy of M. Gilbert Grand, MD.)*

associated with PHPV. The disease, which is unilateral in 90% of cases, may have serious visual consequences. There are usually no associated systemic findings. Anterior, posterior, and combined forms of this developmental abnormality have been described.

Anterior PFV

In anterior PFV, or PHPV, the hyaloid artery remains, and a white vascularized fibrous membrane or mass is present behind the lens. Associated findings include microphthalmos, a shallow anterior chamber, and elongated ciliary processes that are visible around the small lens. Leukocoria is often noted at birth. A dehiscence of the posterior lens capsule may, in many cases, cause swelling of the lens and cataract as well as secondary angle-closure glaucoma. In addition, glaucoma may result from incomplete development of the chamber angle.

The natural course of anterior PFV may lead to blindness in the most advanced cases. Lensectomy and removal of the fibrovascular retrolental membrane will prevent angle-closure glaucoma; however, growth of a secondary cataract is common. Deprivational and refractive amblyopia is a serious postoperative challenge in these patients (Fig 14-9).

Anterior PFV should be considered in the differential diagnosis of leukocoria. Differentiating it from retinoblastoma is particularly important. Unlike for PFV, retinoblastoma is usually not obvious at birth, is more often bilateral, and is almost never associated with microphthalmos or cataract. PFV is anterior in the eye at birth; retinoblastomas do not appear in the anterior fundus until well after birth. Ancillary testing, such as diagnostic echography and x-ray techniques to look for calcification within the retinoblastoma, can be helpful in differentiating the 2 disorders.

Posterior PFV

Posterior PFV, or PHPV, may occur in association with anterior PFV or as an isolated finding. The eye may be microphthalmic, but the anterior chamber is usually normal and the lens typically clear, without a retrolental membrane. A stalk of tissue emanates from

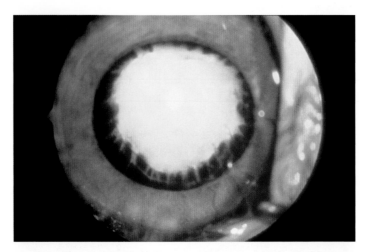

Figure 14-9 PFV in a 4-month-old boy. Note cataract secondary to retrolental mass. Blood vessels on the iris represent persistent vascularized pupillary membranes. *(Courtesy of Jerry A. Shields, MD.)*

the optic disc and courses toward the retrolental region, often running along the apex of a retinal fold that may extend anteriorly from the disc, usually in an inferior quadrant. The stalk fans out circumferentially toward the anterior retina. Posterior PFV should be differentiated from retinopathy of prematurity (ROP), familial exudative vitreoretinopathy, and ocular toxocariasis.

Goldberg MF. Persistent fetal vasculature (PFV): an integrated interpretation of signs and symptoms associated with persistent hyperplastic primary vitreous (PHPV). LIV Edward Jackson Memorial Lecture. *Am J Ophthalmol.* 1997;124(5):587–626.

Mittra RA, Huynh LT, Ruttum MS, et al. Visual outcomes following lensectomy and vitrectomy for combined anterior and posterior persistent hyperplastic primary vitreous. *Arch Ophthalmol.* 1998;116(9):1190–1194.

Hereditary Hyaloideoretinopathies With Optically Empty Vitreous: Wagner and Stickler Syndromes

The hallmark of the group of conditions known as *hereditary hyaloideoretinopathies* is vitreous liquefaction (synchysis) that results in an optically empty cavity except for a thin layer of cortical vitreous behind the lens and threadlike, avascular membranes that run circumferentially and adhere to the retina. Fundus abnormalities include equatorial and perivascular (radial) lattice degeneration (Fig 14-10). The electroretinogram may be subnormal.

These conditions can be classified into 2 main groups: those with ocular signs and symptoms exclusively and those with associated systemic findings. The first group includes *Wagner disease,* which is not associated with retinal detachment and is transmitted as an autosomal dominant trait. Additional ocular abnormalities include myopia, strabismus, and cataract. The second group, conditions with associated systemic abnormalities, includes hereditary arthro-ophthalmopathy (marfanoid variety) of the Stickler syndrome, hereditary arthro-ophthalmopathy with stiff joints (Weill-Marchesani–like variety), and 4 varieties with frank dwarfism.

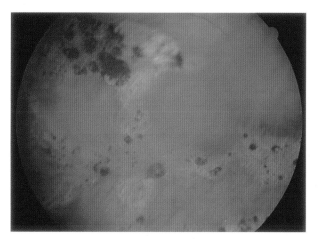

Figure 14-10 Extensive lattice degeneration and pigmentary change in a patient with Stickler syndrome. *(Courtesy of William F. Mieler, MD.)*

Stickler syndrome, the most common variety, is transmitted as an autosomal dominant trait. Most patients with Stickler syndrome have a mutation in the gene encoding type II procollagen, *COL2A1.* Various mutations may produce Stickler syndrome phenotypes of differing severity. Additional ocular abnormalities include myopia, open-angle glaucoma, and cataract. Orofacial findings include midfacial flattening and the Pierre Robin malformation complex of cleft palate (which may be submucosal), micrognathia, and glossoptosis. These abnormalities may be dramatic at birth, requiring tracheostomy, or they may not be obvious at all. Generalized skeletal abnormalities include joint hyperextensibility and enlargement, arthritis, particularly of the knees, and mild spondyloepiphyseal dysplasia. Early recognition of this syndrome is very important because of the high incidence of retinal detachment. Retinal tears were associated with *COL2A1* in 91% of cases in 1 series and retinal detachments in 53%. The detachments may be difficult to repair because of multiple, posterior, or large breaks and because of a tendency toward proliferative vitreoretinopathy. Patients with this condition typically have cortical vitreous condensations firmly adherent to the retina. For this reason, the ophthalmologist should strongly consider prophylactic therapy of retinal breaks. (See Prophylactic Treatment of Retinal Breaks in Chapter 13.)

Blair NP, Albert DM, Liberfarb RM, Hirose T. Hereditary progressive arthro-ophthalmopathy of Stickler. *Am J Ophthalmol.* 1979;88(5):876–888.

Maumenee IH. Vitreoretinal degeneration as a sign of generalized connective tissue diseases. *Am J Ophthalmol.* 1979;88(3 Pt 1):432–449.

Familial Exudative Vitreoretinopathy

Familial exudative vitreoretinopathy (FEVR) is characterized by failure of the temporal retina to vascularize and is phenotypically similar to ROP (Fig 14-11). It is usually inherited as an autosomal dominant trait, but X-linked transmission also occurs. Several different gene loci have been associated with the FEVR phenotype: 3 *(EVR1, EVR2,* and *EVR4)* that are

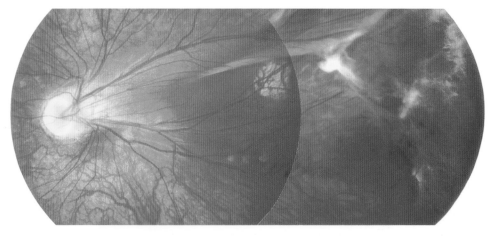

Figure 14-11 Familial exudative vitreoretinopathy. The temporal zone of nonperfusion is horizontally V-shaped, causing a tractional macular fold.

on the "gene-dense" chromosome 11 and are autosomal dominant and 1 *(EVR2)* on chromosome arm Xp that is X-linked. The *EVR2* gene encodes the Norrie disease protein. Retinal folds, peripheral fibrovascular proliferation, as well as tractional and exudative retinal detachment are often associated with FEVR. Temporal dragging of the macula may cause the patient to appear to have exotropia. Late-onset rhegmatogenous retinal detachments may occur. Generally, the earlier the disease presents, the more severe the manifestations.

The condition is frequently bilateral, although the severity of ocular involvement may be asymmetric. Individuals with FEVR, unlike those with ROP, are born full term and have normal respiratory status. In FEVR, the peripheral retinal vessels form numerous parallel fascicles that end abruptly a variable distance from the ora (brush border). Differentiation of FEVR from ROP is also helped by family history and careful examination of all family members. The only finding in some family members with FEVR may be a straightening of vessels and peripheral retinal nonperfusion. Parents of affected children may be mildly affected and asymptomatic. FA with peripheral sweeps is indispensable in examining family members.

Shubert A, Tasman W. Familial exudative vitreoretinopathy: surgical intervention and visual acuity outcomes. *Graefes Arch Clin Exp Ophthalmol.* 1997;235(8):490–493.

Tasman W, Augsburger JJ, Shields JA, Caputo A, Annesley WH Jr. Familial exudative vitreoretinopathy. *Trans Am Ophthalmol Soc.* 1981;79:211–226.

Vitreous Opacities

Asteroid Hyalosis

Minute white opacities composed of calcium-containing phospholipids are found in the otherwise normal vitreous in asteroid hyalosis (Fig 14-12). Clinical studies have confirmed a relationship between asteroid hyalosis and both diabetes and hypertension. Asteroid hyalosis has an overall incidence of 1 in 200 persons, most frequently in those older than 50 years. The condition is unilateral in 75% of cases, and significant decreases in visual acuity are rare. When asteroid hyalosis blocks the view of the posterior fundus and retinal pathology is suspected, FA is usually successful in imaging the abnormalities. Occasionally, vitrectomy may be necessary to remove visually significant opacities or to facilitate treatment of underlying retinal abnormalities such as proliferative retinopathy or choroidal neovascularization.

Bergren RL, Brown GC, Duker JS. Prevalence and association of asteroid hyalosis with systemic diseases. *Am J Ophthalmol.* 1991;111(3):289–293.

Cholesterolosis

Numerous yellow-white, gold, or multicolored cholesterol crystals are present in the vitreous and anterior chamber in *cholesterolosis,* also known as *synchysis scintillans.* This condition appears almost exclusively in eyes that have undergone repeated or severe accidental or surgical trauma causing large intravitreal hemorrhages. The descriptive term *synchysis scintillans* refers to the highly refractile appearance of the cholesterol-containing

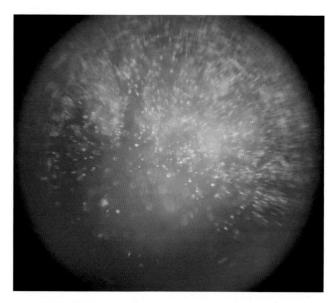

Figure 14-12 Asteroid hyalosis. *(Courtesy of Hermann D. Schubert, MD.)*

crystals. In contrast to eyes with asteroid hyalosis, in which the opacities are evenly distributed throughout the vitreous cavity, eyes with cholesterolosis frequently have a PVD, which allows the crystals to settle inferiorly.

> Spencer WH, ed. *Ophthalmic Pathology: An Atlas and Textbook.* 4 vols. 4th ed. Philadelphia: Saunders; 1996.

Amyloidosis

Bilateral vitreous opacification can occur as an early manifestation of the dominantly inherited form of familial amyloidosis, most commonly associated with a transthyretin mutation (Fig 14-13). Amyloid infiltration of the vitreous is rare in nonfamilial cases. In addition to the vitreous opacification, amyloid can be deposited in the retinal vasculature, the choroid, and the trabecular meshwork.

Retinal findings include hemorrhages, exudates, cotton-wool spots, and peripheral retinal neovascularization. In addition, infiltrations of the orbit, extraocular muscles, eyelids, conjunctiva, cornea, and iris may be present. Nonocular manifestations of amyloidosis include upper and lower extremity polyneuropathy and central nervous system abnormalities. Amyloid can be deposited in multiple organs, including the heart and skin, and in the gastrointestinal tract.

Initially, the extracellular vitreous opacities appear to lie adjacent to retinal vessels posteriorly; they later develop anteriorly. At first, the opacities appear granular with wispy fringes, but as they enlarge and aggregate, the vitreous takes on a "glass-wool" appearance. With vitreous liquefaction or PVD, the opacities may be displaced into the visual axis, causing reduced vision and photophobia.

The differential diagnosis includes chronic (dehemoglobinized) vitreous hemorrhage, lymphoma, sarcoidosis, and Whipple disease. Vitrectomy may be indicated for vitreous opacities when symptoms warrant intervention, but recurrent opacities may develop in

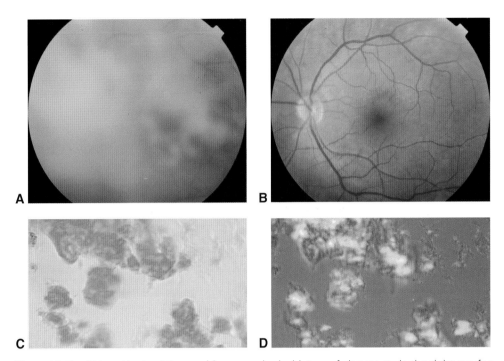

Figure 14-13 This patient, a 57-year-old woman, had a history of vitrectomy in the right eye for floaters. A cataract subsequently developed, and she had a cataract extraction in the right eye. Her vision decreased in the left eye, which she ascribed to a cataract. **A,** She had a dense, vitreous infiltration, no cataract, and marked, elevated intraocular pressure. Review of systems revealed carpal tunnel syndrome in both wrists. She had a vitrectomy **(B),** and the removed material stained with Congo red **(C)** and showed birefringence **(D)**. She was found to have a mutation affecting transthyretin. Glaucoma commonly develops in patients with transthyretin-related familial amyloidotic polyneuropathy. *(Courtesy of Richard F. Spaide, MD.)*

residual vitreous. Histologic examination of removed vitreous shows material with a fibrillar appearance and staining reaction characteristic of amyloid. Birefringence and electron microscopic studies are confirmatory. Immunocytochemical studies have shown the major amyloid constituent to be a protein resembling prealbumin.

> Sandgren O. Ocular amyloidosis, with special reference to the hereditary forms with vitreous involvement. *Surv Ophthalmol.* 1995;40(3):173–196.

Spontaneous Vitreous Hemorrhage

The decreased vision and floaters caused by non–trauma-related, spontaneous vitreous hemorrhages are common causes of emergency visits to ophthalmologists' offices. The most frequent underlying etiology in adults is diabetic retinopathy (39%–54%). Other major causes include

- retinal break without detachment (12%–17%)
- posterior vitreous detachment (7.5%–12.0%)
- rhegmatogenous retinal detachment (7%–10%)
- retinal neovascularization following branch vein and central vein occlusion (3.5%–10.0%)

Peripheral neovascularization of any cause may bleed into the vitreous (see Chapter 6, Table 6-2). In children, trauma should always be considered in the differential diagnosis of a vitreous hemorrhage (see Chapter 15). X-linked hereditary retinoschisis and pars planitis are other causes of vitreous hemorrhage in children as well as in adults.

In most cases of vitreous hemorrhage, the underlying cause can be detected by retinal examination. If the hemorrhage is too dense to permit biomicroscopy, suggestive clues can be obtained from the history and from examination of the fellow eye. Diagnostic echography should be performed to locate any tractional tear (often superotemporally) and to rule out retinal detachment or tumor. If the cause still cannot be determined, bed rest for a few hours to 2 days, with the head of the bed elevated, and bilateral patches may permit the intrahyaloid and retrohyaloid blood to settle. If the etiology still cannot be established, the ophthalmologist should consider frequent reexamination with repeat echography until the cause is found.

Pigment Granules

In a patient without uveitis, retinitis pigmentosa, or a history of surgical or accidental eye trauma, the presence of pigmented cells in the anterior vitreous ("tobacco dust"), known as *Shafer sign,* is highly suggestive of a retinal break (see Chapter 13).

Vitreous Abnormalities Secondary to Surgery

Incarceration of vitreous in the wound during cataract or vitreous surgery can lead to many postoperative complications:

- It contributes to faulty wound closure, possibly permitting entry of microorganisms into the eye and subsequent endophthalmitis.
- An insecure wound may allow epithelial or fibrous ingrowth, with the incarcerated vitreous serving as a scaffold for the proliferating cells, especially in the presence of other complicating factors, such as inflammation and hemorrhage.
- A wound leak may lead to hypotony, partial or complete collapse of the anterior chamber, peripheral anterior synechiae, or secondary glaucoma.

Incarcerated vitreous in the wound and iridovitreal adhesions may cause chronic ocular discomfort with inflammation, cystoid macular edema, and disc edema (Irvine-Gass syndrome). These complications have reportedly been reduced by sectioning discrete anterior vitreous bands with the Nd:YAG laser (vitreolysis) or by vitrectomy. Retinal detachment is another complication caused by contraction of the incarcerated vitreous. Such detachments may be rhegmatogenous or tractional and may require vitrectomy in addition to scleral buckling (see Chapter 17). The risk of complications from vitreous loss can be greatly reduced by careful vitrectomy followed by meticulous closure of all wounds at the time of surgery.

For further discussion of the complications of cataract surgery, see BCSC Section 11, *Lens and Cataract.* For postoperative endophthalmitis, see BCSC Section 9, *Intraocular Inflammation and Uveitis.*

Fankhauser F, Kwasniewska S. Laser vitreolysis: a review. *Ophthalmologica.* 2002;216(2): 73–84.

Fung WE. Vitrectomy for chronic aphakic cystoid macular edema: results of a national, collaborative, prospective, randomized investigation. *Ophthalmology.* 1985;92(8): 1102–1111.

Harbour JW, Smiddy WE, Rubsamen PE, Murray TG, Davis JL, Flynn HW Jr. Pars plana vitrectomy for chronic pseudophakic cystoid macular edema. *Am J Ophthalmol.* 1995;120(3):302–307.

CHAPTER 15

Posterior Segment Manifestations of Trauma

Ocular trauma is an important cause of visual impairment in the United States. The types of posterior segment injuries can be classified as follows:

- blunt trauma (no break in eyewall)
- penetrating trauma (entrance break, no exit break in eyewall)
- perforating trauma (both entrance and exit breaks in eyewall)
- intraocular foreign bodies, penetrating or perforating

Microsurgical techniques have improved the ability to repair corneal and scleral lacerations, and vitrectomy techniques allow management of severe intraocular injuries (see Chapter 17). Ocular trauma is also discussed in BCSC Section 6, *Pediatric Ophthalmology and Strabismus*; Section 7, *Orbit, Eyelids, and Lacrimal System*; and Section 8, *External Disease and Cornea*.

Evaluation of the Patient After Ocular Trauma

Obtaining a complete history, or as complete as possible under the circumstances, is crucial before a patient with ocular trauma is examined. The following important information is needed:

- How and when was the patient injured?
- Was the injury work related?
- What emergency measures were taken (eg, tetanus shot given, antibiotics administered)?
- Are there concomitant systemic injuries?
- When was the patient's last oral intake (in case surgery is required)?
- What was the health status of the eye before the injury?
- Has the patient had previous ocular surgery, including LASIK?
- Is the presence of an intraocular foreign body a possibility?
- Was the patient hammering metal on metal or working near machinery that could have caused a projectile to enter the eye?
- Was the patient wearing spectacles or was he or she close to shattered glass?
- How forceful was the injury?
- Was the patient wearing eye protection?

Caution is required to avoid causing more damage to the eye by examining it. Initial evaluation should try to determine whether there is a closed-globe or open-globe injury. In an open-globe injury, the eyewall has a full-thickness defect. This eyewall defect may be caused by rupture, which is mechanical failure from too much pressure, or by a laceration, which is caused by a sharp object cutting the eyewall. If an open-globe injury is suspected, the eye should be covered with a shield. The physician should avoid prying open the eye of an uncooperative patient. If severe chemosis, ecchymosis, or eyelid edema prevents a thorough examination, it is best postponed until the time of surgery. Examination under anesthesia should be considered for children or anyone unable to cooperate.

If the patient is able to be examined, the clinician should measure the visual acuity of each eye separately and evaluate the pupils for an afferent pupillary defect. Careful slit-lamp examination can reveal an entrance wound, hyphema, iris damage or incarceration, cataract, or other anterior segment pathology, although a scleral entrance wound is sometimes obscured by ecchymosis. Intraocular pressure (IOP) should be checked. Reduced IOP may suggest a posterior scleral rupture; however, normal IOP does not exclude an occult penetration of the globe.

It is important to examine the eye with the indirect ophthalmoscope as soon as feasible. A posterior penetration or an intraocular foreign body may be detected before synechiae, cataract, dispersed vitreous hemorrhage, or infection obscure it. If the examiner suspects that the eye may harbor an intraocular foreign body that is not found on examination, an imaging study should be considered.

Ultrasound examination may be necessary for eyes that exhibit opaque media after trauma, although it may be deferred (ie, to follow surgical repair of the eyewall defect). To increase the efficacy of the ultrasonographic examination, the clinician should assure the patient that the examination is not painful. Sterile gonioscopic gel is used as a coupling agent for the ultrasound. When copious amounts of gel are used, the ultrasonographic examination can be performed with minimal pressure on the closed lid. Intraocular air may cause artifacts that complicate the interpretation of ultrasonography. Computed tomography (CT) is very helpful in evaluating patients suspected of having intraocular foreign bodies. Metal foreign bodies may introduce artifacts that make them appear larger than they really are, making exact localization difficult. On occasion, wood and certain types of plastic may be very difficult to detect by CT. These types of foreign bodies may be identified and localized with magnetic resonance imaging (MRI). However, MRI should be used only after the presence of ferromagnetic foreign bodies has been definitively ruled out because of the possibility that such foreign bodies may be moved by the magnetic field, causing additional damage.

Blunt Trauma

The object that causes the injury in a blunt trauma does not penetrate the eye but may cause rupture of the eyewall. Blunt trauma can have a number of serious sequelae:

- angle recession
- hemorrhage into the anterior chamber (hyphema) or vitreous
- retinal tears or detachment

- subluxated or dislocated lens
- commotio retinae
- choroidal rupture
- macular hole
- avulsed optic nerve
- scleral rupture

See Chapter 13 for discussion of traumatic retinal breaks and retinal detachment and BCSC Section 11, *Lens and Cataract,* for discussion of dislocated lenses.

A complete ophthalmic examination is essential after blunt trauma because an eye with minimal or no anterior segment damage may still harbor a severe posterior injury. For example, a patient without hyphema or iritis may have a large retinal tear, choroidal rupture, or blowout fracture.

Vitreous Hemorrhage

Vitreous hemorrhage can result from damage to blood vessels of the iris, ciliary body, retina, or choroid and can also be caused by retinal tears. A search for the cause of the vitreous hemorrhage should always be undertaken. Sometimes a hemorrhage that is loculated at presentation later becomes diffuse; thus, the eye should be carefully examined with the indirect ophthalmoscope as soon as possible. If the posterior segment cannot be seen because of vitreous hemorrhage, ultrasound examination is indicated. Retinal or choroidal detachment, large retinal tears, and posterior vitreous detachment can be detected by ultrasound techniques. Echographic signs of an occult scleral rupture include vitreous strands that feed into the rupture site.

More often than not, bed rest with elevation of the patient's head enables the hemorrhage to settle sufficiently to allow for more detailed ophthalmoscopic examination. If the source of the hemorrhage still cannot be determined, frequent follow-up visits and repeated ultrasound examinations are indicated until the hemorrhage clears. In the absence of glaucoma, hypotony, retinal detachment, or endophthalmitis, a unilateral hemorrhage can be monitored until it clears. Macular hole, choroidal rupture in the macula, traumatic maculopathy, retinal detachment, or other injuries can limit recovery of vision.

Commotio Retinae

The term *commotio retinae* describes the damage to the outer retinal layers caused by shock waves that traverse the eye from the site of impact following blunt trauma. Ophthalmoscopic examination shows a sheenlike retinal whitening that appears some hours post-injury (Fig 15-1). The retinal whitening occurs most commonly in the posterior pole but may be found peripherally as well. Several mechanisms for the retinal opacification have been proposed, including extracellular edema, glial swelling, and photoreceptor outer segment disruption. With foveal involvement, a cherry-red spot may appear because the cells involved in the whitening are not present in the foveola. Commotio retinae in the posterior pole, also called *Berlin edema,* may decrease visual acuity to as low as 20/200. Fortunately, the prognosis for recovery of vision is good, as the condition clears in 3–4 weeks. In some cases, however, visual recovery is limited by associated macular pigment epitheliopathy, choroidal rupture, or macular hole formation. No effective treatment is known.

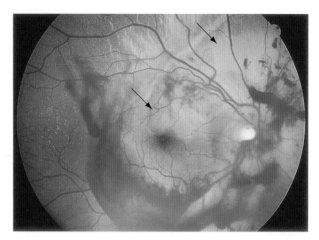

Figure 15-1 Commotio retinae *(arrows)* and vitreous hemorrhage after blunt trauma.

Choroidal Rupture

When the eye is compressed along its anterior-posterior axis, tears may occur in the Bruch membrane, which has little elasticity, as well as in the overlying retinal pigment epithelium (RPE) and fibrous tissue investing the choriocapillaris. Adjacent subretinal hemorrhage is common. Choroidal ruptures may be single or multiple, occurring commonly in the periphery and concentric to the optic disc (Fig 15-2). Ruptures that extend through the fovea may cause permanent visual loss. There is no effective treatment.

Occasionally, choroidal neovascularization (CNV) will develop as a late complication in response to damage to the Bruch membrane (Fig 15-3). A patient with choroidal rupture near the macula should be alerted to the risk of CNV and should be advised to use an

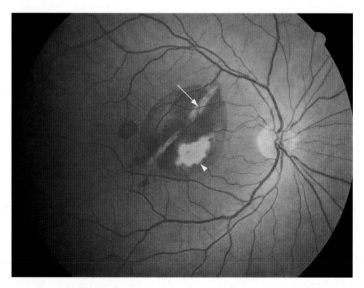

Figure 15-2 Following trauma, this patient had a submacular hemorrhage. The hemorrhage started to clear, revealing a choroidal rupture *(arrow)*. The yellow material located at the inferonasal portion of the macula *(arrowhead)* is dehemoglobinized blood. *(Courtesy of Mark Johnson, MD.)*

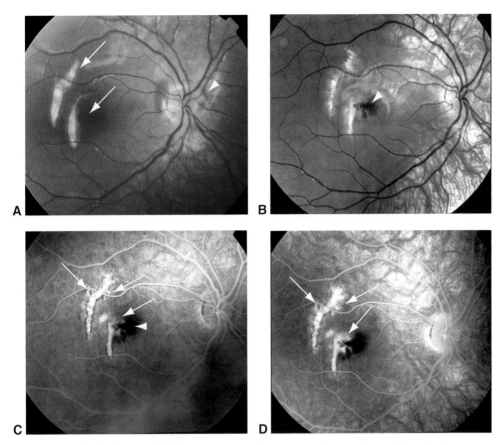

Figure 15-3 **A,** A 10-year-old hit in the eye with a tennis ball sustained choroidal ruptures *(arrows)*. Note the subretinal hemorrhage around the nerve head *(arrowheads)*. The visual acuity was 20/30. **B,** Six weeks later, visual acuity decreased to 20/400. The borders of the choroidal ruptures are more difficult to delineate, and a serosanguineous detachment of the central macula *(arrowhead)* is present. **C,** The early-phase fluorescein angiogram shows multiple fronds of CNV arising from the choroidal ruptures *(arrows);* these fronds leaked during the course of the study. (Image **D** shows corresponding arrows later in the study.) The subretinal blood is shown blocking the background choroidal fluorescence *(arrowhead)*.

(Continued on next page)

Amsler grid for self-testing. Subfoveal CNV, if present, is generally treated with a vascular endothelial growth factor (VEGF) inhibitor, although photodynamic therapy can be used for selected patients. Thermal laser photocoagulation is rarely employed for extrafoveal lesions. Given the effectiveness of anti-VEGF drugs, photodynamic therapy and subfoveal surgery are infrequently used in patients with choroidal rupture complicated by CNV. See Chapter 4 for guidelines on treatment of CNV.

Posttraumatic Macular Hole

The foveola is extremely thin (130 μm), and blunt trauma may cause a full-thickness macular hole by 1 or more mechanisms, including contusion necrosis and vitreous traction

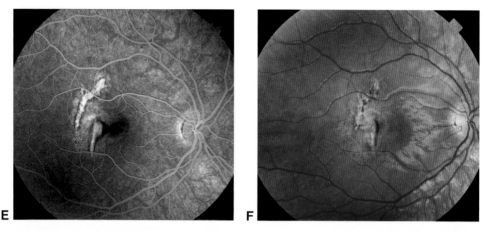

Figure 15-3 *(continued)* **E,** Two weeks after treatment with corticosteroids and photodynamic therapy, the CNV has regressed dramatically. **F,** Six months after treatment, the scarring around the choroidal ruptures obscures their characteristic appearance. Some pigmentary changes have occurred in the macula as well, but visual acuity is 20/25. *(Courtesy of Richard F. Spaide, MD.)*

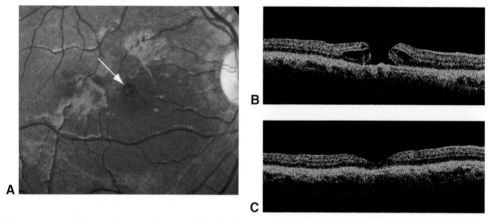

Figure 15-4 **A,** Image from a 16-year-old who bent over to put her phone back in her purse when the car she was traveling in struck a pole. The air bag deployed directly into her face, causing a traumatic macular hole *(arrow)* to develop. Visual acuity was 20/200. **B,** OCT scan showed a full-thickness hole with cystoid changes in the fovea adjacent to the hole. One week after vitrectomy, the hole was closed **(C),** and visual acuity improved to 20/30. *(Courtesy of Richard F. Spaide, MD.)*

(Fig 15-4). Holes may be noted immediately after blunt trauma that causes severe Berlin edema, after a subretinal hemorrhage caused by a choroidal rupture, after severe cystoid macular edema, or after a whiplash separation of the vitreous from the retina. In addition, central depressions, or macular pits (similar to those observed in patients after sun gazing), have been described after blunt trauma to the eye and whiplash injuries. (Lightning and electrical injury can also cause macular holes; patients with these injuries usually have signs of cataract and can have acute peripapillary retinal whitening.) Posttraumatic macular holes may close spontaneously or may be successfully closed with vitrectomy and gas injection, although the prognosis for improved vision may be poorer than for patients with idiopathic macular holes, depending on the degree of collateral damage to the fovea.

Traumatic Chorioretinal Disruption (Retinal Sclopetaria)

An unusual retinal pathology can be produced by high-speed projectile injuries to the orbit. Large areas of choroidal and retinal rupture and necrosis combine with extensive subretinal and retinal hemorrhage, often involving 2 quadrants of the retina. As the blood resorbs, the injured area is repaired by extensive scar formation and widespread pigmentary alteration (Fig 15-5). The macula is often involved, associated with significant loss of vision; curiously, however, secondary retinal detachment rarely develops. The pattern of damage is ascribed to shock waves generated by the deceleration of the projectile passing close to the sclera; a similar fundus appearance may result from blunt trauma to the eyelids from paintball injuries.

Scleral Rupture

Severe blunt injuries can rupture the globe. The 2 most common locations for rupture are at the limbus (under intact conjunctiva) or parallel to and under the insertions of the rectus muscles, that is, regions where the sclera is thinnest. Important diagnostic signs of rupture include marked decrease in ocular ductions, a very boggy conjunctival chemosis with hemorrhage (ecchymosis), deepened anterior chamber, and severe vitreous hemorrhage. The IOP is usually reduced but may be normal or even elevated. Presence of an intraocular foreign body must be ruled out in all cases of ruptured globe. The principles of surgical management of ruptured and lacerated globes are discussed in the following section.

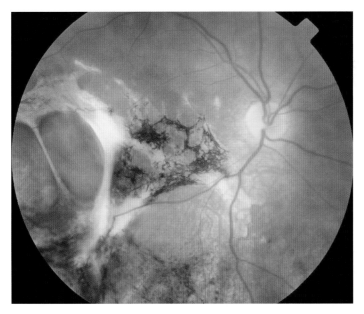

Figure 15-5 Image from a patient shot in the right inferotemporal orbit with a bullet, causing retinal sclopetaria. The bullet's path missed the globe by several millimeters. The patient acutely lost visual acuity. This photograph was taken 2 months after her injury and shows large areas of subretinal proliferation and retinal pigment epithelial hyperplasia. Her visual acuity returned to 20/70. *(Courtesy of Richard F. Spaide, MD.)*

Lacerating and Penetrating Injuries

Lacerating injuries result from cutting or tearing of the eyewall by objects of varying sharpness. A penetrating injury of the globe is a laceration of the eyewall at a single entry site. The prognosis is related to the location and extent of the wound, as well as the associated damage and degree of hemorrhage. Any corneal laceration that crosses the limbus must be explored until its posterior extent has been located. See also BCSC Section 8, *External Disease and Cornea*. If a posterior rupture is suspected, a 360° peritomy should be performed carefully without exerting any pressure on the globe, including exploration underneath the rectus muscles.

The principles of initial management of a penetrating injury include meticulous microsurgical corneoscleral wound repair, in which incarcerated uvea is reposited or excised. Corneal lacerations may be closed with 10-0 nylon interrupted sutures, and scleral wounds may be closed with stronger 7-0 or 8-0 nonabsorbable sutures. Vitreous should be excised from the wound and the anterior chamber re-formed. The ophthalmologist should not apply excessive pressure to the eye during wound closure to avoid extrusion of intraocular tissues. Small posterior wounds may be allowed to heal without treatment because attempts at repair may increase the risk of vitreous incarceration in the wound. BCSC Section 4, *Ophthalmic Pathology and Intraocular Tumors,* discusses wound healing in detail in Chapter 2.

Late complications of a penetrating injury (eg, tractional retinal detachment, cyclitic membrane formation, and phthisis bulbi) result from intraocular cellular proliferation and membrane formation. Removal of the vitreous may reduce the risk of late tractional retinal detachment by eliminating the scaffold on which the contractile membranes grow. The optimal timing of vitrectomy after penetrating injuries is unknown. Some surgeons favor immediate vitrectomy before cellular proliferation can begin; however, most prefer primary repair of the wound to restore the globe and intraocular pressure and decrease the risk of endophthalmitis. Depending on the circumstances, vitrectomy may be postponed for 4–14 days for the following reasons:

- to decrease the risk of intraoperative hemorrhage in acutely inflamed and congested eyes
- to allow the cornea to clear and improve intraoperative visualization
- to permit spontaneous separation of the vitreous from the retina, which facilitates a safer and more complete vitrectomy

Although there are some theoretical reasons for early vitrectomy, the overruling priority at the time of the acute injury is to close the globe. Primary wound closure should not be delayed by the uncertainty of whether an early vitrectomy should be performed. Immediate vitrectomy may be necessary in some circumstances—for example, if examination or history suggests the possibility of infectious endophthalmitis or a retained intraocular foreign body at the time of primary repair. See also Chapter 17.

Mieler WF, Mittra RA. The role and timing of pars plana vitrectomy in penetrating ocular trauma. *Arch Ophthalmol.* 1997;115(9):1191–1192.

Perforating Injuries

Whereas a penetrating injury of the globe has an entrance wound through the eyewall, a perforating injury has both entrance and exit wounds. Perforating injuries may be caused by objects of varying sharpness such as needles, knives, high-velocity pellets, or small fragments of metal. An important iatrogenic cause is needle perforation during retrobulbar anesthesia for cataract surgery. Studies have shown that fibrous proliferation after perforating injuries occurs along the scaffold of damaged vitreous between the entrance and exit wounds. The wounds are often closed by fibrosis within 7 days after the injury, depending on size. Small-gauge injuries with only a small amount of hemorrhage and no significant collateral damage often heal without serious sequelae. Anterior wounds are usually cleared of incarcerated vitreous and closed with sutures, but small very posterior wounds are sometimes left unrepaired to avoid vitreous extrusion through the wound during attempted closure. Vitrectomy may be considered in the following situations:

- the presence of moderate to severe vitreous hemorrhage
- other tissue damage requiring repair
- signs of developing transvitreal traction

Vitrectomy is usually delayed 7 days to allow the posterior wounds to close by proliferation so that posterior suturing will not be necessary.

During vitrectomy, an attempt should be made to separate the posterior cortical gel to prevent later proliferation and contraction that could lead to retinal detachment. Separating the posterior cortical vitreous from the retina may be difficult, however, in children, in young adults, and in eyes with retinal breaks, a retinal detachment, or both. Retinal detachment is frequently caused by the primary injury or by the traction developing as part of proliferative vitreoretinopathy (PVR).

Intraocular Foreign Bodies

In most cases, the intraocular foreign body is suggested because an entry wound is visible, or the intraocular foreign body itself can be seen. Even without such direct evidence, however, an intraocular foreign body should always be suspected and ruled out after ocular or orbital trauma. A detailed history should be taken. Small, high-velocity pieces of steel, such as those that might be broken off in hammering steel on steel or thrown by high-speed machinery, are often overlooked. If a sample of the suspected foreign body material can be located in a timely manner, it may be examined to determine whether it is magnetic, radiopaque, or both. Frontal and lateral skull x-rays usually reveal the presence of radiopaque foreign bodies, although they are less accurate in localizing them. In an eye with opaque media, plain-film x-rays and other imaging studies such as CT or echography are indicated to detect the number, size, and location of foreign bodies (Fig 15-6). CT is better than plain-film x-rays at localizing the radiopaque foreign bodies. CT is also better at detecting and locating less radiopaque foreign bodies. When very small or less radiopaque foreign bodies are suspected, bone-free x-ray studies may be

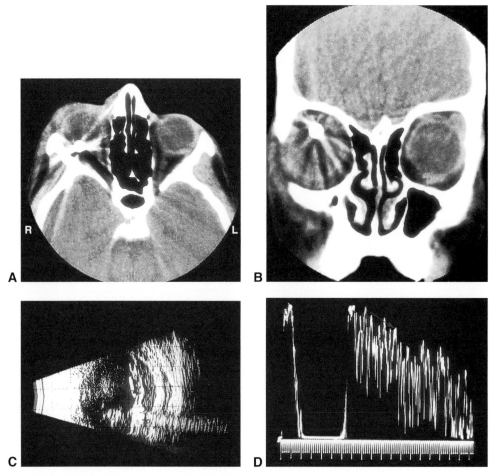

Figure 15-6 Images from a patient with an intraocular BB pellet. Axial **(A)** and coronal **(B)** CT views show the pellet to be in the superior and posterior globe. B-scan echography **(C)** shows retinal detachment *(arrow)* and subretinal hemorrhage *(H)*. A characteristic reverberation of echoes between the front and back surfaces of the round pellet gives a "trail of echoes" artifact that extends posterior to the foreign body on B-scan *(asterisk)* and on A-scan **(D)** *(arrow)*.

helpful. The presence of nonradiopaque foreign bodies and their relationship to intraocular structures may be determined by an experienced ultrasonographer. The possibility of multiple foreign bodies should always be considered. MRI is contraindicated if the foreign body is metallic because the magnetic force may move a metallic foreign body, causing further ocular damage.

Surgical Techniques for Removal of Intraocular Foreign Bodies

The surgical planning for removal of a magnetic intraocular foreign body must include the following:

- location of the foreign body in the eye
- surgeon's ability to see the foreign body

- size and shape of the foreign body
- composition of the foreign body (ferromagnetic vs nonferromagnetic)
- encapsulation of the foreign body

Pars plana vitrectomy allows removal of the vitreous and facilitates extraction of the intraocular foreign body.

A pars plana magnet extraction can be considered for small, nonencapsulated ferromagnetic foreign bodies that can be easily seen in the vitreous cavity, are not embedded in or adherent to retina or other structures, and have no associated retinal pathology such as a retinal tear. After a full-thickness incision is made through the pars plana, the magnet is aligned with its long axis pointing directly at the foreign body and its short blunt tip against the gaping sclerotomy site. When the pulsed magnet is activated, the foreign body will be pulled through the pars plana toward the magnet.

If the media are opaque because of cataract or hemorrhage, if the foreign body is encapsulated and adherent to vitreous or retina, or if the foreign body is large or nonmagnetic, vitrectomy (with lensectomy if necessary) and forceps extraction of the foreign body are indicated. Before forceps extraction is attempted, the foreign body should be freed of all attachments. A small rare-earth magnet may be used to engage and separate the foreign body from the retinal surface. Although small foreign bodies can be removed through the pars plana sclerotomy site, some large foreign bodies may be extracted more safely through the corneoscleral limbus or the initial wound to minimize collateral damage.

Retained Intraocular Foreign Bodies

The reaction of the eye to a retained foreign body varies greatly depending on the chemical composition, sterility, and location of the object. Inert, sterile foreign bodies such as stone, sand, glass, porcelain, plastic, and cilia are generally well tolerated. If such material is found several days after the injury and does not appear to create an inflammatory reaction, it may be left in place provided it is not obstructing vision.

Evaluation for retinal toxicity using electroretinography may be helpful in some cases. Zinc, aluminum, copper, and iron are metals that are commonly reactive in the eye. Of these, zinc and aluminum tend to cause minimal inflammation and may become encapsulated. If very large, however, any foreign body may incite inflammation, causing anterior and posterior proliferative vitreoretinopathy. Epiretinal proliferations, tractional retinal detachment, and phthisis bulbi may result in complete loss of vision. Migration of the foreign body also can occur, especially if it contains copper.

Pure copper (eg, wire, percussion cap) is especially toxic, and prompt removal is required. Copper causes acute chalcosis manifesting itself with severe inflammation, which may lead to loss of the eye. Late removal of copper may not cure the chalcosis, which may increase after surgery in some cases because of dissemination of the metal. If copper is alloyed with another metal for a final copper content of less than 85% (eg, brass, bronze), chronic chalcosis may occur. Copper has an affinity for basement membranes. Typical findings in chalcosis are deposits in Descemet membrane (similar to the Kayser-Fleischer ring of Wilson disease), greenish aqueous particles, green discoloration of the iris, lens capsule ("sunflower" cataract), brownish red vitreous opacities and strand formation, and metallic flecks on retinal vessels and the internal limiting membrane in the macular region.

Iron from intraocular foreign bodies is mostly deposited in neuroepithelial tissues such as the iris sphincter and dilator muscles, the nonpigmented ciliary epithelium, the lens epithelium, the retina, and the RPE. Oxidation and dissemination of ferric ions throughout the eye promotes the Fenton reaction, in which metal ions, particularly iron, catalyze the generation of powerful oxidants such as hydroxyl radicals. These oxidants cause lipid peroxidation, sulfhydryl oxidation, and depolymerization, with cell membrane damage and enzyme inactivation. BCSC Section 2, *Fundamentals and Principles of Ophthalmology,* and Section 9, *Intraocular Inflammation and Uveitis,* discuss these reactions in greater detail, with illustrations.

Retinal photoreceptors and RPE cells are especially susceptible to siderosis (Table 15-1). Electroretinogram (ERG) changes in siderosis include an increased a-wave and normal b-wave during the very early phase of toxicity and diminishing b-wave amplitude in later phases. Eventually, the ERG may become undetectable. Serial ERGs can be helpful in monitoring eyes with small retained foreign bodies. If the b-wave amplitude decreases, removal of the foreign body generally is recommended.

Posttraumatic Endophthalmitis

Endophthalmitis occurs after 2%–7% of penetrating injuries; the incidence is higher in association with intraocular foreign bodies and in rural settings. Posttraumatic endophthalmitis can progress rapidly; its clinical signs include marked inflammation featuring fibrin, hypopyon, vitreous infiltration, and corneal opacification. The risk of endophthalmitis after penetrating ocular injury may be reduced by prompt wound closure and early removal of intraocular foreign bodies. Prophylactic subconjunctival, intravenous, and sometimes intravitreal antibiotics are often recommended.

Bacillus cereus, which rarely causes endophthalmitis in other settings, accounts for almost 25% of cases of traumatic endophthalmitis. Endophthalmitis caused by *B cereus* has a rapid and severe course and, once established, leads to profound vision loss and often loss of the eye. Most commonly, *B cereus* endophthalmitis is associated with soil-contaminated

---

Table 15-1 Symptoms and Signs of Siderosis

Symptoms
 Nyctalopia
 Concentrically constricted visual field
 Decreased vision

Signs
 Rust-colored corneal stromal staining
 Iris heterochromia
 Pupillary mydriasis and poor reactivity
 Brown deposits on the anterior lens
 Cataract
 Vitreous opacities
 Peripheral retinal pigmentation (early)
 Diffuse retinal pigmentation (late)
 Narrowed retinal vessels
 Optic disc discoloration and atrophy
 Secondary open-angle glaucoma from iron accumulation in the trabecular meshwork

injuries, especially those involving foreign bodies. Anterior chamber and vitreous cultures should be obtained, and antibiotics should be injected if endophthalmitis is suspected. *Bacillus cereus* is sensitive to vancomycin or clindamycin injected intravitreally. Gram-negative organisms are frequent pathogens in posttraumatic endophthalmitis, for which ceftazidime may be an effective therapy that avoids the toxicities associated with amino-glycosides. Because recommendations for antibiotic selection change frequently, ophthal-mologists should consult a recent reference for current guidelines.

The role of prophylactic antibiotics in cases without signs of endophthalmitis is con-troversial. Caution should be exercised in their use because of reports of retinal vascular infarction after intravitreal injection of aminoglycoside antibiotics. Intravitreal antibiotics are generally limited to cases at high risk of infection. See also BCSC Section 9, *Intraocular Inflammation and Uveitis.*

Reynolds DS, Flynn HW Jr. Endophthalmitis after penetrating ocular trauma. *Curr Opin Ophthalmol.* 1997;8(3):32–38.

Sympathetic Ophthalmia

If the corneoscleral coat cannot be repaired because of tissue loss or the globe is internally disorganized, that is, there is no hope for visual recovery from no light perception in a recently lacerated or ruptured eye, enucleation should be considered to reduce the risk of sympathetic ophthalmia. Recent estimates suggest the incidence of sympathetic ophthal-mia to be 1 in 500 cases of penetrating injury. Because the extent of intraocular damage is often difficult to determine, it is best to close the wound and restore the eye if that is at all possible. In general, primary evisceration should be performed only if the globe can-not be repaired. After the primary wound repair, management of a severely injured eye that maintains light perception is a matter of careful follow-up. The viability of the globe should be assessed at each visit within the first 7–14 days.

After careful preoperative evaluation, one strategy is to explore the eye using a vit-rectomy approach. If the eye shows potential for anatomical repair and visual recovery, it is repaired and retained. If the eye has no potential for recovery, enucleation should be considered. Enucleation performed within 2 weeks of the initial injury may reduce the risk of sympathetic ophthalmia. The patient and surgeon should discuss and consent to enucleation preoperatively, that is, decide whether enucleation is to be performed at the time of exploratory vitrectomy or in a later surgery. Some patients may be candidates for evisceration, which may carry a higher risk of sympathetic ophthalmia than enucleation but may produce a better cosmetic outcome. See also BCSC Section 9, *Intraocular Inflam-mation and Uveitis.*

A large proportion of patients with sympathetic ophthalmia present between 3 months and 1 year after trauma, but many show initial signs and symptoms of the disease over a very wide time interval. If the injury to the inciting eye is still present, it is common for inflammation to flare up in that eye, followed by signs and symptoms of inflammation in the sympathizing fellow eye. Symptoms can include loss of acuity, loss of accommodation, photophobia, and pain. Signs include panuveitis, multifocal infiltrates at the level of the RPE (Dalen-Fuchs nodules) or choroid, exudative detachment, optic nerve swelling, and thickening of the uveal tract as detected by contact B-scan ultrasonography or optical coherence tomography (OCT). Early, aggressive treatment with high-dose corticosteroids and immunomodulatory drugs is required to save both inciting and sympathizing eyes.

Albert DM, Diaz-Rohena R. A historical review of sympathetic ophthalmia and its epidemiology. *Surv Ophthalmol.* 1989;34(1):1–14.

Power WJ, Foster CS. Update on sympathetic ophthalmia. *Int Ophthalmol Clin.* 1995;35(1): 127–137.

Shaken Baby Syndrome/Nonaccidental Trauma

Severe shaking of infants, a form of nonaccidental trauma, is the cause of shaken baby syndrome. The typical baby is almost always less than 1 year and frequently less than 6 months of age. The presenting sign of child abuse involves the eye in approximately 5% of cases. Systemic signs and symptoms include

- bradycardia, apnea, and hypothermia
- lethargy, irritability, seizures, hypotonia
- signs of failure to thrive
- full or bulging fontanelles and increased head size
- skin bruises, particularly on the upper arms, chest, or thighs
- spiral fractures of the long bones
- subdural and subarachnoid hemorrhages

Ocular signs include

- retinal hemorrhages and cotton-wool spots (Fig 15-7)
- retinal folds
- hemorrhagic schisis cavities

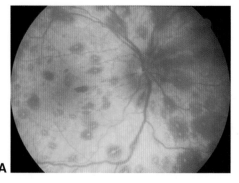 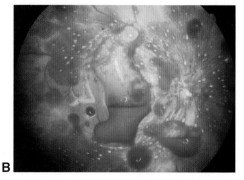

A **B**

Figure 15-7 Images from a patient with shaken baby syndrome with preretinal and retinal hemorrhages. **A,** This photograph was taken several days after hospital admission, by which time many of the smaller hemorrhages had started to resorb. **B,** Numerous hemorrhages are located on and within the retina. There are regions of hemorrhagic retinoschisis centrally. Because the baby was upright, the red blood cells sank down into a dependent position within the larger regions of hemorrhagic retinoschisis. Note that some of the hemorrhages were white-centered, whereas others had reflections of the flash from the fundus camera on them. *(Reproduced with permission from Spaide RF, Swengel RM, Scharre DW, Mein CE. Shaken baby syndrome. Am Fam Physician. 1990;41(4):1145–1152.)*

The retinal hemorrhages in shaken baby syndrome often have a hemispheric contour. They can start to resolve very rapidly; therefore, it is important to examine suspected shaken baby syndrome infants on presentation. The retinopathy may resemble that observed in Terson syndrome or central retinal vein occlusion. None of these conditions is common in infants. Retinal hemorrhages may be caused by trauma, but they are not usually associated with typical accidents, such as falls at home. Any physician who suspects that child abuse might have occurred is required by law in every US state and Canadian province to report the incident to a designated government agency. Vitrectomy for vitreous hemorrhage should be considered if amblyopia is likely to occur but may be deferred if a bright-flash ERG shows loss of the b-wave, indicative of extensive retinal damage. See also BCSC Section 6, *Pediatric Ophthalmology and Strabismus*.

Matthews GP, Das A. Dense vitreous hemorrhages predict poor visual and neurological prognosis in infants with shaken baby syndrome. *J Pediatr Ophthalmol Strabismus*. 1996;33(4):260–265.

Pierre-Kahn V, Roche O, Dureau P, et al. Ophthalmologic findings in suspected child abuse victims with subdural hematomas. *Ophthalmology*. 2003;110(9):1718–1723.

Avulsion of the Optic Disc

A forceful backward dislocation of the optic nerve from the scleral canal can occur under several circumstances, including

- extreme rotation and forward displacement of the globe
- penetrating orbital injury, causing a backward pull on the optic nerve
- sudden increase in IOP, causing rupture of the lamina cribrosa

Total loss of vision characteristically occurs. Findings may vary from a pitlike depression of the optic nerve head to posterior hemorrhage and contusion necrosis (Fig 15-8); however, hemorrhage is usually present acutely.

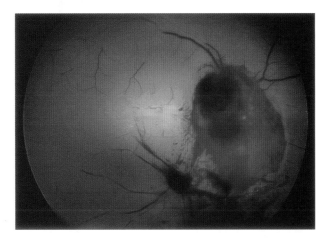

Figure 15-8 Avulsion of the optic nerve. Nerve is obscured by hemorrhage, and a mixed vascular occlusion is present.

Gass JDM. *Stereoscopic Atlas of Macular Diseases: Diagnosis and Treatment.* 4th ed. St Louis: Mosby; 1997.

Photic Damage

The eye has several mechanisms protecting against light damage, including constriction of the pupils, light absorption by melanin in the RPE, and the presence of antioxidants, such as lutein and zeaxanthin, in the macula. Light injures the retina by 3 basic mechanisms:

1. mechanical
2. thermal
3. photochemical

Mechanical injury occurs when the power of the absorbed light is high enough to form gas or water vapor or to produce acoustic shock waves that mechanically disrupt retinal tissues. The absorbed energy may be enough to strip electrons from molecules in the target tissue, producing a collection of ions and electrons referred to as *plasma.* For example, a Q-switched Nd:YAG laser produces its therapeutic effect through mechanical light damage and uses this effect to disrupt a cloudy posterior capsule behind an intraocular lens.

Thermal injury occurs when excessive light absorption by the RPE and surrounding structures causes local elevation of the tissue temperature, leading to coagulation, inflammation, and scarring of the RPE and the surrounding neurosensory retina and choroid. The end result of this temperature elevation is protein denaturation and scar formation. A therapeutic application of thermal light injury is the retinal burn caused by laser photocoagulation. See Chapter 16 for discussion of photocoagulation.

Photochemical injury results from biochemical reactions that cause retinal tissue destruction without elevation of temperature. Photochemical injury is the result of the transfer of light energy to a molecule; the excess energy initiates reactions that cause tissue damage. For photochemical reactions to occur, the energy of the photon must exceed a certain threshold. Damaging reactions can include oxidation, photoisomerization, photochemical cleavage, and electrocyclic reactions. Each may cause damage directly or indirectly through formation of reactive molecules, such as lipofuscin, that are photoreactive. Such changes occur primarily at the level of the outer segments of the photoreceptors, which are more sensitive than the inner segments. Solar retinopathy and photic retinopathy after exposure to operating microscope illumination are examples of photochemical injury.

Mainster MA, Boulton ME. Photic retinopathy. In: Albert DM, Miller JW, Azar DT, Blodi BA, eds. *Albert & Jakobiec's Principles and Practice of Ophthalmology.* 3rd ed. Philadelphia: Saunders; 2008:chap 174.

Mainster MA, Turner PL. Retinal injuries from light: mechanisms, hazards, and prevention. In: Ryan SJ, Hinton DR, Schachat AP, Wilkinson CP, eds. *Retina.* 3 vols. 4th ed. Philadelphia: Elsevier/Mosby; 2006:1857–1870.

Solar Retinopathy

Solar retinopathy, also known as *foveomacular retinitis, eclipse retinopathy,* and *solar retinitis,* is photochemical retinal injury caused by direct or indirect viewing of the sun; it usually occurs after viewing a solar eclipse or gazing directly at the sun. The damage is thought to be the result of exposure to visible blue light and shorter wavelengths of ultraviolet A or near-UV radiation. Younger patients with clearer lenses and patients taking drugs that photosensitize the eye, including tetracycline and psoralens, are at a higher risk of solar retinopathy. Patients with high refractive errors and dark fundus pigmentation are at a slightly lower risk. Patients report decreased vision, central scotomas, dyschromatopsia, metamorphopsia, micropsia, and frontal or temporal headache within hours of exposure. Visual acuity is typically reduced to 20/25–20/100 but may be worse depending on degree of exposure. Most patients recover within 3–6 months, with vision returning to the level of 20/20–20/40, but residual metamorphopsia and paracentral scotomata may remain.

The fundus findings are variable and usually bilateral. The characteristic finding in the first few days after exposure is a yellow-white spot in the fovea, which subsequently changes after several days into a reddish dot, often surrounded by a pigment halo. Mild cases, however, often have no biomicroscopic fundus changes. After approximately 2 weeks, a small, reddish, well-circumscribed, 100–200-μm lamellar hole or depression may evolve that is more apparent on OCT. This lesion may lie at or adjacent to the fovea and is usually permanent. Fluorescein angiography reveals leakage in early stages and window defects in late stages.

It is theorized that solar retinopathy is caused by a photochemical injury, perhaps thermally enhanced. The extent of the damage depends on the duration of the exposure. Histologic studies have shown RPE damage. No known beneficial treatment exists, and prevention through education is critically important.

Phototoxicity From Ophthalmic Instrumentation

The potential for photochemical damage from modern ophthalmic instruments has been studied extensively. Injuries have been reported from operating microscopes and from fiber-optic endoilluminating probes used in vitrectomies. The prevalence of photic retinopathy after cataract surgery has been estimated at 3%–7.4%. The incidence increases with prolonged operating times but can occur even with surgery times as short as 30 minutes. In retinal surgery, photic injury is more likely to occur with prolonged, focal exposure, especially when the light probe is held in close proximity to the retina, as is the case in macular hole and epiretinal membrane procedures. If dyes such as indocyanine green are used for staining of the internal limiting membrane, photochemical damage to neural tissue may occur as a result of the phototoxic properties of the dye. Most patients are asymptomatic; however, some will notice a paracentral scotoma on the first postoperative day. In general, vision returns to normal after a few months. Acutely affected patients may have a deep, irregular, oval-shaped, yellow-white retinal lesion adjacent to the fovea that resembles the shape of the light source. The lesion typically evolves to become a zone of mottled RPE that transmits hyperfluorescence on fluorescein angiography. Although animal studies generally exaggerate clinical exposures, reports of photic macular lesions after cataract surgery and after the use of indocyanine green emphasize the need for prevention. Minimizing exposure, avoiding intense illumination, using oblique illumination when possible during parts of the surgery, filtering out short-wavelength blue light and UV light, and using shielding may help reduce the risk of photic retinopathy during ocular surgery. BCSC Section 11, *Lens and Cataract,* lists several precautions to minimize retinal light toxicity. See also BCSC Section 3, *Clinical Optics,* Chapter 4.

Fuller D, Machemer R, Knighton RW. Retinal damage produced by intraocular fiber optic light. *Am J Ophthalmol.* 1978;85(4):519–537.

Gandorfer A, Haritoglou C, Gandorfer A, Kampik A. Retinal damage from indocyanine green in experimental macular surgery. *Invest Ophthalmol Vis Sci.* 2003;44(1):316–323.

Kleinmann G, Hoffman P, Schechtman E, Pollack A. Microscope-induced retinal phototoxicity in cataract surgery of short duration. *Ophthalmology.* 2002;109(2):334–338.

Pavilack MA, Brod RD. Site of potential operating microscope light-induced phototoxicity on the human retina during temporal approach eye surgery. *Ophthalmology.* 2001;108(2):381–385.

Ambient Light

Although there is much speculation that ambient exposure to UV radiation or visible light may be a potential cause of retinal toxicity or degeneration, further study and documentation are required.

Increased light exposure after cataract surgery has been suggested as a potential cause of the increase in the incidence and progression of age-related macular degeneration (AMD) found by the Beaver Dam Eye Study. Therefore, some authors have been advocating the use of blue-filtering intraocular lenses. However, more recent reevaluation of the Age-Related Eye Disease Study found no statistically significant increase in AMD after cataract surgery.

Furthermore, not only is there still no evidence that filtering out blue light has a protective effect, but doing so may potentially interfere with night vision.

Forooghian F, Agrón E, Clemons TE, et al. Visual acuity outcomes after cataract surgery in patients with age-related macular degeneration: age-related eye disease study report no. 27. *Ophthalmology.* 2009;116(11):2093–2100. Epub 2009 Aug 22.

Klein R, Klein BE, Wong TY, Tomany SC, Cruickshanks KJ. The association of cataract and cataract surgery with the long-term incidence of age-related maculopathy: the Beaver Dam eye study. *Arch Ophthalmol.* 2002;120(11):1551–1558.

Mainster MA. Intraocular lenses should block UV radiation and violet but not blue light. *Arch Ophthalmol.* 2005;123(4):550–555.

Occupational Light Toxicity

Occupational exposure to bright lights can lead to retinal damage. One of the most common causes of occupational injury is arc welding without the use of protective goggles. The damage from the visible blue light of the arc welder leads to photochemical damage similar to that observed in solar retinopathy. Occupational injury from stray laser exposure is also a serious concern. Photic retinal injury has been reported as well after exposure to laser pointers. Robertson and colleagues noted damage after exposing the retina to light from class 3A laser pointers for durations greater than 15 minutes.

Robertson DM, Lim TH, Salomao DR, Link TP, Rowe RL, McLaren JW. Laser pointers and the human eye: a clinicopathologic study. *Arch Ophthalmol.* 2000;118(12):1686–1691.

PART III

Selected Therapeutic Topics

CHAPTER 16

Laser Therapy for Posterior Segment Diseases

Basic Principles of Photocoagulation

Photocoagulation uses a strong light source to coagulate tissue. Light energy is absorbed by the target tissue and converted into thermal energy. When the tissue temperature rises above 65°C, denaturation of tissue proteins and coagulative necrosis occur.

Most surgeons currently perform photocoagulation with lasers spanning the visible light spectrum of 400–780 nm and venturing into the infrared wavelengths. Current posterior segment laser delivery systems include green, red, yellow, and infrared wavelengths. Delivery systems may employ a transpupillary approach with slit-lamp delivery, indirect ophthalmoscopic application, endophotocoagulation during vitrectomy, or transscleral application with a contact probe.

The effectiveness of any photocoagulator depends on how well its light is transmitted by the ocular media and how well that light is absorbed by pigment in the target tissue. Light is absorbed principally by ocular tissues that contain melanin, xanthophyll, or hemoglobin. Figure 16-1 illustrates the absorption spectra of the key pigments found in ocular tissues:

- *Melanin* is an excellent absorber of green, yellow, red, and infrared wavelengths.
- Macular *xanthophyll* readily absorbs blue but minimally absorbs yellow or red wavelengths.
- *Hemoglobin* easily absorbs blue, green, and yellow, with minimal absorption of red wavelengths.

Choice of Laser Wavelength

Depending on the specific goals of treatment, the surgeon considers the absorption properties of the key ocular pigments when choosing the appropriate wavelength of light to selectively deliver focal photocoagulation to target tissues while attempting to spare adjacent normal tissues. However, the *area* (depth and diameter) of effective coagulation is also related directly to the *intensity* and *duration* of the irradiation, and these factors can often supersede the theoretical differences of various wavelengths. For a specific set of laser parameters (spot size, duration, and power), the intensity of the burn obtained depends on the clarity of the ocular media and the degree of pigmentation of the fundus in the individual eye.

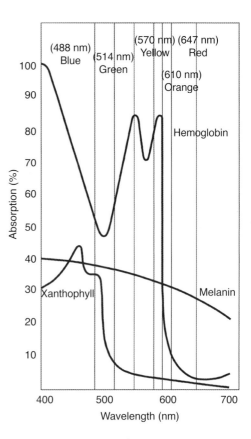

Figure 16-1 Absorption spectra of xantho-phyll, hemoglobin, and melanin. *(Reproduced with permission from Folk JC, Pulido JS. Laser Photo-coagulation of the Retina and Choroid. Ophthalmology Monograph 11. San Francisco: American Academy of Ophthalmology; 1997:9.)*

The *green laser* produces light that is absorbed well by melanin and hemoglobin and less completely by xanthophyll. Because of these characteristics and the absence of blue wavelengths, it has replaced the blue-green laser for the treatment of retinal vascular abnormalities and choroidal neovascularization (CNV).

The *red laser* penetrates through nuclear sclerotic cataracts and moderate vitreous hemorrhages better than lasers with other wavelengths. In addition, it is minimally absorbed by xanthophyll and thus may be useful in the treatment of CNV adjacent to the fovea. The red laser, or diode laser, causes deeper burns with a higher rate of patient discomfort and inhomogeneous absorption at the level of the choroid in the same areas, leading to a focal disruption referred to as a "pop-effect." The *infrared laser* has characteristics similar to those of the red laser, but it offers deeper tissue penetration. For typical laser wavelengths of specific lasers, see BCSC 3, *Clinical Optics*, Chapter 1.

The *yellow laser* has, among its advantages, minimal scatter through nuclear sclerotic lenses, low xanthophyll absorption, and little potential for photochemical damage. It appears to be useful for destroying vascular structures with minimal damage to adjacent pigmented tissue; thus, it may be valuable for treating retinal vascular and choroidal neovascular lesions.

Laser effects on tissue of the posterior segment include photochemical and thermal effects and vaporization. Photochemical reactions can be induced by ultraviolet or visible light that is absorbed by tissue molecules or by molecules of photosensitizing medication (eg, verteporfin) that are then converted into cytotoxic molecules such as free radicals. Absorption of laser energy by pigment results in a 10°C–20°C temperature rise and subsequent protein denaturation. Vaporization is caused by raising the temperature of water above the boiling point and causing microexplosions, as occurs in overly intense argon burns.

Atebara NH, Thall EH. Principles of lasers. In: Yanoff M, Duker JS, eds. *Ophthalmology.* 3rd ed. Edinburgh, UK: Mosby/Elsevier; 2009.

Palanker D, Blumenkranz MS, Weiter JJ. Retinal laser therapy: biophysical basis and applications. In: Ryan SJ, Hinton DR, Schachat AP, Wilkinson CP, eds. *Retina.* 4th ed. Philadelphia: Elsevier/Mosby; 2006.

Practical Aspects of Laser Photocoagulation

Anesthesia

Topical, peribulbar, or retrobulbar anesthesia may be needed to facilitate delivery of laser photocoagulation. The choice of which method to use is often guided by the laser wavelength being used, the duration of treatment, the type of treatment, and the importance of immobilizing the eye.

Lenses

Two types of contact lenses are available to assist in slit-lamp delivery of photocoagulation:

1. negative-power planoconcave lenses
2. high-plus-power lenses

The planoconcave lenses provide an upright image with superior resolution of a small retinal area. Most clinicians favor use of these lenses for macular treatments. Mirrored planoconcave lenses direct photocoagulation more peripherally depending on the angle of the mirror in use. Where these mirrors are positioned, the macula will not be in the surgeon's view; therefore, he or she must be mindful of where the mirror is directing the laser beam in the fundus to avoid accidental photocoagulation of the macula.

High-plus-power lenses provide an inverted image with some loss of fine resolution, but they offer a wide field of view, facilitating efficient treatment over a broad area. The macula may be kept in view while the midperiphery of the retina is being treated, making these lenses ideal for panretinal photocoagulation. The type of contact lens selected affects the actual burn size on the retina. Planoconcave lenses generally provide the same retinal spot size as that selected on the slit-lamp setting, whereas high-plus-power lenses provide a spot size that is magnified over the laser setting size, with the magnification factor depending on the lens used (Table 16-1).

Parameters

Selection of laser setting parameters depends on the intent of the treatment, the clarity of the ocular media, and the fundus pigmentation. As a general rule, smaller spot sizes require less energy than larger spot sizes, and longer-duration exposures require less energy than shorter-duration exposures to achieve the same intensity effects. For further discussion of laser characteristics and techniques, see BCSC Section 3, *Clinical Optics.*

Table 16-1 Magnification Factors for Common Laser Lenses

Lens	Magnification	Laser Spot Magnification
Panretinal photocoagulation lenses		
Ocular Mainster PRP 165	0.51×	1.96×
Ocular Mainster Ultra Field PRP	0.53×	1.89×
Ocular Mainster Wide Field PDT	0.68×	1.50×
Rodenstock Panfunduscope	0.7×	1.43×
Volk Equator Plus	0.44×	2.27×
Volk QuadrAspheric	0.51×	1.97×
Volk SuperQuad 160	0.5×	2.0×
Focal laser lenses		
Goldmann 3-mirror (central)	0.93×	1.08×
Ocular Mainster High Magnification	1.25×	0.80×
Ocular PDT 1.6×	0.63×	1.6×
Ocular Reichel-Mainster 1× Retina	0.95×	1.05×
Ocular Yannuzzi Fundus	0.93×	1.08×
Volk Area Centralis	1.06×	0.94×
Volk PDT Lens	0.66×	1.5×

Other laser delivery systems

Among the slit-lamp delivery systems are pattern scanners that deliver an entire array of laser applications with each foot-pedal depression. Delivery is accomplished by using ultrashort (20–50 millisecond) laser applications at high intensity in rapid succession. This approach possibly increases the efficiency of treatment.

Some systems incorporate real-time retinal image overlay and registration with the laser delivery system. This configuration allows for computer-assisted planning and targeting of the retinal lesions.

Folk JC, Pulido JS. *Laser Photocoagulation of the Retina and Choroid.* Ophthalmology Monograph 11. San Francisco: American Academy of Ophthalmology; 1997.

Ip M, Puliafito CA. Laser photocoagulation. In: Yanoff M, Duker JS, eds. *Ophthalmology.* 3rd ed. Edinburgh, UK: Mosby/Elsevier; 2009.

Indications

Indications for retinal photocoagulation include the following:

- panretinal scatter treatment to ablate ischemic tissue in order to eliminate retinal, iris, and disc neovascularization and to reduce the stimulus that causes continuing damage in proliferative diseases such as proliferative diabetic retinopathy and venous occlusive diseases
- closure of intraretinal vascular abnormalities such as microaneurysms, telangiectasia, and microvascular abnormalities (IRMAs)
- focal ablation of extrafoveal CNV, such as neovascularization associated with ocular histoplasmosis syndrome (OHS) or age-related macular degeneration (AMD)
- creation of chorioretinal adhesions, as in the area surrounding retinal breaks or limited retinal detachment

- focal treatment of pigment epithelial abnormalities, including leakage associated with central serous chorioretinopathy
- to a limited degree, coagulation of selected ocular tumors

Complications of Photocoagulation

Like any other surgical procedure, photocoagulation may occasionally be associated with complications. The most serious complications are caused by use of excessive energy or misdirected light. The surgeon must pay constant attention to the foveal center during any laser treatment to avoid injury to this vital structure. Wide-field lenses make this easier because the fovea is always in the field of view. Proper selection of wavelength, power, exposure time, and spot size is crucial. If appropriate laser settings do not produce the desired tissue effect, the clinician should interrupt the procedure and cautiously vary the laser power and exposure to avoid unnecessary levels of energy or burns that break through the Bruch membrane, which would risk bleeding or future CNV.

Patient preparation is also important in minimizing complications. Careful preoperative explanation of the laser procedure to the patient and proper positioning of patient and surgeon for comfort both help improve the patient's cooperation, steady fixation, and safety.

Among the complications that may be associated with photocoagulation are inadvertent corneal burns, which can lead to opacities. Treatment of the iris may cause iritis and create zones of atrophy. Pupillary abnormalities may arise from thermal damage to the long ciliary nerves in the suprachoroidal space. Absorption by lens pigments may create lenticular burns and resultant opacities. Optic neuropathy may occur from treatment directly to or adjacent to the disc, and nerve fiber damage may follow intense absorption in zones of increased pigmentation or retinal thinning. Chorioretinal complications include foveal burns, Bruch membrane ruptures, creation of retinal or choroidal lesions, and exudative choroidal or retinal detachment.

Accidental foveal burns

The surgeon should take great care to identify the fovea by means of biomicroscopy; comparison with images from fluorescein angiography may aid in the identification. Frequent reference to the foveal center throughout the procedure is helpful to avoid losing track of where, in the fundus, treatment is taking place. Another practical approach to identify the location of the fovea is to discontinue coagulation briefly and to instruct the patient to fixate on the aiming beam, with the treatment beam turned off. Parafoveal marking burns can then be placed a safe distance from the center of fixation. The patient's ability to fixate steadily is important for avoiding foveal burns. In some instances, the risk of foveal burns may be reduced by immobilizing the globe with peribulbar or retrobulbar anesthesia, especially when juxtafoveal treatment is being performed.

Bruch membrane ruptures

Small spot size, high power, and short duration of applications all increase the risk of a rupture in the Bruch membrane, which may subsequently give rise to hemorrhage from the choriocapillaris and development of CNV. Increasing digital pressure on the contact lens is often sufficient to allow for thrombosis and cessation of acute bleeding.

Retinal lesions

Intense photocoagulation may cause full-thickness retinal holes. Similarly, intense treatment may create fibrous proliferation striae and foveal distortion, with resultant metamorphopsia or diplopia. Focal treatment with small-diameter, high-intensity burns may cause vascular occlusion or perforate blood vessels, leading to preretinal or vitreous hemorrhage with resultant loss of vision. In addition, extensive panretinal treatment may induce or exacerbate macular edema.

Choroidal lesions

Treatment of CNV may be complicated by subretinal hemorrhage, choroidal ischemia, and additional CNV or chorioretinal anastomosis. Active subretinal hemorrhage that occurs during treatment should be addressed immediately by increasing digital pressure on the contact lens while continuing to treat the remaining portions of the CNV lesion. Interruption of the treatment may allow the hemorrhage to obscure the surgical landmarks that define the area of treatment, and it may hinder absorption of the laser at the level of the retinal pigment epithelium (RPE) and choroid. Progressive atrophy of the RPE may develop at the margin of photocoagulation scars, resulting in enlarged or even central scotomata. Also, tears of the pigment epithelium may be precipitated by photocoagulation.

Exudative retinal and choroidal detachment

Extensive, intense photocoagulation may result in massive chorioretinal edema, with sensory retinal detachment, choroidal detachment, and narrowing of the anterior chamber angle associated with elevated intraocular pressure (Fig 16-2).

An exudative response of the choroid with retinal or choroidal detachment may occur after intensive photocoagulation of large areas with high numbers of laser spots or the use of large spots. This inflammatory reaction peaks 1–3 days after treatment and resolves spontaneously within a few weeks. Corticosteroids may be helpful to treat massive exudation but are usually not required.

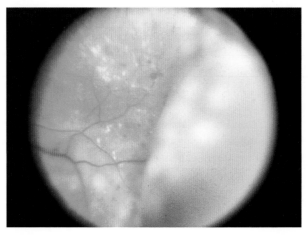

Figure 16-2 Choroidal detachment following panretinal scatter photocoagulation for the management of diabetic retinopathy. *(Courtesy of M. Gilbert Grand, MD.)*

Gass JDM, ed. *Stereoscopic Atlas of Macular Disease: Diagnosis and Treatment.* 4th ed. St Louis: Mosby; 1997.

Palanker D, Lavinsky D, Blumenkranz MS, Marcellino G. The impact of pulse duration and burn grade on size of retinal photocoagulation lesion: implications for pattern density. *Retina.* 2011;31(8):1664–1669.

Transpupillary Thermotherapy

Transpupillary thermotherapy (TTT) acts in a subthreshold manner by slightly raising the choroidal temperature and thus causing minimal thermal damage to the RPE and overlying retina. TTT is administered with an infrared laser (810 nm) with beam sizes from 0.8–3.0 mm, power settings between 250 and 750 mW, and a 1-minute exposure time; the endpoint is no visible change or slight graying of the retina. Results from a phase 3 trial in 303 eyes with occult CNV showed that use of TTT for the treatment of AMD did not result in a statistically significant benefit relative to sham treatment. By contrast, TTT is still of some importance for treating retinal and choroidal tumors. In choroidal melanoma, TTT may be considered a stand-alone treatment for flat tumors. For thicker tumors, a combination of TTT and plaque radiotherapy (the sandwich technique) results in better local tumor control than TTT alone. For patients with uveal melanoma, TTT has been shown to decrease the secondary enucleation rate related to the adverse effects of proton beam radiotherapy such as exudation from the necrotic tumor and glaucoma. However, TTT administered as an isolated treatment for choroidal melanomas has raised concerns because of tumor recurrence and insufficient local tumor control.

Bartlema YM, Oosterhuis JA, Journée-De Korver JG, Tjho-Heslinga RE, Keunen JE. Combined plaque radiotherapy and transpupillary thermotherapy in choroidal melanoma: 5 years' experience. *Br J Ophthalmol.* 2003;87(11):1370–1373.

Chakravarthy U, Soubrane G, Bandello F, et al. Evolving European guidance on the medical management of neovascular age related macular degeneration. *Br J Ophthalmol.* 2006;90(9):1188–1196.

Desjardins L, Lumbroso-Le Rouic L, Levy-Gabriel C, et al. Combined proton beam radiotherapy and transpupillary thermotherapy for large uveal melanomas: a randomized study of 151 patients. *Ophthalmic Res.* 2006;38(5):255–260.

Hussain N, Khanna R, Hussain A, Das T. Transpupillary thermotherapy for chronic central serous chorioretinopathy. *Graefes Arch Clin Exp Ophthalmol.* 2006;244(8):1045–1051.

Subramanian ML, Reichel E. Current indications of transpupillary thermotherapy for the treatment of posterior segment diseases. *Curr Opin Ophthalmol.* 2003;14(3):155–158.

Photodynamic Therapy

Photodynamic therapy (PDT) using the photosensitizing drug verteporfin has been approved by the US Food and Drug Administration for the treatment of the following:

- subfoveal CNV secondary to OHS
- subfoveal CNV secondary to pathologic myopia

- subfoveal, predominantly classic, CNV in AMD
- occult, with no classic, CNV smaller than 4 disc areas, with recent disease progression defined as vision loss, new hemorrhage, or enlargement by at least 10% of the CNV

Other indications are currently under investigation for PDT, including the treatment of ocular tumors and central serous chorioretinopathy. PDT is a 2-step procedure:

1. intravenous administration of the photosensitizing drug that localizes to endothelial cells of vessels present in CNV and tumors
2. local activation of the drug by a laser wavelength preferentially absorbed by the sensitizing drug

The laser does not heat or photocoagulate tissues; instead, the laser energy produces a photochemical reaction that excites the drug into a higher energy state. The activated drug then releases its energy to surrounding oxygen molecules, leading to the formation of reactive oxygen species and free radicals. This process, in turn, leads to endothelial cell damage, platelet adherence, vascular thrombosis, and capillary closure. The technique and clinical studies of PDT are discussed further in Chapter 4.

Photodynamic effects are not selective for neovascular structures and affect physiologic choroidal vessels as well. In particular, PDT induces an increased expression of vascular endothelial growth factor (VEGF) and inflammatory mediators. Corticosteroids such as triamcinolone have a reducing effect on VEGF expression and inflammation. Intravitreal application of triamcinolone alone demonstrated a documented but transient reduction in CNV-related leakage. The combination of verteporfin laser therapy and intravitreal triamcinolone may have an additive effect, improve vision outcome, and reduce the rate of recurrence.

Complications of Photodynamic Therapy

The most serious adverse effects of PDT are photosensitivity reactions that range from mild to second-degree burns of sun-exposed skin. Photosensitivity reactions occurred in 3.5% of patients in the Treatment of AMD with Photodynamic Therapy (TAP) study and in 0.4% in the Verteporfin in Photodynamic Therapy (VIP) study. This complication is easily avoided through patient education to minimize exposure to sunlight and wear protective clothing, special glasses, and a hat during the period of total-body photosensitivity. For verteporfin, this period lasts 48 hours after treatment. Other photodynamic compounds have different precautionary periods. Back, side, and chest pain were reported in 2.2%–2.5% of patients in the studies and was related to infusion of the drug. The pain resolved after the infusion finished, and no treatment was effective in preventing it. In addition, 0.7%–2.2% of patients experienced severe loss of vision within 7 days of treatment with PDT. This complication was more common in eyes with CNV lesions that were minimally classic or those that were occult with no classic component, and it could lead to permanent acuity loss.

CHAPTER **17**

Vitreoretinal Surgery

Pars Plana Vitrectomy

Pars plana vitrectomy is a vitreoretinal surgical technique that is typically used for removing vitreous opacities (eg, nonclearing vitreous hemorrhage), relieving vitreoretinal traction, restoring the normal anatomical relationship of the retina and retinal pigment epithelium (RPE), and accessing the subretinal space. It involves a closed-system approach that usually requires placement of 3 ports 3–4 mm posterior to the surgical limbus. One port is typically dedicated to infusion of balanced salt solution into the vitreous cavity, by which intraocular pressure (IOP) can be maintained at a level determined by the surgeon. The remaining ports are used to access the vitreous cavity with tools such as a fiber-optic endoilluminator to visualize the posterior segment and other instruments to manipulate, dissect, or remove intraocular tissues, fluids, or objects.

Vitrectomy is performed using an operating microscope in conjunction with a contact lens or noncontact viewing system. Direct and indirect visualization are possible, the latter requiring an inverting system to orient the image. The advantages of indirect visualization include a wider viewing angle as well as better visualization through media opacities, miotic pupils, and gas tamponades. The direct viewing systems allow greater magnification and enhanced stereopsis at the expense of a smaller field of view. Many vitreoretinal surgeons utilize both types of viewing systems and make their selection according to the task.

Vitreoretinal surgery is facilitated by various instruments, visualization aids, and vitreous substitutes. Advanced instrumentation includes the following: high-speed vitreous cutter, retinal forceps, endolaser probe, micro-pic, retinal scissors, extrusion cannula, and fragmatome, among others. Examples of visualization aids include indocyanine green (ICG) dye to stain the internal limiting membrane (ILM) and triamcinolone suspension to help identify cortical vitreous. Tamponade of the retina can be achieved with air, gas, or silicone oil as vitreous substitutes. Commonly used gases include sulfur hexafluoride (SF_6) and perfluoropropane (C_3F_8), which have intravitreal half-lives of approximately 1 and 3 weeks, respectively, at nonexpansile (isovolemic) concentrations. Perfluorocarbon liquids are heavier than water and can be used to temporarily stabilize the retina during dissection and allow for anterior drainage of subretinal fluid during retinal detachment repair.

A more recent advance in vitreoretinal surgery has been the development of a smaller gauge, transconjunctival technique for vitrectomy. With these systems, 23- or 25-gauge trocars are placed in lieu of using standard 19- or 20-gauge sclerotomies. Entry sites into the vitreous cavity created using a 23- or 25-gauge technique avoid the need for a conjunctival cutdown procedure or cautery and generally do not require suture closure because of their self-sealing architecture. A 20-gauge sclerotomy is typically 1 mm in diameter, compared with diameters of 0.7 mm and 0.5 mm for the 23- and 25-gauge techniques, respectively. Potential advantages of small-gauge vitrectomy include shortened operative time, increased postoperative patient comfort, and faster visual recovery. Potential disadvantages include an increased risk of postoperative hypotony, endophthalmitis, and retinal tears.

Fujii GY, de Juan E Jr, Humayun MS, et al. Initial experience using the transconjunctival sutureless vitrectomy system for vitreoretinal surgery. *Ophthalmology.* 2002;109(10): 1814–1820.

Spirn MJ. Comparison of 25, 23, and 20-gauge vitrectomy. *Curr Opin Ophthalmol.* 2009;20(3):195–199.

Vitrectomy for Selected Macular Diseases

Macular Epiretinal Membranes

Epiretinal membranes (ERMs) have a variable clinical course; most affected eyes maintain excellent visual acuity and have minimal distortion of central vision. The small percentage of patients who experience marked distortion or loss of central vision may be candidates for pars plana vitrectomy with membrane peeling (Fig 17-1). Patients whose primary complaint is metamorphopsia may derive the most benefit from this surgery.

After surgery, approximately 60%–80% of patients achieve an improvement in visual acuity of 2 or more lines, and improvement often continues for another 6–12 months (Fig 17-2). Potential intraoperative complications include retinal tear or retinal detachment in fewer than 5% of cases. Progressive nuclear sclerosis occurs postoperatively in the majority of phakic patients, and the rate increases over time. See Chapter 14 for further discussion of ERMs.

Vitreomacular Traction Syndrome

Vitreomacular traction (VMT) syndrome is a distinct vitreoretinal interface disorder that is differentiated clinically from typical ERM. Whereas ERM formation is generally associated with complete posterior vitreous detachment, VMT stems from anomalous, incomplete posterior vitreous separation at the macula. VMT may create focal elevation of the fovea (Fig 17-3) and, occasionally, a shallow retinal detachment. VMT syndrome is best diagnosed and differentiated from ERMs with the aid of optical coherence tomography (OCT), which classically shows the hyaloid inserting onto tractionally elevated retina. Symptoms include decreased vision and distortion. VMT syndrome is often progressive and is associated with a greater loss of vision than are ERMs alone. Surgical treatment

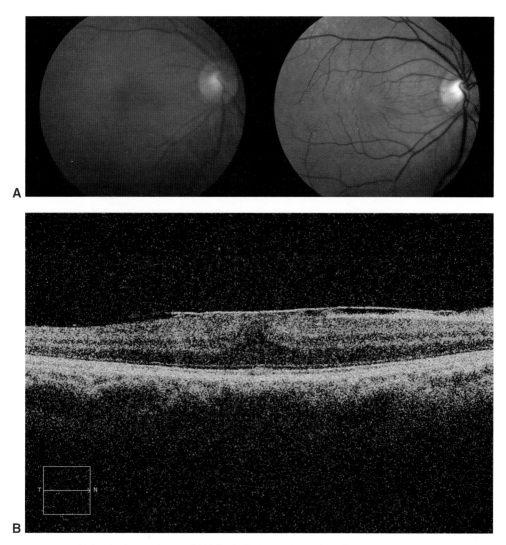

Figure 17-1 Epiretinal membrane (ERM). **A,** Color and red-free fundus photographs showing macular ERM with distortion of foveal architecture and retinal striae. **B,** Corresponding optical coherence tomogram confirms preretinal traction from the ERM, the associated loss of foveal contour, and macular thickening. With a visual acuity of 20/70 and symptomatic distortion, this patient was judged to be a potential candidate for pars plana vitrectomy with membrane peeling. *(Courtesy of Adam A. Martidis, MD.)*

consists of a standard pars plana vitrectomy and peeling of the cortical vitreous from the surface of the retina. Intraoperative use of triamcinolone may aid visualization of the cortical vitreous. See Chapter 14 for further discussion of VMT.

Voo I, Mavrofrides EC, Puliafito CA. Clinical applications of optical coherence tomography for the diagnosis and management of macular diseases. *Ophthalmol Clin North Am.* 2004;17(1):21–31.

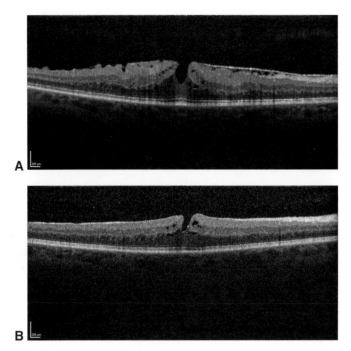

Figure 17-2 ERM forming a pseudohole in a patient with visual distortion and reduced visual acuity (20/100). **A,** Optical coherence tomography (OCT) image corroborates a preretinal membrane distorting the retinal contour and intraretinal edema. **B,** One week after membrane peeling, distortion was substantially reduced, and acuity had increased to 20/60. OCT image shows restoration of normal macular contour, absence of preretinal membrane and traction, as well as mild residual macular edema. *(Courtesy of Matthew T. S. Tennant, MD.)*

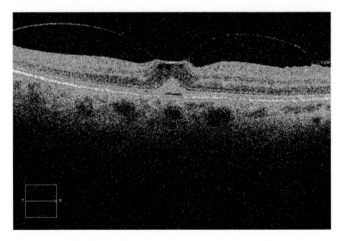

Figure 17-3 Vitreomacular traction (VMT) syndrome in a patient with visual acuity of 20/80 and minimal ophthalmoscopic findings. OCT image shows a partial posterior detachment with persistent hyaloidal insertion at the center of the macula. Note the elevated fovea with complete loss of contour; there is associated intraretinal edema with subtle submacular fluid. Pars plana vitrectomy with membrane peeling led to an improved visual acuity of 20/25 and resolution of symptomatic distortion. *(Courtesy of Adam A. Martidis, MD.)*

Idiopathic Macular Holes

Vitrectomy is indicated for full-thickness macular holes (stages 2, 3, and 4). Because stage 1 macular holes have a relatively high rate of spontaneous resolution and reported studies have not demonstrated a benefit from vitrectomy, surgery is not generally recommended for this stage. However, early intervention for stage 2 or greater holes is important for prognostic reasons: shorter intervals between the development and the closure of macular holes have been associated with improved anatomical and functional outcomes. Surgery for full-thickness macular holes consists of a standard pars plana vitrectomy; the separation and removal of the posterior cortical vitreous, ILM, or both; and the use of an intraocular gas tamponade (or, less frequently, silicone oil) with face-down positioning. ILM peeling has been demonstrated in numerous studies to improve the rate of hole closure, particularly for larger stage 3 or 4 holes. The intraoperative use of dyes (ICG, trypan blue) or other visualization techniques (triamcinolone) to aid in peeling the ILM is widely practiced, although the toxicity of ICG continues to be an issue. Timing of face-down positioning is also debated, with surgeon preferences ranging from a few hours to 4 weeks and averaging approximately 1 week.

The first series of patients undergoing vitrectomy for idiopathic macular holes was reported in 1991. The holes were successfully closed in 58% of cases, and visual acuity improved by 2 lines or more in 42%. Subsequent series have reported hole closure rates after vitrectomy as high as 95% (Fig 17-4).

Complications of macular hole surgery include postvitrectomy nuclear sclerotic cataract, secondary glaucoma, retinal detachment, visual field loss, late reopening of the hole, and others more specifically related to vitrectomy surgery. See Chapter 14 for further discussion of macular holes.

Gass JD. Reappraisal of biomicroscopic classification of stages of development of a macular hole. *Am J Ophthalmol.* 1995;119(6):752–759.

Kelly NE, Wendel RT. Vitreous surgery for idiopathic macular holes. Results of a pilot study. *Arch Ophthalmol.* 1991;109(5):654–659.

Kumagai K, Furukawa M, Ogino N, Uemura A, Demizu S, Larson E. Vitreous surgery with and without internal limiting membrane peeling for macular hole repair. *Retina.* 2004;24(5):721–727.

Submacular Hemorrhage

The clinical course of submacular hemorrhages is variable. Many smaller submacular hemorrhages resolve spontaneously, yielding acceptable visual acuity. However, patients with neovascular age-related macular degeneration (AMD) and larger submacular hemorrhages generally have poor visual outcomes. For removal of thick submacular hemorrhages, pars plana vitrectomy techniques can be considered. The Submacular Surgery Trials (SST) was a randomized, prospective study evaluating the outcomes of observation versus surgery for eyes with submacular hemorrhage due to AMD. The study found that vitrectomy surgery in which the hemorrhage was removed from the subretinal space was no better than observation for improving or stabilizing visual acuity. However, postvitrectomy eyes were more likely than control eyes to avoid severe vision loss despite a higher

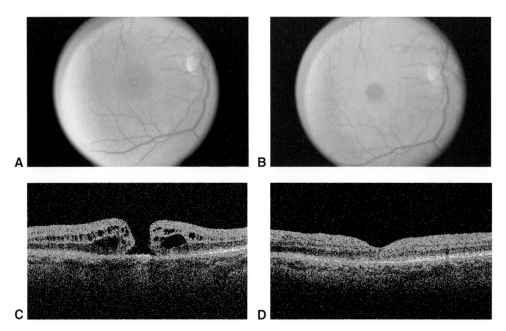

Figure 17-4 Idiopathic macular hole. **A,** Fundus of a patient with macular hole and reduced visual acuity (20/100) for 5 months. **B,** After vitrectomy, membrane peeling, and fluid–gas exchange, the macular hole depicted in **A** closed, and visual acuity improved to 20/25. **C,** Pre-operative OCT image of a full-thickness macular hole with intraretinal cystic degeneration. **D,** Postoperative OCT image shows restoration of normal foveal anatomy. *(Parts A and B courtesy of Harry W. Flynn, Jr, MD; parts C and D courtesy of Mark W. Johnson, MD.)*

complication rate. An alternate vitrectomy technique involves pneumatic displacement of the subretinal blood away from the macular center, without attempting to remove the hemorrhage. With this technique, a standard vitrectomy is performed, subretinal tissue plasminogen activator (tPA) is delivered via a 39- to 41-gauge cannula, and air is instilled into the eye. Postoperative face-down positioning can result in substantial inferior ex-tramacular displacement of blood (Fig 17-5). Finally, office-based intravitreal injection

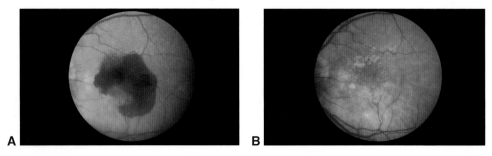

Figure 17-5 Submacular hemorrhage in AMD. **A,** Fundus photograph of a patient with sub-macular hemorrhage for 5 days and counting fingers vision. **B,** After vitrectomy with subretinal infusion of tPA and pneumatic displacement, dry atrophic changes are apparent. Visual acuity is 20/100. *(Courtesy of Nancy M. Holekamp, MD.)*

of expansile gas (eg, SF_6 or C_3F_8) and face-down positioning with or without adjunctive intravitreal tPA administration has been reported.

Bressler NM, Bressler SB, Childs AL, et al; Submacular Surgery Trials (SST) Research Group. Surgery for hemorrhagic choroidal neovascular lesions of age-related macular degeneration: ophthalmic findings. SST report no. 13. *Ophthalmology.* 2004;111(11):1993–2006.

Hassan AS, Johnson MW, Schneiderman TE, et al. Management of submacular hemorrhage with intravitreous tissue plasminogen activator injection and pneumatic displacement. *Ophthalmology.* 1999;106(10):1900–1907.

Subfoveal Choroidal Neovascularization

Pharmacologic therapy has become the predominant method of treatment for patients with subfoveal choroidal neovascularization (CNV). Historically, surgical management options have included pars plana vitrectomy and excision of subfoveal CNV through a small retinotomy or pars plana vitrectomy and macular translocation (Fig 17-6). The SST found vitrectomy surgery to be of no benefit for subfoveal CNV caused by AMD and to be of modest benefit for subfoveal CNV due to ocular histoplasmosis or idiopathic causes if visual acuity was less than 20/100. An alternate surgical treatment for this condition is macular translocation. Two techniques have been described:

1. Limited macular translocation—scleral imbrication allowing redundant retina to be shifted by as much as 1000 μm.
2. Full macular translocation—360° retinotomy at the ora serrata allowing for larger retinal rotation about the optic disc.

The goals of both techniques are to relocate the fovea over healthier RPE that has not been damaged previously by a choroidal neovascular complex. Both techniques are associated with higher complication rates than those of standard vitrectomy procedures, and they are infrequently used in the era of pharmacologic CNV therapy. No prospective, randomized clinical trials evaluating macular translocation surgery have been published.

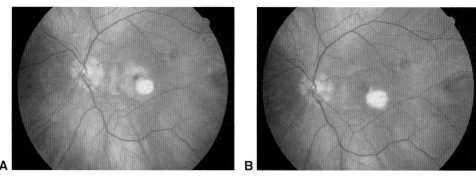

Figure 17-6 Fundus of a 59-year-old man with recurrent CNV from ocular histoplasmosis. **A,** Preoperatively, subfoveal CNV is adjacent to a previous laser scar; visual acuity is 20/300. **B,** One month after pars plana vitrectomy and removal of CNV, visual acuity is 20/25. *(Courtesy of Mark W. Johnson, MD.)*

de Juan E Jr, Loewenstein A, Bressler NM, Alexander J. Translocation of the retina for management of subfoveal choroidal neovascularization. II: A preliminary report in humans. *Am J Ophthalmol.* 1998;125(5):635–646.

Hawkins BS, Bressler NM, Bressler SB, et al; Submacular Surgery Trials Research Group. Surgical removal vs observation for subfoveal choroidal neovascularization, either associated with the ocular histoplasmosis syndrome or idiopathic: I. Ophthalmic findings from a randomized clinical trial. Submacular Surgery Trials (SST) Group H Trial. SST report no. 9. *Arch Ophthalmol.* 2004;122(11):1597–1611.

Hawkins BS, Bressler NM, Miskala PH, et al; Submacular Surgery Trials (SST) Research Group. Surgery for subfoveal choroidal neovascularization in age-related macular degeneration: ophthalmic findings. SST report no. 11. *Ophthalmology.* 2004;111(11):1967–1980.

Mruthyunjaya P, Stinnett SS, Toth CA. Change in visual function after macular translocation with 360 degrees retinectomy for neovascular age-related macular degeneration. *Ophthalmology.* 2004;111(9):1715–1724.

Vitrectomy for Complications of Diabetic Retinopathy

Vitreous Hemorrhage

Vitreous hemorrhage is among the most common vision-threatening complications of proliferative diabetic retinopathy. Vitrectomy is indicated when a vitreous hemorrhage fails to clear spontaneously after approximately 6 weeks to 3 months; timing of surgery is determined by surgeon preference and patient visual requirements. Possible indications for more prompt intervention include bilateral vitreous hemorrhages or ultrasonic evidence of retinal tear, underlying rhegmatogenous retinal detachment, or tractional retinal detachment threatening the macula. During the interval of observation for spontaneous resolution, the examining physician must ascertain that the source of hemorrhage is indeed from proliferative diabetic retinopathy and not an etiology requiring more urgent intervention. In addition, serial ultrasonography is recommended to assess the anatomical condition of the retina in the absence of ophthalmoscopic visualization. If surgery is indicated, treatment involves a standard pars plana vitrectomy with removal of vitreous hemorrhage and release of the hyaloid from fronds of retinal neovascular ingrowth. Vitreoretinal traction at the disc and along the arcade vessels, if present, is addressed at the time of surgery, along with any macular ERMs. Complete panretinal photocoagulation and hemostasis are generally achieved during surgery.

Diabetic Tractional Retinal Detachment

Tractional retinal detachment (TRD) occurs when the hyaloid shrinks but is prevented from separating from the retinal interface by fronds of neovascular ingrowth. The tractional forces are transmitted to full-thickness retina and, in the absence of a retinal break, result in schisis and possibly detachment of the underlying retina from its corresponding RPE (Fig 17-7). Vitrectomy is indicated when progression of a TRD threatens or involves the macula. In certain complex cases, spontaneous breaks also occur in atrophic retina

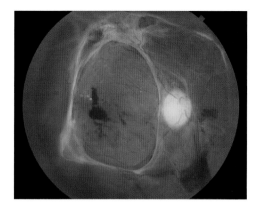

Figure 17-7 Diabetic tractional retinal detachment. Note the fibrovascular proliferation along the retinal arcade vessels causing elevation and distortion of the retinal surface; there is associated hemorrhage due to traction on fronds of neovascular ingrowth. *(Courtesy of Matthew T. S. Tennant, MD.)*

under traction, resulting in traction-rhegmatogenous detachments; this variety of TRD is also a strong indication for surgical intervention. Whenever possible, panretinal photocoagulation should precede vitrectomy; this is sometimes more difficult to accomplish in the presence of vitreous hemorrhage. Some surgeons utilize adjunctive intravitreal injection of an anti–vascular endothelial growth factor (anti-VEGF) drug preoperatively as well. The goal is to induce regression of neovascularization to facilitate dissection and minimize intraoperative bleeding.

Vitrectomy for TRD is performed to relieve vitreoretinal traction that interferes with retinal reattachment. This involves peeling cortical vitreous and posterior hyaloid from the retinal surface, particularly in areas of neovascular ingrowth. Point adhesions of cortical vitreous to surface retinal neovascularization can be addressed with some combination of appropriate scissors, pics, and forceps, using unimanual or bimanual techniques; current vitrectomy probes can now supplant these instruments in many cases, giving surgeons control of flow, cut rate, and duty cycle. Various surgical methods to remove fibrovascular tissue have been described; these include segmentation, delamination, and en bloc and modified en bloc excision.

After tractional membranes are removed, diathermy may be used to treat fibrovascular tufts and achieve hemostasis, and supplementary laser treatment is used in the periphery to complete panretinal photocoagulation. At the end of the surgery, the retina is carefully examined for breaks and treated accordingly with laser therapy and any necessary tamponade.

Eliott D, Lee MS, Abrams GW. Proliferative diabetic retinopathy: principles and techniques of surgical treatment. In: Ryan SJ, ed. *Retina.* Vol 3. 4th ed. Philadelphia: Elsevier Mosby; 2006:2413–2449.

Diabetic Macular Edema

Laser photocoagulation and intravitreal pharmacotherapy are currently the mainstays of treatment for diabetic macular edema. However, recalcitrant cases may be considered for vitrectomy with membrane peeling. In such cases, a standard pars plana vitrectomy is performed with mechanical release of a taut hyaloid, peeling of epiretinal membrane, and stripping of the internal limiting membrane as necessary.

Vitrectomy for Posterior Segment Complications of Anterior Segment Surgery

Postoperative Endophthalmitis

The clinical features of endophthalmitis after anterior segment surgery include marked intraocular inflammation, often with hypopyon, conjunctival vascular congestion, corneal edema, and eyelid edema. Symptoms often include pain and marked loss of vision that is usually profound and out of proportion to typical postoperative visual acuity measured during the first days or weeks after intraocular surgery.

The classification of postoperative endophthalmitis is based on the time of onset and the organisms most frequently isolated:

- acute-onset endophthalmitis (within 6 weeks of intraocular surgery): coagulase-negative *Staphylococcus* species including *S aureus, Streptococcus* species, gram-negative organisms
- chronic (delayed-onset) endophthalmitis (beyond 6 weeks after surgery): *Propionibacterium acnes,* coagulase-negative *Staphylococcus* species, fungi
- bleb-associated endophthalmitis (months or years after surgery): *Streptococcus* species, *Haemophilus* species, gram-positive organisms

Management of postoperative endophthalmitis includes obtaining intraocular cultures and administering intravitreal antibiotics. An anterior chamber specimen is typically obtained by using a 30-gauge needle on a tuberculin syringe, after preparation with povidone-iodine solution. A vitreous specimen can be obtained either by needle tap or by using a vitrectomy instrument. A needle tap of the vitreous is typically accomplished using a 25-gauge, 1-inch needle introduced through the pars plana and directed toward the midvitreous cavity. Neither a conjunctival incision nor suture closure is necessary for the needle tap. A small (0.2–0.5 mL) specimen is obtained and directly inoculated onto culture media. Vitreous specimens are more likely to yield a positive culture result than simultaneously obtained aqueous specimens.

Acute-onset postoperative endophthalmitis

The use of vitrectomy for acute postoperative endophthalmitis is guided by the results of the Endophthalmitis Vitrectomy Study (EVS; Clinical Trial 17-1). In the EVS, patients were randomly assigned to undergo either vitrectomy or vitreous tap/biopsy. Both groups received intravitreal and subconjunctival antibiotics (vancomycin and amikacin). The EVS concluded that vitrectomy surgery was indicated in patients with acute-onset (within 6 weeks of cataract extraction) postoperative endophthalmitis with light perception vision (Fig 17-8). Patients with hand motions visual acuity or better had equivalent outcomes in both treatment groups.

Ceftazidime has largely replaced amikacin in clinical practice, primarily because of concerns of potential aminoglycoside toxicity. Intravitreal dexamethasone may reduce posttreatment inflammation, but its role in endophthalmitis management remains controversial.

CLINICAL TRIAL 17-1

Endophthalmitis Vitrectomy Study (EVS)

Objective: Evaluate the role of pars plana vitrectomy and intravenous antibiotics in management of postoperative bacterial endophthalmitis.

Participants: Patients with clinical signs and symptoms of bacterial endophthalmitis in an eye after cataract surgery or lens implantation with onset of infection within 6 weeks of surgery.

Randomization: Patients were randomly assigned to immediate pars plana vitrectomy or to immediate tap and inject. Patients were randomly assigned to receive systemic antibiotics or no systemic antibiotics and evaluated at regular intervals after treatment.

Outcome measures: Standardized visual acuity testing and media clarity.

Outcomes:

1. No difference in final visual acuity or media clarity whether or not systemic antibiotics (amikacin/ceftazidime) were employed.
2. No difference in outcomes between the 3-port pars plana vitrectomy group and the immediate tap/biopsy group for patients with better than light perception visual acuity at the study entry examination.
3. For patients with light perception visual acuity, much better results in the immediate pars plana vitrectomy group:
   a. Three times more likely to achieve ≥20/40 (33% vs 11%)
   b. Two times more likely to achieve ≥20/100 (56% vs 30%)
   c. Less likely to incur <5/200 (20% vs 47%)

Clinical impact: Study completed in 1995. Revolutionized treatment of post–cataract surgery endophthalmitis by making it an office procedure of tap and inject for most eyes.

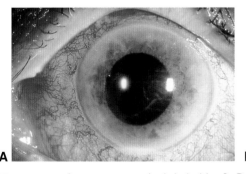
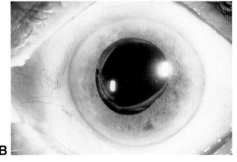

A **B**

Figure 17-8 Acute-onset endophthalmitis. **A,** Patient with marked epibulbar hyperemia, iritis, hypopyon, and endophthalmitis 5 days after cataract surgery. **B,** After needle tap of vitreous and injection of intravitreal antibiotics, inflammation resolved and visual acuity improved to 20/30. *(Courtesy of Harry W. Flynn, Jr, MD.)*

Results of the Endophthalmitis Vitrectomy Study. A randomized trial of immediate vitrectomy and of intravenous antibiotics for the treatment of postoperative bacterial endophthalmitis. Endophthalmitis Vitrectomy Study Group. *Arch Ophthalmol.* 1995;113(12):1479–1496.

Chronic (delayed-onset) endophthalmitis

Patients with chronic endophthalmitis follow a progressive or indolent course over months or years. Endophthalmitis caused by *P acnes* characteristically induces a peripheral white plaque within the capsular bag and an associated chronic granulomatous inflammation. Treatment by injection of antibiotics into the capsular bag or vitreous cavity usually does not eliminate the infection. A preferred approach is pars plana vitrectomy, partial capsulectomy with selective removal of intracapsular white plaque, and injection of intravitreal vancomycin 1 mg adjacent to or inside the capsular bag. If the condition recurs after vitrectomy and subtotal capsulectomy, removal of the entire capsular bag, with removal or exchange of the intraocular lens (IOL) should be considered (Fig 17-9).

Clark WL, Kaiser PK, Flynn HW Jr, Belfort A, Miller D, Meisler DM. Treatment strategies and visual acuity outcomes in chronic postoperative *Propionibacterium acnes* endophthalmitis. *Ophthalmology.* 1999;106(9):1665–1670.

Endophthalmitis associated with conjunctival filtering blebs

Except for the additional sign of a purulent bleb, the clinical features of conjunctival filtering bleb–associated endophthalmitis are similar to those of acute-onset postoperative endophthalmitis. These features include conjunctival vascular congestion and marked intraocular inflammation, often with hypopyon (occurring months or years after glaucoma filtering surgery or cataract surgery resulting in an unintentional bleb). The initial infection may involve the bleb only *(blebitis),* without anterior chamber or vitreous involvement. Blebitis without endophthalmitis can be treated with frequent applications of topical and subconjunctival antibiotics and close follow-up. However, when blebitis

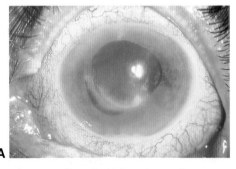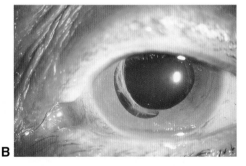

A **B**

Figure 17-9 Chronic (delayed-onset) postoperative endophthalmitis. **A,** Endophthalmitis in a patient with progressive intraocular inflammation 3 months after cataract surgery. **B,** Same patient after pars plana vitrectomy, capsulectomy, and injection of intravitreal antibiotics. Culture results confirmed diagnosis of *Propionibacterium acnes* endophthalmitis. *(Courtesy of Harry W. Flynn, Jr, MD.)*

progresses to bleb-associated endophthalmitis, patients are treated by intravitreal antibiotics with or without vitrectomy. The recommended intravitreal antibiotics are similar to those used in acute-onset postoperative endophthalmitis. However, the most common causative organisms in bleb-associated endophthalmitis (eg, *Streptococcus* or *Haemophilus* spp) are more virulent than the most frequently encountered organisms in endophthalmitis occurring after other intraocular surgeries (such as cataract surgery). Even with prompt treatment, the visual outcomes in bleb-associated endophthalmitis are generally worse than for acute-onset endophthalmitis after cataract surgery (Fig 17-10).

Greenfield DS. Dysfunctional glaucoma filtration blebs. *Focal Points: Clinical Modules for Ophthalmologists.* San Francisco: American Academy of Ophthalmology; 2002, module 4.

Retained Lens Fragments After Phacoemulsification

The incidence of posteriorly displaced lens fragments ranges from 0.3%–1.1% in reported series. Retained lens fragments may cause severe intraocular inflammation and secondary glaucoma. Postoperative intraocular inflammation is generally related to the amount of retained lens material and the induced surgical trauma. Nuclear fragments usually continue to cause chronic intraocular inflammation, whereas cortical remnants may be spontaneously reabsorbed. Eyes with posteriorly retained lens fragments may have incurred substantial trauma during the initial cataract surgery and therefore often have associated corneal edema, retinal detachment, and/or cystoid macular edema (CME). The postoperative inflammation may be exacerbated by the eye's individual inflammatory response to retained lens material.

Use of phacoemulsification in patients with vitreous prolapse into the anterior segment can create excessive vitreoretinal traction that can lead to retinal detachment. Vitreous and any remaining lens fragments should be removed from the anterior segment using a cutting instrument. Attempts at retrieving posteriorly dislocated lens fragments at the time of the initial cataract surgery can lead to further complications and should be avoided in the absence of an experienced vitreoretinal surgeon.

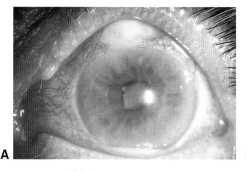
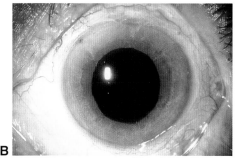

A   **B**

Figure 17-10 Bleb-associated endophthalmitis. **A,** Patient with endophthalmitis who had sudden onset of decreased vision, redness, and pain 2 years after glaucoma filtering surgery. **B,** Same patient after treatment with pars plana vitrectomy and injection of intravitreal antibiotics. *(Courtesy of Harry W. Flynn, Jr, MD.)*

Small fragments of nuclear material may be tolerated in the posterior segment without the need for surgical intervention. However, larger pieces (>2 mm in diameter) almost always require removal (Table 17-1).

Indications for vitrectomy include secondary glaucoma, lens-induced uveitis, and the presence of large nuclear fragments. In the 4 largest reported series, 52% of patients with retained lens fragments had an IOP ≥30 mm Hg before vitrectomy. Removal of the lens fragments reduced this incidence by 50% or more in these series.

The preferred approach is pars plana vitrectomy with or without ultrasonic emulsification (using a fragmatome) to remove harder pieces of the lens nucleus (Fig 17-11). In treating concurrent retinal detachment, perfluorocarbon liquid may be useful in floating the lens material anteriorly while stabilizing the retinal detachment. After the vitreous is removed as completely as possible, the fragmatome can be used to engage the nuclear fragments at a low-power setting. The retinal periphery should be examined for the presence of retinal tears or retinal detachment in these patients.

Reported series with long-term follow-up have found that retinal detachment occurs in about 15% of eyes with retained lens fragments. Aggressive attempts to retrieve posterior lens fragments using a limbal approach are sometimes complicated by retinal detachments caused by giant retinal tears (retinal breaks that exceed 3 contiguous clock-hours or 90°). Giant retinal tears are more commonly found in the inferior quadrants when a superior limbal approach is used for cataract surgery.

The outcomes reported in the literature came from studies that did not exclude patients with preexisting ocular disease, such as glaucoma, diabetic retinopathy, or macular degeneration. Therefore, some unfavorable visual acuity outcomes may reflect retinal

---

Table 17-1 General Recommendations for Management of Retained Lens Fragments

For the anterior segment surgeon
Attempt retrieval of displaced lens fragments only if fragments are readily accessible.
Perform anterior vitrectomy as necessary to avoid vitreous prolapse into the wound.
Insert an intraocular lens if possible.
Close the cataract wound with interrupted sutures.
Prescribe topical medications as needed.
Refer the patient to a vitreoretinal consultant.

For the vitreoretinal surgeon
Observe eyes with minimal inflammation and/or a small lens fragment.
Continue topical medications as needed.
Schedule vitrectomy:
    if inflammation or IOP is not controlled
    if a nuclear fragment is >2 mm in size
Delay vitrectomy if necessary to allow clearing of corneal edema.
Perform maximal core vitrectomy before phacofragmentation.
Start with low fragmentation power (5%–10%) for more efficient removal of the nucleus.
Prepare for secondary intraocular lens insertion if necessary.
Examine the retinal periphery for retinal tears or retinal detachment.

Modified from Flynn HW Jr, Smiddy WE, Vilar NF. Management of retained lens fragments after cataract surgery. In: Saer JB, ed. *Vitreo-Retinal and Uveitis Update: Proceedings of the New Orleans Academy of Ophthalmology Symposium.* The Hague, Netherlands: Kugler; 1998:149, 150.

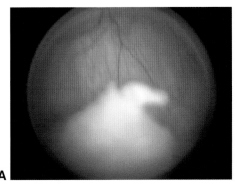
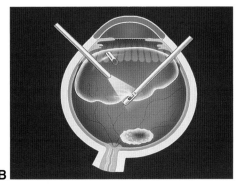

A B

Figure 17-11 Retained lens fragments after phacoemulsification. **A,** Clinical photograph of large lens fragment on the retina. **B,** Schematic shows pars plana vitrectomy for removal of formed vitreous before the lens fragment is approached. *(Reproduced with permission from Smiddy WE, Flynn HW Jr. Managing retained lens fragments and dislocated posterior chamber IOLs after cataract surgery. Focal Points: Clinical Modules for Ophthalmologists. San Francisco: American Academy of Ophthalmology; 1996, module 7.)*

problems not directly caused by retained lens fragments. Overall, approximately 60% of patients in published studies achieved reading vision (≥20/40).

Aaberg TM Jr, Rubsamen PE, Flynn HW Jr, Chang S, Mieler WF, Smiddy WE. Giant retinal tear as a complication of attempted removal of intravitreal lens fragments during cataract surgery. *Am J Ophthalmol.* 1997;124(2):222–226.

Borne MJ, Tasman W, Regillo C, Malecha M, Sarin L. Outcomes of vitrectomy for retained lens fragments. *Ophthalmology.* 1996;103(6):971–976.

Lewis H, Blumenkranz MS, Chang S. Treatment of dislocated crystalline lens and retinal detachment with perfluorocarbon liquids. *Retina.* 1992;12(4):299–304.

Posteriorly Dislocated Intraocular Lenses

Dislocated posterior chamber intraocular lenses (PCIOLs) may not be recognized by the surgeon until the first day after cataract surgery, even though capsular support may have seemed satisfactory at the time of the initial surgery. Factors that should be considered when placing a sulcus-fixated IOL include the presence of zonular dehiscence, total amount of anterior capsular support (eg, >180°), size of the eye, and haptic-to-haptic diameter of the IOL. Foldable IOLs have a 12.5- to 13.0-mm haptic-to-haptic length. This is frequently smaller than the sulcus-to-sulcus diameter into which these haptics must fit and may contribute to subluxation or dislocation of the IOL in the postoperative period. Dislocation of a flexible IOL may also follow Nd:YAG laser capsulotomy that is performed soon after cataract surgery. Late dislocation of the IOL (from several days to decades after surgery) is less common but may occur as a result of trauma or spontaneous loss of zonular support in eyes with pseudoexfoliation syndrome. The options for treatment in such cases include observation only, surgical repositioning, IOL exchange, or IOL removal.

Vitrectomy for posteriorly dislocated IOLs involves removing all vitreous adhesions to the IOL in order to minimize vitreous traction to the retina when the lens is manipulated back into the anterior chamber. The IOL may be placed into the ciliary sulcus provided there is adequate support. If capsular support is inadequate, the IOL may be suture-fixated to either the iris or the sclera. Alternatively, the PCIOL can be removed through a limbal incision and exchanged for an anterior chamber IOL (ACIOL).

Smiddy WE, Flynn HW Jr. Managing retained lens fragments and dislocated posterior chamber IOLs after cataract surgery. *Focal Points: Clinical Modules for Ophthalmologists.* San Francisco: American Academy of Ophthalmology; 1996, module 7.

Cystoid Macular Edema

CME that develops after anterior segment surgery usually resolves spontaneously. Treatment with corticosteroid and nonsteroidal anti-inflammatory drops is the first-line approach for patients with persistent CME. Periocular corticosteroids may be used in recalcitrant cases. Recent case reports suggest that intravitreal triamcinolone or anti-VEGF drugs can be effective in treating post–cataract surgery CME that has not resolved with more conservative measures. For vision loss that is unresponsive to topical therapy and injections, pars plana vitrectomy with removal of obvious vitreous adhesions to anterior segment structures may promote resolution of CME and improve visual acuity (Fig 17-12). An IOL may require repositioning, exchange, or removal if it is deemed to irritate the iris by chafing or capture.

Heier JS, Topping TM, Baumann W, Dirks MS, Chern S. Ketorolac versus prednisolone versus combination therapy in the treatment of acute pseudophakic cystoid macular edema. *Ophthalmology.* 2000;107(11):2034–2039.

Pendergast SD, Margherio RR, Williams GA, Cox MS Jr. Vitrectomy for chronic pseudophakic cystoid macular edema. *Am J Ophthalmol.* 1999;128(3):317–323.

Suprachoroidal Hemorrhage

Suprachoroidal hemorrhage may occur during or after any form of intraocular surgery, particularly glaucoma surgery in which large shifts in IOP are commonplace. By definition,

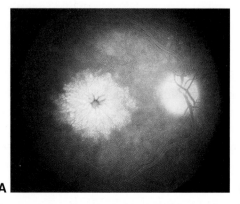
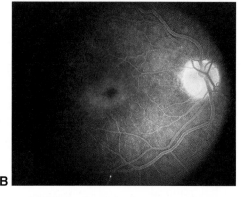

A   B

Figure 17-12 Pseudophakic cystoid macular edema (CME). **A,** Fundus of patient with nonresolving CME, vitreous strands to cataract wound, and dislocated IOL. **B,** Same patient after pars plana vitrectomy, removal of vitreous strands, repositioning of IOL, and periocular administration of corticosteroids. CME has markedly improved. *(Courtesy of Harry W. Flynn, Jr, MD.)*

such hemorrhages accumulate in the supraciliary and suprachoroidal space, a potential space between the sclera and uvea that is modified by uveal adhesions and entries of vessels. Hemorrhages may be limited or massive and involve 1–4 quadrants. When retinal surfaces touch one another, dictated by scleral spur and the entries of the short posterior ciliary vessels and nerves, the choroidal hemorrhage is termed "appositional," or "kissing." These hemorrhages may be further classified as nonexpulsive or expulsive; the latter type involves extrusion of intraocular contents. Reported risk factors for suprachoroidal hemorrhage include

- advanced age
- glaucoma
- myopia
- aphakia
- arteriosclerotic cardiovascular disease
- hypertension
- Sturge-Weber–associated choroidal hemangiomas
- intraoperative tachycardia

Transient hypotony is a common feature of all incisional ocular surgery and, in a small percentage of patients, may be associated with suprachoroidal hemorrhage from rupture of the long or short posterior ciliary arteries.

Surgical management strategies are controversial. Most authors recommend immediate closure of ocular surgical incisions and removal of vitreous incarceration in the wound, if possible; the primary goal is to prevent or limit expulsion. Successful intraoperative drainage of a suprachoroidal hemorrhage is rare, however, as the blood coagulates rapidly. Most surgeons recommend observation of suprachoroidal hemorrhages for 7–14 days to allow some degree of liquefaction of the hemorrhage. Determining the timing of secondary surgical intervention is aided by B-scan ultrasound, through evaluation of echographic features of clot liquefaction. Indications for surgical drainage include recalcitrant pain, increased IOP, retinal detachment, and appositional choroidal detachments (ie, "kissing" choroidals) associated with ciliary body rotation and angle closure. Furthermore, prolonged IOP elevation in the presence of anterior chamber hemorrhage (hyphema) increases the risk of corneal blood staining and is an indication for surgical intervention.

Surgical management of suprachoroidal hemorrhage involves placement of an anterior chamber infusion line to maintain IOP (Fig 17-13). A full-thickness sclerotomy is then placed subjacent to the site of maximum accumulation of blood. After drainage of suprachoroidal blood, pars plana vitrectomy may be performed. Appositional and closed-funnel suprachoroidal hemorrhage, prolonged elevation of IOP, and retinal detachment all portend a poor visual prognosis.

Pollack AL, McDonald HR, Ai E, et al. Massive suprachoroidal hemorrhage during pars plana vitrectomy associated with Valsalva maneuver. *Am J Ophthalmol.* 2001;132(3):383–387.

Scott IU, Flynn HW Jr, Schiffman J, Smiddy WE, Murray TG, Ehlies F. Visual acuity outcomes among patients with appositional suprachoroidal hemorrhage. *Ophthalmology.* 1997;104(12):2039–2046.

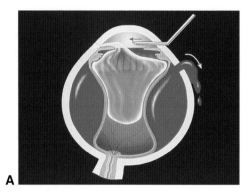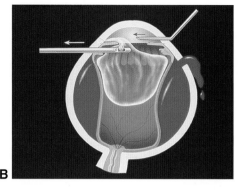

A **B**

Figure 17-13 Suprachoroidal hemorrhage. **A,** Schematic shows anterior infusion and simultaneous drainage of suprachoroidal hemorrhage through pars plana sclerotomy. **B,** Schematic shows pars plana vitrectomy to remove vitreous prolapse as drainage of suprachoroidal hemorrhage continues. *(Courtesy of Harry W. Flynn, Jr, MD.)*

Needle Penetration of the Globe

Factors predisposing to needle penetration of the globe include

- axial high myopia
- posterior staphyloma
- previous scleral buckling surgery
- poor patient cooperation at the time of the injection

Another risk factor may be injection performed by those with limited experience in providing ocular anesthesia.

Management options vary with the severity of the intraocular damage. Often, blood obscures and surrounds the retinal penetration site, making laser treatment difficult. Observation or transscleral cryotherapy may be considered in such cases. When associated retinal detachment is present, early vitrectomy with or without scleral buckling is often recommended. Eyes without retinal detachment have a much better visual prognosis than do eyes with retinal detachment. Posterior pole damage from needle extension into the macula or optic nerve is associated with a very poor visual prognosis (Fig 17-14).

Duker JS, Belmont JB, Benson WE, et al. Inadvertent globe perforation during retrobulbar and peribulbar anesthesia. Patient characteristics, surgical management, and visual outcome. *Ophthalmology.* 1991;98(4):519–526.

Retinal Detachment Surgery

Rhegmatogenous retinal detachment occurs when a retinal break (or multiple breaks) allows ingress of fluid from the vitreous cavity into the subretinal space. Breaks can be atrophic, often associated with lattice degeneration, or they may be tractional, related to vitreous traction on the retina and posterior vitreous detachment (PVD). The incidence of rhegmatogenous retinal detachment (RRD) in the general population is approximately 1 in 15,000 persons. The reported incidence after cataract surgery is less than 1% (Fig 17-15). Patient characteristics that increase the risk of pseuodophakic retinal detachment include

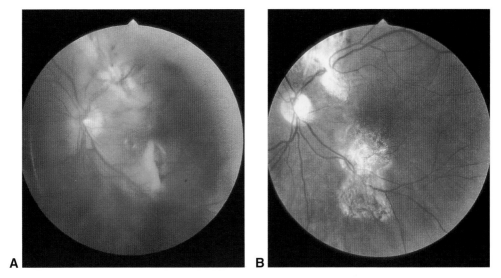

Figure 17-14 Needle penetration of the globe. **A,** Needle penetration of the globe has caused multiple retinal breaks, including damage to the macula. **B,** After retinal detachment occurred, treatment consisted of vitrectomy, fluid–gas exchange, and endolaser photocoagulation of retinal breaks. Retinal reattachment was achieved, but the visual acuity remained very poor. *(Courtesy of Harry W. Flynn, Jr, MD.)*

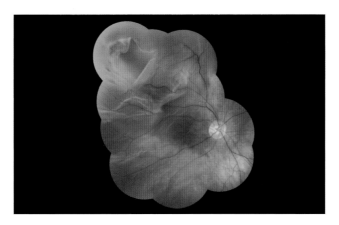

Figure 17-15 Fundus of a patient with symptomatic retinal detachment due to a large superotemporal break after cataract surgery. *(Courtesy of Nancy M. Holekamp, MD.)*

younger age at the time of cataract extraction, male sex, and longer axial length. A surgical complication such as posterior capsular rupture with vitreous loss has been estimated to increase the risk of retinal detachment by as much as 20-fold. By contrast, Nd:YAG laser capsulotomy after uncomplicated phacoemulsification has not been shown to appreciably increase the risk of retinal detachment.

Management options for RRD include laser demarcation of the detachment, pneumatic retinopexy, scleral buckling, and vitrectomy with or without a scleral buckle procedure. Observation can be considered for selected patients with localized retinal detachment and no associated symptoms (subclinical retinal detachment).

Selection of the treatment approach among the modalities available for retinal detachment is surgeon-dependent and remains a topic of debate among retinal surgeons. The precise configuration of the detachment, the location of the breaks, and the phakic status of the eye are all considered carefully before the method of treatment is determined.

Campo RV, Sipperley JO, Sneed SR, et al. Pars plana vitrectomy without scleral buckle for pseudophakic retinal detachments. *Ophthalmology.* 1999;106(9):1811–1816.

Powell SK, Olson RJ. Incidence of retinal detachment after cataract surgery and neodymium:YAG laser capsulotomy. *J Cataract Refract Surg.* 1995;21(2):132–135.

Tuft SJ, Minassian D, Sullivan P. Risk factors for retinal detachment after cataract surgery: a case-control study. *Ophthalmology.* 2006;113(4):650–656.

Techniques for Surgical Repair of Retinal Detachments

Three surgical techniques have been described for patients with primary uncomplicated rhegmatogenous retinal detachment: pneumatic retinopexy, scleral buckling, and primary vitrectomy. These procedures all share the common goals of identifying and treating all causative retinal breaks while providing support of such breaks through external and internal tamponade as needed.

Kreissig I, ed. *Primary Retinal Detachment: Options for Repair.* Berlin: Springer-Verlag; 2005.

Pneumatic retinopexy

The goal of pneumatic retinopexy is to close (or to "cork" or "bouchonade," as coined by the pioneering retinal surgeon Jules Gonin) the retinal breaks using an intraocular gas bubble for a sufficient time to allow the subretinal fluid to reabsorb and a chorioretinal adhesion to form around the causative break(s). The classic indications for pneumatic retinopexy include the following: confidence that all retinal breaks have been identified; retinal breaks confined to the superior 8 clock-hours; a single retinal break or multiple breaks within 1–2 clock-hours; the absence of proliferative vitreoretinopathy (PVR) grade C or D; a cooperative patient who can maintain proper positioning; and clear media. With direct pneumatic occlusion of the causative retinal breaks in acute detachments, subretinal fluid is often completely reabsorbed within 6–8 hours.

The procedure can be performed with topical, subconjunctival, or retrobulbar anesthesia. Transconjunctival cryopexy of the causative retinal breaks can be applied. Alternatively, laser retinopexy may be performed after retinal apposition (a procedure the ophthalmologist Alfredo Domínguez of Spain termed "pneumocausis"). A 5% povidone-iodine solution is applied to the conjunctival cul-de-sac and lid margin. Gas is then injected transconjunctivally through the pars plana. A variety of intraocular gases have been used (eg, air, SF_6, C_3F_8). Frequently, an anterior chamber paracentesis is required to normalize the elevated IOP that results from the gas injection. To close (cork) and push (tamponade) all causative retinal breaks, the patient must maintain a predetermined head posture that places the breaks in the least dependent position (Fig 17-16).

A prospective, multicenter, randomized clinical trial comparing pneumatic retinopexy with scleral buckling demonstrated successful retinal reattachment in 73% of patients who underwent pneumatic retinopexy and in 82% of those who received scleral buckle

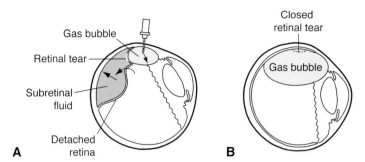

Figure 17-16 Pneumatic retinopexy. **A,** Schematic showing a small, expansile gas bubble being injected into the vitreous cavity. **B,** The bubble enlarges. The patient is positioned so the gas bubble occludes the retinal break, allowing for resorption of subretinal fluid. *(Illustration by Dave Yates.)*

procedures—a difference that was not statistically significant. Among patients who re-quired more than 1 procedure, 99% of those initially receiving pneumatic retinopexy and 98% of those initially receiving the scleral buckle procedure achieved anatomical success.

The final visual outcomes also were equivalent between the 2 groups for retinal de-tachments that did not involve the macula. However, for patients with retinal detachments of recent duration (<14 days) that did involve the macula, pneumatic retinopexy was su-perior to scleral buckling in visual outcomes.

Complications from pneumatic retinopexy include subretinal gas migration, anterior chamber gas migration, endophthalmitis, cataract, and recurrent retinal detachment from the formation of new retinal breaks.

Tornambe PE, Hilton GF. Pneumatic retinopexy. A multicenter randomized controlled clinical trial comparing pneumatic retinopexy with scleral buckling. The Retinal Detachment Study Group. *Ophthalmology.* 1989;96(6):772–784.

Scleral buckling

The goal of scleral buckling is to close retinal breaks through external scleral indentation. Transscleral cryopexy is used to create a permanent adhesion between the retina and RPE at the sites of retinal breaks. The buckling material is then carefully positioned to support the causative breaks by scleral imbrication.

The choice of scleral buckling technique (eg, encircling, segmental, or radial place-ment of the sponge) takes into account the number and position of the retinal breaks, the size of the eye, individual surgeon preference and training, and associated vitreoretinal findings (eg, lattice degeneration, vitreoretinal traction, aphakia) (Fig 17-17).

An increase in the IOP related to compression from the buckling effect may indicate the need for external drainage of the subretinal fluid, anterior chamber paracentesis, or both. Chronic viscous subretinal fluid, fish-mouthing of large retinal breaks, and bullous retinal detachments may necessitate treatment with intraocular gas tamponade, drainage, or both. Complications of scleral buckling include induced myopia, anterior ocular ische-mia, diplopia, ptosis, orbital cellulitis, subretinal hemorrhage from drainage, and retinal incarceration at the drainage site.

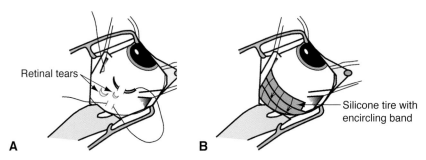

Retinal tears

Silicone tire with encircling band

A　　　　　　　　　**B**

Figure 17-17　Scleral buckle procedure. **A,** Schematic shows placement of mattress-style sutures to bracket retinal breaks in preparation for an encircling scleral buckle. **B,** A solid silicone tire with encircling band is secured in place. *(Illustration by Dave Yates.)*

Primary vitrectomy

Traction on focal areas of adhesion of the vitreous to the peripheral retina (frequently at the posterior vitreous base insertion) may cause retinal breaks and allow for the subsequent migration of intraocular fluid into the subretinal space, leading to retinal detachment. Consequently, the goals of primary vitrectomy are to remove cortical vitreous adherent to retinal breaks, directly drain the subretinal fluid, tamponade the breaks (using air, gas, or silicone oil), and create chorioretinal adhesions around each retinal break with endolaser photocoagulation or cryopexy.

In general, the standard 3-port vitrectomy technique is used, employing 20-, 23-, or 25-gauge instruments. At the discretion of the surgeon, vitrectomy can be combined with a scleral buckle procedure. During vitrectomy, a complete posterior vitreous separation is ensured, and the peripheral cortical vitreous is carefully shaved toward the vitreous base to relieve traction on the retinal breaks (Fig 17-18). To drain the subretinal fluid and achieve intraoperative retinal reattachment, the surgeon can use either an intentional drainage retinotomy or perfluorocarbon liquid technique. If PVR is present, it may be necessary to peel the epiretinal (and, less commonly, subretinal) membranes to facilitate the retinal reattachment. For extensive PVR, a relaxing retinotomy or retinectomy may be required. Once the retina is flattened, chorioretinal laser photocoagulation or cryopexy can be applied. Postoperative tamponade is generally provided by intraocular air or nonexpansile

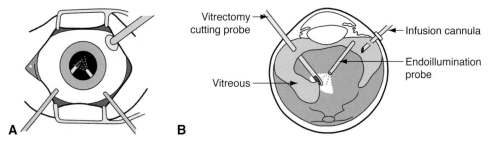

Vitrectomy cutting probe

Infusion cannula

Endoillumination probe

Vitreous

A　　　　　　　　　**B**

Figure 17-18　Vitrectomy. **A,** Schematic of surgeon's view of a 20-gauge, 3-port pars plana vitrectomy. **B,** A cross-sectional view of a vitrectomy, showing an infusion cannula, endoillumination probe, and vitrectomy cutting probe. *(Illustration by Dave Yates.)*

(isovolemic) concentrations of SF_6 or C_3F_8 gas, although complex cases may require the use of silicone oil. Complications of vitrectomy for retinal detachment include postvitrectomy nuclear sclerosis (in phakic eyes), glaucoma, PVR, and retinal redetachment.

Complex retinal detachment includes giant retinal tears, recurrent retinal detachment, vitreous hemorrhage, and PVR. Pars plana vitrectomy is necessary to remove proliferative membranes, unfold the retina, and remove media opacities—features common in patients with PVR (see also Chapter 13). In the past, controversy surrounded the use of long-acting gas versus silicone oil in retinal tamponade for eyes with complex retinal detachment due to advanced grades of PVR; this issue was addressed in the Silicone Study (Clinical Trial 17-2). This prospective, multicenter, randomized study concluded that tamponade with SF_6 was inferior to long-term tamponade with either C_3F_8 or silicone oil. Differences in outcomes from the use of C_3F_8 and silicone oil were statistically insignificant. A lower rate of hypotony was noted in patients treated with silicone oil than in those treated with C_3F_8.

CLINICAL TRIAL 17-2

Silicone Study

Objective: Evaluate the use of various methods of retinal tamponade, together with pars plana vitrectomy techniques, on eyes with complex retinal detachment and advanced PVR.

Participants: Patients aged 18 years or older with grade C3 or greater PVR. Subgroups in the prospective, randomized study included the following:

Group 1 eyes: no previous vitrectomy
Group 2 eyes: one or more previous vitrectomy procedures using gas

Randomization: The study eye was randomly assigned to receive either perfluoropropane (C_3F_8) gas or silicone oil after retinal reattachment was performed by fluid–gas exchange.

Outcome measures: Visual acuity of 5/200 or better and macular reattachment maintained for 6 months after the surgical procedure.

Outcomes: The results showed no statistically significant difference between C_3F_8 and silicone oil in achieving visual acuity of 5/200 or better (43% vs 45%, respectively, for group 1 eyes; 38% vs 33%, respectively, for group 2 eyes) and in complete posterior retinal reattachment (73% vs 64% for group 1; 73% vs 61% for group 2 eyes). The rates of reoperation and keratopathy were similar, whereas hypotony was more prevalent in eyes randomized to perfluoropropane gas (group 2). Either tamponade produced better results that those observed for sulfur hexafluoride gas.

Clinical impact: Study completed in 1992. The results demonstrated that long-term tamponade is beneficial for eyes with retinal detachment and PVR, and that the choice of perfluoropropane versus silicone oil is up to the surgeon after other surgical factors are considered.

Vitrectomy with silicone oil or perfluoropropane gas in eyes with severe proliferative vitreoretinopathy: results of a randomized clinical trial. Silicone Study report 2. *Arch Ophthalmol.* 1992;110(6):780–792.

Vitrectomy with silicone oil or sulfur hexafluoride gas in eyes with severe proliferative vitreoretinopathy: results of a randomized clinical trial. Silicone Study report 1. *Arch Ophthalmol.* 1992;110(6):770–779.

Complications of Pars Plana Vitrectomy

Nuclear sclerotic cataract is the most common complication of vitrectomy. Within 2 years of undergoing vitrectomy, more than 90% of phakic eyes in patients over the age of 50 years will develop visually significant nuclear sclerotic cataract. Evidence suggests that vitrectomy increases the long-term risk of open-angle glaucoma by 10%–20%. Other complications of pars plana vitrectomy include retinal tears and detachment, subretinal perfluorocarbon liquid (when utilized), retinal and vitreous incarceration, endophthalmitis, and recurrent vitreous hemorrhage. Endophthalmitis after vitrectomy is rare (approximately 1 in 2500 cases) but is more commonly found in patients with diabetes and in eyes with retained intraocular foreign bodies. Table 17-2 lists the most common complications of pars plana vitrectomy.

Banker AS, Freeman WR, Kim JW, Munquia D, Azen SP. Vision-threatening complications of surgery for full-thickness macular holes. Vitrectomy for Macular Hole Study Group. *Ophthalmology.* 1997;104(9):1442–1453.

Chang S. LXII Edward Jackson lecture: open angle glaucoma after vitrectomy. *Am J Ophthalmol.* 2006;141(6):1033–1043.

Cherfan GM, Michels RG, de Bustros S, Enger C, Glaser BM. Nuclear sclerotic cataract after vitrectomy for idiopathic epiretinal membranes causing macular pucker. *Am J Ophthalmol.* 1991;111(4):434–438.

Table 17-2 Complications of Pars Plana Vitrectomy

Complications commonly associated with pars plana vitrectomy
Postoperative nuclear sclerotic cataract
Long-term risk of open-angle glaucoma
Intraoperative or postoperative retinal break
Intraoperative or postoperative retinal detachment
Intraoperative cataract
Postoperative vitreous hemorrhage
Postoperative massive fibrin exudation
Postoperative anterior segment neovascularization

Complications associated with silicone oil
Glaucoma
Band keratopathy

Complications of intraocular surgery in general
Endophthalmitis
Sympathetic ophthalmia
Recurrent corneal erosion

Basic Texts

Retina and Vitreous

Albert DM, ed. *Ophthalmic Surgery: Principles and Techniques.* 2 vols. Malden, MA: Blackwell Science; 1999.

Albert DM, Miller JW, Azar DT, Blodi BA, eds. *Albert & Jakobiec's Principles and Practice of Ophthalmology.* 4 vols. 3rd ed. Philadelphia: Elsevier/Saunders; 2008.

Alfaro DV III, Liggett PE, eds. *Vitreoretinal Surgery of the Injured Eye.* Philadelphia: Lippincott Williams & Wilkins; 1998.

Gass JDM. *Stereoscopic Atlas of Macular Diseases: Diagnosis and Treatment.* 2 vols. 4th ed. St Louis: Mosby; 1997.

Guyer DR, Yannuzzi LA, Chang S, et al, eds. *Retina–Vitreous–Macula.* 2 vols. Philadelphia: Saunders; 1999.

Kertes PJ, Conway MD, eds. *Clinical Trials in Ophthalmology: A Summary and Practice Guide.* Philadelphia: Lippincott Williams & Wilkins; 1998.

Meredith TA. *Atlas of Retinal and Vitreous Surgery.* St Louis: Mosby; 1998.

Parrish RK II, ed. *The University of Miami Bascom Palmer Eye Institute Atlas of Ophthalmology.* 2nd ed. Boston: Butterworth-Heinemann; 2000.

Peyman GA, Meffert SA, Conway MD, eds. *Vitreoretinal Surgical Techniques.* 2nd ed. London: Informa Healthcare; 2006.

Regillo CD, Benson WE. *Retinal Detachment: Diagnosis and Management.* 3rd ed. Philadelphia: Lippincott Raven; 1998.

Regillo CD, Brown GC, Flynn HW Jr, eds. *Vitreoretinal Disease: The Essentials.* New York: Thieme; 1999.

Ryan SJ, Hinton DR, Schachat AP, Wilkinson CP, eds. *Retina.* 3 vols. 4th ed. Philadelphia: Elsevier/Mosby; 2006.

Tasman WS, Jaeger EA, eds. *Duane's Ophthalmology on DVD-ROM.* Philadelphia: Lippincott Williams & Wilkins; 2012.

Wilkinson CP, Rice TA. *Michels Retinal Detachment.* 2nd ed. St Louis: Mosby; 1997.

Yannuzzi LA. *The Retinal Atlas: Expert Consult.* Elsevier/Saunders; 2010.

Related Academy Materials

Focal Points: Clinical Modules for Ophthalmologists

Print modules are available through an annual subscription or limited back-year set. Online modules are also available. For more information and a complete list of back issues, visit www.aao.org/focalpoints.

Buggage RR. White dot syndrome (Module 4, 2007).

Coney JM, Miller, DG. Epiretinal membrane (Module 5, 2009).

Do DV, Fallano KA, Adyantha R, Nguyen QD. Neovascular age-related macular degeneration (Module 12, 2010).

Esmaili DD, Loewenstein JI. Retinal arterial occlusions (Module 3, 2010).

Federici TJ. Intravitreal injections (Module 9, 2009).

Foster BS, Bhisitkul RB. OCT: impact on managing retinal disorders (Module 11, 2006).

Fuller JJ, Mason JO. Retinal vein occlusions: update on diagnostic and therapeutic advances (Module 5, 2007).

Hannush S. Sutured posterior chamber intraocular lenses (Module 9, 2006).

Heier JS, Shah SP. Pseudophakic CME (Module 6, 2012).

Mayo GL, Tolentino MJ. Cytomegalovirus retinitis (Module 2, 2007).

Mitchell KT, Lee SY. Current options for retinal detachment repair (Module 9, 2010).

Walker JD, Bressler SB. Update on the management of diabetic retinopathy (Module 5, 2011).

Print Publications

Dunn JP, Langer PD, eds. *Basic Techniques of Ophthalmic Surgery* (2009).

Oetting TA, ed. *Basic Principles of Ophthalmic Surgery.* 2nd ed. (2011).

Russell SR, Rockwood EJ, eds. *ProVision Series 5: Ophthalmic Multiple-Choice Questions With Discussions* (2012).

Wilson FM II, Bloomquist PH, eds. *Practical Ophthalmology: A Manual for Beginning Residents.* 6th ed. (2009).

Academy Maintenance of Certification (MOC)

MOC Exam Review Course; www.aao.org/moc (2011)

Ophthalmic Technology Assessments

Ophthalmic Technology Assessments are available at www.aao.org/ota. Assessments are published in the Academy's journal, *Ophthalmology.*

Ophthalmic Technology Assessment Committee. *Anti-VEGF Pharmacotherapy for Age-Related Macular Degeneration* (2008).

Ophthalmic Technology Assessment Committee. *Indocyanine Green Angiography* (1998; reviewed for currency 2003).

Ophthalmic Technology Assessment Committee. *Laser Scanning Imaging for Macular Disease* (2007).

Ophthalmic Technology Assessment Committee. *Photodynamic Therapy With Verteporfin for Age-Related Macular Degeneration* (2000; reviewed for currency 2006).

Ophthalmic Technology Assessment Committee. *The Repair of Rhegmatogenous Retinal Detachments* (1996; reviewed for currency 2006).

Ophthalmic Technology Assessment Committee. *Single-Field Fundus Photography for Diabetic Retinopathy Screening* (2004; reviewed for currency 2010).

Ophthalmic Technology Assessment Committee. *Small-Gauge Pars Plana Vitrectomy* (2010).

Ophthalmic Technology Assessment Committee. *Surgical Management of Macular Holes* (2001; reviewed for currency 2006).

Preferred Practice Patterns

Preferred Practice Patterns are available at www.aao.org/ppp.

Preferred Practice Patterns Committee, Retina/Vitreous Panel. *Age-Related Macular Degeneration* (2008).

Preferred Practice Patterns Committee, Retina/Vitreous Panel. *Diabetic Retinopathy* (2008).

Preferred Practice Patterns Committee, Retina/Vitreous Panel. *Idiopathic Macular Hole* (2008).

Preferred Practice Patterns Committee, Retina/Vitreous Panel. *Posterior Vitreous Detachment, Retinal Breaks, and Lattice Degeneration* (2008).

Online Materials

Focal Points modules; www.aao.org/focalpoints
ONE Network, Academy Grand Rounds, Retina; www.aao.org/cases
ONE Network, Online Courses, Retina; www.aao.org/courses
Ophthalmic Technology Assessments; www.aao.org/ota
Practicing Ophthalmologists Learning System; www.aao.org/learningsystem
Preferred Practice Patterns; www.aao.org/ppp
Russell SR, Rockwood EJ, eds. *ProVision Series 5: Ophthalmic Multiple-Choice Questions With Discussions* (2012); www.aao.org/provision

---

To order any of these materials, please order online at www.aao.org/store, or call the Academy's Customer Service toll-free number, 866-561-8558, in the U.S. If outside the U.S., call 415-561-8540 between 8:00 AM and 5:00 PM PST.

Requesting Continuing Medical Education Credit

The American Academy of Ophthalmology is accredited by the Accreditation Council for Continuing Medical Education to provide continuing medical education for physicians.

The American Academy of Ophthalmology designates this enduring material for a maximum of 15 *AMA PRA Category 1 Credits™*. Physicians should claim only the credit commensurate with the extent of their participation in the activity.

The American Medical Association requires that all learners participating in activities involving enduring materials complete a formal assessment before claiming continuing medical education (CME) credit. To assess your achievement in this activity and ensure that a specified level of knowledge has been reached, a posttest for this Section of the Basic and Clinical Science Course is provided. A minimum score of 80% must be obtained to pass the test and claim CME credit.

To take the posttest and request CME credit online:

1. Go to www.aao.org/cme and log in.
2. Click on "Review or claim CME online" and then "Report AAO credits."
3. Select the appropriate Academy activity. You will be directed to the posttest.
4. Once you have passed the test with a score of 80% or higher, you will be directed to your transcript. *If you are not an Academy member, you will be able to print out a certificate of participation once you have passed the test.*

To take the posttest and request CME credit using a paper form:

1. Complete the CME Posttest Request Form on page 375 and return it to the address provided. *Please note that there is a $20.00 processing fee for all paper requests.* The posttest will be mailed to you. As of **January 1, 2014,** the paper form will no longer be available; you must take the posttest and request CME credit online.
2. Return the completed test as directed. Once you have passed the test with a score of 80% or higher, your transcript will be updated automatically. To receive verification of your CME credits, be sure to check the appropriate box on the posttest.

   Please note that test results will not be provided. If you do not achieve a minimum score of 80%, another test will be sent to you automatically, at no charge. If you do not reach the specified level of knowledge (80%) on your second attempt, you will need to pay an additional processing fee to receive the third test.

Note: Submission of the CME Posttest Request Form does not represent claiming CME credit.

• **Credit must be claimed by June 1, 2015** •

For assistance, contact the Academy's Customer Service department at 866-561-8558 (US only) or 415-561-8540 between 8:00 AM and 5:00 PM (PST), Monday through Friday, or send an e-mail to customer_service@aao.org.

**AMERICAN ACADEMY
OF OPHTHALMOLOGY**
The Eye M.D. Association

CME Posttest Request Form
Basic and Clinical Science Course, 2013–2014
Section 12

Please note that requesting CME credit with this form will incur a fee of $20.00. (Prepayment required.) Also, as of **January 1, 2014,** you must take the posttest and request CME credit online; paper forms will not be available.

☐ Yes, please send me the posttest for BCSC Section 12. I choose not to report my CME credit online for free. I have enclosed a payment of **$20.00** for processing.

Academy Member ID Number (if known): _____

Name: _____
      First   Last

Address: _____

_____
    City   State/Province   ZIP/Postal Code   Country

Phone Number: _____ Fax Number: _____

E-mail Address: _____

Method of Payment: ☐ Check   ☐ Credit Card   Make checks payable to AAO.

Credit Card Type: ☐ Visa   ☐ MasterCard   ☐ American Express   ☐ Discover

Card Number: _____   Expiration Date: _____

Credit must be claimed by June 1, 2015. Please note that submission of this form does not represent claiming CME credits.

Test results will not be sent. If a participant does not achieve an 80% pass rate, one new posttest will be sent at no charge. Additional processing fees are incurred thereafter.

Please mail completed form to:
American Academy of Ophthalmology, CME Posttest
Dept. 34051
PO Box 39000
San Francisco, CA 94139

Please allow 3 weeks for delivery of the posttest.

Academy use only:

PN: _____   MC: _____

Study Questions

Please note that these questions are *not* part of your CME reporting process. They are provided here for self-assessment and identification of personal professional practice gaps. The required CME posttest is available online or by request (see "Requesting CME Credit"). Following the questions are a blank answer sheet and answers with discussions. Although a concerted effort has been made to avoid ambiguity and redundancy in these questions, the authors recognize that differences of opinion may occur regarding the "best" answer. The discussions are provided to demonstrate the rationale used to derive the answer. They may also be helpful in confirming that your approach to the problem was correct or, if necessary, in fixing the principle in your memory. The Section 12 faculty thanks the Self-Assessment Committee for working with them to provide these self-assessment questions and discussions.

1. What is a posterior extension of the pars plana epithelium onto the retinal side of the ora serrata?
   a. enclosed ora bay
   b. meridional complex
   c. dentate process
   d. peripheral retinal excavation

2. Which of the following diagnostic studies is indicated in the evaluation of age-related macular degeneration (AMD) to detect the presence of choroidal neovascularization (CNV)?
   a. fluorescein angiography
   b. magnetic resonance imaging
   c. corneal topography
   d. computerized axial tomography

3. Which of the following interventions is the most appropriate management of a patient who has undergone fluorescein angiography?
   a. administer aspirin
   b. observe patient for late adverse reactions
   c. advise patient to avoid sunlight for 5 days after the procedure
   d. order urine culture and sensitivity test for urine color change

4. The technique of fluorescein angiography includes which of the following procedures?
   a. intramuscular injection of 5 mL of 10% sodium fluorescein
   b. intravenous injection of 5 mL of indocyanine green solution
   c. intravenous injection of 5 mL of 10% sodium fluorescein
   d. coadministration of oral or intravenous diphenhydramine

5. The electro-oculogram (EOG) is most useful in the diagnosis of which retinal dystrophy or degeneration?

    a. Best disease

    b. rubella retinopathy

    c. pattern dystrophy

    d. fundus flavimaculatus

6. Which agent with potential retinal toxicity may be associated with an irreversible abnormal electroretinogram (ERG) result?

    a. hydroxychloroquine

    b. canthaxanthine

    c. sildenafil

    d. talc

7. Which of the following findings constitutes a pertinent clinical feature of neovascular AMD?

    a. subretinal fluid

    b. geographic retinal pigment epithelium (RPE) atrophy

    c. drusen

    d. RPE pigmentary changes

8. The most appropriate workup for ocular histoplasmosis includes which one of the following components?

    a. C-reactive protein measurement

    b. white blood cell count with differential count

    c. erythrocyte sedimentation rate determination

    d. thorough examination for CNV

9. Which of the following patients has been determined to benefit from Age-Related Eye Disease Study (AREDS) vitamin supplementation?

    a. 40-year-old man with numerous large drusen

    b. 14-year-old girl with Stargardt disease

    c. 62-year-old man with geographic atrophy in 1 eye

    d. 78-year-old patient with previous bilateral CNV

10. Which of the following statements about patients who inherit sickle cell hemoglobin (Hb SC) is *least* accurate?

    a. "Salmon patch" lesions, "black sunburst" lesions, and "sea fans" are all signs of proliferative sickle cell retinopathy.

    b. Those with hemoglobin SS have the most severe systemic complications.

    c. Those with hemoglobin C and sickle cell thalassemia have the most serious ocular complications.

    d. Sickling of red blood cells occurs under conditions of decreased oxygen tension.

11. Which of the following statements does *not* accurately describe the use of indirect ophthalmoscopy to screen for retinopathy of prematurity (ROP)?

    a. Screening should be performed on all premature neonates of less than 30 weeks gestation.

    b. Screening should be repeated biweekly on neonates who demonstrate ROP on initial examination.

    c. Screening should be performed before hospital discharge, or by 4–6 weeks of age.

    d. Screening should be performed on all premature neonates with a birth weight <1500 g.

12. Which of the following factors is an important risk factor for ocular toxoplasmosis?

    a. consumption of undercooked meat

    b. exposure to ticks

    c. exposure to mosquitoes

    d. living in the Ohio River Valley

13. A 25-year-old woman recently received a diagnosis of pars planitis. Her visual acuity is 20/20 OD, 20/50 OS. Examination reveals vitreous cells and cystoid edema in the left eye. Which of the following options is the most appropriate management plan?

    a. argon laser treatment of the peripheral retina in the left eye

    b. sub-Tenon steroid injection in the left eye

    c. oral methotrexate administration

    d. pars plana vitrectomy in the left eye

14. What is a clinical feature of the multiple evanescent white dot syndrome (MEWDS)?

    a. RPE scarring

    b. gray-white, poorly demarcated, patchy, outer-retinal lesions

    c. severe vitreous cellular reaction

    d. gray, granular pigmentation of the fovea

15. The parents of a 2-year-old girl report that she has had "bobbing eyes" and light sensitivity since birth. In your office, the girl shows good visual attention but has bilateral pendular nystagmus and squints in bright light. The retina appears normal, but the foveal reflex is blunted. Dark-adapted scotopic ERG responses are normal, but light-adapted photopic signals are greatly diminished. No relatives are similarly affected. What condition does this patient most likely have?

    a. Stargardt disease

    b. congenital stationary night blindness

    c. Leber congenital amaurosis

    d. achromatopsia

16. Acetazolamide is most beneficial when used to treat cystoid macular edema (CME) associated with which of the following disorders?

a. retinitis pigmentosa

b. central retinal vein occlusion

c. hypotony

d. vitreomacular traction syndrome

17. Which of the following tests most often yields a normal result in Best disease?

a. optical coherence tomography (OCT)

b. ERG

c. fluorescein angiography

d. EOG

18. Which of the following diagnostic procedures is most likely to reveal a carrier for Best disease?

a. EOG

b. OCT

c. ERG

d. fluorescein angiography

19. Which of the following disorders would be *least* likely to be considered in the differential diagnosis of chloroquine phosphate and hydroxychloroquine toxicity?

a. AMD with geographic atrophy

b. Stargardt disease

c. Tay-Sachs disease

d. cone dystrophy

20. What predisposing factor contributes to an accelerated development of hydroxychloroquine maculopathy?

a. adolescence

b. northern European ancestry

c. lean body weight

d. renal and/or hepatic disease

21. A patient taking thioridazine complains of blurred central vision. Macular evaluation reveals pigmentary stippling. What is the preferred management?

a. switch medication to trifluoperazine hydrochloride

b. switch medication to chlorpromazine

c. decrease dosage of thioridazine

d. discontinue use of thioridazine

22. An atypical form of CME may be seen as an adverse effect of which of the following medications?

    a. sildenafil

    b. amiodorone

    c. hydroxychloroquine

    d. niacin

23. For a patient with a diabetic midperipheral tractional retinal detachment, what complication is of primary concern in the application of initial panretinal photocoagulation?

    a. rhegmatogenous retinal detachment

    b. cortical cataract

    c. retinal neovascularization

    d. tractional macular detachment

24. Which of the following scenarios offers the strongest indication for prophylactic treatment (cryopexy or laser surgery) to prevent rhegmatogenous retinal detachment?

    a. high myopia and lattice degeneration with new onset of floaters in a phakic patient

    b. lattice degeneration in a pseudophakic patient with a family history of retinal detachment

    c. an atrophic hole in a phakic patient whose other eye developed a retinal detachment

    d. an asymptomatic flap tear in an eye with a cataract that is about to be rendered pseudophakic

25. A 42-year-old man has a total retinal detachment and a circumferential, 150° peripheral retinal tear with an inverted flap. What surgical approach would be most appropriate?

    a. intravitreal injection 0.3 mL of sulfur hexafluoride (SF_6) gas

    b. 360° peripheral laser photocoagulation

    c. pars plana vitrectomy, retinal reattachment with perfluorocarbon liquid, laser photocoagulation, and complete fluid–gas exchange

    d. scleral buckle with intravitreal injection of SF_6 gas

26. In the repair of an acute-onset rhegmatogenous retinal detachment that involves the macula, what period of delay between diagnosis and surgery has been shown to worsen visual prognosis?

    a. 3 weeks

    b. 1 day

    c. 1 month

    d. 1 week

27. If pars plana vitrectomy is performed on a patient whose fundus has a macular epiretinal membrane, what is the most likely postsurgical complication to occur?

    a. nuclear sclerosis

    b. retinal tear/detachment

    c. endophthalmitis

    d. macular pucker

28. What are the characteristics of a stage 3 macular hole?

    a. small, perifoveal hole with no posterior vitreous separation

    b. full-thickness hole with surrounding subretinal fluid and no posterior vitreous separation

    c. reopened stage 2 macular hole

    d. full-thickness hole with surrounding subretinal fluid and a posterior vitreous separation

29. An epiretinal membrane developed in a 63-year-old woman over several years after scatter laser treatment for a branch retinal vein occlusion. You are preparing to counsel her regarding potential pars plana vitrectomy and membrane peeling. Which of the following complications associated with surgery need not be addressed?

    a. cataract

    b. high rates of epiretinal membrane recurrence

    c. retinal pigment epithelial disturbance

    d. macular edema

30. Which of the following choices has been reported as a complication of face-down positioning after macular hole surgery?

    a. compressive optic nerve injury

    b. ulnar neuropathy

    c. cyclodialysis cleft

    d. cavernous sinus thrombosis

31. What is the preferred treatment for *Bacillus cereus* endophthalmitis?

    a. intravitreal vancomycin or clindamycin

    b. intravitreal amphotericin B

    c. intravitreal ganciclovir

    d. intravitreal gentamicin or tobramycin

32. What condition should be suspected in an 8-month-old baby presenting with lethargy, seizures, bruises on the upper arms, retinal hemorrhages, and cotton-wool spots?

    a. shaken baby syndrome

    b. sickle cell retinopathy

    c. retinopathy of prematurity

    d. von Hippel–Lindau disease

33. What is a benefit of red laser photocoagulation compared with other wavelengths?
    a. better penetration through nuclear sclerotic cataracts
    b. less patient discomfort
    c. reduced risk of a "pop effect" from inhomogeneous absorption at the level of the choroid
    d. maximal absorption by xanthophyll

34. What laser wavelength is best absorbed by xanthophyll?
    a. blue
    b. red
    c. yellow
    d. infrared

35. What parameter increases the risk of Bruch membrane ruptures during application of laser photocoagulation?
    a. small spot size
    b. long duration
    c. low intensity
    d. green wavelength

36. In the immediate postoperative period after vitrectomy, which of the following findings is most commonly observed?
    a. elevation of intraocular pressure
    b. acceleration of cataract development
    c. hyphema
    d. retinal detachment

37. The risk of hemorrhagic choroidal detachment is increased by which one of the following factors?
    a. younger age
    b. hyperopia
    c. elevated intraocular pressure during surgery
    d. hypertension

38. Development of an epiretinal membrane is most commonly associated with which one of the following findings?
    a. glaucoma
    b. posterior vitreous detachment
    c. cataract
    d. facial clefts

39. Panretinal photocoagulation therapy is used in a young patient with poorly controlled diabetes mellitus and arcade tractional retinal detachments, moderate subhyaloid hemorrhage, and retrolenticular blood. Which of the following complications could result in irreversible loss of vision after such treatment?

    a. aggravation of hyperglycemia

    b. cortical cataract

    c. new vitreous hemorrhage

    d. tractional retinal detachment involving the fovea

Answer Sheet for Section 12 Study Questions

Question	Answer	Question	Answer
1	a b c d	21	a b c d
2	a b c d	22	a b c d
3	a b c d	23	a b c d
4	a b c d	24	a b c d
5	a b c d	25	a b c d
6	a b c d	26	a b c d
7	a b c d	27	a b c d
8	a b c d	28	a b c d
9	a b c d	29	a b c d
10	a b c d	30	a b c d
11	a b c d	31	a b c d
12	a b c d	32	a b c d
13	a b c d	33	a b c d
14	a b c d	34	a b c d
15	a b c d	35	a b c d
16	a b c d	36	a b c d
17	a b c d	37	a b c d
18	a b c d	38	a b c d
19	a b c d	39	a b c d
20	a b c d		

Answers

1. **a.** A dentate process is an anterior extension of retinal tissue that separates adjacent ora bays in pars plana and is aligned with but does not reach a minor ciliary process. A meridional complex is a hyperplastic dentate process that extends across the entire length of the pars plana and merges with a ciliary process. A peripheral retinal excavation is a small, oval retinal depression posterior to the ora and is often aligned with a meridional fold or complex. It is excavated because of hypoplasia of inner retinal layers, similar to lattice degeneration.

2. **a.** Fluorescein angiography is indicated in the evaluation of age-related macular degeneration (AMD) to detect the presence of choroidal neovascularization (CNV).

3. **b.** Allergic reactions to fluorescein dye may occur immediately or several hours after the administration of the dye. Adverse effects of the dye are usually mild but in rare cases can be serious or even fatal.

4. **c.** Fluorescein angiography involves intravenous injection (or, less commonly, oral administration) of fluorescein dye, followed by photography of the retinal vasculature. Intramuscular administration of fluorescein is never appropriate. Indocyanine green (ICG) is used intravenously in ICG angiography. Diphenhydramine may be used if an allergic reaction to fluorescein is anticipated.

5. **a.** The electro-oculogram (EOG) is most specific as a test for Best disease, which produces a severely reduced light-peak, dark-trough (Arden) ratio. In fundus flavimaculatus and pattern dystrophy, the light–dark ratio is normal or only mildly subnormal. In rubella retinopathy, the retinal pigment epithelium (RPE) can be diffusely altered, but the EOG pattern is normal.

6. **a.** The full-field electroretinogram (ERG) response is a test of the mass response of the retina and is not a direct test of macular function. It is important for diagnosing and following diffuse diseases, such as retinal dystrophies, retinal degenerations, central retinal artery occlusion, and retinal drug toxicities, including some cases of hydroxychloroquine retinal toxicity. The multifocal ERG has been shown to be more specific than the full-field ERG in the diagnosis of hydroxychloroquine retinal toxicity. The ERG response is less likely to be affected by more focal diseases such as macular holes, epiretinal membranes, branch retinal vein occlusions, or regional uveitis damage. The retinal toxicity associated with canthaxanthine, sildenafil, and talc has not been shown to result in an irreversible abnormal ERG result.

7. **a.** Neovascular AMD is characterized by the development of CNV. This exudative neovascular complex commonly results in the accumulation of subretinal fluid, blood, and lipid. Drusen, RPE pigmentary changes, and geographic RPE atrophy are characteristics of nonneovascular AMD.

8. **d.** There are 4 signs of ocular histoplasmosis: "punched-out" chorioretinal scars, juxtapapillary pigmentary changes, no vitritis, and CNV. Untreated CNV may lead to severe and permanent loss of vision.

9. **c.** Patients at the time of enrollment into the Age-Related Eye Disease Study (AREDS) were 55–80 years old. The AREDS showed a 25% reduction in the risk of progression to advanced AMD for patients with advanced unilateral AMD who were randomly assigned to the combination supplement group.

10. **a.** "Salmon patch" and iridescent spot lesions represent areas of intraretinal hemorrhage, while "black sunburst" lesions are localized areas of intra- and subretinal hemorrhage and arise from hyperplasia and intraretinal migration of the RPE. "Sea fans" are fronds of neo-vascularization that extend from the retina into the vitreous and are therefore signs of pro-liferative retinopathy. A prospective clinical trial has demonstrated the efficacy of argon laser scatter photocoagulation therapy for proliferative sickle cell retinopathy. Prolonged loss of visual acuity and vitreous hemorrhage were reduced in treated eyes compared with control eyes. Scatter photocoagulation proved to be effective and safe in the treatment of patients with sea fan neovascularization.

11. **b.** Several risk factors have been associated with the development of retinopathy of pre-maturity (ROP) in premature neonates, including low birth weight, low gestational age, oxygen therapy apnea, sepsis, and others. Premature infants with a birth weight of 1500 g or less, of gestational age of 30 weeks or less, or who require supplemental oxygen are particularly at risk of developing ROP. Initial examination of the peripheral retina by in-direct ophthalmoscopy in these neonates is recommended before hospital discharge, or by 4–6 weeks of postnatal age (or within the 31st to 33rd week of postconceptional or postmenstrual age, whichever is later). Retinal examinations are repeated every 1–2 weeks until the retina becomes fully vascularized or ROP is noted. If ROP develops, weekly ex-aminations should be performed to watch for possible progression to threshold disease.

12. **a.** Consumption of undercooked or raw meat or of substances contaminated with cat feces is a risk factor for ocular toxoplasmosis. Exposure to ticks increases the risk of Lyme dis-ease, whereas exposure to mosquitoes increases the risk of acquiring various infectious disease–causing organisms (eg, parasites that cause malaria and West Nile virus). The Ohio River Valley is endemic for the ocular histoplasmosis syndrome.

13. **b.** Sub-Tenon steroid injection is a local treatment that is effective in managing inflam-mation and macular edema associated with pars planitis, especially when only 1 eye is involved. Immunomodulation is reserved for persistent or refractory cases. Argon laser treatment is utilized for peripheral retinal neovascularization associated with the disease. Pars plana vitrectomy is reserved for serious complications such as retinal detachment, advanced uveitis, cataract, and/or severe cystoid macular edema (CME) unresponsive to corticosteroid therapy.

14. **b.** Multiple evanescent white dot syndrome (MEWDS) is characterized by the presence of multiple small gray-white dots at the level of the deep retina/RPE in the posterior pole. Foveal granularity, when present, appears as tiny yellow-orange dots. Vitritis may or may not be present, but it is not severe. RPE scarring is not a feature, as the condition typically resolves spontaneously over 2–6 weeks.

15. **d.** The early onset of photophobia and nystagmus points to a congenital cone dysfunction. The loss of photopic ERG response, including photopic flicker response, and the patient's essentially normal rod function confirm the generalized cone abnormality. Although con-genital stationary night blindness (CSNB) can reduce visual acuity and cause nystagmus, the congenital loss of night vision from rod system abnormalities would cause an abnor-mal scotopic ERG response. CSNB is frequently an X-linked recessive trait that affects males. In Leber congenital amaurosis, overall vision is very limited because of generalized retinal dysfunction that causes loss of both rod and cone ERG responses. Stargardt disease often becomes evident during the grade school and teenage years and typically shows a nearly normal rod and cone ERG response. Achromatopsia causes total color blindness as

a result of a congenital absence of cone photoreceptors. It has an autosomal recessive inheritance pattern, and its appearance in more than the current generation is rare. Ultimate visual acuity ranges from 20/100 to 20/200 and is best in dimmer light or with sunglasses.

16. **a.** Acetazolamide has been shown to reduce CME in patients with hereditary retinal degeneration (retinitis pigmentosa). CME caused by a central retinal vein occlusion can be treated with intravitreal injections of steroids or anti–vascular endothelial growth factor drugs. Underlying causes of hypotony should be treated to reduce CME. In patients with CME caused by vitreomacular traction, surgery may be indicated to relieve the traction on the retina.

17. **b.** In patients with Best disease, the optical coherence tomogram and fluorescein angiogram can help delineate the structure of vitelliform lesions, and the EOG is often abnormal. The ERG pattern, however, does not usually reveal any characteristic defects.

18. **a.** EOG is most helpful in identifying patients with, or carriers of, Best disease. Results of optical coherence tomography, ERG, and fluorescein angiography are typically normal in carriers of the disease.

19. **c.** AMD, Stargardt disease, and cone dystrophy can all cause RPE changes similar to those found in chloroquine and hydroxychloroquine toxicity. Tay-Sachs disease typically causes a cherry-red–spot appearance of the macula, related to intraretinal storage of ganglioside.

20. **d.** The coexistence of renal and/or hepatic disease represents a risk factor for the development of hydroxychloroquine maculopathy; youth, lean body weight, and northern European ancestry do not.

21. **d.** The other medications can also cause pigmentary retinopathy. Thus, the recommendation is to discontinue thioridazine as soon as toxicity is suspected. Late atrophic changes of the macula can occur after discontinuation.

22. **d.** Niacin can cause a form of CME in which no late leakage is apparent on the fluorescein angiogram. The other medications listed are not associated with an atypical CME.

23. **d.** In proliferative diabetic retinopathy, panretinal photocoagulation may result in the contraction of fibrovascular tissue, exacerbating tractional retinal detachment, resulting in macular detachment. Although this may also result in retinal breaks and combined tractional-rhegmatogenous retinal detachment, this is uncommon. Panretinal photocoagulation reduces retinal neovascularization and has no known direct impact on cortical cataract formation.

24. **d.** The subject of prophylaxis for rhegmatogenous retinal detachment is an area of some controversy among vitreoretinal specialists. As with any surgical decision, the decision to treat must rest on an educated assessment of the risks of treatment versus the risks of leaving the patient untreated, as well as on knowledge of how much the treatment can actually reduce the risk of detachment. A thorough exploration is beyond the scope of this discussion, but factors that prompt treatment are evidence of acute onset of symptoms and the presence of vitreous traction. Less compelling indications are a history of detachment in the other eye and imminent cataract surgery, but the combination of the latter with evidence of traction becomes a strong indication to treat.

25. **c.** Retinal detachments from giant retinal tears, tears of greater than 90°, have a high redetachment rate due to proliferative vitreoretinopathy. Because of the high risk of failure, the preferred approach would usually include pars plana vitrectomy, use of perfluorocarbon

liquid, laser photocoagulation demarcation, and complete fluid–gas exchange. The other options, performed alone, would not be likely to temporarily flatten or reattach the retina.

26. **d.** Repair for acute retinal detachment soon after diagnosis is important to optimize outcome. Retrospective studies have shown a worsened prognosis in cases for which surgery was delayed for about 7 days or more from the time of diagnosis. However, compared with emergency (same-day) surgery, scheduled surgery has been associated with similar outcomes and complication rates, and with lower cost. Nevertheless, because no prospective randomized studies have addressed this topic, clinical judgment must be exercised. Eyes with attached maculae or recently detached maculae may benefit from earlier surgery. In addition, detachments associated with acute giant retinal tears or superior bullous detachments with the macula remaining attached should be repaired as soon as possible. A good peripheral examination at diagnosis of retinal detachment is important to assess for these factors.

27. **a.** Pars plana vitrectomy is indicated for patients with an epiretinal membrane/macular pucker that produces metamorphopsia or a significant decrease in visual acuity. Visual acuity improves in most eyes after surgery but usually does not return to normal. Complications after pars plana vitrectomy for epiretinal membrane/macular pucker include peripheral retinal break formation (4%–6%); retinal detachment (3%–6%), which may occur immediately postoperatively or months after surgery; endophthalmitis (1%); recurrent macular pucker that affects visual acuity (5%); and progression of nuclear sclerosis (12%–68%).

28. **b.** The staging system applies only to idiopathic macular holes, not traumatic or disorder-associated macular holes. A stage 2 macular hole is defined as a perifoveal or "can-opener"–like hole. A stage 3 idiopathic macular hole is characterized by an adjacent annulus of subretinal fluid without a posterior vitreous separation. A stage 4 macular hole is a full-thickness hole with a posterior vitreous separation. Occasionally, idiopathic macular holes that have been repaired surgically will reopen spontaneously or in relation to cataract surgery. However, hole reopening is not included in the staging system.

29. **b.** Vitrectomy for removal of epiretinal membranes is a highly successful surgery. The procedure is associated with improvement in visual acuity, reduction in metamorphopsia, and low rates of recurrent membrane formation. Accelerated cataract development is the most common complication after vitrectomy for epiretinal membrane removal. Other postoperative risks include atrophy, hypertrophy, and migration of RPE cells, macular edema, glaucoma, and retinal breaks. Hypotony is a rare postoperative complication. However, when present, it is usually due to decreased aqueous production or a wound leak rather than increased trabecular filtration. RPE disturbances are reported after successful vitrectomy and membrane peeling. Indistinguishable RPE changes may develop after long-standing venous occlusive disease. Cautioning the patient regarding these postoperative complications would be appropriate given the clinical setting.

30. **b.** Commonly reported complications of macular hole surgery include retinal tear, retinal detachment, cataract, phototoxicity, and visual field loss. Cavernous sinus thrombosis, compressive optic nerve injury, and cyclodialysis cleft have not been reported. In 1999, Holekamp and colleagues reported 7 cases of ulnar neuropathy from face-down positioning after macular hole surgery. All patients had positioned themselves with elbows flexed for at least 1 week. The proposed mechanism was compression of the ulnar nerve while the nerve was stretched in the condylar groove plus entrapment of the nerve in a narrowed cubital tunnel during elbow flexion. At least 3 additional cases of this complication have been reported as the result of face-down positioning after vitrectomy.

31. **a.** *Bacillus cereus*, which rarely causes endophthalmitis in other settings, accounts for almost 25% of cases of traumatic bacterial endophthalmitis. Endophthalmitis caused by *B cereus* has a rapid and severe course if untreated but is sensitive to intravitreal vancomycin or clindamycin. Amphotericin B is an antifungal drug. Ganciclovir is an antiviral drug. Although *B cereus* may be sensitive to gentamicin and tobramycin, the risk of retinal toxicity from these drugs precludes their use in the treatment of this condition.

32. **a.** Shaken baby syndrome is a form of nonaccidental trauma, typically in a baby less than a year old, frequently less than 6 months of age. Systemic signs include bradycardia, apnea, hypothermia, lethargy, seizures, and bulging fontanelles. Skin bruises may be present, particularly on the upper arms, chest, or thighs, as may long-bone fractures and subdural and subarachnoid hemorrhages. Ocular signs include retinal hemorrhages, cotton-wool spots, retinal folds, and hemorrhagic schisis cavities.

33. **a.** The red laser penetrates through nuclear sclerotic cataracts better than other wavelengths. It is minimally absorbed by xanthophyll, possibly reducing the risk of thermal damage in the treatment of CNV adjacent to the fovea. It causes deeper burns with a higher rate of patient discomfort and a higher risk of a "pop effect."

34. **a.** Macular xanthophyll readily absorbs blue but minimally absorbs yellow, red, and infrared wavelengths. Therefore, the blue wavelength should be avoided during macular laser photocoagulation in order to minimize thermal retinal damage.

35. **a.** Small spot size, high intensity, and short duration of laser applications all increase the risk of a Bruch membrane rupture. The red laser causes deeper burns with a higher risk of inhomogeneous choroidal absorption and focal disruption.

36. **a.** Immediate postoperative elevation of intraocular pressure is not uncommon after pars plana vitrectomy, especially in gas-filled eyes. Although cataract progression is the most common complication of vitrectomy, the onset occurs over months, with 90% of eyes in patients over age 50 years showing visually significant nuclear sclerosis within the 2 years following surgery. Hyphema is not commonly observed after vitrectomy. Retinal detachment occurs in 1%–5% of vitrectomy cases overall; the presentation is generally not immediate owing to the time involved for tear formation as well as the time involved between tear formation and subretinal fluid accumulation.

37. **d.** Hypertension is the only risk factor for choroidal detachment listed; additional risk factors include advanced age, glaucoma, myopia, aphakia, cardiovascular disease, Sturge-Weber–associated choroidal hemangioma, and intraoperative tachycardia. Transient hypotony during surgery may cause rupture of a posterior ciliary or choroidal artery.

38. **b.** Idiopathic epiretinal membrane formation is associated with posterior vitreous detachment involving an abnormality of the vitreoretinal interface in which retained cortical vitreous contracts and distorts the underlying retina.

39. **d.** The patient described represents a difficult challenge to the clinician. Panretinal photocoagulation may result in contraction and regression of epiretinal and disc neovascularization that has a fibrovascular component. The resulting traction may aggravate or initiate tractional retinal detachments. If the fovea becomes detached, the vision loss may not be reversible with vitrectomy and membrane peeling. Vitreous hemorrhage may follow scatter photocoagulation but does not cause irreversible vision loss and may present an indication for pars plana vitrectomy. Photocoagulation does not aggravate hyperglycemia. Cortical cataract may result from absorption of laser energy at the posterior lens surface, or by hemorrhage adjacent to the posterior capsule. Most photocoagulation-related crystalline lens laser burns occur within the anterior cortex and in preexisting cataractous areas. Regardless, any associated vision loss is reversible with cataract surgery.

Index

(*f* = figure; *t* = table)

A2E, in fundus autofluorescence, 30
a-wave, of electroretinogram, 34, 34*f. See also*
     Electroretinogram
ABC. *See* ATP binding cassette (ABC) transporters
ABCA4 gene
     in cone–rod dystrophy, 233
     in Stargardt disease, 233, 234
ABCC6 gene, in pseudoxanthoma elasticum, 84
Abetalipoproteinemia, 260–261
Absorption, light, spectra of, for visual pigments,
     337, 338*f*
Abuse, child, ocular trauma and, 330–331, 330*f*
Acetazolamide, for cystoid macular edema, 143
     in retinitis pigmentosa, 230, 230*f*
Achromatopsia (monochromatism), 214–215, 214*t*
     blue-cone, 214, 214*t*, 215
         ERG patterns in, 36*f*
     rod, 214*t*, 215
     Sloan test for, 50
Acute idiopathic maculopathy, 193
Acute macular neuroretinopathy (AMN), 193
Acute posterior multifocal placoid pigment epitheliopathy
     (APMPPE), 185–187, 186*t*, 187*f*
Acute retinal necrosis, 201–202, 202*f*
Acute retinal pigment epitheliitis (ARPE/Krill disease),
     193–194
Acute zonal occult outer retinopathy (AZOOR), 186*t*,
     192–193, 192*f*
Acyclovir, for acute retinal necrosis, 201
ADA. *See* American Diabetes Association
Adaptation, dark, testing, 46, 47*f*
     in congenital stationary night blindness, 215, 216*f*
Adaptometer, Goldmann-Weekers, for dark adaptation
     testing, 46, 47*f*
Adenomatous polyposis, familial (Gardner syndrome),
     retinal manifestations of, 255, 255*f*
Adrenoleukodystrophy, neonatal, 250*t*, 254, 261, 261*f*
ADRP. *See* Retinitis pigmentosa, autosomal dominant
Adult-onset foveomacular vitelliform dystrophy,
     237–238, 238*f*
     age-related macular degeneration differentiated from,
         69, 69*f*
Adult-onset vitelliform lesions, 237–238, 238*f*, 239*f*
AF. *See* Autofluorescence
Aflibercept. *See* VEGF Trap
Age/aging
     angioid streaks and, 84
     ERG affected by, 36
     macular changes associated with, 55–56, 56*f*
     macular holes and, 304
     posterior vitreous detachment and, 274
     vitreous changes and, 297
Age-Related Eye Disease Study (AREDS), 61–63
Age-related macular degeneration/maculopathy, 55–80
     antiangiogenic agents for, 72–73
     central serous chorioretinopathy differentiated from,
         60, 70, 71*f*
     choroidal neovascularization in, 23*f*, 63–64,
         64–65*f*, 65–68, 66*f*, 67*f. See also* Choroidal
         neovascularization

clinical studies in, 61–62, 72, 74, 75, 75*f*, 76–77, 78. *See*
     also specific study
drusen associated with, 57–58, 57*f*
fluorescein angiography in, 59–60, 64
genetic factors in, 56–57
hyperfluorescent lesions in, 59
hypofluorescent lesions in, 59
incidence/prevalence of, 55
management of, 60–63, 71–80, 75*f*
neovascular (wet/exudative), 63–80
     choroidal neovascularization and, 63–64, 64–65*f*,
         65–68, 66*f*, 67*f*
     differential diagnosis of, 68–70, 68*t*, 69*f*, 70*f*, 71*f*
     management of, 71–80, 75*f*
     signs and symptoms of, 64
nonneovascular (dry/nonexudative), 57–63
     differential diagnosis of, 60
     management of, 60–63
     signs and symptoms of, 57–60, 57*f*, 59*f*
photocoagulation for, 71, 340
     ineffectiveness of, 63
photodynamic therapy for, 71–72, 78, 79, 344
retinal pigment epithelium abnormalities associated
     with, 57, 58–59, 59*f*
risk factors for, 56
submacular hemorrhage in, 349, 350*f*
AIM. *See* Acute idiopathic maculopathy
Ala69Ser *(LOC387715)* gene, in age-related macular
     degeneration, 56
Alagille syndrome, 250*t*
Albinism, 257–259, 258*t*, 259*f*
Albinoidism, 258
Allergic reactions
     to fluorescein, 24–25
     to indocyanine green, 26
ALMS1 gene mutation, in cone–rod dystrophy, 233
Alpha-galactosidase A gene, in Fabry disease, 262
Alport disease/syndrome, renal disease and, 254
Alström syndrome
     cone–rod dystrophy and, 233
     renal disease and, 254
Aluminum, foreign body of, 327
Amacrine cells, 12, 14*f*
Amaurosis
     fugax, in central retinal artery occlusion, 139
     Leber congenital (congenital/infantile/childhood
         retinitis pigmentosa), 229, 251–252
Ambient light toxicity, 334
Amblyopia, persistent fetal vasculature and, 308
AMD. *See* Age-related macular degeneration/maculopathy
American Diabetes Association, 89
Amikacin, for endophthalmitis, 354
Amino acids, disorders of metabolism of, retinal
     degeneration and, 264–265
AMN. *See* Acute macular neuroretinopathy
Amniotic fluid embolism, Purtscherlike retinopathy and,
     154, 155*t*
Amphotericin B, for fungal endogenous endophthalmitis
     Aspergillus/mold, 204
     Candida/yeast, 203

Amsler grid testing
in age-related macular degeneration, 60, 64
in chloroquine/hydroxychloroquine toxicity
screening, 267
for choroidal rupture self-testing, 321
Amyloidosis/amyloid deposits, 312–313, 313*f*
Anaphylactic hypersensitivity reactions, fluorescein
angiography and, 24
Anaphylactoid reactions, fluorescein angiography and, 24
Anatomical reattachment surgery, for retinal
detachment, 290–291
ANCHOR (Anti-VEGF Antibody for the Treatment of
Predominantly Classic Choroidal Neovascularization
in AMD) study, 73–74, 75, 75*f*
Ancylostoma caninum, diffuse unilateral subacute
neuroretinitis caused by, 210
Anemia
diabetic retinopathy and, 94
sickle cell. *See* Sickle cell disease
Anesthesia (anesthetics)
ERG affected by, 40
for photocoagulation, 339
Aneurysmal telangiectasia (type 1 parafoveal retinal
telangiectasia), 145*f*, 146
Aneurysms
Leber miliary, 146
retinal arterial
idiopathic vasculitis and neuroretinitis and
(IRVAN), 141
macroaneurysms, 147–148, 147*f*
age-related macular degeneration differentiated
from, 68–69, 69*f*
microaneurysms, in diabetes mellitus
in diabetic macular ischemia, 103
in nonproliferative diabetic retinopathy, 104, 104*f*
Angiogenesis
in age-related macular degeneration/choroidal
neovascularization, 72
in retinopathy of prematurity, 162
Angiographic cystoid macular edema, 143
Angiography, retinal, 20–26, 23*f*, 24*f*. *See also* Fluorescein
angiography; Indocyanine green angiography
Angioid streaks, 84–85, 84*f*
in pseudoxanthoma elasticum, 84, 84*f*
in sickle cell hemoglobinopathies, 84, 120
Angiokeratoma corporis diffusum (Fabry disease),
262–263, 264*f*
Angiomas (angiomatosis)
racemose (Wyburn-Mason syndrome), 151
retinal, 148–151, 149*f*, 150*f*. *See also* Retinal
angiomatosis
Angle closure/angle-closure glaucoma
central retinal vein occlusion and, 129, 130
persistent fetal vasculature and, 308
retinopathy of prematurity and, 163
Annular gap, 8
Anomaloscope, red-green color defects tested with, 47, 50
Anomalous trichromatism, 213, 213–214
Anterior chamber, in persistent fetal vasculature, 308
Anterior chamber angle, neovascularization of, in diabetes
mellitus, 108–109
Anterior cortical gel, 7
Anterior segment surgery, vitrectomy for posterior
segment complications of, 354–362
Anterior vitreous detachment, 297

Antiangiogenic agents. *See also specific agent*
for age-related macular degeneration, 72–73
Antibiotics
for blebitis, 356–357
intravitreal administration of, for postoperative
endophthalmitis, 354
prophylactic, for endophthalmitis, 329
Anticoagulant therapy, in central retinal vein
occlusion, 131
Antienolase antibodies, retinopathy associated
with, 256
Antimicrobial prophylaxis, for endophthalmitis, 329
Antioxidants
age-related macular degeneration and, 61–62
retinitis pigmentosa and, 231
Antiphospholipid syndrome, choroidal perfusion
abnormalities and, 179
Antiplatelet therapy, for central retinal vein
occlusion, 131
Antirecoverin antibodies
cancer-associated retinopathy and, 256, 257
retinitis pigmentosa and, 257
Antiretroviral therapy, CMV retinitis and, 201
Anti-VEGF agents
for age-related macular degeneration/choroidal
neovascularization, 72–79, 75*f*, 86–87, 87–88
combination treatment and, 78
photodynamic therapy and, 78, 79, 344
for branch retinal vein occlusion, 127
for central retinal vein occlusion, 131, 132*f*
for diabetic macular edema, 100, 101*f*
for parafoveal (juxtafoveal) retinal telangiectasia, 147
for proliferative diabetic retinopathy, 106
for retinopathy of prematurity, 169
Anti-VEGF Antibody for the Treatment of Predominantly
Classic Choroidal Neovascularization in AMD
(ANCHOR) study, 73–74, 75, 75*f*
AP3B1 gene, in Hermansky-Pudlak syndrome, 258*t*
Aphakia
posterior vitreous detachment and, 275
prophylactic treatment of retinal breaks and, 285
APMPPE. *See* Acute posterior multifocal placoid pigment
epitheliopathy
Arc welding, occupational light injury and, 334
Arden ratio, 43
in Best disease, 237
Area centralis, 8, 9*f*, 9*t*. *See also* Macula
Area of Martegiani, 7*f*, 8
in posterior vitreous detachment, 274, 274*f*, 297
AREDS (Age-Related Eye Disease Study), 61–63
Areolar choroidal dystrophy, central, 245, 245*f*
Arginine restriction, in gyrate atrophy, 244
Argon laser therapy. *See also* Photocoagulation
for age-related macular degeneration, ineffectiveness
of, 63
for branch retinal vein obstruction, 124–125
for diabetic retinopathy/macular edema, 101–103
ARN. *See* Acute retinal necrosis
ARPE. *See* Acute retinal pigment epitheliitis
ARRP. *See* Retinitis pigmentosa, autosomal recessive
Arterial occlusive disease
carotid. *See* Carotid occlusive disease
retinal. *See* Occlusive retinal disease, arterial
Arteriohepatic dysplasia (Alagille syndrome), 250*t*
Arteriovenous malformations, congenital retinal, 151

Arteritis, giant cell
  central retinal artery occlusion and, 139
  choroidal perfusion abnormalities and, 177–179, 179f
Arthro-ophthalmopathy. *See also* Stickler syndrome
  hereditary hyaloideoretinopathy with optically empty
      vitreous and, 309
  pigmentary retinopathy and, 250t
Aspergillus (aspergillosis), endogenous endophthalmitis
      caused by, 203–204, 205f
Aspirin, for diabetic retinopathy/macular edema, 98
Asteroid hyalosis, 311, 312f
Ataxia
  Friedreich, pigmentary retinopathy and, 250t, 254
  with neuropathy and retinitis pigmentosa, 265
Atherosclerosis
  central retinal artery occlusion and, 139
  ocular ischemic syndrome and, 133
ATP binding cassette (ABC) transporters, mutations in, in
      Stargardt disease, 233, 234
Atrophic retinal holes, 271
  lattice degeneration and, 278, 278f
    treatment of, 284–285, 284t
  treatment of, 283, 284, 284t
Atrophy, gyrate, 243–244, 244f
Autofluorescence, fundus, 22
  in central serous chorioretinopathy, 173–174
  near-infrared, 31
Autoimmune retinopathy, 256
Autosomal dominant inheritance, of pigmentary
      retinopathies, 250t
  retinitis pigmentosa, 228
Autosomal recessive inheritance, of pigmentary
      retinopathies, 250–251t
  retinitis pigmentosa, 228, 229
AZOOR. *See* Acute zonal occult outer retinopathy

b-wave, of electroretinogram, 34, 34f. *See also*
      Electroretinogram
  vascular disease and, 40, 41f
Bacillus
  endogenous endophthalmitis caused by, 202
  traumatic endophthalmitis caused by, 328
Background diabetic retinopathy. *See* Diabetic
      retinopathy, nonproliferative
Bacteria, endogenous endophthalmitis caused by,
      202–203, 202f
Bardet-Biedl syndrome, 250t, 252–253, 252f
  pigmentary retinopathy and, 250t, 252, 252f
  renal disease and, 254
Bartonella henselae, cat-scratch disease caused by,
      206, 207f
Basal lamina (basal cell layer), drusen of (cuticular
      drusen), 60, 239–240
  age-related macular degeneration differentiated from,
      60, 69
  vitelliform exudative macular detachment and,
      238, 238f
Basal laminar deposits, 55, 56f, 57
Basal linear deposits, 55, 56f, 57
Batten disease, 251t, 254, 259–260, 260f
Baylisascaris procyonis, diffuse unilateral subacute
      neuroretinitis caused by, 210
BDUMP. *See* Bilateral diffuse uveal melanocytic
      proliferation
Bear tracks (grouped pigmentation of retina), 282

BEAT-ROP (Bevacizumab Eliminates the Angiogenic
      Threat of Retinopathy of Prematurity) Cooperative
      Group, 169
Behçet disease, 194–195
Berger space, 7
Bergmeister papilla, 307
Berlin edema (commotio retinae), 319, 320f
Best disease/Best vitelliform dystrophy, 236–237, 237f
  electro-oculogram in, 44, 237
Best1 (VMD2) gene, 236
Bestrophin, mutations in, 236
Beta (β) carotene, for age-related macular
      degeneration, 61–62
Beta (β)-thalassemia, angioid streaks in, 84
Bevacizumab
  for age-related macular degeneration/choroidal
      neovascularization, 78, 86, 87
  for branch retinal vein occlusion, 127
  for central retinal vein occlusion, 131, 132f
  for diabetic macular edema, 100
  for proliferative diabetic retinopathy, 106
  for retinopathy of prematurity, 169
Bevacizumab Eliminates the Angiogenic Threat of
      Retinopathy of Prematurity (BEAT-ROP) Cooperative
      Group, 169
Biconvex indirect lenses, for slit-lamp
      biomicroscopy, 19–20
Bietti crystalline corneoretinal dystrophy/
      retinopathy, 250t
Bilateral diffuse uveal melanocytic proliferation, 183, 183f
Binocular indirect ophthalmoscope (BIO), in retinal
      examination, 19
Biomicroscopy, slit-lamp. *See* Slit-lamp biomicroscopy/
      examination
Bipolar cells, 12, 14f
Birdshot retinochoroidopathy (vitiliginous
      chorioretinitis), 186t, 190–191, 190f
Birth weight, retinopathy and, 157, 163, 164, 166. *See also*
      Retinopathy, of prematurity
Black sunburst lesions, in sickle cell disease, 118, 119f
Bleb-associated endophthalmitis, 354, 356–357, 357f
Blebitis, 356–357
Blind spot, idiopathic enlargement of, 190
Blindness
  color. *See* Color vision, defects in
  day (hemeralopia), in cone/cone–rod dystrophies, 232
  diabetic retinopathy causing, 89, 90
  ocular ischemic syndrome causing, 134
  persistent fetal vasculature causing, 308
  in retinitis pigmentosa, 229, 230, 231
  in retinopathy of prematurity, 157
BLOC1S3 gene, in Hermansky-Pudlak syndrome, 258t
Bloch-Sulzberger syndrome (incontinentia pigmenti),
      251t, 255
Blocked fluorescence, 22
Blood–retina barrier, 249
Blue-cone monochromatism/achromatopsia, 214,
      214t, 215
  ERG patterns in, 36f
Blue-yellow color vision defects, 47, 214t
  tests for, 49
Blunt trauma, 318–323, 320f, 321–322f, 322f, 323f. *See
      also* Trauma
  retinal breaks/detachment caused by, 272
  in young patients, 272–273

Blurred vision/blurring, in central serous chorioretinopathy, 171
Bone, Paget disease of, angioid streaks in, 84
Borrelia burgdorferi, 210
Brachytherapy, retinopathy after, 151–153, 153*f*
Branch retinal artery occlusion, 136–137, 136*f*, 137*f*
Branch retinal vein occlusion, 121–127, 122*f*, 125*f*
    evaluation/management of, 124–127, 125*f*
    neovascularization in, 123
    risk factors for, 123
    visual prognosis in, 123
Branch Retinal Vein Occlusion (BRAVO) study, 127
Branch Vein Occlusion Study (BVOS), 124–125, 125*f*
BRAO. *See* Branch retinal artery occlusion
BRAVO (Branch Retinal Vein Occlusion) study, 127
Breaks (retinal). *See* Retinal breaks
Breast feeding, fluorescein dye transmission to breast milk and, 25
Bright-flash electroretinogram, 35, 37
    in hereditary retinal/choroidal dystrophies, 224*t*
Bruch membrane, 16*f*, 17
    age-related macular degeneration/choroidal neovascularization and, 55, 56*f*, 57, 63–64, 64–65*f*, 65, 66*f*, 87, 88*t*
    drusen and, 55, 56*f*, 57
    rupture of, 320
        photocoagulation causing, 341
BRVO. *See* Branch retinal vein occlusion
Bull's-eye maculopathy
    chloroquine/hydroxychloroquine causing, 266, 266*f*
    in cone dystrophies, 232, 233*f*
    differential diagnosis of, 235, 236*t*
    in Stargardt disease, 235
Butterfly pattern dystrophy, 240, 240*f*
BVOS (Branch Vein Occlusion Study), 124–125, 125*f*

C3 complement, in age-related macular degeneration, 56
C$_3$F$_8$
    for retinal detachment, 367
    for submacular hemorrhage, 350–351
C-reactive protein, in giant cell arteritis, central retinal artery occlusion and, 139
c-wave, of electroretinogram, 37. *See also* Electroretinogram
CACD. *See* Central areolar choroidal dystrophy
Cancer, retinopathy associated with, 256–257, 256*f*
Candida (candidiasis), endogenous endophthalmitis caused by, 203
Canthaxanthine, crystalline maculopathy caused by, 268*f*, 269
Capillary hemangioblastoma, retinal, 148–151, 149*f*, 150*f*
Capillary nonperfusion. *See* Retinal capillary nonperfusion
Capillary plexus, retinal, 12
Capillary retinal arteriole obstruction, 135–136, 135*f*. *See also* Cotton-wool spots
Capsulotomy, Nd:YAG laser, retinal detachment and, 363
CAPT (Complications of Age-Related Macular Degeneration Prevention Trial), 63
CAR. *See* Cancer, retinopathy associated with
Cardiac glycosides, retinopathy caused by, 269
Cardiovascular disorders
    central retinal artery occlusion and, 139
    ocular ischemic syndrome and, 134

Carotenoids (xanthophylls)
    absorption spectrum for, 337, 338*f*
    in macula, 8
    age-related macular degeneration and, 62
Carotid cavernous fistula, choroidal perfusion abnormalities and, 176
Carotid endarterectomy, for ocular ischemic syndrome, 134–135
Carotid occlusive disease
    central retinal artery occlusion and, 139
    diabetic retinopathy and, 94
    ocular ischemic syndrome and, 133–135, 134*f*
    retinopathy of, 133–135, 134*f*
        central retinal vein occlusion differentiated from, 130, 133
Cat-scratch disease, 206, 207*f*
Cataract
    diabetic, surgery for, 111
    ERG and, 41
    persistent fetal vasculature and, 308, 308*f*
    postvitrectomy, 368
    in retinitis pigmentosa, 225–226, 230
    sunflower, in chalcosis, 327
Cataract surgery
    cystoid macular edema and, 142, 143, 360
    in diabetes mellitus, 111
    needle penetration/perforation of globe and, 325
    retained lens material and, 357–359, 358*t*, 359*f*
    retinal detachment after, 314, 362–363, 363*f*
        Nd:YAG laser capsulotomy and, 363
        retained lens material and, 357, 358
    retinal light toxicity and, 333, 334
    in retinitis pigmentosa, 230
    vitreal complications/vitreous abnormalities and, 314
        posterior vitreous detachment, 275, 297
CATT (Comparison of Age-Related Macular Degeneration Treatments Trials), 78
Cavernous hemangioma
    cerebrofacial. *See* Sturge-Weber syndrome
    of retina, 151, 152*f*
Cavernous sinus, carotid artery fistulas and, choroidal perfusion abnormalities and, 176
CD4$^+$ T cells, cytomegalovirus retinitis control and, 200, 201
Ceftazidime, for endophthalmitis, 355
Cellophane maculopathy, 300
Central areolar choroidal dystrophy, 245, 245*f*
Central nervous system
    lymphoma of (intraocular lymphoma), 199, 199*f*
        central serous retinopathy differentiated from, 174
    metabolic abnormalities of, retinal degeneration and, 259–264
Central retinal artery, 12, 135
    angiography and, 21
    occlusion of, 138–140, 138*f*, 139*f*
        ERG in evaluation of, 40*f*
        in sickle cell hemoglobinopathies, 119
Central retinal vein, occlusion of, 127–133, 127*f*, 128*f*, 129*f*, 132*f*
    cilioretinal artery occlusion and, 137–138
    ERG in, 40, 41*f*, 128
    evaluation and management of, 130–131
    iris neovascularization in, 128–129
        photocoagulation for, 132
    ischemic/nonperfused, 127, 128, 129*f*

nonischemic/perfused, 127, 128, 128*f*
risk factors for, 129–130
treatment of, 131–133, 132*f*
Central Retinal Vein Occlusion (CRUISE) study, 131
Central serous chorioretinopathy/retinopathy/
 choroidopathy, 171–176, 173*f*
 age-related macular degeneration differentiated from,
  60, 70, 71*f*
 fluorescein angiography in, 23, 24*f*, 172–173, 173*f*
 photocoagulation for, 175, 176, 341
Central Vein Occlusion Study (CVOS), iris
 neovascularization in central retinal vein occlusion
 and, 128
Ceramide trihexoside, in Fabry disease, 262–263
Cerebellar hemangioblastoma, with retinal angiomatosis
 (von Hippel–Lindau disease), 150
Cerebrohepatorenal (Zellweger) syndrome, 251*t*,
 254, 261
Ceroid lipofuscinosis, 251*t*, 254, 259–260
CFH (complement factor H) gene
 in age-related macular degeneration, 56
 in basal laminar/cuticular drusen, 240
Chalcosis, 327
Charcot-Marie-Tooth disease, 250*t*, 254
Chédiak-Higashi syndrome, 259
Cherry-red spot
 in central retinal artery occlusion, 138, 138*f*
 in lysosomal metabolism disorders, 262, 263*f*
 myoclonus and, 262
Cherry-red spot myoclonus syndrome, 262
Children
 Coats disease in, 143–145, 144*f*
 ERG in, 40, 41*f*
 ocular trauma in, 272–273
  abuse and, 330–331, 330*f*
 retinal degeneration onset in, 251–252
Chloroquine, toxicity of, 266–267, 266*f*
 age-related macular degeneration differentiated
  from, 60
 EOG in evaluation of, 44
 multifocal ERG tracing in, 38*f*
Chlorpromazine, retinal degeneration caused by, 267
CHM (Rab escort protein) gene mutation, in
 choroideremia, 242
Cholesterol emboli (Hollenhorst plaques)
 in branch retinal artery occlusion, 136, 137*f*
 in central retinal artery occlusion, 139
Cholesterolosis, vitreous involvement in, 311–312
Choriocapillaris, 12, 17–18, 17*f*
 angiography and, 21
 atrophy of (choroidal dystrophy), 242–246, 243*f*,
  244*f*, 246*f*
 in choroideremia, 242–243, 243*f*
 in gyrate atrophy, 244
 perfusion abnormalities and, 171
Chorioretinal disruption, traumatic (sclopetaria),
 323, 323*f*
Chorioretinal edema, in photocoagulation, 342
Chorioretinal scarring
 ocular histoplasmosis and, 81, 82*f*
 prophylactic treatment of retinal breaks and, 283
 toxoplasmic chorioretinitis and, 207, 208*f*
Chorioretinitis
 in syphilis, 205–206, 207*f*
 toxoplasmic, 206–209, 208*f*, 208*t*

vitiliginous (birdshot retinochoroidopathy), 186*t*,
 190–191, 190*f*
 in West Nile virus infection, 211
Chorioretinopathy
 central serous, 171–176, 173*f*
  age-related macular degeneration differentiated
   from, 60, 70, 71*f*
  fluorescein angiography in, 23, 24*f*, 172–173, 173*f*
  photocoagulation for, 175, 176, 341
 infectious, 200–211
 noninfectious, 185–199
Choroid, 17–18, 17*f*
 anatomy of, 17–18, 17*f*
 dark, in Stargardt disease, 234–235, 235*f*
 detachment of, photocoagulation causing, 342, 342*f*
 diseases of. *See also specific disorder*
  dystrophies, 242–246, 243*f*, 244*f*, 245*f*
  inflammatory, 185–211. *See also* Chorioretinitis;
   Chorioretinopathy; Choroidopathy
   infectious, 200–211
   noninfectious, 185–199
  noninflammatory, 171–183
 gyrate atrophy of, 243–244, 244*f*
 hemangiomas of, 180–182, 181*f*
  age-related macular degeneration differentiated
   from, 70
  in Sturge-Weber syndrome, 181
 hypertension affecting, 114–115, 115*f*, 116*f*,
  176–177, 178*f*
 ischemia of, 176–180, 177*f*, 178*f*, 179*f*, 180*f*
 melanoma of
  age-related macular degeneration differentiated
   from, 70
  transpupillary thermotherapy for, 343
 neovascularization of. *See* Choroidal neovascularization
 photocoagulation causing lesions/detachment of,
  342, 342*f*
 photocoagulation for disorders of, 71, 340
  complications of, 342, 342*f*
 rupture of, 320–321, 320*f*, 321–322*f*
 tumors of, age-related macular degeneration
  differentiated from, 70
 vasculature of, 17–18, 17*f*
  fluorescein angiography in study of, 21, 22–23, 23*f*
  indocyanine green angiography in study of, 26
  insufficiency of, central retinal artery occlusion and,
   138, 139*f*
  perfusion abnormalities and, 176–180, 177*f*, 178*f*,
   179*f*, 180*f*
Choroidal hemorrhage. *See* Choroidal/suprachoroidal
 hemorrhage
Choroidal neovascularization, 23*f*, 63–64, 64–65*f*, 65–68,
 66*f*, 67*f*, 80–88, 88*t*. *See also* Neovascularization
 in age-related macular degeneration, 23*f*, 63–64,
  64–65*f*, 65–68, 66*f*, 67*f*
  photocoagulation and, 63, 71, 340
 angioid streaks and, 84–85, 84*f*
 antiangiogenic agents in management of, 72–73
 central serous chorioretinopathy and, 174–175
 choroidal rupture and, 320–321, 321–322*f*
 classic, 23*f*, 66, 67, 67*f*, 68
 conditions associated with, 87, 88*t*
 fellow eye considerations and, 79
 fluorescein angiography in, 22, 23*f*, 65–68, 67*f*
 idiopathic, 83

indocyanine green angiography in, 25–26
in myopia, 86–87
occult, 23*f*, 66, 67, 67*f*, 68
in ocular histoplasmosis syndrome, 80–83, 82*f*, 351, 351*f*
pathologic (high/degenerative) myopia and, 86–87
photocoagulation for, 71, 340
complications of, 342, 342*f*
wavelength selection and, 338
photodynamic therapy for, 71–72, 78, 79, 343–344
poorly defined/demarcated, 67*f*, 68
in punctate inner choroidopathy, 192
in Sorsby macular dystrophy, 241, 242*f*
subfoveal, 351, 351*f*
transpupillary therapy for, 79, 343
treatment of, 71–80, 75*f*
combination, 72, 78–79
vitrectomy for, 351, 351*f*
well-defined/demarcated, 68
Choroidal/suprachoroidal hemorrhage, 360–361, 362*f*
Choroidal vasculopathy, polypoidal (posterior uveal bleeding syndrome)
age-related macular degeneration differentiated from, 69–70, 70*f*
central serous chorioretinopathy differentiated from, 174, 175
Choroideremia, 242–243, 243*f*
ERG in evaluation of, 40
Choroiditis
multifocal
and panuveitis (MCP), 186*t*, 191–192, 191*f*
West Nile infection causing, 211
solitary idiopathic, 194
Choroidopathy
central serous, 171–176, 173*f*
age-related macular degeneration differentiated from, 60, 70, 71*f*
fluorescein angiography in, 23, 24*f*, 172–173, 173*f*
photocoagulation for, 175, 176, 341
hypertensive, 114–115, 115*f*, 116*f*, 176–177, 178*f*
lupus, 195
punctate inner (PIC), 186*t*, 192, 192*f*
serpiginous (geographic/helicoid), 186*t*, 188–189, 188*f*
Chronic progressive external ophthalmoplegia (CPEO), 251*t*, 254, 265
CHRPE. *See* Congenital hypertrophy of retinal pigment epithelium
CHS. *See* Chédiak-Higashi syndrome
Ciliary arteries, 12, 17, 17*f*
Ciliobursal canal, 7*f*, 8
Cilioretinal artery, 12, 15*f*, 135
macular preservation in central retinal artery occlusion and, 138
occlusion of, 137–138
11-*cis*-retinaldehyde, 15
Clarin-1, in Usher syndrome, 253
Clindamycin, for endophthalmitis, 329
Clinically significant diabetic macular edema, 90, 97, 98, 99*f*
photocoagulation for, 97, 98, 99*f*, 101–103, 102*t*
Cloquet canal, 307
CME. *See* Cystoid macular edema
CMV. *See* Cytomegalovirus
CNGA3 gene, in achromatopsia, 215
CNGB3 gene, in achromatopsia, 215

CNV. *See* Choroidal neovascularization
Coats disease, 143–145, 144*f*
retinal detachment and, 143, 144, 144*f*
Coats reaction, 143, 144*f*
Cobblestone (paving-stone) degeneration, 281–282, 281*f*
Cocaine abuse, choroidal perfusion abnormalities and, 176–177
Coherence tomography, optical. *See* Optical coherence tomography
COL2A1 gene
retinal tears/detachment and, 310
in Stickler syndrome, 310
Collagen
in sclera, 18
in vitreous, 7, 297
Collagen-vascular diseases, Purtscherlike retinopathy and, 154, 155*t*
Color blindness. *See* Color vision, defects in
Color plate testing, pseudoisochromatic, 48, 48*f*
Color vision, 46–50
defects in, 47, 213–215, 214*t*. *See also specific type*
achromatopsia (monochromatism), 214–215, 214*t*
blue-cone, 36*f*, 214, 214*t*, 215
rod, 214*t*, 215
acquired, 214, 214*t*, 231
assessment of, 47, 48–50, 48*f*, 49*f*
in cone dystrophies, 232
congenital, 213–214, 214*t*
genetic basis of, 213–214, 214*t*
testing, 48–50, 48*f*, 49*f*
Comma sign, in sickle cell hemoglobinopathies, 120
Commotio retinae, 319, 320*f*
Comparison of Age-Related Macular Degeneration Treatments Trials (CATT), 78
Complement, Purtscher/Purtscherlike retinopathy and, 154
Complement C3, in age-related macular degeneration, 56
Complement factor B/complement component 2, in age-related macular degeneration, 56
Complement factor H *(CFH)* gene
in age-related macular degeneration, 56
in basal laminar/cuticular drusen, 240
Complement inhibitors, for age-related macular degeneration, 63
Complications of Age-Related Macular Degeneration Prevention Trial (CAPT), 63
Computed tomography (CT scan), in foreign-body identification, 318, 325, 326*f*
Cone dystrophies/degenerations, 232–233, 233*f*
ERG in, 36*f*, 232
visual field testing in, 232
Cone inner segments, 10, 11*f*, 13*f*. *See also* Cones
Cone outer segments, 10, 11*f*, 13*f*. *See also* Cones
Cone response, single-flash (photopic/light-adapted electroretinogram), 34, 34*f*, 35, 36*f*
in cone dystrophies, 232
in hereditary retinal/choroidal dystrophies, 224*t*
Cone–rod dystrophies/degenerations, 233–234. *See also* Retinitis pigmentosa
ERG in, 36*f*, 233
visual field defects in, 234
visual field testing in, 223
Cone–rod homeobox-containing *(CRX)* gene, 222
cone-rod dystrophy and, 233

Cones, 10, 12, 13*f*, 14*f*
  abnormalities of, 213–215, 214*t*. *See also* Color vision,
    defects in
Confluent drusen, 58
Confocal scanning laser ophthalmoscopy, 29–30
  in fundus autofluorescence, 30
  in indocyanine green angiography, 25
Congenital hypertrophy of retinal pigment epithelium
  (CHRPE), 255*f*, 282
Congenital night blindness
  with normal fundi, 215–217, 216*f*, 217*f*
  with prominent fundus abnormality, 217–219,
    218*f*, 219*f*
  stationary, 215–217, 216*f*, 217*f*
    ERG patterns in, 36*f*, 216, 217, 217*f*
Congenital retinal arteriovenous malformations, 151
Conjunctivitis, follicular, in Lyme disease, 210
Contact lens electrode, corneal, for electroretinogram, 35
Contact lenses
  for slit-lamp biomicroscopy, 19
  for slit-lamp delivery of photocoagulation, 339, 340*t*
Contraceptives, oral, central retinal vein occlusion
  and, 129
Contrast sensitivity, 50, 51*f*
  testing, 50–52, 51*f*
Contrecoup mechanism, in blunt trauma, retinal breaks
  caused by, 272
Contusion injury. *See also* Blunt trauma; Trauma
  retinal breaks caused by, 272, 273*f*
Copper
  foreign body of, 327
  sunflower cataract in chalcosis and, 327
Cornea
  lacerations of, 324
  verticillata, in Fabry disease, 263, 264*f*
Corneal contact lens electrode, for electroretinogram, 35
Cortical gel, anterior, 7
Cortical potentials, 44–45, 45*f*
  electrically evoked, 45
  visually evoked, 44–45, 45*f*
Corticosteroids (steroids)
  for branch retinal vein occlusion, 126
  for central retinal vein occlusion, 131
  in central serous chorioretinopathy, 172
  for cystoid macular edema, 143, 360
  for diabetic macular edema, 100
  for giant cell arteritis, central retinal artery occlusion
    and, 139
  for multifocal choroiditis and panuveitis syndrome, 191
  with photodynamic therapy, 344
  for punctate inner choroidopathy, 192
  for toxocariasis, 209–210
  for toxoplasmosis, 208–209, 208*t*
  for Vogt-Koyanagi-Harada (VKH) syndrome, 198
Cotton-wool spots, 135–136, 135*f*
  in capillary retinal arteriole obstruction,
    135–136, 135*f*
  in central retinal vein occlusion, 128, 128*f*
  in diabetic retinopathy, 104
  in hypertensive retinopathy, 113, 114*f*
  in Purtscher retinopathy, 154, 154*f*
  in systemic lupus erythematosus, 195
Coup mechanism, in blunt trauma, retinal breaks caused
  by, 272
CRAO. *See* Central retinal artery, occlusion of

CRUISE (Central Retinal Vein Occlusion) study, 131
CRVO. *See* Central retinal vein, occlusion of
CRX gene, 222
  cone–rod dystrophy and, 233
CRYO-ROP (Cryotherapy for Retinopathy of
  Prematurity) study, 166–167
Cryotherapy
  for Coats disease, 145
  for retinal angiomatosis, 150
  for retinal breaks, 283
  for retinopathy of prematurity, 166–167, 167–168, 169*f*
Cryotherapy for Retinopathy of Prematurity Cooperative
  Group, 164
Cryotherapy for Retinopathy of Prematurity (CRYO-
  ROP) study, 166–167
Crystalline maculopathy/retinopathy, 268–269,
  268*f*, 269*t*
  Bietti, 250*t*
  drug toxicity causing, 268–269, 268*f*, 269*t*
CSC. *See* Central serous chorioretinopathy
CSDME. *See* Clinically significant diabetic macular edema
CSNB. *See* Congenital night blindness, stationary
CSR (central serous retinopathy). *See* Central serous
  chorioretinopathy
Cushing syndrome, central serous chorioretinopathy
  and, 172
Cuticular (basal laminar) drusen, 60, 239–240
  age-related macular degeneration differentiated from,
    60, 69
  vitelliform exudative macular detachment and, 238, 238*f*
CVOS (Central Vein Occlusion Study), iris
  neovascularization in central retinal vein occlusion
  and, 128
Cyclitic membrane formation, after penetrating
  injury, 324
Cysteamine, for cystinosis, 265
Cystic retinal tufts, 278, 279*f*
Cystine accumulation/crystals, in cystinosis, 264
Cystinosis, 264–265
Cystoid degeneration, peripheral, 282
  reticular, 282, 293
  typical, 282, 292
Cystoid macular edema, 142–143, 142*f*
  angiographic, 143
  corticosteroids for, 143, 360
  in pars planitis, 196
  postoperative, 360, 360*f*
    cataract surgery and, 142, 143, 360
  in retinitis pigmentosa, 225, 230, 230*f*
  vitrectomy for, 360, 360*f*
Cytomegalovirus, retinitis caused by, 200–201, 200*f*

D-15 test, 48–50, 49*f*
  in anomalous trichromatism, 214
Dalen-Fuchs nodules, in Vogt-Koyanagi-Harada (VKH)
  syndrome, 197
Dark adaptation testing, 46, 47*f*
  in congenital stationary night blindness, 215, 216*f*
Dark-adapted electroretinogram, 33, 34*f*, 35, 36*f*
  in hereditary retinal/choroidal dystrophies, 224*t*
Dark choroid, in Stargardt disease, 234–235, 235*f*
Day blindness (hemeralopia), in cone/cone–rod
  dystrophies, 232
DCCT (Diabetes Control and Complications Trial), 91,
  92, 94*f*

Deafness (hearing loss), pigmentary retinopathy and, 251*t*, 253
Degenerations
  choroidal
    diffuse, 242–244, 243*f*, 244*f*
    regional and central, 244–246, 245*f*
  peripheral cystoid, 282
    reticular, 282, 293
    typical, 282, 292
  retinal. *See also specific type and* Dystrophies, retinal
    hearing loss and, 251*t*, 253
    systemic disease and, 249–270, 250–251*t*
  retinal pigment epithelium, 58
Degenerative (high/pathologic) myopia, 85–87, 86*f*
  choroidal neovascularization and, 86–87
Degenerative retinoschisis, typical and reticular, 293–294, 293*f*
DENALI study, 79
Dentate processes, 8, 10*f*
  enclosed ora bays and, 8
  meridional folds and, 280, 281*f*
Dermatologic disorders, retinal degeneration and, 255
Desferrioxamine, retinopathy caused by, 269
Deutan defects (deuteranopia), 47, 49, 50
Deuteranomalous dichromatism, 214*t*
Deuteranomalous trichromatism, 213, 214*t*
Dexamethasone, for endophthalmitis, 354
Dexamethasone implant, for branch or central retinal vein occlusion, 126
DHA. *See* Docosahexaenoic acid
Diabetes Control and Complications Trial (DCCT), 91, 92, 94*f*
Diabetes mellitus
  cataracts associated with, surgery for, 111
  glycemic control and, retinopathy incidence and progression affected by, 91–94
    Diabetes Control and Complications Trial, 91, 92, 94*f*
    United Kingdom Prospective Diabetes Study, 91, 92, 93
  ophthalmic examination timetables and, 111–112, 112*t*
  retinopathy of. *See* Diabetic retinopathy
  terminology used in, 89
  type 1 (insulin-dependent/IDDM/juvenile-onset), 89
  type 2 (non–insulin-dependent/NIDDM/adult-onset), 89
Diabetic macular edema, 95–103, 96*f*, 97*f*, 99*f*, 101*f*
  clinically significant, 90, 97, 98, 99*f*
  treatment of, 98, 98–103, 101*f*, 102*t*
    pharmacologic treatment, 100–101, 101*f*
    photocoagulation/laser treatment, 97, 98, 99*f*, 101–103, 102*t*
    surgical treatment, 101–103, 102*t*, 353
Diabetic macular ischemia, 103
Diabetic nephropathy, glycemic control/diabetic retinopathy and, 94
Diabetic retinopathy, 89–112
  anterior chamber angle neovascularization and, 108–109
  background. *See* Diabetic retinopathy, nonproliferative
  cataract surgery and, 111
  classification of, 89–90
  conditions associated with vision loss from, 95
  cotton-wool spots in, 104

epidemiology of, 90
glycemic control affecting, 91–94
    Diabetes Control and Complications Trial, 91, 92, 94*f*
    United Kingdom Prospective Diabetes Study, 91, 92, 93
  iris neovascularization and, 108–109
  macular edema and, 95–103, 96*f*, 97*f*, 99*f*, 101*f*, 102*t*, 353
  medical management of, 91–94
  nonproliferative (background), 89–90, 95–104, 105*f*.
      See also Diabetic macular edema; Diabetic macular ischemia
    severe, 104, 104*f*, 105*f*
  ophthalmic examination timetables and, 111–112, 112*t*
  pathogenesis of, 90–91, 91*f*
  photocoagulation for
    in nonproliferative retinopathy/macular edema, 97, 98, 99*f*, 101–103, 102*t*
    in proliferative retinopathy, 106–108, 108*f*, 109*f*, 340
  preproliferative, 104
  proliferative, 90, 91*f*, 105–111, 106*f*, 108*f*, 109*f*
    nonsurgical management of, 106
    surgical management of, 106–109, 108*f*, 109*f*
    vitrectomy surgery for complications of, 109–111, 352–353, 353*f*
  retinal detachment and, 110–111, 291
    vitrectomy for, 110–111, 352–353, 353*f*
  stages/progression of, 90, 91
  terminology used in, 89–90
  vitrectomy for, 109–111, 352–353, 353*f*
  vitreous detachment in, 110
  vitreous hemorrhage in, 105, 106*f*, 313
    vitrectomy for, 110, 352
Diabetic Retinopathy Clinical Research Network (DRCR.net), 100, 103
Diabetic Retinopathy Study (DRS), 105, 107–108, 109*f*
Diabetic Retinopathy Vitrectomy Study (DRVS), 110
Dialyses, 271, 272, 273*f*
    treatment of, 284*t*
Dichromatism/dichromacy, 213, 214*t*
Differential membrane filtration (rheopheresis), for nonneovascular age-related macular degeneration, ineffectiveness of, 63
Diffuse unilateral subacute neuroretinitis (DUSN), 210–211
Digitalis, retinopathy caused by, 269
Diode laser, 338
Direct ophthalmoscopy. *See* Ophthalmoscopy
Disc sign, in sickle cell hemoglobinopathies, 120
Disciform scar, in choroidal neovascularization, 64, 64–65*f*, 66, 68, 83
Disseminated intravascular coagulation, choroidal perfusion abnormalities and, 179
Diuretics, central retinal vein occlusion and, 129
DME. *See* Diabetic macular edema
DNA, mitochondrial, retinal degeneration associated with deletions/mutations of, 251*t*, 265, 265*f*
Docosahexaenoic acid, supplementary, in retinitis pigmentosa, 231
Dominant (familial) drusen, 239–240, 239*f*
Dot-and-flame hemorrhages, in central retinal vein occlusion, 128
Doyne honeycombed dystrophy, 239
DRCR.net (Diabetic Retinopathy Clinical Research Network), 100, 103

DRS (Diabetic Retinopathy Study), 105, 107–108, 109f
Drugs, ocular toxicity and
    age-related macular degeneration differentiated
        from, 60
    ERG in evaluation of, 41
    retinal degenerations caused by, 266–270, 266f, 268f, 269t
Drusen
    in age-related macular degeneration, 57–58, 57f
    classification of, 58
    confluent, 58
    cuticular (basal laminar), 60, 239–240
        age-related macular degeneration differentiated
            from, 60, 69
        vitelliform exudative macular detachment and,
            238, 238f
    familial (dominant), 239–240, 239f
    hard, 58
    refractile, 59
    regressed, 59
    soft, 57, 57f, 58
    drusenoid RPE detachment and, 57, 238, 239f
Drusenoid retinal pigment epithelial detachment, 57,
    238, 239f
DRVS (Diabetic Retinopathy Vitrectomy Study), 110
DTNBP1 gene, in Hermansky-Pudlak syndrome, 258t
Duchenne muscular dystrophy, pigmentary retinopathy
    and, 254
Dural arterial malformation, choroidal perfusion
    abnormalities and, 176
DUSN. See Diffuse unilateral subacute neuroretinitis
Dystrophies. See also specific type
    choroidal, 242–246, 243f, 244f, 245f
    hereditary, 221–248
    macular, 234–242. See also specific type
    pattern, 240–241, 240f, 241f
        adult-onset foveomacular vitelliform, 237–238, 238f
        age-related macular degeneration differentiated
            from, 60, 69
        butterfly, 240, 240f
    retinal. See also specific type and Degenerations, retinal
        ERG in evaluation of, 39–41, 40f, 41f
        hereditary, 221–248
            diagnostic and prognostic testing in, 223, 224t
        inner, 246–248
        photoreceptor, 223–234
    vitreoretinal, 246–248
        Goldmann-Favre, 219, 248
Dystrophin, mutations in gene for, in Duchenne muscular
    dystrophy, 254

Eales disease, 141
Early receptor potentials, 37, 37f
Early Treatment Diabetic Retinopathy Study (ETDRS), 97,
    98, 101–102, 104
    scatter laser treatment and, 98, 102, 107, 108f
Early Treatment for Retinopathy of Prematurity (ETROP)
    study, 160, 166–167
ECCE. See Extracapsular cataract extraction
Eclampsia, choroidal perfusion abnormalities and,
    176, 178f
Eclipse (solar) retinopathy, 332–333
Ectasia
    parafoveal (juxtafoveal), 145–147, 145f, 146f
    retinal, 143–145, 144f. See also Coats disease
        arterial macroaneurysms, 147–148, 147f

Edema
    macular. See Macular edema
    retinal
        in branch retinal artery occlusion, 136
        in central retinal artery occlusion, 138, 138f
        in central retinal vein occlusion, 128, 129f
        in clinically significant diabetic macular edema,
            97, 99f
        in cystoid macular edema, 142–143, 142f
EDI. See Enhanced depth imaging
EFEMP1 gene, 239
EGF-containing fibrillinlike extracellular matrix protein
    (EFEMP1) mutations, 239
Ehlers-Danlos syndrome, angioid streaks in, 84
Electrically evoked potentials, 45
Electro-oculogram, 42–44, 42f, 43f
Electrophoresis, hemoglobin, in sickling disorders, 116
Electrophysiologic testing, of retina, 33–45. See also
    specific test
    in Leber congenital amaurosis, 229
Electroretinogram, 33, 33–41
    in achromatopsia, 36f, 214
    aging affecting, 36
    applications and cautions for, 39–41, 40f, 41f
    in birdshot retinochoroidopathy, 190
    in blue-cone monochromatism, 36f, 214
    bright-flash, 35, 37
        in hereditary retinal/choroidal dystrophies, 224t
    c-wave, 37
    in choroideremia, 40
    in cone dystrophies, 36f, 232
    in cone–rod dystrophies, 36f, 233
    in congenital stationary night blindness, 36f, 216,
        217, 217f
    dark-adapted. See Electroretinogram, scotopic
    in Duchenne muscular dystrophy, 254
    early receptor potential, 37, 37f
    focal, 37
    foveal, 37
    in fundus albipunctatus, 218
    in glaucoma evaluation, 39
    in hereditary retinal and choroidal dystrophies,
        223, 224t
    in infants/newborn, 36, 40, 41f
    interpretation of, 35–36, 36f
    in Leber congenital amaurosis, 229
    in macular disorders, 39, 40f
    multifocal, 37, 38f
    in multiple evanescent white dot syndrome, 190
    negative
        in congenital stationary night blindness, 216, 217f
        in hereditary retinal/choroidal dystrophies, 224t
    in ocular ischemic syndrome, 133
    in older patients, 36
    pattern, 38–39, 39f
    pediatric, 40, 41f
    photopic/light-adapted, 34, 34f, 35, 36f
        in cone dystrophies, 232
        in hereditary retinal/choroidal dystrophies, 224t
    recording, 33–35, 34f
    in retinal disease, 33–41
    in retinitis pigmentosa, 40f, 226
    scotopic/dark-adapted, 33, 34f, 35, 36f. See also Dark
        adaptation testing
        in hereditary retinal/choroidal dystrophies, 224t

in siderosis, 328
specialized types of, 37–39, 37f, 38f, 39f
in X-linked retinoschisis, 36f, 247
Elevated intraocular pressure
central retinal artery occlusion and, 140
central retinal vein occlusion and, 129, 130
in ocular ischemic syndrome, 133
in Terson syndrome, 155
in Valsalva retinopathy, 153
Ellipsoid, photoreceptor, 10
ELM. See External limiting membrane
ELOVL4 gene, in Stargardt disease, 234
Elschnig spots, 114, 115f, 177
Emboli
branch retinal artery occlusion and, 136, 137
central retinal artery occlusion and, 139
cholesterol (Hollenhorst plaques)
in branch retinal artery occlusion, 136, 137f
in central retinal artery occlusion, 139
choroidal perfusion abnormalities and, 179
Purtscherlike retinopathy and, 154, 155t
retinal vasculitis and, 141
Encephalofacial cavernous angiomatosis (Sturge-Weber
syndrome), choroidal hemangioma in, 181
Endarterectomy, carotid, for ocular ischemic
syndrome, 134–135
Endophthalmitis
endogenous
Aspergillus/molds causing, 203–204, 205f
bacterial, 202–203, 202f
Candida/yeasts causing, 203, 204f
fungal, 203–204, 204f
postoperative, 354–357, 355f, 356f, 357f
acute-onset, 354, 354–356, 355f
bleb-associated, 354, 356–357, 357f
chronic (delayed-onset), 355, 356, 356f
after vitrectomy, 368
vitrectomy for, 354–357, 355f, 356f, 357f
posttraumatic, 328–329
Endophthalmitis Vitrectomy Study (EVS), 354, 355
Enhanced depth imaging, in central serous
chorioretinopathy, 173
Enhanced S-cone/blue-cone syndrome, 218–219,
219f, 248
Enolase antibodies, retinopathy associated with, 256
Enucleation, for sympathetic ophthalmia prevention,
198–199, 329
EOG. See Electro-oculogram
Epidermal growth factor–containing fibrillin-
like extracellular matrix protein (EFEMP1)
mutations, 239
Epiretinal membrane, 298–301, 302f, 346, 347f, 348f
vitrectomy for, 301, 346, 347f, 348f
Epitheliitis, acute retinal pigment (ARPE/Krill
disease), 193–194
Epitheliopathy, acute posterior multifocal placoid pigment
(APMPPE), 185–187, 186t, 187f
Equatorial retina, 8
ERG. See Electroretinogram
ERM. See Epiretinal membrane
ERP. See Early receptor potentials
Erythema migrans, in Lyme disease, 210
Erythrocyte sedimentation rate, in giant cell arteritis,
central retinal artery occlusion and, 139
ESCS. See Enhanced S-cone/blue-cone syndrome

ETDRS (Early Treatment Diabetic Retinopathy Study), 97,
98, 101–102, 104
scatter laser treatment and, 98, 102, 107, 108f
ETDRS visual acuity chart, 102
in branch retinal vein occlusion, 127
in central retinal vein occlusion, 131
Ethylene glycol, crystalline maculopathy caused by, 269
ETROP (Early Treatment for Retinopathy of Prematurity)
study, 160, 166–167
Evisceration, sympathetic ophthalmia and, 329
Evoked cortical potentials, 44–45, 45f
electrical, 45
visual, 44–45, 45f. See also Visually evoked cortical
potentials
EVR1/EVR2/EVR4 genes, in familial exudative
vitreoretinopathy, 310–311
EVS (Endophthalmitis Vitrectomy Study), 354, 355
Examination, ophthalmic
age-related macular degeneration follow-up and, 60
for chloroquine/hydroxychloroquine toxicity, 267
in diabetes mellitus, timetables for, 111–112, 112t
in retinitis pigmentosa, 230
for retinopathy of prematurity, 164–165
EXCITE study, 76
Expansile dot pattern, in central serous chorioretinopathy,
172, 173f
External-beam radiation, retinopathy after, 151–153
External limiting membrane, 10, 11f, 12, 13f, 14f
Extracapsular cataract extraction (ECCE)
cystoid macular edema and, 143
posterior vitreous detachment and, 275
Exudates, hard, in diabetic macular edema, 96, 97f, 99f
Exudative retinal detachment. See Retinal detachment
Exudative retinopathy, retinopathy of prematurity and, 164
Exudative vitreoretinopathy, familial, 310–311, 310f
Eye
injury to. See Trauma
phthisical (phthisis bulbi)
after penetrating injury, 324
retained foreign body and, 327
Eye Disease Case-Control Study
in branch retinal vein occlusion, 123
in central retinal vein occlusion, 129

FA. See Fluorescein angiography
Fabry disease (angiokeratoma corporis diffusum),
262–263, 264f
Famciclovir, for acute retinal necrosis/herpetic
retinitis, 201
Familial adenomatous polyposis (Gardner syndrome),
retinal manifestations of, 255, 255f
Familial amyloidosis, vitreous opacification in,
312–313, 313f
Familial (dominant) drusen, 239–240, 239f
Familial exudative vitreoretinopathy, 310–311, 310f
Familial juvenile nephronophthisis, retinal degeneration
and, 254
Family history/familial factors, in hereditary dystrophies,
221, 221–222
FAP. See Familial adenomatous polyposis
Farnsworth-Munsell 100-hue test, 48
Farnsworth Panel D-15 test (Farnsworth Dichotomous
Test for Color Blindness), 48–50, 49f
in anomalous trichromatism, 214
Fat embolism, Purtscherlike retinopathy and, 154, 155t

FAZ. *See* Foveal avascular zone
Fellow eye. *See also* Sympathetic ophthalmia
    in patient with choroidal neovascularization
        age-related macular degeneration and, 79
        ocular histoplasmosis and, 82–83
    in patient with macular hole, 305
    in patient with retinal detachment, 285
Fenton reaction, 328
Fetal vasculature, persistent. *See* Persistent fetal vasculature
FEVR. *See* Familial exudative vitreoretinopathy
Fibroplasia, retrolental. *See* Retinopathy, of prematurity
Fibrovascular pigment epithelial detachment, 66–67
Filling defect, vascular, 22
Filtering bleb, endophthalmitis associated with, 354,
    356–357, 357*f*
FIPTs. *See* Focal intraretinal periarteriolar transudates
Fistulas, carotid cavernous sinus, choroidal perfusion
    abnormalities and, 176
Flap tears (horseshoe tears), 271, 272, 273*f*
    treatment of, 283, 284, 284*t*
Flashing lights. *See* Photopsias
Fleck retina of Kandori, 218
Flicker response
    30-Hz, 34, 34*f*, 35, 36*f*
    vascular disease and, 40, 41*f*
Floaters
    in posterior vitreous detachment, 275
    in rhegmatogenous retinal detachment, 286
    in spontaneous vitreous hemorrhages, 313
Fluconazole, for *Candida* endophthalmitis, 203
Fluocinolone implant
    for birdshot retinochoroidopathy, 191
    for branch retinal vein occlusion, 126
    for diabetic macular edema, 100
Fluorescein, 20–21
    allergic reactions to, 24–25
    angiography with. *See* Fluorescein angiography
Fluorescein angiography, 20–25, 23*f*, 24*f*
    in acute posterior multifocal placoid pigment
        epitheliopathy (APMPPE), 187, 187*f*
    in acute retinal pigment epitheliitis, 194
    adverse effects of, 24–25
    in age-related macular degeneration, 59–60, 64
    in birdshot retinochoroidopathy, 190
    in branch retinal vein occlusion, 122*f*, 123, 125*f*
    in cavernous hemangioma, 151, 152*f*
    in central retinal vein occlusion, 128, 128*f*, 129*f*
    in central serous chorioretinopathy, 23, 24*f*, 172–173, 173*f*
    in choroidal neovascularization, 22, 23*f*, 65–68, 67*f*
    in choroidal perfusion abnormalities, 176, 177*f*, 180*f*
    in Coats disease, 143, 144*f*
    in cystoid macular edema, 142, 142*f*
    in diabetic macular edema, 95–96, 97*f*
    in diabetic retinopathy, 90, 91*f*
    extravasation of dye and, 25
    in hypertensive choroidopathy, 115, 116*f*
    in juxtafoveal/parafoveal retinal telangiectasia, 145*f*,
        146*f*, 147
    in macular holes, 305
    in multiple evanescent white dot syndrome, 189, 189*f*
    in ocular ischemic syndrome, 134
    in pars planitis, 196
    in radiation retinopathy, 152–153, 153*f*
    in retinal hemangioblastoma, 150, 150*f*
    in solitary idiopathic choroiditis, 194

    in Stargardt disease, 234, 235*f*
    in uveal effusion syndrome, 182, 182*f*
    in Vogt-Koyanagi-Harada (VKH) syndrome, 198, 198*f*
    in West Nile virus chorioretinitis, 211
Fluorescent treponemal antibody absorption (FTA-ABS)
    test, in syphilitic chorioretinitis, 205–206
Focal electroretinogram, 37
Focal intraretinal periarteriolar transudates (FIPTs),
    113, 114*f*
Folinic acid, for toxoplasmosis, 208–209, 208*t*
Follicular conjunctivitis, in Lyme disease, 210
Foreign bodies, intraocular, 325–328, 326*f*, 328*t*
    endophthalmitis and, 328
    retained, 327–328
        siderosis and, 328, 328*f*
    surgical techniques for removal of, 326–327
Forster-Fuchs spots, 86
Foscarnet
    for acute retinal necrosis, 201
    for CMV retinitis, 200
4:2:1 rule, 104
Fovea (fovea centralis), 8, 9*f*, 9*t*, 10
    in albinism, 258, 259*f*
Foveal avascular zone, 8
Foveal burns, photocoagulation causing, 341
Foveal electroretinogram, 37
Foveal pseudocyst, 304, 305*f*
Foveal retinoschisis, 246, 246*f*
Foveola, 8, 9*f*, 9*t*
Foveomacular retinitis (solar retinopathy/
    retinitis), 332–333
Foveomacular vitelliform dystrophy, adult-onset,
    237–238, 238*f*
    age-related macular degeneration differentiated from,
        69, 69*f*
Friedreich ataxia, 250*t*, 254
FTA-ABS (fluorescent treponemal antibody absorption)
    test, in syphilitic chorioretinitis, 205–206
Fucosidosis, 263
Fundus
    in albinism, 258, 259*f*
    albipunctatus, 218, 218*f*
    in congenital night blindness
        abnormalities of, 217–219, 218*f*, 219*f*
        normal, 215–217, 216*f*, 217*f*
    flavimaculatus (Stargardt disease/juvenile macular
        degeneration), 234–236, 235*f*, 236*t*
        ABC transporter mutations causing, 233, 234
        cone–rod dystrophy and, 233
        gene for, 222, 233, 234
    pulverulentus, 240
    in retinitis pigmentosa, 225, 225*f*
    in solitary idiopathic choroiditis, 194
    sunset-glow, in Vogt-Koyanagi-Harada (VKH)
        syndrome, 197
Fundus autofluorescence, 22
    in central serous chorioretinopathy, 173–174
    near-infrared, 31
Fundus near-infrared autofluorescence, 31
Fungi, endophthalmitis caused by, 203–204, 204*f*

Galactosialidoses, cherry-red spot in, 262
Ganciclovir
    for acute retinal necrosis/herpetic retinitis, 201
    for CMV retinitis, 200

Ganciclovir implant, for CMV retinitis, 200
Ganglion cells, retinal, 8, 10, 11*f*, 12, 14*f*
Gangliosidoses, retinal degeneration and, 262–264, 263*f*, 264*f*
Ganzfield stimulus, electroretinogram evoked by, 35
Gardner syndrome (familial adenomatous polyposis), retinal manifestations of, 255, 255*f*
Gas retinal tamponade, in retinal detachment, 290, 345, 364–365, 365*f*, 366–367
Gastrointestinal disease, retinal degeneration associated with, 255, 255*f*
Gaucher disease, 262
GCL (ganglion cell layer). *See* Ganglion cells, retinal
Generalized gangliosidosis (GM₁ gangliosidosis type I), cherry-red spot in, 262
Genetic/hereditary factors
    in age-related macular degeneration, 56–57
    in retinitis pigmentosa, 228–229, 230
Genetic testing/counseling, in retinitis pigmentosa, 230
Genital ulcers, in Behçet disease, 194
Geographic atrophy, of retinal pigment epithelium, 58–59, 59*f*
    patient education/follow-up and, 60
Geographic choroiditis/choroidopathy (serpiginous/helicoid), 186*t*, 188–189, 188*f*
Geranylgeranyl transferase Rab escort protein, in choroideremia, 242
Gestational age, retinopathy and, 157, 162, 164, 166. *See also* Retinopathy, of prematurity
Giant cell arteritis
    central retinal artery occlusion and, 139
    choroidal perfusion abnormalities and, 177–179, 179*f*
Giant retinal tear, 271
    retained lens fragments after phacoemulsification and, 358
Glaucoma
    central retinal vein occlusion and, 129, 130
    pattern electroretinogram in identification of, 39
    persistent fetal vasculature and, 308
    retained lens fragments after phacoemulsification and, 357
    retinopathy of prematurity and, 163
    uveal effusion syndrome and, 182
    vitrectomy and, 368
Globe
    evaluation of injury to, 318
    open injury of, 318
    penetrating and perforating injuries of, 324, 325
        needle penetration/perforation and, 325, 362, 363*f*
    rupture of, 323
Glomerulonephritis, retinal degeneration and, 254
Glycemic control, retinopathy incidence and progression affected by, 91–94
    Diabetes Control and Complications Trial, 91, 92, 94*f*
    United Kingdom Prospective Diabetes Study, 91, 92, 93
GM₁ gangliosidosis type I (generalized), cherry-red spot in, 262
GM₁ gangliosidosis type IV (Goldberg-Cotlier syndrome), retinal degeneration and, 262
GM₂ gangliosidosis type I (Tay-Sachs disease), 262, 263*f*
GM₂ gangliosidosis type II (Sandhoff disease), cherry-red spot in, 262
GNAT2 gene, in achromatopsia, 215
Goldberg-Cotlier syndrome (GM₁ gangliosidosis type IV), retinal degeneration and, 262

Goldmann-Favre disease/syndrome, 219, 248
Goldmann perimetry
    in hereditary retinal/choroidal degenerations, 223
    in photoreceptor dystrophies, 223, 225*f*
Goldmann-Weekers adaptometer, 46, 47*f*
Gonioscopy, in central retinal vein occlusion, 130
GPR143 gene, in ocular albinism, 258*t*
Granulomas
    in toxocariasis, 209, 209*f*
    in tuberculosis, 205, 205*f*
Granulomatosis, Wegener, choroidal perfusion abnormalities and, 179, 180*f*
Green lasers, 338
Grid pattern photocoagulation, in central retinal vein occlusion, 131
Grönblad-Strandberg syndrome. *See* Pseudoxanthoma elasticum
Grouped pigmentation of retina (bear tracks), 282
Growth factors, in retinopathy of prematurity, 157
Guanylate cyclase activator 1A, in cone dystrophies, 232
GUCA1A gene, in cone dystrophies, 232
GUCY2D gene
    in cone dystrophies, 232
    in cone–rod dystrophies, 233
Gyrate atrophy, 243–244, 244*f*

Haemophilus, bleb-associated endophthalmitis caused by, 354, 357
Haller layer, 17
Halos, macular, in Niemann-Pick disease, 262, 263*f*
Haltia-Santavuori syndrome, 251*t*, 260
Harada disease, 197, 198*f*
HARBOR study, 77
Hard (hyaline) drusen, 58
Hard exudates, in diabetic macular edema, 96, 97*f*, 99*f*
Hardy-Rand-Rittler color plates, 48
Harmonin gene, in Usher syndrome, 253
Head trauma
    Purtscher retinopathy and, 154, 154*f*, 155*t*
    retinal breaks and, 272–274, 273*f*
Hearing loss (deafness), pigmentary retinopathy and, 251*t*, 253
Helicoid choroidopathy (serpiginous/geographic), 186*t*, 188–189, 188*f*
HELLP syndrome, choroidal perfusion abnormalities and, 178*f*
Hemangioblastomas
    cerebellar, with retinal angiomatosis (von Hippel–Lindau disease), 150
    retinal, 148–151, 149*f*, 150*f*
Hemangiomas (hemangiomatosis)
    of choroid, 180–182, 181*f*
        age-related macular degeneration differentiated from, 70
    in Sturge-Weber syndrome, 181
    of retina, cavernous, 151, 152*f*
Hemeralopia (day blindness), in cone/cone–rod dystrophies, 232
Hemispheric (hemicentral) retinal vein occlusion, 127, 127*f*
Hemoglobin, absorption spectrum for, 337, 338*f*
Hemoglobin A₁c, glycemic control and, 92, 94*f*
Hemoglobin AS (sickle cell trait), 116, 117*t*
Hemoglobin C, mutant, 115, 116

Hemoglobin C trait (hemoglobin AC), 117*t*
Hemoglobin CC, 117*t*
Hemoglobin electrophoresis, in sickling disorders, 116
Hemoglobin S, mutant, 115, 116
Hemoglobin SC disease, 116, 117*t*
Hemoglobin SS, 116, 117*t*
Hemoglobinopathies, sickle cell. *See* Sickle cell disease;
    Sickle cell retinopathy
Hemorrhages
    intracranial, Terson syndrome caused by, 155
    retinal
        in arterial macroaneurysms, 147–148
        in branch retinal vein occlusion, 123
        in central retinal vein occlusion, 128, 128*f*, 129*f*
        in diabetic retinopathy, 104, 104*f*
        in shaking injury, 330, 330*f*, 331
        in Terson syndrome, 155
    salmon patch, in sickle cell disease, 118, 118*f*, 119*f*
    submacular, 349–351, 350*f*
    suprachoroidal, 360–361, 362*f*
    vitreous, 313–314, 319
        blunt trauma causing, 319
        in branch retinal vein occlusion, 123, 125, 126
        in diabetic retinopathy, 105, 106*f*, 310, 313, 352
        in pars planitis, 196
        in posterior vitreous detachment, 275, 313
        retinal cavernous hemangioma causing, 151
        spontaneous, 313–314
        vitrectomy for, in diabetes mellitus, 110, 352
Hemorrhagic retinopathy (severe/ischemic CRVO), 127,
    128, 129*f*
Heparan sulfate, in mucopolysaccharidoses, retinal
    dystrophy and, 262
Hereditary dystrophies, 221–248. *See also specific type*
    choroidal, 242–246, 243*f*, 244*f*, 245*f*
    diagnostic/prognostic testing in, 223, 224*t*
    inner retinal, 246–248
    macular, 234–242
    photoreceptor (diffuse), 223–234
    vitreoretinal, 246–248
Hereditary hyaloideoretinopathies with optically empty
    vitreous, 309–310, 309*f*
Hermansky-Pudlak syndrome, 258*t*, 259
Herpes simplex virus, retinitis caused by, 201–202, 202*f*
Herpes zoster, retinitis caused by, 201–202, 202*f*
Hexosaminidase, defective/deficiency of, in
    gangliosidoses, 262
High (pathologic/degenerative) myopia, 85–87, 86*f*
    choroidal neovascularization and, 86–87
High-plus-power lenses
    for slit-lamp biomicroscopy, 19–20
    for slit-lamp delivery of photocoagulation, 339
Histiocytic lymphoma. *See* Intraocular lymphoma
Histo spots, 81
Histoplasma capsulatum (histoplasmosis), ocular,
    80–83, 82*f*
History
    in hereditary dystrophies, 221–222
    in intraocular foreign body, 325
    in trauma, 317
HIV infection/AIDS
    CMV retinitis in, 200–201
    toxoplasmic chorioretinitis in, 208
    tuberculosis and, 205
HLA. *See* Human leukocyte antigens

Holes
    macular, 304–306, 305–306*f*, 349, 350*f*
        idiopathic, 304–306, 305–306*f*, 349, 350*f*
            vitrectomy for, 305–306, 349, 350*f*
        impending, 304, 305*f*
        posterior vitreous detachment and, 298,
            304–306, 305–306*f*
        posttraumatic, 321–322, 322*f*
        treatment of, 305–306, 349, 350*f*
    retinal
        atrophic, 271
            lattice degeneration and, 278, 278*f*
                treatment of, 284–285, 284*t*
            treatment of, 283, 284, 284*t*
        lattice degeneration and, 276, 277*f*, 278, 278*f*
        operculated, 271
            treatment of, 283, 284*t*
        photocoagulation causing, 342
        retinal breaks and, 271
Hollenhorst plaques (cholesterol emboli)
    in branch retinal artery occlusion, 136, 137*f*
    in central retinal artery occlusion, 139
Homeobox (cone–rod homeobox-containing/*CRX*)
    gene, 222
    cone–rod dystrophy and, 233
Homocystinuria, pigmentary retinopathy and, 250*t*
HORIZON study, 77
Horizontal cells, 12, 14*f*
Horseshoe tears (flap tears), 271, 272, 273*f*
    treatment of, 283, 284, 284*t*
Hot spots, focal, in indocyanine angiography, 25–26
HPS. *See* Hermansky-Pudlak syndrome
HPS1/HPS3/HPS4/HPS5/HPS6 genes, in Hermansky-
    Pudlak syndrome, 258*t*
Hruby lens, for slit-lamp biomicroscopy, 20
HTRA1 gene, in age-related macular degeneration, 56
Human leukocyte antigens (HLA)
    in Behçet disease, 194
    in birdshot retinochoroidopathy, 190
    in Vogt-Koyanagi-Harada (VKH) syndrome, 197
Hunter syndrome, 251*t*, 262
Hurler syndrome, 250*t*, 262
Hyaline (hard) drusen, 58
Hyaloid artery/system, persistence/remnants of, 307, 308.
    See also Persistent fetal vasculature
Hyaloideoretinopathies, hereditary, with optically empty
    vitreous, 309–310, 309*f*
Hyalosis, asteroid, 311, 312*f*
Hyaluronan/hyaluronic acid, in vitreous, 7, 297
Hydroxychloroquine, retinal toxicity of, 266–267, 266*f*
    EOG in evaluation of, 44
    multifocal ERG tracing in, 38*f*
Hyperfluorescence, angiographic, 22–23, 23*f*, 24*f*
    in age-related macular degeneration/choroidal
        neovascularization, 23*f*, 59, 66, 67, 67*f*
    in angioid streaks, 84
    in central serous chorioretinopathy, 23, 24*f*, 172, 173*f*
    in multiple evanescent white dot syndrome, 189
Hyperglycemia, diabetic retinopathy incidence and
    progression and, 90
    Diabetes Control and Complications Trial, 91, 92, 94*f*
    United Kingdom Prospective Diabetes Study, 91, 92, 93
Hyperopia, uveal effusion syndrome and, 182, 183
Hyperpigmentation, of retinal pigment epithelium, in
    age-related macular degeneration, 58

Hyperplasia, of retinal pigment epithelium, 282
Hypertension, 113
    choroidal perfusion abnormalities and, 114–115, 115f, 116f, 176–177, 178f
    in diabetic retinopathy, 94
        United Kingdom Prospective Diabetes Study, 92
    retinal arterial macroaneurysms and, 148
    retinal disease associated with, 113–115, 114f, 116f, 117f
Hypertensive choroidopathy, 114–115, 115f, 116f, 176–177, 178f
Hypertensive optic neuropathy, 115, 117f
Hypertensive retinopathy, 113–114, 114f, 117f
Hyperviscosity, retinopathy and, central retinal vein occlusion differentiated from, 129–130
Hyphema, sickle cell disease and, 120
Hypofluorescence, angiographic, 22
    in age-related macular degeneration, 59
    in multiple evanescent white dot syndrome, 189–190
    in serpiginous choroidopathy, 188, 188f
    in uveal effusion syndrome, 182, 182f
Hypopyon, in Behçet disease, 194
Hypotony, during/after surgery, suprachoroidal hemorrhage and, 361

Iatrogenic abnormalities, choroidal ischemia caused by, 180
ICCE. See Intracapsular cataract extraction
ICG. See Indocyanine green
Ichthyosis, retinal degeneration and, 255
ICROP (International Classification of ROP), 157, 158t
Idiopathic choroidal neovascularization, 83
Idiopathic enlargement of blind spot syndrome (IEBSS), 190
Idiopathic macular hole, 304–306, 305–306f, 349, 350f
    posterior vitreous detachment and, 298, 304–306, 305–306f
    vitrectomy for, 305–306, 349, 350f
Idiopathic polypoidal choroidal vasculopathy. See Polypoidal choroidal vasculopathy
Idiopathic retinal vasculitis/aneurysms/neuroretinitis (IRVAN), 141
IEBSS. See Idiopathic enlargement of blind spot syndrome
ILM. See Internal limiting membrane
Immune recovery uveitis, 201
Immunocompromised host
    endogenous mold (Aspergillus) endophthalmitis in, 203
    progressive outer retinal necrosis in, 201
    toxoplasmic chorioretinitis in, 208
Immunomodulatory therapy/immunosuppression
    for birdshot retinochoroidopathy, 190–191
    for multifocal choroiditis and panuveitis syndrome, 191
    for serpiginous choroidopathy, 188–189
    for Vogt-Koyanagi-Harada (VKH) syndrome, 198
Impending macular holes, 304, 305f
Implicit time (τ), in electroretinogram, 34, 34f
Incontinentia pigmenti (Bloch-Sulzberger syndrome), 251t, 255
Indocyanine green, 25
    allergic reactions to, 26
    angiography with. See Fluorescein angiography
    phototoxicity and, 333
Indocyanine green angiography, 25–26
    adverse effects of, 26
    in age-related macular degeneration, 64
    in central serous chorioretinopathy, 174

in choroidal hemangioma, 181, 181f
in choroidal neovascularization, 25–26
in choroidal perfusion abnormalities, 176, 177f
in multiple evanescent white dot syndrome, 189–190, 189f
Infantile Refsum disease, 261
Infants
    ERG in, 36, 40, 41f
    retinal degeneration onset in, 251–252
        peroxisomal disorders/Refsum disease and, 254, 261
    shaking injury and, 330–331, 330f
Infection (ocular). See also specific agent and disease
    retinal and choroidal, 200–211
Infectious chorioretinopathies, 200–211
Inflammation (ocular)
    age-related macular degeneration differentiated from, 70
    choroidal and retinal, 185–211
Inflammatory vasculitis, 194–196. See also Vasculitis
Infrared lasers, 338
    for SD-OCT, 30–31, 31f
    for transpupillary thermotherapy, 343
Infrared reflectance imaging, 30–31, 31f
Injection drug use, endogenous mold (Aspergillus) endophthalmitis and, 203
INL. See Inner nuclear layer
Inner nuclear layer, 10, 11f
Inner plexiform layer, 10, 11f, 12
Inner segments, photoreceptor, 10, 11f, 13f. See also Cone inner segments; Rod inner segments
Insulinlike growth factor I, in retinopathy of prematurity, 166
Intermediate uveitis, 196
Internal limiting membrane, 10, 11f, 12, 14f
    in Valsalva retinopathy, 153–154
International Classification of ROP (ICROP), 157, 158t
Intracapsular cataract extraction (ICCE)
    cystoid macular edema and, 143
    vitreous changes/detachment and, 275
Intracranial hemorrhage, Terson syndrome caused by, 155
Intraocular foreign bodies. See Foreign bodies
Intraocular lenses (IOLs)
    cystoid macular edema and, 143, 360
    in retinitis pigmentosa patient, 230
    vitrectomy for dislocation of, 359–360
Intraocular lymphoma, 199, 199f
    central serous retinopathy differentiated from, 174
Intraocular pressure
    in central retinal artery occlusion, 140
    in central retinal vein occlusion, 129, 130
    in ocular ischemic syndrome, 133
    in ocular trauma, 318
    in rhegmatogenous retinal detachment, 286
Intraocular specimens, for endophthalmitis diagnosis, 354
Intraretinal microvascular abnormalities (IRMAs)
    in diabetic retinopathy, 104, 105f
    photocoagulation for, 340
Intraretinal periarteriolar transudates, focal (FIPTs), 113, 114f
Intravenous drug use, endogenous mold (Aspergillus) endophthalmitis and, 203
Intravitreal medications
    for birdshot retinochoroidopathy, 190–191
    for branch retinal vein occlusion, 126, 127
    for central retinal vein occlusion, 131

for macular edema, 143, 360
with photodynamic therapy, 344
for postoperative endophthalmitis, 354
IOLs. *See* Intraocular lenses
IPL. *See* Inner plexiform layer
Iridocyclitis, in Lyme disease, 210
Iris, neovascularization of (rubeosis iridis)
in branch retinal vein occlusion, 124
in central retinal artery occlusion, 140
in central retinal vein occlusion, 128–129
photocoagulation for, 132
in diabetes mellitus, 108–109
in ocular ischemic syndrome, 133, 134, 134*f*
Iritis, in Behçet disease, 194
IRMAs. *See* Intraretinal microvascular abnormalities
Iron, foreign body of, 328
siderosis caused by, 328, 328*t*
IRVAN. *See* Idiopathic retinal vasculitis/aneurysms/
neuroretinitis
Irvine-Gass syndrome, 142, 314
Ischemia
choroidal, 176–180, 177*f*, 178*f*, 179*f*, 180*f*
macular, in diabetes mellitus, 103
ocular (ocular ischemic syndrome), 94, 133–135, 134*f*
Ishihara color plates, 48
in anomalous trichromatism, 213
Isotretinoin, retinopathy caused by, 269
IU. *See* Intermediate uveitis

Jansky-Bielschowsky disease, 251*t*, 260
Juvenile macular degeneration (Stargardt disease/fundus
flavimaculatus), 234–236, 235*f*, 236*t*
ABC transporter mutations causing, 233, 234
cone–rod dystrophy and, 233
gene for, 222, 233, 234
Juvenile nephronophthisis, retinal degeneration and, 254
Juxtafoveal/parafoveal retinal telangiectasia, 145–147,
145*f*, 146*f*

Kandori, fleck retina of, 218
Kearns-Sayre syndrome, 251*t*, 265, 265*f*
Kinetic perimetry. *See also* Visual field testing
in hereditary retinal/choroidal degenerations, 223
in photoreceptor dystrophies, 223, 225*f*
Krill disease (acute retinal pigment epitheliitis/
ARPE), 193–194

L cones, absent/defective
in achromatopsia, 214
in dichromacy, 213
Lacerations, posterior segment, 324
Lacquer cracks, in pathologic myopia, 84, 86, 86*f*
Lactation, fluorescein dye transmission to breast milk
and, 25
Lake-Cavanagh disease, 251*t*, 260
Laser capsulotomy (Nd:YAG), retinal detachment
and, 363
Laser ophthalmoscopy, 29–30
in fundus autofluorescence, 30
in indocyanine green angiography, 25
Laser pointers, retinal injury caused by, 334
Laser therapy (laser surgery). *See also* specific procedure
and Photocoagulation; Photodynamic therapy
for posterior segment disease, 337–344
for retinopathy of prematurity, 167–168, 168*f*

Lasers
occupational light injury and, 334
photic damage in therapeutic mechanism of, 332, 337
visual pigment absorption spectra and, 337, 338*f*
wavelengths used in, for photocoagulation, 337–339
Lattice degeneration, 276–278, 277*f*, 278*f*
in hereditary hyaloideoretinopathies with optically
empty vitreous, 309, 309*f*
treatment of, 283, 284–285, 284*t*
LCA. *See* Leber congenital amaurosis
Leakage, fluorescein, 22–23, 23*f*, 24*f*. *See also*
Hyperfluorescence
in central serous chorioretinopathy, 24*f*, 172–173, 173*f*
in choroidal neovascularization/age-related macular
edema, 23*f*, 67, 67*f*
in cystoid macular edema, 142, 142*f*
in diabetic macular edema, 95–96, 97*f*
in hypertensive choroidopathy, 115, 116*f*
Leber congenital amaurosis (congenital/infantile/
childhood retinitis pigmentosa), 229, 251–252
Leber miliary aneurysm, 146
Lens (crystalline), retained, cataract surgery and,
357–359, 358*t*, 359*f*
Lenses, for slit-lamp biomicroscopy, 19–20
Leopard spot fluorescence pattern, in uveal effusion
syndrome, 182, 182*f*
Leukocoria
in Coats disease, 144
in persistent fetal vasculature, 308
Lifestyle modification, in age-related macular
degeneration, 63
Ligament of Wieger, 7, 7*f*
Light-adapted electroretinogram, 34, 34*f*, 35, 36*f*
in hereditary retinal/choroidal degenerations, 224*t*
Light–dark (Arden) ratio, 43
in Best disease, 237
Light response, of standing potential, 42–43, 43*f*
Light toxicity/photic damage/phototoxicity, 332–334
age-related macular degeneration and, 63
ambient exposure to ultraviolet or visible light and, 334
cataract surgery and, 333, 334
occupational, 334
ophthalmic instrumentation causing, 333–334
retinal, 332–334
in retinitis pigmentosa, 231
solar retinopathy and, 332–333
Limiting membrane
external, 10, 11*f*, 12, 13*f*, 14*f*
internal, 10, 11*f*, 12, 14*f*
in Valsalva retinopathy, 153–154
middle, 10, 11*f*, 12, 14*f*
Lincoff rules, 286, 288*f*, 289*f*
Lipofuscin granules, accumulation of, in Best disease, 236
Lipofuscinlike material, in Stargardt disease, 235, 235*f*
Lipofuscinosis, neuronal ceroid, 251*t*, 254, 259–260
LOC387715 (Ala69Ser) gene, in age-related macular
degeneration, 56
Long-chain polyunsaturated fatty acids, age-related
macular degeneration and, 62
Low birth weight, retinopathy and, 157, 163, 164, 166. *See
also* Retinopathy, of prematurity
Low vision aids
in age-related macular degeneration, 79
in cone dystrophies, 232
in retinitis pigmentosa, 230

Lupus choroidopathy, 195
Lupus erythematosus, systemic
  choroidal perfusion abnormalities and, 179
  retinal manifestations of, 195–196, 195*f*
Lupus vasculitis, 195–196, 195*f*
  choroidal perfusion abnormalities and, 179
Lutein, in macula, 8
  age-related macular degeneration and, 62
Lyme disease/Lyme borreliosis, 210
Lymphomas, intraocular, 199, 199*f*
  central serous retinopathy differentiated from, 174
Lysosomal storage disorders, retinal degeneration and,
    262–264, 263*f*, 264*f*
  mucopolysaccharidoses, 250*t*, 251*t*, 262
Lysosomes, in outer segment phagocytosis, 15
LYST gene, in Chédiak-Higashi syndrome, 258*t*

M cones, absent/defective
  in achromatopsia, 214
  in dichromacy, 213
Macroaneurysms, retinal arterial, 147–148, 147*f*
  age-related macular degeneration differentiated from,
    68–69, 69*f*
Macula/macula lutea, 8, 9*f*, 9*t*. *See also under Macular*
  age-related changes in, 55–56, 56*f*. *See also* Age-related
    macular degeneration
  anatomy of, 8, 9*f*, 9*t*
  choroidal neovascularization in. *See* Age-related
    macular degeneration
  detachment of, visual acuity after reattachment surgery
    and, 291
  diseases of. *See also specific type*
    ERG in evaluation of, 39, 40*f*
    vitrectomy for, 346–352
  vitreous attachment to, 7*f*, 8
    posterior vitreous detachment and, 298, 302–304, 303*f*
Macular atrophy
  chloroquine/hydroxychloroquine causing, 266, 266*f*
  in cone dystrophies, 232, 233*f*
  in Stargardt disease, 235, 235*f*
Macular degeneration
  age-related. *See* Age-related macular degeneration
  juvenile (Stargardt disease/fundus flavimaculatus),
    234–236, 235*f*, 236*t*
    ABC transporter mutations causing, 233, 234
    cone–rod dystrophy and, 233
    gene for, 222, 233, 234
  vitelliform
    adult-onset, 237–238, 238*f*
      age-related macular degeneration differentiated
        from, 69, 69*f*
    Best disease, 236–237, 237*f*
      electro-oculogram in, 44, 237
Macular detachment
  optic pits and, 295, 295*f*
  vitelliform exudative, 238, 238*f*
Macular dystrophies, 234–242. *See also specific type*
  hereditary, 234–242
  North Carolina, 245–246, 245*f*
  Sorsby, 241–242, 242*f*
  vitelliform. *See* Macular degeneration, vitelliform
Macular edema
  in branch retinal vein occlusion, 123
    photocoagulation for, 124, 125*f*
  in central retinal vein occlusion, 128
    grid pattern photocoagulation for, 131

  cystoid, 142–143, 142*f*
    angiographic, 143
    corticosteroids for, 143, 360
    in pars planitis, 196
    postoperative, 360, 360*f*
      cataract surgery and, 142, 143, 360
    in retinitis pigmentosa, 225, 230, 230*f*
  diabetic, 95–103, 96*f*, 97*f*, 99*f*, 101*f*, 102*t*
    clinically significant, 90, 97, 98, 99*f*
    treatment of, 98, 98–103, 101*f*, 102*t*
      pharmacologic treatment, 100–101, 101*f*
      photocoagulation/laser treatment, 97, 98, 99*f*,
        101–103, 102*t*
      surgical treatment, 101–103, 102*t*, 353
  diffuse, 96, 97*f*
  focal, 95–96, 97*f*
Macular epiretinal membrane. *See* Epiretinal membrane
Macular fibrosis, preretinal, 300
Macular halo, in Niemann-Pick disease, 262, 263*f*
Macular holes, 304–306, 305–306*f*, 349, 350*f*
  idiopathic, 304–306, 305–306*f*, 349, 350*f*
    vitrectomy for, 305–306, 349, 350*f*
  impending, 304, 305*f*
  posterior vitreous detachment and, 298,
    304–306, 305–306*f*
  posttraumatic, 321–322, 322*f*
  treatment of, 305–306, 349, 350*f*
Macular ischemia, diabetic, 103
Macular neuroretinopathy, acute, 193
Macular Photocoagulation Study (MPS), 71, 81, 85, 86
Macular pits, trauma causing, 322
Macular pucker, 300
Macular translocation procedures, for age-related macular
  degeneration/choroidal neovascularization, 79
Maculopathies
  acute idiopathic, 193
  bull's-eye
    chloroquine/hydroxychloroquine causing, 266, 266*f*
    in cone dystrophies, 232, 233*f*
    differential diagnosis of, 235, 236*t*
    in Stargardt disease, 235
  cellophane, 300
  crystalline, drug toxicity causing, 268–269, 268*f*, 269*t*
  optic pit, 294–295, 295*f*
    central serous chorioretinopathy differentiated
      from, 174
Magnetic resonance imaging (MRI), in foreign-body
  identification, 318, 326
Malattia Leventinese, *EFEMP1* gene defects causing, 239
Malignant hypertension, choroidal perfusion
  abnormalities and, 116*f*, 176
Mannosidosis, pigmentary retinopathy and, 250*t*
MAR. *See* Melanoma-associated retinopathy
MARINA (Minimally Classic/Occult Trial of the Anti-
  VEGF Antibody Ranibizumab in the Treatment of
  Neovascular AMD), 73, 74, 75*f*
Martegiani
  area of, 7*f*, 8
  in posterior vitreous detachment, 274, 274*f*, 297
Masquerade syndromes, 199, 199*f*
  retinal vasculitis and, 141
Matrix metalloproteinases, in Sorsby dystrophy, 241
Maximal combined response, in electroretinogram, 33,
  34*f*, 35, 36*f*
MCP. *See* Multifocal choroiditis and panuveitis syndrome
Medical history, in hereditary dystrophies, 221–222

Melanin
  absorption spectrum for, 337, 338*f*
  defective synthesis of, in albinism, 257
  in retinal pigment epithelium, hypertrophy and, 282
Melanocytic proliferation, bilateral diffuse uveal,
  183, 183*f*
Melanoma-associated retinopathy, 256, 257
Melanomas
  choroidal
    age-related macular degeneration differentiated
      from, 70
    transpupillary thermotherapy for, 343
  retinopathy associated with, 256, 257
Melanosomes, in retinal pigment epithelium, 15
MELAS (mitochondrial myopathy with encephalopathy/
  lactic acidosis/strokelike episodes) syndrome, 265
Meridional complex, 8, 10*f*, 281*f*
Meridional folds, 8, 10*f*, 280, 281*f*
Metabolic disorders. *See also specific type*
  retinal manifestations of, 257–265
Metalloproteinases, matrix, in Sorsby dystrophy, 241
Metamorphopsia
  in age-related macular degeneration, 64
  in central serous chorioretinopathy, 171, 175
  in epiretinal membrane, 301, 346
  in macular holes, 304
Methoxyflurane, crystalline maculopathy caused by, 269
MEWDS. *See* Multiple evanescent white dot syndrome
Microaneurysms, retinal, in diabetes mellitus
  in diabetic macular ischemia, 103
  in nonproliferative diabetic retinopathy, 104, 104*f*
Micronutrients, in age-related macular degeneration
  management, 61–63
Microphthalmia (microphthalmos), persistent fetal
  vasculature associated with, 308
Micropsia, in central serous chorioretinopathy, 171
Microscope, operating, phototoxicity and, 333
Microvascular abnormalities, intraretinal (IRMAs)
  in diabetic retinopathy, 104, 105*f*
  photocoagulation for, 340
Microvascular disease, diabetic. *See* Diabetic retinopathy
Middle limiting membrane, 10, 11*f*, 12, 14*f*
Midget bipolar cell, 12
Migraine headache, branch retinal artery occlusion
  and, 136
Miliary aneurysm, Leber, 146
Minimally Classic/Occult Trial of the Anti-VEGF
  Antibody Ranibizumab in the Treatment of
  Neovascular AMD (MARINA), 73, 74, 75*f*
Mitochondrial DNA, retinal degeneration associated with
  deletions/mutations of, 251*t*, 265, 265*f*
Mitochondrial myopathy, 251*t*, 265, 265*f*
  with encephalopathy/lactic acidosis/strokelike episodes
    (MELAS), 265
Mittendorf dot, 307
Mizuo-Nakamura phenomenon, 218, 219*f*, 233
MLM. *See* Middle limiting membrane
Molds, endogenous endophthalmitis caused by,
  203–204, 205*f*
Monochromatism/achromatopsia, 214–215, 214*t*
  blue-cone, 214, 214*t*, 215
    ERG patterns in, 36*f*
  rod, 214*t*, 215
  Sloan test for, 50
Monoclonal antibodies, for age-related macular
  degeneration/choroidal neovascularization, 78

MPS (Macular Photocoagulation Study), 71, 81, 85, 86
MPS I H. *See* Hurler syndrome
MPS I S. *See* Scheie syndrome
MPS II. *See* Hunter syndrome
MPS III. *See* Sanfilippo syndrome
MPSs. *See* Mucopolysaccharidoses
Mucolipidoses, retinal degeneration and, 262
Mucopolysaccharidoses, 250*t*, 251*t*, 262. *See also specific*
  type
  pigmentary retinopathy and, 250*t*, 251*t*, 262
Müller cells/fibers, retinal, 12, 14*f*
Multifocal choroiditis, West Nile infection causing, 211
Multifocal choroiditis and panuveitis syndrome (MCP),
  186*t*, 191–192, 191*f*
Multifocal electroretinogram, 37, 38*f*
Multiple evanescent white dot syndrome (MEWDS), 186*t*,
  189–190, 189*f*
Muscular dystrophy, Duchenne, pigmentary retinopathy
  and, 254
Mycobacterium tuberculosis, 204–205
Mydriasis/mydriatics, for retinal examination, 19
Myoclonus, cherry-red spot in, 262
Myoid, photoreceptor, 10
Myopathies, mitochondrial, 251*t*, 265, 265*f*
  with encephalopathy/lactic acidosis/strokelike episodes
    (MELAS), 265
Myopia
  choroidal neovascularization in, 86–87
  lattice degeneration and, 276, 278
Myosin gene mutations, in Usher syndrome, 253
Myotonic dystrophy, pigmentary retinopathy and,
  250*t*, 254

Nagel anomaloscope, 50
NARP (neurogenic muscle weakness/ataxia/retinitis
  pigmentosa) syndrome, 265
National Health and Nutrition Examination Survey III, 90
NCL. *See* Neuronal ceroid lipofuscinosis
Nd:YAG laser, mechanical light damage caused by, 332
Nd:YAG laser therapy
  capsulotomy, retinal detachment and, 363
  for cystoid macular edema, 143
Near-infrared fundus autofluorescence, 31
Near-infrared reflectance imaging, 30–31, 31*f*
Near periphery, 8
Necrotizing retinitis/retinopathy, herpetic, 201–202, 202*f*
Needle penetration/perforation of globe, 325, 362, 363*f*
Nematodes, diffuse unilateral subacute neuroretinitis
  caused by, 210
Neodymium:ytrium-aluminum-garnet laser. *See* Nd:YAG
  laser
Neonatal adrenoleukodystrophy, 250*t*, 254, 261, 261*f*
Neonates. *See also* Infants
  ERG in, 36
Neovascular glaucoma, central retinal vein occlusion
  and, 130
Neovascularization
  of anterior chamber angle, in diabetes mellitus, 108–109
  in branch retinal vein occlusion, 123
    photocoagulation for, 124–126, 125*f*
  in central retinal artery occlusion, 140
  in central retinal vein occlusion, 128, 130
    photocoagulation for, 132
  choroidal. *See* Choroidal neovascularization
  in diabetes mellitus, 105, 106*f*, 108–109. *See also*
    Diabetic retinopathy, proliferative

of iris (rubeosis iridis)
  in branch retinal vein occlusion, 124
  in central retinal artery occlusion, 140
  in central retinal vein occlusion, 128
    photocoagulation for, 132
  in diabetes mellitus, 108–109
  in ocular ischemic syndrome, 133, 134, 134*f*
  in ocular histoplasmosis syndrome, 80–83, 82*f*,
    351, 351*f*
  in ocular ischemic syndrome, 133, 134, 134*f*
  optic disc (NVD), in diabetic retinopathy, 105, 106*f*
  in pars planitis, 196
  peripheral retinal, 121, 122*t*
    vitreous hemorrhage and, 313, 314
  in punctate inner choroidopathy, 192
  in radiation retinopathy, 153, 153*f*
  in retinopathy of prematurity, 157, 163
  sea fan, in sickle cell disease, 119, 119*f*
Nephronophthisis, juvenile, retinal degeneration
  and, 254
Nephropathy, diabetic, glycemic control/diabetic
  retinopathy and, 94
Nerve fiber layer, 10, 11*f*, 12
  infarcts of. *See* Cotton-wool spots
Neurogenic muscle weakness/ataxia/retinitis pigmentosa
  (NARP) syndrome, 265
Neuromuscular disorders, pigmentary retinopathy and, 254
Neuronal ceroid lipofuscinosis, 251*t*, 254, 259–260
Neuroretinitis
  diffuse unilateral subacute (DUSN), 210–211
  idiopathic retinal vasculitis/aneurysms and
    (IRVAN), 141
Neuroretinopathy, acute macular, 193
Neurosensory retina, 8–13, 9*f*, 9*t*, 10*f*, 11*f*, 13*f*, 14*f*, 15*f*. *See
  also* Retina
Neurotomy, radial optic, for central retinal vein
  occlusion, 133
Neurotrophic factor, ciliary, for age-related macular
  degeneration, 63
Newborns. *See also* Infants
  ERG in, 36
NFL. *See* Nerve fiber layer
NIA imaging. *See* Near-infrared fundus autofluorescence
Niemann-Pick disease, 262, 263*f*
Night blindness
  in choroideremia, 242, 243
  congenital
    with normal fundi, 215–217, 216*f*, 217*f*
    with prominent fundus abnormality, 217–219,
      218*f*, 219*f*
    stationary, 215–217, 216*f*, 217*f*
      ERG patterns in, 36*f*, 216,
        217, 217*f*
  dark adaptometry in evaluation of, 46, 47*f*
  in gyrate atrophy, 244
Night-vision abnormalities, 215–219. *See also* Night
  blindness
NIR reflectance imaging. *See* Near-infrared reflectance
  imaging
Nonaccidental trauma. *See* Trauma, in children, shaking
  injury and
Non–contact lenses, for slit-lamp biomicroscopy, 19–20
Noncystic retinal tufts, 278, 279*f*
Nongeographic atrophy (degeneration), of retinal pigment
  epithelium, 58

Non–Hodgkin lymphoma, of CNS (intraocular
  lymphoma), 199, 199*f*
  central serous retinopathy differentiated from, 174
Nonperfused/ischemic central retinal vein occlusion, 127,
  128, 129*f*
Nonperfusion, capillary. *See* Retinal capillary
  nonperfusion
Nonproliferative diabetic retinopathy (NPDR). *See*
  Diabetic retinopathy, nonproliferative
Nonproliferative sickle cell retinopathy (NPSR). *See* Sickle
  cell retinopathy, nonproliferative
Nonrhegmatogenous retinal detachment. *See* Retinal
  detachment
Nonsteroidal anti-inflammatory drugs (NSAIDs), for
  cystoid macular edema, 143
Norrie disease, gene for, X-linked familial exudative
  retinopathy and, 311
North Carolina macular dystrophy, 245–246, 245*f*
NPDR. *See* Diabetic retinopathy, nonproliferative
NPSR. *See* Sickle cell retinopathy, nonproliferative
NR2E3 gene, in enhanced S-cone/blue-cone and
  Goldmann-Favre syndromes, 219, 248
Nuclear cataracts, postvitrectomy, 368
Nuclear layer
  inner, 10, 11*f*
  outer, 10, 11*f*
Nursing (breast feeding), fluorescein dye transmission to
  breast milk and, 25
Nutritional supplements
  in age-related macular degeneration
    management, 61–63
  in retinitis pigmentosa management, 231
NVD. *See* Optic disc (optic nerve head),
  neovascularization of
Nyctalopin, in congenital stationary night
  blindness, 216
Nystagmus
  in albinism, 258
  in color blindness, 215
NYX gene, in congenital stationary night
  blindness, 216

OA1 (albinism), 258*t*
OAT (ornithine aminotransferase) gene, mutations/
  defects of, in gyrate atrophy, 243
OCA1 (albinism), 258*t*
OCA2 (albinism), 258*t*
OCA2 gene (*P* gene), in albinism, 258*t*
OCA3 (albinism), 258*t*
OCA4 (albinism), 258*t*
Occlusive retinal disease
  arterial, 135–140
    branch retinal artery occlusion, 136–137, 136*f*, 137*f*
    capillary retinal arteriole occlusion, 135–136, 135*f*
    central retinal artery occlusion, 138–140, 138*f*, 139*f*
  ocular ischemic syndrome/retinopathy of carotid
    occlusive disease and, 133–135, 134*f*
  venous, 121–133. *See also* Retinal vein occlusion
    branch retinal vein occlusion, 121–127, 122*f*, 125*f*
    central retinal vein occlusion, 127–133, 127*f*, 128*f*,
      129*f*, 132*f*
Occupation, light toxicity and, 334
OCT. *See* Optical coherence tomography
Ocular albinism, 258, 258*t*
Ocular examination. *See* Examination

Ocular histoplasmosis syndrome, 80–83, 82f
   choroidal neovascularization in, management of,
      81–83, 351, 351f
   photocoagulation for, 340
Ocular ischemia (ocular ischemic syndrome), 94,
   133–135, 134f
Ocular (intraocular) surgery
   cystoid macular edema after, 360, 360f
   endophthalmitis after, 354–357, 355f, 356f, 357f
      acute-onset, 354, 354–356, 355f
      bleb-associated, 354, 356–357, 357f
      chronic (delayed-onset), 355, 356, 356f
   needle penetration/perforation of globe and, 325,
      362, 363f
   retinal detachment after, 314, 362–363, 363f
   suprachoroidal hemorrhage and, 360–361, 362f
   sympathetic ophthalmia and, 198
   vitrectomy for complications of, 354–362
Ocular trauma. See Trauma
Oculocutaneous albinism, 257–258, 258t, 259f
Oculodentodigital dysplasia/syndrome (Meyer-
      Schwickerath and Weyers syndrome), 250t
Oculodigital reflex, in Leber congenital amaurosis, 229
Oculoglandular syndrome, Parinaud, 206
Oguchi disease, 218, 219f
OHS. See Ocular histoplasmosis syndrome
Olivopontocerebellar atrophy, pigmentary retinopathy
      and, 250t, 254
Omega-3 fatty acid supplements
   age-related macular degeneration and, 62
   retinitis pigmentosa management and, 231
OMIM (Online Mendelian Inheritance in Man),
      221, 249
100-hue test (Farnsworth-Munsell), 48
ONL. See Outer nuclear layer
Online Mendelian Inheritance in Man (OMIM),
      221, 249
Opacities, vitreous, 311–314
   amyloidosis causing, 312–313, 313f
   in asteroid hyalosis, 311, 312f
   in cholesterolosis, 311–312
   hemorrhage causing, 313–314
   pigment granules and, 314
Open-angle glaucoma. See also Glaucoma
   central retinal vein occlusion and, 129
   vitrectomy and, 368
Operating microscope, phototoxicity and, 333
Operculated holes, 271
   treatment of, 283, 284t
Ophthalmia, sympathetic, 198–199, 329–330
Ophthalmic artery, occlusion of, 140
   chronic, ocular ischemic syndrome and, 133
Ophthalmic examination. See Examination
Ophthalmic instrumentation, phototoxicity
      from, 333–334
Ophthalmic vein, 18
Ophthalmoplegia, progressive (chronic progressive)
      external, 254
Ophthalmoscopy
   direct, in retinal examination, 19
   indirect
      in ocular trauma, 318
      in posterior vitreous detachment, 276
      in retinal examination, 19
      in retinopathy of prematurity, 164

laser, 29–30
   in fundus autofluorescence, 30
   in indocyanine green angiography, 25
OPL. See Outer plexiform layer
Optic atrophy, in cone dystrophies, 232
Optic disc (optic nerve head)
   avulsion of, 331–332, 331f
   cavernous hemangioma of, 151
   edema of
      in central retinal vein occlusion, 128
      in cystoid macular edema, 142
   neovascularization of (NVD), in diabetic retinopathy,
      105, 106f
   vasculitis of (papillophlebitis), 128
Optic nerve, avulsion of, 331–332, 331f
Optic neuropathy, hypertensive, 115, 117f
Optic neurotomy, radial, for central retinal vein
      occlusion, 133
Optic pits (optic nerve pits), 294–295, 295f
   central serous chorioretinopathy differentiated
      from, 174
Optical coherence tomography, 26–29, 27f, 28f
   in central serous chorioretinopathy, 173, 173f
   in cystoid macular edema, 142
   in epiretinal membrane, 300
   in idiopathic macular hole, 304, 305, 305–306f
   in posterior vitreous detachment, 298, 299f
   ranibizumab therapy for AMD guided by, 74–76
   in vitreomacular traction syndrome, 302, 346, 348f
Optotypes, for contrast sensitivity testing, 51–52, 51f
Ora bays, 8, 10f
   enclosed, 8, 280, 281f
Ora serrata, 8, 10f
Oral contraceptives, central retinal vein occlusion and, 129
Oral ulcers, in Behçet disease, 194
Orbit, trauma to, sclopetaria and, 323, 323f
Ornithine, elevated serum levels of, in gyrate atrophy,
      243, 244
Ornithine aminotransferase (OAT) gene mutations, in
      gyrate atrophy, 243
Oscillatory potentials, 34, 34f, 35
   vascular disease and, 40, 41f
Outer nuclear layer, 10, 11f
Outer plexiform layer, 10, 11f, 12
Outer segments, photoreceptor, 10, 11f, 12, 13f. See also
      Cone outer segments; Rod outer segments
   shed, retinal pigment epithelium phagocytosis of,
      12, 15
Oxygen therapy, retinopathy of prematurity and, 165–166

P gene (OCA2 gene), in albinism, 258t
Paget disease of bone, angioid streaks in, 84
Pancreatitis, Purtscherlike retinopathy and, 154, 155t
Panel D-15 (Farnsworth) test, 48–50, 49f
   in anomalous trichromatism, 214
Panel tests of color vision, 48–50, 49f
   in anomalous trichromatism, 213–214
Panophthalmitis, tuberculous, 204
Panretinal photocoagulation. See also Photocoagulation;
      Scatter laser treatment
   for branch retinal vein occlusion, 124–125, 125f
   for central retinal artery occlusion, 140
   for central retinal vein occlusion, 132
   for diabetic retinopathy, 106–108, 108f, 109f
      DRS/ETDRS, 107–108, 108f, 109f

indications for, 340
lenses for, 339, 340t
for lupus vasculitis, 195
for ocular ischemic syndrome, 134
Panuveitis, 196–199. *See also specific cause and* Uveitis
multifocal choroiditis and (MCP), 186t, 191–192, 191f
sarcoid, 196–197, 197f
sympathetic ophthalmia and, 198–199
in Vogt-Koyanagi-Harada (VKH) syndrome,
197–198, 198f
Papillae, Bergmeister, 307
Papillophlebitis, 128
Paracentral scotoma
in age-related macular degeneration, 64, 79
in central serous chorioretinopathy, 171
Parafovea, 8, 9f, 9t
Parafoveal/juxtafoveal retinal telangiectasia, 145–147,
145f, 146f
Paraneoplastic disorders
bilateral diffuse uveal melanocytic proliferation, 183, 183f
retinopathies, 256–257, 256f
Parinaud oculoglandular syndrome, 206
Pars plana magnet extraction, of foreign body, 327
Pars plana vitrectomy, 345–346. *See also* Vitrectomy
for branch retinal vein occlusion, 126
for choroidal neovascularization, 351, 351f
for CMV retinitis, 201
complications of, 368, 368t
for cystoid macular edema, 143
postoperative, 360, 360f
for diabetic retinopathy complications, 109–111,
352–353, 353f
macular edema, 103, 353
tractional retinal detachment, 110–111,
352–353, 353f
vitreous hemorrhage, 110, 352
for endophthalmitis
Aspergillus/mold, 204
Candida/yeast, 203
postoperative, 354–357, 355f, 356f, 357f
acute-onset, 354, 354–356, 355f
bleb-associated, 354, 356–357, 357f
chronic (delayed-onset), 355, 356, 356f
endophthalmitis after, 368
for epiretinal membranes, 301, 346, 347f, 348f
for foreign-body removal, 327
for idiopathic macular hole, 305–306, 349, 350f
for macular diseases, 346–352
open-angle glaucoma after, 368
for pars planitis, 196
for postoperative endophthalmitis, 354–357, 355f,
356f, 357f
for retained lens fragments after phacoemulsification,
357–359, 358t, 359f
for retinal detachment, 290
complex detachment, 367
in diabetes mellitus, 110–111, 352–353, 353f
for subfoveal choroidal neovascularization, 351, 351f
for submacular hemorrhage, 349–351, 350f
for suprachoroidal hemorrhage, 360–361, 362f
Pars planitis, 196
Patellar fossa, 7
Pathologic myopia, 85–87, 86f
age-related macular degeneration/choroidal
neovascularization and, 86–87

Patient education, in age-related macular degeneration, 60
Pattern dystrophies, 240–241, 240f, 241f
adult-onset foveomacular vitelliform, 237–238, 238f
age-related macular degeneration differentiated from,
60, 69
butterfly, 240, 240f
Pattern electroretinogram, 38–39, 39f
Pattern scanners, for photocoagulation, 340
Paving-stone (cobblestone) degeneration, 281–282, 281f
PCIOLs. *See* Posterior chamber intraocular lenses
PDR. *See* Diabetic retinopathy, proliferative
PDT. *See* Photodynamic therapy
Peau d'orange, in pseudoxanthoma elasticum, 84, 84f
PED (pigment epithelial detachment). *See* Retinal
pigment epithelium (RPE), detachment of
Pediatric electroretinogram, 40, 41f
Pegaptanib
for age-related macular degeneration/choroidal
neovascularization, 73
for diabetic macular edema, 100
Pelizaeus-Merzbacher disease, pigmentary retinopathy
and, 251t
Pelli-Robson chart/test, 51–52, 51f
Penetrating injuries, 324. *See also* Trauma
endophthalmitis after, 328–329
needle penetration/perforation and, 362, 363f
retinal breaks caused by, 272
sympathetic ophthalmia and, 198, 329–330
tractional retinal detachment and, 291, 324
Perfluoropropane (C_3F_8)
for retinal detachment, 367
for submacular hemorrhage, 350–351
Perforating injuries. *See also* Trauma
needle penetration/perforation and, 325, 362, 363f
posterior segment, 325
retinal breaks caused by, 272
Perfused/nonischemic central retinal vein occlusion, 127,
128, 128f
PERG. *See* Pattern electroretinogram
Periarteriolar transudates, focal intraretinal (FIPTs),
113, 114f
Perifovea, 8, 9f, 9t
Perifoveal telangiectasia (type 2 parafoveal retinal
telangiectasia), 14, 146f
Perifoveal vitreous detachment, posterior, 298
Perimetry
Goldmann
in hereditary retinal/choroidal degenerations, 223
in photoreceptor dystrophies, 223, 225f
kinetic
in hereditary retinal/choroidal degenerations, 223
in photoreceptor dystrophies, 223, 225f
Peripheral cystoid degeneration, 282
reticular, 282, 293
typical, 282, 292
Peripheral retina, 8
excavations of, 280
neovascularization of, 121, 122t
vitreous hemorrhage and, 313, 314
Peripheral retinal tufts, 278, 279f, 280f
Peripherin, 228
Peripherin/*RDS* gene mutations, 222
in adult-onset vitelliform lesions, 237
in central areolar choroidal dystrophy, 245
in pattern dystrophies, 240

in retinitis pigmentosa, 226, 228
in Stargardt disease, 234
Peroxisomal disorders, 261–262
pigmentary retinopathy in, 254, 261–262
Persistent fetal vasculature (persistent hyperplastic
primary vitreous), 307–309, 308f
Persistent hyaloid artery/system, 307, 308. *See also*
Persistent fetal vasculature
Personality/personality disorders, in central serous
chorioretinopathy, 172
PFV. *See* Persistent fetal vasculature
Phacoemulsification, retained lens fragments after,
357–359, 358t, 359f
Phagocytosis, by retinal pigment epithelium, 12, 15
Phakomatoses, 148–151, 149f, 150f, 152f. *See also specific
type*
Phenothiazines, retinal degeneration caused by,
267–268, 268f
Phosphenes, in electrically evoked cortical potential, 45
Photic damage/phototoxicity/light toxicity, 332–334
age-related macular degeneration and, 63
ambient exposure to ultraviolet or visible light and, 334
cataract surgery and, 333, 334
occupational, 334
ophthalmic instrumentation causing, 333–334
retinal, 332–334
in retinitis pigmentosa, 231
solar retinopathy and, 332–333
Photo-ROP Cooperative Group, 165
Photochemical injury, 332
laser effects/photocoagulation and, 339
occupational light toxicity and, 334
ophthalmic instrumentation causing, 333–334
in photodynamic therapy, 344
in solar retinopathy, 332–333
Photocoagulation, 337–343
for age-related macular degeneration, 71
ineffectiveness of, 63
anesthesia for, 339
for angioid streaks, 85
for branch retinal vein occlusion, 124–126, 125f
for central retinal artery occlusion, 140
for central retinal vein occlusion, 131–132
for central serous chorioretinopathy, 175, 176, 341
choroidal lesions caused by, 342
for choroidal neovascularization
in age-related macular degeneration, 63, 71, 340
in myopia, 86
in ocular histoplasmosis, 81–82
choroidal perfusion abnormalities caused by, 180
for clinically significant diabetic macular edema, 97,
98, 99f, 101–103, 102t
for Coats disease, 145
complications of, 341–343
for diabetic retinopathy
in nonproliferative retinopathy/macular edema, 97,
98, 99f, 101–103, 102t
in proliferative retinopathy, 106–108, 108f, 109f
for diffuse unilateral subacute neuroretinitis, 210
indications for, 340–341
laser wavelengths used in, 337–339
lenses for, 339, 340t
for lupus vasculitis, 195
for macroaneurysms, 148
for ocular histoplasmosis, 81–82

for ocular ischemic syndrome, 134
for parafoveal (juxtafoveal) retinal telangiectasia, 147
parameter settings for, 339
practical aspects of, 339–340, 340t
principles of, 337–343
prophylactic, in acute retinal necrosis, 202
for retinal angiomas, 150
for retinal breaks, 283
retinal/choroidal detachment caused by, 342, 342f
for retinopathy of prematurity, 167–168, 168f
for sickle cell retinopathy, 120–121
thermal light injury caused by, 332, 337
Photodynamic therapy, 343–344
for central serous chorioretinopathy, 175
for choroidal hemangioma, 182
for choroidal neovascularization, 71–72, 78,
79, 343–344
in age-related macular degeneration, 71–72, 78,
79, 344
angioid streaks and, 85
combination treatment and, 72, 78, 79
complications of, 344
in myopia, 86, 343
choroidal perfusion abnormalities caused by, 180
for retinal hemangioblastoma, 150
Photophobia
in albinism, 258
in cone dystrophies, 232
Photopic/light-adapted electroretinogram, 34, 34f,
35, 36f
in cone dystrophies, 232
in hereditary retinal/choroidal dystrophies, 224t
Photopsias
in posterior vitreous detachment, 275
in rhegmatogenous retinal detachment, 286
Photoreceptor dystrophies, 223–234. *See also* Cone
dystrophies/degenerations; Cone–rod dystrophies/
degenerations; Retinitis pigmentosa
Photoreceptor inner segments, 10, 11f, 13f. *See also*
Photoreceptors
Photoreceptor outer segments, 10, 11f, 12, 13f. *See also*
Photoreceptors
shed, retinal pigment epithelium phagocytosis of,
12, 15
Photoreceptors, 10–12, 11f. *See also* Cones; Rods
age-related changes in, 55
density/distribution of, 10
in macular degeneration, 57, 58, 64f, 66f
Photosensitivity, photodynamic therapy and, 344
PHPV (persistent hyperplastic primary vitreous). *See*
Persistent fetal vasculature
Phthisis bulbi (phthisical eye)
after penetrating injury, 324
retained foreign body and, 327
Phytanic acid storage disease. *See* Refsum disease/
syndrome
PIC. *See* Punctate inner choroidopathy
PIER study, 74, 75f
Pierre Robin malformation, Stickler syndrome
and, 310
PIGF. *See* Placental-like growth factor
Pigment, visual. *See* Pigments, visual
Pigment epithelium. *See* Retinal pigment epithelium
Pigment granules, in vitreous ("tobacco dust"/Shafer
sign), 286, 314

Pigmentary retinopathy, 223–224, 249. *See also* Retinitis pigmentosa
  in Bardet-Biedl syndrome, 250*t*, 252
  hearing loss and, 251*t*, 253
  in neuromuscular disorders, 254
  secondary/systemic disease and, 224, 249, 250–251*t*
  X-linked, 251*t*
Pigmentations/pigment deposits, retinal/retinal pigment epithelium, 249. *See also* Pigmentary retinopathy
  in age-related macular degeneration, 58
Pigments, visual, 15
  absorption spectra of, 337, 338*f*
Pits, optic (optic nerve pits), 294–295, 295*f*
  central serous chorioretinopathy differentiated from, 174
Placental-like growth factor, in VEGF Trap mechanism of action, 77
Planoconcave lenses
  for slit-lamp biomicroscopy, 20
  for slit-lamp delivery of photocoagulation, 339
Plaques
  Hollenhorst (cholesterol emboli)
    in branch retinal artery occlusion, 136, 137*f*
    in central retinal artery occlusion, 139
    in indocyanine green angiography, 25
Plasma (ions/electrons), mechanical light injury and, 332
Plexiform layer
  inner, 10, 11*f*, 12
  outer, 10, 11*f*, 12
Plus disease, retinopathy of prematurity and, 160, 161*f*
Plus-power lenses
  for slit-lamp biomicroscopy, 19–20
  for slit-lamp delivery of photocoagulation, 339
Pneumatic retinopexy, for retinal detachment, 290, 364–365, 365*f*
POHS. *See* Presumed ocular histoplasmosis syndrome
Polyarteritis nodosa, choroidal perfusion abnormalities and, 179
Polydactyly, in Bardet-Biedl syndrome, 252, 252*f*
Polypoidal choroidal vasculopathy (posterior uveal bleeding syndrome)
  age-related macular degeneration differentiated from, 69–70, 70*f*
  central serous chorioretinopathy differentiated from, 174, 175
Polyposis, familial adenomatous (Gardner syndrome), retinal manifestations of, 255, 255*f*
Pooling, fluorescein, 23, 24*f*
  in central serous chorioretinopathy, 23, 24*f*, 172, 173*f*
  in cystoid macular edema, 142, 142*f*
PORN. *See* Progressive outer retinal necrosis
Posterior chamber intraocular lenses, dislocated, 359–360
Posterior ciliary arteries, 12, 17, 17*f*
Posterior pole, 9*f*, 9*t*. *See also* Macula
  in uveal effusion syndrome, 182
Posterior segment
  complications of anterior segment surgery and, vitrectomy for, 354–362
  hereditary dystrophies of, 221–248. *See also* Hereditary dystrophies
  trauma to, 317–334. *See also* Trauma
    blunt trauma, 318–323, 320*f*, 321–322*f*, 322*f*, 323*f*
    child abuse and, 330–331, 330*f*
    endophthalmitis and, 328–329

    foreign bodies, 325–328, 326*f*, 328*t*
    lacerating and penetrating injuries, 324
    optic disc avulsion and, 331–332, 331*f*
    patient evaluation after, 317–318
    perforating injuries, 325
    photic damage and, 332–334
    shaken baby syndrome and, 330–331, 330*f*
    sympathetic ophthalmia and, 329–330
Posterior uveal bleeding syndrome (polypoidal choroidal vasculopathy)
  age-related macular degeneration differentiated from, 69–70, 70*f*
  central serous chorioretinopathy differentiated from, 174, 175
Posterior vitreous detachment, 200*f*, 274–276, 274*f*, 275*f*, 297–306, 299*f*, 301*f*, 362
  in diabetic retinopathy, 110
  epiretinal membranes and, 298–301, 302*f*
  macular holes and, 298, 304–306, 305–306*f*
  perifoveal, 298
  vitreomacular traction syndrome and, 298, 302–304, 303*f*
  vitreous hemorrhage and, 275, 313
Postoperative endophthalmitis, 354–357, 355*f*, 356*f*, 357*f*
  acute-onset, 354, 354–356, 355*f*
  bleb-associated, 354, 356–357, 357*f*
  chronic (delayed-onset), 355, 356, 356*f*
  after vitrectomy, 368
  vitrectomy for, 354–357, 355*f*, 356*f*, 357*f*
Posttraumatic endophthalmitis, 328–329
Posttraumatic macular hole, 321–322, 322*f*
Postvitrectomy cataract, 368
Potentials, cortical, 44–45, 45*f*
  electrically evoked, 45
  visually evoked, 44–45, 45*f*
Precortical vitreous pocket, 7*f*, 8
Prednisone, for toxoplasmosis, 208–209, 208*t*
Preeclampsia, choroidal perfusion abnormalities and, 178*f*
Pregnancy
  diabetic retinopathy affected by, 94
    timetable for ophthalmic examination and, 111, 112*t*
  fluorescein angiography during, 25
  toxoplasmosis during, 206–207
Prehypertension, 113
Premacular bursa, 7*f*, 8
Premacular hole, 304
Prematurity, retinopathy of. *See* Retinopathy, of prematurity
Preoperative preparation for photocoagulation, 341
Prepapillary vascular loops, 307, 307*f*
Preretinal macular fibrosis, 300
Preretinal tract, 8
Presumed ocular histoplasmosis syndrome, 80–83, 82*f*
Primary vitreous, persistent hyperplasia of. *See* Persistent fetal vasculature
Progressive (chronic progressive) external ophthalmoplegia, 254
Progressive outer retinal necrosis (PORN), 201
Proliferative diabetic retinopathy (PDR). *See* Diabetic retinopathy, proliferative
Proliferative sickle cell retinopathy (PSR). *See* Sickle cell retinopathy, proliferative
Proliferative vitreoretinopathy, 286–288, 289*f*, 289*t*
PrONTO study, 76–77

Propionibacterium acnes, endophthalmitis caused by, 354, 356
Prostaglandin analogues, cystoid macular edema and, 143
Protan defects (protanopia), 47, 49, 49*f*, 50, 213
Protanomalous dichromatism, 214*t*
Protanomalous trichromatism, 213, 214*t*
PRP. *See* Panretinal photocoagulation
Pseudocyst, foveal, 304, 305*f*
Pseudoisochromatic plates, 48, 48*f*
Pseudophakia, prophylactic treatment of retinal breaks and, 285
Pseudoxanthoma elasticum
    angioid streaks in, 84, 84*f*
    Bruch membrane affected in, 17
    peau d'orange fundus changes in, 84, 84*f*
PSR. *See* Sickle cell retinopathy, proliferative
Psychophysical testing, 33, 45–52. *See also specific test*
Punctate inner choroidopathy (PIC), 186*t*, 192, 192*f*
Pupillary block, retinopathy of prematurity and, 163
Pupils, dilation of. *See* Mydriasis/mydriatics
Purpura, thrombotic thrombocytopenic, choroidal perfusion abnormalities and, 179
Purtscher/Purtscherlike retinopathy, 154–155, 154*f*, 155*t*
PVD. *See* Posterior vitreous detachment
PVR. *See* Vitreoretinopathies, proliferative
PXE. *See* Pseudoxanthoma elasticum
Pyridoxine (vitamin B₆), for gyrate atrophy, 244
Pyrimethamine, for toxoplasmosis, 208–209, 208*t*

Rab escort protein *(CHM)* gene mutation, in choroideremia, 242
Race
    central serous chorioretinopathy and, 171
    sickle cell hemoglobinopathies and, 116
Racemose angioma/hemangioma (Wyburn-Mason syndrome), 151
Radial optic neurotomy, for central retinal vein occlusion, 133
Radial peripapillary network, 12
Radiation retinopathy, 151–153, 153*f*
RADICAL (Reduced Fluence Visudyne Anti-VEGF-Dexamethasone in Combination for AMD Lesions) study, 78
Radioactive plaque therapy (brachytherapy), retinopathy after, 151–153, 153*f*
Radiography, in foreign-body identification, 325–326
Ragged red fibers, 265
Ranibizumab
    for age-related macular degeneration/choroidal neovascularization, 73–77, 75*f*, 87–88
        combination treatment and, 78, 79
    for branch retinal vein occlusion, 127
    for central retinal vein occlusion, 131
    for diabetic macular edema, 100, 101*f*
Ranibizumab for Edema of the Macula in Diabetes 2 (READ-2) trial, 100, 101*f*
Rapid plasma reagin (RPR) test, in syphilitic chorioretinitis, 205
RDS/peripherin gene mutations, 222
    in adult-onset vitelliform lesions, 237
    in central areolar choroidal dystrophy, 245
    in pattern dystrophies, 240
    in retinitis pigmentosa, 226, 228
    in Stargardt disease, 234

READ-2 (Ranibizumab for Edema of the Macula in Diabetes 2) trial, 100, 101*f*
Reattachment surgery. *See* Retinal detachment, surgery for
Recoverin (CAR antigen), 256, 257
Red-green color vision defects, 47, 49*t*
    testing for, 47, 50
Red infarct, 147–148
Red lasers, 338
Reduced Fluence Visudyne Anti-VEGF-Dexamethasone in Combination for AMD Lesions (RADICAL) study, 78
Reflectance imaging, infrared/near-infrared, 30–31, 31*f*
Refractile bodies/spots
    in parafoveal/juxtafoveal retinal telangiectasia, 145, 146*f*
    in sickle cell retinopathy, 118, 118*f*, 119*f*
Refractile drusen, 59
Refsum disease (phytanic acid storage disease), 251*t*, 254, 261–262, 261*f*
    ichthyosis and, 255
    infantile, 261
    pigmentary retinopathy and, 251*t*, 254, 261–262, 262*f*
Regressed drusen, 59
Renal disease
    congenital, retinal degeneration and, 254
    diabetic retinopathy and, 94
    fluorescein angiography in patient with, 25
Renal–retinal dysplasias, 254
Retained lens material, cataract surgery and, 357–359, 358*t*, 359*f*
Reticular degenerative retinoschisis, 293–294
Reticular dystrophy, 240, 241*f*
Reticular peripheral cystoid degeneration, 282, 293
Reticulum cell sarcoma. *See* Intraocular lymphoma
Retina
    amyloidosis affecting, 312
    anatomy of, 8–13, 9*f*, 9*t*, 10*f*, 11*f*, 13*f*, 14*f*, 15*f*
    angiography in examination of, 20–26, 23*f*, 24*f*
    arteriovenous anastomoses/malformations in, 151
    blood supply of, 12, 15*f*
        angiography and, 21–22, 23*f*, 24*f*
    capillary hemangioblastoma of, 148–151, 149*f*, 150*f*
    cavernous hemangioma of, 151, 152*f*
    congenital disorders of, 213–219
    contrast sensitivity in disorders of, 50
    degenerations of. *See* Retinal degenerations
    detachment of. *See* Retinal detachment
    diabetes affecting. *See* Diabetic retinopathy
    dystrophies of. *See* Retinal dystrophies
    electrophysiology of, 33–45. *See also specific test*
    equatorial, 8
    examination of, 19–20
    fleck, of Kandori, 218
    gyrate atrophy of, 243–244, 244*f*
    imaging techniques in evaluation of
        angiography, 20–26, 23*f*, 24*f*
        fundus autofluorescence, 22, 30
            near-infrared, 31
        infrared reflectance imaging, 30–31, 31*f*
        OCT, 26–29, 27*f*, 28*f*
        scanning laser ophthalmoscopy, 29–30
    infection/inflammation of, 185–211. *See also specific disease and* Retinitis
    layers of, 10, 11*f*

mechanical injury of, light causing, 332
necrosis of
    acute, 201–202, 202f
    progressive outer, 201
neovascularization of
    disorders of, in retinopathy of prematurity,
        157, 163
    peripheral, 121, 122t
        vitreous hemorrhage and, 313, 314
neurosensory, 8–13, 9f, 9t, 10f, 11f, 13f, 14f, 15f
    vascular elements of, 12, 15f
OCT in examination of, 26–29, 27f, 28f
peripheral (anterior), 8
photic injury of, 332–334
    in retinitis pigmentosa, 231
photochemical injury of, 332
    occupational light toxicity and, 334
    ophthalmic instrumentation causing, 333–334
    in photodynamic therapy, 344
    in solar retinopathy, 332–333
photocoagulation causing lesions of, 342
physiology and psychophysics of, 33–52
radiation affecting, 151–153, 153f
scanning laser ophthalmoscopy in evaluation of,
    29–30
systemic disease affecting, 249–270, 250–251t
in systemic lupus erythematosus, 195–196, 195f
thermal injury of, light causing, 332
thickness of, mapping with OCT, 28f, 29
vitreous attachment to, 7f, 8
    posterior vitreous detachment and, 274–276, 274f,
        275f, 297–306, 362
Retinal angiography, 20–26, 23f, 24f. See also Fluorescein
    angiography; Indocyanine green angiography
Retinal angiomatosis (von Hippel/von Hippel–Lindau
    disease), 148–151, 149f, 150f
Retinal arteriole obstruction, capillary, 135–136, 135f. See
    also Cotton-wool spots
Retinal artery
    central, 12, 135
        angiography and, 21
    macroaneurysms of, 147–148, 147f
        age-related macular degeneration differentiated
            from, 68–69, 69f
    microaneurysms of, in diabetes mellitus
        in diabetic macular ischemia, 103
        in nonproliferative diabetic retinopathy, 104, 104f
    occlusion of. See Retinal artery occlusion
Retinal artery occlusion, 135–140
    branch, 136–137, 136f, 137f
    central, 138–140, 138f, 139f
        ERG in evaluation of, 40f
    in sickle cell hemoglobinopathies, 119
Retinal blood vessels, 12, 15f
    angiography and, 21–22, 23f, 24f
Retinal breaks, 271–274, 273f. See also Retinal tears
    in acute retinal necrosis/herpetic retinitis, 201
    asymptomatic, treatment of, 284, 284t
    lattice degeneration and, 276
        treatment of, 283, 284–285, 284t
    management of, 289–290, 290f
    paving-stone (cobblestone) degeneration and, 282
    photocoagulation for, 283
    in posterior vitreous detachment, 298, 362
    prophylactic treatment of, 282–285, 284t

retinal detachment and, 271, 286, 288f, 289f, 362, 363f
    prophylaxis of, 282–285, 284t
    symptomatic, treatment of, 283–284, 284t
    traumatic, 272–274, 273f
    vitreous hemorrhage and, 313
    vitreous traction and, 274, 275f
Retinal capillary nonperfusion
    in Coats disease, 143, 144f
    in diabetic retinopathy, 90, 91f, 103
    in radiation retinopathy, 152, 153f
Retinal degenerations. See also specific type and
    Pigmentary retinopathy; Retinal dystrophies
    in Bardet-Biedl syndrome, 250t, 252–253, 252f
    in cancer, 256–257, 256f
    in dermatologic disease, 255
    drug toxicity and, 266–270, 266f, 268f, 269t
    ERG in evaluation of, 39–41, 40f, 41f
    in gastrointestinal disease, 255, 255f
    hearing loss and, 251t, 253
    infantile to early childhood–onset, 251–252
    lattice, 276–278, 277f, 278f
        in hereditary hyaloideoretinopathies with optically
            empty vitreous, 309, 309f
        treatment of, 283, 284–285, 284t
    in metabolic diseases, 257–265
    in neuromuscular disorders, 254
    paving-stone (cobblestone), 281–282, 281f
    peripheral cystoid, 282
        reticular, 282, 293
        typical, 282, 292
    renal disease and, 254
    retinal pigment epithelium and, 58
    systemic disease and, 249–270, 250–251t
Retinal detachment, 286–292, 287t, 362–368
    in acute retinal necrosis/herpetic retinitis, 201–202
    after blunt trauma, in young patient, 272–273
    in branch retinal vein occlusion, 123
    after cataract surgery, 314, 362–363, 363f
        Nd:YAG laser capsulotomy and, 363
        retained lens material and, 357, 358
    in central serous chorioretinopathy, 171, 172–173, 173f
    choroidal perfusion abnormalities and, 176, 178f, 179
    classification of, 286, 287t
    in CMV retinitis, 201
    in Coats disease, 143, 144, 144f
    COL2A1 gene and, 310
    complex, 367
    in diabetic retinopathy, 110–111, 191, 352–353, 353f
    diagnostic features of, 287t
    differential diagnosis of, 286, 292–294, 293f, 294t
    enclosed ora bays and, 280
    exudative, 286, 287t, 291–292, 292f
        in Coats disease, 143, 144, 144f, 292
        photocoagulation causing, 342
    familial exudative vitreoretinopathy and, 311
    fellow eye in patient with, 285
    in intraocular lymphoma, 199
    lattice degeneration and, 276–278, 278f
        treatment of, 283, 284–285, 284t
    lesions not predisposing to, 281–282, 281f
    lesions predisposing to, 276–280, 277f, 278f, 279f,
        280f, 281f
    management of, 289–291, 290f, 362–368, 363f,
        365f, 366f
    meridional folds and, 280

after Nd:YAG laser capsulotomy, 363
nonrhegmatogenous (secondary), 286, 287*t*
in pars planitis, 196
peripheral retinal excavations and, 280
pneumatic retinopexy for, 290, 364–365, 365*f*
posterior vitreous detachment and, 274, 275*f*, 362
postoperative, 314, 362–363, 363*f*
proliferative vitreoretinopathy and, 286–288, 289*f*, 289*t*
in punctate inner choroidopathy, 192, 192*f*
in retinal angiomatosis 148–149, 149*f*
retinal breaks and, 271, 286, 288*f*, 289*f*, 362, 363*f*
in retinopathy of prematurity, 157, 158, 160*f*, 163, 164
retinoschisis and, 294, 294*t*
rhegmatogenous, 286, 286–291, 287*t*, 288*f*, 289*f*,
    289*t*, 290*f*
    management of, 289–291, 290*f*, 362–368, 363*f*,
        365*f*, 366*f*
    in retinopathy of prematurity, 164
scleral buckle for, 289–290, 290*f*, 365, 366*f*
    sickle cell retinopathy and, 121
secondary (nonrhegmatogenous), 286, 287*t*
in sickle cell retinopathy, 119, 119*f*, 121
    vitreoretinal surgery for, 121
Stickler syndrome and, 310
subclinical, 285
surgery for, 289–291, 290*f*, 362–368, 363*f*, 365*f*, 366*f*
    anatomical reattachment, 290–291
    pneumatic retinopexy, 290, 364–365, 365*f*
    primary vitrectomy, 290, 291, 366–368, 366*f*
    in retinopathy of prematurity, 170
    scleral buckle, 289–290, 290*f*, 365, 366*f*
    techniques for, 364–368
    visual acuity after, 291
tractional, 286, 287*t*, 291, 362
    in diabetic retinopathy, 110–111, 191, 352–353, 353*f*
    in pars planitis, 196
    after penetrating injury, 191, 324
    in retinopathy of prematurity, 157, 163
traumatic, 291
    in young patient, 272–273
vitrectomy for, 290, 291, 366–368, 366*f*
    in diabetes mellitus, 110–111, 352–353, 353*f*
vitreoretinal tufts and, 278
vitreous hemorrhage and, 313, 314
in young patient, 272–273
Retinal dialyses, 271, 272, 273*f*
    treatment of, 284*t*
Retinal disease
    angiography in, 20–26, 23*f*, 24*f*. See also Fluorescein
        angiography; Indocyanine green angiography
    chloroquine/hydroxychloroquine toxicity and, 38*f*,
        266–270, 266*f*, 268*f*, 269*t*
    color vision/color vision testing and, 46–50, 48*f*, 49*f*
    congenital, 213–219
    contrast sensitivity testing and, 50–52, 51*f*
    cortical evoked potentials in, 44–45, 45*f*
    dark adaptation testing in, 46, 47*f*
    degenerative. See Retinal degenerations
    in diabetes. See Diabetic retinopathy
    diagnostic approach to, 19–32
    electrically evoked potentials in, 45
    electro-oculogram in, 42–44, 42*f*, 43*f*
    electrophysiologic testing in, 33–45. See also specific test
    ERG in, 33, 33–41
    evoked cortical potentials in, 44–45, 45*f*

inflammatory, 185–211. See also specific disorder and
    Retinitis
    infectious, 200–211
    noninfectious, 185–199
in metabolic disorders, 257–265
OCT in, 26–29, 27*f*, 28*f*
photocoagulation causing, 342
psychophysical testing in, 33, 45–52. See also specific
    test
scanning laser ophthalmoscopy in, 29–30
stationary, 213–219
vascular, 89–112, 113–155. See also specific type
    arterial occlusion, 135–140. See also Retinal artery
        occlusion
    Behçet disease and, 194–195
    carotid occlusive disease and, 133–135, 134*f*
    Coats disease and, 143–145, 144*f*
    cystoid macular edema and, 142–143, 142*f*
    in diabetes. See Diabetic retinopathy
    ERG in evaluation of, 40, 41*f*
    hypertension and, 113–115, 114*f*, 116*f*, 117*f*
    lupus vasculitis, 195–196, 195*f*
    macroaneurysms, 147–148, 147*f*
        age-related macular degeneration differentiated
            from, 68–69, 69*f*
    microaneurysms, in diabetes mellitus
        in diabetic macular ischemia, 103
        in nonproliferative diabetic retinopathy,
            104, 104*f*
    ocular ischemic syndrome, 133–135, 134*f*
    parafoveal (juxtafoveal) telangiectasia, 145–147,
        145*f*, 146*f*
    peripheral neovascularization and, 121, 122*t*
    phakomatoses, 148–151, 149*f*, 150*f*, 152*f*
    Purtscher/Purtscherlike retinopathy, 154–155,
        154*f*, 155*t*
    radiation retinopathy, 151–153, 153*f*
    in sickle cell retinopathy, 115–121, 117*t*, 118*f*,
        119*f*, 120*f*
    Terson syndrome, 155
    Valsalva retinopathy, 153–154
    vasculitis and, 140–141, 141*f*
    venous occlusion, 121–133. See also Retinal vein
        occlusion
visually evoked potentials in, 44–45, 45*f*
Retinal dystrophies. See also specific type and Retinal
    degenerations
    ERG in evaluation of, 39–41, 40*f*, 41*f*
    hereditary, 221–248
        diagnostic and prognostic testing in, 223, 224*t*
        inner, 246–248
        photoreceptor, 223–234
Retinal edema
    in branch retinal artery occlusion, 136
    in central retinal artery occlusion, 138, 138*f*
    in central retinal vein occlusion, 128, 129*f*
    in clinically significant diabetic macular edema, 7, 99*f*
    cystoid macular edema, 142–143, 142*f*
Retinal excavations, peripheral, 280
Retinal hemorrhages
    in arterial macroaneurysms, 147–148
    in branch retinal vein occlusion, 123
    in central retinal vein occlusion, 128, 128*f*, 129*f*
    in diabetic retinopathy, 104, 104*f*
    in ocular ischemic syndrome, 133, 134*f*

in shaking injury, 330, 330*f*, 331
in Terson syndrome, 155
Retinal holes
    atrophic, 271
        lattice degeneration and, 278, 278*f*
            treatment of, 284–285, 284*t*
        treatment of, 283, 284, 284*t*
    lattice degeneration and, 276, 277*f*, 278, 278*f*
    operculated, 271
        treatment of, 283, 284*t*
    photocoagulation causing, 342
    retinal breaks and, 271
Retinal neovascularization
    peripheral, 121, 122*t*
        vitreous hemorrhage and, 313, 314
    in retinopathy of prematurity, 157, 163
Retinal pigment epithelium (RPE), 14–16, 16*f*
    age-related changes in, 55
    in age-related macular degeneration, 57, 58–59, 59*f*
    anatomy of, 14–16, 16*f*
    angiography and, 21
    atrophy of, 58–59, 59*f*, 243–244, 244*f*
        photocoagulation and, 342
    in choroideremia, 242–243, 243*f*
    degeneration of, 58
    detachment of
        in age-related macular degeneration/choroidal
            neovascularization, 57, 66–67
        in central serous chorioretinopathy, 23, 24*f*, 171,
            173, 174
        choroidal neovascularization and, 65
        drusenoid, 57, 238, 239*f*
        fibrovascular, 66–67
        multiple recurrent serosanguineous (polypoidal
            choroidal vasculopathy)
            age-related macular degeneration differentiated
                from, 69–70, 70*f*
            central serous retinopathy differentiated from,
                174, 175
    dystrophies of, age-related macular degeneration
        differentiated from, 60, 69
    electro-oculogram and, 42–44, 42*f*, 43*f*
    fundus autofluorescence in evaluation of, 30
    geographic atrophy of, 58–59, 59*f*
        patient education/follow-up and, 60
    in gyrate atrophy, 243–244, 244*f*
    hyperpigmentation of, in age-related macular
        degeneration, 58
    hyperplasia of, 282
    hypertrophy of, 282
        congenital, 255*f*, 282
    inflammation of (acute retinal pigment epitheliitis/
        ARPE/Krill disease), 193–194
    nongeographic atrophy (degeneration) of, 58
    phagocytosis by, 12, 15
    in Stargardt disease, 234, 235*f*
Retinal sclopetaria, 323, 323*f*
Retinal striae, 300
Retinal tears. *See also* Retinal breaks
    COL2A1 gene and, 310
    enclosed ora bays and, 280
    flap (horseshoe), 271, 272, 273*f*
        treatment of, 283, 284, 284*t*
    giant, 271
        retained lens fragments after phacoemulsification
            and, 358

lattice degeneration and, 278, 278*f*
    treatment of, 283, 284–285, 285*t*
    meridional folds and, 10*f*, 280
    paving-stone (cobblestone) degeneration and, 282
    retinal breaks and, 271
    Stickler syndrome and, 310
    vitreous traction and, 274, 275*f*
Retinal telangiectasia, 143–145, 144*f. See also* Coats
    disease
    parafoveal (juxtafoveal), 145–147, 145*f*, 146*f*
Retinal thickness map, OCT producing, 28*f*, 29
Retinal tufts, 278, 279*f*, 280*f*
Retinal vasculitis, 140–141, 141*f*
    in Behçet disease, 194–195
    inflammatory, 194–196
    in systemic lupus erythematosus, 195–196, 195*f*
Retinal vein occlusion, 121–133
    branch, 121–127, 122*f*, 125*f*
        evaluation/management of, 124–127, 125*f*
        neovascularization in, 123
        risk factors for, 123
        visual prognosis in, 123
    central, 127–133, 127*f*, 128*f*, 129*f*, 132*f*
        cilioretinal artery occlusion and, 137–138
        ERG in, 40, 41*f*, 128
        evaluation and management of, 130–131
        iris neovascularization in, 128–129
            photocoagulation for, 132
        ischemic/nonperfused, 127, 128, 129*f*
        nonischemic/perfused, 127, 128, 128*f*
        risk factors for, 129–130
        treatment of, 131–133, 132*f*
    hemispheric (hemicentral), 127, 127*f*
Retinaldehyde, in retinal pigment epithelium, 15
Retinitis
    CMV, 200–201, 200*f*
    foveomacular (solar retinopathy/retinitis), 332–333
    herpetic, necrotizing, 201–202, 202*f*
    pigmentosa. *See* Retinitis pigmentosa
    punctata albescens, 218, 226, 226*f*
    solar (solar retinopathy/foveomacular
        retinitis), 332–333
Retinitis pigmentosa, 223–232
    autosomal dominant, 228
    autosomal recessive, 228
    cataract/cataract surgery in patients with, 225–226, 230
    central, 228
    clinical features of, 225–227, 225*f*, 226*f*
    congenital/infantile/childhood (Leber congenital
        amaurosis), 229, 251–252
    contrast sensitivity testing in, 50
    counseling patients with, 229–230
    cystoid macular edema and, 225, 230, 230*f*
    definition of, 223–224
    diagnosis of, 225–227, 225*f*, 226*f*
    differential diagnosis of, 227
    ERG in, 40*f*, 226
    genetics of, 228–229
    hearing loss and, 253. *See also* Usher syndrome
    management/therapy of, 229–232, 230*f*
    multiplex, 228
    with neuropathy and ataxia, 265
    pericentral, 228
    primary, 224
    regional variants of, 227–228, 227*f*
    sectorial, 227–228, 227*f*

simplex, 227
sine pigmento, 225, 225f
unilateral, 228
visual field testing/defects in, 226, 228
X-linked, 228, 229
    ocular findings in carriers of, 226, 228
Retinoblastoma, persistent fetal vasculature differentiated
    from, 308
Retinochoroiditis, *Toxoplasma* causing, 206–209, 208f, 208t
Retinochoroidopathies, birdshot (vitiliginous
    chorioretinitis), 186t, 190–191, 190f
Retinoid inhibitors, for age-related macular
    degeneration, 63
Retinopathy
    acute zonal occult outer (AZOOR), 186t, 192–193, 192f
    autoimmune, 256
    cancer-associated, 256–257, 256f
    canthaxanthine, 268f, 269
    of carotid occlusive disease, 133–135, 134f
        central retinal vein occlusion differentiated from,
            130, 133
    central serous, 171–176, 173f
        age-related macular degeneration differentiated
            from, 60, 70, 71f
        fluorescein angiography in, 23, 24f, 172–173, 173f
        photocoagulation for, 175, 176, 341
    in child abuse, 331
    chloroquine/hydroxychloroquine causing, 38f,
        266–270, 266f, 268f, 269t
    crystalline, 268–269, 268f, 269t
        Bietti, 250t
        drug toxicity causing, 268–269, 268f, 269t
    diabetic. See Diabetic retinopathy
    drug-related, 266–270, 266f, 268f, 269t
    eclipse (solar), 332–333
    exudative, retinopathy of prematurity and, 164
    hemorrhagic (severe/ischemic CRVO), 127, 128, 129f
    hypertensive, 113–114, 114f, 116f
    hyperviscosity, central retinal vein occlusion
        differentiated from, 129–130
    isotretinoin, 269
    melanoma-associated, 256, 257
    in ocular ischemic syndrome, 133–135, 134f
    paraneoplastic, 256–257, 256f
    pigmentary, 223–224, 249. See also Retinitis
        pigmentosa
        in Bardet-Biedl syndrome, 250t, 252
        hearing loss and, 251t, 253
        in neuromuscular disorders, 254
        secondary/systemic disease and, 224, 249, 250–251t
        X-linked, 251t
    of prematurity, 157–170
        classification of, 157–160, 158t, 159f, 160f
        conditions associated with, 163–164
        epidemiology of, 157
        extent of involvement and, 160, 161f
        familial exudative vitreoretinopathy and, 310
        fundus photography/screening in, 164, 165
        glaucoma and, 163
        management of, 166–170
        natural course of, 163
        pathogenesis of, 162–164
        prevention/risk factors for, 165–166
        screening examinations for, 164–165
        sequelae and complications of, 163–164
        stages of, 158–160, 158t, 159f, 160f

terminology used with, 160–161, 161f
        zones of involvement and, 158, 158t, 159f, 161
    Purtscher/Purtscherlike, 154–155, 154f, 155t
    radiation, 151–153, 153f
    in shaken baby syndrome, 331
    sickle cell. See Sickle cell retinopathy
    solar (foveomacular/solar retinitis), 332–333
    surface-wrinkling, 300
    tamoxifen, 268, 268f
    thioridazine, 267–268, 268f
    Valsalva, 153–154
    venous stasis, 127, 128, 128f
    vitamin A deficiency, 260–261
Retinopexy, pneumatic, for retinal detachment, 290,
    364–365, 365f
Retinoschisin, in X-linked retinoschisis, 247
Retinoschisis, 246, 292–294, 293f, 294t
    reticular degenerative, 293–294
    retinal detachment and, 294, 294t
    typical degenerative, 293, 293f
    X-linked (congenital/juvenile), 246–247, 246f
        ERG in, 36f, 247
RetNet website, 221, 228, 233, 253
Retrolental fibroplasia. See Retinopathy, of prematurity
Rhegmatogenous posterior vitreous detachment, 297. See
    also Posterior vitreous detachment
Rhegmatogenous retinal detachment. See Retinal
    detachment
Rheopheresis (differential membrane filtration), for
    nonneovascular age-related macular degeneration,
    ineffectiveness of, 63
Rhodopsin gene mutations, 222
    in congenital stationary night blindness, 215
    in retinitis pigmentosa, 228, 231
Rifabutin, uveitis caused by, 269
RLF (retrolental fibroplasia). See Retinopathy, of
    prematurity
Rod–cone dystrophies/degenerations. See also Retinitis
    pigmentosa
    choroideremia as, 242
    ERG patterns in, 36f
    visual field testing in, 223
Rod inner segments, 10, 11f, 13f
Rod monochromatism, 214t, 215
Rod outer segments, 10, 11f, 12, 13f. See also Rods
    shed, retinal pigment epithelium phagocytosis of, 12, 15
Rod response, 33, 34f, 35, 36f. See also Dark adaptation
    testing
Rods, 10, 12, 13f, 14f
    abnormalities of, 215–219. See also Night blindness
ROP. See Retinopathy, of prematurity
RP. See Retinitis pigmentosa
RP12 phenotype, 229
RPE. See Retinal pigment epithelium
RPR (rapid plasma reagin) test, in syphilitic
    chorioretinitis, 205
RRD (rhegmatogenous retinal detachment). See Retinal
    detachment
RS1 gene, in X-linked retinoschisis, 247
Rubeosis iridis (iris neovascularization)
    in branch retinal vein occlusion, 124
    in central retinal artery occlusion, 140
    in central retinal vein occlusion, 128–129
        photocoagulation for, 132
    in diabetes mellitus, 108–109
    in ocular ischemic syndrome, 133, 134, 134f

Ruby laser, photocoagulation for central serous chorioretinopathy with, 175
Rush (plus) disease, retinopathy of prematurity and, 160, 161*f*

S cones, enhanced, 218–219, 219*f*, 248
SAILOR trial, 77
Salmon patch hemorrhages, in sickle cell disease, 118, 118*f*, 119*f*
Sandhoff disease (GM₂ gangliosidosis type II), cherry-red spot in, 262
Sandwich technique, 343
Sanfilippo syndrome, 250*t*, 262
Sarcoidosis, panuveitis and, 196–197, 197*f*
Sarcoma, reticulum cell. *See* Intraocular lymphoma
Sattler layer, 17
SCA7 gene, cone–rod dystrophy and, 233
Scanning laser ophthalmoscopy (SLO), 29–30
  in fundus autofluorescence, 30
  in indocyanine green angiography, 25
Scatter laser treatment. *See also* Panretinal photocoagulation; Photocoagulation
  for branch retinal vein occlusion, 124–125, 125*f*
  for central retinal vein occlusion, 132
  for diabetic retinopathy, 106–108, 108*f*, 109*f*
  indications for, 340
  for nonproliferative diabetic retinopathy/macular edema, 102
    ETDRS, 98, 102
  for ocular ischemic syndrome, 134
  for proliferative diabetic retinopathy, 106–108, 108*f*, 109*f*
    DRS/ETDRS, 107–108, 108*f*, 109*f*
  for retinopathy of prematurity, 167–168, 168*f*
  for sickle cell retinopathy, 120–121
Scheie Classification of Hypertension Retinopathy, Modified, 114
Scheie syndrome, 250*t*, 262
Schubert-Bornschein form of congenital stationary night blindness, 216
Sclera, 18
  anatomy of, 18
  rupture of, 323
Scleral buckle
  for retinal detachment, 289–290, 290*f*, 365, 366*f*
    sickle cell retinopathy and, 121
  for retinopathy of prematurity, 170
Sclopetaria, 323, 323*f*
SCORE (Standard Care Versus Corticosteroid for Retinal Vein Occlusion) trial, 100, 126, 131
Scotomata
  in acute zonal occult outer retinopathy, 192
  in age-related macular degeneration, 64, 79
  in central serous chorioretinopathy, 171
  in choroideremia, 243
  in cone–rod dystrophies, 234
  paracentral, 64, 79
  in photoreceptor dystrophies, 223, 225*f*
  physiologic (blind spot), idiopathic enlargement of, 190
  in retinitis pigmentosa, 225*f*, 228
  in serpiginous choroidopathy, 188
  in Stargardt disease, 235
Scotopic/dark-adapted electroretinogram, 33, 34*f*, 35, 36*f*
  in hereditary retinal/choroidal dystrophies, 224*t*
Screening/diagnostic tests, for retinopathy of prematurity, 164–165

SD-OCT. *See* Spectral-domain OCT
Sea-blue histiocyte syndrome, 262, 263*f*
Sea fan neovascularization, in sickle cell disease, 119, 119*f*, 120*f*
Serpiginous choroidopathy/choroiditis (geographic/helicoid), 186*t*, 188–189, 188*f*
Serratia, endogenous bacterial endophthalmitis caused by, 202
SF₆
  for retinal detachment, 367
  for submacular hemorrhage, 351
Shafer sign ("tobacco dust"), 286, 314
Shaken baby syndrome, 330–331, 330*f*
Sheathotomy, arteriovenous, for branch retinal vein occlusion, 126
Sialidoses, cherry-red spot in, 262
Sickle cell disease (sickle cell anemia), 115–121, 117*t*
  ophthalmic manifestations of, 115–121, 117*t*, 118*f*, 119*f*, 120*f*. *See also* Sickle cell retinopathy
    angioid streaks, 84, 120
    traumatic hyphema and, 120
Sickle cell hemoglobin (SC), 116, 117*t*
Sickle cell preparations, 116
Sickle cell retinopathy, 115–121, 117*t*, 118*f*, 119*f*, 120*f*
  angioid streaks in, 84, 120
  management of, 120–121
  nonproliferative, 118–119, 118*f*, 119*f*
  proliferative, 119, 119*f*
    photocoagulation for, 120–121
    vitreoretinal surgery for, 121
Sickle cell thalassemia, 116, 117*t*
Sickle cell trait (hemoglobin AS), 116, 117*t*
Siderosis, 328, 328*t*
Siegrist streaks, 114–115, 177
Sildenafil, ocular effects of, 269
Silicone oil, for tamponade in retinal detachment, 345, 366, 366*f*, 367
Silicone Study, 367
Simplex retinitis pigmentosa, 227
Single-flash cone response (photopic/light-adapted electroretinogram), 34, 34*f*, 35, 36*f*
  in cone dystrophies, 232
  in hereditary retinal/choroidal dystrophies, 224*t*
Sjögren-Larsson syndrome, ichthyosis in, 255
Skin, disorders of, retinal degeneration and, 255
SLC45A2 gene, in OCA4, 258*t*
Slit-lamp biomicroscopy/examination
  in diabetic macular edema, 95
  in macular holes, 304
  in ocular trauma, 318
  in posterior vitreous detachment, 276, 297–298
  in retinal examination, 19–20
Slit-lamp delivery systems, for photocoagulation, 340
SLO. *See* Scanning laser ophthalmoscopy
Sloan achromatopsia test, 50
Small-gauge vitrectomy, 346
SmartSight patient handout/website, 60, 231
Smokestack, in central serous chorioretinopathy, 172, 173*f*
Snowballs
  in intermediate uveitis/pars planitis, 196
  in sarcoidosis, 197
Snowbanks
  in intermediate uveitis/pars planitis, 196
  in sarcoidosis, 197
Snowflakes, in typical degenerative retinoschisis, 293

Soft drusen, 57, 57f, 58
   drusenoid RPE detachment and, 57, 238, 239f
Soft exudates. *See* Cotton-wool spots
Solar retinopathy/retinitis (foveomacular
   retinitis), 332–333
Solitary idiopathic choroiditis, 194
Sorsby macular dystrophy, 241–242, 242f
Spatial frequency, contrast sensitivity testing and, 50, 51f
Spectral-domain OCT, 27
   in central serous chorioretinopathy, 173
   near-infrared spectrum scanning laser and, 30–31, 31f
Spielmeyer-Vogt disease, 251t, 260
Spinocerebellar degenerations
   cone–rod dystrophy and, 233
   pigmentary retinopathy and, 254
Spontaneous vitreous hemorrhage, 313–314
SS. *See* Sickle cell disease
SST (Submacular Surgery Trials), 79, 249–250
Staining, fluorescein, 23, 23f, 24f
Standard Care Versus Corticosteroid for Retinal Vein
   Occlusion (SCORE) trial, 100, 126, 131
Standing potential, 42, 42f
Staphylococcus aureus
   endogenous endophthalmitis caused by, 202
   postoperative endophthalmitis caused by, 354
Stargardt disease (juvenile macular degeneration/fundus
   flavimaculatus), 234–236, 235f, 236t
   ABC transporter mutations causing, 233, 234
   cone–rod dystrophy and, 234
   gene for, 222, 233, 234
Stationary night blindness, congenital, 215–217, 216f, 217f
   ERG patterns in, 36f, 216, 217, 217f
Stationary retinal disease, 213–216
Steinert disease, pigmentary retinopathy and, 250t
Stent placement, carotid artery, for ocular ischemic
   syndrome, 134–135
STGD4 gene, in Stargardt disease, 234
Stickler syndrome (hereditary progressive arthro-
   ophthalmopathy), 250t, 309, 309f, 310
   pigmentary retinopathy and, 250t, 309f
STOP-ROP (Supplemental Therapeutic Oxygen for
   Prethreshold ROP) study, 166
Streptococcus
   in bleb-associated endophthalmitis, 354, 357
   in endogenous endophthalmitis, 202
   in postoperative endophthalmitis, 354
Striae, retinal, 300
Stroke, ocular ischemic syndrome and, 134
Sturge-Weber syndrome, choroidal hemangioma in, 181
Subclinical retinal detachment, 285
Submacular hemorrhage, 349–351, 350f
Submacular surgery
   for age-related macular degeneration, 79
   for hemorrhage, 349–351, 350f
   for ocular histoplasmosis syndrome, 82, 351
Submacular Surgery Trials (SST), 79, 349–350
Subretinal fluid, in central serous chorioretinopathy, 172,
   173, 173f, 174
Substance abuse disorders, endogenous mold (*Aspergillus*)
   endophthalmitis and, 203
Sugiura sign, 197
Sulfadiazine, for toxoplasmosis, 208–209, 208t
Sunburst lesions, black, in sickle cell disease, 118, 119f
Sunflower cataract, in chalcosis, 327
Sunset-glow fundus, in Vogt-Koyanagi-Harada (VKH)
   syndrome, 197

Supplemental Therapeutic Oxygen for Prethreshold ROP
   (STOP-ROP) study, 166
Suprachoroidal/choroidal hemorrhage, 360–361, 362f
Surface-wrinkling retinopathy, 300
Susac syndrome, 141
SUSTAIN trial, 77
Sympathetic ophthalmia, 198–199, 329–330
Synchysis, 297
   in cholesterolosis, 311–312
   in hereditary hyaloideoretinopathies with optically
      empty vitreous, 309
Synchysis scintillans, 311–312
Syneresis, 297
   in posterior vitreous detachment, 274
   in young eyes, 272
Syphilis, chorioretinitis in, 205–206, 207f
Systemic lupus erythematosus
   choroidal perfusion abnormalities and, 179
   retinal manifestations of, 195–196, 195f

Tamoxifen, retinopathy caused by, 268, 268f
Tap/biopsy of vitreous, for specimen collection, 354
TAP (Treatment of Age-Related Macular Degeneration
   with Photodynamic Therapy) Study, 72, 75f, 344
Tapetal retinal reflex, in cone dystrophies, 232, 233
τ (implicit time), in electroretinogram, 34, 34f
Tay-Sachs disease (GM$_2$ gangliosidosis type I), 262, 263f
Telangiectasias, retinal, 143–145, 144f. *See also* Coats
   disease
   parafoveal (juxtafoveal), 145–147, 145f, 146f
Terson syndrome, 155
Thalassemia
   β, angioid streaks in, 84
   sickle cell, 116, 117t
Thermal injury (burns), retinal, light causing, 332
Thermal laser photocoagulation. *See* Photocoagulation
Thermotherapy, transpupillary, 343
   for age-related macular degeneration/choroidal
      neovascularization, 79, 343
   for melanoma, 343
Thioridazine, retinal degeneration caused by,
   267–268, 268f
30-Hz flicker response, 34, 34f, 35, 36f
   vascular disease and, 40, 41f
Thorazine. *See* Chlorpromazine
Threshold disease, in retinopathy of prematurity, 163
Thrombocytopenic purpura, thrombotic, choroidal
   perfusion abnormalities and, 179
Thrombosis/thrombotic disorders
   branch retinal artery occlusion and, 136–137, 136f, 137f
   central retinal artery occlusion and, 139
   choroidal perfusion abnormalities and, 179
   retinal vasculitis and, 141
Thrombotic thrombocytopenic purpura, choroidal
   perfusion abnormalities and, 179
Ticks, Lyme disease transmitted by, 210
Tight junctions (zonulae occludentes), in retinal pigment
   epithelium, 14
TIMP3 gene/TIMP3 protein mutation, in Sorsby
   dystrophy, 241
Tissue plasminogen activator
   for central retinal vein occlusion, 133
   for submacular hemorrhage, 350, 350f
"Tobacco dust" (Shafer sign), 286, 314
Toxocara (toxocariasis), 209–210, 209f
   diffuse unilateral subacute neuroretinitis caused by, 210

Toxoplasma (toxoplasmosis), chorioretinitis caused by, 206–209, 208*f*, 208*t*

tPA. *See* Tissue plasminogen activator

Traction retinal tufts, zonular, 278, 280*f*

Tractional retinal detachment. *See* Retinal detachment

11-*trans*-retinaldehyde, 15

Transconjunctival vitrectomy technique, 346

Transient ischemic attacks, central retinal artery occlusion and, 139

Transient visual loss, in central retinal artery occlusion, 139

Transillumination, in retinal examination, 20

Transmission (window) defect, of fluorescence, 23, 23*f*
   in angioid streaks, 84
   in macular holes, 305

Transplantation, organ, endogenous mold *(Aspergillus)* endophthalmitis after, 203

Transpupillary thermotherapy, 343
   for age-related macular degeneration/choroidal neovascularization, 79, 343
   for melanoma, 343

Transpupillary Thermotherapy for Choroidal Neovascularization (TTT4CNV) study, 79

Transthyretin mutation, amyloidosis and, 312, 313*f*

Trauma, 317–334. *See also* Blunt trauma; Lacerations; Penetrating injuries
   in children
      retinal breaks and, 272–273
      shaking injury and, 330–331, 330*f*
   endophthalmitis after, 328–329
   ERG in evaluation of, 41
   foreign bodies and, 325–328, 326*f*, 328*t*
   macular holes associated with, 321–322, 322*f*
   optic disc avulsion and, 331–332, 331*f*
   patient evaluation after, 317–318
   photic damage and, 332–334
   Purtscher retinopathy and, 154–155, 154*f*, 155*t*
   retinal breaks caused by, 272–274, 273*f*
   retinal detachment and, 291
      in young patients, 272–273
   sympathetic ophthalmia and, 198, 329–330

Traumatic hyphema, sickle cell disease and, 120

Traumatic retinal breaks, 272–274, 273*f*

Treatment of Age-Related Macular Degeneration with Photodynamic Therapy (TAP) Study, 72, 75*f*, 344

Triamcinolone
   for cystoid macular edema, 143, 360
   intravitreal (IVTA)
      for branch retinal vein occlusion, 126
      for central retinal vein occlusion, 131
      for macular edema, 100
      with photodynamic therapy, 344
   with photodynamic therapy, 344
   PVD visualization in vitrectomy and, 298, 301*f*

Trichromatism/trichromacy, 213, 214*t*
   anomalous, 213, 213–214

Trimethoprim-sulfamethoxazole, for toxoplasmosis, 209

Tritan defects (tritanopia), 47, 213
   tests for, 49

Tritanomalous congenital defects, 213, 214*t*

TTT. *See* Transpupillary thermotherapy

TTT4CNV (Transpupillary Thermotherapy for Choroidal Neovascularization) study, 79

Tubercles, choroidal, in tuberculosis, 205

Tuberculosis, choroidal involvement in, 204–205, 205*f*

Tunica vasculosa lentis, remnant of, 307

Typical degenerative retinoschisis, 293, 293*f*

Typical peripheral cystoid degeneration, 282, 292

Tyr402His
   in age-related macular degeneration, 56
   in basal laminar/cuticular drusen, 239–240

Tyrosinase gene mutations, in albinism, 258, 258*t*

TYRP1 gene, in OCA3, 258*t*

UKPDS (United Kingdom Prospective Diabetes Study), 91, 92, 93

Ultrasonography/ultrasound (echography)
   in foreign-body identification, 325, 326, 326*f*
   in ocular trauma, 318
   in posterior vitreous detachment, 276, 298
   in vitreous hemorrhage, 110, 314
   in Vogt-Koyanagi-Harada (VKH) syndrome, 198

Ultraviolet light (ultraviolet radiation), eye disorders/injury associated with, 332–334. *See also* Light toxicity
   age-related macular degeneration, 63
   ambient exposure and, 334
   in retinitis pigmentosa, 231
   solar retinopathy, 332–333

Ultra-wide-angle fundus photography, for screening in retinopathy of prematurity, 165

Umbo, 8, 9*f*, 9*t*

United Kingdom Prospective Diabetes Study (UKPDS), 91, 92, 93

Urticaria, from fluorescein angiography, 24, 25

USH2A gene, 222

USH3A gene, 253

Usher syndrome, 251*t*, 253
   gene for, 222, 253

Usherin, in Usher syndrome, 253

Uvea, bilateral diffuse melanocytic proliferation of, 183, 183*f*

Uveal (posterior) bleeding syndrome (polypoidal choroidal vasculopathy)
   age-related macular degeneration differentiated from, 69–70, 70*f*
   central serous retinopathy differentiated from, 174, 175

Uveal effusions/uveal effusion syndrome, 182–183, 182*f*
   central serous chorioretinopathy differentiated from, 174

Uveitis
   in Behçet disease, 194
   immune recovery, 201
   intermediate, 196
   masquerade syndromes and, 199, 199*f*
   sarcoidosis and, 196–197, 197*f*
   in toxocariasis, 209
   in toxoplasmosis, 206
   Vogt-Koyanagi-Harada (VKH) syndrome and, 197–198, 198*f*

Valacyclovir, for acute retinal necrosis, 201

Valganciclovir, for CMV retinitis, 200

Valsalva retinopathy, 153–154

Vancomycin, for endophthalmitis, 356

Vaporization, 339

Vascular endothelial growth factor (VEGF)
   in age-related macular degeneration/choroidal neovascularization, 72–73
   agents inhibiting. *See* Anti-VEGF agents
   in diabetic retinopathy, 104

Vascular filling defect, 22

Vascular loops, prepapillary, 307, 307*f*

Vasculitis
  lupus, 195–196, 195f
    choroidal perfusion abnormalities and, 179
  optic disc (papillophlebitis), 128
  retinal, 140–141, 141f
    in Behçet disease, 194–195
    idiopathic, aneurysms and neuroretinitis and
      (IRVAN), 141
    inflammatory, 194–196
    in systemic lupus erythematosus, 195–196, 195f
Vasculogenesis, in retinopathy of prematurity, 162
Vasculopathy
  polypoidal choroidal (posterior uveal bleeding
    syndrome)
    age-related macular degeneration differentiated
      from, 69–70, 70f
    central serous chorioretinopathy differentiated from,
      174, 175
  primary occlusive, 141
Vasoproliferative tumor, 148
VDRL (Venereal Disease Research Laboratory) test, in
    syphilitic chorioretinitis, 205
VECP. See Visually evoked cortical potentials
VEGF. See Vascular endothelial growth factor
VEGF Inhibition Study in Ocular Neovascularization
    (VISION), 75f
VEGF Trap
  for age-related macular degeneration/choroidal
    neovascularization, 77–78
  for central retinal vein occlusion, 131
VEGF Trap-Eye: Investigation of Efficacy and Safety
    in Wet Age-Related Macular Degeneration 1 and 2
    (VIEW 1 and 2) studies, 77–78
Venereal Disease Research Laboratory (VDRL) test, in
    syphilitic chorioretinitis, 205
Venous beading, in diabetic retinopathy, 104, 104f
Venous occlusive disease, retinal, 121–133. See also
    Retinal vein occlusion
  branch retinal vein occlusion, 121–127, 122f, 125f
  central retinal vein occlusion, 127–133, 127f, 128f,
    129f, 132f
  photocoagulation for, 340
Venous outflow disorders, choroidal perfusion
    abnormalities and, 176
Venous stasis retinopathy, 127, 128, 128f, 133
VEP/VER. See Visually evoked cortical potentials (visual
    evoked response)
Verteporfin, photodynamic therapy with, 343–344
  in age-related macular degeneration/choroidal
    neovascularization, 72, 78, 79
  in central serous chorioretinopathy, 175
  in choroidal hemangioma, 182
  combination treatment and, 72, 78, 79
  in retinal hemangioblastoma, 150
Verteporfin in Photodynamic Therapy (VIP) Trial, 72, 344
VIEW 1 and 2 (VEGF Trap-Eye: Investigation of Efficacy
    and Safety in Wet Age-Related Macular Degeneration
    1 and 2) studies, 77–78
VIM (Visudyne in Minimally Classic CNV) Trial, 72
VIP Pathologic Myopia Trial, 86
VIP (Verteporfin in Photodynamic Therapy) Trial, 72,
    344
VISION (VEGF Inhibition Study in Ocular
    Neovascularization), 75f
Vision rehabilitation
  in age-related macular dystrophy, 79

  in cone dystrophies, 232
  in retinitis pigmentosa, 230
Visual acuity
  in acute macular neuroretinopathy, 193
  in acute posterior multifocal placoid pigment
    epitheliopathy (APMPPE), 187
  in age-related macular degeneration, 55, 79
  in albinism, 258
  in birdshot retinochoroidopathy, 190
  in branch retinal vein occlusion, 123, 124, 127
  in central areolar choroidal dystrophy, 245
  in central retinal artery occlusion, 138
  in central retinal vein occlusion, 128, 131
  in central serous chorioretinopathy, 171, 175
  in choroidal neovascularization, 65, 79
  in cone dystrophies, 232
  in congenital stationary night blindness, 215
  in diabetic retinopathy/diabetic macular edema, after
    photocoagulation, 102
  in epiretinal membrane, 301, 346
  in Leber congenital amaurosis, 229
  in macular holes, 304, 349
  in multiple evanescent white dot syndrome, 189
  in North Carolina macular dystrophy, 246
  in ocular histoplasmosis syndrome, 81
  posterior segment trauma evaluation and, 318
  after retinal detachment surgery, 291
  in rod monochromatism, 215
  in Stargardt disease, 236
Visual evoked response. See Visually evoked cortical
    potentials
Visual field defects
  in acute zonal occult outer retinopathy, 192, 193
  in branch retinal artery occlusion, 136
  in chloroquine/hydroxychloroquine toxicity, 266
  in cone dystrophies, 232
  in cone–rod dystrophies, 223, 232
  in photoreceptor dystrophies, 223, 225f
  in retinitis pigmentosa, 225f, 228
  in Stargardt disease, 235
Visual field testing
  in chloroquine/hydroxychloroquine toxicity
    screening, 267
  in cone dystrophies, 232
  in hereditary retinal and choroidal dystrophies,
    223, 225f
  in photoreceptor dystrophies, 223, 225f
  in retinitis pigmentosa, 225f, 226
Visual loss/impairment
  in acute macular neuroretinopathy, 193
  in acute posterior multifocal placoid pigment
    epitheliopathy (APMPPE), 185, 187
  in acute zonal occult outer retinopathy, 192, 193
  in birdshot retinochoroidopathy, 190
  in branch retinal vein occlusion, 123
  in central retinal artery occlusion, 138
  in central retinal vein occlusion, 128
  in central serous chorioretinopathy, 171, 175
  in cone dystrophies, 232
  in diabetic retinopathy, 95
  in Leber congenital amaurosis, 229
  in macroaneurysms, 147–148
  in macular holes, 304, 349
  in multiple evanescent white dot syndrome, 189
  in ocular histoplasmosis syndrome, 81
  in ocular ischemic syndrome, 133

in pars planitis, 196
after photodynamic therapy, 344
in retinitis pigmentosa, 225f, 228, 229, 230, 231
in retinopathy of prematurity, 157
in serpiginous choroidopathy, 188
in sickle cell retinopathy, 117
in Stargardt disease, 235
in toxoplasmosis, 207
Visual pigments, 15
absorption spectra of, 337, 338f
Visually evoked cortical potentials (visual evoked
response), 44–45, 45f
Visudyne in Minimally Classic CNV (VIM) Trial, 72
Vitamin A
for abetalipoproteinemia, 260
deficiency of, retinopathy caused by, 260–261
for retinitis pigmentosa, 231
Vitamin B$_6$ (pyridoxine), for gyrate atrophy, 244
Vitamin C (ascorbic acid), for age-related macular
degeneration, 61–62
Vitamin E
abetalipoproteinemia and, 260
age-related macular degeneration and, 61–62
for retinitis pigmentosa, 231
Vitamin supplements
in age-related macular degeneration
management, 61–63
in retinitis pigmentosa management, 231
Vitelliform degenerations, 236–238. See also Adult-onset
vitelliform lesions; Best disease
Vitelliform exudative macular detachment, 238, 238f
Vitiliginous chorioretinitis (birdshot
retinochoroidopathy), 186t, 190–191, 190f
Vitiligo, in Vogt-Koyanagi-Harada (VKH)
syndrome, 197
Vitrectomy, 345–368
for amyloidosis, 312–313, 313f
for branch retinal vein occlusion, 126
cataract caused by, 368
for choroidal neovascularization, 351, 351f
for CMV retinitis, 201
complications of, 368, 368t
for cystoid macular edema, 143
postoperative, 360, 360f
for diabetic retinopathy complications, 109–111,
352–353, 353f
macular edema, 103, 353
tractional retinal detachment, 110–111,
352–353, 353f
vitreous hemorrhage, 110, 352
for dislocated posterior chamber intraocular
lenses, 359–360
for endophthalmitis
Aspergillus/mold, 204
Candida/yeast, 203
postoperative, 354–357, 355f, 356f, 357f
acute-onset, 354, 354–356, 355f
bleb-associated, 354, 356–357, 357f
chronic (delayed-onset), 355, 356, 356f
endophthalmitis after, 368
for epiretinal membranes, 301, 346, 347f, 348f
for foreign-body removal, 327
for idiopathic macular hole, 305–306, 349, 350f
for macular diseases, 346–352
after needle penetration/perforation of globe,
362, 363f

open-angle glaucoma after, 368
for pars planitis, 196
after penetrating injury, 324
after perforating injury, 325
phototoxicity and, 333
for posterior segment complications of anterior
segment surgery, 354–362
for posterior vitreous detachment, 276, 289, 301f
for postoperative endophthalmitis, 354–357, 355f,
356f, 357f
primary, 366–368, 366f
for retained lens fragments after phacoemulsification,
357–359, 358t, 359f
for retinal detachment, 290, 291, 366–368, 366f
complex detachment, 367
in diabetes mellitus, 110–111, 352–353, 353f
in retinopathy of prematurity, 170
tractional, 110–111, 191
for retinopathy of prematurity, 170
in sickle cell retinopathy, 121
small gauge technique for, 346
for subfoveal choroidal neovascularization,
351, 351f
for submacular hemorrhage, 349–351, 350f
for suprachoroidal hemorrhage, 360–361, 362f
sympathetic ophthalmia and, 329
transconjunctival technique for, 346
for vitreomacular traction syndrome, 302–303,
346–347, 348f
Vitreomacular traction syndrome, 298, 302–304, 303f,
346–347, 348f
vitrectomy for, 302–303, 346–347, 348f
Vitreoretinal dystrophies, 246–248
Goldmann-Favre, 219, 248
Vitreoretinal interface, diseases of, 297–315. See also
specific type
Vitreoretinal surgery, 345–368. See also Vitrectomy
in sickle cell retinopathy, 121
Vitreoretinal tufts, 278, 279f, 280f
Vitreoretinopathies
familial exudative, 310–311, 310f
proliferative, 286–288, 289f, 289t
Vitreoschisis. See Vitreous detachment
Vitreous, 7–8, 7f
amyloidosis involving, 312–313, 313f
anatomy of, 7–8, 7f
cataract surgery complications and, 314
posterior vitreous detachment, 275, 297
developmental abnormalities of, 307–309, 307f, 308f
disorders of, 297–315. See also specific type
hyaluronan/hyaluronic acid in, 7, 297
macular attachment to, 7f, 8
posterior vitreous detachment and, 298,
302–304, 303f
opacification of, 311–314
in amyloidosis, 312–313, 313f
in asteroid hyalosis, 311, 312f
in cholesterolosis, 311–312
hemorrhage causing, 313–314
pigment granules and, 314
optically empty, hereditary hyaloideoretinopathies
with, 309–310, 309f
pigment granules in ("tobacco dust"/Shafer sign),
286, 314
primary, persistent hyperplasia of. See Persistent fetal
vasculature

retinal attachment to, 7f, 8
posterior vitreous detachment and, 274–276, 274f,
275f, 297–306, 362
specimen collection from, 354
Vitreous base, 7, 7f, 274
avulsion of, 272, 273f
posterior vitreous detachment and, 297
Vitreous detachment
anterior, 297
posterior, 200f, 274–276, 274f, 275f, 297–306, 299f,
301f, 362
in diabetic retinopathy, 110
epiretinal membranes and, 298–301, 302f
macular holes and, 298, 304–306, 305–306f
perifoveal, 298
vitreomacular traction syndrome and, 298,
302–304, 303f
vitreous hemorrhage and, 275, 313
Vitreous hemorrhage, 313–314, 319
blunt trauma causing, 319
branch retinal vein occlusion and, 123, 125, 126
central retinal vein occlusion and, 130
diabetic retinopathy and, 105, 106f, 110, 313, 352
pars planitis and, 196
posterior vitreous detachment and, 275, 313
retinal cavernous hemangioma and, 151
retinopathy of prematurity and, 157, 163, 164
spontaneous, 313–314
vitrectomy for, in diabetes mellitus, 110, 352
Vitreous membrane, tractional retinal detachment and, 291
Vitreous pocket, precortical, 7f, 8
Vitreous tap, for specimen collection, 354
Vitreous traction
in posterior vitreous detachment, 298, 302–304,
303f, 362
in retinal break/tear formation, 274, 275f
retinal cavernous hemangioma and, 151
Vitritis
in acute zonal occult outer retinopathy, 192
in birdshot retinochoroidopathy, 190
in cystoid macular edema, 142
in Lyme disease, 210
in multifocal choroiditis and panuveitis
syndrome, 191
in pars planitis, 196
in Vogt-Koyanagi-Harada (VKH) syndrome, 197
VKH. See Vogt-Koyanagi-Harada (VKH) syndrome
VMD2 (Best1) gene, 236
VMT. See Vitreomacular traction syndrome
Vogt-Koyanagi-Harada (VKH) syndrome, 197–198, 198f
central serous chorioretinopathy differentiated
from, 174
von Hippel lesions, 150
von Hippel–Lindau disease/syndrome, 150, 150f
Voriconazole, for fungal endogenous endophthalmitis
Aspergillus/mold, 204
Candida/yeast, 203
Vortex veins, 18

Waardenburg syndrome, pigmentary retinopathy
and, 250t
Wagner disease/Wagner hereditary vitreoretinal
degeneration, 250t, 309

Wavelength, laser, for photocoagulation, 337–339
Wegener granulomatosis, choroidal perfusion
abnormalities and, 179, 180f
Weight, IGF, neonatal ROP (WINROP) algorithm, 166
Weiss ring, 274, 274f, 297–298, 304
Welding, occupational light injury and, 334
WESDR (Wisconsin Epidemiologic Study of Diabetic
Retinopathy), 90
West Nile virus, chorioretinitis caused by, 211
White dot syndromes, 185–193, 186t. See also specific
type
multiple evanescent (MEWDS), 186t, 189–190, 189f
White infarct, 147
Wide-angle fundus camera, for screening in retinopathy
of prematurity, 165
Wieger ligament, 7, 7f
Window (transmission) defect, of fluorescence, 23, 23f
in angioid streaks, 84
in macular holes, 305
WINROP (weight, IGF, neonatal ROP) algorithm, 166
Wisconsin Epidemiologic Study of Diabetic Retinopathy
(WESDR), 90
Wyburn-Mason syndrome (racemose angioma/
hemangioma), 151

X-linked disorders
albinism, 258
blue-cone monochromatism, 214t, 215
choroideremia, ocular findings in carriers of, 243
color vision deficiency, 214, 214t, 215
cone dystrophies, 233
congenital stationary night blindness, 215
familial exudative vitreoretinopathy, 310, 311
pigmentary retinopathies, 251t
retinitis pigmentosa, 228, 229
ocular findings in carriers of, 226, 228
retinoschisis (congenital/juvenile retinoschisis),
246–247, 246f
ERG in, 36f, 247
Xanthocoria, in Coats disease, 143
Xanthophylls (carotenoids)
absorption spectrum for, 337, 338f
in macula, 8
age-related macular degeneration and, 62
XLM. See External limiting membrane
XLRP. See X-linked disorders, retinitis pigmentosa
XLRS. See X-linked disorders, retinoschisis

Yeasts, endogenous endophthalmitis caused by,
203, 204f
Yellow lasers, 338

Zeaxanthin, in macula, 8
age-related macular degeneration and, 62
Zellweger (cerebrohepatorenal) syndrome, 251t,
254, 261
Zinc
in age-related macular degeneration
management, 61–62
foreign body of, 327
Zonulae occludentes (tight junctions), in retinal pigment
epithelium, 14
Zonular traction retinal tufts, 278, 280f